THE EXPLODING EYE

THE SUNY SERIES
CULTURAL STUDIES IN CINEMA/VIDEO

Wheeler Winston Dixon, editor

THE EXPLODING EYE

*A Re-Visionary History
of 1960s
American Experimental Cinema*

WHEELER
WINSTON
DIXON

STATE UNIVERSITY OF NEW YORK PRESS

Front cover photo: Warren Sonbert projecting one of his films at
Andy Warhol's Factory, 33 Union Square West, Spring 1969.
Photostrip by Wheeler Winston Dixon.

Published by
State University of New York Press, Albany

For information, address State University of New York Press,
State University Plaza, Albany, N.Y., 12246

Production by Marilyn P. Semerad
Marketing by Dana E. Yanulavich

Library of Congress Cataloging-in-Publication Data

Dixon, Wheeler, W., 1950–
     The exploding eye : a re-visionary history of 1960s American
     experimental cinema / Wheeler Winston Dixon.
          p.   cm. — (SUNY series, cultural studies in cinema/video)
     Includes bibliographical references and index.
          ISBN 0-7914-3565-2 (hc : alk. paper). — ISBN 0-7914-3566-0 (pb :
     alk. paper)
          1. Experimental films—United States—History and criticism.
     I. Title. II. Series.
     PN1995.9.E96D55 1997
     791.43'022—dc21
                                                                97-11382
                                                                CIP

10 9 8 7 6 5 4 3 2 1

For Gwendolyn

CONTENTS

LIST OF
ILLUSTRATIONS

■■

ACKNOWLEDGMENTS

———————— ▘▘ ————————

For the use of the photographs in this volume, I wish to thank Robert Haller of Anthology Film Archives; David Sherman and Dominic Angerame of Canyon Cinema; as well as the individual filmmakers Gordon Ball, Bert Deivert, Michael Snow, Jud Yalkut, Jerome Hiler, Nathanael Dorsky, Ernie Gehr, Michael Mideke, David Curtis, Keewatin Dewdney, David Secter, Vivienne Dick, Terry Cannon (for materials on Sara Kathryn Arledge), St. Clair Bourne, William Greaves, and many others. Credits for each individual still appear throughout the work as part of the caption material. My thanks to all for their help in providing the rare illustrative materials for this volume.

For letters and individual reminiscences, I would like to thank Ernie Gehr, Freude Bartlett, Michael Snow, Michael Mideke, Nathanael Dorsky, Jerome Hiler, Taylor Mead, David Sherman, Dominic Angerame, Gordon Ball, and Vivienne Dick. For services above and beyond the call of obligation in typing and collating this manuscript, I wish to sincerely thank Dana Miller. For their continued insights and inspiration I would like to acknowledge the collegial advice and counsel of David Desser, Scott Stark, Lloyd Michaels, Mark Reid, Tony Williams, Marcia Landy, Anna Everett, Deac Rossell and many others, whose critical works continually challenge me, and provoke new insights.

For her support in securing release time to complete this volume, I thank Linda Ray Pratt, Chair of the Department of English at the University of Nebraska, Lincoln; I would also like to thank my colleagues within the department for providing a stimulating and invigorating intellectual environment. Clay Morgan, Marilyn Semerad, and the staff of the State University of New York Press helped me immeasurably in the preparation of this volume, as did the reviewers who offered their suggestions and emendations during the final process of textual revision.

CHAPTER ONE

■■

Introduction

In the words of Rosalind Krauss, "the historical period that the Avant-Garde shared with modernism is over" (170). And yet the films of the 1960s American independent cinema movement continue to have enormous repercussions in contemporary cinema practice, even if only in the most superficial way: the scratched titles for the feature film *Se7en* (1995); the ostentatiously hand-held camera of the television series *Law and Order* or *ER*; or the jagged, fragmented visual style of a typical MTV video. Commercials inundate us with meaningless flash frames, light flares, and skewed camera angles reminiscent of the '60s Avant-Garde, often created through digital imaging rather than direct photographic processing. But the originators of these techniques, and more importantly, the concepts and ideological constructs inhabiting and made manifest by these external stylistic manifestations, are often ignored or overlooked. As Habermas notes, "at the end of the twentieth century . . . philosophical thought appears withdrawn, cocooned in esotericism" (118). In the 1960s, however, it was quite a different matter; the entire fabric of human existence was being called into question, and discourse in both the arts and abstract philosophical inquiry was being practiced in the open, as part of the social economy of everyday existence.

In this examination of experimental cinema practice in the American experimental cinema of the 1960s, I want to consider primarily (but not exclusively) those filmmakers whose works have escaped into the phantom zone of the absent signifier through the exi-

1

gencies of poor distribution, lack of initial acclaim during "first runs" (the reception period of new cinema, until the advent of home video, had been characterized by a notoriously short "shelf life"), the reclusiveness of the filmmaker her- or himself, or a variety of other mitigating factors. Thus, certain cinematic works become historical commonplaces, while others, lacking critical champions, recede into the depths of individual memory. At the same time, I want to acknowledge the debt owed to more widely known cinema/video artists, as viewers/practitioners/scholars, in presenting the vision of the Avant-Garde to the general public. Most categorically, I want to allow each film to speak for itself, and each filmmaker (wherever possible) to speak for her- or himself through her or his writings, and to refrain, for the most part, from imposing an external ideological grid on the works discussed within this text.

It should be readily seen by now that all value judgments, however universally accepted (in either the positive or negative sphere), are almost entirely subjective, particularly when dealing with a cinema that set itself the preordained task of abolishing all the established rules of film/video syntax and structure. It seems to me that the only aesthetic rule that we should respect within the independent cinema is the rule of the filmmaker her- or himself, since this is the sole rule that governs production within this sphere of cinematic endeavor. Our reception of the spectacle that we collectively witness as viewers is an altogether different (and often tangential, or inconsequential) matter; many of these films were made with no expectation of winning an audience, and some were created for the sole purpose of alienating and/or marginalizing the viewer, and the concomitant demand for spectatorial pleasure implicit within the construct of the dominant narrative cinema. Certainly, any number of valuative strategies will insidiously seep in at the margins of my discussion, as such a priori assumptions have a way of doing, but my guiding principle in creating this text was to admit (and this was also one of the founding principles of the New American Cinema, when the non-censorial, non-selective Filmmakers' Cooperative was originally formed) all possible filmic (and occasionally, video) visions created during the rough time span of the 1960s, with occasional extensions into the 1940s or into the early 1970s. The fifth chapter, or "coda" of the work, suggests some of the ways in which these multiple visions are being carried forward by a new generation of experimental film and video artists.

One of the key aspects of the American Experimental cinema during the 1960s remains the *uniqueness* of each individual artist's vision; it is no more possible to confuse a film by Bruce Conner with a film by Stan Vanderbeek (for example) than it is to mistakenly conflate the writings of Anais Nin and Paul Bowles from the same period. The voice of each filmmaker remained hers or his alone, and during a period when filmmaking was cheap, and a short B/W film could be made for as little as one hundred dollars (complete with an optical track and a final release print), there were few constraints on one's personal vision. Nor, I would hasten to add, has the independent cinema collapsed into a black hole of nonexistence within the confines of contemporary cinema. As Trinh T. Minh-ha observed in her study *Framer Framed*, "as a filmmaker it is odd to read so many commentaries bemoaning the demise of experimental cinema. A lot of this is misleading, because what is really happening is that people are speaking in a generational way, and are feeling a passage. They see the passing, and also the diminishing, through derivative work, of what they trust and found expansive" (246).

It requires an enormous amount of energy and resolve to continue the practice of experimental cinema in an atmosphere that is not entirely complementary to the values that alternative cinema espouses, or the questions that it inevitably poses. Many of the artists discussed in this book are now retired from active filmmaking, or taking an extended hiatus from their work; some are dead; others continue their work unabated. What Trinh T. Minh-ha terms "generational" is certainly a factor in the continuing "plate-shifts" of independent cinema practice. What is new cannot be eternally new; what is past comes back to us, recycled and reified through reinterpretation, restatement, and other derivative practices. The independent cinema is a figurative ground of contestation, in which ideas, gender roles, metaphoric/iconic/metatextual concepts and gestures of overt defiance form much of the text of the discourse. As Todorov observes, with the dissemination of new ideas through easily distributed mediums (books in the Gutenberg era; 16mm film in the prevideo era; VHS tapes in the 1980s; digital satellite dishes in the present), "populations, and thus cultures, that had been previously isolated from one another come into contact through [new] encounters" (78); it was this spreading of new ideas, new ways of looking at contemporary culture, which most shaped independent filmmaking practice in the 1960s.

That said, I should also acknowledge that as much as I might like to, I cannot possibly include (even parenthetically) the work of every independent filmmaker who was working during the period under discussion; this text is primarily a work of recovery and regeneration. Concomitantly, since much has been written on several of the artists I consider within this text, I have examined their work briefly, without in any way intending or desiring to diminish their importance within the canon of experimental cinema, in order to include the lives and works of lesser-known artists. Thus we should consider anew the accomplishments and values espoused by these Avant-Garde American pioneer cinema artists; in a fresh consideration of their works, we may find new clues as to the origins of these important films, and new insights into the loose-knit community which brought about their creation.

In addition, this book seeks to present a newer, more unified history of the experimental cinema during this period, which returns to the egalitarian spirit of the era in which these films were produced. This is not an easy task; as Marcia Landy points out, "common-sense historicizing offers a seemingly unified narrative by relying on a sense of individual agency and of history as the final ground of moral and religious judgment. But through a critical lens, common-sense reconstruction of the past dissolves into a melange of competing perspectives, a multifaceted, polysemic representation of scenes, actors, and events" (129). In creating this text, then, I seek to avoid such an artificially unified narrative, organizing my text in roughly alphabetical order, but at every juncture seeking to privilege the voice of each artist above all other considerations, and allowing the leakage of discourse to flow freely from one film, and one filmmaker, to another.

At the same time, I seek to guard against the modular singularity of any one interpretation of these films as material artifacts, known to so few, and to de-center my own narrative within this text. Jacques Derrida noted that

> I don't believe one can retranslate ones own utterances in an exhaustive fashion. It's better to produce texts that leave and don't come back altogether, but that are not simply and totally alienated or foreign. One regulates an economy with ones texts, with other subjects, with ones family, children, desire. They take off on their own, and one then tries to get them to come back a little even as they remain outside, even as they remain the other's speech. This is what happens when one writes a text . . . You think it's talking to you, that you are talking in it, but in fact it talks by itself. (157)

And thus, for the most part, I have desired to allow these films and filmmakers to speak for themselves within the time period they were originally created in, as autonomous texts and entities requiring little translation for contemporary readers.

Mainstream cinema seeks to uphold the status quo; it has always been the domain of experimental cinema to seek to disrupt this artificially enforced order. The experimental cinema of the 1960s sought to question the legal and moral representations created in the dominant cinema practice. In the creation of these new works, experimental filmmakers embraced the notion that, "in regard to both time and space, the effect of the techniques of cinema is to pry perception loose from the larger world of which it is a part, subject it to extreme temporal and spatial condensation, and hold it suspended, floating in a seemingly autonomous set of dimensions" (Buck-Morss, 49). It is this autonomy of vision that was most prized by the '60s experimentalists, and their work covered a wide range of social, sexual, political and/or artistic concerns. The will to action in all human endeavor is that which seeks to celebrate the self; "in the will to suppress pain, we are led to action, instead of limiting ourselves to dramatization" (Bataille, 11).

The experimental cinema in the United States in the 1960s was nothing less than a call to decisive action to free the self from the dreams of the state, from the Orientalist strategies then pursued by the government in the prosecution of the war in Vietnam, from the neo-colonialist sign/system exchange apparatus ruthlessly applied by the dominant media. This new cinema was embraced by the transalterity of those for whom there has previously been no effective agency; it sought to escape the tyranny of history, and the commodification of the future in the mainstream cultural industry, through the abdication of all conventional standards of photographic representationalism. What was sought above all other considerations was a new way of apprehending the visual world, and of disseminating this vision to the widest possible audience. Financial gain was not a primary motive. What was at sake was nothing less than the care of the soul. What follows, then, is a compendium of those who worked within the cinema in the 1960s as an extension of their personal positionality within the social and cultural milieu of the 1960s, with commentary and interviews. It is not intended to be exclusive, but, hopefully, it will begin the process of historical renewal which this period so necessarily requires.

CHAPTER TWO

■■

Adachi to Higgins

One of the early figures of the Japanese Avant-Garde, **Masao Adachi**, made *Wan (Rice Bowl)* in 1962, a 10-minute 16mm sound film described by Donald Richie as "an exercise in surrealism involving a rice ceremony, black robes, a ceremonial sword, and a white-robed sacrifice" (Filmmakers' Cooperative [FMC] 1967, 7). Adachi then went on to direct *The Holeless Vagina*, a feature film released in Japan in 1963. As Adachi noted at the time, the film was initially impounded by the Japanese authorities on the grounds of obscenity, and was never screened commercially. Adachi, born in 1940, studied at the Nippon University Film School, graduating in 1963 (FMC 1967, 7). His work is simultaneously audacious and resonantly poetic, incorporating Adachi's sense of mystical involvement with the condition of human corporeality, and a gentle sense of a remembrance of childhood innocence.

Rudy Albers created a series of lyrical meditations on shape, color, and form, including *Cycle* (1966) and *Silent Music* (1966), "a film experimenting with the use of multiple exposed colored lights evoking the mystery of creation, stars and planets, atoms and electrons, souls and spirits" (FMC 1967, 7). In the summer of 1968, Rudy presented a multiple projector show of his work at the Filmmakers' Cinematheque at 125 West 41st Street. In addition to a battery of projectors mounted on stationary platforms at variable distances from the screen, Rudy operated two projectors independently, hand-held, melding the various images into a newly congruent whole of imagistic expression.

The poet **Daisy Aldan** (who brought Gerard Malanga into the world of experimental filmmaking) directed a beautifully evocative and impressionist documentary, *Once Upon an El*, in 8mm color with a 7 1/2 ips tape soundtrack. The 15-minute film's cast included John Ashberry, James Broughton, Chester Kallman, Frank O'Hara, Olga Petroff, Kermit Sheets, and other luminaries of the Avant-Garde; the soundtrack was composed by the noted filmmaker Storm de Hirsch. *Once Upon an El* documented the activities of "a group of artists, writers and composers [. . .] [demonstrating] against the demolition of New York's Third Avenue" elevated railway (FMC 1967, 7–8), which was demolished anyway.

Cinematographer **Nestor Almendros** was also an early supporter of the independent film movement, releasing his 10-minute short B/W sound film *Gente en la Playa* through the Filmmakers' Cooperative in 1967. **Maurice Amar** made *Concerto Flamenco* (1964), *The World of Guillermo Nunez* (1966), and *Discotheque U.S.A.* (1966). **Eric Andersen's** 8mm films included *Opus 49* and *Opus 53*. **Thom Andersen** made an early structuralist/minimalist film *Melting*, which in six minutes depicted "the natural monostructural disintegration of a strawberry sundae" (FMC 1967, 8), accompanied by a glissando soundtrack that prefigures Michael Snow's *Wavelength*, made several years later. **Yvonne Andersen**, working with **Red Grooms, Dominic Falcone**, and **the Yellow Ball Workshop** (a children's creativity center in Lexington, Massachusetts), created *The Amazing Colossal Man* (1964), *The Yellow Ball Cache* (1965), and *Spaghetti Trouble* (1963), all in 16mm sound. These films exhibit a childlike playfulness and a sense of disorganized spontaneity entirely in keeping with the spirit of the Yellow Ball Workshop.

An African-American filmmaker whose work during the 1960s has been unjustly marginalized is **Madeline Anderson**, who began working in December, 1958, for a company called Andover Productions (which was co-owned by filmmaker Ricky Leacock). For the *Omnibus* television series, Anderson and Leacock created *Bernstein in Europe*, following the legendary composer/conductor during his travels overseas, and also a series of science films for MIT. In December, 1960, Anderson left Andover Productions, and produced and directed *Integration Report One*, a film chronicling the Civil Rights struggle of the period. From 1963 to 1970, Ms. Anderson worked for WNET television (Channel 13) in New York City, as well as serving as an assistant editor on a number of feature films. At WNET, she worked on (according to her own notes), "the Black Journal series," where she became film editor, writer, and producer-director during the years this series won an Emmy and the NATRA awards. Anderson went on to produce, direct, edit, and write a half-hour film, *I Am Somebody*, for the Hospital Workers Union, Local 1199. This film won both national and international acclaim.

Anderson also worked at the Children's Television Workshop (CTW) on "Sesame Street" and the Electric Company. In 1987 Anderson was the senior producer of *Al Manaahil*, an award-winning Arabic literacy series produced by CTW International on location in Amman, Jordan. The series was broadcast in Jordan, Egypt, Morocco, Yemen, and Tunisia. In the '70s Anderson was the executive producer of *Infinity Factory*, a television series for eight to twelve year olds. The show taught children how to use math by problem-solving in everyday events. The target audience was inner-city children with an emphasis on African-Americans and Latinos. With this series Anderson became the first African-American woman to executive-produce a television series which aired nationally on PBS. The show was broadcast on over 256 stations.

In addition to producing and directing in film and television, Anderson has taught at the Columbia Graduate School of the Arts, Howard University and Delaware University, and has lectured at various colleges over the years. She has received many honors and awards: in 1976, the Woman of the Year (Sojourner Truth Festival of the Arts) award; in 1985, the Indie Award for Life-Long Achievement and Contributions to the Arts of Film and Television (the Association of Independent Filmmakers, AIFV); in 1991, she was one of the twelve honorees chosen by Miller Brewing Company for the Gallery of Great Black Filmmakers Calendar; and in 1992 she was inducted into the Black Filmmakers Hall of Fame. In a letter to William Greaves dated August 11, 1995, Anderson expressed great satisfaction that her work was still remembered; she is certainly one of the most important (and yet curiously underappreciated) talents of 1960s African-American independent cinema.

Kenneth Anger emerged as a major filmmaker in the underground during this period, with his most important films being *Fireworks* (1947), *Inauguration of the Pleasure Dome* (1954), and *Scorpio Rising* (1963). Of *Fireworks*, Jean Cocteau wrote that the film "comes from the beautiful night from which emerge all true works;" Anger himself says "this flick is all I have to say about being 17, the United States Navy, American Christmas and the Fourth of July" (both quotes as cited in *Canyon Cinema* 1992, 4). *Puce Moment* (1949) is a fragment of an abandoned feature film, *Puce Woman*. *Eaux D' Artifice* (1953) is a brief, abstract mood piece shot in Italy. *Inauguration of the Pleasure Dome* is an unbelievably lavish costume drama based on the writings and performances of Crowley. *Scorpio Rising* intercuts footage of motorbikers with stock scenes from a low-budget life of Christ and other materials, evoking the tribalism of outlaw biker society, cut to a sound track of early 1960s pop songs. *Kustom Kar Kommandos* (1965) was to follow this film, but was abandoned after funding ran out; all that survives is a 3 1/2-minute fragment of the intended film. In 1972, Anger completed *Rabbit's Moon*, a 7-minute short film using footage shot earlier in Paris.

Of *Invocation of My Demon Brother* (1969), I noted in 1969 that

> Kenneth Anger . . . has just completed a new film, *Invocation of My Demon Brother*, featuring Mick Jagger and Keith Richards of the Rolling Stones, and with an original soundtrack composed on the Moog synthesizer by Jagger. The 15 minute color film is the first work Anger has completed in five years, after the roughcut original for his projected feature *Lucifer Rising* was stolen from a locked trunk at the Straight Theatre in San Francisco after a benefit screening to help complete that work. Adding insult to injury, a few days later Anger's Bolex camera was stolen from his apartment in the Haight, and he took advertisements in underground newspapers pleading for the return of the film and his equipment. Nothing happened. Bitter and enraged, Anger took another series of full page ads in the papers, this time announcing his own death as a filmmaker, and vowing never again to make another film. Then he disappeared to France and nobody heard from him except close friends, and even they had only American Express for an address.
>
> But as might be expected, Anger could not put abandon the medium forever, and *Invocation of My Demon Brother* is a dazzling piece of cinema. The main character is a blood-robed sorcerer (Anger himself) who streaks around an altar in speeded-up motion, performing an invocation to raise a spirit, intercut with glimpses of bodies, eyes, tapestries, and the London Hell's Angels. There is also footage of the Brian Jones Memorial Concert put on by the Rolling Stones in Hyde Park, and a brief shot of Mick Jagger descending a staircase in stop-motion photography, heavily made-up. Jagger's score for the film is a real surprise, a sort of slicing drone that repeats endlessly with variations in texture and volume, like a John Cage tape loop piece. (Dixon papers, 1969)

Since this period, Anger has turned his attention to two very successful volumes of Hollywood gossip, *Hollywood Babylon I and II* (which also spawned a syndicated television series starring Tony Curtis), and his final (to date) 16mm experimental film, the resurrected *Lucifer Rising* (1974).

Sara Kathryn Arledge is one of the earliest unsung pioneers of the American experimental cinema, although her work is now undergoing a posthumous renaissance, thanks in large measure to the efforts of

FIGURE 1. Composite still from *Fireworks* by Kenneth Anger. Courtesy David Curtis.

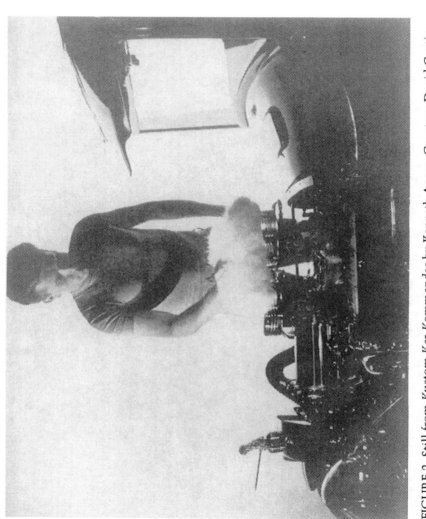

FIGURE 2. Still from *Kustom Kar Kommandos* by Kenneth Anger. Courtesy David Curtis.

Terry Cannon, who provided the stills of her work and other archival materials reprinted within this text. Her 1958 film *What Is a Man?* is an early exploration of the relationships between women and men in life and art; *Introspection* (1941–46) is an even earlier film created with the most primitive equipment, a worthy contemporary of Maya Deren's exactingly metaphoric cinema. In her films, Arledge seems to be examining the truth aptly set forth by Michel de Certeau, when he states that "a body is itself defined, delimited, and articulated by what writes it" (139). Arledge's camera seeks to abstract, and yet simultaneously demystify the human body, bringing the contested site of the human corpus into play with the cinematographic apparatus she utilizes in her work.

In an essay entitled "Speaking About the Art in Film," Arledge comments on her craft and ambition within the world of cinema:

> by improper direction and use of technical advances; by improper education; and, overall, by improper goals, we have created patterns of society and counter-patterns of living that are so dull that they can only be animated, temporarily, by sensationalism, which we find in the media, in politics, and in our sex lives. This sensationalism provides us with an excitement disconnected from the true significance of living. This shallow excitement moves our blood around and sometimes even passes for art. But it is the opposite of the function of art.
>
> The function of art is to awaken in us an understanding of our true potential. Sensationalism stunts growth and development of the most recently evolved part of the human mind—not only stunts it by the media, but by the usual school system's utter neglect of the right brain. People with active right hemispheres should be sought out for this training of our young. The old Roman letters carved in cement on the proscenium arch of universities, "Where there is not vision, the people perish," state a fact. We are facing the results of that fact now. While a way of seeing called "vision" animates artists' communications at times, true vision is non-transferable. Each human may discover her/his own, which also contains elements common to all of us. (Arledge n.d.)

Born in Mojave, California, September 28, 1911, Arledge obtained her education from the University of California in Los Angeles, graduating with a Bachelor of Education degree in Art in 1936. Arledge also attended Columbia University in New York in the summer of 1934, and obtained a grant from the Barnes Foundation to support her work as a painter and plastic visual artist from October 1934 to May 1935. She was a member of the faculty in the Department of Art at the University of Oklahoma from 1943 to 1944, and then at the University of Arizona–Tucson from 1945 to 1946, as well as the San

FIGURE 3. Production still from *What Is a Man?* by Sara Kathryn Arledge. Courtesy Terry Cannon.

FIGURE 4. Feminist film pioneer Sara Kathryn Arledge, March 4, 1980. Photograph by Barbara Hammer. Courtesy Canyon Cinema.

Francisco School of Advertising Art from 1947 to 1948, and the Oakland College of Arts and Crafts from 1948 to 1949, where she taught the art of making transparencies on glass. In addition to her work from 1941 to 1946 on *Introspection* (16mm color, sound, 6 minutes long) and her 1958 production of *What Is a Man?* (16mm, color, sound, 10 minutes), Arledge's later works include the 1978 films *Tender Images* (16mm color, 6 minutes), *Interior Garden I* (16mm color film, 7 minutes) and *Interior Garden II* (16mm color, 7 minutes), as well as the 1980 film *Iridum Sinus (Cave of the Rainbow)* (16mm color) and the 1983 film *What Do Two Rights Make?* (16mm, color, 15 minutes). Her paintings were exhibited at the Metropolitan Museum in New York, the Chicago Art Institute, the Los Angeles County Museum, the Art Exhibition of San Francisco World's Fair, the San Francisco Museum of Art, and the Aarnum Gallery in Pasadena, California, where Arledge was given a retrospective show of her entire body of work in 1978.

Sara Kathryn Arledge lived the last years of her productive life in Pasadena, California, and she was able to appreciate a revival of interest in her art through the concerted efforts of filmmaker Barbara Hammer and others who championed Arledge's pioneering work in cinema. Along with Maya Deren and Marie Menken, Sara Kathryn Arledge is one of the foremothers of the American experimental cinema, who worked tirelessly to perfect her art during the span of several decades when she was one of the few practitioners of independent cinema.

William Ault's *The Movie Set*, shot in 35mm "with an old hand-operated 35mm Pathé camera [. . .] as used to film [D. W. Griffith's] *Intolerance* [1916]" (FMC 1967, 11), is an attempt at "*re-seeing* or *re-visiting* [. . .] the set [. . .] of the Babylonian sequence from [. . .] *Intolerance* [using] a 15″ x 23″ still photograph [of the set] made from the original 8″ x 10″ negative taken back in the winter of 1915-16" (FMC 1967, 11). Thus, the film looks forward to Ken Jacobs's *Tom, Tom, the Piper's Son* (1969), which rephotographs (and thus "re-visits," or re-examines) a 1905 film "shot and probably directed by G. W. Billy Bitzer" (FMC 1989, 270), and can again be seen as a forerunner of the structuralist/formalist movement which would manifest itself more abundantly in the late 1960s, and the early to late 1970s.

Bruce Baillie, still one of the most active and pastoral of independent filmmakers, began creating a series of gorgeously transcendent films during the early days of the Canyon Cinema Cooperative (which Baillie helped found), with *On Sundays* (1960–61), *Mr. Hayashi* (1961), *The Gymnasts* (1961), *Have You Thought of Talking to the Director?* (1962), and *A Hurrah for Soldiers* (1962–63), this last film "dedicated to Albert Verbrugghe, whose wife was killed in Katanga by U. N. soldiers" (FMC 1967, 12). Baillie went on to international acclaim with the highly complex and multitextural films *To Parsifal* (1963), *Mass for the Dakota Sioux* (1963–64), and *Quixote* (1964–65). *Mass* won the Grand Prize at the Ann Arbor Film Festival in 1964, and firmly established Baillie's international reputation.

Later Baillie films, such as *Yellow Horse* (1965), *Scrambles* (1965), *Tung* (1966), *All My Life* (1966), *Still Life* (1966), *Show Leader* (1966), and particularly *Castro Street* (1966), consolidated Baillie's achievement within the cinema. More recently, he has created *Termination* (1966), *Valentin de Las Sierras* (1967), *Quick Billy* (1967–70)—a multi-part meditation on the mythos and structure of the Western film—and *Roslyn Romance (Is It Really True?)* (1974)—a sort of ecstatic diary film in the best tradition of the Beat(ific) sensibility. Baillie has had to work hard all his life to obtain financing for his independent films, as almost all filmmakers must; in 1964, he applied for (but did not win) a Ford Foundation Grant to support his work. Reflecting on his unsuccessful candidacy, he wrote in response to a questionnaire provided by *Film Comment* that he had intended to make "a 35mm work—material from over the U.S.—men and what they are doing—the land—the myths that can sometimes be seen, or heard, flowing beneath the land—a living museum of gesture, textures, etc., Andre Malraux's museum, in film," a work that in all probability became *Quixote*. Baillie noted also noted at the time that he had created "twelve motion pictures (16mm)—writing, directing, editing, financing, sound, etc.; four years' hard work, not much help" (12), a situation which is still very much the rule with independent film and video artists today.

Gordon Ball was born in Paterson, New Jersey, on December 30, 1944. His preschool education took place at Parkersburg, West Virginia; from ages five to seventeen, he went to school in Tokyo, Japan; he received his bachelor's degree from Davidson College in North Carolina. After this, he moved to New York and became involved in the Filmmakers' Cooperative, where he worked for a number of years. His first film was the 1966 production of *Georgia*, followed by apprentice work for Jonas Mekas. Then came seven years away from film and involving farming, editing books, entering graduate school. Ball returned to filmmaking in 1977, and completed four new films during the next three years. He received a Ph.D. in English in December, 1980.

Among Ball's best-known films are *Enthusiasm* (1979) and *Mexican Jail Footage* (1980). *Enthusiasm* is described by the filmmaker as "an elegy for my mother, the conditions of her dying, particularized &

detailed in terms of our individual personal & family experience; the
assumption being that there is something universal in all this—I
wanted to make a statement about our essential condition, & felt very
strongly that it must be direct and honest to the bone. Art must have
some spiritual information in some form or another; here I feel it's at
the heart." Ball describes *Mexican Jail Footage* as

> images from 1968 events combined with 1980 voice recollection. Para-
> noid surreptitious camera records daily events & posturings of 25 *grin-
> gos* jailed without charge—& fellow Mexican prisoners—prior to 1968
> Mexico City Olympics. Was there a larger collusion behind this? We
> were never told, but this was at height of Nixon-Agnew national polar-
> ization effort, when American tourists in Mexico were shocked to find
> more of the youths they thought they'd left behind—*and* when Mexican
> govt. was administering national preening in its own paranoiac antici-
> pation of international Olympics exposure 6 months later. [. . .] the
> soundtrack narration [is] culled from a much longer account I wrote of
> the event; it's told as directly as I could tell it [. . .] I'm not interested in
> technical polish or "smoothness" but in technical sincerity; the form of
> the film must take shape from the heart of the experience which engen-
> dered it. There are so many "smooth" films made now anyway that
> there should be room for those which are direct, honest, unique, and
> absolutely the representation of the soul of their maker. (letter to the
> author, 1995)

Other films by Gordon Ball include *Father Movie* (1977), *Millbrook* (1985), and *Do Poznania (To Poznan): Conversations in Poland*
(1990). *Father Movie* is a 10-minute silent film "made spontaneously
with news of my father's death—I kept a friend's Instamatic Super 8
in coat pocket as I headed to Winston-Salem and the rest home where
my father had died of a sudden stroke overnight. I filmed on highway,
in his abandoned rest home room, then drove weeping and filming at
the same time, one hand on wheel, other on camera, past the houses—
my sisters, his own—he and my mother had lived in after retirement
from life's work abroad." In regards to *Millbrook* (1985), with a running time of 9 minutes in color and sound Ball notes

> for aeons it's been the human family around a fire constructing and
> refiguring its basis myths: it's our earliest family or tribal "movie." So
> *Millbrook* recounts a mythical "true story," a life-changing event told
> against fire, the emblem of consumption and renewal: in the enormous
> forested estate once used by Timothy Leary, a young couple lose indi-
> vidual identity, merge with decaying leaves & are consumed by maggots
> as entire universe undergoes entropy, revives as it regenerates, and are
> saved from death by mysterious familiar stranger.

FIGURE 5. Childhood's afternoons in *Enthusiasm* by Gordon Ball. Courtesy Gordon Ball.

Do Poznania is a 17-minute color, sound 16mm film created out of

> personal glimpses of Polish life immediately preceding *glasnost*. Filmed during my two month-long visits (1986, 1988) as American Literature and Culture Specialist at Adam Mickiewicz University, it offers everyday street scenes, crumbling building facades; remains of death camps Auschwitz & Birkenau; Solidarity monument at Gdansk's Lenin Shipyard; and traveling shots of idyllic countryside, all in a handheld camera style: personal, raw, rapid, eccentric, intense—the opposite of Lowell Thomas or PBS. Charging the rapidly fleeting images are gists of conversations with Poles in which I took part, recreated back in Chernobyl; food; Communists; anti-Semitism; "free" education and work under Soviet socialism. The "voices" I re-present are urgent & multiple, and enrich the images with ambiguity, contradiction, and personal history. This film is an unpretentious, unconventional, unimposing, & uncompromising record of life in the last (& in some ways worst) days of a regime whose loss of power was just around the corner. (letter to the author, 1995)

The film was presented at the April Six Conference, Jagiellonian University, Krakow, Poland, on April 15, 1993.

Of his work as a filmmaker, Ball recently wrote to me that

> my approach to filmmaking is as old as that of the Lumieres nearly a century ago, when they recorded the feeding of baby and their workers leaving the factory. Except: I'm concerned not with recording objectively but subjectively. My work's autobiographical, diaristic, personal, non-professional, and my impressions and perceptions and fleeting glimpses are central. *Do Poznania* is not a film "on" Poland in the sense that many documentaries and educational films are; it doesn't strive for objectivity.
>
> This determines its style. I don't direct actors and actresses or interview people in home or street or office. I don't plan in the usual sense. I shoot (and can't re-shoot) according to my impressions and situations at the moment, and the style, with lots of quick cutting in a small handheld Super 8 (small format) camera, reflects that. This wedding of visual "insights" and circumstances of shooting (e.g., walking with friends to the Solidarnosc monument in Gdansk; hurrying toward or onto a train, having been warned not to shoot in stations; shooting fields at sunset out the window of a moving vehicle with only a few feet of film left, and utterly no knowledge of if there'll be another roll, or where it might come from) means that shots may appear awkward or brief—but in that failing they bear the diaristic stamp of my life.
>
> Why anyone else might be interested in a film with such features would be beyond me, but added dimensions can be given the images by the soundtrack. It consists of my "re-creation" of conversations (based

on memory and on written diary records) I had with Poles in two month-long summer work visits, 1986 and 1988. But the relationship of word and image is diffuse: often, at any one moment, there may appear to be no specific relation between the one and the other. At other times, it's one of contrast, irony: it's not, typically, the customary one-to-one ratio where if we hear, for example, "Kraków" on the soundtrack we should expect to see, say, the square in Stary Rynek (Rynek Glowny) or Jagiellonian University. This may seem contradictory, but the film is in a sense my efforts to come to grips with impressions of Poland.

So *Do Poznania* contains ambiguity and contradiction in the various views of a country and people it presents. It also reflects at least one bias on my part as well: I wanted to do something to express my love for the Polish people, for their ways of life in the face of centuries of difficulties, for the aesthetics of their daily lives, for the endurances of their spirit. Thus the soundtrack dedication at the film's outset, thus especially, perhaps, the movie's ending sequence. (notes in letter to the author, 1995)

Gordon Ball continues to work as a filmmaker and teacher at the Virginia Military Institute, and his work constitutes a resonant body of personal filmmaking wedded to his deepest humanist concerns as an artist.

Paul Bartel, who later made a reputation for himself as a "cult" commercial director with such films as *Eating Raoul* (1982) and *Scenes from the Class Struggle in Beverly Hills* (1989), began his career as a filmmaker with *Progetti* (*Plans*), shot in Rome in 35mm in the spring of 1962, and *The Secret Cinema* (1966), about a phantasmal film theater and its bizarre denizens, which Bartel later remade as an episode of Steven Spielberg's television series, *Amazing Stories*.

In San Francisco, the late video/film artist **Scott Bartlett** made a series of challenging and evocative films in the mid to late 1960s, fusing video and film techniques in such early classics as *Metanomen* (1966), *Off/On* (1967), and *Moon 1969* (1969). *Metanomen* used black and white high contrast cinematography to create a hauntingly bleak boy-meets-girl anti-narrative, set to a sitar soundtrack. *Off/On* was the first really pioneering film/video mix to come out of the underground, with the exception of the early work of Stan Vanderbeek in this area; the assault of imagery and the blasting electronic soundtrack combine to create a harrowing vision of the future of cinema/video constructs. Often imitated, the film remains one of the most effective examples of the genre. Although anthologized in numerous film archives around the world, *Off/On* still has not been accorded the full measure of attention it so clearly deserves; the film is comprised, for the most part, of a series of film loops which Bartlett manipulates through various rephotographing and video colorization techniques, to create an intense cybernetic journey which elevates both the consciousness and the external sensibilities of the viewer.

Moon 1969 explores the sensory limits of the viewer: the beginning moves slowly from complete blackness and blankness to glaring white, with aerial footage of an airport runway at night slowly washing in and out. It proceeds through a series of tempo changes until it reaches stroboscope intensity in the final minutes, and then caps everything with a long shot of the sun reflected in the sand at the edge of a beach. *Moon 1969* broke new ground, challenging then-existing preconceptions about videotape filmmaking and about humanist perception thresholds. Bartlett, in these films, seems to be asking "how much can the eye assimilate and the brain still understand?" Seen today, *Moon 1969* remains a remarkable achievement because it bypasses the mind and goes straight to the eye. "As soon as it admits the existence of the point, *the mind is an eye*" (Bataille, 118; original emphasis); in his resolutely non-linear, excessively spectacular kinesthetic works, Bartlett seeks to integrate the spectator-subject into the fabric of the visual construct being presented. The viewer, subjected to a benevolent aural/visual tyranny within the empire of the senses, becomes a willing receptacle of autosuggestion, inhabiting a space characterized by a mutuality of address between filmmaker and viewer/subject, a realm of visual/tactile sublimity. Bartlett's strongest films are those in which the artificial concerns of narrative are abandoned for sensation; it is in being for itself that we can best view *Off/On*, *Metanomen*, and *Moon 1969*.

Later Bartlett films included *Lovemaking* (not to be confused with the similarly titled film by Stan Brakhage; 1970), *Serpent* (1971), *1970* (1970), and *Medina* (1971). Bartlett's brief and explosive career as a filmmaker epitomized a certain style of West Coast cinema prefiguring the incipient merging of cinema and video imagery; in his embrace of a new sort of kinesthetic construction of image and sound, Bartlett single-handedly pushed film/video as a combinatory medium into the forefront of public consciousness. But despite his intense concern with the mechanics of vision, Bartlett's films retain a hold on the emotions and human memory. Bartlett was a romantic figure, whose marginalization is perhaps a consequence of his desire to cross-pollinate film and video into an ineffably complex hybrid medium, unlike the stripped-down essentialist cinema discourse which became the dominant form of cinema practice in the 1970s. In his embrace of the cinema/video construct, Bartlett was in many ways ahead of most of the other members of his generation, who insisted on a "purity" of image supposedly inherent in a strict adherence to either film, or alternatively video, practice.

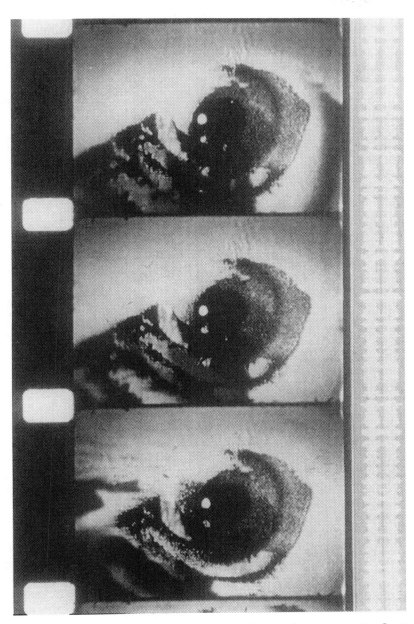

FIGURE 6. The panopticonic eye confronts the viewer in Scott Bartlett's *Off/On*. Courtesy David Curtis.

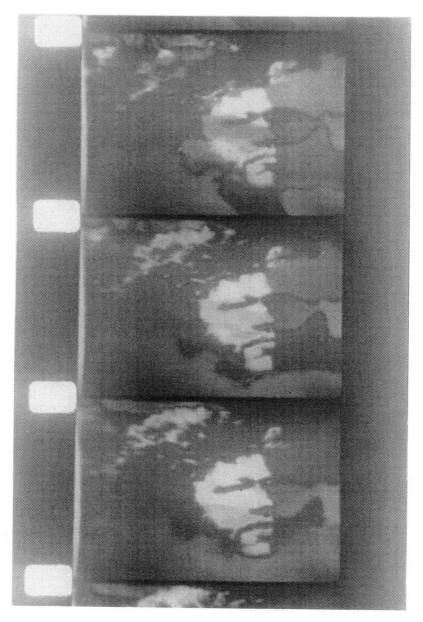

FIGURE 7. Video/cinema portrait of Scott Bartlett in his film *Moon*.
Courtesy David Curtis.

Bartlett rejected the then-prevalent notion of the video image as the landscape of death, of flesh transfigured into a matrix of multicolored pixels for material consumption by the passive viewer. Arthur and Marilouise Kroker refer to the "harvesting of the human flesh" (87) by the televisual apparatus, as it draws the viewer into its mechanism until the human body becomes a recombinant extension of the machine, rather than an auditor of it (the image before the flesh), but it is precisely this which Bartlett seeks to avoid. Bartlett's intensity of imagery and sound *mixage* alienates some viewers, who find his vision of the cybernetic image bank cold, or forbidding; in direct opposition to this, Bartlett himself invests his images (video and/or film) with an overwhelming plethora of humanist concerns, in which the human is always served by the visiotemporality of the electronic sign/system exchange.

Paul Beattie, whose films are apparently no longer in distribution, directed the 8-minute short *A Thimble of Goodbye* in 16mm B/W sound in the early 1960s, and followed this with *The T Cross, L, The 8th House, Finger-Water-Light ("F-W-L"), O, V,* and *Clarion;* these brief, epigrammatic and evocative films comprise an important contribution to the history of the early independent cinema.

David Bienstock, who tragically took his own life during one of the most successful periods of his career (he was curator of film at the Whitney Museum of American Art at the time), created two short films that present some measure of the work that he would have accomplished. *Nothing Happened This Morning* (1965) and *Brummer's* (1966), both of which were highly regarded and honored with numerous prizes and awards upon their initial release. Bienstock served for a time as the curator of film for the Whitney Museum of American Art, and the energy and vibrance of his personal vision is sorely missed in the world of contemporary American experimental cinema. What Bienstock might have accomplished had he chosen to live is a matter of absolute conjecture; his work is so absolutely original that his loss to the world of film is felt all the more keenly.

African-American producer/director/writer **St. Clair Bourne** began his career in American public television. His films have concentrated on the cutting edge of changing cultural and political themes, a focus he continues to explore in his work. As an independent filmmaker and head of the Chamba Organization, his production company, Bourne has more than thirty-three productions to his credit, including documentaries for public television in education and industry in collaboration with clients like *Sesame Street,* the American Institute of Architecture and the College Entrance Examination Board; network programs like NBC White Paper Special Report *Amer-*

ica: Black and White, which won the Monte Carlo TV Film Festival's Documentary Award; political films like *The Black and the Green,* in which African-American activists meet the IRA in Northern Ireland; and *On the Boulevard,* a dramatic short for television about two unemployed entertainers in Hollywood.

St. Clair Bourne's break with traditional television journalism and his change in direction toward more personal narrative films started with *Let the Church Say Amen!* (1973), a film chronicling the maiden voyage into the secular world of a young minister. Bourne then made his entrance into theatrical feature films as the co-producer of *The Long Night,* which premiered at New York's Museum of Modern Art's New Directors, New Films series. Based on Julian Mayfield's novel, the film had an American theatrical release as well as foreign broadcasts.

Bourne also produced a one-hour narrative performance documentary for the PBS *Voices and Visions* series; *The Gullah Connection,* dealing with the impact of tourism on the African "Gullah" culture of the South Carolina Sea Island people; and *Making "Do the Right Thing,"* Bourne's narrative documentary about the making of Spike Lee's controversial feature, which was invited to the Munich, Hawaii, Los Angeles, Amiens (France), Popoli, and Turino (Italy) film festivals and received national theatrical distribution.

Bourne's other films include *Soul, Sounds, and Money* (1969) a film examining Black musicians in the record industry, including Smokey Robinson, Isaac Hayes, and Gladys Knight and the Pips; *Big City Blues* (1981), showcasing a new generation of blues musicians in Chicago; *On the Boulevard* (1984), Bourne's first fiction film, which stars Lawrence Hilton-Jacobs as an unemployed musician who falls in love with a dancer on the streets of Hollywood; *In Motion: Amiri Baraka* (1983), examining the past and present of the famed Black poet and writer; *Langston Hughes: The Dream Keeper* (1986), with commentary from James Baldwin, Amiri Baraka, Gwen Brooks, Leopold Senghor, and Max Roach; *The South: Black Student Movements* (1969), a pioneering look at Black campus activism in the American south; *Malcolm X Liberation University* (1969) which tells the story of Black students leaving a White university to start their own school; *The Nation of Common Sense* (1970) on the Black Muslims, with an appearance by the Hon. Elijah Muhammed; and *Afro-Dance* (1970) on the Black dance movement, with Eleo Pomare and Percival Borde.

Bourne continues working in the documentaries for a six-part BBC series with Catalyst TV, a London-based company. Entitled *Will to Win,* the series explores the political impact of African and African-American athletes on international sports. He is currently preparing

FIGURE 8. Actualizing the self; St. Claire Bourne at work. Courtesy St. Claire Bourne.

to shoot a documentary about the role of African-Americans in the American West. Bourne is also developing three dramatic feature projects: *The Bride Price*, a contemporary romantic thriller set in Senegal about the romance between an African-American Peace Corps Volunteer and an African holy man's daughter; *Deacons*, a story of love and friendship strained over the role of Black armed self-defense during the 1960s Civil Rights period in the American south; and *Exiles*, the story of the expatriate community of U.S. Army deserters in Stockholm, Sweden, during the Vietnam War in the 1970s.

Bourne has designed and taught film courses at Cornell University and Queens College, served as guest lecturer at UCLA's Film and Theatre Arts Department and was a film consultant for the African Festival of Arts and Culture in Nigeria. He has given filmmaking seminars at Spike Lee's 40 Acres & a Mule Seminars and at Atlanta's Image Media Art Center. Most recently, he was invited by the Canadian National Film Board to give a seminar on documentary filmmaking at the Canadian Film Centre for the Canadian Black Film/Video Network. Bourne has received several fellowships from the National Endowment for the Arts, a Film/Video Fellowship from the Rockefeller Foundation and a Revson Fellowship from Columbia University. There have been retrospectives of Bourne's work at the Whitney Museum of Art in New York City, the Kennedy Center in Washington, D.C., and at the Cineclub Estacao in Rio de Janeiro, Brazil. St. Claire Bourne thus emerges as a very important African-American filmmaker, whose works deserve even greater public attention and screening. In all his projects, Bourne seeks what bell hooks correctly describes as "spaces of agency" (116), a strategy shared by many other marginalized members of the Avant-Garde cinema. These "spaces of agency" are ultimately areas to which one may lay definitive claim, spaces which allow one to make a statement in opposition to the dominant culture.

Filmmaker **Stan Brakhage** was born January 1, 1933, in Kansas City, Missouri, and was adopted as a child. He grew up in Denver, attending South High School as an A student. He went on to Dartmouth, but left after three months because of a minor nervous breakdown. Brakhage started attending art theaters in Denver and became intrigued by Roberto Rossellini's films. Motivated by the vision presented in Rossellini's raw, metanarrativistic works, Brakhage bought some war-surplus 16mm film, borrowed some cameras, and wrote and directed a film called *Interim*, a brief romantic narrative (25 minutes) which was simultaneously crude and vital. *Interim* was produced in 1953, and Brakhage has been making films ever since. Brakhage subsequently attended the California School of Fine Arts for one term to learn the fundamentals of camera work, and later moved to a log house in the mountains of Colorado beyond the small town of Rollinsville, where he lived and worked quietly with his wife, Jane, and five children during the 1960s and '70s. Now remarried, Brakhage teaches, and continues to produce films at the University of Colorado.

Brakhage became one of the most highly regarded of the new filmmakers, especially after *Dog Star Man*, his epic creation of the universe, was released to almost universal critical and audience acclaim. Several of his earlier films won prizes in Brussels, Uruguay, and Bergamo in 1958 and 1964; but when Brakhage himself finally judged a festival he began to turn against competitive festivals. In a previously unpublished interview in 1969, Brakhage noted that he "disapprove[d] of competition. This filmmaking must be the individual working out of his own necessities. Otherwise you undermine the process. There's a bad effect if [the filmmaker] loses a prize, and it's even worse if [the filmmaker] wins" (Dixon papers). Implicit in all of Brakhage's work as a filmmaker is an empirical connection with the spectator-subject as a paradigmatic force within the film being screened, rather than the consumerist recognition of perceptual relativity which serves as the foundation of dominant consumerist moving image constructs.

Brakhage's other films during this period include *My Mountain Song 27*, one in a series of 8mm films, documenting the weathers and seasons in stop motion, single frame photography; *Lovemaking* (1968), a 16mm 40-minute film about four visions of sexual loving which Brakhage described as "an American Kama Sutra and love's answer to filmic pornography"; *The Horseman, the Woman and the Moth* (1968), a 26-minute 16mm film employing numerous serially repeated hand-painted frames, inspired by the harpsichord sonatas of Scarlatti; and *Scenes from Under Childhood* (1967–70). *Scenes from Under Childhood* was originally conceived as the first chapter of a longer film called *Book of the Film*, a work evolving around incidents of daily living. In the late 1960s, Brakhage had been collecting and shooting for twelve years on the whole *Book of the Film*, and assumed that would be working on it most of the rest of his life.

Brakhage was an early advocate of home viewing of experimental films, and some of his films were offered in the late 1960s and early 1970s in 8mm format to subscribers through Grove Press. At the time, Brakhage presciently commented that "to be as an art form, [film] needs to be in the home. 8mm reduces the price to that of an art book. It should be feasible in the future to put 8mm into cassettes to give people a balanced film library. Otherwise you are stuck with the situation of an art form in which you have to make it with one screening in a public auditorium" (Dixon papers).

Brakhage continues to turn out films at a torrential pace today; his other films (to mention just a very few of the literally hundreds of films Brakhage has created during his lifetime of work) include *Desist-film* (1954), 7 minutes; *The Way to Shadow Garden* (1954), 10 minutes; *In Between* (1955), 10 minutes; *Reflections on Black* (1955), 12 minutes; *The Wonder Ring* (1955), 6 minutes; *The Dead* (1960), 11 minutes; *Thigh Line Lyre Triangular* (1961), 5 minutes; *Blue Moses* (1962), 11 minutes; *Oh Life, A Woe Story, The A-Test News* (1963), 5 minutes; *Mothlight* (1963), 4 minutes; *Dog Star Man: Complete* (1961–1964), 78 minutes; *Three Films: Bluewhite, Blood's Tone, Vein* (1965), 10 minutes; *Fire of Waters* (1965), 10 minutes; *Pasht* (1965), 5 minutes; *Two: Creeley/McClure* (1965), 5 minutes; *Scenes from Under Childhood Section #1* (1967), 25 minutes; *Scenes From Under Childhood Section #2* (1969), 40 minutes; *Western History* (1971), 8 minutes; *Sexual Meditation: Room With View* (1972), 4 minutes; *Purity, and After* (1978), 5 minutes; *Sincerity III* (1978), 35 minutes; *Sluice* (1978), 6 minutes; *Aftermath* (1981), 8 minutes; *Flesh of Morning* (1956; re-edited 1986), 25 minutes; *Caswallon Trilogy* (1986), 10 minutes; *Confession* (1986), 27 minutes; *The Loom* (1986), 50 minutes; *Glaze of Cathexis* (1990), 3 minutes; *Vision in Meditation #3: Plato's Cave* (1990), 18 minutes; *Vision in Meditation #4: D. H. Lawrence* (1990), 19 minutes; and *First Hymn to the Night—Novalis* (1994), 3 minutes. Brakhage's energy continues unabated to the present day; if anything, he is at the peak of his career as an artist, and his energy and audacious tenacity of vision mark him as one of the major artists of the twentieth century in any medium.

The free-spirited **Bob Branaman**, better known as a painter, worked for years in standard 8mm, eventually releasing a 30-minute reel of his silent work through the Filmmakers' Cooperative in 1966. These unnamed films involve much use of superimpositions and flash frames, all created within the camera. It is a minor miracle that even this sparse reel of 8mm footage survives; for much of the '50s and '60s, Branaman lived in a beach shack in Big Sur, California, and after an extended trip he returned to the shack one day to find most of his films and equipment stolen. Despondent, Branaman felt that he might never be capable of creating any new films, and it is only through the efforts of Anthology Film Archives that we have any copies of Branaman's films at all. Those images which have been saved offer us a tantalizing glimpse of a major talent at work. We might wish that Branaman had given us more to look at, but the materials he *has* gifted us with are remarkably tough, kinetic chunks of raw cinematic energy.

Interviewing animator **Robert Breer** during the late 1960s, I took away these impressions:

Robert Breer's films, with a few exceptions, are almost entirely single frame stop motion animations. Since 1952, Breer has made over twenty films that explore the visual effects achieved by juxtaposing, twenty-four times a second, independent visual images. Occasionally, the images have continuity, and some of his films have live action, such as *Pat's Birthday* and *Homage to Jean Tinguely's Homage to New York*. But these are side trips from his main aesthetic concern: the exploration of retinal persistence of vision. Born in 1926 in Detroit, Breer had a rather uneventful high school education, and entered Stanford in 1943. Unsure of his life's work, he was persuaded by his father to take up engineering (his father, also an engineer, designed the Chrysler Air-Flow, the first streamlined car). He studied engineering for a while, but soon switched to art. World War II interrupted his studies, and he served two years in the army at various posts around the states. He painted signs, did portraits of personnel, designed syphilis posters. Discharged, he returned to Stanford, and took up art with a new enthusiasm. Graduating in 1949, he left for Paris and spent a decade there, painting and beginning films in 1952. His first completed film was *Form Phases I* (1953), then *Form Phases II, III* and *IV* through 1954. His first film using unrelated, continuous images was *Images by Images I* (1954). Ten seconds long, the film is a succession of 240 stills. Breer cut it into a loop, and ran the film through the projector. Intrigued by the result, he continued his experiments in this area through 1956, also making some short line animations.

Jamestown Baloos (1957) marked the culmination of his work during this period and was followed by *Par Avion, A Man and His Dog Out for Air* (both 1957 line animations), and *Eyewash* (1958–59) which incorporates live action photography and film tinting. *Homage to Jean Tinguely's Homage to New York* (1968) is essentially a document of Jean Tinguely's self-destructing sculpture performance in the sculpture garden of the Museum of Modern Art. But through careful editing and photography, the film becomes a separate work of art as well. Following this, Breer returned to line animations with *Inner and Outer Space* (1960), and unrelated image-collage films with *Blazes* (1961). These were followed by *Horse Over Teakettle* (1962), *Pat's Birthday* (1962), of which he says, "Things happen after each other in the film only because there isn't room for everything at once," and *Breathing* (1963), *Fist Fight* (1964), and *66* (1966). His newest film, *69* (1969), is one of his most accomplished works. Basic geometric shapes are rotated against a background of changing (twenty-four times per second) colors. The drawings intertwine, forming new configurations, somewhat like an eggbeater's blades do. This is interspersed with chunks of black leader to space the film into stylistic segments.

Married in 1955 to Frances Foote, whom he met in Paris, the Breers live with their three children, Sophia, Emily and Julia, in a small house in Sneden's Landing. His garage has been converted for film work: it contains his animation apparatus, as well as an improvised projection

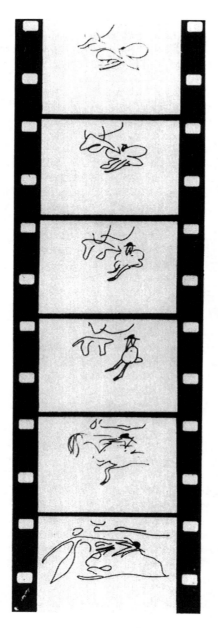

FIGURE 9. Minimalist lines gather to form the construct of Robert Breer's *A Man and His Dog Out for Air*. Courtesy David Curtis.

room. Up a hill from his house he rents a barn for his sculpture work. He has been devoting more and more time to sculpture, fabricating "floats," small crescents, half circles and other basic geometric shapes which move at about six inches a minute so that they move almost imperceptibly, and seem to change position without moving. They are powered by small battery motors that change direction when they bump into a wall or another object. He has built floating columns, a mylar sheet with motors inside it so that it slowly tumbles across the floor, as well as mutoscopes, rotating stovepipe constructions, and gilded license plates mounted on a stand with rackets. His sculpture has been exhibited a number of times at the Bonino Gallery in New York, located at 7 West 57th Street.

When he started, Breer had an income of "zero." However, he works quite inexpensively: he built his animation stand from a 16mm Bolex and a frame and table, and by skill and care he manages to use almost everything he shoots. [In 1969, Breer created] a sculpture project for the Pepsi-Cola pavilion at the upcoming Osaka world's fair. (Dixon papers, 1969)

Breer went on in the 1970s to the present day to produce the animated short films *69* (1968), *70* (1970), *Gulls and Buoys* (1972), *Fuji* (1973), *Rubber Cement* (1975), *77* (1977), *Lmno* (1978), *T.Z.* (1979), *Swiss Army Knife with Rats and Pigeons* (1987), *Trial Balloons* (1982), and *Bang!* (1986). Breer's daughter Emily is now an established filmmaker in her own right, with such films as *Chicken* (1981), *Stork* (1982), *Fluke* (1982), and *Spiral* (1987).

David Brooks, who "died on February 26, 1969 at the age of 24" (FMC 1971, 47), created *Jerry* (1963), *Nightspring Day Star* (1964), *Winter* (1964–66), *Letter to D. H. in Paris* (1967), *The Wind Is Driving Him Toward the Open Sea* (1968), and *Eel Creek* (1968), a serious of dazzlingly poetic considerations on the vicissitudes of human existence. Brooks left behind a plethora of unedited footage which was subsequently edited and released by his wife Carolyn as *Carolyn and Me (Parts One, Two, and Three)*, with a total running time of more than 90 minutes in 16mm color with an accompanying taped soundtrack, as well as two half-hour reels entitled *Late Fragments (1963–66 and 1966–69)*.

James Broughton was one of the most productive San Francisco filmmakers in the late 1940s and '50s. His films *Mother's Day* (1948), *Adventures of Jimmy* (1950), *Loony Tom, The Happy Lover* (1951), *Four in the Afternoon* (1951), *The Pleasure Garden* (1953), and perhaps most notably *The Bed* (1968), are suffused with a gentle eroticism and a tender sense of Chaplinesque comedy. Later films, such as *Nuptiae* (1969), *The Golden Positions* (1970), *This Is It* (1971), *Dreamwood*

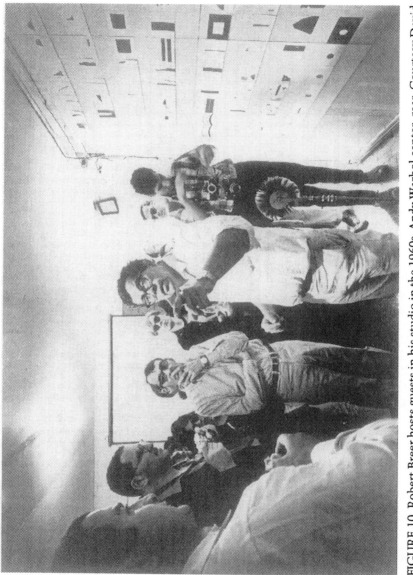

FIGURE 10. Robert Breer hosts guests in his studio in the 1960s; Andy Warhol center, rear. Courtesy David Curtis.

(1972), *High Kukus* (1973), *Testament* (1974), *The Water Circle* (1975), *Erogeny* (1976), *Together* (1976), *Windowmobile* (1977), *Song of the Godbody* (1977), *Hermes Bird* (1979), *The Gardener of Eden* (1981), *Shaman Psalm* (1981), *Devotions* (1983), and *Scattered Remains* (1988) continue Broughton's lifelong quest for (in the filmmaker's own words) "a world where men have forsaken rivalry and taken up affection, thereby creating a society that relishes a variety of comradely devotions" (FMC 1989, 86).

Rudy Burckhardt, whose son Jacob is also a filmmaker, created an entire series of films beginning in the late 1930s, including *Haiti* (1938, a 16-minute B/W documentary of that country on the eve of World War II); *The Pursuit of Happiness* (1940); *Montgomery, Alabama* (1941, a 4-minute color film of Burckhardt's reactions to the city while in the military); *The Climate of New York* (1948, in collaboration with William Flanagan; this film was described as "perceptive, stark, [. . .] sharp and memorable" by A. H. Weiler in *The New York Times*, as cited in FMC 1989, 89); *The Aviary/ Nymphlight/A Fable for Fountains* (1955–57); *The Automotive Story* (in collaboration with Kenneth Koch and Frank O'Hara); *East Side Summer* (1959); *Under Brooklyn Bridge* (1953); *What Mozart Saw on Mulberry Street* (1956); *Mounting Tension; Millions in Business and Usual; How Wide Is Sixth Avenue*; and in the 1960s, *Miracle on the BMT* (1964, in collaboration with Mimi Gross, Red Grooms, and Ken McIntyre), *Lurk* (1965, a Frankenstein parody starring Red and Mimi Grooms and Edwin Denby, with music coordinated by Frank O'Hara and narration by Denby), *Goodmorning, Hyacinth and Junction* (1966), and *Daisy* (1966).

More recently, Burckhardt has persevered with his craft despite the ever-mounting costs of film production to create a gallery of personal films such as *Square Times* (1967), *Money* (1968), *Tarzan* (1969, starring the legendary comedian Taylor Mead in the title role), *Summer* (1970), *Made in Maine* (1970), *Doldrums* (1972), *Caterpillar* (1973), *Slipperella* (1973), *City Pasture* (1974), *Default Averted* (1975), *Saroche* (1975), *The Bottle of the Bulge* (1975), *Dwellings* (1975), *Sodom and Gomorrah, New York 10036* (1976), *Good Evening, Everybody* (1977), *Alex Katz Painting* (1978), *Sonatina and Fugue* (1980), *All Major Credit Cards* (1982), *Indelible, Inedible* (1983), *The Nude Pond* (1985), *In Bed* (1986), and *Zipper* (1987).

In an article originally written in English, but published only in a German language anthology of film history and theory, critic Catrina Neiman discussed the ground-breaking work of experimental filmmaker **Mary Ellen Bute** (I quote from the original English manuscript provided to me by archivist Terry Cannon; the page numbers and German citation of this work will be found in the bibliography):

FIGURE 11. External space and asynchronous non-interaction in *Mother's Day* by James Broughton. Courtesy Anthology Film Archives.

Bute is said to have been the first American to make abstract films and the first filmmaker anywhere to use electronically generated images (photographed off a cathode ray oscilloscope). Beginning in 1933, she produced 12 animated films and then turned in the late '50s to making dramatic features, the last of which was *Passages from Finnegan's Wake* (1967). Directing features, she complained, was "2% creative and 98% hard work," but she had said the same about animation. Before she discovered the oscilloscope, each of her animate films, just 6–9 minutes long, required making 7000 photographs, after doing all the drawings. Bute was assisted by her husband and co-producer, the skilled cameraman Ted Nemeth, who shot her earliest films and taught her how to use the camera: thereafter she did her own photography.

Bute's goal, even as a young painter, was the synthesis of light and movement, color and sound. She was frustrated by what she thought of as the "inflexibility" of painting—the confines of the frame, the flatness of the surface and, above all, its insistent muteness. "There were so many things I wanted to say, stream-of-consciousness things, designs and patterns while listening to music. I felt I might be able to say [them] if I had an unending canvas." Bute set herself the goal of developing "kinetic art" and pursued it with the drive and curiosity of a scientist. The most advanced field at the time, she said, was stage lighting, which she learned at Yale Drama School, operating its "fabulous switchboard." In New York in 1929 she sought out Thomas Wilfred, who had developed the Clavilux light-organ, an early light-show instrument used for entertainment in convention halls and to accompany religious meditation at St. Mark's-in-the-Bowerie church. The following year she apprenticed herself to electronic music pioneer Leon Theremin, conducting experiments in the "use of electronics for drawing," and studied at the same time with the musicologist, Joseph Schillinger, whose methods for composing music with mathematics she applied to painting, "using form, line and color, as counterparts to compositions in sound." Still hungering for "a medium in which movement would be the primary design factor," Bute put off turning to film, at first thinking it too commercial. It was Oskar Fischinger's *Hungarian Rhapsody* that convinced her she could do anything she wanted with it [. . .] (see Neiman, 111–126)

William Cannon's 87-minute feature film *The Square Root of Zero* (1966), photographed by Sheldon Rochlin (who later made the beautiful feature film *Vali*, 1966), and featuring music by Elliot Kaplan, was shot in 35mm "on a small island off the coast of Maine" (FMC 1967, 33) when Cannon was only twenty-five years old. It received favorable reviews during its initial release from *Film Daily* ("rare offbeat satire") and Leonard Lyons in the *New York Post* ("displays a flair for tenderness without sentimentality and parody without pettiness," as cited in FMC 1967, 33), but has not been exhibited for a number of years. *The Square Root of Zero* remains a ground-breaking satire in the tradition of Jonas Mekas's *Guns of the Trees* (1962), and Robert Downey Sr.'s *Babo 73* (1964) and *Chafed Elbows* (1966).

During this same period, **Adolf Centeno** made the beautiful cinematic fantasy *End of a Day* in 1966. This 15-minute B/W sound film has been compared to the early works of the French Surrealist filmmakers. In addition, **Myrna Changes** made the post-slapstick comedy *The Neighborhood* in 1966. The completed 20-minute film was shown to receptive audiences at the 1966 San Francisco Film Festival and elsewhere, but has since been unjustly forgotten. **Pola Chapelle** created *A Matter of Baobab* in 1967. This extremely brief (50-second) film featured cameos by Jonas Mekas, filmmaker Louis Brigante, Storm de Hirsch, Contessa Angela Maria Andreacci Castiglione and Adolfas Mekas, and was prized at the Montreal Film Festival in 1967.

Martin Charlot's feature film *Apocalypse 3:16*, starring Myron van Brundt and Tom Kealiinohomoko, was completed in 1966 and had a commercial theatrical run in New York City in the summer of 1968; *Boxoffice* (a commercial journal not generally known for its keen artistic insight, being more concerned [as its name implies] with the commercial aspects of cinema) cited the film as "a piercing piece of film that combines shocking horror and tender beauty, violence rich in unrelenting quiet and a strange quietness oozing with tension . . .," while *Die Tat* in Zurich hailed the film as "strong and new [. . .] Charlot has brought out a true Avant-Garde pioneer work" (as cited in FMC 1967, 35). *Apocalypse 3:16* is remarkable both for its relaxed, nearly anarchic construction, and the beauty and transfiguring ferocity of its imagery; it stands as one of the most important and simultaneously most neglected of the many experimental feature films produced during this era.

Mention should certainly be made here of the work of two key artists who began their careers in the 1960s, whose output was carefully considered and compactly presented. **Tom Chomont's** filmmaking began in the mid 1960s with *Flames* (1965), *Night Blossoms* (1965), *Anthony* (1966), and *Mona Lysa* (1966). Chomont continues to work in cinema to the present day, more recently creating *Phases of the Moon* (1968), *Love Objects* (1971), *Abda/Rebirth* (1974), *Space Time Studies* (1977), and *Minor Revisions* (1979). **Dan Clark's** anarchic and deeply personal films during the early 1960s, all in 8mm, included *Garbage* (1961–63), *Rebirth* (1963), *Blood* (1964), *Twelve Loops* (1965), and *One to One* (1963–66); *One to One* is a full length feature, with a running time of 121 minutes.

Before she made *The Connection* in 1960, *The Cool World* in 1963, and *Portrait of Jason* in 1967 (all feature length films), which

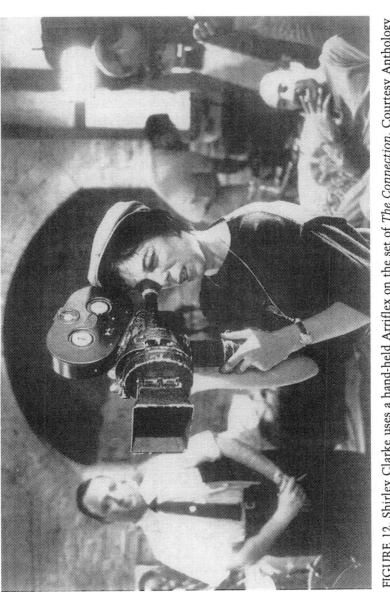

FIGURE 12. Shirley Clarke uses a hand-held Arriflex on the set of *The Connection*. Courtesy Anthology Film Archives.

have been examined extensively elsewhere, filmmaker **Shirley Clarke** made a series of sensuous and evocative short films including *Dance in the Sun* (1953), *In Paris Parks* (1954), *Bullfight* (1955), *Moment in Love* (1957), *Brussels Loops* (1958; these brief film loops, designed to be run repeatedly through a series of film projectors, were ultimately "destroyed by the U. S. State Department" [FMC 1967, 37]), *Bridges-Go-Round* (1958, with music by Teo Macero), and *Skyscraper* (1959). Of all these films, perhaps *In Paris Parks* strikes me the most forcefully as a film of indefatigable romanticism and gently nostalgic mimesis. Clarke's feature films are an altogether different matter: while *The Cool World* is a rather conventionally straightforward narrative, *Portrait of Jason* is a Warholian marathon exercise in cinematic voyeurism, in which Clarke photographed cabaret artist Jason Holliday for many hours, and then edited the result down into a brutally compact indictment of society's indifference to Jason's plight as a gay African-American, whose ambitions of nightclub stardom were ultimately never realized. *The Connection*, based on a stage play by Jack Gelber, chronicles the drifting nonexistences of a group of junkie jazz musicians waiting for a fix; Clarke's camera restlessly prowls the loft where the hapless addicts wait for their daily injection of heroin to arrive. The film is both convincingly realistic and unflinchingly detailed; Arthur Knight, writing in the *New York Times*, said of *The Connection* that "as in Antonioni's films, the camera insists that we look" (as cited in FMC 1967, 38); indeed, the power of the prolonged gaze seems to be at the center of all of Clarke's most powerful work.

Kip Coburn worked at the perimeters of filmic consciousness with a group of intensely personal, yet modest 8mm films. *Cocaine, Flesh, Hitchiker, Johns Doll, Trips, Stoned,* and *Colors,* all 8mm shorts from the early 1960s with running times between 8 and 20 minutes when projected at 16 fps, document an intense odyssey through varying states of altered consciousness with unabashed directness and naturalism, displaying a Carnivalesque dualism in their construction which belies the simplicity of their porphryic origins.

The figure of **Kathleen Collins** represents yet another unjustly marginalized figure in cinematic discourse; this gifted African-American filmmaker created a compelling body of original and transcendent work during the brief span of her life, from 1942 to 1988. Born in Jersey City, New Jersey, Kathleen Conway Collins Prettyman received her B.A. in Philosophy and Religion from Skidmore; after studying in France in French literature and cinema, she received her M.A. and Ph.D. from Middlebury. From 1967 to 1974, Collins worked as an editor for National Educational Television on such programs as

FIGURE 13. Jason Holliday in Shirley Clarke's *Portrait of Jason*. Courtesy Anthology Film Archives.

American Dream Machine, The 51st State, and *Black Journal.* She later worked for the BBC, the United States Information Agency, and William Greaves Productions, among others, before accepting a post at the City College of New York in the Theatre Arts Department, teaching courses in the theory and production of film.

As a filmmaker, Collins's most important works are undoubtedly *The Cruz Brothers and Miss Malloy* (1980), and *Losing Ground* (1982), both completed only after heroic measures by Collins and her cast and crew. Indeed, *The Cruz Brothers* was begun with an initial investment of a mere $5,000 and *Losing Ground* began principal photography with only $25,000 of the film's $125,000 final production cost in place. As recounted by Phyllis Rauch Klotman, before her death Collins "completed six plays, all of which were produced or published, four screenplays, numerous short stories, and a novel" in addition to her work as a filmmaker (123). Collins's untimely death robbed the American cinema of one of its most original and innovative talents. For more on Collins's works, the reader is directed to Klotman's *Screenplays of the African American Experience,* which is still the foremost text on Collins's life and work (see especially 123–185 in Klotman's study).

Poet **Gregory Corso** made a 20-minute silent B/W "film in progress" with Jay Socin, entitled *Happy Death;* Jonas Mekas observed that the vision the film presents "is not a very happy death [. . .] it is more decay than death" (FMC 1967, 40). Although Corso's major contribution to the culture of the 1960s is unquestionably his work as a textual poet, this lone film work represents a challenging and disturbing contribution to his extensive and influential body of work as a writer. Another unique talent during this period was filmmaker and occasional Filmmakers' Cinematheque projectionist **Robert Cowan**, who created a series of violently beautiful films (often working with the Kuchar Brothers' star, Donna Kerness), in *Child, Summer Dance, Evocation, Solo* (all 1965), *River Windows* (1966), *Academy Luncheon* (1967), and most notably in the horrific *Soul Freeze* (1967), of which critic D. J. Ben Levi said "from *Soul Freeze* there is no escape, only an endless embrace of hell" (FMC 1967, 41). For many years, Cowan also wrote incisive film criticism for the critical journal *Take One.*

Storm De Hirsch was one of the true pioneers of the underground cinema, although her work is often neglected today. Aside from her superb 35mm feature *Goodbye in the Mirror* (1964), shot in luminous black and white on location in Rome (with her husband, Louis Brigante, functioning as assistant director), De Hirsch also created several books of poetry including *Twilight Massacre, The Shape of Change,* and *The Atlantean Poems,* as well as the film *Journey Around a*

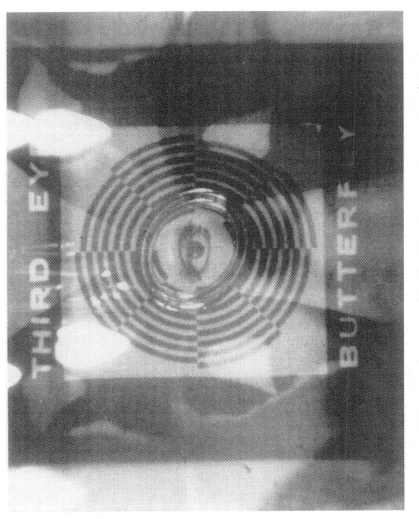

FIGURE 14. Still from Storm De Hirsch's *Third Eye Butterfly*. Courtesy David Curtis.

Zero (1963), 3 minutes, B/W. The aforementioned 35mm feature *Goodbye in the Mirror* (1964), an 80-minute, B/W feature of unparalleled sensual beauty, starred Rosa Pradell, Franco Volpino, Diane Stainton, Barbara Apostal, and Charlotte Bradley. Photographed by Giorgio Turi, with songs arranged and sung by Pola Chapelle, the film centers on the lives of three American expatriates in Rome, who search for some new meaning in their lives through a series of tangled relationships and uncertain alliances. The film is shot, for the most part, with a hand-held camera, and post-dubbed, but the technical crudity of the execution of the film in no way mars the finished work's impact, much in the same way that Ron Rice's *The Flower Thief* paradoxically benefits from its impoverished, even desperate production circumstances. Other De Hirsch films include *The Color of Ritual, The Color of Thought* (1964–67); *Divinations* (1964), 5 1/2 minutes; *Peyote Queen* (1965), 9 minutes; *Shaman, A Tapestry for Sorcerers* (1967), 12 minutes; *Newsreel: Jonas in the Brig*, 5 minutes, B/W, silent (24FPS); *Sing Lotus* (1966), 14 minutes; *Cayuga Run. Hudson River Diary: Book I* (1967), 18 minutes; the abstract animation film *Trap Dance* (1968), 1 1/2 minutes, B/W, in which the images are scratched directly onto the film itself with surgical instruments; the two-screen projection film *Third Eye Butterfly* (1968), 10 minutes; *The Tattooed Man* (1969), 35 minutes; and many other works. De Hirsch also created the film *An Experiment in Meditation* (1971), 18 1/2 minutes, B/W, Silent (24FPS). Her personal and poetic images constitute an important addition to the literature of the experimental cinema in the 1960s.

Maya Deren's work is well known, even among members of the general public. Although her main period of work was during the 1940s and '50s, her influence is too pervasive not to provide a few words here on her hypnotic, sensuous work. Much has been written on Deren, but an unfortunate canonical side effect of this plethora of material is that Deren's work has been allowed to overshadow the films produced by other feminist artists during this period of cinematic endeavor, marginalizing the equally important films of Sara Kathryn Arledge and Mary Ellen Bute. Deren's classic experimental short dream film, *Meshes of the Afternoon* (made in 1943, with music by Teiji Ito, who also created several soundtracks for Marie Menken's films), was one of the key films of 1940s American Avant-Garde cinema. *Meshes of the Afternoon* was co-made with Deren's then-husband Alexander Hammid; some revisionist critics have even gone so far as to claim that the film is primarily Hammid's, but this claim seems difficult to substantiate.

FIGURE 15. Storm De Hirsch gestures during a lecture. Courtesy Anthology
Film Archives.

FIGURE 16. Maya Deren filming with her Bolex in 1946. Courtesy Anthology Film Archives.

Of Maya Deren's life, critic Gwendolyn Foster notes that

Deren's father was a Russian-Jewish psychiatrist from whom Deren learned a great deal of Freudian theory and an interest in ontological investigations. [Deren] was educated in Switzerland and went to college at Syracuse University and New York University. She earned a Master of Fine Arts degree from Smith College, where she wrote on the French symbolists' influence on imagist poetry. Deren then moved to Greenwich Village, where she wrote poetry and began a book on modern dance theory in collaboration with choreographer Katherine Dunham [. . .] Deren went to Los Angeles in 1941, where she met Czechoslovakian documentarist Alexander Hammid, with whom she collaborated on various projects and whom she later married. (Foster, 111)

Deren's work as a filmmaker, poet, and dancer subsequently continued in Los Angeles and New York, and she traveled on location to Haiti for her posthumously released feature *Divine Horsemen: The Living Gods of Haiti*. Tragically, Deren died of a cerebral hemorrhage in 1961 at the age of 44.

Deren's films, including *At Land* (1944), *A Study in Choreography for Camera* (1945), *Ritual in Transfigured Time* (1946), *Meditation on Violence* (1948), *Divine Horsemen: The Living Gods of Haiti* (a 54-minute feature shot by Deren on location from 1947 to 1951, and completed after Deren's death by Teiji Ito and Cherel Ito in 1977), and *The Very Eye of Night* (1958) are all heavily influenced by Deren's interest in dance theory, psychology, dreams, and the work of those experimental filmmakers who came before her. Deren's work is highly polished, and lulls the viewer into a receptive trance where images of death, erotic desire, and sexual urgency are played out in intricately choreographed dance sequences. Her documentary *Divine Horsemen: The Living Gods of Haiti* is one of the most effective examples of a filmmaker being at one with the subjects of her film, as Deren photographs the ritual religious ceremonies of a group of Haitians with an easy confidence born of a complete immersion in the subject. Deren's work is the subject of numerous books and essays; perhaps the most comprehensive survey of her work can be found in *The Legend of Maya Deren*, an anthology of Deren's writings, and other critical materials on her work, edited by Anthology Film Archives.

Keewatin Dewdney is the maker of a series of brief, early structuralist films in the late 1960s, including *Malanga* (1967), which documents the poet Gerard Malanga reading his poems and dancing to the music of the Velvet Underground in increasingly short bursts of image and sound, until the sound and image alternate on a frame-by-

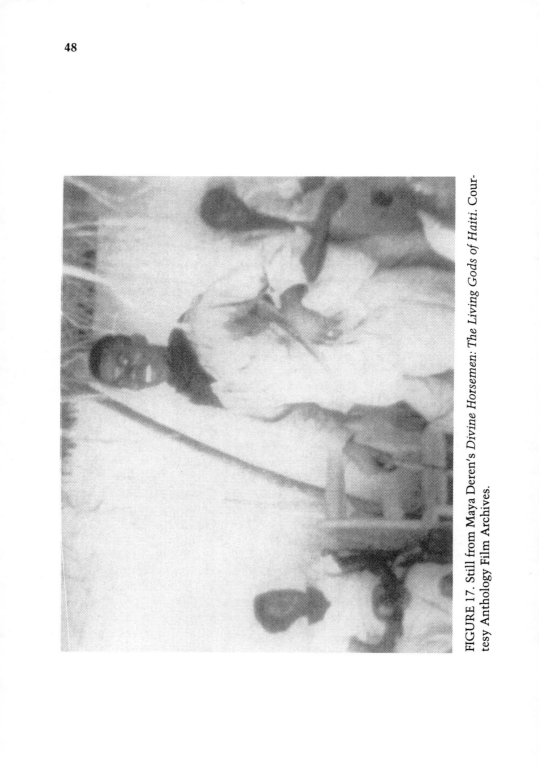

FIGURE 17. Still from Maya Deren's *Divine Horsemen: The Living Gods of Haiti.* Courtesy Anthology Film Archives.

frame basis, much in the manner of Paul Sharits's work; *The Maltese Cross Movement* (1967), in which a series of objects are gathered into the structure of the film, only to be broken down into the syllabic structures which comprise their taxonomy, and then reassembled in a variety of surprising combinations; as well as *Scissors* (1967), Dewdney's first animation film; and *Four Girls* (1967), in which images of four young women are intercut with the commodifying image-structures which dominated "fashion" in clothing during the period. In a rare interview conducted via e-mail on February 26, 1996, Dewdney offered these thoughts on his life and work:

> I was born on August 5, 1941 in London, Ontario, just 120 miles up the road from Detroit. This was why it was so natural for me to drift across the border to do graduate work in Ann Arbor, Michigan. My films are as much about the 1960s (now that I think about it) as they were about anything else. Everybody wanted to redefine themselves, some through imagery. My father was a painter, by the way, so I grew up thinking in images. I began to make films in Ann Arbor Michigan while a graduate student in math. It was the 1960s and the world was coming apart at the seams, but in a most interesting way. "There has to be more to life than math and science," I said to myself, so I enrolled in George Manupelli's filmmaking course for one semester in 1966. I purchased a Bolex camera and began to work on single frame animations, producing *Scissors* in about a month of work at home with an animation frame built out of 2 x 4s. I became fascinated with rapid-fire imagery. The idea that led to *The Maltese Cross Movement* was a synthetic approach blending sound and visual imagery, pushed by the syllabic process, the pressure that causes us to shorten words when we make syllables out of them on the way to hieroglyphic writing. That's why you see a certain amount of Egyptian and Middle Eastern symbolism in the movie.
>
> In all I made six movies. The movie I always wanted to make, but never did, was an animation involving real objects. Take a circle. You can find circles in a lot of places, like hubcaps, shower heads, pupils of eyes, door knobs, and so on. Shoot, say, two frames of each circular object and make sure that each new subject has its circle in the same place (or nearly so—therein lies the art). The effect would be stupendous! *The Maltese Cross Movement* won the Canadian Artists '68 award for Non-Narrative Film. The pressure of teaching computer science pretty well blew away the filmmaking career. I'm not involved with film any more, except at the moment I'm a consultant for a project with IMAX (the big screen guys) who are making a movie based (loosely) on one of my books, *The Planiverse*, about a whole world of 2-dimensional beings. (e-mail interview with the author)

Dewdney's films remain an early link to the structuralist film practice of the late 1960s through the 1980s, and as such, an important part of

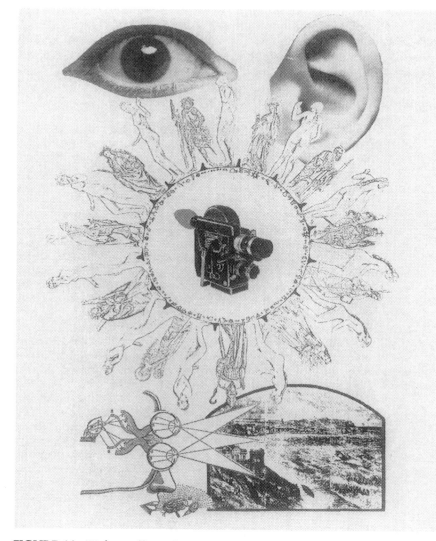

FIGURE 18. "Bolex collage" by Keewatin Dewdney from *The Maltese Cross Movement*. Courtesy Keewatin Dewdney.

the heritage of the American independent cinema. Recent university screenings of Dewdney's works demonstrate that they have lost little of their power, and continue to fascinate and enthrall contemporary audiences, as they did when first released.

Bert Deivert is another filmmaker who created a series of sensuous and original films in the early 1970s through the 1990s, and now does work with futurists Arthur and Marilouise Kroker, along with pioneering work programming on the World Wide Web. Deivert graciously consented to a series of interviews on his life and work over the Internet on November 28, December 1 and 10, 1995, from his present home in Karlstad, Sweden, where he is Senior Lecturer in Film Studies at the University of Karlstad. Deivert shared these thoughts on his films:

> *Deja Vu* (1970) was the first film I ever made, and was influenced by Dali and Buñuel. My film instructor, Warren Bass, helped me a lot on this one. All the people in the film were students at the college, and some of them were asked by Anna Bass, Warren's wife, to come to be in a student film that evening. Just picked right off the campus! Others were theatre majors and friends. I was 19 when we shot it and 20 when it hit the festivals. This spurred me on to the decision of becoming a filmmaker/teacher and giving up theatre [. . .] *John* (1971) was an actor improvisation film which started out in an acting class with these two classmates of mine [. . . a] totally improvised film which was formed in the editing process.
>
> *Lamentations IV: Black Kristian* (1995) is a culmination of thoughts about masculinity/femininity, eyes, colors and their opposites, sexuality, my older films, color/black and white, and an impressionistic interpretation of Steve Gibson's composition. For me, it was like a catharsis . . . I freed myself from a lot of frustration of NOT being able to do film for years because of no money or access to equipment. I was able to deal with that, my past, my former films, and start moving in a new filmic direction. That the film was made for performance makes it slightly less interesting as a stand-alone, but I feel it is very much in line with what I used to do, and is a logical progression for me. By the way, talk about low budget . . . I made *Lamentations IV* for less than 100 dollars, the cost of the BETA videotapes! I filmed the 16mm material projected on a wall into the Betacam camera because the cost of scanning at the lab was 400 dollars an hour! I was pleased with the quality.
>
> *Lamentations IV: Black Kristian* was chosen for screening at the performance of "Hacking the Future" with Arthur and Marilouise Kroker, Steve Gibson (composer of the soundtrack), David Kristian and Mark Bell at the International Symposium on Electronic Art in Montreal, ISEA 95. The next film will be going somewhere else, but using computer graphics, and mix between video and 16mm. (e-mail interview with the author, Nov. 28, Dec. 1, 10, 1995)

FIGURE 19. "Rocket collage" by Keewatin Dewdney from *The Maltese Cross Movement*. Courtesy Keewatin Dewdney.

Bert Deivert's Web Page can be found at: <http://www.hks.se/~bertd/toc.html>.

My own independent filmmaking career began in the early 1960s. I was a member of the Filmmakers' Cooperative from 1966 on, making 16mm films, working on an informal basis at the Cooperative, and screening my work at various theaters and festivals. I later taught at Rutgers University, Livingston College, and the New School for Social Research. Of my personal films made during the late 1960s and early 1970s, my favorites remain *Tight Rope* (1972), *Serial Metaphysics* (1972), *London Clouds* (1970), *Numen Lumen* (1973), *A Devotion for Travellers* (1969), *The DC Five Memorial Film* (1969), *Wedding* (1968), *Quick Constant and Solid Instant* (1969), *Dave's Fantastic Fifties Rock Group* (1968), *Gaze* (1974), *Damage* (1974), and *Stargrove* (1974).

Of my film *Serial Metaphysics*, on the occasion of the film's projection at the Whitney Museum of American Art, then-curator Bruce Rubin commented: "**Wheeler Winston Dixon** is a masterful film editor. His sensitivity to the movement within the frame and of the camera itself allows for a fluidity in his editing that is exuberant and refreshing. He is skillful not only in manipulating the flow of images but the flow of ideas as well [. . .] even the mundane world we so readily accept beings to look somehow dreamlike and unreal." And of my short film *Tight Rope*, Stan Brakhage wrote that

> [it is] an unusually balanced film, a very simple film (but, then, one which knows itself), an evolution of feeling poised (occasionally) on a single pinpoint of light, its two "halves" like two thought processes which counter each other without ever encountering. Light is the subject matter, beginning in sun & ending at fireplace: but this continuity is not permitted to disturb the singular emotion of the film. I am especially intrigued by the stops and starts within zoom and pan movements—these metaphoring eye-movement more exactly than the usual smoothness [. . .] thus keeping the work most carefully personal. (FMC 1975, 71)

Singly or in one-person shows, my films have been screened at the Museum of Modern Art, the Whitney Museum of American Art, the Museum of the Moving Image at the National Film Theatre, London, the Filmmakers' Cinematheque, the Elgin Theatre, the Amos Eno Gallery, the Gallery of Modern Art, the Oberhausen Film Festival, Yale University, Rutgers University, and elsewhere.

As the 1970s progressed, I began working at Rainbow Special Effects with William Nemeth (brother of Ted Nemeth, who was married to Mary Ellen Bute), and created the films *Un Petit Examen, And*

FIGURE 20. Dreams of the absent empire in *The DC Five Memorial Film*. Courtesy Canyon Cinema.

FIGURE 21. Wheeler Winston Dixon in 1969. Photo by Bruce Nadelson. Courtesy Canyon Cinema.

Not So Damned Petit, Either, or the Light Shining Over the Dark (1974), *An Evening with Chris Jangaard* (1974; the film was shot in a single night on outdated black and white high-speed film stock, and documents the life of a friend of mine who was being forced to leave the country), *Dana Can Deal* (1975), and *Madagascar, or Caroline Kennedy's Sinful Life in London* (1974). These films were followed by *The Diaries* (1986), a split-screen compilation of my filmic diaries up to that point in my life. After these personal projects, I concentrated on working within the industry in Los Angeles, eventually becoming involved with Michael Shamberg's TVTV Group as an editor on various projects. By the time I returned to personal 16mm filmmaking with the Postfilm narrative *What Can I Do?* (1993), a feature film starring Anna Lee which premiered at Anthology Film Archives and the Museum of Modern Art in 1993/94, I was more active as a critic than a filmmaker, although I continued to make new films as funding permitted. This new emphasis on critical/theoretical production has culminated with my most recent feature film, the 80-minute French-language *Squatters* (1994), shot in Super 16mm sync-sound outside of Paris in the summer of 1994. On May 24, 1997, the Millennium Film Workshop in New York City presented a retrospective of my work, screening roughly fifteen of my early films from 1969–1972.

Nathanael Dorsky is one of the most accomplished practitioners of the independent cinema, who has managed over the years to juggle a masterful career as an independent filmmaker with many commercial editing assignments, usually as a post production supervisor, on *Frontline* and other television series for PBS. Nathanael's personal films, dating from the earliest days of the New York experimental film scene, include *Ingreen* (1964), 16mm, sound, color, 12 minutes; *A Fall Trip Home* (1965), 16mm, sound, color, 11 minutes; *Summerwind* (1965), 16mm, sound, color, 14 minutes; and *Hours for Jerome* (1966–82), 16mm, silent at 24 FPS, color, 50 minutes. Dorsky notes that the footage for *Hours for Jerome* "was shot from 1966 to 1970 and edited over a two year period ending in July 1982. *Hours for Jerome* (as in a Book of Hours) is an arrangement of images, energies, and illuminations from daily life. These fragments of light revolve around the four seasons. Part One is spring through summer; Part Two is fall and winter."

Pneuma (1976–83) is a 16mm, silent, color film running 29 minutes, and designed to be shown at 18 FPS, which Dorsky describes by noting that

> in Stoic philosophy "pneuma" is the "soul" or fiery wind permeating the body, and at death survives the body but as impersonal energy. Similarly the "world pneuma" permeates the details of the world. The images in this film come from an extensive collection of outdated raw

FIGURE 22. The landscape of memory in *A Devotion for Travellers*. Courtesy Canyon Cinema.

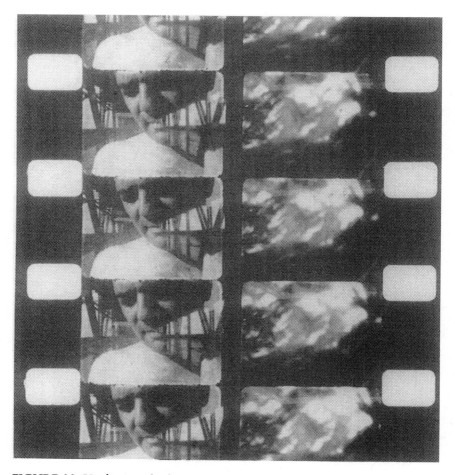

FIGURE 23. Unslit Standard 8mm footage creates multiple frame imagery in *17 Reasons Why* by Nathanael Dorsky. Courtesy Nathanael Dorsky.

stock that has been processed without being exposed, and sometimes rephotographed in closer format. Each pattern of grain takes on its own emotional life, an evocation of different aspects of our own being. A world is revealed that is alive with the organic deterioration of film itself; the essence of cinema in its before-image, preconceptual purity. With the twilight of reversal reality this collection has become a fond farewell to those short-lived but hardy emulsions. (letter to the author, summer 1995)

Dorsky's next independent films were *Ariel* (1983) 16mm, silent, 18 FPS, color, 16 minutes; *Alaya* (1976–87) 16mm, silent, 18 FPS, color, 28 minutes; and *17 Reasons Why* (1985–87) 16mm, silent, 18 FPS, color, 20 minutes—a film that Dorsky describes as being ". . . photographed with a variety of semi-ancient regular 8 cameras and is projected unslit as 16mm. These pocket-sized relics enabled me to walk around virtually 'unseen,' exploring and improvising with the immediacy of a more spontaneous medium. The four image format has built-in contrapuntal resonances, ironies, and beauty, and in each case gives us an unpretentious look at the film frame itself . . . the simple and primordial delite of luminous Kodachrome and rich black and white chugging through these time worn gates" (letter to the author, summer 1995).

Nathanael Dorsky and Jerome Hiler have been working within the cinema for more than thirty years, and their work continues to impress one with its visual audacity and the uncompromising integrity of its vision. Unlike Jerome Hiler, Nathanael Dorsky makes meticulously "timed" (color-corrected) prints of his work, and regularly screens his films at museums and film festivals. The precise control of stop-framing, light, grain texture, and color in *Hours for Jerome* (to select just one of Dorsky's many evocative and deeply personal films) directly reflects the patience and craft that Dorsky brings to all his work. The silence of many of Dorsky's films is the perfect accompaniment for a complete appreciation of the images he creates; any sort of a soundtrack would detract from the overall impact of the film's imagistic construction.

In his work, Dorsky harnesses the fabric of light and daily existence, as filtered through the lens of the cinematographic apparatus, and creates a new vision of life as we would like to live it, the sublime moments of existence when all elements seem to coexist in perfect harmony and balance. In his considerations of the qualities of film grain and the characteristics of reversal film, he is a structuralist possessed of a great warmth and humanity, and even his most austere films have a romantic and subtly quixotic visual structure. Nathanael Dorsky's films constitute a unique and compelling body of work

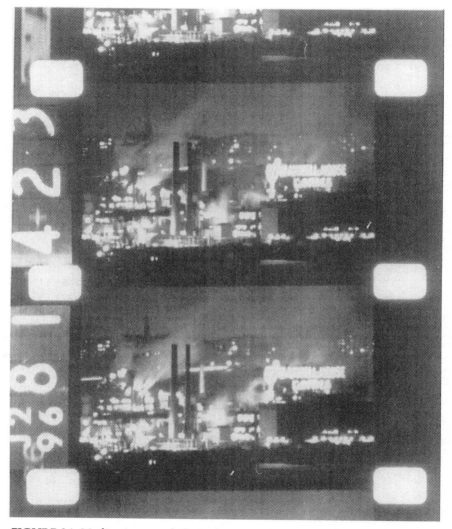

FIGURE 24. Meditations on daily existence in *Hours for Jerome* by Nathanael Dorsky. Courtesy Nathanael Dorsky.

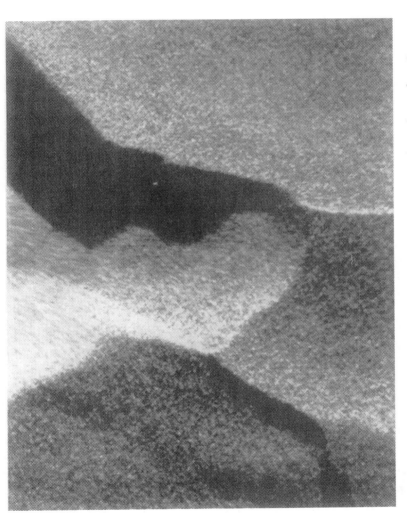

FIGURE 25. Film grain becomes the image in *Alaya* by Nathanael Dorsky. Courtesy Nathanael Dorsky.

within the contemporary American independent cinema, and it is to his credit as a filmmaker than he continues to create films today, even in the face of rising film production costs and disappearing lab facilities. Dorsky's films are works of what Vivian Sobchack has termed *"transcendental determinism*—based on the belief in the film object as *meditation-in-itself"* (18; original emphasis). One sees an equally meditational vision in the films of Gehr, Snow, and Frampton. Dorsky's apprehension of the apparatus of the cinema considers certain inimical filmic characteristics (grain, light, the passage of time, the inevitability of decay, changing color dyes and granular patterns) as the central concerns of his investigations.

Robert Downey, Sr. emerged as one of the most prolific and audacious satirists in the New American Cinema in the 1960s with *Balls Bluff* (1963; Downey later incorporated this footage into his 16mm pastiche film, *No More Excuses* [1968]), *Babo 73* (1964), and *Chafed Elbows* (1966). *Babo 73* stars Taylor Mead as "a newly elected President of the United Status (sic) . . . [featuring] bold swipes at, among other targets, the Catholic Church, the Civil Rights Movement, international diplomacy, *Time*, God, shoe-fetishism, psychiatry, the South, the North, the East, and the West [. . .] Mead looks like a cross between a zombie and a kewpie and speaks as if his mind and mouth were full of marshmallow" (Brendan Gill, the *New Yorker*, as cited in FMC 1967, 46). *Chafed Elbows* was described by Downey as a film "about a man who marries his mother, they go on welfare, and it all breaks into a musical" (FMC 1967, 46). *Chafed Elbows* was an enormous commercial success. Downey Sr. went on to direct the feature films *Putney Swope* (1969)—a brutal satire on advertising—along with *Pound* (1970), *Is There Sex After Death* (1971), *Greaser's Palace* (1972), *Rented Lips* (1988), and *Too Much Sun* (1991), a purposefully tasteless and cheerfully offensive feature film starring his son, the actor Robert Downey, Jr. In all of Downey Sr.'s work as a filmmaker, one finds a cheerful and confident glee in the manner in which he deconstructs the sites of power in 1960s cultural production, both as consumerist and/or colonialist zones of haptic transcendence, in which the self may triumphantly reassert its individuality outside the realm of social constraint.

Ed Emshwiller's work as a filmmaker arose out of his long career as a science-fiction illustrator, and he brought a fine sense of discipline and professionalism to his craft after he embraced the medium of the cinema. Emshwiller won a Ford Foundation grant in 1964, which he used to create the epic consideration of the human condition entitled *Relativity* (1966); before that, he built a considerable reputation on a series of elegantly crafted short films with meticulous attention to detail and judiciously glossy production values, including *Dance Chromatic* (1959), *Lifelines* (1960), *Thanatopsis* (1962), *Totem* (1963), *Scrambles* (1964), and *George Dumpson's Place* (1965). *Relativity*, a 38-minute inner voyage in which, as Emshwiller described it, "a man wonders, measures, views relationships, people, places, things, time, himself" (FMC 1989, 153), was an international success, and allowed the director to create *Image, Flesh and Voice* (1969), *Carol* (1970), *Film with Three Dancers* (1970), *Branches* (1970), *Choice Chance Woman Dance* (1971), *Scape-Mates* (1972), *Chrysalis* (1973), *Sunstone* (1979), and other films in the latter part of his career. Since his death, with the assistance of Emshwiller's widow, Carol, Emshwiller's work has been screened on numerous occasions at Anthology Film Archives, including a complete retrospective cycle of his films.

Edward English's *The Family Fallout Shelter* (1962) won the Screen Director's Guild Award for that year as best experimental short film. *The Fugs* (1963) documents the life and work of the pioneering rock group, the Fugs, as they pursue their art and craft amid the sights and sounds of the lower East Side of Manhattan. **Shirley Erbacher** created a series of lyrical Cine-poems in 8mm, each about 3 minutes long, all silent (run at 16 FPS) and in color, including *Playground* (1963), *Snow* (1965), *Dawn* (1966), *Kyle* (1972), and the *Dance* series (nos. 1–8, 1966–1972). She emerged as one of the most gifted and unpretentious creative artists of the early New York Avant-Garde, working on the fringes of cinematographic representationalism. Erbacher continues her work today; she was recently given a screening at Anthology Film Archives of her most recent works.

The Fluxus Group, spearheaded by **George Maciunas**, presented a 96-minute program of short silent experimental film works in the summer of 1966, featuring films by **Eric Andersen** ("*Opus 74, Version 2*—Color. Single Frame Exposure: 1 min."), **Chieko Shiomi** ("*Disappearing Music for Face* . . . transition from smile to no-smile within 12 min. Shot at 2000 ft./sec."), **John Cale**, better known as a member of the rock group the Velvet Underground, and now a composer of scores for feature films ("*Police Car*—Color: 1 min."), **Paul Sharits** ("*Sears Catalogue, Dots, Wrist Trick*—Single Frame Exposures: 10 sec."), **George Landow** ("*The Evil Faerie*—2 min."), **Yoko Ono** ("*Match Striking and Burning.* Shot at 2000 ft./sec.: 5 minutes"), **Wolf Vostel** ("*Sun In Your Head*—5 min."), **James Riddle** ("*9 minutes*—Exact time given each second if projected at 24 ft./sec. Good test film to check accuracy of projector") and others (FMC 1967, 51). The compilation won "The Moss Tent Award (a lightweight high-count Poplin Moss Mountain Tent)" (FMC 1967, 50), when it was screened in competition at the Ann Arbor Film Festival in 1966, and epitomizes the anarchic freedom of individual artistic expression in the 1960s.

The poet and lithographer **Charles Henri Ford** produced *Poem Posters*, a 20-minute color sound film, to document an exhibition of his work at the Cordier and Ekstrom Gallery. The film features camerawork by Charles Boltenhouse, Charles Henri Ford, Gregory Markopolous, Marie Menken, Ed Sanders, Stan Vanderbeek, Andy Warhol, Bud Wirtschafter and others; appearing in the film are "Jayne Mansfield, Frank O'Hara, Ruth Ford, Ned Rorem, Virgil Thomson, Claes Oldenburg, Roy Lichtenstein, William Burroughs, Andy Warhol, Rudy Gernreich, Jonas Mekas" and other luminaries (FMC 1967, 52) of the New York art world during this period.

The late **Hollis Frampton** was one of the most noted and prolific filmmakers of the 1970s independent cinema scene; in the early to late 1960s, he was still finding his voice as a filmmaker. Early films such as *Manual of Arms* (1966), *Information* (1966), *Process Red* (1966), *States* (1967/70), *Heterodyne* (1967), *Snowblind* (1968), *Maxwell's Demon* (1968), *Surface Tension* (1968), *Palindrome* (1969), *Carrots and Peas* (1969), *Lemon* (1969), and other short works paved the way for the epic *Zorn's Lemma* (1970), and the complete *Hapax Legomena* series (1971–72). The series is a 3-hour-and-22-minute work comprised of numerous sections, including *Nostalgia* (1973), *Poetic Justice* (1972), *Critical Mass* (1971), *Traveling Matte* (1971), and other formalist exercises. Frampton's unique sensibility forces the viewer to question both the known limits of perception and that which is unknown. In *Surface Tension*, a series of seemingly disconnected episodes coalesce into a mysteriously satisfying metanarrative structure; *Lemon* concentrates on the tactile empiricism of a common, everyday fruit with remarkably contemplative results; *Zorn's Lemma* pushes the viewer through a rigorous series of precisely timed shots toward a surprisingly serene apotheosis; *Hapax Legomena*, too rich to take in even after several viewings, meditates on the act of seeing, or not seeing, and on what happens within and outside of the film frame.

Later Frampton films attacked equally ambitious themes. *The Red Gate* (1976) and *The Green Gate* (1976), from *The Magellan: At the Gates of Death* series, confront the filmmaker's own mortality in movingly metaphoric terms. For much of his life, Frampton was physically ill, and he seemed driven, impelled to create his films in the face of his impending demise with ever increasing rapidity. Rigorous, austere, and yet darkly playful, Hollis Frampton's unique investigations into the cinematographic process are a unique testament to his own sensibility as a filmmaker; it is somehow fitting that his works come near the end of the period under discussion.

Robert Frank, who has worked as a still photographer, painter, collagist, sculptor and filmmaker, who would later create the moving documentary *Me and My Brother* (1969), as well as the elusive and legendary *Cocksucker Blues*, documenting a 1971 tour by the Rolling Stones, began his filmmaking career with the short film *Pull My Daisy* (1959), a 30-minute, 35mm B/W sound film starring Allen Ginsberg, Gregory Corso, Peter Orlovsky and Larry Rivers, with narration by Jack Kerouac. In view of the film's legendary cast, *Pull My Daisy* has become something of a cult classic for aficionados of the Beat era, and was most recently revived in 1995 at the Whitney Museum of American Art as part of a show curated by critic Raymond Carney. Frank followed this film with *The Sin of Jesus* (1961), a dark and brooding 40-minute film, described by Jonas Mekas as a document of the "pessimism, [. . .] desolation, doom, or despair [which is] the inner landscape of modern man, a place that is cold, cruel, heartless, stupid, lonely, desolate . . ." (FMC 1967, 52), before turning to longer films in the late 1960s.

Two widely disparate visions in 1960s experimental cinema were offered by Japanese filmmaker **Kazutomo Fujino** and **Edd Dundas**. Fujino's film *An Eater* (1963) is a 20-minute Japanese film described by scholar Donald Richie as a "very funny surrealist extravaganza" (FMC 1967, 54); at the same, expatriate filmmaker Dundas, working in Japan, created a riveting film entitled *The Burning Ear* (1964), chronicling a young man's spiritual search through the landscape of modern Tokyo. Both Dundas and Fujino were resolutely individual talents of the era, and their work deserves to be widely screened, and restored to its rightful place within in the canon of 1960s experimental cinema practice.

Arnold Gassan, originally a still photographer, created several short films in the early 1960s, including *The Doors* (1963; no relation to the rock group of that name), *American Dreams* (1964), and the documentary *Brakhage on Film* (1966). My own favorite of Gassan's works is *Marsyas* (1962), with Don Crawford, which effectively blends positive and negative footage, silence and sound, to convey the torment of a young African-American seeking to establish a personal identity within a hostile society. No less an authority than Stan Brakhage called *Marsyas* "a positively beautiful work of cinema art" (FMC 1967, 53). In the film, a young African-American wakes from a troubled sleep to face a nightmarish vision of the American metropolis. The man flees to the country as the phantoms of civilization pursue him. At length, exhausted, he falls to the ground, and Gassan presents several vivid scenes of an animal being virtually castrated. Back in his apartment again, as the film cycles in upon itself, the African-

American reawakens to discover that he has been transformed into a White male during his sleep. Peering at his new visage in the bathroom mirror, the young man realizes that White American civilization seeks to assimilate him, and destroy his racial identity. Not shown since 1966, the film has recently been revived in university screenings to considerable acclaim.

Filmmaker **Ernie Gehr** was born in the Midwest in 1945. Gehr traveled around the states for a while, finally settling in New York in 1966. He started going to Cinematheque screenings when the theater was located on 41st Street, and eventually decided to make films of his own. Gehr bought a cheap 8mm camera, and began filming short studies. In all, he shot about twenty-five reels, and edited some of them into films, *Wind* and *Mosquito Towers* among them. At this point, he was more or less experimenting from style to style—baking the film, scratching it, painting it, et cetera. His early films resembled the early work of Stan Brakhage: dark, somber, lighting; hand-held camera work; intense montage editing. Gradually, however, Gehr began to use fewer of these devices and concentrate more on the abstract qualities of objects, animate and inanimate. Gehr's camera became more controlled, and he did most of his editing in the camera.

In September, 1967, Gehr switched to 16mm. His first 16mm film was a home movie thing with some friends in Vermont. He was by this time moving the camera very little, leaving it fixed most of the time on a tripod, and editing almost entirely within the camera. During this period, he had been listening to the music of Karlheinz Stockhausen, the electronic composer, and had been intrigued by Stockhausen's interest in intensities of tone, fragmentation, tonal durations, and dissonances. Gehr set about to translate this to film, and hit upon the use of f-stops as comparable to the pitch of the notes. From here, he began to map out an entire aesthetic for film as music. In December, 1967, he shot his first film using this framework, *Wait*. By opening and closing the camera iris (over and under exposing the film), frame by frame, he produced a flicker effect of rather startling quality. The film was shot in color, and as Gehr used this process, the variations in light would alter the colors the film stock produced in the final print. Coupled with the use of slow zooms, pans, time exposures, and straight shots without the "flicker effect," Gehr produced a completely new visual look for the new American cinema.

Since this auspicious beginning, Gehr has pursued a kinesthetic sensibility in his subsequent works, playing with audience perceptions of time, space, memory, and image retention. Gehr's superbly compact *Serene Velocity* (1970) is a tour de force voyage down an empty institutional hallway achieved entirely through the zoom lens

FIGURE 26. Light transforms the internal landscape in *Wait* by Ernie Gehr. Courtesy Ernie Gehr.

of a stationary camera. *Signal - Germany on the Air* (1982–85) is a meditation on inhabited and open/isolated spaces, merging formalist concerns with a spirit of humanist inquiry. *Side/Walk/Shuttle* (1991) represents a perceptual *trompe de oeil* which confounded and delighted critics upon its initial release. Gehr's complete filmography (furnished to the author in a letter dated August 26, 1995) is as follows: *Morning* (1968), 4 1/2 min., color, silent; *Wait* (1968), 7 min., color, silent; *Reverberation* (1969), 25 min., B/W, sound; *Transparency* (1969), 11 min., color, silent; *History* (1970), 40 min., B/W, silent; *Field* (1970), 19 min., B/W, silent; *Field* (short version) (1970), 9 1/2 min., B/W, silent; *Serene Velocity* (1970), 23 min., color, silent; *Three* (1970), 4 min., B/W, silent; *Still* (1969–71), 55 min., color, sound; *Eureka* (1974), 30 min., B/W, silent; *Shift* (1972–74), 9 min., color, sound; *Behind the Scenes* (1975), 5 min., color, sound; *Table* (1976), 16 min., color, silent; *Untitled* (1977), 5 min., color, silent; *Hotel* (1979), 15 min., B/W, silent; *Mirage* (1981), 12 min., color, silent; *Untitled, Part One* (1981), 30 min., color, silent; *Signal - Germany on the Air* (1982–85), 37 min., color, sound; *Listen* (1986–91), 12 min., B/W, sound; *Rear Window* (1986–91), 10 min., color, sound; *This Side of Paradise* (1991), 14 min., color, sound; *Side/Walk/Shuttle* (1991), 40 min., color, sound; *Daniel Willi* (work in progress), color, sound; *Untitled* (work in progress), color, sound.

Working with documentary and "found" footage, **Peter Gessner** created a brutally effective tract against the Vietnam War with his 12-minute black and white compilation film *Time of the Locust*, a film that blends atrocity footage and pop songs into a devastating indictment of United States involvement in Vietnam. The film used "American newsfilm, combat footage shot by the National Liberation Front of South Vietnam, and suppressed film taken by Japanese cameramen" to create what journalist I. F. Stone described as "a poem in film of agony and protest [. . .] not propaganda [but] an expression of agony" (FMC 1967, 55). Prized at Mannheim in 1966, Leipzig in 1966, Tours in 1967, the Festival dei Populi in 1967, and presented at the 1966 Robert Flaherty International Film Seminar, Gessner's *Time of the Locust* remains one of the most powerful films to come out of this painful period in American history, and a film that is every bit the equal of Alain Resnais's *Night and Fog* (1956) in its evocation of a time of pain, crisis, and intense human suffering.

Peter Emmanuel Goldman's *Echoes of Silence* (1965) is a stunning dramatic feature shot entirely on location in New York with the barest of equipment and production facilities; the 75-minute film was much prized when it was first released, but has since been marginalized by current canonical practice. The entire feature film was shot silent, with music added later from some extremely scratched records. Like the '60s other epic feature film construct, Rice's *The Flower Thief* (although Rice's film is in a much lighter vein), Goldman's work is uncompromising in its execution, rough, and brutally tender. Goldman later moved to Paris, and completed work on a little-seen but highly influential feature film, *Wheel of Ashes* (1969–70).

Victor Grauer's *Angel Eyes* (1965), *Archangel* (1966), and *Seraph* (1966) are films which transmute colored light into stroboscopic patterns to elevate the audience into a serenely pacific state of heightened consciousness; *Archangel* was shown as part of the Special Events Program Section at the 1966 New York Film Festival. Grauer's films can been seen as having a good deal in common with the work of his contemporaries Tony Conrad and Paul Sharits. Grauer's work should be revived and shown so that it can be appreciated by a new group of responsive viewers; these gentle and evocative films form a unique legacy in the domain of 1960s American experimental cinema, and thus deserve a wider audience.

African-American director, producer, and writer **William Greaves** began his career as a featured actor on Broadway, in television, and in films, and is one of few African-American experimental filmmakers active in the 1960s. His work behind the camera as an independent filmmaker has earned him more than seventy international film festival awards, an Emmy, and four Emmy nominations. In 1980 he was inducted into the Black Filmmakers Hall of Fame and was the recipient of a special "homage" at the first Black American Independent Film Festival in Paris that same year. Greaves is also the recipient of an Indie Special Life Achievement Award from the Association of Independent Video and Filmmakers, a nationwide organization. Executive producer for the mainstream feature motion picture *Bustin' Loose*, starring Richard Pryor and Cicely Tyson, Greaves has also produced, wrote, and directed three other feature films: *The Marijuana Affair*, *Symbiopsychotaxiplasm: Take One*, and *Ali, The Fighter*, starring Muhammad Ali and Joe Frazier. Most recently, Greaves produced, directed, and wrote *Ida B. Wells: A Passion for Justice*, featuring Toni Morrison, for the PBS television series *The American Experience*. This last film has received more than twenty film festival awards and two citations for excellence. He has made more than two hundred documentary films, and for two years was executive producer and co-host of the network television series *Black Journal*.

Writing in *Premiere* magazine, critic Jim Hoberman noted that

> *Symbiopsychotaxiplasm* draws on the post-Warhol sense that life itself is a "movie" and the related recognition that to record something with

the camera is to necessarily alter it. The movie opens with a close-up of a woman complaining about all the abortions she's had to get, then—as the screen splits into two slightly different images—cursing her husband as a "fag." It's not long before Greaves and a film crew appear onscreen as well. "Don't take me seriously," the director remarks, delegating one cameraman to film the film that's being filmed—and whatever else happens to occur. When a cop wanders by, the crew puts him on-camera as well, Greaves blandly explaining that they're making "a feature-length we-don't-know-what." As moviemaking, *Symbiopsychotaxiplasm* is raw and profligate. The film runs out, the mechanism jams, the mikes go dead, the actors get upset, but the camera just keeps grinding on [. . .] Like John Cassavetes's *Faces*, first shown in 1968, *Symbiopsychotaxiplasm* is an attempt to redefine the notion of acting "naturally." The fact that Greaves is directing a largely white cast and crew puts a further spin on his self-consciousness. As an experiment in self-reflexive filmmaking, *Symbiopsychotaxiplasm* belongs with Jim McBride's *David Holzman's Diary*, Norman Mailer's *Maidstone*, and Yoko Ono's *Rape*. Scarcely the least of these, it's a movie that enters American history so decisively it seems like it's always been there. (33)

Other films by Greaves include *Just Doin' It*, which is described by Greaves as "a [1976] portrait of a traditional gathering place in the black community for the collecting of news and information, philosophizing, and socializing—the neighborhood barbershop" (letter to the author); *Malcolm X*, 115-minute 1969 short film produced by Greaves and directed by Madeline Anderson; *Booker T. Washington: The Life and the Legacy* (1982) and *Frederick Douglass: An American Life* (1984), two docudramas in which Greaves intertwines dramatic passages with vintage photographs, and *That's Black Entertainment* (1989), a compilation of rare and historic footage from African-American films of the thirties and forties. Greaves remains extraordinarily active today; along with St. Claire Bourne and a few other African-American practitioners of American independent cinema, Greaves continues to stake out an imagistic territory that is decisively his own.

It is sad, but nevertheless apparently true, that only a few African-American filmmakers were working in the 1960s. There was a pioneering Boston-based Black Film Collective which was also making 16mm sound shorts in the late 1960s, but their films (and all the catalogues of their works) seems to have vanished, and thus no prints of their works could be found for screening. Thus, it is all the more essential that the works of Greaves, Collins, Bourne and other African-American pioneering cinema artists are screened as widely as possible. It must also be noted that the works of African-American

FIGURE 27. 1960s African-American consciousness at work; William Greaves filming *Symbiopsychotaxiplasm*. Courtesy William Greaves.

filmmakers might be said to operate from a site of double-alterity; even outside of the mainstream cinema, one sees in certain canonical enterprises within the experimental cinema a desire to privilege one work artificially over another. As with the dominant cinema, "in order to exercise and elaborate its own power, a regulatory regime will generate the very object it seeks to control" (Butler 1993, 86). This might explain why certain styles of cinema practice wax and wane within the confines of the academic film environment at the expense of other methodologies and practitioners. The recent reclamation of Greaves's work is a spectacular instance of the contemporary re-writing of canon.

Amy Greenfield is another film/video/dance artist whose work deserves greater attention: her visual constructs (either in film or video) include *4 Solos for 4 Women* (1980), *Red Dervish* (1972/83), *Duets (For Television), Woman In a Room* (A Videodance Improvisation) (1984/87), *Image to Remind Me* (1968), *For God While Sleeping* (1970), *Dirt* (1971), *Transport* (1971), *Encounter* (1970), *One-O-One* (1976), and *Tides* (1982). As critic Robert Haller noted of Greenfield's work,

> Greenfield is a member of that generation of filmmakers who came to cinema in the 1960s, taking advantage of the technological developments that made film, and later, video cameras lightweight and portable. With these new tools it was possible to extend the realm of cinema *inward* into the personal lives of the filmmakers, and *outward* to locations and places where it had only rarely ventured previously [. . .]
>
> In 1982 [Greenfield] released *Tides*, which had been in production since 1979, and which incorporates images and ideas from many of the films, tapes, and holograms of the previous ten years, most particularly the opening image of a woman (Greenfield) rolling in slow motion across the sand on a beach, and then being enveloped by the sea. This archetypal image appeared, in different forms, in the hologram *The Wave*, in *Videotape For A Woman and A Man*, and suggests, also, *Element*, Greenfield's 1973 film where she appears as a solitary figure in a tidal mud basin. If, in *Element*, the impression the spectator departs with is of a Sisyphus-like struggle against implacable nature, *Tides* is a reply from the other direction. Greenfield is depicted not in conflict with the sea, but in a kind of exalted communion where space, light, and even time are in flux. The universe of *Tides* is volatile and visionary—a domain of the artist's imagination yet also of powers larger than any single person [. . .]
>
> Since 1984 Greenfield has focused all of her attention on a single project, reconstructing and filming Sophocles's play *Antigone*. Two to three times as long as any of her previous works, particularly daunting in that the play is a revered classic and is known only through words—

which Greenfield wished to translate into images—*Antigone* is at once a new direction for Greenfield and the climax of much of her previous work [. . .] a feature film that explicitly deals with the mythic themes that she has so often alluded to in her earlier films and tapes, a narrative work that dares to turn Sophocles's words into images but remain faithful to his most profound intent, *Tragedy of Antigone* will locate what T. S. Eliot had in mind when he wrote of the "concrete visual and emotional actuality [. . .] behind the dialogue of Greek drama." This 80 minute film, with major actors like Bertram Ross and Janet Eilber, should make Greenfield's special visual language accessible to a much broader public. (Haller, program notes)

Red Grooms, better known as the creator of cartoon-like oversize museum installation environments, collaborated with filmmaker Rudy Burckhardt to create *Shoot the Moon* (1964), an homage to George Méliès. He then went on to make *Fat Feet* (1966), a "living comic strip" using his sculptures and human actors, and manipulating their movements through stop-frame animation, and *Ruckus Shorts*, "a stable full of ruckus films to shorten your program [. . .] including *Washington's Wig Whammed*, *Before an After*, *The Big Sneeze*, *Man or Mouse* [and] *Spaghetti Trouble*" (FMC 1967, 59).

Walther Grunwald's *March 31* (1965), and his two-part *To America with Love* (August and September 1965, respectively), offer a riveting vision of the kaleidoscopic effect of '60s culture, combining "beach-scapes (black-and-white), light compositions (color) with Tchaikovsky's violin concerto and African tribal music [and the sounds of] Ray Charles, Country and Western music, JFK speeches [with images of the] Bronx, FDR Drive, Times Square, Harlem, Coney Island [. . .] Fifth Avenue parades, Wall Street after five, Harlem Sunday morning" (FMC 1967, 59). Together with Grunwald's *Uh Uh Uh* (November, 1965) and *Three* (April, 1965), these films form a most impressive body of work, shot in a brief period of time. Unhappily, these films are apparently no longer in distribution.

Another interesting but critical marginalized filmmaker, **David Hanson**, whose films were screened at the Moscow Film Festival, the Edinburgh Film Festival, the Tours Film Festival, the Oberhausen Film Festival and the Museum of Modern Art in the early 1960s, made two quiet and lyrical films in the mid '60s, *Minnesota Summer 1964* and *California Spring 1965*. Both movies are silent, color, and 5 minutes in length. Together, these two films represent an idyllic strain of transcendental contemplative cinema at its purest and most affecting.

Other filmmakers created compact but unique bodies of work within the context of 1960s cinema: **Taylor Hardwick's** *Three Film Poems* (1964–65) and *Pariah* (1966) are highly personal film poems

FIGURE 28. The body in space; Amy Greenfield shooting *Transport* (two men hold woman in air; Greenfield on ground with Bolex). Photo by Sam Robbins. Courtesy Anthology Film Archives.

that use lush color cinematography to create a sense of loss and nostalgia; both films are compact and economically constructed, running 22 minutes and 29 minutes respectively. **Hilary Harris**, better known as a cinematographer, created the brief newsreel *The Draft Card Burners* in 1966, and commented that "the film shows draft card burning demonstrations that took place in New York City during the fall of 1965, relating these incidents to the protests against the draft system and the war in Vietnam" (FMC 1967, 61).

John H. Hawkins, who often worked with Willard Maas and Marie Menken, created three brief films between 1964 and 1967: *LSD Wall* (1964–65), *A Valentine for Marie* (1965, with a soundtrack by Teiji Ito, who worked not only with Marie Menken, but filmmaker Maya Deren as well), and *Gingerbread* (1967). *LSD Wall*, a "clay animation" film which "attempt[ed] to reproduce some visual hallucinations while on a trip" (FMC 1967, 61) is perhaps the most successful of these efforts, although *A Valentine for Marie*, co-made with Willard Maas, is an undeniably poetic "'catch me if you can' game between two real hearts" (FMC 1967, 61).

Piero Heliczer, born in 1937, was one of the founders of the underground film movement in the very early 1960s, and a staunch proponent of standard 8mm film in most of his works. He created a bizarre gallery of low-budget spectacles, using Angus MacLise, Jack Smith, La Monte Young, Mario Montez, Harry Smith, Gerard Malanga, Andy Warhol, Charles Henri Ford, Sally Kirkland, and others as an informal stock company of actors. His films include *The Autumn Feast*, shot in Brighton, England; *The Soap Opera, Dirt, Satisfaction, Venus in Furs*, and *Joan of Arc*. Heliczer preferred to work in standard 8mm because it was (then) inexpensive, lightweight, and, as he put it, "as narrow as a gauntlet." Heliczer's films were much admired by his fellow pioneers in the early 1960s underground; of *The Autumn Feast*, Jack Smith noted that "it rubs the very noses of our mannequins in our own mold and sends us spinning into the street—undone and toothless" (FMC 1967, 61). *Dirt* and *Joan of Arc* were both 8mm "epics," each film running 40 minutes in length for each film.

All of these films were shot silent with separate tape soundtracks (some featuring the Velvet Underground) created by Heliczer to accompany the images in his cheerfully anarchic and yet "personal lyrical" (Jonas Mekas, cited in FMC 1967, 63) works. Heliczer's films were, for the most part, "insider" films, originally shown in subscription screenings. Later came screenings at the Bridge Theatre, and in 1969 a one-person show of films as part of the Eight and 1/2 New York Film Festival, an event organized by Jonas Mekas at New York City's Elgin Theatre. Heliczer died in 1993; his works are an important and too often forgotten part of the New American Cinema.

Dick Higgins is another important figure in the early New American Cinema. His epic feature *The Flaming City* is a 135-minute, 16mm color sound film made in 1963. It is described by Higgins as "an anti-semantic love story about a marvelous part of New York City and the people who lived there—as the city is destroyed, so are they, except that both are indestructible" (FMC 1967, 63). As influential in its time as Ron Rice's better known *The Flower Thief, The Flaming City* is almost never revived today. The film should be screened by a new generation of viewers, so that it can take its rightful place as one of the key narrative films of 1960s experimental American cinema.

CHAPTER THREE

∷

Hiler to Machover

The films of **Jerome Hiler** occupy a unique position within the canon of experimental cinema. Alone among his contemporaries, Hiler refuses to make prints of his films, or to release them, or to screen them in public—in short, his is the vocation of the truly personal filmmaker, that of a person who makes films solely for his own gratification and amusement. Hiler has been making films since the early 1960s, and during that time he has shot and roughly edited some fifty hours of completed film work. Most of it is color, all of it is shot on reversal film, and all of it is silent. Most of the material is mounted on 1600' (45 minutes) reels stored in a warehouse in San Francisco; there are also numerous shorter works, including a fairly recent addition which has been informally named *Acid Rock*.

Shot in early 1990 on outdated Ektachrome reversal stock, *Acid Rock* exists only in the original (that is, Hiler has never made a print of it), and consists of three 100' reels of film unedited, straight from the camera, joined together solely by three splices into a 9-minute film of dazzling beauty and incandescent imagery. What Jerome Hiler accomplishes with this brief film is little short of alchemy. Everyday objects, places, things, and people are transformed into integers of light, creating a sinuous tapestry of restless imagistic construction. *Acid Rock* (so named because a huge rock with the word "acid" emblazoned on it drifts briefly past the camera during the opening moments of the film) displays the best qualities of abstract expressionist experimental cinema in that it transmutes perceptual reality into a zone of ineluctable transcendence, causing the images to perceptibly burst forth from the surface of the screen.

In a 1995 interview, Hiler offered these thoughts on his life and work:

I was born in Jamaica, Long Island, on March 27, 1943. My very first film experiences were terrifying; no matter what the film I went to was, it was a totally frightening experience. The first film I ever saw was *White Zombie*. So I was introduced to this new medium, in which you went into a very dark room, and there were other people in the room—you couldn't see them, but you could hear them rustling around. I was just a child, of course; this was about 1948. And on the screen were images of zombies accidentally slipping into giant grinders. This was explained to me with the words "they're being made into sugar," and needless to say, I went right under the seat. And every time I got up and looked at the screen, there would be another terrifying image; a giant close-up of Bela Lugosi or something. So I was traumatized for weeks.

Then, after a while, I would get my courage up, and go back to the movies, and *this* time when I wandered into that big, dark room, I found an equally terrifying scene. It was the Three Stooges. They were even more horrifying. Here were three men, with scary haircuts, hitting each other and gouging each other's eyes out on the screen. And this time, the theatre was full to capacity with screaming people, emitting these high-pitched wails; hundreds of voices all at once. And on the screen, one of the Stooges has his head stuck between the leaves of a table from underneath, and the other two are pushing the table together, with him in the middle. And it was just like *White Zombie* all over again—a completely horrifying experience. And I thought, "this medium is the most powerful thing I've ever experienced." And of course, I've loved horror movies and the Three Stooges ever since. But I wasn't making any movies at the time.

Later, I made a few 8mm films in which I ineptly attempted to imitate Hitchcock's framing—getting under lampshades, you know—Hitchcock's a real lampshade queen. But this was much later, around 1963. Before that, I was into drawing comic strips of movies that I saw. Then I got into painting, had a loft in downtown New York, and had a falling out with the people I was living with, and put all my paintings into storage. And then all my paintings were stolen—everything, all my paintings and equipment. And so I moved into a very seedy men's hotel in the Bowery while I waited for something to happen, and there I ran into, of all people [experimental filmmaker] Gregory Markopolous. Gregory came to this rundown hotel I was living with at the suggestion of a friend of mine, who had been cast by Gregory as Icarus in his film *The Illiac Passion*. I don't know why, but he decided to introduce Gregory to me in these circumstances. Gregory was having a fight with his roommate, who was leasing the apartment they shared.

So here I am in this derelicts' hotel in the Bowery, and here's elegant Gregory standing in this seedy men's hotel, looking like a well-tai-

FIGURE 29. Nathanael Dorsky and Jerome Hiler in 1976. Courtesy Nathanael Dorsky.

lored statue, hoping not to contaminate himself from any of the dust and germs in the room. He just looked at me for a few moments and then said, "Would you like to live in *better* circumstances?" And at the same time I had just seen Stan Brakhage's *Dog Star Man Pt. I* for the first time, and Brakhage more than anyone else convinced me that it would be wonderful to have a camera, to make the kind of images he did. When I looked at the screen, I just remembered that my eyes were more open, more receptive, than they ever had been watching a film in a theatre, in which someone was telling a *story*. I was completely taken by his vision, by the saturated colors of his images. So there I was. I had lost all my paintings, I had no place to live, I met Gregory and he said that I could borrow his camera, a 16mm Bolex. So all of these circumstances tipped my hand into becoming completely involved in film. So I'd buy a few rolls of film, and walk around the city late at night photographing the fountains, the street lights—this was about 1964. Gregory lived on 11th Street between 5th and 6th Avenues, and for a time everything went along well. But Gregory was always reminding me that I didn't live up to his high standards of male physical perfection, and when I would joke about taking the role of one of the Greek gods in Gregory's movies, he'd look me up and down and say, "You just don't have the *figure*, old man."

So I lasted there about six to ten months, until I found another apartment at 162 East Broadway. I was working as a projectionist for the Filmmakers' Cinematheque, which was then located in the basement of the now demolished Wurlitzer Building, at 125 W. 41st Street. Robert Cowan was the other projectionist, and he couldn't do it all the time, and they were desperate, so they took me. By this time I was shooting a lot of material, because film was very cheap back then, and so I accumulated a number of 1600' reels of images I'd shot on the streets of New York. It just absorbed *all* my money. You went to work and earned a living, and then whatever money you had after rent and food went to film. So I shot a lot of film—it was my sole passion in life. My favorite labs were Du Art and Lab TV. I only shot reversal [positive image] film. I wanted my thrills on the spot. I was previously a painter, you have to understand, and there's an incredible amount of *waiting* in film making. First the film is in the box and then you shoot it, and then you have to go to the lab, so who wants to fool around with negative, and then have to wait for a print. No, reversal film by all means.

I first met Nathanael Dorsky in September, 1964. Gregory Markopolous had set me up for an interview with a photographer to work as his assistant. At that time, I had zero money, so I thought, "I guess I can walk from 162 East Broadway up to 31st and Lexington," where the Filmmakers' Cooperative was located, "and borrow money for a subway the rest of the way from Leslie Trumbull" [then secretary of the cooperative]. So when I got to the Coop, Nathanael was there, being interviewed by Leslie for a job. I had no idea who Leslie was talking to, but then I looked over on a table and saw a film can he'd been carrying, labeled *Ingreen* [a film Nathanael Dorsky made in 1964]. As luck would have it, I had just been to see *Ingreen* the night before with Gregory at the Washington Square Gallery. So I went up to Nathanael and said, "Oh, did you make *Ingreen?*," and that was our initial introduction.

Now [in 1995] I'm working in stained glass, and that's going to be my direction from now on. It's something I always desired to do, and in fact a lot of my 16mm footage used stained glass windows as new material, but with the camera moving around in such a way as to obscure that fact, so it would just be swirls of color. So that's always been a love of mine, but the other thing is that film has just gotten too expensive . . . too expensive! So that's basically what happened. I've been a very good lover to Madame Cinema, but she just raises her price for each session. I have a lot of footage, though, that I'm working on now, but it's really hard to say how much, because I don't think in those terms. I used to mount my footage on 1600' reels with bits of black leader in between, but I think I've decided that the nature of my kind of images should be taken in less copious doses. Nathanael Dorsky said that 20 minutes was the maximum before you just wanted to take a break, turn on the lights, and then put something else on, or at least it seemed that way in 1990, that it kind of taxed the eye. So I don't put on these big long rolls anymore—I mean, you're a friend, you could watch this stuff forever, but most people aren't like that.

Acid Rock is about the last thing I did. That was shot on some old Ektachrome reversal you sent me, and the finished film is only 300 feet—it's only three rolls of film. It's presented almost exactly as it was shot; in other words, there are flareouts between reels, and it's really just spliced together. I left it as a separate film in response to "public demand": people told me to leave it just as it was, and I did. I've never made a print; it's just the original, three reels spliced together, and the only artistic aspect of it is that I never remembered what the previous shot was when I was filming it. But it works out perfectly. So much of the time, I find that outside circumstances, coincidence, things that aren't products of my mind are far more brilliant than any amount of pre-planning. But then it's true, I have to admit it: I still don't release my films, or print them, or distribute them. I'll screen them from time to time for a few people—that's how you saw *Acid Rock*, and I screen my stuff for Nathanael, or Stan Brakhage, or a few other people, but that's it. I think I tend to be entirely too self-critical, and things are never in the shape I'd like them to be. The only reason *Acid Rock* exists as a separate film is that people have threatened me if I do anything to it. It's the same thing with the rest of my work. I've never been satisfied with it, never been happy with it, and I'm always thinking "Oh, I'll put this together in a better way" or something like that, but it never happens.

But having said all that, I'm pretty damned near right now to getting some material I haven't seen since 1980 into sections that are ready to print up, and I find that I relate to my footage in a much better way now that I've had this gap. I don't have any kind of a strong emotional connection to the images. I can just be ruthless, or loving, and I'm experiencing a spontaneity during the editing process that I never felt before. In my particular case as a filmmaker, I've been way too timid, all over, whether it's handling the film, or having it shown. So now that I care *less*, I can see what I'm doing more clearly. I have a bit more freedom to move, and simply to finalize what I'm doing. And so I'm thinking of printing some of the stuff up, and putting it in Canyon Cinema for distribution, after all this time.

Any kind of art, be it painting, cinema, poetry, or even a craft, these are the tools for living. You don't just live your life by begging food, or begging clothing and shelter. You should *do* something with life. And film for me was a tool, and a tool I felt very fortunate to have. With film, you're able to put down images from your life and reflect upon them, mold them, into a coherent vision of existence. But now I can't afford that, and I feel kind of bad about it. I'd still be making films if it was more affordable. Wherever I went in the 1960s, 1970s, even in the 1980s, part of my attire was always a backpack with a Bolex in it. That's how I stepped out on to the street.

Although walking around is much lighter now, it's a little sadder. When I see things now, I can just look and appreciate them. But there was a sort of fun about catching it in a black box and bringing it home. Being a filmmaker the way I was is like someone who remembers their dreams, little images and things that take place. They might be forgotten, but with film, you have a dream journal, and you've recorded it for all time. So as a filmmaker, I was editing a dream journal, shooting things that mattered to me, editing it in the camera as I went along. I think all of our experiences have a dreamlike quality, in that we can't really *remember* our lives as we live them. You remember certain specific incidents—happy or unhappy—but daily existence is often lost. Some of the stronger experiences I have are in my dreams, and in a way, life and dreams start to become equal. So in that sense, film has been my dream journal. I've captured little fragments of my life, and my dreams, on film. (Dixon interview, 1995)

In the winter of 1995, Jerome Hiler presented the first public screening of his work at the San Francisco Cinematheque. The reception was enthusiastic; we can hopefully look forward to more shows of Hiler's work in the future.

Jerome Hill, who, by virtue of his family fortune, was often able to lend a helping hand to perpetually impoverished experimental filmmakers, created a series of documentary films (*Grandma Moses* [1950], *Albert Schweitzer* [in association with filmmaker Erica Anderson; 1957]) and the lyrical semi-documentary *The Sand Castle* (1961), before directing the feature film *Open the Door and See All the Peo-*

ple in 1964, with a cast including everyone from Alec Wilder and Maybelle Nash to Gwen Davis and Taylor Mead. The 82-minute feature was shot in 35mm, and chronicled the misadventures of twin sisters Alma and Thelma, both played by Maybelle Nash. Alma is a free spirit, who leads an unfettered existence with little concern for money; Thelma is a paupered millionaire. Taylor Mead holds the film together as a sort of itinerant junk collector, wandering through the film and collecting discarded props. Hill also made an excellent short film, the 2-minute mini-short comedy *Death in the Forenoon, or Who's Afraid of Ernest Hemingway?* (FMC 1967, 64–65), which mixes live action and animation with darkly humorous results. (Parenthetically, further mention should be made here of Hill's collaborator, cinematographer/filmmaker **Erica Anderson**, who did much of the work on Hill's production of *Albert Schweitzer*. Anderson later founded the Albert Schweitzer Friendship Center in Connecticut, and spent the rest of her long career as a filmmaker, still photographer, and political activist working for world peace.)

Katsumi Hirano's *Conversation Between a Nail and a Stocking* (1958) was a 25-minute surrealist film completed with the assistance of the students of the Nippon University Film Makers Group. Takahiko Iimura called the film "a monumental post-war work in Japanese student filmmaking" (FMC 1967, 65). Hirano's film is yet another exemplar of the prolific Japanese underground cinema scene of the early 1960s, and as with many of his contemporaries, Hirano's work demands revival and reassessment within the context of today's cinema practice.

As a filmmaker in his own right, **Takahiko Iimura** was intensely active in the early 1960s, and remains so today. In the early 1960s he created such films as *Ai (Love)* in 8mm (with a 16mm blowup) in 1962, featuring a tape soundtrack created by Yoko Ono; and *Iro* (1962), *6x6* (1962), *Desade* (1962), and *Dada '62* (1962), all in standard 8mm. These films were followed by a second wave of 8mm films from Iimura, including *Junk* (1962), *Sakasama* (1963; edited by Tony Cox, who would later collaborate with Yoko Ono on her 1964 film, *Bottoms*), *The Masseurs* (1963), and *Ukiyo Ukare* (1964). Nearly all of these early 8mm works are meditations on the human body, or dance studies, or semi-documentary interpretations of contemporary Japanese painting and/or sculpture.

Onan (1963), with music by Yasunao Tone, was Iimura's first work created directly in 16mm. In *Onan*, as described by Iimura himself, "a young man (Natsuyuki Nakanishi) lies naked in a bed and burns holes in the breasts and pubic regions of pictures of girls taken from magazines" (FMC 1967, 68). As the film progresses, the young man apparently gives birth to a totemic stone idol, and runs through the streets until he meets a young woman (Akiko Kodaira), and drops the stone in front of her. For one version of the film, Iimura punched holes in the film itself as it was being run through the projector; *Sight and Sound* described the end result as "a strange shocker," while *Films in Review* called *Onan* a "skillful sexual fantasy" (as cited in FMC 1967, 68). The 7-minute film was Iimura's first international success, and created a storm of controversy when it was exhibited at the Third International Experimental Film Festival in Brussels in 1963. Iimura followed this film with *The Fact* (1964), *Inside and Outside* (1964), *A Dance Party in the Kingdom of Lilliput* (1964), *Yomei-Mon* (1966), *Ama-Ata* (*A Ghanian in Boston*, 1966), *Why Don't You Sneeze* (1966; an homage to Marcel Duchamp), *Rose Colored Dance* (1966), *I Saw the Shadow* (1966), and *Schelter 9999* [sic] (1966).

Many of these works were created in standard 8mm, which was then a relatively inexpensive production format, readily accessible to both artists and the general public. Iimura continued making films throughout the 1960s and into the present, but in his later films he became more interested in considerations of filmic structure than issues of human sexuality, as in his first films. Of Iimura's early work, one might especially recommend *Iro*, *Ai*, *Onan*, and *A Dance Party in the Kingdom of Lilliput*; Iimura's later, more rigorous films include *White Calligraphy* (1967), *Face* (1968–69), *Filmmakers* (1968–69, shot during Iimura's first visit to the United States in 1966–68), *Film Strips I & II* (1966–70), *Buddha Again* (also known as *Cosmic Buddha*, 1969–70), *In the River* (1969–71), the "Tony Conradesque" *Shutter* (1971, a flicker film of hylomorphic intensity), *1 to 60 Seconds* (1973), *Parallel* (1974), *One Frame Duration* (1977), *Sync Sound* (1975–78), *24 Frames per Second* (1975–78), and *Talking Picture: The Structure of Film Viewing* (1981–83). In these spare, often brutally economical films, Iimura is questioning the very process of film construction itself, and in his later works Iimura recalls the rigor and spatial clarity of his colleagues Michael Snow, Ernie Gehr, Hollis Frampton, and Joyce Wieland (FMC 1989, 263–268).

During the early 1960s, **Ken Jacobs** created a beautiful compendium of short vignettes entitled *Little Stabs at Happiness*, an 18-minute, color film in 16mm featuring brief segments titled "In the Gold Room," "It Began to Drizzle," "The Spirit of Listlessness," et cetera. Jacobs's later films are, as with Iimura, more formal in nature, and include *Window* (1964), *Airshaft* (1967), *Soft Rain* (1968), *Tom, Tom, the Piper's Son* (1969), *Nissan Ariana Window* (1969), and other works. *Tom, Tom, the Piper's Son* is a rephotographing of a 1905 Billy Bitzer film, as previously mentioned in this text, and at 115 minutes

FIGURE 30. Takahiko Iimura in the East Village in the late 1960s. Courtesy Canyon Cinema.

is one of the longest of Jacobs's films. *The Sky Socialist* (1964–65) is a 90-minute feature with a somewhat more traditional narrative, reminiscent of Ron Rice or Jack Smith. *The Winter Footage*, shot in 1964 but completed in 1984, offers views of Bob Fleischner, Robert Cowan, Florence Jacobs, Storm de Hirsch, Louis Brigante and others from the early days of the American experimental cinema. Jacobs's most notorious film is probably *Blonde Cobra* (1959–1963), a film Jacobs edited from footage originally shot by Bob Fleischner, featuring Jack Smith. Jacobs has also created a "found film," which he dubbed *Perfect Film* (1968), consisting of old TV news footage he found in a junk bin on Canal Street in New York. Even as his later films have become more vigorous and reflexive, Jacobs has not abandoned the lyrical savagery of his first motion pictures (*Blonde Cobra, Little Stabs at Happiness*), and he remains an original and iconoclastic cinema visionary today.

Lewis Jacobs, author of the pioneering study *The Rise of the American Film*, also produced a series of 16mm documentaries and experimental films dating back to the late 1930s, including *From Tree Trunk to Head* (1937), *Lincoln Speaks at Gettysburg* (1951), *The Raven* (1954), *Face of the World* (1960), and his most ambitious film, *Another Time: Another Voice* (1964), described by Lewis Jacobs himself as "the story of a man who has a rendezvous with memory and desire; a man who can neither escape from his present [or] his past" (FMC 1989, 274). *Another Time: Another Voice* won the Diploma of Merit, Gran Premio Bergamo, 1964, and was presented at the San Francisco Film Festival the same year. Featuring a sensuous musical score by Jo Scianni, the film is a vigorous and original piece of American cinematic art.

Mike Jacobson created a gorgeous series of loop variations, the first of which was *Esprit de Corps* in 1965, featuring camerawork and a performance by filmmaker Saul Levine. Jacobson's most accomplished works include *Sunspots* (1967), *Dracula's Wedding Day* (1967), and *No Title* (1968), all 16mm silent films designed to be projected either forwards or backwards, at any speed. Jacobson's loop work reached its apotheosis with *Loop Variations from the Seventh Voyage of Sinbad* (1969), a 45-minute, three-part film composed of segments from Nathan Juran's 1958 film, manipulated into a dazzling series of visual mosaics.

Motoharu Jonouchi created *Pou Pou* (1960), another pioneering Japanese surrealist effort in which "a mob of children enact a burial rite; the place of the 'corpse' is taken by one of the rebellious youths" (FMC 1967, 71).

Larry Jordan, who would become a major figure in the Avant-Garde in the late 1960s and early 1970s, began his career with *Cen-*

tennial Exposition, a 4½-minute silent exercise which was incorporated into his film *Duo Concertantes* (1964). Later films included *Hamfat Asar* (1965), *Gymnopedies* (1965), and *Our Lady of the Sphere* (1969), all involving manipulated steel engravings animated against a variety of phantasmagorical backgrounds. In the 1970s, Jordan created the animated films *Orb* (1973), *Once Upon a Time* (1974), and *The Rime of the Ancient Mariner* (1977). *Rime* is a 40-minute epic film, with narration by Orson Welles, using Coleridge's poem and Gustave Dore's engravings to create an homage to and reinterpretation of Coleridge's doom-laden narrative. *Ancestors* (1978) is a briefer animated work, while *Cornell, 1965* (1978) documents Jordan's period of apprenticeship to the late Joseph Cornell in the mid '60s; Jordan's material is the only live action footage of the pioneer collagist and "box artist" Joseph Cornell at work. Jordan's other films include *Moonlight Sonata* (1979), *Carabosse* (1980), *Finds of a Fortnight* (1980), *Masquerade* (1981), and the live action *Magenta Geryon* (1983). Jordan has also recently released three films from the 1940s, produced in collaboration with Joseph Cornell: *Cotillion*, *The Midnight Party*, and *Children's Party*.

Norman Kamerling's *Too Bazooka* (1964) is an absurdist slapstick comedy. **Howard S. Kaplan's** *Thanks a Lot* (1964) won first prize in the Experimental Documentary Section at the 1964 Venice Film Festival, and participated in the Edinburgh, Mannheim, and Brussels film festivals in the same year. *Thanks a Lot* presents, in Kaplan's words, "the endless, never-to-be-broken cycle of birth, childhood, manhood, and the ever present awaiting Army" [a clear reference to the Vietnam era, in which conscription likely meant active duty overseas] (FMC 1967, 72).

Laurence Kardish, now Curator of Film at the Museum of Modern Art, created the beautiful and dreamlike narrative feature *Slow Run* in the late 1960s. Structured around a monologue by Saul Rubinek, it is linked to a disparate variety of evocative and haunting visual sequences, with the images and soundtrack functioning independently of each other. The film received an admiring notice from Philip Strick on the occasion of its premiere at the 1968 Toronto Film Festival, with Strick commenting that the film "packs a sardonic punch." Jonas Mekas, in the *Village Voice* of October 10, 1968, also praised *Slow Run*, saying that "I was surprised to see how good a film it was [. . .] I would have to see it once more to write about *Slow Run* with any intelligence [. . . Kardish lets] the images run their own way, and the soundtrack its own—and then put[s] the two together [. . .] Kardish [does this] in a big, sweeping way, consciously, as a formal, aesthetic principle of the film. And it works [. . .]" (FMC 1989, 283).

Max Katz's pioneering *Wisp* (1963) is a virtuoso display of film editing, using a simple date between a man and a woman as the pretext for its Vertovian extravagance in the service of associative montage. Katz's major work, *Jim the Man*, is a 77-minute 16mm color sound feature created in the mid 1960s, with a script by Herbert Gold and starring Scott Beach. As with *Wisp*, Katz anchors *Jim the Man* in a world of "violent montage effects, starkly beautiful photography, and a unique story construction that ends in a startling eruption of psychological images," as Katz himself noted upon the initial release of the film (as cited in FMC 1967, 72). *Jim the Man* remains a gorgeously epigrammatic and stylishly formal semi-autobiographical exercise, and a window into the personal, social, and sexual construction of heterosexualist masculinity as it was perceived/received in the 1960s.

Stanton Kaye's first film, *Georg*, was completed in February of 1964. Photographed by Detlev Wiede, and featuring Lynn Averill, Mark Cheka, and Stanton Kaye, the film was enthusiastically received. It won first prize at the Second Los Angeles Film-Makers' Festival, and was selected for the "direct cinema" program at the Film Centre, the Gallery of Modern Art, New York, 1964. It was also a major prize winner at the 1965 Ann Arbor Film Festival, and was included as one of the key works on the Ann Arbor tour for that year. Kaye described the film to me in a 1969 interview as "an hour long neo-realistic account of a war-torn German soldier, who, after having emigrated to America, finds he cannot live within any civilization, but he cannot live without it either." For the next four and a half years, Kaye worked on a feature film, *Brandy in the Wilderness*, which was released in 1968.

Born in 1943 in Hollywood, Kaye lived in New York during the late 1960s, although he wasn't overly fond of Manhattan. "Anybody who has any sense of the land can't possibly like New York," he noted.

> I always had Hollywood people around me . . . my father worked for René Clair once, as an assistant director on *It Happened Tomorrow*. My first film work was with Jimmy Sherwood, who wrote *Stradella*. We were all 16, all doing what our parents did. We'd been working on this script: *Riders to the Sea*. We went out on some cliffs and got our picture published in the *Hollywood Reporter*. That was when I was in Hollywood High School and it was part of our dramatic seminar. A woman I knew gave me a small movie studio because she thought I had a good aura floating around my head, but I never got to use it because I was too busy writing the screenplay for *Georg*.
>
> I dropped out of high school, and got some money together. About two years later I went out into the desert with some friends of mine to

FIGURE 31. Stanton Kaye at home in 1969. Courtesy Anthology Film Archives.

shoot the film in 120 degree heat. The whole thing collapsed, though, because there were a lot of older people and I didn't know how to handle them. I was about 18 then. Anyway, after a lot of hassles, I finally shot *Georg* [. . .] *Brandy in the Wilderness* is done in the same style as *Georg*, first-person film narrative, but it's done not as trickily, and it's much more honest. The budget was twelve grand, took four years, shot in 16mm. I got the money wherever I could: fifteen hundred from a grant, and I sold my life for the rest for three years to finish it. And then you think it's not worth it . . . life's too much fun for it . . . but on the other hand so are movies, so you do it again. Cinema is Josef Von Sternberg, it's Erich Von Stroheim, it's Jean Renoir . . . cinema is control. It is not merely experimentation. My films are considered experimental, but I don't consider them experimental . . . it's just something I've *got* to say. (Dixon papers, 1969)

Kaye listed Pirandello, Strindberg, and Brecht as his major literary influences; in film, he admired Ozu, Bresson, Chaplin, and Buñuel. In trying to strike a balance between these two mediums, Kaye used the device of having the characters in his movies film their own lives: thus, his films are presented as the fictional character's "home movies." This technique was also used in Jim McBride's experimental feature *David Holzman's Diary*, although *Georg* precedes McBride's film by a number of years. Kaye in the late 1960s looked forward to continuing his work in the cinema, and concluded our interview with the thought that "the ultimate film for me is a distillation of all the elements that go into making it, so they can be recognized and understood" (Dixon papers, 1969).

Poet **Weldon Kees** is not often thought of as an American independent filmmaker, but his work *Hotel Apex* (1952), which Kees entirely produced, photographed and directed, and his musical score for James Broughton's *Adventures of Jimmy* (1951) are admirable additions to his work in other areas. Kees also created *The Bridge* (1956), a short film co-directed with Bill Heick. *The Bridge* is a tone poem evoking the majestic span of San Francisco's Golden Gate Bridge—ironically, the identical bridge from which Kees presumably jumped to his death in July of that same year. Kees's melancholic sensibility comes across most clearly in *Hotel Apex*, which Kees photographed in an abandoned flophouse scheduled for imminent demolition. Shooting only 800 feet of black and white film with a simple, hand-held, spring-wound camera, Kees indelibly evoked the sense of despair and loss associated with the structure's erstwhile inhabitants. Kees's major interests as a creative artist clearly lay in other areas, particularly his poetry and his film criticism, and he also worked on a variety of commercial projects in a number of varying capacities. But it is

FIGURE 32. Still from *Georg* by Stanton Kaye. Courtesy of Anthology Film Archives.

in his own, independent films that Kees's spirit comes out most directly. According to Kees authority Steven Shively, prints of *Hotel Apex* (along with the printing originals for the film) still survive today, housed in the Heritage Room of the Bennett Martin Public Library in Lincoln, Nebraska.

George Kling's 30-minute 16mm sound film *Vacuous Vicinity* (1963) was conceived by the filmmaker as "an attack/study of the modern business man, his values, beliefs, rituals, etc. . . . the film shows the destruction of a person caught in the whirlpool of group-thinking, committee decisions, materialism" (FMC 1967, 73). Kling's other films include *The Sower* (1964) and *Result* (1965), both in 16mm color and sound. *Result* is an anti-war film shot in black and white with sepia tints, intermixed with reversal color imagery.

Robert Kramer produced a series of apocalyptic feature narratives, including *In the Country* (1965), *The Edge* (1967), *Ice* (1969), and *Milestones* (1975), the last film co-directed with John Douglas. The first three films are radical political tracts; *Milestones* is an elegy to a past era of social commitment, with a running time of three and a half hours. Vincent Canby in the *New York Times* described *Milestones* as "a vast mosaic of a movie [. . . Robert Kramer] is one of our most original and gifted filmmakers [. . . the film] bursts with unexpected life" (as cited in FMC 1989, 302).

One of the most original and iconoclastic personalities of the New American Cinema did his work in the early 1970s, and as such does not strictly belong within the scope of this book. But the work of **James Krell** is simultaneously so important and so unknown, that his inclusion here is more than justified. Beginning in the early 1970s, James Krell created a series of rigorous and mysterious films that defy written description—perhaps that is why he offers no commentary on the films he distributes through the Filmmakers Cooperative. During the 1970s, I had the opportunity to watch him at work on several occasions. What always impressed me (or perhaps "astonished" is a better word) concerning Krell's shooting methods was the intrinsic speed and seemingly random technique he brought to his work.

For one of his films, Krell descended into a storm drain with a spring-wound Bolex and a box of railroad flares; while shooting in the darkened tunnel, he threw lighted flares in front of him, illuminating the viaduct with rings of flaming red. For a projected film on the Patty Hearst kidnapping which was never completed, Krell shot two hours of sync-sound footage in a single weekend, creating a film that worked both as a fictive narrative and a deconstruction of the events that led up to the Hearst affair. For *Finally a Lamb*, Krell documented a performance piece by German artist Hermann Nitsch of the Orgies/Mysteries theatre, in which a dead sheep's carcass was disemboweled in front of a stunned audience. In *Paper Palsy*, one of his earliest films, archival footage of an amateur night performance at the Apollo Theatre in New York was superimposed over blown-up Super 8mm footage of scraped, baked, and chemically treated unexposed film stock, causing huge multi-colored blotches to interrupt the visual terrain of the Apollo Theatre material at regular intervals. The sound track was a live recording of dolphins mating in the depths of the Atlantic Ocean, played in reverse.

For *The Shoreline of China*, Krell shot two rolls of footage of a young woman walking up and down a beach on the coast of New Jersey at dawn, creating fades and dissolves in the camera during shooting. He then printed the color positive and negative footage on top of each other on the A and B rolls, with the images flipped so that they crossed over into each other in the center of the frame, to create a disquieting vision of an alien landscape. For another film, Krell shot the shadow of a curtain on the floor of his New York loft for 30 minutes with ancient black and white 1/2" Portapack video equipment; the resultant video imagery was then remastered onto black and white negative stock with a professional film chain to achieve astonishing results in contrast, frame sizing, and the arbitrary duration of this reductive image.

Optical effects in Krell's films were commissioned in a similarly haphazard manner, or so it seemed to most external observers. Krell would give several hundred feet of film to the Oxberry technician, and ask only that it be stopped and started at random intervals, with any inadvertent mistakes or "frame rips" left in the completed footage. Soundtracks were composed out of found materials, or created electronically by Krell working with a homemade synthesizer. Krell's films, silent or sound, would take a full evening to project, and have never received a fraction of the attention and critical commentary that they deserve.

Because Krell's works are so seldom seen, it is important to list them all: his first 16mm film was *Paper Palsy* (1972), followed by *The Shoreline of China* (1973), *Wolverine Kills T.V.* (1975), *Coda/M.C.* (1975), *Fur (But Less Fun)* (1976), *Action Past Compassion* (1976), *Alpine Lookout # One* (1976), *Alpine Lookout # Two* (1977), *Alpine Lookout # Three* (1978), *30 Days: Speed or Gravity?* (1976), *Four Rolls (Rarely Pre-Dated; Tribute to Marcel Duchamp)* (1976), *Finally a Lamb* (1976), *Ram's Photos* (1977), *Shame, Shame: Dallas Diary, 1964* (1977), *Thank You/Your Receipt* (1977), *All Area* (1978), *Kay Serra Serra/The Mirror (New Paltz Diary, 1975* (1978), *(Kozo Okamoto's Quote)* (1979), *Second Thoughts* (1980), and *On the Count of Love*

(*Indian Lake Diary, 1977* (1980). All of Krell's films are in 16mm.

Some of these films are silent, some have optical soundtracks; they vary in length from 2½ minutes to nearly an hour. In all cases, the films are engaging to the viewer's mind and eye because of the undeniable intelligence and intuitive sensibility apparent in every aspect of their construction. Krell's films form a body of work that is so subterranean that only the most dedicated observers of the New American Cinema are aware of its existence, but this does not detract from the distinct and utterly original beauty of the films in question. Made on a shoestring budget, with materials and raw stock obtained on a haphazard basis, James Krell has created in his films a transformed and rigorously structured vision of an entirely alternative modality of seeing. Working within the highly idiosyncratic world of experimental film, Krell has made films that are entirely his own, works which are utterly without formal or thematic precedent in the cinema.

Peter Kubelka, whose work has been well documented elsewhere, created a series of intricately crafted minimalist movies, starting with *Mosaik Im Vertrauen* (1954–55), *Adebar* (1956–57), *Schwechater* (1957–58), *Arnulf Rainer* (1958–60), and culminating in *Unsere Afrikareise* (1961–66). Kubelka's films are carefully calculated, frame by frame, and display a rigorous contrapuntal interplay between sound and image. *Arnulf Rainer* is a black and white flicker film; *Adebar* is a restructured dance film; *Schwechater* was originally commissioned as a beer commercial. Since most of Kubelka's films are extremely brief, Kubelka mounts them on reels of 2 and 5 prints, to encourage the viewer to appreciate and apprehend his works to the fullest possible extent. Of all of Kubelka's works, perhaps *Unsere Afrikareise* is his most ambitious and accomplished film, deconstructing documentary footage of an African safari into a 12-minute commentary on the politics of colonialism, the commodification of the colonized subject's body, the rape of the African landscape and its people by external interests, and the slaughter of numerous innocent animals in the name of sport. Densely structured, deeply felt, and brutally economical in its execution, *Unsere Afrikareise* looks forward to the films of Trinh T. Minh-ha, Safi Faye and others, who would later examine the Colonial instinct in international social/cultural/political/economic discourse.

The Kuchar Brothers, George and **Mike,** began their career with a series of ultra low-budget, steamy, Sirkian melodramas, many featuring Robert Cowan and Donna Kerness, and all shot in garish color using standard 8mm equipment. Some of these films, notably *Pussy on a Hot Tin Roof*, survive today in 16mm blowups, with their original tape soundtracks transferred to a 16mm optical track. Others, such as *Born of the Wind*, *A Town Called Tempest*, *Lust for Ecstasy*, *I Was a Teenage Rumpot*, and *The Lovers of Eternity* are more difficult to see. After these early films, the brothers split up to create a long series of separate films, including George Kuchar's *Corruption of the Damned* (1965) and his elegantly graceless *Hold Me While I'm Naked* (1966), a 17-minute featurette which remains one of the most famous films of the New American Cinema. Mike Kuchar created *Sins of the Fleshapoids* (1965), a 50-minute color sound 16mm featurette starring Robert Cowan and Donna Kerness, followed by *Green Desire* (1965) and *The Secret of Wendell Samson* (1966). More recently, George Kuchar has directed *Leisure* (1966), *Mosholu Holiday* (1966), and *Encyclopedia of the Blessed* (1968); and, more recently, *The Devils Cleavage* (1975), *Wild Night in El Reno* (1977), *Blips* (1979), and *Ascension of the Demonoids* (1986; this last film constitutes a sort of return to the past for the director). Mike Kuchar has been less preoccupied with production, creating only a few films (*The Craven Slucks*, *Variations*, *Dwarf Star* and *Faraway Places* [all 1974]) since the duo's breakup.

George Landow, who later changed his name to Owen Land, has continually revised, retitled, and reedited his works during his long career as a filmmaker. Landow was one of the first filmmakers to treat the medium of the cinema directly in his earliest standard 8mm works, including *Are Era* (1963), *Richard Kraft at the Playboy Club* (1963), *Fleming Faloon Screening* (1963), *Not a Case of Lateral Displacement* (1964), and *Adjacent Yes, But Simultaneous?* (1965). These very short films, ranging in length from 1½ minutes (or twenty-five 8mm feet) to 8 minutes, were mounted together as a one-reel show by the filmmaker, but have since been withdrawn from circulation. *Fleming Faloon* (1963–64), an absurdist structuralist collage film was produced in 16mm. Critic Noel Burch cited *Fleming Faloon* as "the freshest film" of the 1964 International Exposition of the New American Cinema (FMC 1967, 81). But Landow's major breakthrough came with *Film in Which There Appear Sprocket Holes, Edge Lettering, Dirt Particles, Etc.* (1965–66), a 4½-minute film manufactured as a "ready-made" in the spirit of Marcel Duchamp out of "China Doll" timing leader, which is used to grade the colors and density of film prints in the laboratory. As Landow himself noted, "this film takes the view that certain defining characteristics of the medium, such as those mentioned in the title, are visually 'worthy'" (FMC 1967, 81). *Film in Which* . . . was also presented in a 20-minute "wide-screen" version, using two 16mm projectors to create a double-paneled incarnation of the film. *Bardo Follies* (later cut from 45 minutes to 7 minutes by the filmmaker, and retitled *Diploteratology*) (1967), in which a loop of a carnival float repeatedly passing in front of the camera gradually degenerates through reprinting, burning, and raw stock manipulation, further consolidated Landow's reputation as one of the most individual and iconoclastic talents of the New American Cinema. Landow's later films take the form of instructional, or educational movies (such as *Remedial Reading Comprehension* [1970] and *Institutional Quality* [1969]), and become ever more mysterious and self-knowing as they shrink in length. *Thank You Jesus for the Eternal Present* (1973) is 5³/₄ minutes; *No Sir, Orison* runs 2³/₄ minutes in its entirety. Landow's most recent work is the perversely humorous *On the Marriage Broker Joke As Cited by Sigmund Freud in Wit and Its Relation to the Unconscious, or Can the Avant-Garde Artist Be Wholed?* (1980).

Interviewing Landow in the late 1960s, I noted that

George Landow was born in New Haven, Connecticut, in 1944. He attended public schools in the area, and while in high school borrowed a friend's camera: "It was an old Kodak home movie camera. I made about three or four kinds of ambitious films; they were more traditionally Avant-Garde. Brakhage and Markopolous were my main influences then: I was doing psychodrama stuff. I never released them; I don't even know where they are right now; I think they're with my family out in Indiana. That was around 1960, when I was 17."

"After that, I got into painting a lot, and for a couple of years I did no film work at all. I've never studied film formally; I think the films I make are much more related to painting than to film as taught commonly." He attended the Pratt Institute and the Art Students League, where he studied painting, sculpture, graphic and design arts from 1962 to 1965. "I was an art student, and I guess the modern technique of teaching art is to try a little of everything. When I went back to films, I had a new orientation, which was much more plastic. I did a series of 8mm films which culminated in *Fleming Faloon*. The series of 8mm studies were applications of ideas from painting transferred to film."

"I didn't want to make films that were narrative; I found the whole traditional narrative approach was really non-visual. This transference of mediums (painting into film) gave birth to a new film aesthetic, film in the purest sense of the word. The 8mm studies (*Are Era, Richard Kraft at the Playboy Club, Fleming Faloon Screening, Not a Case of Lateral Displacement,* and *Adjacent Yes, But Simultaneous?*) are progressively removed by steps: the first is a television MC photographed off a flickering screen; the second is the same thing with a real face superimposed over the TV image; the third is a film of a film being projected, shot off the screen; and so on."

Following these brief studies, Landow made his first 16mm film, *Fleming Faloon.* For *Fleming Faloon,* Landow combined all his previous

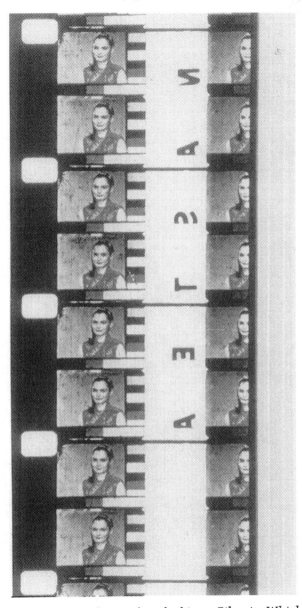

FIGURE 33. Film as found object: *Film in Which There Appear Sprocket Holes, Edge Lettering, Dirt Particles, Etc.* by George Landow (Owen Land). Courtesy Anthology Film Archives.

FIGURE 34. George Landow in his apartment, 1969. Courtesy Anthology Film Archives.

"studies" by using unslit 8mm copies of them, shot off a screen, and then superimposing a copy of *that* copy shot off the screen. *Fleming Faloon* was shown at the 1964 International Exposition of New American Cinema, and attracted considerable critical attention. Next, Landow made a 16mm loop film of some "China Doll" test leader, an image of a young woman blinking her eye repeatedly, which was to be projected continuously for 11 minutes, interrupted by a commercial, and then run for 11 minutes more. When the film was shown at the Cinematheque, the audience reacted violently and the screening was cut short. Landow printed the loop optically into a 4-minute film entitled, *Film in Which There Appear Sprocket Holes, Edge Lettering, Dirt Particles, Etc.* Of the film, Landow says: "The film takes the view that certain defining characteristics of the medium, such as those mentioned in the title, are visually 'worthy.'" Following this, Landow prepared a 20-minute, split-screen expansion of the same loop, which he calls "a gaze fixing meditation piece, which brings to life any plane surface. It looks better because it's more of a horizontal film than a vertical film; you look *across* it, not *into* it. It also brings the blinking more into focus."

"Then I did some more 8mm things, but at that time I was studying art, and I didn't really have that much time to work on film. The next film that I released then was *Diploteratology, or Bardo Follies* (1967–68). A friend of mine was very interested in The Tibetan Book of the Dead, and he got me interested in it. If you accept the Tibetan sense, we're all here because of follies in the Bardo (a spirit-life state). Also, I was living across from the Bowery Follies at the time, so that may have something to do with it." The film is in three sections: in the first third of the film, a young woman in garish 1930s Technicolor, repeatedly waves goodbye to a passing banana boat; in the second section, the same scene is repeated simultaneously on three small screens inside the main screen; the final portion of the film shows the loop burning, frame by frame, suggesting both the destruction of the cinematic image, and the loss of desire and memory itself.

Landow's next work was *Film Which Rises to the Surface of Clarified Butter* (1968) which shows a young woman drawing an unspecified extinct animal, which comes to life and does a little dance, as the woman points to it with a gesture of distress, or urgency. This is repeated several times, and then a man goes through the same actions. With each successive repetition, the film gets fainter and fainter: a copy, then a copy of a copy, and so on. "I wanted a kind of imagery that didn't refer to anything in our visual vocabulary, and also was so non-objective that it didn't refer to anything. I never know if something's going to work until I've done it; my films are more or less intuitive. The thing I'm working on now is more conventional, it has more to do with structure."

"There are a lot of filmmakers whom I admire, like Len Lye and Ed Emshwiller, but as far as aesthetics, there are very few filmmakers I admire; thinking aesthetically, I think people in other areas are much

FIGURE 35. Death and regeneration: three frames from George Landow's *Bardo Follies* (*Diploteratology*). Courtesy Anthology Film Archives.

more advanced, like Claes Oldenburg and Jim Rosenquist. I'm interested in that type of thinking which is involved with seeing the object, and then seeing it again in an entirely different way. A reinterpretation of seeing. The point of my films is not to involve the spectator . . . emotionally in a situation; it's to keep the distance, so s/he's aware of the situation, where s/he is, and who s/he is, keeping her/him in present time. The point is to sharpen the sensibilities and increase the eye's awareness, to ultimately bring about a spiritual awareness . . ." (Dixon papers, 1969)

David Larcher's epic *Mare's Tail*, a 163-minute film that structures itself very much after the fashion of Jean-Isidore Isou's *Venom and Eternity*, caused a sensation in the early 1970s on the museum and university film screening circuit, yet it is all but forgotten today. Disjointed, fragmented, and willfully self-destructive, the film assaults the viewer with each new frame, seemingly losing control of itself even as it seeks to establish visual primacy over the spectator. In films such as these, "what inspires the cinematic spectator is a passion for that very loss of control, that abjection, fragmentation, and subversion of self-identity that psychoanalytic theory so dubiously classifies under the rubrics of lack and castration" (Shaviro, 57); one gives one's self over to the film entirely by the mere fact of watching it unspool. "The self is repetitively shattered" (Shaviro, 56) by the brutal anti-narrative tactics of such films as *Mare's Tail* and *Venom and Eternity*; indeed, the filmmakers in each case demand that the viewer aggressively confront the film, either submitting to the visual assault constituted by its ragged imagery, or rejecting the film, and one's abjection to it, outright.

Standish Lawder, who coordinated the Yale Film Festival for many years in the 1960s and '70s while serving as Professor of Cinema at Yale, created a series of delicate meditations on the human condition, including *Necrology* (1969), a 12-minute take of a group of bone-tired commuters descending on an escalator at the end of the work day. Other Lawder films, such as *Runaway* (1969), which manipulates a scrap of an old cartoon through a variety of printing and video techniques, and *Corridor* (1968–70), with a soundtrack composed by Terry Riley, are romantic yet formal evocations of the artistic impulse as mediated by the exigencies of modern existence. Lawder now lives and teaches in California, where he continues to make films and videos. Lawder is also responsible for restoring the films of pioneering abstract filmmaker Hans Richter to general distribution.

Dov Lederberg created *The Lilaku*, or *Lilith Cycle*, between April 1963 and June 1964. Mixing Beatles' music and Rilke, these three highly personal visions (*Tree*, 9 minutes; *Mother*, 7 minutes; and

Handheat, 17 minutes) coalesce into a coherent and cohesive whole. Lederberg also created a burlesque on the life of Vincent van Gogh, *Eargogh* (made between June 1964 and June 1965) starring Jack Smith as Van Gogh, with Marie Menken as the madame of a particularly debauched brothel. The film was shot in 16mm color, with a running time of 35 minutes. Lederberg also kept an 8mm diary, *Trips*, which he would only project in person, using his own equipment (much as the Kuchar brothers insisted upon, presenting their early standard 8mm films only under their own immediate auspices).

Francis Lee created a superb 3-minute compendium of classic experimental cinema clips in his *Filmmakers' Showcase* (1963), a color and sound "trailer" for a series of weekly screenings in the early 1960s at New York's Gramercy Arts Theatre. Seen today, the film effortlessly evokes the energy and egalitarian spirit that informed both the production and exhibition of 1960s experimental cinema, and works quite effectively as a piece of highly kinetic cinema in its own right. Incorporating behind-the-scenes clips of Gregory Markopolous directing one of his films and of Robert Breer working at his animation stand, interspersed with scenes from numerous early experimental classics, this is a film that should be a regular (and highly compact) introduction to any study of the works of this era.

Alfred Leslie, who collaborated with Robert Frank on *Pull My Daisy* (cited earlier in this text), also directed the bizarre narrative *The Last Clean Shirt* (1964), a 40-minute film that presents the same sequence three times, but from three different points of view. The dialogue for the film was written by the poet Frank O'Hara, and the film was screened at the New York Film Festival in 1964, with a rather hostile audience reception. Nevertheless, the film was singled out for praise by critic Philip Hartung in *Commonweal* who found *The Last Clean Shirt* "fascinat[ing] [. . .] I applaud Alfred Leslie's intention in telling the same story three times" (FMC 1967, 84). Leslie also produced and directed *Philosophy in a Bedroom* (1966), a film which was released in two versions, one 70 minutes long and one 40 minutes long. *Philosophy in a Bedroom* featured dialogue by Frank O'Hara and Alfred Leslie, with contributions by "Alexis de Tocqueville [and the] Marquis de Sade"; among the members of the cast were "Miles Forst, Dorothea Rockburn [and] Bill de Kooning" (FMC 1967, 84).

Charles Levine collaborated with Warhol associate Paul Morrissey on the short film *Peaches and Cream* (1964), which examined the paintings of artist Stanley Fisher. On his own, Levine produced *Andy's White Holes* (1965), *Shooting Guns* (1966, a "news-reel" of Jonas Mekas shooting his film *Guns of the Trees*), *The Sound of*

Chartreuse (1967), *Frost Free Forever* (1967), *Si See Sunni* (1967), *Siva* (1967), *Bessie Smith* (1968), *Apropos of San Francisco* (1968, featuring filmmaker Ben Van Meter in a rare on-screen appearance), *Horseopera* (1970), *Steps* (1976), and *Levine's Mother* (1980). *Levine's Mother* appeared in two versions. One version is an hour in length, black and white, with sound; the other edition is thirty minutes long, and silent. Critic Lenny Lipton described Levine's *Bessie Smith* as "the best film I've seen this year [. . .] a masterpiece" (FMC 1989, 333). **Naomi Levine** created a series of rigorously beautiful films, beginning in the early 1960s, such as *Yes* (1963), *Jeremelu* (1964), *Prismatic* (1968), *From Zero to 16* (1969), *Premoonptss* (1969), *At My Mother's House* (1970), and numerous other works.

Saul Levine, working in 8mm and 16mm, began his work as a filmmaker with *Salt of the Sea, Ivan's Scarf, The Queen of Night, Gotta Box of Light* (featuring Vivian Kurz, Andrew Meyer and René Ricard), *Tear/Or* (1967), *Cats Cradle Harp Wind Lock Heart* (1967), *The Big Stick* (1967–73), *Saul's Scarf, Note One, Note to Pati, Lost Note, Not Even a Note, Starfilm* (1975), *New Left Note* (1968–1972), *Charlatan* (1976–77), *On Guard* (1977–78), *Bopping the Great Wall of China Blue, A Few Tunes Going Out* (1979–84), *Raps and Chants* (1981–82), *Note to Poli* (1982–83), *Four Films* (1984), *Unemployment*, and many other works. Not all of Saul Levine's works can be precisely dated. The best of Levine's films are deeply personal diary films, or portraits, chronicling Levine's own odyssey as a poet and filmmaker, a person who works entirely on his own uncompromising terms as an independent artist.

Bob Liikala, whose contribution the experimental cinema of the 1960s is often overlooked, created the early pop art films in *Fatem/In the Labyrinth/Now* (1966–67), a three-part film chronicling a Happening staged in New York City in the early 1960s, intercut with a mixture of stock footage and other found material, and *Boxed In* (1965), which was described as "a study in Camp Sadism. Old vaudeville jugglers phallically toss chromium pins in contrast to voyeuristic vignettes of black laced, high-heeled women boxers . . ." (FMC 1967, 86).

The late **Carl Linder**, whose work is almost completely marginalized today, created a series of violently surreal films in the early 1960s, which were highly celebrated at the time of their original release. In a statement from the mid 1960s on his work, Linder stated his objective in all his films:

> I try to debase my art, to violate it, to impregnate it. Often you will notice an image which deflates—or a gesture that castrates. The impor-

tance of image in my art is in its special nature. It represents neither a tree nor any known being—for the image is personal, but personal like the fall of a garment over one's shoulders. The image can be *read but not labeled*. It is almost supernatural—it is a totemic, occult and devilish thing. It overpowers with ugliness. And it defends itself like the devil against innocuousness. Thus, when one of my films ends, it is the final removal of obstruction to this image, however sinister it may be. The image may be manifest as an attitude even—but one that has been shaped, hammered, in short, named. (FMC 1967, 86)

Thus, such early Linder films as *The Devil Is Dead* (1964), *Skin* (1964), *Overflow* (1966), *Detonation* (1966), and *Womancock* (1965), along with a series of films released and then withdrawn by the filmmaker (including *Apocalypse, Mother's Little Helper, Going, The Black and White Peacock, The Telephonic Dolls*, and *The Allergist*), are composed of a series of violent and intentionally disturbing images that directly confront and/or assault the viewer. Jonas Mekas dubbed Linder's films "neo-surrealist poetry" in a *Village Voice* review of January 28, 1965, and went on to comment that "*The Devil Is Dead* wasn't an accident. His new film *Skin* is very, very good [. . .] a beautiful film to look at" (as cited in FMC 1967, 86). Carl Linder continued working in cinema right up until his untimely death. His films certainly deserve a retrospective screening in view of the contemporary revival of interest in the New American Cinema.

Lenny Lipton was active as a part of Canyon Cinema during the cooperative's early years; he also wrote film criticism for the *Berkeley Barb*. Among his films are *Happy Birthday, Lenny* (1965), *We Shall March Again* (1965), *The Dunes of Truro* (1966), *Memories of an Unborn Baby* (1966), *Powerman* (1966), *Below the Fruited Plane* (1966), *Ineluctable Modality of the Visible* (1966), *Let a Thousand Parks Bloom* (1969), and *People* (1969). Filmmaker **Carla Liss** created *The Kiss*, a one-minute B/W silent film documenting an instant of evocative romance. Liss was also active as an administrator and writer during this period.

Jock Livingston's *Zero in the Universe*, shot in 35mm in the early 1960s in Amsterdam, was directed by George Moorse and produced by Livingston from a script by Livingston and Moorse. The 85-minute film was described by Livingston as "a comedy, a cryptogram—a message in code to the viewer. Who is Zero? What universe? What is the opposition of Zero and his arch enemy, Steinmetz? [. . .] the film presents abundant clues, but the answers are never stated [. . .]" Critical reception was rapturous: "the film is sometimes comic, sometimes poetic, sometimes both, and frequently beautiful," said *The Villager*, while the *Glasgow Herald* called *Zero in the*

Universe "a glorious spoof [. . . on] the whole climate of life today."
The East Village Other cited the film as "the first truly expanded consciousness on celluloid." Seymour Krim commented that he was "baffled the first time. The second time I relaxed and enjoyed it. The third
time I plan to get high and sneak right into the bizarre action. How
many flicks do you want to see three times in three different ways?"
(all as cited in FMC 1967, 88–89). Awarded a special prize for cinematography at the Mannheim Film Festival in 1966, *Zero in the Universe* is one of the key early '60s "beat consciousness" films, whose
accomplishment has somehow been obscured through the machina-
tions of the canonical process.

Other filmmakers who created original and individual films
during this period include **Roy Loe**, whose *321* (1966) was photographed at the Jewish Museum, and documents the sculpture of
Jean Tinguely. Loe also created *Temporalysis* (1966), a 12-minute
silent loop film. **Stephen Lovi's** *A Portrait of the Lady in the Yellow
Hat* was described by Stan Brakhage as "one of the finest visually-ori-
ented slapstick comedies I've ever seen [. . .] a cross between
Broughton, Breer, Vanderbeek and Emshwiller" (FMC 1967, 89).
Gavin MacFayden and **Charles Leigh-Bennett** created *Rubbish People* in 1966, a 17-minute black and white 16mm documentary on the
plight of a group of tenants in a London slum. The film was shown at
film festivals in Salerno, Mannheim, Leipzig, Oberhausen, and Cairo
in 1966, and was well received in all cases; it was cited as the "best
information film" at Salerno. It was also screened at the Museum of
Modern Art in New York City. **Leroy McLucas** made the beautiful
documentary of life and work in the sugar cane fields, *Dulce
Domingo Dulce*, a 16mm sound B/W film of ten minutes' length.
Jonas Mekas noted that McLucas's "temperament and [. . .] eyes are
those of a poet" (FMC 1967, 90).

Willard Maas, co-founder of the Gryphon Group with his wife
and fellow filmmaker Marie Menken, created a beautiful series of
experimental narratives starting with the feature film *Narcissus*,
which Maas co-produced with Ben Moore. *Geography of the Body*,
with commentary by the poet George Barker, followed. Other Maas
films include *The Mechanics of Love, Image in the Snow* (co-directed
with Marie Menken), *A Valentine for Marie* (co-directed with John
Hawkins), *Andy Warhol's Silver Flotations* (1966, documenting the
show of Warhol's floating silken pillow sculptures at the Leo Castelli
Gallery), and *For Leo Castelli* (1966, a documentary of Castelli and his
more celebrated artists, such as Roy Lichtenstein, James Rosenquist
and Warhol). Maas's last two films were *Orgia* and *Excited Turkeys*.
His death created a void in the ranks of the original founders of the

American Avant-Garde. In his early years, Maas was better known as a poet, and was "the author of two books of verse and winner of *Poetry* magazine's Guarantor's Prize[. . . . Maas] was chairman of the first symposium on 'Poetry and Film' at Cinema 16, in which Dylan Thomas, Maya Deren, Arthur Miller and Parker Tyler appeared" (FMC 1989, 374). Maas and Menken are truly two of the most influential and important cinema artists of the first wave of the New American Cinema.

Robert Machover directed the nihilist documentary *Troublemakers* with Norman Fruchter; the 54-minute film, photographed by Machover, was "about community organizing in a Newark, New Jersey ghetto," according to Machover, and Jonas Mekas called *Troublemakers* "the only film I know that preaches revolution." *Troublemakers* was also screened at the Fourth Annual New York Festival to enthusiastic notices, and was cited as "perhaps the best film of the New American Left [. . .] avoiding both liberal clichés and propaganda" (FMC 1967, 92). As a document of its time, the film is unsurpassed in relating the reality and tension of the political climate during this turbulent era, and the film is yet another overlooked and undervalued work which pressingly merits our immediate attention as viewers, critics, and cultural historians. More than that, it is a call to action, for "art is contemplation and conceptualization, the ritual exhibitionism of primal mysteries. Art makes order of nature's cyclonic brutality. Art, I said, is full of crimes" (Paglia, 34).

CHAPTER FOUR

■■

Malanga to Snow

Gerard Malanga is familiar to most historians as Andy Warhol's assistant, and the "Prime Minister" of the Warhol Factory scene from its inception through 1970. In addition to his work as a filmmaker and his many years with Warhol, Gerard is also a poet of international standing, whose interviews, articles and book reviews have appeared in the *New Yorker, Partisan Review, Poetry,* the *Paris Review, Art and Literature, Lugano Review, New York,* the *Sunday Herald Tribune Magazine,* the *World Journal Tribune, Chicago Review, Status and Diplomat,* and the Italian edition of *Vogue.* Although Warhol's work is well known, Gerard's aggressively Romantic films have never received the acclaim or attention due them, and this is one of the canonical defects the present volume hopes to correct. Making it all the more difficult is the fact that Gerard has withdrawn all of his films from circulation; hopefully, Malanga will see fit to redistribute them in the near future, and thus allow contemporary viewers access to his unique and elegant vision. Interviewing Malanga during 1968 and 1969, I took these notes:

> Of his films, Gerard Malanga notes that "I want to make films as though films were to have the form its content involved, as though not only the eye but the mind was to be its measurer, as though the intervals of its superimpositions (i.e., natural fade-ins and fade-outs) could be so carefully spaced as to be precisely the intervals of its registrations upon one another. Form is never any more than an extension of content, for it is impossible to proceed to the form (structure) of film, or poems

for that matter, without preparing the content on which the form is to be placed. For the eye, which once had the burden of memory to quicken it, can now again be the threshold of projective film [. . .] the reason why I have turned to film as a means of artistic expression is because previously to my venture in filmmaking I had no other device in life but poetry, and when I thought poetry had failed me, or that I had failed it, I turned to film to reenact experience [. . .]"

Gerard Malanga was born March 20, 1943. A native New Yorker, he went to school at the School of Industrial Arts, which is now the School of Art and Design, where his classmates included the Kuchar Brothers (underground filmmakers to be) and Donna Kerness (Kuchar superstar-to-be). "We all majored in advertising," he says. When he was a teenager, Malanga danced on the Alan Freed Show, until the payola scandal closed it down. When he was a senior in high school, he met the poet Daisy Aldan, who was then running a poetry workshop. Through her, Gerard got interested in poetry and began meeting members of the New York literary Avant-Garde. Eventually, he met Marie Menken, wife of Willard Maas (also a poet and filmmaker) and began to get interested in filmmaking, although at this time he had shot nothing. At a party at Marie's, he ran into Andy Warhol. Gerard, at this point, had just quit Wagner College and needed a job, so Andy gave him a job as his assistant. "It started out as a summer job, and it's lasted since then."

Gerard had by this time gotten himself a small but growing reputation as a poet, and he presented a series of poetry readings entitled *Screen Tests*, consisting of the silent projection of 16mm film portraits of various Factory "superstars" shot by Warhol, to the accompaniment of live poetry readings by Malanga of his works. These poems and frames from the Warhol "screen tests" were later gathered into a book of poetry, also titled *Screen Tests*, which was published by Kulchur Press in 1967. Malanga subsequently borrowed Warhol's Bolex and began shooting his own films. He had been watching Andy working, and had been in some of his early films. "I realized . . . I saw how easy it was. So, if I'm doing it for him and it's so easy, I should be doing it for myself, too." In 1964 he shot his first film, *Portraits of the Artist As a Young Man*, of which he says: "It's a secret film, I've never shown it. It's screen tests of Andy."

At this point Malanga was more or less experimenting with the film medium, shooting reels of his friends working and experimenting with zooms, pans, and light exposures. During this period he shot a batch of rolls and just kept them, editing them into 1600' reels of raw footage in no particular order. Malanga's next finished film was *Academy Leader*, which consisted of 45 minutes of academy leader (the countdown numbers before a film), while a friend of his, David Murray, read his journals on the soundtrack. That was in early 1965, and he made no other films until *Mary for Mary*, a 12-minute portrait of Mary Woronov and her friends in Cambridge, Massachusetts, during January of 1966. In July of 1966 Malanga shot *Cambridge Diary*, another short film incorporating more footage of his friends and associates. In the same month, Malanga shot *Prelude to International Velvet Debutante*, a 35-minute Warhol static shot film of Susan Bottomly (renamed *International Velvet*) making up in front of a mirror. Malanga still considers all of these films unfinished.

Malanga's first major work, winner of the 1967 Gran Premio Bergamo Internazionale del Film D'Autore and honored at the Chicago Film Festival, was *In Search of the Miraculous* (*Alla Ricerca Del Miracoloso*). This 35-minute, B/W and color film represents a radical departure from all his previous films. B/W and color footage are superimposed in a fantastic mosaic. It tells the story of Malanga's love for model Benedetta Barzini, and of her father's search for her. It was shot over a period of more than a year, went through over four versions of editing before a final print was struck, and combines footage shot by Malanga, Warren Sonbert, Andy Warhol, and Andy Meyer. Of *Alla Ricerca Del Miracoloso*, Malanga says that "as I was making the film, more ideas came; it grew. It's like the idea of one perception leading to another; Charles Olson said that. I wasn't ready to stop the film until I realized I had expanded it to the end. I was searching . . . at the same time as I was making a movie of a search, so I was searching through the film and outside the film."

Following this, Gerard began work on *Pre-Raphaelite Dream*, a 60-minute 16mm split screen color/sound film which took him from April to May, 1968, to shoot, and incorporates three smaller films that he extensively reedited for their inclusion in the film: *Lou Lou Dove Lace, Mother's Day* (not to be confused with James Broughton's film of the same name), and *John Wiener's Trilogy Parts 1 and 3*. Originally, he had planned to present the film on two separate 2000' reels with both images superimposed, but found that the images washed each other out, so he tried running them side by side. "During my one man show at the Cinematheque, I separated the two projectors, just for the fun of it, to see what it looked like; this was just an experiment, a chance, and it looked better than before, the images weren't blocked out, so that's the way *Pre-Raphaelite Dream* became split screen." This pleased him for a time, but the final version has one screen inside the other in the lower right-hand corner. "The large image becomes a concentrated image, the smaller image is a focal point." Malanga feels that he needs to get a print made up of this "inserted screen" version, and so for the present the film is unreleased.

Malanga also shot some footage in 35mm Techniscope and Technicolor in Rome during February to March of 1968 which was to have been called *The Recording Zone Operator*, but it remains unfinished due to lack of funds. The film was screened in 35mm silent black and white work print format on several occasions, at the Elgin Theatre in New York and at Rutgers University with an accompanying tape soundtrack, but a final color composite print has never been struck. Featuring Anita Pallenberg, Tony Kinna, and members of the Living Theatre

FIGURE 36. The Romantic impulse: Gerard Malanga in his film *In Search of the Miraculous*. Courtesy Anthology Film Archives.

troupe, the film is an interesting prefiguration of Wim Wenders's *Wings of Desire*, and deserves to be presented in final format in the near future.

In 1969, Malanga received a grant from the American Film Institute for $5,000 for a short film of children at war called *Children*, dealing with the contrasts between children in America and children in Vietnam, which was projected to run 15 minutes in the final version, but the film was never completed. Gerard feels that only his finished works should be shown: he is dissatisfied with his incomplete projects. He admires Warhol's films, as well as the work of Luchino Visconti, Robert Enrico, and filmmakers Piero Heliczer, Warren Sonbert (in whose films he has appeared a number of times, and vice versa), and David Brooks. His favorite poets are Leonard Cohen, Michael McClure, St. Geraud [aka Bill Knott], and Charles Olson. As a cinema artist, Malanga makes films primarily for himself, like most independent filmmakers, and he says: "If someone doesn't like or appreciate my work that's too bad, but people have been misunderstanding one another since the world began. Either people accept my work or they totally dismiss it. There is no middle." The one theme that runs through all of his work is "a life outside my life: the idea of immortality through my work. My life as one work, and my works as another life." (Dixon papers, 1968–69)

Seen from the vantage point of the virus conscious 1990s, one senses that in all his films, Malanga seeks to create a unified posthuman body, a site of Romantic discourse reminiscent of Halberstam and Livingston's assertion that "posthuman bodies do not belong to linear history [but rather] thrive in subcultures [such as Warhol's Factory]." In their discussion of "voguing," Halberstam and Livingston identify the central activity of many of the Warhol stars and starlets, and, by extension, the "poses" adopted by Malanga and his performers (Barzini, Woronov, Ricard, Sonbert and others) in Malanga's films. In no way can this be seen as a parodic extension of the rites of conventional performance theory, which both Warhol and Malanga disdained; Halberstam and Livingston hold that "to identify voguing as parasitical on Big Culture [. . .] would be as reductive as to try to understand voguing as Romantic Creativity" (4). Malanga's contribution to Warhol's cinematic pantheon was the concept of the self as a work of art, posed and preened to perfection in a series of highly stylized tableaux. Indeed, the work Malanga accomplishes in his films is nothing less than allowing his performers the luxury of self-actualization through attitude in the loosely scripted sequences Malanga creates; taken as a whole, Malanga's cumulative cinematic corpus constitutes one of the major achievements of the Romantic independent cinema in the 1960s.

Lawrence Marinelli's *From the Unknown* and *With Stronger Reason* are both 17-minute, 16mm color sound films with strong fantastic and/or surrealist content. **Eugene and Carole Marner** created *Phyllis and Terry* (1964–65), a 36-minute black and white documentary chronicling the lives of two young African-American women living on the lower East Side of Manhattan. *Cahiers du Cinéma* singled *Phyllis and Terry* out for special praise in 1965 as "precisely the type of human exploration that only cinema can do" (as cited in FMC 1967, 352). The heartbreaking intensity of this *cinema verité* is still affecting and engaging for contemporary audiences, while simultaneously offering the audience a collective window to a past era of lost innocence, when most of the problems facing humanity seemed capable of being solved, no matter how pressing.

Gregory Markopolous created a long series of epic features beginning in the late 1940s, although his first released film was his 1942 version of Charles Dickens's *A Christmas Carol*, made when Markopolous was only twelve years old. Subsequently, Markopolous began production on an ambitious trilogy, *Du Sang de la Volupte et de la Mort*. The first segment of the trilogy, *Psyche*, was produced in 1948 in 16mm color and sound, with music by Ralph Vaughn Williams. This 25-minute film was followed in the same year by the second portion of the trilogy, *Lysis*, a 30-minute color film with music by Arthur Honegger. *Charmides* (1948) completed the trilogy, a 15-minute meditation on the social education of a young man divorced from the social institutions that seek to force him to conform to post World War II society. In 1949, Markopolous began producing a 35mm feature, *The Dead Ones*, dedicated to Jean Cocteau, using a Mitchell studio camera and war surplus B/W negative film stock to economize on production expenses. The film was never finished, and for many years was considered lost, until Markopolous tracked it down at a film laboratory. He had a 16mm reduction print made, and subsequently released it, without revision, in 1966.

Also in 1949, Markopolous produced *Flowers of Asphalt*, a 10-minute silent film, and *Eldora*, a 7-minute color film originally shot in 8mm and then blown-up to 16mm. *Swain* (1950) was Markopolous's next major work, "a personal rendering of the Hyacinthus myth" according to critic P. Adams Sitney (FMC 1967, 95). *Serenity*, a 35mm color film released in two versions, one 90 minutes and one 70 minutes, followed *Swain*, and was perhaps Markopolous's most advanced narrative to that time, with a soundtrack in four languages. *Twice a Man* was completed in 1963, starring Paul Klib, Olympia Dukakis, Albert Torgesen, and Violet Roditi. The 49-minute color 16mm film won the Prix Lambert at the 3rd International Film Competition in Knokke-Le Zoute, Belgium, 1964. The reception of this deeply personal film was rapturous: one critic asserted that "had we been permitted to see only *Twice a Man*, the Festival at Knokke would have justified itself;" Elliot Stein of the *London Financial Times* felt that "one was especially glad to see *Twice a Man* among the prize winners [. . .] both the passion and stature of tragedy was carried out by Markopolous in a technique so advanced and intricate in design it would require certainly more than one viewing before one could claim to really understand it." Bruce Frier in *The Daily Princetonian* claimed that "anyway you see it [. . .] *Twice a Man* is one of the most significant movies of the past decade" (all cited in FMC 1967, 96). *The Death of Hemingway* (1965), based on the play by George Christopoulos, was Markopolous's next project, a 12-minute 35mm short "filmed in 32 hours in Eastman Color in an abandoned theatre in Brooklyn [. . . which attempts] to display the mental state of Ernest Hemingway prior to his suicide" (FMC 1967, 97).

Galaxie (1966) was a departure from Markopolous's penchant for the reinterpretation of classical myth, consisting of thirty film portraits, each 100′ in length. The resultant 90-minute color film is thus thirty 100′ reels edited together with no other external editorial manipulation of the footage. To make *Galaxie*, Markopolous ran each reel of film through the camera multiple times, sometimes executing as many as ten exposures for a single reel. The portraits were usually shot at the apartments of the various subjects, and "all fades, dissolves, single frames here [were] literally conceived and executed during the" production. For his subjects, Markopolous assembled a gallery of some of the most influential figures of twentieth-century art, an undertaking unparalleled in any other American experimental film. Beginning with Parker Tyler, Markopolous created portraits of Storm de Hirsch, Amy Taubin, Jasper Johns, W. H. Auden, Jerome Hill, Allen Ginsberg and Peter Orlovsky, Gregory Battcock, Jan Cremer, Maurice Sendak, Susan Sontag, Gian Carlo Menotti, and many others (FMC 1967, 97). The film has been called a "motionless movie" by some, in that the superimpositions, in conjunction with the minimalist soundtrack, create a series of subtly changing, evanescently subliminal "static" portraits, in which the posed subjects seem to simply exist in front of the lens. But, as with Warhol's early works, a sort of *reducto ad absurdum* is at play here, and as one becomes accustomed to the ever-shifting tapestry of shimmering superimpositions created by Markopolous in *Galaxie*, one gets a strong sense of both personality and place. *Galaxie* was enormously successful, and was followed by *Ming Green* (1966), a portrait of Markopolous's apartment, and *Through a Lens Brightly: Mark Turbyfill* (1966), a brief work in the style of *Galaxie*. Markopolous closed out the decade with the feature film *Himself as Herself* (1966), shot in fourteen days in

Boston; *Eros, O Basileus* (1966), a 45-minute meditation on "the lone-liness of Eros himself"; and *The Divine Damnation* (1967), a 60-minute feature film shot in Chicago.

However, shortly after the completion of *The Divine Damnation*, Markopolous withdrew all of his work from commercial distribution, and moved to Europe to continue making films, and occasionally directing for television. Until his recent death, Markopolous was something of a reclusive figure, seemingly wishing to disassociate himself from the New York independent filmmaking community. The current unavailability of Markopolous's films is lamentable, and hopefully they will be re-released in the near future, so that they may enrich and inspire a new generation of viewers.

In 1964, writing in *Film Comment*, Markopolous summed up his quest as a personal filmmaker: "[I wish] to recreate the essence, the universal meanings, found in the legend not only of Prometheus Bound, but also many of the other ancient legends[. . . .] I do not consider myself a professional. I consider myself as an amateur, that is, a lover of film. My first concern is film [, and I plan] to continue working in film as film as I feel, see, and hear it" (Hitchens 26). In the creation of his films, Markopolous seems to echo the sentiments of Camille Paglia, when she describes the spectator within art as a voyeur "at the perimeters of art . . . art is a scandal, literally a stumbling block to all moralism." In the works of Markopolous, Bill Vehr, Jack Smith, José Rodriguez-Soltero, and others, "there is a sado-masochistic sensuality in our responses to" (35) the works in question. A classicist by disposition, Markopolous was nevertheless a sensualist at the core of his works, more a part of the world of fabrics and flesh-tones inhabited by the "decadents" of the Underground *maudit* than he would have readily admitted. Recently, many of Markopolous's films were screened as part of an extensive retrospective of the artist's work at the Whitney Museum of American Art.

Joseph Marzano created a series of beautifully sensuous films starting in the late 1950s: *While They Sleep* (1957), *Erostratus* (1958), *Trilogy* (1960–61), *The Dancer and the Photographer* (1961), *From Inner Space* (1961), *You or I* (1963), *Barbara* (1963), the feature film *Man Outside* (1965), and *Just Too Precious* (1966). Marzano's best-known short film is probably *From Inner Space*, a bizarre comedy in which a group of unruly coat hangers gang up on an unsuspecting victim. Marzano's feature film *Man Outside* was described by filmmaker Lloyd Michael Williams as "magnificent and truly human," and praised by critic Judith Crist on *The Today Show* on NBC during a review of the film—a reminder that in the early 1960s, experimental films had viable distribution outlets, and access to even the most mainstream media (FMC 1967, 107).

Although not strictly a 1960s independent filmmaker, the late **Curt McDowell's** pioneering hard-edged gay aesthetic marks him as the Queer successor to the luxuriant yet hypersensual world of Jack Smith. His films include *Dora Myrtle*, *Peed Into the Wind*, *Tasteless Trilogy*, *Truth for Ruth* (all made in the late 1960s), and the subsequent work *Pornografollies* (1970), a catalogue of a series of lewd sideshow routines, including, in McDowell's words, the: "Peckernose Act; The Cooking and the Washing Act; Spin Your Little Clothes Off Act; Tea Break; The Spinning Nuns; Balancing Prick Act; The Dirty Hummers; Spanish Dancer Act; The Whora; Picking a Winner; The Poop Chute Act; Waiting and Worrying Nude Act; The Tapping Tennies; The Disappearing Milk and Sandwich Act; The Flower Magician; Fart Chorus; The Whirlwinds; The Paper Bags on the Heads Act; The Belly Dancer; Cheek to Cheek; Head Job Act; Tweeting Prick Act; Fanny Dancer; Back Words Act; Betsy the Cussing Doll; And . . . The Singing Twat" (Canyon Cinema 1992, 233), all in thirty minutes.

This film was followed by *A Visit to Indiana* (1970), a bizarre critique of life in the Midwest; *Confessions* (1971), which McDowell, then "a graduate student at San Francisco Art Institute, opens [. . .] with a confession to his mother and father, listing in exhausting detail his sins of the flesh," (Canyon Cinema 1992, 233); *Wieners and Buns Musical* (1971); *Ronnie* (1972), in which, in McDowell's works "a naked hustler tells his story non-stop" (Canyon Cinema 1992, 233); *Siamese Twin Pinheads* (1972); *A Night with Gilda Peck* (1973); *Boggy Depot* (1974), a seriously demented musical; *Naughty Words* (1974); *Stinkybutt* (1974); *True Blue and Dreamy* (1974); and *Fly Me to the Moon* (1975). *Nudes: A Sketchbook* (1975) was, in a number of respects, McDowell's breakthrough film into the established canon of experimental cinema; James Broughton, among others, praised the film's "real feeling for the subject" (Canyon Cinema 1992, 234). It paved the way for *Thundercrack* (1975) and *Loads* (1980), perhaps McDowell's best-known film. Reacting to *Loads*, David Ehrenstein observed that "San Francisco–based Curt McDowell has always been a pioneer in sexual frankness, but his new film, *Loads*, goes far beyond his earlier all-out efforts and puts such big-time dabblers in eroticism as Bernardo Bertolucci and Nagisa Oshima decidedly in the shade" (as cited in Canyon Cinema 1992, 234).

Working on the fringes of parody, yet possessed with a core of serious social commentary, McDowell's films are uniquely his own, although the influence of his friend George Kuchar (no stranger to cin-

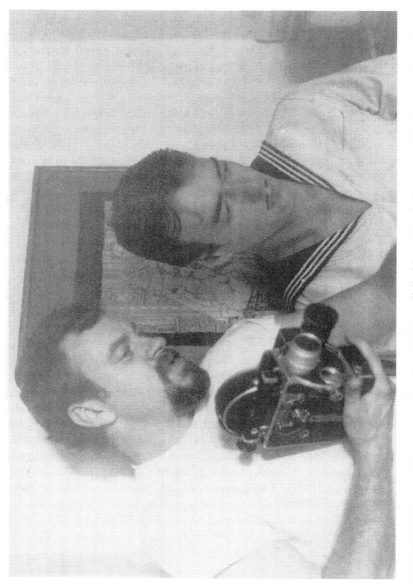

FIGURE 37. Queer Cinema practice: Curt McDowell (holding Bolex). Photograph by Stewart Bass. Courtesy Canyon Cinema.

ematic excess) can readily be discerned in McDowell's earlier efforts. By the time McDowell created his final works, his vision had become raw, uncompromising, and bereft of any sense of parodic camouflage. *Loads*, in particular, is the work of an artist possessed of an acute social vision, but then again, McDowell was never a filmmaker to shy away from controversy.

As Jack Bubuscio wrote of *Thundercrack* (1975) in the *London Gay News*, "*Thundercrack* is the hardest of hard-core pictures—the most sexually explicit movie I've ever viewed in Britain: solo, lesbian, heterosexual and mixed male couplings are viewed with a remorseless camera. This is, in short, a steamy spoof filmed with a sure and witty grasp of genre conventions whose prevailing mood is one of buoyancy and exhilaration. *Thundercrack* is, simply, pro-sex—of all sorts: try it, you'll like it—that's its theme . . ." (Canyon Cinema 1992, 234). McDowell's films acknowledge Fredric Jameson's assertion that "the visual is *essentially* [Jameson's emphasis] pornographic [. . .] the most austere films necessarily draw their energy from the attempt to repress their own excess . . ." (1). In McDowell's work, repression has been banished as a primary condition of the film's initial conception, thus concomitantly freeing the spectator to participate in the sexual spectacle McDowell so insistently (re)presents.

Taylor Mead is best known for his brilliant improvisatory comic acting in numerous independent films of the 1960s to the present. His work in numerous films of Andy Warhol, Ron Rice, Paul Morrissey, Lloyd Michael Williams, Robert Downey, and others is documented elsewhere through this book. But he also made two personal diary films in 16mm color, using a 50' cartridge loading Keystone camera and shooting "single frame" for most of the time to conserve raw film stock, which even then cost $10 for a 50' cartridge. *My Home Movies* (1964) covers Mead's travels in Mexico City, New York, and Malibu; *European Diaries* (1966) follows Mead's wanderings through Europe during this tumultuous decade. As a filmmaker, Mead brings his own pixilated comic imprint to the visual blitz of images he creates. Critics Jean-Jacques Lebel and Noel Burch called *My Home Movies* a "masterpiece"; Julian Beck, co-founder of the Living Theatre with Judith Malina, noted that "after seeing Taylor Mead's diaries I can't look around myself anymore. There is so much to see! So now I sit with my back to nature, like Gertrude Stein" (as cited in FMC 1967, 102).

In 1964, Mead described his plans for future films for the journal *Film Comment*:

[. . . I hope] to continue with my home movies (random unedited in 16mm color) until I get enough backing to make my first self-directed,

self-starred, self-edited opus—*Taylor Mead Sings and Dances, Sort Of*
[. . .] plans at present call for opening shots of New York to Debussy's
La Mer—camera swings down to a long shot of some creature lurking in
a decadent doorway doing something—close-up shows him surrepti-
tiously scribbling "Taylor Mead Taylor Mead Taylor Mead" (introduction to film—further titles just as imaginative), then commence swing
up into sky and down through a maze of fire-escapes and windows (a
vast dissolve) to T. M. sitting in a window on fire escape with guitar and
he does inimitable (questionable) rendition of *Moon River*—camera to
"crossing you in style someday"—cut to rowboat in Central Park or a
Rolls Royce or whatever is available for a dance, another song, or a pastiche of friends, acquaintances, melee and much raw strange talent,
which I have among my friends, in various lofts, apartments and outdoor locations—over last ten months I have written down titles of
music I especially want to relate to (while I was wandering streets with
my portable FM)—even long dances down streets [. . .] in course of film
there would be considerable variation from myself and much of it I want
open to suggestion from the moment, surroundings, music, whatever is
floating in the air. (Hitchens 27)

In a letter to the author dated July 15, 1995, Mead remembered
working with Ron Rice in the early 1960s:

Looking at the picture [see still on page 119]—on the left we have Jerry
Joffen with his hand raised holding a cigarette. He is or was a filmmaker
who had us spend hours putting on costumes and makeup (like Jack
Smith) and then would put a veil over the camera nearly obliterating
us—very frustrating. But several critics including Jonas praised him and
he was an interesting person. Jack Smith was even more meticulous
about makeup. [I remember] at least . . . one occasion where after many
hours . . . I walked out [because] . . . Jack never got around to filming.
But at least Jack didn't usually cover up the lens with a veil. I didn't
speak to Jack the last several years of his life even though he lived a
block away—he was too insulting on occasion. And too SLOW! (Meticulous? Crazy?) (Multiple choice.) The film Ron and I [are] looking at was
probably *Queen of Sheba Meets the Atom Man*—1962—my favorite of
the nearly 100 films I've been in. In the center of the Xerox photo page
is Ron Rice and Jack Smith in a photo booth session. (letter to the
author)

Mead remains active as an actor and writer to this day, making frequent appearances at benefits, and lending his unique presence to a
myriad of independent film and video projects.

Abbott Meader produced a beautiful series of daily meditations
in 16mm silent films documenting the circumstances of his daily
existence. *Oct.* (1962), *A Looking for Summer* (1963), *Bone* (1963), *An*

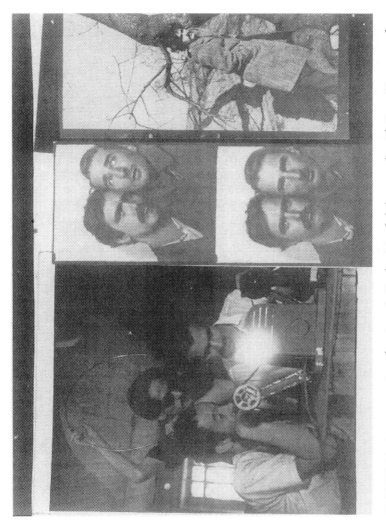

FIGURE 38. A community of artists: 1. Taylor Mead, left, seated, with Ron Rice, seated, at film viewer during editing of *Queen of Sheba Meets the Atom Man*; Jerry Joffen stands in background; 2. A photo-booth strip of Ron Rice, left, and Jack Smith; 3. Ron Rice standing next to a tree. Courtesy Anthology Film Archives.

Interior (1963), *Gain Again* (1964), *The Elms* (1964), *Summer Storm Passage* (1964–65), *Vigil* (1965), and *Departure* (1965) are all brief, silent films, with running times ranging from 5 to 10 minutes. In their quiet and patient construction, and their devotion to the details of light, textures, fabrics, and the changing seasons, Meader's films are akin to Nathanael Dorsky's *Hours for Jerome* or Joseph Seigh's *The Dream Reel*. Meader's only sound film, *Celebration #1* (1966), has a soundtrack by Bach, Handel, Mingus, Sonny Stitt and Joan Baez, and carries forward the concerns of his earlier lyrical works with grace and assurance.

Jonas Mekas's influence as a writer and theoretician of the New American Cinema is incontestable, but his career as a filmmaker predates, and extends beyond, his work as a critic. Mekas's first feature, *Guns of the Trees*, was shot in 35mm in 1962; the members of the creative unit working on the film included the late Allen Ginsberg (who wrote and recited poetry for the soundtrack), Sheldon Rochlin, Ben Carruthers, Louis Brigante, George Maciunas, and many others. Mekas's next film was the summer, 1963, production of *Film Magazine of the Arts*, a 20-minute color and black and white newsreel of (in Mekas's words) "Shakespeare in the park; Marisol; Warhol; Jasper Johns; Sardi's; Jerry Joffen; Eric Hawkins; Lucia Dlugoszewski; A Happening by Whitman" (FMC 1989, 360). Storm de Hirsch composed some music for the soundtrack; Ed Emshwiller, David Brooks, and Mekas served as cinematographers for the project; final editing was completed by Mekas and filmmaker Barbara Rubin. The film was originally commissioned by *Show* magazine (now defunct), but the editors of *Show* apparently weren't happy with the result, and kept the original printing materials for the film. Mekas eventually released the work print of the film to general distribution.

Other films followed in rapid succession. One night in 1964, Mekas filmed the Living Theater's production of *The Brig*, from the play by Kenneth Brown, after the theatrical production had been closed down by the police. Using two stationary cameras and one hand-held machine, Mekas shot the play in a series of 400' bursts, and edited the footage into a harrowing 68-minute document which won the Grand Prize at the Venice, Italy, Documentary Festival in 1964. Later films included numerous editions of his film diaries, including *Walden* (filmed between 1964 and 1968, edited in 1968–69), documenting Mekas's early days in the New American Cinema; *Reminiscences of a Journey to Lithuania* (1971–72); *Lost, Lost, Lost* (1976); *He Stands In a Desert Counting the Seconds of His Life* (1969–1985), and many other works. Mekas also organized the Filmmakers Cooperative in the early 1960s, and founded (along with colleagues Ken Kelman,

James Broughton, P. Adams Sitney and Peter Kubelka) Anthology Film Archives in 1970.

The late **Andrew Meyer** created a group of memorable short films as part of the early 1960s New York independent movement, before he went to Los Angeles and directed several features for Roger Corman (*Night of the Cobra Woman* [1973], *Tidal Wave* [1975]). *Shades and Drumbeats* (1964) was shot in 8mm, entirely silent. It deals with the lives of a number of young people drifting through their lives in search of hope, or love. *Annunciation* (1964), also in 8mm silent format, is a brief autumnal elegy. Another short film, *1x1* (1965), followed, this time in 16mm, although Meyer withdrew it from distribution almost immediately. It is for *Match Girl* (1966) and *An Early Clue to the New Direction* (1966) that Meyer is most fondly remembered. The first film is nominally based on the Hans Christian Andersen fairy tale; Vivian Kurz appeared as the match girl, while Gerard Malanga essayed the role of Prince Charming. Andy Warhol also made a brief appearance in the film.

Of even more interest and subtlety is Meyer's *An Early Clue to the New Direction*, with a fabulously non-synchronous soundtrack featuring music by the pioneering feminist garage-rock band, the Unidentified Flying Objects. Joy Bang, a performer gifted with natural screen presence, is here teamed with Prescott Townsend, a fixture in the Boston/Cambridge scene of the 1960s, while René Ricard appears in a brief cameo. The plot of the film is slight: Joy visits Prescott Townsend's flat in search of René, and despite Townsend's initial suspicious reserve, the two disparate individuals become fast friends. By the end of the film, René has ceased to figure in the narrative. Prescott and Joy bicycle through the streets of Boston in a trance of blissed-out goodwill, as the camera, somewhat unsteadily, follows them in a tracking shot accomplished by the use of an automobile. Technical polish is entirely lacking in the film, but somehow it doesn't matter. In this half-hour film, which won first prize at the 1967 Ann Arbor Film Festival, Meyer has afforded the viewer a lasting vision of a simpler, kinder universe. Meyer subsequently made two more experimental shorts before abandoning independent filmmaking for Hollywood: 1967's *Flower Child* (again with Joy Bang), and the feature film *The Sky Pirate* (1969).

Michael Mideke is another marginalized filmic voice from the 1960s. His works include *Paths of Fire* (1975, 3½ minutes, color, silent; co-made with Neelon Crawford), described by the filmmaker as "an abstract kinetic film derived from fireworks images which have been subjected to a variety of contact and optical printing permutations; resulting in symmetrical, streaming, frozen and otherwise modified images"; *The Veiled Forest* (1977, 4 minutes, color, silent) of which Mideke notes, "this film was made with a modified camera. The camera shutter was removed and replaced so that a part of the exposure was made while the film was in motion, providing a synchronized superimposition of registered and unregistered images. The film consists of a series of slow movements through forest textures. The viewer's attention is constantly moving back and forth between the literal and abstract levels of the film"; *Goats* (1977, 7 minutes, B/W, silent), described as a film that "accompanies a herd of goats during an afternoon's browse in the forest. It is an investigation of goat forms, goat movement and goat time. A brief excursion into an alien culture"; *Shadowgame* (1967, 7 minutes, B/W, silent), which Mideke characterizes as "a thing of light and dark, of rhythm and motion and the play of forms one against another. Although its images are derived from nature (sometimes very directly by the process of contact printing leaves and plants directly onto the film) the construction of the film is abstract. In its abstraction it comes close to laying bare some of the fundamental dynamics of film"; as well as *Twig* (1966, 3 minutes, B/W, silent), *Scratchdance* (1972, 7 minutes, B/W, silent), *Flight of Shadows* (1973, 7 minutes, B/W, silent), *Phi Textures* (1975, 4 minutes, B/W, silent), *Impressions of My Right Hand* (1976, 4½ minutes, B/W, silent), *Rapid Transit* (1962), *Search for Icarus* (1963), *Ming-I* (1964), *Nightride* (my personal favorite of all of Mideke's work that I've seen; 1964), *Aasis* (1965–66), *Mantra* (1966), *Bronze* (1967–68), *Plastic Stone* (1968), *Secret of the Golden Flower* (1968), *Zone 413* (1969–70), *Infinity is 5.4* (1968–69), *Autumn-Winterfilm* (1968–69), *Twelves* (1969), and *Devil's Canyon* (1972–77, 40 minutes, color, silent), "a modular film built up out of a number of short titled sequences. It represents a variety of film responses and explorations inspired by the wilderness area where I live. I see the film as a sort of a walk through a number of places and a number of thoughts on and about film [. . .] I am concerned with particularizing the initially uniform seeming texture of the forest. I am working to produce a film vision which encompasses the subject rather than confronting it . . ." (letter to the author, fall 1995).

Marie Menken was one of the major figures of the American independent cinema during the 1940s through the early 1970s, working with her husband Willard Maas as part of the Gryphon Group, and separately with her own gentle and poetic films. Menken worked for many years as a night teletype operator at *Life* magazine to support the activities of the Gryphons; she also appeared in a number of films by Andy Warhol, particularly *The Chelsea Girls* (1966), in which she portrayed Gerard Malanga's mother. The role was not without its real-life resonance. Menken had functioned as a sort of second mother to Gerard during his early days in the New York underground, and Warhol was quick to capitalize on this fact.

The beauty and brevity of Marie Menken's films is a mark of the simplicity of her vision as an artist. There is nothing remotely pretentious or forced about Menken's films, which seem more than the works of any other artist to possess the crystalline beauty of objects found in nature. The perfection of Menken's films is also a reflection of the generosity of her own spirit as a person; when one looks at a film by Marie Menken, one is acutely aware of the individual consciousness behind the creation of each frame of the film, and one trusts this sensibility instinctively.

Critic Catrina Neiman notes that

from 1941–45 [Marie Menken] worked as a special effects expert for the Signal Corps, making training films and war documentaries. She built and photographed miniature sets simulating, for example, a region of Italy where paratroopers were to land. In this capacity she also provided assistance to other experimental filmmakers: for Deren she animated the chess sequence in *At Land* and "plotted the moving constellations" of stars for *The Very Eye of Night*: for Willard Maas, her husband, she photographed *Geography of the Body* (1943) and *Image in the Snow* (1951), and constructed the miniature set of the Emperor's Court for [Maas's] *Narcissus* (1955).

Of the eighteen films [Menken] made on her own, all are under 11 minutes long (her motto was "Make them short—always!") except [*Andy*] *Warhol* (1965), a time-lapse document of the artist at work (22 min[utes]). Many are in the form of "notes" or sketches in that they embody a single visual idea [. . .] a work like *Drips and Strips* (1961), a simple record of "what happens with paint on glass when it responds to gravity," transformed the notion of what a film could be [. . .] *Dwightiana* (1959) [is] an amusing vision of "stones, beads, pencils, brushes, shells" moving snake-like over the surface of a Dwight Ripley painting, or pixillation, as in *Moonplay* (1962), a dance of the moon in the black sky, filmed "over a period of years from midnight on, always at full moon only" [. . . Menken described] *Go! Go! Go!* (1962–64) [as] "my major film, showing the restlessness of human nature and what it is striving for, plus the ridiculousness of its desires" [The film can best be described as] a time-lapse record of a day in the life of a city [. . .] *Hurry! Hurry!* [1957] attains the austerity and symbolic resonance of Greek tragedy. It is composed of just three elements: sperm cells (so large that one fills the whole frame) struggling to reach an egg and dying one by one, to the sound of bombs exploding, and the whole piteous contest is viewed through the slowly pulsating flame of a candle. (see Neiman, 111–126)

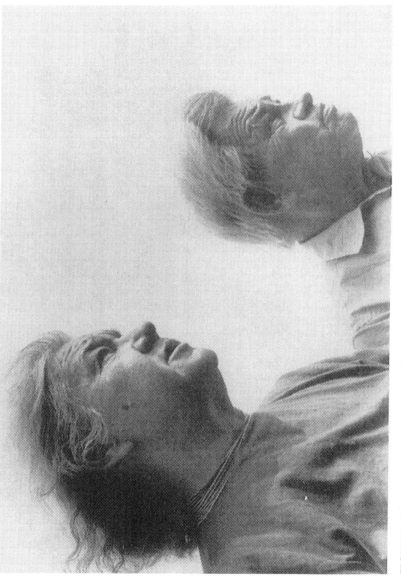

FIGURE 39. Marie Menken and Willard Maas. Photo by John Hawkins. Courtesy Anthology Film Archives.

My own favorite of all of Menken's films is the lyrical and graceful
Glimpse of the Garden (1957), in which Menken's camera sweeps
through a small backyard garden as if imitating the point of view of a
bird; the soundtrack of the film, in fact, is composed of nothing more
or less than continual bird song.

The prolific filmmaker **Gunvor Nelson** gives this biographical
information on the early years of her life: "[She was] born in 1931 in
Stockholm, Sweden. After living in both England and Holland she
returned to her native Sweden and attended Stockholm's famed 'Kon-
stfakskolan.' She immigrated to the U. S. in 1953 and since then she
has earned her Master of Fine Arts degree, become a naturalized citizen, and pursued a career in painting [. . .] *Schmeerguntz* marks her
completed transition from painter to film-maker" (FMC 1967, 115).
Co-made with **Dorothy Wiley**, *Schmeerguntz* is a brief B/W 16mm
short which burst on the then-phallocentric Independent Cinema
landscape with the force of a bombshell, although it was immediately
recognized, perhaps because of the unrelenting brutality of its
imagery, as a major work. The film was a prize winner at the Ann
Arbor Film Festival in 1966, and went on to win additional awards at
the Webster College Film Festival, the Chicago Art Center Festival,
and the Milwaukee Film Festival. Writing in *Film Quarterly*, critic
Ernest Callenbach described the film as "one long raucous belch in
the face of the American home[. . . .] A society which hides its animal
functions beneath a shiny public surface deserves to have such films
as *Schmeerguntz* shown everywhere—in every PTA, every Rotary
Club, every Garden Club in the land. For it is brash enough, brazen
enough, and funny enough to purge the soul of every harried American woman" (as cited in FMC 1975, 193).

This film was followed by *Fog Pumas* (1967)—also co-made with
Dorothy Wiley—a 25-minute film that further consolidated Nelson's
reputation as an innovative and spontaneously contentious film artist.
Contemporary critic Don Lloyd described the film as "[. . .] an updating
of surrealism. It really teases the viewer because you *know* something
is happening, but you don't know what it is. Some of the carefully composed shots are just long enough to allow involvement, and others just
quick enough to be concerned with abstract graphics. The sound track
has the admirable quality of being an integral part of the film" (FMC
1975, 193). The film won awards at the Belgium International Film Festival at Knokke Le Zoute in 1968, and was shown during international
Short Film Week at the British Film Institute in the same year, as well
as being screened at the Oberhausen International Film Festival.

Nelson took a major step forward as a filmmaker with *My Name
Is Oona* (1969), a 10-minute film starring Nelson's daughter, Oona.

FIGURE 40. Sequence
of frames from Marie
Menken's *Glimpse of
the Garden*. Courtesy
Anthology Film
Archives.

FIGURE 41. Guerrilla tactics: Gunvor Nelson (with cigarette) and Dorothy Wiley. Photo by Robert Nelson. Courtesy Canyon Cinema.

The film shows a young child (Oona) riding around on a horse amidst a phantasmagorical landscape of fabrics, superimpositions, and Gustav Klimt–like trees at twilight, coupled with an incantatory and mesmerizing soundtrack by Steve Reich, in which Oona repeats her name as a sort of mantra ("My name is Oona . . . my name is Oona") until the sound of her speech collapses into a dreamlike series of reverberations effected through the use of tape delay mechanisms. Nevertheless, the film is still constructed with a certain element of chance in its design, as images from the "A" and "B" roll melt together to create a vision of childhood unhampered by the artificial "poetry" of more calculated evocations of childhood. Writing in the *Village Voice*, Amos Vogel commented that "*My Name Is Oona* captures in haunting, intensely lyrical images fragments of the coming to consciousness of a child girl. A series of extremely brief flashes of her moving through night-lit space or woods in sensuous negative, separated by rapid fades into blackness, burst upon us like sweet firework clusters, caught by a beautifully fluid camera. Staccato shots of playful, ultimately almost erotic contact with a friend, are followed by the girl, in flowing garment, riding atop a horse along an indistinct landscape, much like a fairy-tale princess [. . .]" (as cited in FMC 1975, 193).

Nelson's next film was *Take Off* (1972), a 10-minute B/W film in which a strip-tease dancer literally deconstructs herself before the gaze of the audience, gradually removing her body parts one by one, until all that is left is the blank space of the returned gaze of the fetishistic viewer. *Moon's Pool* (1972) is a 15-minute color film described by filmmaker Freude Bartlett as a "[. . .] search for identity and resolution of self. Photographed under water, live bodies are intercut with natural landscapes [,] creating powerful mood changes and images surfaced from the unconscious" (FMC 1975, 194). *Trollstenen* (1973–76), an ambitious two-hour feature film, concerns itself with Nelson's home life in Sweden, and is a deeply personal, autobiographical work. *Before Need* (1979) represented another collaboration with Dorothy Wiley; the 70-minute film is a consideration of aging, of lost dreams and hopes, of a future which is suddenly finite after the seemingly endless horizon afforded by youth. Other films are *Red Shift* (1983), *Frame Line* (1983), and *Kirsa Nicholina*, a poetic examination of childbirth, rendered in a style which is at once personal and intimate, yet at the same time mysteriously driven by sexual passion.

Robert Nelson was born in 1930 in San Francisco. He graduated from San Francisco State College, then completed post-graduate work at the San Francisco Art Institute and Mills College, eventually receiving a Master of Fine Arts degree in painting. For several years Nelson lived in France and Spain. Returning to the United States, he taught in the San Francisco School District, San Quentin Prison, and the San Francisco Art Institute. Nelson's first film was the primitive *Plastic Haircut* (1963), a 15-minute B/W "funk" short thrown together from a large quantity of material that Nelson shot of himself and his friends Ron Davis and William Wiley. With its bizarre, *Caligari*esque sets and a crudely constructed audio montage by Steve Reich on the soundtrack, the film is one of the most rigorous of Nelson's works, simultaneously mysterious and inaccessible. This film was followed by *Oh Dem Watermelons* (1965), an 11-minute film which has become something of an underground classic, featuring members of the San Francisco Mime Troupe, with a rough narrative devised by Nelson, Davis, and Saul Landau. The film was originally conceived as a silent work, but several early screenings of the film for even the most partisan audiences proved that it didn't work without a sound-track. Subsequently, Steve Reich created a *mixage* of Stephen Foster songs and a repetitive "Oh Dem Watermelons" chant to accompany the film. The film became an overnight success, and perhaps Nelson's most visible work.

Oh Dem Watermelons begins with a long shot of a watermelon on a football field, as punch holes and leader marks drift by; for a long time, nothing seems to happen. Suddenly a voice on the track announces, "OK, everybody, follow the bouncing watermelon!," and a series of crude "bouncing ball" lyrics (using, in this case, a "bounc-ing watermelon") take the audience through a ragged chorus of Stephen Foster's ultra-racist "Massa's In the Cold, Cold Ground," which segues into Reich's chanted chorus. The film then drifts into a series of intentionally outrageous sight gags: a watermelon is opened to reveal animal intestines bursting forth from inside; a nude women smears herself with a crushed watermelon in a parody of sexual frenzy; various members of the Mime Troupe chase each other through the city streets holding watermelons on their heads, in a bru-tal parody of offensive American ante-bellum imagery. *Oh Dem Watermelons* stills shocks and offends today, which is precisely its intent; and yet the stylistic innocence of the film has recently led some viewers to attack it as an unconsciously racist construct that reinforces the very stereotypes it seeks to deconstruct.

Oh Dem Watermelons was followed by a barrage of similarly constructed, intentionally crude films, including *Thick Pucker* (1965) and *Oiley Peloso the Pumph Man* (1965). *The Great Blondino* (1967), a 45-minute featurette that Nelson co-made with William Wiley, was Nelson's most ambitious film of the period, using intricate sets and multilayered superimpositions to evoke the tale of the nineteenth-century tightrope walker Blondin, who won international notoriety

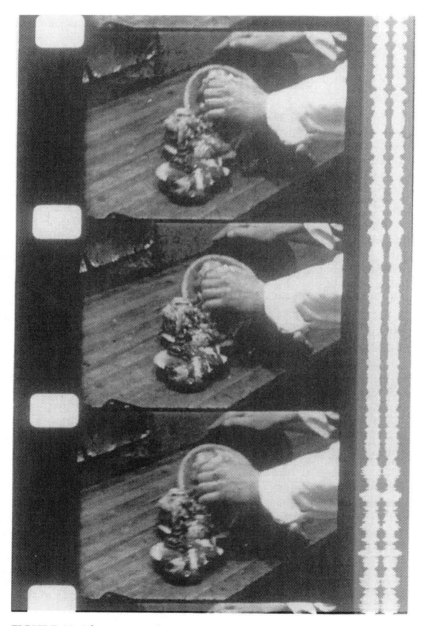

FIGURE 42. The watermelon as eviscerated corpus in Robert Nelson's *Oh Dem Watermelons*. Courtesy Anthology Film Archives.

for walking over Niagara Falls on a tightrope. The film gestures towards a consideration of Blondin, or Blondino, rather than attempting to chronicle in a straightforward manner the events of his life; often, the narrative is suspended for long periods of time, so that Nelson can indulge himself in long bursts of multicolored light flares (outtakes from this material later wound up in his short compilation film, *Half Open and Lumpy* [1967]). A drone-like musical soundtrack by the group Moving Van Walters and His Truck accompanies the dreamlike footage, which seems to float evanescently off the screen and into the individual consciousness of the viewer.

Nelson's *Super Spread* (1967) is a 13-minute multi-screen light-show film, with an original soundtrack performed by the Grateful Dead. In *The Awful Backlash* (1967), Nelson and co-maker William Allan take 14 minutes to untangle a long length of fishing line in one continuous take. *Penny Bright and Jimmy Witherspoon* (1967) is a 3-minute loop film that recycles one image of a man in a bunker repeatedly pointing a gun at the camera/viewer, in conjunction with a similarly repetitive soundtrack; Nelson once loaned this film to a young man who was seeking to obtain conscientious objector status during the Vietnam War, and wanted to show the film to his draft board as supplementary evidence of his convictions. Nelson let him have the film for free, and apparently, the young man's appeal was successful. *Hot Leatherette* (1967) is a brief and funny film in which a 1952 pickup truck flies off the edge of a cliff and rolls endlessly down a hill to its destruction, using primitive re-photography to lengthen the truck's final slide into oblivion. *Half Open and Lumpy* (1967) is a very funny 2-minute short incorporating all of Nelson's trims from earlier movies, accompanied by the sound of a pop tune played at double-speed. *The Off-Handed Jape* (1967), co-made with William Wiley, is a brief comic performance film. Nelson continued his work as a filmmaker in the 1970s and '80s; perhaps his most famous later film is the semi-structural *Bleu Shut* (1970).

Born in Santa Fe, New Mexico, 1943, **Andrew Noren** began taking still photographs in 1958, but didn't get seriously interested in film until 1961, when he saw Jean Cocteau's *Blood of a Poet* and Kenneth Anger's *Scorpio Rising* on a double bill. At this point, he was just getting out of high school; borrowing some money from his parents, Noren took off on an extended tour of Western Europe. He eventually arrived back in New York, and spent a couple of months doing odd jobs and seeing a lot of films. From New York he moved to Boston, got into the Yale Film School, and dropped out after six months. Returning to New York, he got a job working for the ABC network as a film editor. There he met filmmaker Louis Brigante. Eventually, Noren left

ABC and began working at the Filmmakers' Cooperative.

Noren borrowed an Auricon camera from filmmaker Ken Jacobs and began shooting numerous reels of film with direct sync optical sound. During this period, Noren made *Say Nothing, Die, The Unclean* (which consists of various friends of his taking baths), *The Trouble with Harry*, and *New York Miseries Parts I & II*. Each of these films ran about 35 minutes, with no editing, except *The Unclean*, which consisted of several 400' (12-minute) reels strung together. During this period, Noren began to refine his zooms and pans, and eventually started editing. Eventually buying a Bolex, Noren began shooting 100' rolls (about 3 minutes each) and doing a great deal of in-camera editing, superimpositions, fades, and dissolves. His camerawork became more controlled, simpler. He began to make shorter films, of 5 or 6 minutes' duration, which were briefly distributed, and then incorporated into longer works. For a time, Noren also abandoned soundtracks, because he felt that they often detracted from the images and encouraged visual laziness on the part of both filmmaker and audience. Later films include *Kodak Ghost Poems Part One: The Adventures of the Exquisite Corpse* (1969), *Scenes From Life: Golden Brain Mantra* (1972; a double-projector film), and *The Wind Variations* (1969). In these later works, Noren is moving toward a sort of "meditative ecstasy" as Ernie Gehr put it (FMC 1975, 198), in which the daily aspects of existence take on the glow of eternal existence.

Although she achieved a degree of notoriety through her work with John Lennon, **Yoko Ono's** work with the Fluxus Group, and as an independent artist, goes back to the early 1960s, and in many ways helped to shape the nascent independent cinema scene in New York. Shuttling between New York and London, Ono created such intriguingly minimalist films as *No. 4 (Bottoms)* (1964), *Wink* (1966), *Match* (1966), *Shout* (1966), *Eyeblink* (1966) and other works, before teaming up with Lennon to create *Apotheosis* (1971), *Fly* (1970), *Erection* (1970) and other key works in the New American Cinema. All of Ono's films display a disarming simplicity of concept and execution, which often serves to mask a seriousness that borders on the melancholic. For example, *No. 4 (Bottoms)* is a film in which a series of buttocks are seen walking on a treadmill, recorded in close-up scrutiny by a simple Bolex camera; the film can readily be seen as an examination of the human instinct to commodify the body into "zones" of visual address.

Apotheosis is a simply structured, sync-sound film in which a camera drifts into the sky in the basket of a hot air balloon. *Erection* views the construction of a building in stop-frame pixillation. *Fly* presents the spectacle of an ordinary housefly crawling slowly across the body of a nude woman. *Smile (No. 5)* (1968) stretches a brief grin on John Lennon's face into an hour-long meditation on the human physiognomy through the agency of a Milliken high speed camera, shooting at many thousands of frames per second. *Rape* (1969) and *Rape II* (1969) document a woman being tailed by an aggressively remorseless camera crew; perhaps this last film comments not only on the objectification of the feminine in world society, but also upon the continual surveillance brought about by the mechanism of fame.

Ono has also pursued a career as a recording artist (recording *Walking on Thin Ice*, 1981; she also created a video to accompany the song), and continues to create sculptures, video installations, and other works of performance art. In all her work, Ono seeks what she describes as "a fusion of all sensory perceptions . . . [I wish] to create a sensory experience isolated from other sensory experiences, which is something rare in daily life" (Haskell and Hanhardt, 39).

One of the most extravagant and individual talents of the early New American Cinema was undoubtedly **Ron Rice**. Rice's most famous film is arguably *The Flower Thief* (1960), an experimental feature film starring Taylor Mead, shot on surplus 16mm B/W World War II aerial gunnery film loaded into 50' cartridges. The film appeared in a number of versions before finally coalescing into the print presently available. All of the footage was improvised, with Mead occupying center stage in what is arguably the greatest performance of his long and distinguished career. The vision that the film presents is extravagant and hyperreal, mirroring its creator's own existence. Ron Rice, from all accounts, lived a lifestyle that was at once hard and ecstatic, and he died a needlessly premature death as a consequence. As Bruce Baillie recounted in a recent memoir in the *Canyon CinemaNews*: "Ron Rice came through [San Francisco] with two ladies. It was to be his last run. They needed a room and some editing equipment, en route to Mexico[. . . .] I visited them one evening, Ron editing in a corner, hanging his film on lines of women's undies strung across the room. He shot 50' rolls of surplus machine-gun film. He never returned from Old Mexico" (11). Rice died in December, 1964, in Acapulco, Mexico, of complications arising from bronchial pneumonia. He had been living there with his wife, Amy, who shortly thereafter gave birth to the couple's son, Christopher.

Of *The Flower Thief*, Eugene Archer in the *New York Times* observed that "Rice, by deliberately flouting established moviemaking traditions, reveals himself primarily as a professional rebel rather than the leader of a new movement. But in the highly specialized area of experimental films, he has produced a major work" (FMC 1989, 406). Rice's *Senseless* (1962), is described by David Brooks as "a poetic

134

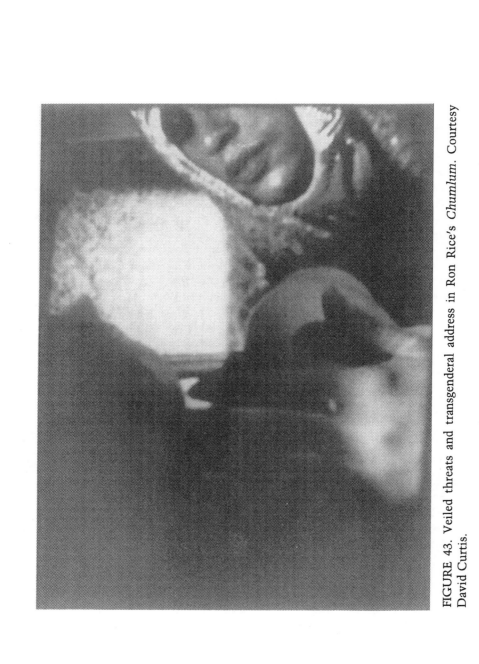

FIGURE 43. Veiled threats and transgenderal address in Ron Rice's *Chumlum*. Courtesy David Curtis.

stream of razor-sharp images[. The] overt content of *Senseless* portrays
ecstatic travelers going to pot over the fantasies and pleasures of a trip
to Mexico . . . highly effective cutting subtly interweaves the contrapuntal development of themes of love and hate, peace and violence,
beauty and destruction." *Chumlum* (1964) starred (among other
notable personages) Jack Smith, Beverly Grant, Mario Montez, Francis
Francine, and Gerard Malanga. Critic René Micha said in *Chumlum*,
"in a house that one could believe was created just for the purpose,
Rice gives us an infinite spectacle, superimposing bodies swinging in
hammocks, back and forth through diaphanous gossamer draperies
that slow the movements, and suspend them on the edge of the
abyss." *The Queen of Sheba Meets the Atom Man* is a 90-minute
rough-cut feature which has since been reconstituted more or less as
Rice imagined it before his untimely death. Of this film, Alberto
Moravia noted that the "the film describes, poetically, a way of living.
The film is a protest which is violent, childish, and sincere—a protest
against an industrial world based on the cycle of production and consumption" (all quotes as cited in FMC 1975, 208).

Rice also left behind several 100' reels of film that became
known as *The Mexican Footage*, a 10-minute sampling of color and
black and white footage shot by Rice in the days and weeks of his life.
Among Rice's unfinished projects, described for the journal *Film
Comment*, were a film he planned in late 1963 concerning "the
shocker or cattle-probe used on Negro demonstrators in the United
States today [,which] should be abolished by federal law. My intended
project was to be a film which would point up the horrors of using this
high-voltage electrical device on humans." Rice also hoped to create
"a film of the life of Sri Ramakrishna, the Hindu mystic" (Hitchens
29). Rice's anarchic vision informed much of the free-form narrative
filmmaking that followed his work in the mid to late 1960s; among
the many who owe him a profound stylistic and thematic debt are
Carl Linder and Gregory Markopolous.

José Rodriguez-Soltero created the beautiful and fantastic film *El
Pecado Original (The Original Sin)* in 1964, a 12-minute 16mm film in
black and white and color with sound, which won the Grand Prize,
International Suncoast Film Festival, Florida, 1965. This was followed
by *Jerovi* (1965), a 16mm, 10-minute, color, silent film which attracted
considerable attention when first released. *Jerovi* was described in a
review in the *New York Post* as "a sexual probe of the Narcissus myth.
[The film's] beautiful male subject [,] clothed at first in rich brocade,
but later nude, is photographed lingeringly in a lush garden. If sensual
self-love in practice doesn't offend you, you'll find some vivid camera
imagery" (as cited in FMC 1975, 212). Later films included the short

FIGURE 44. The eternal nymph (Taylor Mead) in *Queen of Sheba Meets the Atom Man* by Ron Rice. Courtesy Anthology Film Archives.

silent film *Rinon* (1966) and *Lupe* (1966), a 50-minute color, sound film starring Mario Montez, Bill Vehr, Charles Ludlam, and Charles Levine in "an improvised film which supposedly was to depict the rise, fall, and assumption of Lupe Velez, as played by Mario Montez" (FMC 1975, 212). This film was followed by his production of *The Human Voice* (1966), based on Jean Cocteau's monologue *La Voix Humaine*, but the film was unfortunately never completed.

Perhaps Rodriguez-Soltero's most effective film was *Dialogue with Ché* (1968), starring Taylor Mead and Rolando Pena. The film was shot on a sync-sound Auricon using outdated black and white DuPont Superior 2 negative film. Presented at the Cannes and Berlin Film Festivals in 1969, *Dialogue with Ché* aroused a storm of controversy because of its offhand violence, including a scene in which Taylor Mead listens to a radio as a number of "political prisoners" are tortured behind him. Soltero's camerawork in the film is wild and improvisatory, engaging the subject with a ceaseless series of zooms and pans in the manner of Warhol's *Chelsea Girls*. Originally, as with *Chelsea Girls*, the film was projected as two images, side by side, although in the case of *Dialogue with Ché*, the images were identical, but one image was slightly staggered to run behind the other. In all of his works, Rodriguez-Soltero seeks to displace the normative with a radical alterity that liberates the sexual unconscious from the prison of gender roles. As Dollimore notes, "more than any other kind, modern civilization demands high levels of sexual repression, the energy of the sexual instincts being 'displaced' . . . or sublimated into increased or higher cultural activity and development" (1991, 186). It is the repression of this "modern civilization" that Rodriguez-Soltero is opposed to, and in *Jerovi*, *Lupe*, and his other works, he offers a positive alternative to the constraints imposed by the dominant culture.

The late **Barbara Rubin** was another master of the early New American Cinema. Her most famous film is undoubtedly *Christmas on Earth*, a 30-minute 16mm split-screen film designed for simultaneous, two-projector screening. In instructions for projection, Rubin noted that

> the film is on two reels. Both reels must be projected simultaneously. Two projectors are needed. The first projector fills the screen; the image of the second projector is approximately 1/3 smaller and fills only the middle of the screen, superimposing on the first image. This can be done either by using different lenses or by placing one projector closer to the screen. It doesn't matter which reel is on which projector. During the screening, the projectionist is asked to play with color changes by holding colored filters in front of the lens of one or the other projector, or both. Moreover, the film has neither head nor tail—it can be projected either way. (FMC 1967, 129)

The overt randomness of this projection scheme epitomizes the relaxed, free-form participatory nature of film performance/presentation in the 1960s; Rubin here is quite willing to embrace the (unknown) projectionist as a fellow collaborator in the final public version of her work. Concomitantly, each projection of *Christmas on Earth* is thus unique, and irreproducible. The fact that "the film has neither head nor tail" also means that the film may be projected right-side-up or upside-down, without any violation of the film's artistic intent; the use of colored filters at random intervals by the projectionist is a final acknowledgment of the ephemerality of filmic presentation.

Astonishingly, Rubin made this film when she was only eighteen years old; and the subject matter of the film is equally audacious, being a surreal and abstractionist deconstruction of the human body as the site of heterosexual desire. Jonas Mekas described the film as containing images of "a woman; a man; the black of the pubic hair; the cunt's moon mountains and canyons. As the film goes on, image after image, the most private territories of the body are laid open for us, now an abstracted landscape; the first shock changes into silence, then is transposed into amazement. We have seldom seen such down-to-earth beauty, so real as only a terrible beauty can be: terrible beauty that man, that woman is, are, that Love is" (in *East Side Review* No. 1; as cited in FMC 1967, 129–130).

Rubin's method of shooting and editing *Christmas on Earth* was equally informal, open to chance and random operations in the spirit of John Cage or Yoko Ono. She described making the film thus: "[I] shoot up down around back over under and shoot over and over speedily slow back and front end, the subject chosen by the creeping souls of the moment cocks and cunts, love supreme can believe to fantasy I then spent 3 months chopping the hours and hours of film up into a basket and then toss and toss flip and toss and one by one absently enchanted destined to put it together and separate onto two different reels and then project one reel half the size inside the other reel and then show it and someone tells me what a good editing job I did well God bless you God Bless You" (FMC 1967, 130).

Nor did Rubin believe in making copies (nor could she afford to make copies) of the film. She projected the originals, and when she first released the film, she simply placed the original camera materials in film cans and let them be rented by anyone, until the film was withdrawn in the early 1970s and subsequently copied and released through the Filmmakers' Cooperative, as restored by Anthology Film Archives. *Christmas on Earth* is both an elegy to an age of shamelessness and bodily freedom which now seems lost beyond recall (our

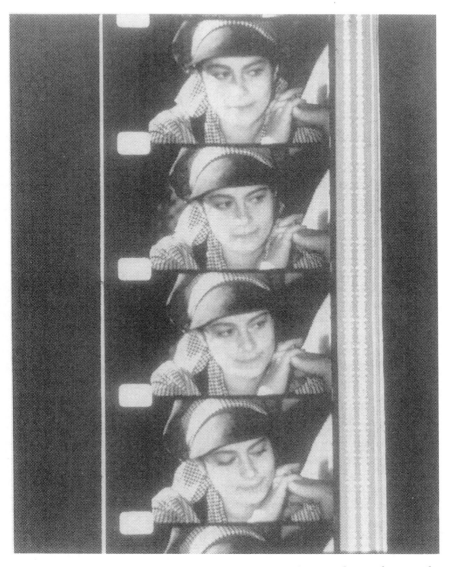

FIGURE 45. Radical heterosexual filmmaker Barbara Rubin. Filmstrip by Jonas Mekas. Courtesy Anthology Film Archives.

"pre-viral consciousness" period of sexual expression; see Rothleder, 206), and a pioneering feminist radical heterosexual document, as is Carolee Schneemann's *Fuses*. Both films are the result of an intense personal consideration of the condition of being human, sexed and/or gendered; both films seek to disrupt the Victorian representationalism then overwhelmingly propagated by the mainstream media. Georges Bataille holds that "what the desire to be happy means [is] suffering and the desire to escape" (43); in *Christmas on Earth*, one can see Rubin's pain, but also her release from the constraints of social integration, as she celebrates the transalterity of her radical heterosexual being in a transgenderal, post-narrative, Gramscian work of random, anarchic elegance.

Rubin made two other films which were briefly released. *The Day the Byrds Flew Into the Factory and I Went Out* is a 15-minute short which Rubin described as "four reels from London, the Summer of 1965 [. . .] tossed and shot thru the hands of some of the angels passing thru. Shot and re shot passed on to anyone who felt like shooting and then left for rediscovery in the New Year 1966, and developed by the grace of Andy [Warhol] and shown to the Byrds the day they flew into the [F]actory and I went out [. . .] they remain unedited tampered or arranged except thru the spirit of love by whom they were shot and the reality of the film processing at their development" (FMC 1967,130). At the same time, she made another brief film documenting the lives of Allen Ginsberg and Peter Orlovsky entitled *Allen for Allen, London, Is Peter*. To the best of my knowledge, both of these films existed only in original materials, and were withdrawn from release shortly after their completion. Rubin's fame thus rests on a single work, but the strength of that work is more than sufficient to ensure her reputation. Barbara Rubin was one of the earliest and most aggressively Romantic of the New York independent filmmakers, and it is gratifying to note that her finest work can still be seen today.

Carolee Schneemann's most famous (and/or notorious) film is certainly *Fuses* (1964–68), a 22-minute silent color film designed to be projected at sound speed, correctly described by the filmmaker as "the first explicit feminist erotic film confronting traditional sexual taboos. An homage to a relationship of ten years, filmed by Schneemann while participant in the action [. . .] *Fuses* is structured in rhythmic layers of collaged imagery; hand-painting to intensify color sequences, cutting, staining, overlapping durations of A and B rolls" (FMC 1989, 423). As Schneemann and her lover engage in lovemaking (filmed by Schneemann with a borrowed spring-wound Bolex), the camera drifts over to show curtains blowing in a window frame, and shows images of Schneemann's cat watching as the two people make love. Schneemann came under intense attack in the 1970s for a perceived lack of political correctness in the construction of this film, which, like Barbara Rubin's *Christmas on Earth*, celebrates the beauty of the female and male body without shame or censorship, with a freedom at once casual and (to some viewers) terrifying. As Donna Haraway notes, "always radically historically specific, bodies have a different kind of specificity and effectivity, and so they invite a different kind of engagement and intervention" (208). In *Fuses*, Schneemann views the body as a produced, constructed entity. Time has not erased the shock of sensation created by the film, as the viewer is confronted with the corporeal reality of human existence.

Writing in the 1970s on *Fuses*, which had by that time become an international cause célèbre, Schneemann noted that "we are equally, interchangeably subject and object. As woman (image) and as image-maker I reclaim, establish and free my image and my will" (FMC 1975, 220). It was exactly this sort of intense personal voyage that created the beautiful, relaxed, and dreamily sensual imagery of *Fuses*; freed from the specific grounding of a soundtrack, the film seems to exist outside of time and societal constraints, constructing a visual domain entirely of its own design. *Fuses* is graphic, yet gently erotic, but it is entirely absent of the objectificational discourse present in pornographic representations of the female or male body; it is a merging of two individual identities into an ecstatic series of moments. The best indication of the spiritual purity of *Fuses* is that the film, despite being the object of heated debate for nearly thirty years, retains its identity as a personal sexual vision operating beyond the realm of censorship, an act of care for the soul and body that escapes the tyranny of history through the tactile sublimity of its intense spectator-subject cultural negotiation. Schneemann's other films include *Plumb Line* (1968–72) and *Ft. Lauderdale: A Portrait* (1968). *Plumb Line* is a 15-minute film comprised of "scrap diary footage shot in 8mm, hand printed as 16mm. *Plumb Line* is a moving and powerful subjective chronicle of the breaking up of a love relationship" (Schneemann). Critic David Curtis described the film as "beautiful, laying open even more than *Fuses*—a very public private film—and as clear as crystal" (FMC 1989, 423).

David Secter's innovative feature film *Winter Kept Us Warm* (1968) was an 81-minute film that opened to almost universal critical acclaim. Set on the campus of the University of Toronto, the film documents the ripening friendship between two young men, both of whom take their identity as heterosexuals as an assumption of their social discourse. As the film progresses, one of the young men finds himself attracted to his male friend, in a plot twist that at the time

142

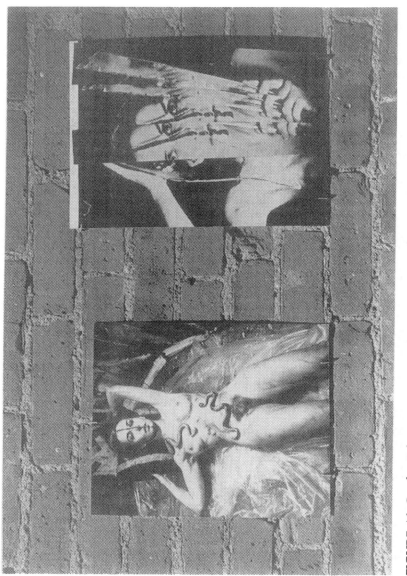

FIGURE 46. Carolee Schneemann in a performance piece from the 1960s. Photo by Robert Haller. Courtesy Anthology Film Archives.

was both unexpected and yet (within the structure of the film) entirely plausible. The *London Times* called *Winter Kept Us Warm* "easily the most appealing of all the North American entries at Cannes [. . .] tells simply yet subtly of an ambiguously close campus friendship between two very different young men, not only convincing but hits on an unconventional truth"; Frances Herridge in the *New York Post* described the film as "an amateur movie that should be the envy of many professionals [. . .] more character perception, better plotting nuance and livelier dialogue than many Hollywood productions"; Laurence Kardish, writing in *Eye Magazine*, described the film as "a triumph of resourcefulness [. . .] one of the most affecting and honest films ever produced on campus life" (FMC 1975, 223–224).

In an interview conducted in January of 1996, Secter offered this third-person account of the film's turbulent genesis:

> On October 30, 1964 in the University of Toronto's *Varsity* newspaper, David Secter announced his intention to write, direct and produce a full-length feature film before the end of the school year. This was greeted with widespread skepticism for several valid reasons, such as: 1. Canada had no feature film industry—most years one could count the full-length fiction films on the fingers of one hand with digits to spare; 2. Secter was 21 and in his senior year of a demanding English Honors course with every expectation of graduating in the spring; 3. He had no training in film production (none was available in Canada at the time) and virtually no experience (he had produced an 8 minute silent short *Love with the Proper Guppy* on a budget of $31.88 over the summer); 4. He had no script and no money; 5. The movie's autobiographical theme dealt with an unlikely attachment between two males in a campus dormitory, at a time when the subject of homosexuality was totally taboo and had rarely been presented on film.
>
> However, the very novelty of the project captured sufficient interest that University College offered a meeting room and a number of students volunteered their services. The venture reached a level of reality when Ryerson Polytechnic Institute (now a University) agreed to provide technical support. At the time Ryerson had no film department but still photography students were introduced to motion picture production in their final year and they formed the crew. Soon the company had a name, Varsity Films (U of T would not permit use of the University's name) and the movie had a title, *Winter Kept Us Warm*, borrowed from the opening lines of T. S. Eliot's poem *The Waste Land*.
>
> Secter cast the film with student actors and hammered out a script with input from the cast and a revolving set of writers, with dialogue often written as cameras and lights were being set up. Cast and crew went through many changes in the first few weeks as early recruits realized the demands the movie would make on their studies and social lives. The two lead roles were played by John Labow and Henry Tar-

FIGURE 47. Joy Tepperman, John Labow, and Henry Tarvainen in David Secter's *Winter Kept Us Warm*. Courtesy David Secter.

vainen, and since John was already married and had a young son, rehearsals often doubled with baby-sitting duty. The first scenes were shot by the end of November and a demo reel was assembled to attract backers. Though no angels emerged, the group received grants of several hundred dollars from various student councils, and loans of equipment and short ends of raw stock from the city's film labs and production companies.

Despite constant obstacles and setbacks, the crew continued to shoot, results steadily improved, and solutions were found to most problems. When one of the supporting players broke his leg during Christmas break, it was quickly written into the script. Production continued till late March, when the cast and crew demanded a break to complete overdue assignments and cram for final exams. Shooting resumed within minutes after the last exam, in a mad scramble to complete the movie before the actors dispersed for the summer. Meanwhile, the production had generated considerable coverage in the Canadian press and some news crossed the Atlantic. Based on positive reports from people who had seen the work-in-progress, *Winter Kept Us Warm* was invited to open the Commonwealth Film Festival in Cardiff, Wales in September. This opportunity was too tempting to pass up and post-production went into high gear: various teams commuted between borrowed editing rooms after hours, missing dialogue and sound effects were recorded, titles were shot, and an original music score recorded as the negative was cut and timed.

Secter was determined to get to Cardiff for the movie's world premiere, as was the film's Welsh-born cameraman Bob Fresco, although neither could afford the airfare and no travel grants materialized. However, they managed to get on a flight to Britain with the Balmy Beach Rugger Club, picking up a work print from the lab sight-unseen en route to the airport. They raced for Cardiff by rented car, arriving almost on time to find the festival audience already seated, waiting for the world premiere of an 81 minute 16 millimeter black and white feature film.

Winter Kept Us Warm received respectable reviews but no distribution offers, and when all the bills came in Secter found himself over $6,000 in debt. Fortunately this was recouped when the film had its initial hometown ten-day run at the Royal Ontario Museum. This was followed by limited bookings at art houses and campus theaters across Canada and a few screenings in the United States. The movie's big break came in 1966 when it was invited to the Cannes Film Festival's Critics Week (the section for first features). There it was enthusiastically reviewed by the world press and launched onto the international film festival circuit. Though it never received commercial distribution, the movie had several successful engagements in art houses, including a six-week run in Manhattan in 1968.

Secter moved to New York in 1968, where he worked as a writer, director and producer in film, theater and television until 1990 when he moved his home base to California. In June, 1996 the University of

Toronto Alumni Association screened *Winter Kept Us Warm* at Spring
Reunion in honor of the Thirtieth Anniversary of the film's production.
(letter to the author from David Secter, January 23, 1996)

Secter remains active in both film and video production to the present
day; a listing of many of his works can be found at various sites on the
World Wide Web.

The late **Greg Sharits**, brother of the better-known filmmaker
Paul Sharits, managed the Filmmakers' Cinematheque from 1967 to
1969; the theater was then located at 125 West 41st Street. Greg Sharits's tenure at the Cinematheque arguably reached its zenith in the
summer of 1967, during which time Sharits presented an ambitious
schedule of experimental films, light shows, performance pieces, and
other works, seven days a week. Jerome Hiler and Robert Cowan
served as projectionists; Donna Kerness and her companion Hope
Morris created costumes for a number of the performance pieces, as
well as appearing in them; rock groups such as the Group Image and
the Velvet Underground appeared on the small theatre stage, and
dance concerts were regularly interspersed with more traditional film
screenings of works by Bruce Conner, Andy Warhol, Steve Anson (perhaps best remembered for his excellent Super 8mm film *Membrane*),
Warren Sonbert, Martin Charlot, Gerard Malanga, Charles Levine, Jud
Yalkut and many others. Even these more organized screenings were
still remarkably informal; filmmakers would often drop by with
works-in-progress, which would be added to the bill at the last
minute. Warhol's *The Chelsea Girls* played there, along with the complete films of Kenneth Anger (*The Magick Lantern Cycle*), and a benefit screening for Jack Smith, featuring yet another revised version of
In the Grip of the Lobster Man.

The light show poster by Greg Sharits reproduced within this
text should give the reader some indication of the energy and passion
that Greg brought to his job as program director and manager of the
Cinematheque. For this particular show, in addition to all of the
advertised participants, a roving group of French light show artists
arrived unannounced during the evening with a battery of projectors,
films, and slides. Greg rummaged behind the stage and found an old
door, with the hinges still attached, which he used as an improvised
projection platform. Clearing several seats in the back row of the theater, Greg helped the light show artists set up their equipment as the
scheduled performance continued on stage. Within minutes, the additional imagery generated by these performers was incorporated as part
of the scheduled entertainment. As the evening drew to a close, the
members of the visiting troupe packed up their equipment and van-

FIGURE 48. Poster designed by Greg Sharits for a multimedia presentation at the Filmmakers' Cinematheque. Collection of the author.

ished without a word, departing as mysteriously as they had arrived.

In addition to his activities as manager of the Cinematheque, Greg Sharits also produced a series of beautiful 8mm films, which have only recently been released to the public. In May, 1983, the Collective for Living Cinema presented a series of films by Greg Sharits, all standard 8mm silent. *Transfer*, a 17-minute film made by applying strips of graphics directly to the film, is perhaps his best film. Other titles include *Transit* (another transfer pattern film, 20 minutes); *Travelogue* (again using applied graphic strips over existing imagery, as well as stretches of clear leader, 17 minutes); as well as *Self-Portrait* (1980), *Ode to Communism* (1980), and *Flowers for Tara Shevchenko* (1980), calmer and more meditative films made in the last year of his life. These films were all made in and around Berkeley, California, many of them in the small hotel room where he lived. In addition to these films, Greg also shot numerous reels of standard 8mm film (again using plastic transfer strips directly pasted on to clear or imaged film) during his stay in New York at the Filmmakers' Cinematheque.

The late **Paul Sharits** was born in Denver, Colorado, in 1943. As he wrote to me in a letter in the late 1960s, his "most affectionate and affecting memories of early childhood were those evenings when relatives would gather in his Grandfather's living room to delight in their grainy black and white projections from his Uncle's home movies" (letter to the author, 1969). While acquiring a Bachelor of Fine Arts in painting at the University of Denver, Sharits began making films, got married, and founded the Denver Experimental Film Society. While Sharits worked for a Master of Fine Arts in visual design at Indiana University, his son was born, and he founded the Indiana University Experimental Cinema Group. Sharits then guided a film workshop at the Aspen School of Contemporary Art, in the summer of 1968, and taught courses in personal filmmaking and experimental design at the Maryland Institute of Art, Baltimore, beginning in 1967.

Sharits's films have been shown at the Filmmakers' Cinematheque, the Museum of Modern Art, the 5th Annual Avant-Garde Festival, the Tokyo National Museum of Modern Art, the Fourth International Experimental Film Competition, Knokke Le Zoute and elsewhere. His films survive in the collections of the New York Museum of Modern Art and the Royal Film Archive of Belgium. Paul Sharits's films during the early to mid 1960s include *Piece Mandala/End War* (1966), on which filmmaker Stan Brakhage commented "[. . .] it IS that/cut to the bone of some matter that does really concern me: how a man and woman meet nakedly head-on among the colors [. . .] lovely: I can hardly wait to see the entirety of that vision . . ."; Takahiko Iimura said that "I never imagined that Go Ko

FIGURE 49. Paul Sharits maps the terrain of his body with a series of segmented photographs in the late 1960s. Courtesy David Curtis.

(the back light which illuminates the spirit of Buddha) could really happen as it does in this film."

Sharits also created the 14-minute sprocket-hole soundtrack film *Ray Gun Virus* (1966), which caused Brakhage to comment that "[. . .] I really do think you have a very fine film there of magnificent subtlety in its by-play with the texture of film and eye's grain"; and *Word Movie (Fluxfilm 29)* (1966), which Sharits described as "words optically-conceptually fuse[d] into one $3^3/_4$ minute long word." *Razor Blades* (1965–68) was Sharits's most ambitious film during this period. Produced with the help of a grant from the American Film Institute, the 25-minute-long work is a two-screen film for two projectors and stereo sound, described by Sharits as "a mandala [opening] to the other side of consciousness." This film was followed by *N:O:T:H:I:N:G* (1968), of which Brakhage noted that "the screen, illuminated by Paul Sharits's *N:O:T:H:I:N:G*, seems to assume a spherical shape, at times—due, I think, to a pearl-like quality of light his flash-frames create . . . a baroque pearl, one might say—wondrous!"; and *T,O,U,C,H,I,N,G* (1968), described by the filmmaker as "an uncutting and unscratching mandala" (all as cited in FMC 1975, 224–226).

Sharits continued to make films into the 1980s, including such works as *S:tream:S:S:ection:S:ection:S:S:ectioned* (1968–71); *Inferential Current* (1971), described by the filmmaker as "A mapping of an image of the linear passage of '16mm film frames' and 'emulsion scratches' onto an actual 16mm film strip (the unperceived film 'print')/the aural word 'miscellaneous' is extended to a length of 8 minutes by serial fragmentation, looping, staggering & overlaying/a variational but non-developmental strand thru time./Dedicated to Lynda Benglis"; *Analytical Studies I: The Film Frame* (1971–76), 25 minutes, silent (24 FPS); *Analytical Studies II: Un-Framed Lines* (1971–76), 30 minutes, silent (24 FPS); *Analytical Studies III: Color Frame Passages* (1973–74), $21^1/_2$ minutes, silent (24 FPS); *Apparent Motion* (1975), 28 minutes, silent (18 FPS); *Color Sound Frames* (1974), $21^1/_2$ minutes; *Analytical Studies IV: Blank Color Frames* (1975–76), $19^1/_2$ minutes, silent (18 FPS); *Epileptic Seizure Comparison* (1976), 34 minutes; *Tails* (1976), $4^1/_2$ minutes, silent; *Declarative Mode* (1976–77); *Episodic Generation* (1977–78), 30 minutes; *3rd Degree* (1982), $23^1/_2$ minutes; *Synchronousoundtracks* (1973–74) (two-screen projection, sound on both reels), $32^1/_2$ minutes; *Shutter Interface* (1975) (two-screen projection, sound on both tracks); *Dream Displacement* (1976) (two-screen projection, stereo sound); *Brancusi's Sculpture Ensemble at Tirgu Jiu* (1977–84), 21 minutes, silent (24 FPS); and finally *Bad Burns* (1982), $5^3/_4$ minutes, silent (24 FPS). In all

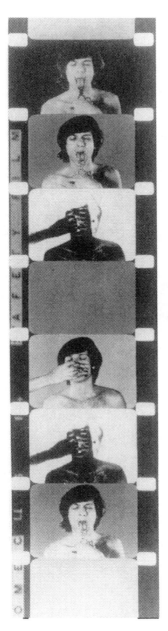

FIGURE 50. Filmstrip from Paul Sharits's *T,O,U,C,H,I,N,G*; the performative body fragmented by single frame intercutting. Courtesy David Curtis.

his work, Sharits seeks to force the viewer into new ways of apprehending the cinematic experience, both as a production and/or reception mechanism. Sharits's best films operate on the margins of visual representationalism; particularly in his double-screen, single-frame images, the viewer is bombarded with forty-eight disparate and individual glyphs with each passing second, forcing the spectator to entirely reevaluate her/his conception of what it is to fully assimilate a non-narrative, resolutely abstractional cinematic construct.

Harry Smith was the creator of a series of brilliantly hallucinatory animation films, most famously *Early Abstractions* and *The Heaven and Earth Magic Feature*. Of his works, Smith said:

> My cinematic excreta is of four varieties:—batiked abstractions made directly on film between 1939 and 1946; optically printed non-objective studies composed around 1950; semi-realistic animated collages made as part of my alchemical labors of 1957 to 1962; and chronologically superimposed photographs of actualities formed since the latter year. All these works have been organized in specific patterns derived from the interlocking beats of the respiration, the heart and the EEG Alpha component and should be observed together in order, or not at all, for they are valuable works, works that will live forever—they made me gray. No. 1: Hand-drawn animation of dirty shapes—the history of the geologic period reduced to orgasm length. No. 2: Batiked animation, etc., etc. The action takes place either inside the sun or in Zurich, Switzerland. No. 3: Batiked animation made of dead squares, the most complex hand-drawn film imaginable. No. 4: Black and white abstractions of dots and grillworks [sic] made in a single night. No. 5: Color abstraction. Homage to Oscar Fischinger—a sequel to No. 4. No. 7: Optically printed Pythagoreanism in four movements supported on squares, circles, grill-work and triangles with an interlude concerning an experiment. No. 10: An exposition of Buddhism and the Kaballa in the form of a collage. The final scene shows Aquaric mushrooms (not in No. 11) growing on the moon while the Hero and Heroine row by on a cerebrum. No. 12: The first part depicts the heroine's toothache consequent to the loss of a very valuable watermelon, her dentistry and transportation to heaven. Next follows an elaborate exposition of the heavenly land in terms of Israel, Montreal and the second part depicts the return to earth from being eaten by Max Muller on the day Edward the Seventh dedicated the Great Sewer to London. No. 14: Superimposed photographs of Mr. Fleischman's butcher shop in New York, and the Kiowa around Anadarko, Oklahoma—with Cognate Material. The strip is dark at the beginning and end, light in the middle, and is structured 122333221. I honor it the most of my films, otherwise a not very popular one before 1972. If the exciter lamp blows, play Bert Brecht's "Mahogany."
>
> For those who are interested in such things: No. 1 to 5 were made under pot; No. 6 with schmeck (—it made the sun shine) and ups; No. 7

FIGURE 51. Filmstrip
from Harry Smith's
Early Abstractions.
Courtesy Anthology
Film Archives.

with cocaine and ups; Nos. 8 to 12 with almost anything, but mainly deprivation, and 13 with green pills from Max Jacobson, pink pills from Tim Leary, and vodka; No. 14 with vodka and Italian Swiss white port. (FMC 1967, 137–138)

In addition to *Early Abstractions*, Harry Smith also produced the films *Late Superimpositions* and *Mirror Animations*. For many years, he lived at the Chelsea Hotel, where I visited him on a number of occasions. Harry was always working on a new project right up until the end of his life; now that he is gone, his works have become all the more valuable through their scarcity, and the singularity of their vision. Impossible, persistent, brilliant, and occasionally menacing, Smith was one of those who pushed the limits of conventional animation beyond the known into the domain of the hyperglyphic. The economy of Smith's sign/system exchange as exhibited in *Heaven and Earth Magic Feature*, for example, is made all the more compelling by the stark black and white tacticity of its stripped-down visual empiricism.

Jack **Smith**, one of the most volatile and original members of the New American Cinema, worked with the bare minimum of equipment and materials to complete such films as the early Queer/transgenderal classic *Flaming Creatures* (1963), perhaps his most famous film. As aptly described by critic Richard Dyer,

> *Flaming Creatures* consists of a series of sequences loosely hung together, performed by a group of people who are sometimes clearly male or female but more often ambiguous—transvestite, hermaphrodite, hormone assisted. It was shot on outdated raw film stock, giving the image a washed out, overexposed or occasionally murky look. Clothes, props and music all refer to Montez's notions of Hollywood glamour and femininity and of what Spain, China and Arabia are like. The bleachy, grainy look and the Hollywoodiana all make it look like an old B-movie that has been run too many times through projectors. At the same time, it is nothing like a Hollywood movie. (Dyer, 147)

Smith's ground-breaking black and white featurette (45 minutes) was shot on outdated film purloined from the Camera Barn in New York, which was then processed as color reversal film using leftover Kodak home movie mailers Smith had somehow obtained; this accounts for the film's somewhat misty overall look (Dixon interview). Smith had grandiose plans for all his work, and in 1964 stated to *Film Comment* that his future plans included the production of "an Arabian Nights movie in Tangiers" (Hitchens 30–31). Always in dire need of financial assistance to create his iconoclastic films, Smith was also a highly opinionated and mercurial individual who brooked very little interference from others in the creation of his films. Smith's work as an artist extended beyond his own films as a director. As Dyer notes,

> Apart from appearing in his own films and theatre pieces, he also appeared in, among other things, *Queen of Sheba Meets the Atom Man* (1963) and *Chumlum* (1964), both directed by Ron Rice, *Batman Dracula* (1964) (Smith plays the former) and *Camp* (1965) by Andy Warhol, and Markopoulos's *The Illiac Passion* (1964–66). In many of the films Smith appears in tacky drag; in *Queen of Sheba* he plays Hamlet. The quality of the performance veers between a wild-eyed, hysterical intensity and a lolling-about playfulness: in the opening sequence of [Ken Jacobs's] *Little Stabs [at Happiness]*, he gobbles at a plastic doll's crotch before gleefully stubbing a lighted cigarette into its eye, yet in the final section, "The Spirit of Listlessness," he dawdles about in Pierrot costume, itself redolent of floppy inconsequentiality, idly sucking on or playing with different coloured balloons. (Dyer, 146)

Smith died of AIDS in September, 1989. As Howard Guttenplan of the Millennium Film Workshop noted in the program notes on the occasion of a 1995 retrospective of Smith's work, the filmmaker "left behind a large amount of material—films, slides, audio tapes, drawing, and writings. Many of [Smith's] films were shown as works-in-progress and some were unlabeled. Jerome Tartaglia and others have managed to organize and pull together some of this material so that it can be screened for the public." Smith's films shown for that retrospective included "The Cobra Dance of Maria Montez in *Cobra Woman* (20 min.), *Scotch Tape* (3 min.), *Flaming Creatures* (45 min.) [and the] Slide/Audio Presentation—*At the Moonpool* (Jack Reading & Rehearsing his Stars) (30 min.), [along with the] Restored version of *Normal Love* (60 min.), [and a] Restored Addendum Reel of *Normal Love*, featuring Tiny Tim (20 min.), [and finally the] Restored Early film *Overstimulated*, featuring Jerry Sims & Bob Fleischner (10 min.)" (Millennium Program Notes, spring 1995).

In the 1990's sexual wilderness of what Dianne Rothleder has referred to as "viral consciousness" (206), Smith's extravagant vision of human sexuality as a celebratory part of the life force is both hopelessly Romantic and a reminder of the freedom afforded by the pre-AIDS era. In the 1960s, sexual experimentation was an accepted fact of human existence, to be encouraged and fostered. In the late 1990s, we live in an era where every act of sex is ineluctably linked with the possibility of infection, or death; sex has become first and foremost a transmission medium, a means of translating desire into the decadence, transforming the human body from a site of pleasure into a carrier of fatal illness. How can we possibly look back on the transgenderal freedom and sense of positive play afforded by Smith's films without succumbing to a nostalgic longing for our past bodies?

Michael Snow's film *Wavelength* won the top prize at the Belgian Film Festival in 1968; in 1969, he finished two new films: *One Second in Montreal* and *´ (Back and Forth)*. Both had their public premiere at the Whitney Museum in May of that year. Snow's primary concern is with time/space relationships, and he uses pans, zooms, and long static takes to explore this. Unlike Warhol, who uses people as the primary element in his current film work, Snow is primarily concerned with camera movement and other wholly filmic/spatial concerns. "I'm interested in doing something that can't be explained," he told me in 1968. "Ultimately, I would like to make a film of complete purity."

In *Wavelength*, a camera zooms excruciatingly slowly across a room for 45 minutes. A series of filters is used, different film stocks, superimpositions; Snow is fascinated by the textural changes of the light flooding through the window. The jagged progress of Snow's zoom is interrupted by four actions: a cabinet is brought into the room; two women enter and listen to "Strawberry Fields Forever" on the radio; a man (Hollis Frampton) enters the frame-space and then crumples to the floor, dead; finally a young woman walks into the room, sees the man on the floor, and calls a friend to find out what she should do. The zoom continues to a photograph of waves on the wall, then the image becomes diffuse and fades out. Throughout this there is a rising electronic pitch, described by Snow as a "glissando," mixed in with the live sound.

Snow's complete filmography includes the following works, all of which have been screened internationally to unanimous critical acclaim at numerous museums, film festivals, and galleries: *A to Z* (1956, 7 minutes, "blue & white silent," as Snow describes it); *New York Eye and Ear Control* (1964, 34 minutes, B/W); *Short Shave* (1965, 4 minutes, B/W, silent); *Standard Time* (1967, 8 minutes, color); *Wavelength* (1967, 45 minutes, color); *´ (Back and Forth)* (1968–69, 50 minutes, color); *One Second in Montreal* (1969, 26 minutes, B/W, silent); *Dripping Water* (co-directed by Michael Snow and his then-wife Joyce Wieland, 1969, 12 minutes, color); *Side Seat Paintings Slides Sound Film* (1970, 20 minutes, color); *La Région Centrale* (1971, 3 hours, color); *Breakfast (Table Top Dolly)*, (1972–76, 15 minutes, color, silent); *Rameau's Nephew by Diderot (Thanx to Dennis Young) by Wilma Schoen* (1974, 4½ hours, color); *Presents* (1980–81, 90 minutes, color); *So Is This* (1982, 43 minutes, color, silent); *Funnel Piano* (1984, 3 minutes, color, sound, Super 8 mm); *Seated Figures* (1988, 42 minutes, color); *See You Later (Au Revoir)* (1990, 18 minutes, color); and *To Lavoisier, Who Died in the Reign of Terror* (1991, 53 minutes).

FIGURE 52. Time stretched into a spatial dimension. *See You Later (Au Revoir)* by Michael Snow. Courtesy Michael Snow.

Other works that Snow created involving film include *Little Walk*, a 1965, 8mm, color, silent film, which Snow projected on a cut-out Walking Woman figure during a gallery show; *Right Reader* (1965), a performance piece with audio tape, suspended Plexiglas sheet, projected light, screen, performer (Snow), and props; *Sink* (1970), 80 35mm color slides, combined with a color photographic print; *A Casing Shelved* (1970), a single 35mm slide presented in conjunction with a 40-minute audio cassette, to be presented as a "single-frame film"; *Untitled Slidelength* (1969–71), 80 35mm color slides; *De La* (1969–71), aluminum and steel mechanical sculpture with electronic controls, television camera, and four video monitors mounted on a wooden base; *Breakfast (Table Top Dolly)* (1972), videotape of three versions of film of the same name, which was exhibited once and then destroyed; *Two Sides to Every Story* (1974), 16mm color sound films, two projectors, and a painted aluminum screen in a room—the two films are projected synchronously on the two sides of the screen; *Intérêts* (1982), video installation created for Art Video Rétrospectives et Perspectives, Palais des beaux-arts de Charleroi, Belgium; *#720* (1970–88), slide installation, projected images from underground comics by Robert Crumb; and *Recombinant* (1992), a piece for slide projector, 80 slides, cylindrical painted plastic stand, and painted wood wall relief. Working in cinema, sculpture, photography and video, Snow continues to create a torrent of original and captivating work which, for many, defines the essence of the experimental cinema of the 1960s.

CHAPTER FIVE

∎∎

Sonbert to Zimmerman

The late **Warren Sonbert** was the supreme Romantic diarist of the cinema, in the tradition of Jonas Mekas and others who have worked within this highly personal genre. His early films were basically diaries: quiet, lyrical records of his friends going through their lives, involved in daily occurrences, shot without pre-planning, organization, or logical sequence. The core of Sonbert's early craft is that he created, without complicated camera choreography, editing, or a pronounced story line, films in which one is never conscious of anything but pure emotion. More than any other new American filmmaker of the mid to late 1960s, Sonbert creates people who are living and vibrant, reaching out of the screen to enfold the audience in their seductively indolent lives. Sonbert's early cinema was one of intimacies and personal glimpses of the young artists at work in New York. Understated and low key, Sonbert's films stay with you. As a filmmaker, Sonbert knew instinctively which moments to film, and his glamorous protagonists thus emerge as genuine personalities existing outside the world of the film.

Born in 1947 in New York City, Warren described his childhood in a 1969 interview as "quiet and uneventful." He had no inclination to make films, and although there was an 8mm camera around the house, he never used it. When he was fifteen, he started going to the Bleecker Street Theatre. One day, during a screening of *Potemkin* and *L'Avventura*, Sonbert found a large manila envelope sitting on the seat next to him, full of issues of *Film Culture*, *Films in Review*, and

159

other film magazines. He took them home, read them, and began seeing films twelve times a week. Attracted to the work of Howard
Hawks and Alfred Hitchcock, Sonbert wrote an angry letter to the
manager of the Bleecker Street Theatre, protesting that their work was
almost never shown there. Surprisingly, the manager wrote him a letter back, and as the months went by they became good friends. Sonbert got a job as usher at the Bleecker Street, but he spent most of his
time meeting filmmakers through the manager. When he was seventeen, Sonbert met Gregory Markopolous, who loaned him his Bolex
camera and encouraged him to make films. Although he shot a couple
of 100' rolls of 16mm film, Sonbert was still reluctant to begin filmmaking, feeling himself inadequately tutored.

     To rectify this, upon graduation from high school Sonbert
enrolled at New York University to study film. In his second year at
NYU, Sonbert made his first 16mm movie, *Amphetamine*, an early
gay-themed film centering around the lives of two friends of Sonbert's
who shared a predilection for injecting speed. The film was screened
publicly at the Bleecker Street for a number of critics and filmmakers
who were enthusiastic in their praise of the film, and Sonbert's career
was truly launched. The film was shot over a weekend in February
1966 at Sonbert's apartment with borrowed equipment and outdated
black and white film stock; the film begins with shots of several
young men shooting up amphetamine, talking, laughing, and drinking
soda. This is followed by a long shot of rippling light (actually footage
from an aborted documentary on the denizens on 42nd Street in New
York; the film got jammed in the camera during shooting and was
considered unusable, until Sonbert realized that it could be employed
as a segue for this film), and then a shock cut to two boys passionately
kissing, as the camera swoops ecstatically around them.

     Edited to a soundtrack of the 1960s pop group the Supremes, the
total effect was electrifying. *Amphetamine* was acclaimed by critic
James Stoller as "a heart-stopping film [. . .] completely symptomatic
of the film-making revolution [. . .] it seems paradoxically to come to
terms with its subject in a way which might be seen as 'cinematic' in
the essence despite its forthright rejection of much of the apparatus of
traditional film-making[. . . . T]he result is beautiful and pure: behind
the bald surface we feel, first, that many inessentials have been
cleared away, and then, that the *need* for them has been cleared
away." This film was followed by *Where Did Our Love Go* (shot in
June, 1966), a 15-minute color film with a taped soundtrack, which
Stoller described as "both a valentine and a farewell to a generation,
as well as being simply a portrait which is tender, distant, accurate,
somewhat high, and sad. In one brief and emblematic image near the

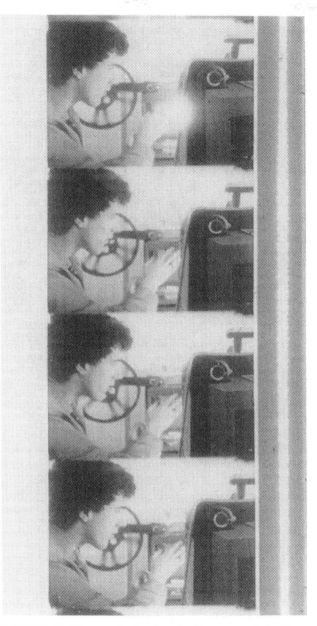

FIGURE 53. Warren Sonbert projecting one of his films at Andy Warhol's Factory, 33 Union Square West, Spring 1969. Photostrip by Wheeler Winston Dixon.

end, a group of kids huddles happily in a semi-circle on a sofa, neither really touching nor completely apart, and you can feel all the ambiguity and the uncertain liveliness of the teenyboppers in the street, the generation probably no one understands but which Sonbert, in a series of tender and moving moments, has revealed to us. I could watch this film a hundred times; it made me feel old, older than I am, but also it opened my eyes and my heart" (FMC 1967, 141).

Next came *Hall of Mirrors* (shot in October, 1966) a 7-minute film in color and black and white. The film opens with, in Sonbert's words, "Fredric March and Florence Eldridge lost in a 1948 hall of mirrors," and then segues into a one reel sequence of poet/artist René Ricard crying in a dimly lit apartment. The final sequence shows Gerard Malanga walking through a mirror sculpture in a New York art gallery. The soundtrack consists of two pop songs, "What Becomes of the Broken Hearted?" and "Walk Away Renee" and ends with a section of Georges Delerue's score for Jean-Luc Godard's film *Contempt* (FMC 1975, 236).

Where Did Our Love Go? was shot in color, and documented his friends going to movies, eating, and shopping for clothes. From this point on, Sonbert abandoned any pretense at narrative, and began to carry the camera with him as he went about, shooting whatever seemed to him to be worth recording. Except for *Hall of Mirrors*, all of Sonbert's early films are presented as a succession of largely unedited reels, straight from the camera, presented with a backdrop of pop music. In this style, he made *The Tenth Legion* (1966), *Truth Serum* (shot in April, 1967), *The Bad and the Beautiful* (shot in October, 1967), and *Holiday* (shot in February, 1968). Sonbert had several highly successful shows at the Cinematheque of these films, as well as screenings at the Jewish Museum and the Elgin Theatre. With this money, and a graduation gift from his mother, Warren left the country for Morocco in April of 1969. Before leaving, he withdrew almost all of his work from distribution. It was re-released in the early 1970s. For the rest of his life, Warren kept his film diary, and presented various versions of footage old and new in a series of revised, silent films, which won him even greater respect from members of the New York Avant-Garde. These films include *Carriage Trade* (1968–72), *Rude Awakening* (1972–76), *Divided Loyalties* (1975–78), *Noblesse Oblige* (1978–81), *A Woman's Touch* (1981–83), *The Cup and the Lip* (1986), *Honor and Obey* (1988), and several other works, films which often used extensive sections from Sonbert's earlier works.

By 1973, Sonbert began working in a new direction in his films, and was in the process of cutting up his early films and restructuring them into silent films such as *Carriage Trade* (1971). As is well

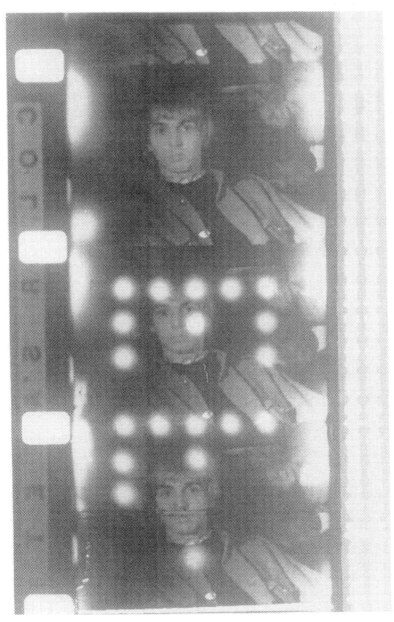

FIGURE 54. Care of the soul. René Ricard in Warren Sonbert's *Hall of Mirrors*. Courtesy Anthology Film Archives.

known, Sonbert never used work prints. Since all of his material was color reversal film, he would project the materials, make notes, and then edit, and re-edit, the footage until he was satisfied with the result.

Sonbert died of complications due to AIDS on May 31, 1995. In an obituary in the *Canyon Cinemanews*, Warren was described by Timoleon Wilkins as "a prolific filmmaker and fearless champion of Avant-Garde and experimental film. Most recently, he had been writing a wide range of film reviews for the local gay press; one could always count on him for up-front insights usually lacking in mainstream movie criticism[. . . .] Sonbert continued to produce beautiful and sensuous [films], and [his work] has been honored around the world, including retrospectives at the Whitney [Museum of American Art in Manhattan] and [The Museum of Modern Art] in New York. [The] San Francisco Cinematheque held a tribute to Sonbert on June 22 [1995]" (Wilkins, 6). There was also a memorial to Sonbert and his work on June 28, 1995, at the Walter Reade Theater in Manhattan.

In his article "Saint Warren," David Ehrenstein had this to say of Sonbert's early, and, some would argue, most evocative and personal work: "that which is most appealing in Warren Sonbert's films has little to do with 'subject' or 'technique,' but rather concerns certain aspects of Sonbert's personality as expressed through his films—specifically his goodness. Warren Sonbert possesses a sensibility both of its time and outside it. Of it for its manifestations of contemporary preoccupations (drugs, clothes, sex, etc.), and outside it because of Sonbert's purity of documentation, innocence of regard—saintliness [. . . . To quote Lorenzo Mans,] 'It would be nice if life were like a Warren Sonbert movie'" (19).

One of the most prolific and, ironically, one of the most neglected practitioners of the New American Cinema was the late **Stan Vanderbeek**, recipient of a $10,000 Film-Maker's Grant from the Ford Foundation in 1964 (along with Kenneth Anger, Bruce Conner, and several other important early filmmakers). Vanderbeek was born in New York City, and studied at Cooper Union and Black Mountain College in North Carolina. Vanderbeek anticipated many of the techniques we now take for granted in the cinema: computer imagery, the use of specialized projection environments in which to show his films and videotapes, collage animation from newspaper and magazine cutouts (which later became a staple on the *Monty Python* series) and compilation filmmaking, to name just a few of his contributions to the technological advancement of cinema.

Vanderbeek even went so far as to build his own film theater, which he dubbed "the Moviedrome," a spherical structure in the

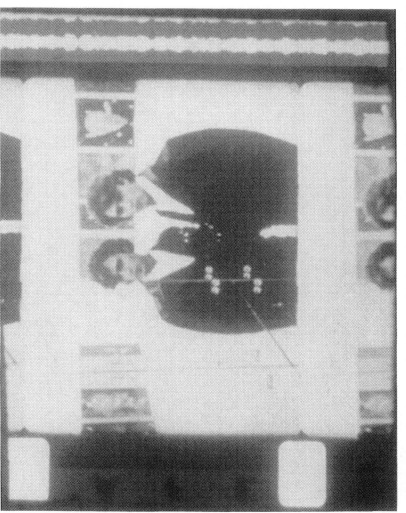

FIGURE 55. A landscape of endless reflection. Gerard Malanga in Warren Sonbert's *Hall of Mirrors*. Courtesy Anthology Film Archives.

FIGURE 56. The cybernetic future of the human visage: solarized/ video portrait of Stan Vanderbeek. Courtesy David Curtis.

woods near Stony Point, New York, where multiple-projector presentations of his works played for rapt audiences in the late 1960s. Using up to six screens of 16mm imagery at one time, in conjunction with slide projectors, overhead projectors, and other image sources to create a cacophonous yet coherently raucous vision of the vast underbelly of American consumer society, Vanderbeek created an intensely vibrant visual environment for his viewers, using the entire interior ceiling space of the Moviedrome as an extended projection area.

While the movie was ideally suited to Vanderbeek's more ambitious projects in video and computer created imagery, the filmmaker's first public impact was a result of his work as a collage animator. Vanderbeek began his career working as an animator on the old *Winky Dink* television series in the early 1950s. Fired from the show, Vanderbeek came back at night for several months afterward, using the 35mm camera and animation stand to create his first independent film works. Writing in the *Village Voice* during this period, Dick Bergman stated that "Vanderbeek manipulates twentieth century American images and idols—gadgets, rockets, satellites, television sets. He selects slick magazine illustrations and animates them, combining and recombining them with comic or satiric purpose. Rockets become automobiles; a car rides over terrain which is a giant woman's chest; a sleek car is frantically propelled by the feet of the driver. These double-meanings and juxtapositions gain effect from Vanderbeek's agitated motions and quick cutting, and in turn become vehicles for his satire" (FMC 1967, 146).

Vanderbeek's early films included *What Who How* (1957), *Mankinda* (1957) *One* (1957), *Astral Man* (1957), *Ala Mode* (1958), *Three-Screen-Scene* (1958), and *Science Fiction* (1959), the last film a 9-minute color film shot in 35mm (as were all the early works), which won the Award of Distinction from the Creative Film Foundation, was prized at the West German and Bergamo International Film Festivals, and selected for special presentation at the Museum of Modern Art.

Vanderbeek described the film as "A social satire aimed at the rockets, scientists, and competitive mania of our time." This film was followed by *Wheeeels #2* (1959), *Achoo Mr. Keroochev* (1959), a less-than-two-minute B/W sound film lampooning Nikita Khrushchev in a violent series of tableaux (whenever Khrushchev starts to speak during a parade, or at the United Nations, he gets hit over the head with a hammer); *Skullduggery* (1960); and *Blacks and Whites, Days and Nights* (1960), described by David Holmstrom as "a 'drawn' film, with images that are constantly changing; drawings of landscapes that keep escaping, traces of faces, everything is almost what it is but never

FIGURE 57. Stan Vanderbeek in the Moviedrome multiple film/video projection facility. Photo by R. Raderman. Courtesy Anthology Film Archives.

stays that way. The soundtrack punches out a wild monotone of dirty, nonsense limericks to the accompaniment of hand-drawn images related only in their complementary rhythm" (FMC 1967, 147).

Next came a document of a Claes Oldenburg Happening, which Vanderbeek entitled *Snapshots of the City* (1961). This was followed by *Summit* (1963), *Breathdeath* (1964), *Wheeeels #1* (1959–1965), *Yet* (1957–1965), *Dance of the Looney Spoons* (1965), *Phenomenon #1* (1965), and *Panels for the Walls of the World* (1966–67, which Vanderbeek described as "an experiment in video tape control, an electric collage that mixes the images by way of electronic mattes, superimpositions, and other electronic means of integrating as many as eight separate images onto one screen. A film commissioned by [. . . CBS Television], it is the first such attempt to examine the almost unlimited graphic and visual possibilities of video tape inter-mix" [FMC 1975, 251]).

Vanderbeek continued to create films at a prodigious pace throughout the later 1960s, including *See, Saw, Seems* (1965), in which a series of images seem to melt into each other in a nonstop profusion of continually self-transformed imagery; *Computer Art* (1965), described by the filmmaker as "a study in computer generated images, where the computer is programmed to produce an alphabet of images and forms in motion, [and] an examination of the possibilities of the computer as a new graphic tool"; *The Human Face Is a Monument* (1965); *Birth of the American Flagg* (1966); *Room Service* (1965); and *Spherical Space Number One* (1967), described by the filmmaker as "a dance film made with Elaine Summers, in which the nude figure is placed against nature, in this case a particular and spherical sense of nature as produced by a special lens . . . (that takes in 195 degrees of sight on film)" (FMC 1967, 149).

As the 1960s ended, Vanderbeek continued to create new and dazzling films, but in most cases these multiple-projector films required specialized projection by Vanderbeek himself, and consequently his shows at the Filmmakers' Cinematheque in the late 1960s dwindled to one a year. During this period, Vanderbeek continued his exploration of computer generated and video imagery with such films as *Man and His World* (1967), *The History of Motion in Motion* (a brilliantly compact summary of motion picture art from the 1890s to *Breathless*, accomplished in less than 10 minutes), *Found Film Number One, Film Form Number One, Computer Generation, Newsreel of Dreams Numbers One and Two, Oh, Poem Field Numbers One, Two, Five and Seven, Super-Imposition, Symmetricks, Transforms, Videospace* (all created between 1967 and 1972, with varying dates of inception and completion that are difficult to trace), and many other

FIGURE 58. Stan Vanderbeek in front of the Moviedrome. Courtesy Anthology Film Archives.

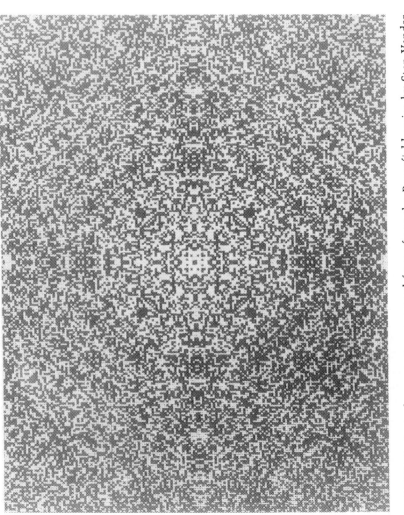

FIGURE 59. A single computer generated frame from the *Poemfield* series by Stan Vander-beek. Courtesy David Curtis.

works, named and unnamed. The vision that Vanderbeek ultimately embraced was a theory of mechanisms, an excess of spectacle identifying the cultural industry that simultaneously ruptures and sutures our collective consciousness as viewers. In Vanderbeek's world of endless advertisements and dualistic causality, all is based on a mutuality of exchange, the automatism of cultural negotiation which signals the occularcentricism of our telecultural alterity. Indeed, it is Vanderbeek's Gramscian insistence on the inherent symbolic capital of his consumerist visions that forces his visual constructs into the zone of haptic rupture; Vanderbeek's world is one in which the commodification of all, including the future of any work of art/commerce, is engaged in a scopic battle for dominance over the neo-canonical apparatus of "being for itself," the domain that the work inhabits despite any attempts to compromise it, or, paradoxically, to install it within the artificial confines of canon.

Vanderbeek's mordant view of the human body as an inverted extension of the cybernetic landscape foreshadows the writings of futurists Arthur and Marilouise Kroker, who note that "in the '60s, McLuhan theorized that the technological media of communication were in his term, 'extensions of man' [. . .] but that was then, and this is now[; . . . it is no longer] technology as an extension of the human sensorium, but the human species as a hotwired extension of digital reality" (139). In his brightly colored, violent assemblages of the future's cybernetic, computer-driven social order, Vanderbeek offers us an unpleasant taste of things to come, sugar-coated with a thin veneer of satire to make his message more palatable. But make no mistake about it. Vanderbeek's Swiftian cultural vision is dark, savage, and ultimately despairing. Perhaps his films are so little seen today because they tell us much about ourselves that we do not wish to know.

Inasmuch as the 1990s comprises the zone in which our corporeal consciousness is ruled by the memory of the body, the films of San Francisco artist **Ben Van Meter** occupy a unique place in experimental cinema history. These films from the early 1960s pursued what Rosi Braidotti later described as "the politics of radical heterosexuality . . . [positing that] the mystery of alterity, of relationship to the other and especially to the Other that is the Divine Being, is summed up in the other who is sexually different from one, that is to say the other sex for each sex" (Braidotti, 133). Thus such radical heterosexualist films as Barbara Rubin's *Christmas on Earth* or Carolee Schneemann's *Fuses* celebrate the finding of the self within the other, just as surely as José Rodriguez-Soltero's *Jerovi* or Ron Rice's *Chumlum* celebrates the self-liberation of an androgynous, pan-sexual universe, and the films of Warhol's Factory espoused the new ethos of gay consciousness as a matter of everyday existence. Van Meter's films *The Poon Tang Trilogy* (1964), *S. F. Trips Festival: An Opening* (1966), and particularly *Acid Mantra* (1966–68), a 47-minute avalanche of images culminating in a free-for-all orgy situated against a pastoral backdrop, celebrate a world of comparative sexual freedom and liberation, an ethos possible only in the era before AIDS and other sexually transmitted diseases mushroomed to epidemic proportions. Ben Van Meter's vision of a society of adventurous yet egalitarian sexual experimentation is too vivid for contemporary audiences, who view the nomadic alterity of 1960s society through the unreliable filter of nostalgic memory.

The Poon Tang Trilogy (1964, B/W, sound) is a brief film composed of three 3-minute segments: in the first tableau, footage of the Hindenburg disaster is projected on the nude body of a young woman; in the second section, Civil Rights protesters are dragged away into police vans to the accompaniment of the '50s r&b hit "I Just Love Your Sexy Ways"; in the final portion of the film, another young woman attempts to remove a floating black bar which seeks to obliterate from the spectator's gaze various portions of her anatomy. For 1964, the film was a revolutionary commentary on the censorship of images within the United States. When the film was being printed in the lab, the owner of the facility viewed the film and, without consulting Van Meter, contacted the FBI and sent Van Meter's footage directly to the FBI headquarters in Washington, D.C. When Van Meter arrived at the lab, he was told that his film had been confiscated, and only a prolonged legal battle enabled Van Meter to recover his original negative (Deivert archives).

The Poon Tang Trilogy was followed by *Colorfilm* and *Olds-mobile*. In 1965–66, Van Meter created the brilliant political poetic documentary *Up Tight, L.A. Is Burning . . . Shit* (20 minutes, color, sound) which won first prize at the Ann Arbor Film Festival in 1966; *Some Don't* (1966), an 8-minute B/W sound film, exposing the staged commodification and banality of the American "beauty contest" with color overlays of fireworks in reverse-motion; and *Nico* (1966), a 4½-minute color sound meditation on the erstwhile Warhol superstar. Van Meter then embarked upon the creation of one of the most sensuous and beautiful films of the 1960s San Francisco Avant-Garde, *S. F. Trips Festival, An Opening*, a hallucinatory documentary of the Trips Festival staged in the Bay Area during the early months of 1966. Van Meter described his 9-minute work, which was shot "silent" with a spring-wound Bolex, and subsequently presented with a densely manipulated soundtrack thus:

174

FIGURE 60. Ben and Sandra Van Meter, 1989. Photo courtesy Bert Deivert.

The Trips Festival was a seminal event of the sixties scene in San Francisco. Held in the Longshoreman's Hall over one three day weekend in February 1966 it was produced by Bill Graham, Stewart Brand and Roland Jacopetti. Freaks came from all over the Bay Area to present their trips and dig what others were doing[, including the] Open Theater, from Berkeley, Brand's America Needs Indians Lightshow, rock and roll with Big Brother and the Grateful Dead (then the Warlocks). Kesey and the Merry Pranksters were there with acid spiked Kool Aid. I could afford only three 100' rolls of 16mm film, [so I] exposed each roll once each of the three nights. The resulting impressionistic vision can be best described as a documentary from the point of a goldfish in the Kool Aid bowl. (Deivert archives)

Of all of Van Meter's films, except for *Acid Mantra, S. F. Trips Festival* is perhaps the most hypnotic and evocative. Van Meter's instinctive control of multiple exposure imagery is striking, as faces, bodies, strips of images from Cocteau's *Blood of a Poet* (1930), and a sound mix of hypermanipulated, sped-up tribal chanting combine to create a dazzling display of virtuosity, made all the more remarkable by the fact that the entire film was composed from memory, in the camera. As with Jerome Hiler's *Acid Rock*, there are only three splices in the entire film, and these joins serve merely to string the three rolls together into a 9-minute cornucopia of sound and image.

Van Meter's major work in the 1960s came to its culmination in *Acid Mantra* (1966–68, 47 minutes, color and B/W, sound), one of the most ambitious and overpowering films of the '60s Avant-Garde, comparable in its intensity to Paul Sharits's split-screen stereo-sound *Razor Blades* (1965–68). The film was widely seen and enormously influential, garnering national news coverage. Thomas Albright described *Acid Mantra* in the May 11, 1968, issue of *Rolling Stone* as follows:

Acid Mantra mixes as many as six different exposures, sometimes adding triple-exposed color to triple-exposed black and white in a light-show-like spectacle of the rock sub-culture, Baroque texture, momentum and soaring sweep, over a sound-track of incessant drumbeats combined with electronic effects . . . contains an extraordinary mixture of location rock dance and Lightshow scenes, crowds on downtown streets, footage from a country party hosted by the Grateful Dead. They build a multi-textured, propulsive structure of sprawling power. (Deivert archives)

Indeed, one of the most remarkable aspects of *Acid Mantra* is its celebration of human sexuality and play as a function of the sacred, as opposed to the commercialized visions of "free love" bequeathed to our collective consciousness by such mainstream films as Michael Wadleigh's *Woodstock* (1969) and Arthur Dreifuss's *The Love-Ins* (1967), both films made long after the initial wave of experimentation and euphoria had passed. In *Acid Mantra*, we see people dancing and congregating in a San Francisco dance hall, with black and white and color images simultaneously competing for our attention, as the soundtrack provides a mesmerizing counterpoint to the visuals we are witnessing. As the film progresses, the scene shifts to a party in the California hills, as nude men, women, and children swim, dance, and play with unabashed abandon. It is of particular importance here to note that Van Meter's camera work documents the spectacle of the nude body with egalitarian élan. Glimpses of full frontal male and female nudity drift across the screen in a haze of visual splendor reminiscent of Botticelli; the light (natural sunlight, for the most part) shines off the bodies of the celebrants as if sanctifying their paean to human sexuality. As the film continues, couples fall to the earth and begin coupling ecstatically, as Van Meter drips blobs of red and green paint directly on the film to suggest an approximation of their orgasmic energy. Yet the couples are photographed as part of an overall exquisite blur, and are never distinct; we cannot be certain as to what we are witnessing. As the film concludes, we again see men and women, separately or together, with or without children, strolling or reclining in the nude underneath the sun. *Acid Mantra* is a joyous expression of the life force that flourished in the very early days of the 1960s in San Francisco, before drugs and decay (and the commercialization of spectacle) were allowed to dominate imagistic film/video discourse, as is the case (for the most part) today. Indeed, what is most remarkable about *Acid Mantra* is its overwhelming innocence of vision and execution; authentically primitive and infinitely complex, it captures in an endlessly shifting tapestry the grandeur and ephemeral beauty of a vanished age, an era almost beyond authentic recall.

Bill Vehr's grandiose costume epics, in the style of Jack Smith's works, included *Avocada*, a 30-minute, color, silent film described by Smith himself as ". . . a study of high-art writhing. Carole Morell writhes as if she were born to writhe in movies; writhes like a movie star among flickering candles and smoldering camera movement. *Avocada* has a percussive Peruvian sound track. It is steeped in blue-green shadows. It is incomparable and nutritiously beautiful. It is a film possessed of gilded glamour" (FMC 1967, 150). *Brothel* is a 45-minute color silent film starring Mario Montez, Jack Smith, Piero Heliczer, Tosh Carillo, and Francis Francine. Filmmaker Carl Linder was especially taken with Vehr's film, describing the film's protagonists as "neo-romantic, Beardsley-esque-phantoms from an Oscar Wilde garden" (FMC 1967, 150).

In the magnificent stasis that informs the construction of these two remarkably similar films (*Brothel* was originally conceived as the first portion of much longer project), Vehr's heavily costumed and ornately decorated performers inhabit a space in which the serial repetition of acts of engenderment is the primary function of the film's anti-narrative. Through excessive repetition, the performers in Vehr's films also constitute a performative rupture of the hegemonic styles of sexual discourse proscribed by the dominant culture. In their tacky and gaudy splendor, and their easy transgenderal, pansexual address, Vehr's films seem the perfect Technicolor complement to Jack Smith's more celebrated films, but they have not been readily available to the public for screening for a number of years. A screening of Vehr's works (in new prints, with the tape soundtracks made into optical tracks for integrated projection) would be an archival project of considerable value.

Filmmaker **Jon Voorhees** created *Shoveling* (1970), a 7-minute black and white silent film that was, said Jonas Mekas ". . . first shot on 8mm, then refined on 16mm. Loop variations of a man shoveling snow. Good use of film grain. In this film (as in Gehr's *Reverberation*) the film image qualities merge almost unrecognizably with the video image qualities" (FMC 1975, 257). Voorhees followed the creation of this film with many other works, all suffused with his own particular visual romanticism, including *Patience* (1970), *Perfectly Normal* (1971), *Serving Time* (1972), *Rivers of Darkness/Rivers of Light* (1972), *Whispers Delaying Grace* (1973), and *Destiny . . . The Universal Fantasy* (1974).

The films of **Andy Warhol** have been amply covered in numerous other texts on the prolific painter, sculptor, performance artist, and film and video maker. I will discuss him only briefly. Warhol was, during his lifetime, the most financially astute and commercially successful of all the members of the New American Cinema. As has been noted of Warhol's early films as documents of an expanding gay consciousness, "*Couch, Blow Job* and the other early films are thus not just about breaking the taboo on seeing gayness, but exposing some of the aesthetic mechanisms of the proscription and the lifting of it" (Dyer, 157). These first films were designed primarily as artistic statements, rather than projects calculated to return a profit at the box office. Other Warhol films during this period included *Kiss* (1963–64); *Sleep* (1963–64), a 6½-hour silent record of a man peacefully slumbering; *Haircut* (1964); *Empire* (1964), an 8-hour meditation on the Empire State Building; *Couch* (1965); *Henry Geldzahler* (1965); *Shoul-*

der (1965); and the sync-sound features *Vinyl* (1965), *Horse* (1965), *Camp* (1965), *Kitchen* (1966), *My Hustler* (1966), *The Velvet Underground and Nico* (1966), all shot in rapid succession. These films, which remain refreshing, raw, and crude when viewed today, were nevertheless commercial successes on a modest scale when released to the public, particularly *The Chelsea Girls* (1966), Warhol's 3½-hour marathon slice-of-life, documenting the dreams and ambitious of those who worked with him during this period of intense artistic ferment.

All of these films have been dealt with elsewhere extensively; indeed, Warhol possessed an undeniable genius for publicity, as a painter, filmmaker, graphic designer, and "pop" personality (including his work as an expanded media artist with his creation of the Exploding Plastic Inevitable troupe), and his mark on the consciousness of the international art world remains secure today. Later Warhol films, such as *Lonesome Cowboys*, were frankly commercial affairs. *Lonesome Cowboys* was made on a twenty thousand dollar investment, and grossed over a million dollars, although much of this was kept by the distribution company. *The Chelsea Girls* was made for less than a fifteen hundred dollar outlay, and eventually grossed a million dollars as well; since that film was initially distributed through the Filmmakers Distribution Center (a now-defunct arm of the Filmmakers Cooperative), Warhol received a considerable share of the proceeds. In 1967, Warhol shot the never-released *San Diego Surf*, jokingly described by Warhol during a 1969 interview with the author as "a quietly, leisurely drama of social domestic life." The plot of *San Diego Surf* is both simple and familiar: Viva and Taylor Mead are married, and have two sons and a couple of over-furnished beach houses in La Jolla, California. A roving band of surfers shows up (roughly the same group of actors as in *Lonesome Cowboys*). For the rest of the film, the surfers chase after Viva, and Taylor Mead chases after the surfers. Due to editing problems, the film was never completed.

In late 1969, Warhol's *Blue Movie* (originally entitled *Fuck*) opened at the Andy Warhol Garrick Theatre (which Warhol had leased to keep control of the box office, and avoid overcharging by distributors), but police closed the film down within a week. At a clandestine pre-release screening of the film at the Factory, Michaelangelo Antonioni watched the film intently, and then commented that "It's not one of Andy's best, but it's quite interesting. And I thought the color in the second reel, the blues and whites, were beautiful" (Dixon interview, 1969). Warhol continued making films and videotapes until his death in 1987. The major collection of his work is housed at the Andy Warhol Museum in Pittsburgh, Pennsylvania, which recently opened to the public.

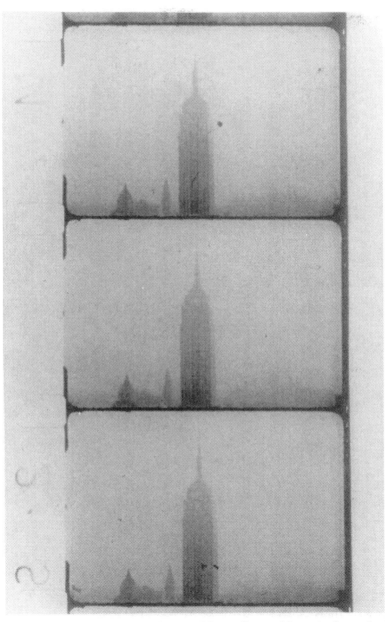

FIGURE 61. "Homage to the World's Tallest": filmstrip from Andy Warhol's *Empire*. Courtesy Anthology Film Archives.

FIGURE 62. Andy Warhol shooting the never-released *San Diego Surf*. Courtesy Anthology Film Archives.

The elder **Whitney Brothers, James** and **John**, were two of the most important and influential film artists of the 1950s and '60s, whose early works with computer generated imagery prefigured much of the work being accomplished in that field today. John Whitney created three abstract films with an overhead projector in the early 1950s, including *Celery Stalks at Midnight* and *Hothouse*. John Whitney then produced three animated films for UPA, *Lion Hunt*, *Blues Pattern*, and *Performing Painter*, and then a documentary film, *Day of the Dead*. Whitney also produced some of the visual effects for Alfred Hitchcock's film *Vertigo*, and created two personal films, *Motion Graphics Number One* and *Permutations*. James Whitney's most well-known film remains *Lapis*. It has won thirty film festival awards including one each at the Ann Arbor Film Festival, New York Film Festival, and the London Film Festival.

The younger **Whitney Brothers, John Jr.** and **Michael**, have been making films since 1965, some together and some as independent works. Michael and John made a three-screen film in 1967, which was initially shown at the Monterey Pop Festival, then at the Aspen Design Conference, at Expo '67, and at the Museum of Modern Art in New York. The brothers use computers exclusively to make their films, and have primarily relied on the mechanical analogue computer designed by their father. Even in the late 1960s, the Whitneys foresaw the future of computer animation. In a previously unpublished 1969 interview, Michael Whitney observed that the "current vogue of attempting to bring together art and technology is absurd. The artist of the future will just have to be a technologist [. . .] I think the computer will become a great artistic aid and will dispel the connotative fear that goes with computerism. Most products of technology are presently negative. There is a positive side yet to come out" (Dixon papers). Indeed, computers have become an indispensable part of contemporary filmmaking, offering greater ease of execution and flexibility than most people dreamed of in the early days of experimental cinema. The work of the Whitneys thus prefigured our current immersion in the era of computer graphic design, in which every raw image is fodder for computer generated enhancement within the dominant Hollywood cinema; it also pointed the way to our current routine and domestic use of computers to create digital mini-movies for use on the World Wide Web.

Joyce Wieland, a Canadian filmmaker who lived in the United States for many years and created some of her most important works here, was one of the major filmmakers of the 1960s Avant-Garde cinema. Her many films include *Barbara's Blindness* (which she co-made with Betty Ferguson), described by Wieland as "a collage film. We

182

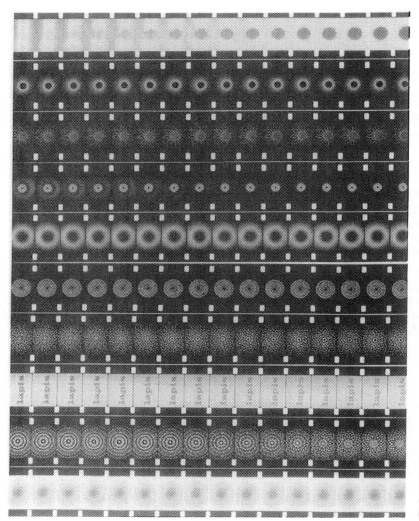

FIGURE 63. Sequences of computer generated imagery from *Lapis*. Courtesy Canyon Cinema.

started out with a dull film about a little blind girl named Mary and ended up with something that made us get crazy"; *Water Sark*, an abstract domestic film with music by Carla Bley, Mike Mantler, and Ray Jessel; and *1933* (1967), a 4-minute structural film in which shots from a fire escape looking down at the street below are interspersed with sections of blank, purplish-tinted clear leader, as the superimposed title "1933" appears and disappears over the image.

Sailboat (1967) is a 3-minute loop film in which a sailboat continually passes in front of the spectator's eyes along the horizon of the shore; *Hand Tinting* (1967) is a silent 5-minute short film comprised of "outcuts from a Job Corps documentary which features hand-tinted sections. The film is full of small movements and actions, gestures begun and never completed. Repeated images, sometimes in color, sometimes not. A beautifully realized type of chamber-music film whose sum-total feeling is ritualistic" (Robert Cowan, *Take One*, as cited in FMC 1975, 261).

Wieland's next work, *Catfood* (1967–68), is a 13-minute film which "studies the eating habits of a luxuriously furred cat devouring separately five fish just arrived from the market. The viewpoint is always as though the camera were held at the edge of a table while the cat operates on top against a black backdrop. It is filled with supreme succulent color, sometimes recalling Manet in the silvery glints of the fish scales, and, as in the *Rat Life* picture, getting the deep, ovular splendor of a Caravaggio"; this film was followed by the allegorical *Rat Life and Diet in North America* (1968), a 16-minute film in which "a band of revolutionary gerbils escape their cat jailers and journey up the Hudson where they hide out at a millionaire's estate and perfect their tactics as guerrilla fighters" (both quotes from a review by Manny Farber in *Artforum*, as cited in FMC 1975, 262). *La Raison Avant La Passion* (1968–69) was perhaps Wieland's most ambitious project, an 80-minute feature film about her homeland. As an artist, Wieland was deeply involved in the creation of this particular film, a consideration of the positive values inherent in Canadian society, as opposed to life within the relatively repressive social fabric of the United States.

Dripping Water (1969) is a 10-minute meditation on the image of water slowly dripping on a plate; *Pierre Vallieres* (1972) is a 30-minute film described by Wieland as "a film about a Quebec revolutionary who spent three years in jail without trial. The film was made in April 1972, when Pierre was working with workers, raising consciousness, in Mount Laurier, Quebec. He was then writing a book about Quebec [. . .]" (FMC 1975, 263); throughout the film, Vallieres speaks in French, as English subtitles flash across the screen. Wieland frames

FIGURE 64. Joyce Wieland's *1933*; structure and sensibility. Courtesy Anthology Film Archives.

her subject closely, so that only his mouth is visible. Other brief Wieland films include *Patriotism*, a 4-minute film blown-up from an 8mm original; *Solidarity* (1973), a film about a women's strike action; and *A & B in Ontario* (1966/1984), a 16-minute B/W film co-made with the late Hollis Frampton. *A & B in Ontario* was shot in 1966 and then abandoned until Wieland completed it after Frampton's death; it is an elegiac farewell to the past, and to the communal energy created by Frampton, Snow, and Wieland during their work in New York in the 1960s.

Paul Wigger was another interesting filmmaker from the 1960s, whose *Jimmy Bugger* (1969) achieved a variety of startling effects through superimposition of negative and positive imagery "staggered" by a few frames through the film's brief running time. Born on October 23, 1942, in Massena, New York, Wigger earned his Bachelor of Science at the State University of New York at Buffalo in 1965 and then went on to receive a Master of Arts in Creative Photography from the University of Iowa in 1968, and also a Master of Fine Arts in Creative Photography and Painting from the University of Iowa in the same year. Wigger's exhibitions include "Light" (presented at the Massachusetts Institute of Technology) and "Vision and Expression" (at the George Eastman House, Rochester, New York). His work is in the permanent collections of the Art Institute of Chicago, M.I.T., George Eastman House, and the Art Department of the University of Iowa.

Lloyd Michael Williams is another major figure of the New American Cinema, whose most famous films are probably *Line of Apogee* (1964–68) and *Wipes* (1963). Williams was the recipient of a Fulbright Fellowship in 1964, to study cinematography in France. In that same year, Williams made this statement to *Film Comment* about his work as a filmmaker, and particularly about *Line of Apogee*, which was then in production

> *Line of Apogee* will be a free form of creativity which, due to its content, should not be limited to standard forms of filmic structure. Its subject is an astronomer at the moment of truth. As he looks at the constellations, he is reminded of incidents from his past. The filmic vehicle is that of the dreaming mind with its total freedom, especially from the inhibitions of the body. Here there is no limit to time or space. Images and sounds materialize and then disperse. Familiar objects are placed in unfamiliar settings. Technically, it could be termed as an experiment of special effects for the purpose of clearly and immediately communicating a visual message to the audience. The nature of this film will allow a great degree of technical and creative freedom and growth. Its central idea is built on pessimism and a sense of futility; the timelessness and loneliness of every man's life; and life's solitary reward which is depth. (Hitchens, 32)

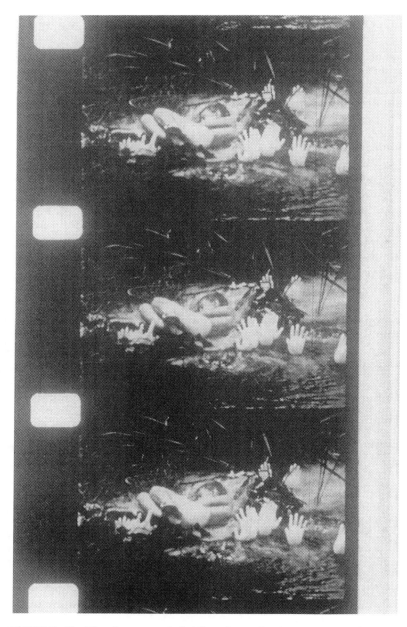

FIGURE 65. The domain of childhood in Lloyd Michael Williams's
Line of Apogee. Courtesy Anthology Film Archives.

Williams's other films include *The Free Pass* (1955), *Rhapsody in Blue* (1956), *Gospel in Chalk* and *The Fungus Among Us* (both 1957), *Les Poissons* (1958), *Jabberwock* and *They're Off* (both 1959), *Ursula* (1960), *The Creation* and *Opus #5* (both 1961), along with *The Inflation of the Air Mattress* (starring the ubiquitous Taylor Mead), *The Creation*, and *Two Images for a Computer Piece* (with an Interlude), with music by Vladimir Ussachevsky.

Bud Wirtschafter, who operated the Auricon camera for many of Warhol's early 16mm Auricon sound films, created *I'm Here Now* (1965–66), a 28-minute 16mm documentary shot in the summer of 1965 in New York, documenting the "Summer in the City" outreach program. He also created the landmark film *What's Happening* (1963), a 13-minute newsreel of "a series of happenings, taking place at George Segal's farm [featuring] Allan Kaprow, Chuck Ginnever, Wolf Vostel, Yvonne Rainer, [La Monte] Young [and] Dick Higgins"; (FMC 1975, 266). As a vision of an artistic past that can never be recreated, the film is of inestimable historic value; it is also an excellent example of Wirtschafter's pure, non-judgmental documentary style. More recently, Wirtschafter has made *Snow Job* (1966) and *Glance* (1970); *Glance* is a brief two-projector film which involves the audience in its performance narrative.

Ray Wisniewski created the performance film *Doomshow* in the mid 1960s, and lost the original for the film on the New York subway; miraculously, the film was returned to Wisniewski by a thoughtful patron of the "D" train. The film documents a Happening created by Wisniewski, photographed in a basement apartment in grainy black and white, to the cacophonous accompaniment of police sirens and other grating noises; the end result is a hellish and brutal document of the early American Avant-Garde.

One of the most influential filmmakers making experimental cinema in New York in the 1960s was **Jud Yalkut**. I interviewed Yalkut in the late 1960s, and wrote at the time that

> Yalkut can best be described as a kinetic filmmaker. His films are studies of Intermedia projects: some are by himself, some are by other artists. But rather than being documents, his films use a wide range of techniques which create a new experience, separate but related to the subject. In 1961, Yalkut began working with an 8mm camera seriously, although he had been shooting home movies for a long time before. Yalkut shot experimental studies and documentaries about New York for two years, and finally in 1963 pulled together enough money to get a 16mm camera. During this period, he was attending classes at the City College of New York and McGill University. After three years of formal education, Yalkut took off on a long rambling odyssey across the entire

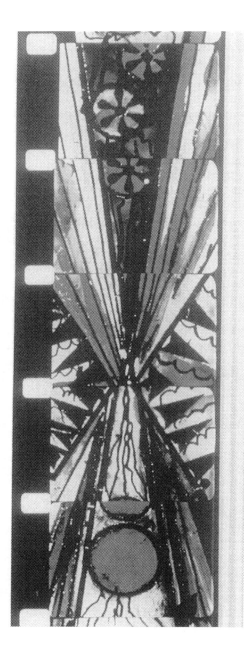

FIGURE 66. Lloyd
Michael Williams's
Wipes; an explosion
of light and color.
Courtesy Anthology
Film Archives.

United States for three more years. One of those years was spent at Big Sur, California, where Yalkut stayed in a commune for a full year. Yalkut stopped doing any kind of work and relaxed; he ultimately felt that this year of "spiritual meditation" in Big Sur was probably more valuable to him than the three years he spent in school.

From Big Sur, Yalkut went back to New York and got involved with USCO, a pioneer experimental multi-media group that put on light shows (a combination of slides, films, moiré projections, overhead machines, sculptures, light constructions, sound either live, taped or both, and actors) in various venues. USCO stands for "Us Company," and the members of the group agreed to adopt a policy of anonymity. All projects, films, anything, were simply labeled USCO; no individual credits were ever given. Nevertheless, two dominant personalities emerged from the group: Gerd Stern and Yalkut. Yalkut's first 16mm films of USCO were rather primitive: *Diffraction Film, Clarence,* and numerous other three and four minute pieces were resilient, mostly single exposure films that were intended not as individual films but as parts of USCO light shows and presentations. With *Turn, Turn, Turn,* Yalkut achieved a new level of sophistication: the superimpositions became extremely controlled, sound tracks were added, and these films were intended as individual presentations rather than parts of a group effort.

It was about this time that Yalkut began to come into his own and break away from USCO, although USCO continued to present media works, pieces and presentations in galleries and museums. Jud began to present one man shows at the Filmmakers' Cinematheque in New York City, and continued producing films. Recently, Yalkut has branched off into still photography and graphics, writing, painting, poetry, and music. Yalkut hopes to combine all these disparate mediums into a newly congruent whole in which each complements the other, much as the instruments of an orchestra create patterns of harmony, counterpoint and dissonance, and together form a unified experience. Yalkut is particularly interested in projection/reception environments: he has designed a theatre which is completely spherical, where the audience would be suspended in air cushioned seats that would gently drift about the globe, while projectors of every variety bombarded all sides of the sphere (which would be translucent) with patterns and shapes. In this fashion, the viewer would become one with the environment, and there would be no sense of up, down, right or left, and no irregularities in the sphere to give the viewer points of visual (and therefore orientational) reference. S/he would become one with the piece: normative visual barriers would be removed. (Dixon interview, 1969)

Since then, Yalkut has gone on to consolidate an enviable reputation as one of the most important metamedia artists in the American independent cinema.

FIGURE 67. Portrait of kinetic filmmaker Jud Yalkut, 1969. Courtesy Anthology Film Archives.

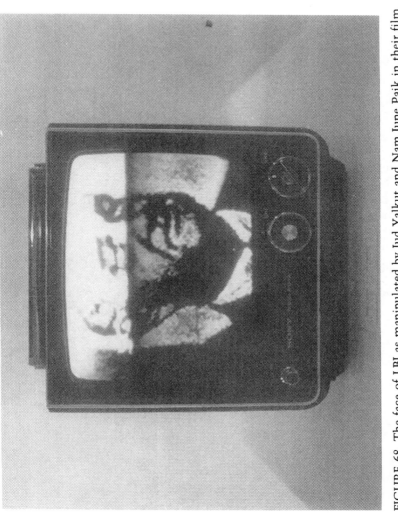

FIGURE 68. The face of LBJ as manipulated by Jud Yalkut and Nam June Paik in their film *Videotape Study No. 3*, here seen on videotape as a performance installation in 1975. Courtesy Jud Yalkut.

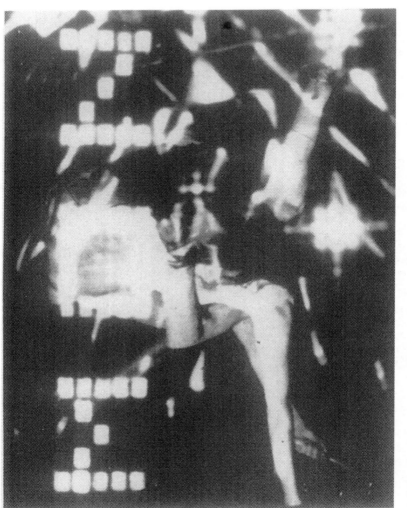

FIGURE 69. Composite still of *Turn, Turn, Turn* and *Yin-Yang Shiva Shakti* from 1969 USCO multimedia installation by Jud Yalkut. Courtesy Jud Yalkut.

Yalkut's many cinematic/video works include *Diffraction Film* (1965), 16mm, color, silent, 10 minutes; *Turn, Turn, Turn* (1966), 16mm, color, sound, 10 minutes; *US Down by the Riverside* (1966), 16mm, color, sound, 3 minutes; *Clarence* (1965–68), 16mm, color, sound, 10 minutes; *Le Parc* (1966), 16mm, color, sound, 4½ minutes; *Moondial Film* (1966), 16mm, B/W, sound, 4 minutes; *D.M.T.* (1966), 16mm, color, sound, 4 minutes; *US* (1967), 16mm, color, silent, 15 minutes (unreleased); *Metamedia: A Film Journal of Intermedia and the Avant-Garde 1966–1970* (1966–71), 16mm, color, silent, 50 minutes; *Kenyon Film* (1969–72), 16mm, color, silent (24 FPS), 10 minutes; *Beatles Electroniques* (1966–69), 16mm, color and B/W, sound, 3 minutes; *Videotape Study No. 3* (1967–69), 16mm, B/W, sound, 4 minutes; *P+A-I(K)* (1966), 16mm, color, sound, 10 minutes; *Electronic Yoga* (1966–94), 16mm, B/W, 8 minutes (released in 3/4" video with sound in 1994); *The Godz* (1966), 16mm, color, sound, 10 minutes; *Kusama's Self-Obliteration* (created in collaboration with the performance artist Yayoi Kusama; 1967), 16mm, color, sound, 23 minutes; and *Aquarian Rushes* (1970), 16mm, color, sound, 50 minutes, which documents the 1969 concert at Woodstock.

Kusama's Self-Obliteration is perhaps of particular interest to contemporary audiences, in that it documents the work of the legendary Japanese performance artist whose best-known activity was covering everyone with painted dots to make them "invisible." Yalkut's film documents Kusama at work painting water lilies in a pond, then intercuts stock footage of various public monuments (such as the Statue of Liberty) covered with punch-hole dots, and finally depicts a full-scale orgy in graphic detail, during which Kusama calmly wanders about the room covering the participants with more painted dots, even as the air is charged with nascent sexual energy. The film was one of the major prize winners at the Fourth International Experimental Film Competition in Knokke Le Zoute, Belgium, in 1968, the same year that Michael Snow's *Wavelength* was first screened for the public (and also walked off with a major prize at the festival). Of *Kusama's Self-Obliteration*, fellow performance artist Yoko Ono observed that "of all the films in the competition, I like best *Wavelength* and *Self-Obliteration*" (FMC 1975, 272). Yalkut's most recent work is *Electronic Super Highway: Nam June Paik in the 1990s*, a 40-minute catalogue/portrait on the work of the internationally known video artist executed in 1" video. Yalkut now lives and works in Ohio, where he continues his explorations into the frontiers of the methodology and theory of the electronic/cinema construct.

The last artist from the 1960s whose work I will discuss is **Vernon Zimmerman**. Zimmerman's *Lemon Hearts* (1960) is a 30-minute

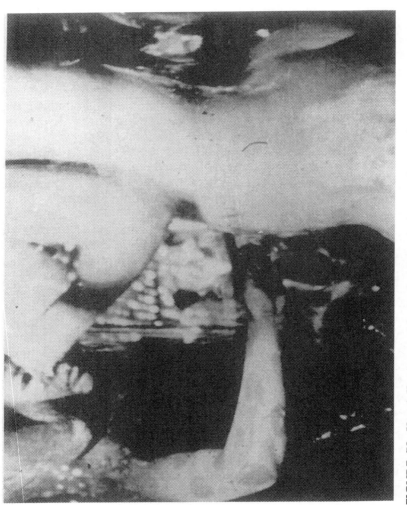

FIGURE 70. Yayoi Kusama paints a man's penis in Kusama's *Self-Obliteration* by Jud Yalkut. Photo by Gideon Bachmann. Courtesy Jud Yalkut.

film comedy set in San Francisco, featuring Taylor Mead in eleven different roles; the film is crude and primitive, with cuts made in the film after the composite optical soundtrack was added, so that the image sometimes precedes the sounds it is supposed to be synchronized with. Nevertheless, the film precedes and largely prefigures Ron Rice's *The Flower Thief,* and while not as grandiose and successful as Rice's work, the film deserves to be recognized as an early classic of Beat-era filmmaking, produced on a minuscule budget.

Other Zimmerman films include *To L. A. . . . With Lust* (1961), a 25-minute film starring Ingrid Lothigius, with supporting performances by Taylor Mead and Eric "Big Daddy" Nord (Nord would later appear in Rice's *The Flower Thief* as one of Taylor Mead's tormentors), and the hour-long documentary film *The College* (1963). *Scarface and Aphrodite* (1963) is a 15-minute film record of a Happening staged by artist Claes Oldenburg, and won a Special Jury Commendation at the Third International Experimental Film Festival (1963–64) in Knokke-Le-Zoute, Belgium. Zimmerman's last experimental film to date is the brief comic short *America Au Gratin;* he has since gone on to a long career in Hollywood.

CHAPTER SIX

■■

Epilogue

As the 1970s dawned, new filmmakers came on the scene, carrying forward the traditions of the 1960s in a variety of ways. As one example of this performative energy, **Vivienne Dick's** proto-punk work offered an alternative to the highly structured films then comprising the dominant mode of alternative cinema practice. Dick worked in Super 8mm with a variety of collaborators in New York from 1974 onwards, starting out as an apprentice for Jack Smith, taking slides for some of Smith's theatrical extravaganzas. Her early vibrant and rough-edged Super 8mm sound films, such as *Beauty Becomes the Beast* (1979), *She Had Her Gun All Ready* (1978) and *Guerrilla Talks* (1978), established her as a force to be reckoned with in the New York punk scene of the 1970s. Dick screened her films in clubs, storefronts, anywhere she could set up a Super 8mm projector and get an audience. Now living in London, Dick wrote me that "I am still making films, using Hi-8 transferring to Betacam (and maybe 16mm too), experimenting a bit with feeding images and sequences into [a] computer and manipulating material." In the notes for a recent retrospective of Dick's work at the London Filmmakers Cooperative, Rod Stoneman wrote that

> Vivienne Dick's Super 8 films dating from the mid-1970s in New York, through *London Suite* to the recent *A Skinny Little Man Attacked Daddy* (1994), plot points on the itinerary of an Irish filmmaker, born in rural Donegal, who has worked in two of the world's largest metropolises.

197

In these different places she explores the cultural dislocations of individuals oscillating in unstable identities, creating a kind of urban ethnography of different groups living at the edge of the city. She has been enshrined in the (largely American) textbooks as "post-feminist punk New York underground" and there are interesting shifts between the Super 8 American films, produced on no budget, and those produced in England, in terms of the different contexts of production (more consistent funding and 16mm) and reception (college screenings and television transmission) [. . .] The construction of *London Suite* and *New York Conversations* (1991) gives rise to an underlying oxymoron: exact looseness. Despite its often digressive movement, there is a real precision in the films' underlying structure and editing. Like the unattached narratives of German filmmaker Alexander Kluge, stories slide into stories, seemingly unfocussed dialogue dissolves into interview, anecdote and parable[. . . .] *Rothach* (1985) is most immediately an observation of a harsh Irish countryside, however, an evocative soundtrack pushes the images into unknown territory. *Rothach* repositions the ways in which the Irish landscape has been traditionally imaged.

London Suite (*Getting Sucked In*) (1989) draws a telling picture of modern London through a mixture of narrative action and people talking straight-to-camera. Dick extends her observational camera into a dramatic context. *London Suite* complicates our expectations of the boundaries of documentary (and drama), however, it is not an overtly formalist film—it taps directly into the energy of life in the conurbation called London. *New York Conversations* (1991) is a document of New York people's lives and work. Quite simply constructed, the video is nevertheless complex in its presentation of modern urban life. It does not attempt to describe the city of New York. Rather, *New York Conversations*, by having people speak quite personally about themselves, allows an audience a chance to experience a sense of place beyond the conventional representations of the Big Apple. *A Skinny Little Man Attacked Daddy* (1994) is a video about a return to the family home. From this starting point a journey through Dick's family history allows a narrative to be constructed about personal identity. In this video, Dick's observational camera contends with her active voice to produce some profoundly moving scenes. But this is not simply a personal, internal work—*A Skinny Little Man* investigates in a significant way the development of the individual subject. (*LFMC Retrospective*, June 16, 1995, program notes, included as part of letter from Vivienne Dick to the author)

Of her early days as a filmmaker, Dick wrote that

[in] 1974 [I was] liv[ing] in New York. [I] worked with Jack Smith for a while taking slides[. . . . I] started to ma[ke] S-8 films in '77 on very low budgets. New York was the right place for me to be because this would never have happened [in London] at the time. [I was] very inspired by emerging punk scene and the women involved in it. Films were initially

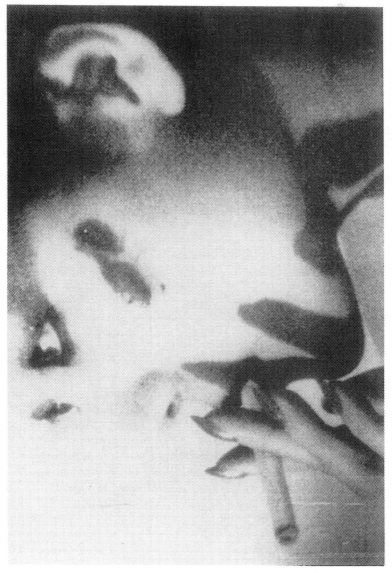

FIGURE 71. Anya Phillips in Vivienne Dick's *Guerrilla Talks*; shot on Super 8mm and blown up to 16mm. Courtesy Vivienne Dick.

shown in music venues between bands and later at independent film venues. Quite a lot of screenings across the US in colleges and other places (Anthology Archives, The Collective, Max's Kansas City, Tier 3, Millennium, Boston, Tampa, Kent State, Pasadena Film Forum [. . . By 1982, I had moved back to Europe, where I] taught film in Rathmines College, Dublin. In 1985, my son, Jesse, [was] born in London. [My films and videos include, in reverse chronological order] *A Skinny Little Man Attacked Daddy* (1994), *New York Conversations* (1991), *London Suite* (1989), *Two Pigeons* (1989), *Rothach* (1985), *Like Dawn to Dust* (1983), *Trailer* (1983), *Loisadia* (1983), *Visibility: Moderate* (1981), *Liberty's Booty* (1980), *Beauty Becomes the Beast* (1979), *She Had Her Gun All Ready* (1978), *Staten Island* (1978), [and others]. (letter to the author, fall 1995)

Much of Dick's early work was shot in Super 8mm, and she still works in that medium today, along with work in Betacam video. She had moved beyond her early punk roots (working with artists such as Lydia Lunch) to create more controlled and accessible works, but she has not lost touch with the anarchic vision that first brought her to prominence.

Other important voices working in cinema and video in recent years include **Barbara Hammer, Phil Solomon, Peggy Ahwesh, Leslie Thornton,** and **Lynne Sachs.** Barbara Hammer is one of the most prolific and influential filmmakers of the 1970s to the present; among her many films are *A Gay Day* (1973), described by the filmmaker as "A satire on lesbian monogamy" (Canyon Cinema 1992, 150); *Sisters* (1973), "a celebration and collage of lesbians including footage of the Women's International Day march in S.F. and joyous dancing from the last night of the second Lesbian Conference where Family of Woman played; as well as images of women doing all types of traditional 'men's' work" (150–51); *Dyketactics* (1974), one of Hammer's most popular works; *Jane Brakhage* (1974), "a documentary on the pioneer woman, her wisdom, philosophy and common sense; Jane Brakhage as herself is the viewpoint rather than Jane Brakhage, wife of the filmmaker, Stan Brakhage," (151); *Women's Rites of Truth Is the Daughter of Time* (1974); *X* (1974); *Psychosynthesis* (1975); *Superdyke* (1975); *Moon Goddess* (1976); *Women I Love* (1976); *The Great Goddess* (1977); *Multiple Orgasm* (1977); *Double Strength* (1978); *Sync Touch* (1981); *Audience* (1982); *Pond and Waterfall* (1982); *Bent Time* (1983); *New York Loft* (1983); *Stone Circles* (1983); *Doll House* (1984); *Parisian Blinds* (1984); *Pearl Diver* (1984); *Tourist* (1984–85); *Optic Nerve* (1985); *Place Mattes* (1987); *No No Nooky T.V.* (1987); *Endangered* (1988); *Still Point* (1989); *Sanctus* (1990); and *Vital Signs* (1991).

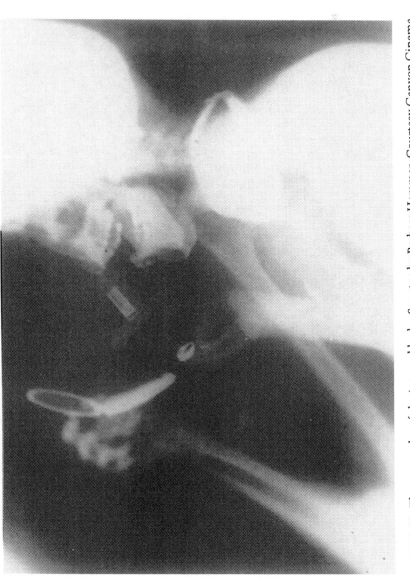

FIGURE 72. The geography of the internal body. *Sanctus* by Barbara Hammer. Courtesy Canyon Cinema.

Hammer's intense productivity places her on the scale of Brakhage or Warhol as a major force in the independent cinema; Hammer neatly inverts the patriarchal forces implicitly and often "invisibly" at work in independent cinema practice. Hammer's early work was marked by a direct address to the lesbian and/or transgendered viewer, and by the filmmaker's insistence on the primacy of lesbian desire as the informing structure behind the images in her works. As Hammer notes of her initial films, specifically in her comments on *Optic Nerve* (1985),

> I am returning to personal imagery, female representation, and emotional content as well as continuing my interest in formal and perceptual concerns: An expressionist use of the optical printer shows the fragility of the image slipping away (my 97 year old grandmother in a nursing home) and my attempt to reach her and imbue her with the faculties she is losing. *Optic Nerve* recognizes film as a vertical strip that slips away frame by frame similarly to the one optic nerve left functioning for my artist-grandmother and recognizes the nerve optically. I took to print this process-apparent film of my subjective interpretation of her approaching death in a solitary and sterile world peopled only with our shared memories of the past. (FMC 1989, 235)

Hammer's most recent works are increasingly ambitious in both form and content; her latest productions include the 58-minute *Tender Fictions* (1995), *Nitrate Kisses* (1992), a feature length documentary using found footage of lesbian and gay life from the 1930s to the present; and *Out in South Africa* (1995), a chronicle of lesbian and gay desire within the discourse of everyday African life.

Phil Solomon's films include *The Passage of the Bride* (1979–80), *Nocturne* (1980–89), *What's Out Tonight Is Lost* (1983), *The Secret Garden* (1988), *The Exquisite Hour* (1989), and *Remains to Be Seen* (1989), in addition to other works. Of *The Passage of the Bride*, Manohla Dargis has written that

> Solomon's work—some of the best of contemporary experimental film—is difficult. Its optical and moral density eludes language, as if the films, which are often dark and cracked were a palimpsest of obscured meaning. His *Passage of the Bride* is dedicated to Duchamp's alter ego, Rose Selavy—the title recalls Duchamp's "The Bride Stripped Bare by the Bachelors, Even"—and is itself a ready-made, composed entirely from a 100-foot roll of wedding footage and what appears to be the honeymoon. *Bride* is hypnotic, dreamy. Solomon compulsively repeats recognizable images until they melt like distilled essences of the originals: The bride's run across a lawn, her climb into a car, a man (her husband?) emerging from a swim all become undulating black and white swirls of grain, ripples of water . . . (as cited in Canyon Cinema 1992, 317)

Filmmaker **Scott Stark's** *The Flicker Pages*, a web site for current American independent cinema (address: <http://www.sirius.com/ ~sstark/welcome.html>), offers a platform for stills, images, and video clips from the work of **Peggy Ahwesh, Dominic Angerame, Eric Saks, Rebecca Barten**, and many other younger filmmakers and video artists. Peggy Ahwesh is best known for such films as *Martina's Playhouse* (1989), *Trick Film* (1996), and *The Trilogy of Plato's Cave* (1996). Her films have been described by Mark McEllhatten as

> unparalleled documents and beautifully distilled essays about ruptures in human continuities. In the contrasts posed between childhood, adolescence and adulthood, we experience the beauty and pain, the consequence of knowledge and the submersion into the social. Ahwesh's films penetrate to the heart of American ritual in an unprecedented way. Some of the short stories of Nathaniel Hawthorne were able to reach into the transfiguring moments when an ossified Puritanism spilled over into shocking carnival—exposing the hidden order of things and the true nature of its celebrants. Ahwesh comes at similar concerns from a unique perspective, unearthing the subterranean roots of sandbox antics, doll playing, bedroom dalliance and tantrums, tourist attractions, social gatherings and the S/M rodeo of love relationships. (McEllhatten, *Flicker Pages*)

Dominic Angerame has been the Director of Canyon Cinema since 1980. Since 1969, Angerame has produced more than twenty films, including *Voyeuristic Tendencies* (1984), *Continuum* (1987), *Deconstruction Sight* (1990) and *Premonition* (1995). Of his work, Angerame has written that:

> my approach to filmmaking has evolved from a casual impressionism, a sort of personal diary style (as seen in *A Ticket Home* and *I'd Rather Be In Paris*), to the almost passionate abstraction of the highly imagistic recent films as *Continuum* (1987) and *Deconstruction Sight* (1990). These late titles are the first two films of a quartet of films that focus upon rich black and white images of construction and destruction of modern structures in the urban environment. These two works deal with ritualization of manual labor, construction activities, the human cycle of building, tearing down, replacing with rebuilding, and maintenance of structures as seen in the contemporary urban world. *Continuum* centers around the people performing hard manual labor, such as tarring roofs, etc. The ritualization and visual aesthetics are explored in rich details. *Deconstruction Sight* shows how in the modern methods of construction activities men and women have seemed to become insignificant behind mammoth tools of destruction. The machines have taken over and the persons running the equipment are no more than minor players in the arena. The third part of this quartet is *Premonition* (1995) in which the concrete world of the American infra-structure and

its demise are made strangely poetic in this expressionist documentary which shows the vacant San Francisco Embarcedero Freeway after it had outlived its usefulness, before its destruction. In an atmosphere of daylight, mystery, I reveal how the past is encircled by the future. Lyrical, ominous, comic, *Premonition* works on the attentive viewer like a remembrance of something that is yet to happen, a silent, telling daydream. (Angerame, *The Flicker Pages*)

Scott Stark, proprietor of *The Flicker Pages*, has created more than forty films and videos in the last fifteen years, including *I'll Walk with God* (1994), *Unauthorized Access* (1993), *Acceleration* (1993), *Don't Even Think* (1992), *Satrapy* (1988), *Hotel Cartograph* (1983), and numerous other works. In addition to this work, Stark notes that

he has created a number of gallery and non-gallery installations using film and video, and created elaborate photographic collages using large grids of images. Born and educated in the Midwest, he has always been interested in aggressively pushing his work beyond the threshold of traditional viewing expectations, challenging the audience to question its relationship to the cinematic process; yet he also tries to build into the work elements of whimsy and incongruity that allow the viewer to laugh and reconnect while maintaining a critical distance. Both a passionate purist and a cynical skeptic, he likes to emphasize the physicality of film while humorously cross-referencing it to the world outside the theater, attempting to lay bare the paradoxes of modern culture and the magical nature of the perceptual experience. (Stark, *The Flicker Pages*)

I'll Walk with God is entirely composed of static images taken from "emergency information cards" taken from airplanes during Stark's travels. These images of fictional disaster (which serve as totemic glyphs for actual destruction) are manipulated through grain, repetition, and editorial juxtapositioning, set to a soundtrack that alternates between complete silence and the emotional voice of Mario Lanza. Watching the film, one doesn't know whether to laugh or cry; the images are at once absurd and yet immutably serious, depictions of imminent death and disaster transformed into transcendental mundanity through serial repetition.

Hotel Cartograph documents, for a single 400' 16mm camera magazine's duration, the intricate designs in the carpet of a downtown luxury hotel, with a resolutely spare sync-sound track serving as the sole counterpoint to Stark's "found" imagery. In an interview on April 2, 1996, Stark observed that:

I'll Walk with God is supposed to be both passionate and a little cynical; I guess I like having it both ways, where you can laugh at the absurdity of it and still enjoy it on a purely sensual, spiritual or emotional level. That is, I think the images are rather odd and even silly but at the same time they're exquisitely beautiful and the music and structure push them over the top into something transcendent. That goes along with an aesthetic philosophy that there are many ways to perceive any given event or object, and they are not mutually exclusive, one can laugh and cry at the same time, and that is also why my work has a lot to do with levels, physical levels between the surface of the screen, the surface of the film, what's happening at various levels in front of the camera, spiritual, formal and conceptual levels, and how all the levels talk to each other. The works I appreciate best leave room for many interpretations. (e-mail interview with the author, April 2, 1996)

Lately, Stark has been involved in what he calls "the chromesthetic response series," described by the filmmaker as "the condition whereby one sees a color or shape and experiences a sensation of taste, smell or hearing . . . [these films] were made by shooting 16mm film in a 35mm still camera and printed onto optical sound 16mm print stock. Each of the four consists of a succession of 35mm still images which flicker, collage-like, through the 16mm projector gate, and because the images spill over onto the optical soundtrack area of the film, the variations in image density actually generate their own peculiar sounds. For example, pictures of zebras (in *Protective Coloration*) create a success of odd musical notes." The films include *Chromesthetic Response* (1987), color, sound, 5 minutes, described by Stark as "A collage of human-created worldly surfaces—sidewalks, streets, storefronts—that evoke subtle and mysterious noises," and *The Sound of His Face* (1988), color, sound, 5 minutes, which Stark calls "a filmed biography of Kirk Douglas—literally. Pages of a book—the lines of text, and the tiny dots comprising the half-tone photographs—create off musical notes, which are edited into a pounding rhythm. This film examines the molecular fabric of Hollywood superficially." *Satrapy* (1988) and *Protective Coloration* (1990) are the other films in this series (quotes from letter to the author, March 18, 1996).

Rebecca Barten's works include *Human Flies* (1987), *You (be) You* (1989), *Seventeen Typewriter Films* (1989), and *700 Measured Sprays* (1993); in addition to her work as a filmmaker, Barten is co-director of the Total Mobile Home MicroCinema, which presents the films of numerous Bay Area artists on a regular basis in a pleasantly intimate setting. The theater's other director is **David Sherman**, whose film *Revolver* (1993) also represents the new spirit of the American independent cinema in the age of cyberspace. In a letter dated February 1, 1996, Sherman spoke of the work that he and Barten hope to accomplish with their new theater:

Total Mobile Home MicroCinema is a screening space that I founded with Rebecca Barten in the summer of 1995 [. . .] we wanted to create a space that would allow for a presentation of work in an intimate context outside of the array of pre-fabricated institutionalized venues. We [. . .] converted an unused basement space into a 30 seat MicroCinema equipped with a projection booth, sound and lighting system, and a video grotto. [Since then, the theater has presented] over 75 shows that range from epic—Hans Jurgen Syberberg's 7 hour *Our Hitler*, to more modest participatory events—pairing 3 minute camera rolls with sushi eating. We have hosted artists from as far away as Japan, Germany, and London. And of course, our own city provides a steady array of interested film-makers. Our space has a disarming quality that encourages artists to want to show works in varying stages of progress; dialogue develops and the distance between maker and viewer seems to almost disappear.

TMH has also become a workshop for our own investigations as artists. Some of our collaborative works that have come out of TMH include: The "Home Mail Project"; a video installation "Double Empire" (from a documentation of S.F.'s only screening of Warhol's 8 hour *Empire*); a film recreation of Guy Debord's *Howls in Favor of Sade*, many performance oriented "TOTAL" shows, i.e. "Total Artist Monster," "Total War," "Total Skeletons in the Closet." My own film work spans a variety of subjects and formal concerns. A short sampling: *Adobe Noise* (1987) is a look at friends left behind after being shot with a broken Bolex; *Rose and Rose Elaine* (1988–90) is a loving confrontation with my family genealogy; *Revolver* (1993) utilizes pin-hole lenses and diary montage to explore tensions of natural vision and urban exhaustion. (letter to the author, February 1, 1996)

In New York City, the Filmmakers' Cooperative under the direction of **M. M. Serra** has also been responsive to new work. An entire new generation of film and video artists has grown up in the past fifteen years, including **Gary Adelstein** (*St. Theresa* [1983], *Kore/Kouros* [1987], and *More Italian Places* [1989]), **Rachel Amodeo** (*What About Me?* [1993]), **Martin Arnold** (*piece touchée* [1989], *Passage a l'acte* [1993]), **Colin Barton** (*Images of Broken Face* [1993]), **Dietmar Brehm** (*Blicklust* [1992]), **Matthew Buckingham** (*The Truth About Abraham Lincoln* [1992]), **Abigail Child** (*Eight Million* [1993]), **Chrystel Egal** (*Tribal* [1993] and *Kirili* [1995]), **Janie Geiser** (*The Red Book* [1994]), **Johannes Hammel** (*Black Sun* [1992]), **Lana Lin** (*I Begin to Know You* [1992]), **Julie Murray** (*Fuck Face* [1986]), and **Ralf Palandt** (*Life Is a Trouble-Feature* [1992]).

M. M. Serra's most famous work is perhaps *Five Films 1984–1988*. Of Serra's *Five Films* Barbara Hammer commented: "M. M. Serra has produced a remarkable series of short films . . . within a few years. Her cinema is marked by a lush sensuality, a concern for

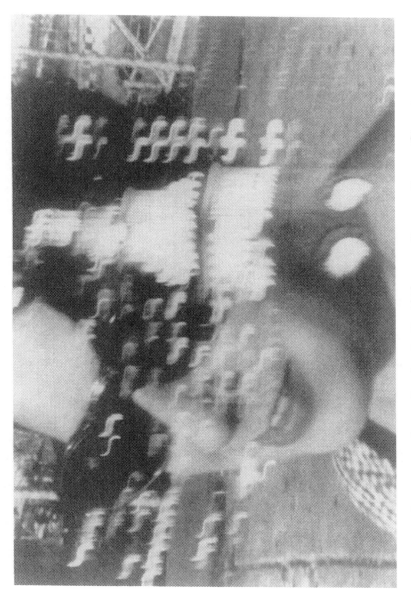

FIGURE 73. The past as prologue. *Revolver* by David Sherman. Courtesy Canyon Cinema.

light, play and artfully woven soundtrack" (as cited in FMC 1989, 512). Joanna Kiernan, writing in *Parabola*, described M. M. Serra as

> a lyric poet filmmaker with a vividly different eye and ear. In *PP2* [one of Serra's *Five Films* series], [a] soundtrack of layered, rhythmic sound accompanies shots of an intensely blue beach at tilting angles, people on the beach wearing red and other diarist images, with a heap of red ribbon which appears in variously unraveling positions, sewing a kinetic mosaic of color, light, and shape.
>
> In *Nightfall* [also in *Five Films*], a black and white film, a flashlight flickers across a fence and long grass while a French text is read by a woman (it turns out to be from Sartre's "The Words") with all the lingering phonetic pronouncement the French give to speech. The flashlight illuminates fleshy white orchids that seem to grow out of the darkness into the spots of light, and then even more strangely, stones which have words such as LAWN, HOUSE, and TREE etched on them. Mysterious, elliptical, extremely slim and delicate in their making—yet bursting with energy—these films seem to elaborate a particularly feminine aesthetic of sensuality and pleasure. (FMC 1989, 512)

Serra has also created *L'Amour Fou* (1992), which Manohla Dargis called "a curious meditation on the pleasures and terrors of S/M, in which interviews with enthusiasts collide with choice porn clips . . . the results are compelling; this film lingers, never once slipping into hype or deadly cool" (FMC 1993, 55).

Taken as a widely disparate group, these new artists are pushing the boundaries of cinematic expression to new extremes. Although the distribution and exhibition mechanism of the American independent cinema has been radically altered by time and technological change, the cinema/video artists of the 1990s continue to transgress upon the limits of our accepted liminal consciousness, delineating new, transgendered modes of address for contemporary viewers that challenge the dominant structures of mainstream cinema. In addition, this book has not had the space to consider numerous other film and video artists of the 1960s whose works deserve wider attention, such as **Anthony Scott**, whose pioneering *The Longest Most Meaningless Movie in the Whole Wide World* (1968) was composed of hundreds of reels of 35mm photographic material—commercials, outtakes, still photograph negative strips, timing leader, porn films, and other castoff fragments of cinematic detritus (Curtis 1971, 168).

In the summer of 1968 in London at the New Arts Lab in Drury Lane, Scott presented a ten-hour section of the film to the public; the screening came to an abrupt and incomplete conclusion when the projector lamp blew out in front of an audience of several hundred spectators. In a sense, Anthony Scott's film may be seen as a metaphoric emblem for independent cinema production, both in the 1960s and in the present day. With the rising cost of raw film stock and lab facilities, even 16mm film has become a luxury. Artists today are forced, more than ever, with Super 8mm, VHS video, Pixelvision cameras and a variety of outdated film stocks and substandard-brand videotapes to create their works, often using (as was done in the past) the jettisoned leftovers of more ambitious productions to create their deeply marginal, deeply personal, deeply disruptive works. We should celebrate the fact that despite all the obstacles of cost and indifference thrown in its collective path, the independent cinema continues to survive, as a new group of *cinéastes* refuse to be bound by the artificial constraints of traditions.

What was valuable then is valuable now: the need to create that which cannot be seen elsewhere, the desire to manufacture a series of personal testaments which simultaneously empower and give voice to those whom mainstream imagistic production/distribution/reception seeks to deny agency. It is this impulse that continues to drive the best of the current Avant-Garde cinema, and that will inform the creation of new works in film, video, or on the Internet, as we approach the dawn of the twenty-first century. The medium in which these works will be created is of little import; it is the essence of the quest that is paramount. If one grounds one's actions in liberty, and in the pursuit of new and transgressive modes of expression that celebrate the nomadic alterity and abundance of the Carnivalesque in human experience, one ineluctably operates within the zone of the taboo, and seeks, through semantic anti-description, to will into existence a new modality of visual mechanisms through the realm of probable sensation within the aural/visual.

BIBLIOGRAPHY

———— ∷ ————

Allen, Richard. "Representation, Illusion and the Cinema." *Cinema Journal* 32.2 (Winter 1993): 21–48.

Anderson, Madeline. Letter to William Greaves dated August 22, 1995, with detailed biographical information; forwarded to the author by William Greaves's office on August 29, 1995.

Anthology Film Archives. *The Legend of Maya Deren*. New York: Anthology Film Archives, 1988.

Arledge, Sara Kathryn. "The Experimental Film: A New Art in Transition." *Arizona Quarterly* (Summer 1947): 101–112.

———. "Brief Statements," *Canyon CinemaNews* 1980/6–1981/1: 5.

———. "Speaking About the Art in Film," Program notes, Terry Cannon Papers, n.p., n.d.

Artaud, Antonin. *The Theatre and Its Double*. Trans. Mary Caroline Richards. New York: Grove Press, 1958.

———. *Collected Works, Vol. 3*. Trans. Alastair Hamilton. London: Calder and Boyars, 1972.

Arthur, Paul. "Beauty, Flesh, and the Empire of Absence; *Resighting Warhol*." *The Independent* (December 1988): 20–23.

Aspinall, Sue. "The Space for Innovation and Experiment." *Screen* 25.6 (November–December 1984): 73–87.

Baillie, Bruce. Letter to Wheeler Winston Dixon, May 26, 1968.

———. "From Bruce Baillie." *Canyon CinemaNews* 95.1 (January 1995): 4–14.

Bakhtin, M. M. *The Dialogic Imagination*. Trans. Caryl Emerson and Michael Holquist. Ed. Michael Holquist. Austin: University of Texas Press, 1981.

211

Bandy, Mary Lea, and John G. Hanhardt, eds. *The Films of Andy Warhol: An Introduction.* Catalogue for a retrospective of Andy Warhol's films at the Whitney Museum of American Art, New York: April 5–June 5, 1988. New York: Whitney Museum of American Art, 1988.

Banes, Sally. *Greenwich Village 1963: Avant-Garde Performance and the Effervescent Body.* Durham, NC: Duke University Press, 1993.

Barret-Barger, Candace. "Seizing the Moment." *The Paper* (December 6, 1990): 19–22.

Bataille, Georges. *Inner Experience.* Trans. Leslie Anne Boldt. Albany: SUNY Press, 1988.

Battcock, Gregory. *The New American Cinema.* New York: Dutton, 1967.

Baudrillard, Jean. "The Precession of Simulacra." In *Art After Modernism: Rethinking Representation,* ed. Brian Wallace. New York: The New Museum of Contemporary Art, 1984, 253–282.

Baudry, Jean-Louis. "The Apparatus: Metapsychological Approaches to the Impression of Reality in Cinema." In *Narrative, Apparatus, Ideology: A Film Theory Reader,* ed. Philip Rosen. New York: Columbia University Press, 1986, 299–318.

——— . "Ideological Effects of the Basic Cinematic Apparatus." *Narrative, Apparatus, Ideology: A Film Theory Reader,* ed. Philip Rosen. New York: Columbia University Press, 1986, 286–298.

Bauman, Zygmunt. *Intimations of Postmodernity.* London: Routledge, 1992.

Beauvais, Yann. "Interview with Barbara Hammer." *Spiral* 6 (January 1968): 33–38.

Bellour, Raymond. "Segmenting/Analyzing." In *Narrative, Apparatus, Ideology,* ed. Philip Rosen. New York: Columbia University Press, 1986, 66–92.

——— . "Believing in the Cinema." in *Psychoanalysis and Cinema,* trans. Dana Polan and ed. E. Ann Kaplan. New York: Routledge, 1990, 98–109.

Benjamin, Walter. *Illuminations.* New York: Harcourt, 1968.

Berg, Gretchen. "Nothing to Lose: An Interview with Andy Warhol." *Cahiers du Cinema in English* 10 (May 1967): 38–42.

Bourdon, David. *Warhol.* New York: Abrams, 1989.

Braidotti, Rosi. *Nomadic Subjects: Embodiment and Sexual Difference in Contemporary Feminist Theory.* New York: Columbia University Press, 1994.

Brakhage, Stan. Interview with Wheeler Winston Dixon, summer, 1969.

——— . *Film at Wit's End: Eight Avant-Garde Filmmakers.* Kingston, NY: McPherson, 1989.

Broughton, James. "The Necessity of Living Poetically in an Electronic Age." *Film Culture* 61 (1975): 19–27.

Buck-Morss, Susan. "The Cinema Screen as Prothesis of Perception: A Historical Account." In *The Senses Still: Perception and Memory as Material Culture in Modernity*, ed. C. Nadia Seremetakis. Boulder: Westview Press, 1994: 45–62.

Burckhardt, Rudy. "Warren Sonbert." *Film Culture* 70/71 (1983): 176.

Butler, Judith. *Gender Trouble: Feminism and the Subversion of Identity.* New York: Routledge, 1990.

———. "Sexual Inversions." In *Foucault and the Critique of Institutions*, ed. John Caputo and Mark Yount. University Park: Pennsylvania State University Press, 1993, 81–100.

Camhi, Gail. "The Films of Andrew Noren." *Film Culture* 70/71 (1983): 100–111.

Camper, Fred. "*Remedial Reading Comprehension* by George Landow." *Film Culture* 52 (Spring 1971): 73–77.

Canyon Cinema. Update 1986. San Francisco: Canyon Cinema, 1986.

———. *Canyon Cinema Catalogue No. 7.* San Francisco: Canyon Cinema Collective, 1992.

———. No. 7. San Francisco: Canyon Cinema, 1992.

Cathcart, Linda. "An Interview with Paul Sharits." *Film Culture* 65/66 (1978): 103–108.

Caws, Mary Ann. *The Eye in the Text: Essays on Perception, Mannerist to Modern.* Princeton: Princeton University Press, 1981.

Chadwick, Whitney, and Isabelle de Courtviron, eds. *Significant Others: Creativity and Intimate Partnership.* London: Thames and Hudson, 1993.

Cham, Mbye B., and Claire Andrade-Watkins, eds. *Blackframes: Critical Perspectives on Black Independent Cinema.* Cambridge, MA: MIT Press, 1988.

Chin, Daryl. "Walking on Thin Ice: The Films of Yoko Ono." *Independent* (April 1989): 19–23.

Cornwell, Regina. "Works of Ernie Gehr from 1968 to 1972." *Film Culture* 63/64 (1976): 29.

Coutros, Peter. "Offbeat Artist-Producer Used Girls as Film Props." *The New York Daily News*, June 4, 1968: 3.

Curtis, David. *Experimental Cinema: A Fifty-Year Evolution.* New York: Delta, 1971.

————, ed. *A Directory of British Film and Video Artists*. Luton, Bedfordshire: John Libbey, 1996.

Dargis, Manohla. "Trying to Mix It Up." *Village Voice*, March 16, 1993: 37.

de Certeau, Michel. *The Practice of Everyday Life*. Trans. Steven F. Rendell. Berkeley: University of California Press, 1984.

Deivert, Bert. Fax dated November 30, 1995, on the films of Ben Van Meter, along with archival taped materials on Van Meter's films and serial e-mail interview on Van Meter's life and work.

Delabre, Patrick. "Acting/Being on the Surface of Film: Conversation with Nathanael Dorsky." *Cinematograph* 1 (1985): 96–100.

de Lauretis, Teresa. *Alice Doesn't: Feminism, Semiotics, Cinema*. Bloomington: Indiana University Press, 1984.

Deren, Maya. *An Anagram of Ideas on Art, Form and Film*. Yonkers, NY: Alicat Book Shop Press, 1946.

————. "Cinema As an Art Form." *New Directions* 9 (1946): 111–120.

Dewdney, Keewatin. E-mail to author dated February 26, 1996.

Dick, Vivienne. Letter to Wheeler Winston Dixon, dated November 9, 1995, with detailed film descriptions attached.

Dixon, Wheeler Winston. Interviews with Gerard Malanga, George Landow, Jack Smith, Stanton Kaye, Ed Emshwiller, Robert Breer, Andrew Noren, Harry Smith, Ernie Gehr, Michaelangelo Antonioni, Hollis Frampton, Gordon Ball, Andy Warhol, Michael Snow, Joyce Wieland, Willard Maas, Stan Brakhage, Jud Yalkut, Marie Menken, and others, 1967–1969.

————. "The Early Films of Andy Warhol." *Classic Images* 214 (April 1993): 38–40.

————. *It Looks at You: Notes on the Returned Gaze of Cinema*. Albany: SUNY Press, 1995.

————. Telephone interview with Jerome Hiler in San Francisco, June 30, 1995.

————. E-main interview with Bert Deivert, November 28, 1995.

Dollimore, Jonathan. "The Dominant and the Deviant: A Violent Dialectic." *Critical Quarterly* 28.1/2 (Spring–Summer 1986): 179–182.

————. *Sexual Dissidence: Augustine to Wilde, Freud to Foucault*. Oxford: Clarendon, 1991.

Dubler, Linda. "Gordon Ball—Portrait of a Filmmaker." *The Arts Journal* (July 1981): 23–25.

Dyer, Richard. *Now You See It: Studies on Lesbian and Gay Film*. London: Routledge, 1990.

Ehrenstein, David. "Saint Warren." *Film Culture* 46 (Autumn 1967): 19.

Everett, Anna. "Africa, the Diaspora, Cinema and Cyberspace: Are We Ready for the 21st Century?" *Screening Noir* 1.1 (Spring 1995): 1, 10.

Faso, Frank, Martin McLaughlin, and Richard Henry. "Andy Warhol Wounded by Actress: He's on Critical List; She Gives Up to Cop." *The New York Daily News*, June 4, 1968: 3, 32.

Feldman, Shoshana. *Literature and Psychoanalysis; The Question of Reading: Otherwise*. Baltimore: Johns Hopkins University Press, 1989.

Filmmakers' Cooperative. *Filmmakers' Cooperative Catalogue No. 4*. New York: New American Cinema Group, 1967.

———. *Filmmakers' Cooperative Catalogue No. 5*. New York: New American Cinema Group, 1971.

———. *Filmmakers' Cooperative Catalogue No. 6*. New York: New American Cinema Group, 1975.

———. *Filmmakers' Cooperative Catalogue No. 7*. New York: New American Cinema Group, 1989.

———. *Filmmakers' Cooperative Catalogue Supplement*. New York: Filmmakers Cooperative, 1993.

Fish, Stanley, Walter Jackson, and Edward Said. "Profession Despise Thyself: Fear and Self-Loathing in Literary Studies." *Critical Inquiry* 10.2 (December 1983): 349–373.

Foreman, Richard. "On Ernie Gehr's Film *Still*." *Film Culture* 63/64 (1978): 27–28.

Foster, Gwendolyn Audrey. *Women Film Directors: An International Bio-Critical Dictionary*. Westport, CT: Greenwood Press, 1995.

Freeman, Judi. *The Dada and Surrealist Word-Image*. Cambridge, MA: MIT Press, 1989.

Gauthier, J. D., trans. "Michel Foucault: The Ethic of Care for the Self as a Practice of Freedom: An Interview." In *The Final Foucault*, ed. James Bernauer and David Rasmussen. Cambridge, MA: MIT Press, 1988, 1–20.

Gavronsky, Serge. "Warhol's Underground." *Cahiers du Cinema in English* 10 (May 1967): 46–49.

Gehr, Ernie. Letter to Wheeler Winston Dixon, August 26, 1995.

Gidal, Peter. *Andy Warhol: Films and Paintings*. London: Studio Vista/Dutton, 1971.

———. "The Anti-Narrative (1978)." *Screen* 20.2 (Summer 1979): 73–93.

———. "Against Sexual Representation in Film." *Screen* 25.6 (November–December 1984): 24–30.

———. *Materialist Film*. London: Routledge, 1989.

Greenfield, Amy. "Dance as Film." *The Filmmakers' Newsletter* 2.3 (January 1969): 1, 2, 27.

Habermas, Jürgen. *The Past as Future*, interview by Michael Haller. Trans. and ed. Max Pensky. Foreword by Peter Hohendahl. Lincoln: University of Nebraska Press, 1994.

Halberstam, Judith, and Ira Livingston. "Introduction: Posthuman Bodies." In *Posthuman Bodies*, ed. Judith Halberstam and Ira Livingston. Bloomington: Indiana University Press, 1995: 1–19.

Haller, Robert. "Films at the Harbor: Amy Greenfield." Program notes for screening March 27–28, 1987; offset typescript manuscript, 9 pages.

Hammer, Barbara. "Sara Kathryn Arledge." *Canyon CinemaNews* 1980/6–1981/1: 3–4.

———. "The Politics of Abstraction." In *Queer Looks: Perspectives on Lesbian and Gay Film and Video*, ed. by Pratibha Parmar, Martha Gever, and John Greyson. New York: Routledge, 1993, 70–75.

Hanhardt, John G. "The Films of Andy Warhol: A Cultural Context." In *The Films of Andy Warhol: An Introduction*. New York: Whitney Museum of American Art, 1988: 7–13.

Haraway, Donna J. *Simians, Cyborgs and Women: The Reinvention of Nature*. New York: Routledge, 1991.

Haskell, Barbara, and John G. Hanhardt. *Yoko Ono: Arias and Objects*. Layton, UT: Peregrine Smith, 1991.

Heath, Stephen. "Repetition Time: Notes around 'Structuralist/Materialist Films.'" *Wide Angle* 2.3 (1978): 4–11.

Hendricks, John. *Fluxus Codex*. New York: Abrams, 1988.

Hill, Jerome. "Brakhage's *Eyes*." *Film Culture* 52 (Spring 1972): 43–46.

Hitchens, Gordon, ed. "Survey Among Unsuccessful Applicants for the Ford Foundation Grants." *Film Comment* 2.3 (Summer 1964): 10–32.

Hoberman, Jim. "A Context for Vivienne Dick." *October* (Spring 1982): 5–6.

———. "Yoko Ono." *Village Voice*, March 14, 1989: 57.

———. "It's Déjà Vu All Over Again." *Premiere* (July 1992): 31–33.

Hoekzema, Loren, Michael Fleishman, and Barbara Klinger. "Evolution of a Style: An Interview with Kathy Rose." *Wide Angle* 2.3 (1978): 60–66.

hooks, bell. *Black Looks: Race and Representation*. Boston: South End Press, 1992.

Hope, Ted. "Indie Film Is Dead." *Filmmaker* (Fall 1995): 18, 54–58.

Horak, Jan-Christopher, ed. *Lovers of Cinema: The First American Film Avantgarde*. Madison: University of Wisconsin Press, 1995.

Indiana, Gary. "I'll Be Your Mirror." Spring Art Supplement 3.1, *The Village Voice*, May 5, 1987: centerfold section, 2–3.

International Forum of New Cinema. Notes of Barbara Hammer's *Tender Fictions*, February 23, 1996. Web address: <http://www.b.shuttle.de/forum-ifb/film041e.html>

Jacoby, Roger. "Willard Maas and Marie Menken: The Last Year." *Film Culture* 63/64 (1976): 119–124.

Jameson, Fredric. *Signatures of the Visible*. New York: Routledge, 1990.

Jarman, Derek. *Queer Edward II*. London: BFI Publishing, 1991.

Jenkins, Bruce. "Frampton Unstructured: Notes for a Metacritical History." *Wide Angle* 2.3 (1978): 22–27.

Juno, Andrea, and V. Vale. *Re/Search #13: Angry Women*. San Francisco: Re/Search Publications, 1991.

Kay, Karyn, and Gerald Peary, eds. *Women and the Cinema: A Critical Anthology*. New York: Dutton, 1977.

Klotman, Phyllis Rauch. *Screenplays of the African American Experience*. Bloomington: Indiana University Press, 1991.

Knee, Adam. "*Symbiopsychotaxiplasm: Take One*; Film History Revised." *Sightlines* (Fall 1992): 10–12.

Knee, Adam, and Charles Musser. "William Greaves, Documentary Film-Making, and the African-American Experience." *Film Quarterly* 45.3 (Spring 1992): 13–25.

Krauss, Rosalind E. *The Originality of the Avant-Garde and Other Modernist Myths*. Cambridge, MA: MIT Press, 1985.

Krauss, Rosalind, and Jane Livingston. *L'Amour Fou: Photography and Surrealism*. New York: Abbeville Press, 1985.

Kroker, Arthur, and Marilouise Kroker. *Hacking the Future: Stories for the Flesh-Eating '90s*. New York: St. Martin's, 1996 (with accompanying audio CD).

Kruger, Barbara. "Adoration." Spring Art Supplement 3.1, *The Village Voice*, May 5, 1987: centerfold section, 10–11.

Landy, Marcia. *Film, Politics and Gramsci.* Foreword by Paul Bové. Minneapolis: University of Minnesota Press, 1994.

Le Grice, Malcolm. *Filmmaking: A Practical Guide.* Englewood Cliffs, NJ: Prentice-Hall, 1976.

——— . *Abstract Film and Beyond.* Cambridge: MIT Press, 1977.

Lopate, Phillip. "The Films of Warren Sonbert." *Film Culture* 70/71 (1983): 177–184.

MacCabe, Colin, ed. *High Theory/Low Culture: Analyzing Popular Television and Film.* Manchester: Manchester University Press, 1986.

MacDonald, Scott. *A Critical Cinema: Interviews with Independent Filmmakers.* Berkeley: University of California Press, 1988.

——— . "Avant-Garde Films: Cinema as Discourse." *Journal of Film and Video* 40.2 (Spring 1988): 33–42.

——— . "Putting All Your Eggs in One Basket: The Single Shot Films as Cinematic Meditation." *Afterimage* 16 (March 1989): 10–16.

——— . "From Zygote to Global Cinema via Su Friedrich's Films." *Journal of Film and Video* 44.1/2 (Spring-Summer 1992): 30–41.

——— . "Sunday in the Park with Bill: William Greaves' *Symbiopsychotaxiplasm: Take One.*" *The Independent* (May 1992): 24–29.

——— . *Avant-Garde Film: Motion Studies.* Cambridge: Cambridge University Press, 1993.

——— . "Visiting Filmmakers: Why Bother?" *Journal of Film and Video* 46.4 (Summer 1995): 3–13.

MacDougall, David. "When Less Is Less—The Long Take in Documentary." *Film Quarterly* 46.2 (Winter 1992–93): 36–46.

Malanga, Gerard. "A Letter to Warren Sonbert." *Film Culture* 46 (Autumn 1967): 20–21.

——— . "The Secret Diaries" (excerpt). *Cold Spring* 9 (January 1976): 4–10.

——— . "Working with Warhol." *Art New England* (September 1988): 6–8.

——— . Letter to Wheeler Winston Dixon, September 30, 1990.

——— . Letter to Wheeler Winston Dixon, October 20, 1990.

Malanga, Gerard, and Andy Warhol. *Screen Tests/A Diary.* New York: Kulchur Press, 1967.

McCreadie, Marsha. *Women on Film: The Critical Eye.* New York: Praeger, 1983.

McShine, Kynaston. *Andy Warhol: A Retrospective*. New York: Museum of Modern Art, 1989.

Mead, Taylor. Letter to Wheeler Winston Dixon, July 15, 1995.

Mekas, Jonas. "Index to the Work of Gregory Markopolous." *Film Culture* 52 (Spring 1971): 47–53.

———. *Movie Journal: The Rise of the New American Cinema*. New York: Collier, 1972.

———. "Warren Sonbert Filmography." *Film Culture* 70/71 (1983): 199.

Mellencamp, Patricia. "Situation and Simulation." *Screen* 26.2 (March–April 1985): 30–41.

———. *Indiscretions: Avant-Garde Film, Video and Feminism*. Bloomington: Indiana University Press, 1990.

Meyers, Ellen, and Toni Armstrong, Jr. "A Visionary Woman Creating Visions: Barbara Hammer." *Hot Wire* 7.2 (May 1991): 42–44.

Mideke, Michael. "Nick Dorsky: Notes and Recollections." *Cantrill's Filmnotes* 65/66: 48–52.

———. Letter to Wheeler Winston Dixon dated August 4, 1995, with detailed film descriptions attached, 15 pages.

Miller, Debra. *Billy Name: Stills From the Warhol Films*. Munich: Prestel, 1994.

Minh-ha, Trinh T. *Framer Framed*. New York: Routledge, 1992.

Moore, Steve. "Gerard Malanga, Andy Warhol's Longtime Assistant, Brings His Films and Poetry to Simon's Rock College." *Berkshires Week*, October 12, 1990: 4–5.

Moore-Gilbert, Bart, and John Seed, eds. *Cultural Revolution?: The Challenge of the Arts in the 1960s*. London: Routledge, 1992.

Mueller, Roswitha. *Valie Export: Fragments of the Imagination*. Bloomington: Indiana University Press, 1994.

Murphy, J. J. "Christopher MacLaine—Approaching *The End*." *Film Culture* 70/71 (1983): 88–99.

———. "The Films of David Brooks." *Film Culture* 70/71 (1983): 206–212.

Myers, Louis Budd. "Marie Menken Herself." *Film Culture* 45 (Summer 1967): 37–39.

Neiman, Catrina. "Women Pioneers of the American Experimental Film: Bute, Arledge, Menken, Deren, Schneemann." English version of paper provided to the author by Terry Cannon, 25 pages. Published as "Pionierinnen des Amerikanischen Experimentalfilms: Bute, Arledge, Menken, Deren, Schneemann," in *Medienkunst von Frauen: Feministische*

Streifzüege Durch's Punkte-Universum, ed. Heidi Hutschenreuter and Claudia Schurian. Dortmund: Edition Filmwerkstatt, 1993, 111–126.

Nicholson, David. "Conflict and Complexity: Filmmaker Kathleen Collins." *Black Film Review* 2.3 (1986): 16–17.

Ono, Yoko. "On Yoko Ono." *Film Culture* 48–49 (Winter–Spring 1970): 32–33.

Paglia, Camille. *Sexual Personae: Art and Decadence from Nefertiti to Emily Dickinson*. New York: Random House, 1990.

Paik, Nam June. "Adios 20th Century." *Point of Contact* 3.3 (April 1993): 104–109.

Perlmutter, Ruth. "Lizzie Borden: An Interview." *Post Script* 6.2 (Winter 1987): 2–11.

Pines, Jim. "The Cultural Context of Black British Cinema." In *Blackframes: Critical Perspectives on Black Independent Cinema*, ed. Mybe B. Cham and Claire Andrade-Watkins. Cambridge, MA: MIT Press, 1988, 26–36.

Podesta, Patti. *Resolution: A Critique of Video Art*. Los Angeles: LACE, 1986.

Probyn, Elspeth. *Sexing the Self: Gendered Positions in Cultural Studies*. London: Routledge, 1993.

Rabinovitz, Lauren. *Points of Resistance: Women, Power, and Politics in the New York Avant-Garde Cinema, 1943–1971*. Urbana: University of Illinois Press, 1991.

Rainer, Yvonne. "Narrative in the (Dis)Service of Identity: Fragments Toward a Performed Lecture Dealing with Menopause, Race, Gender and Other Uneasy Bedfellows in the Cinematic Sheets; Or, How Do You Begin to Think of Yourself as Lesbian." *Review of Japanese Culture and Society* 4 (December 1991): 46–52.

Reveaux, Tony. Previously unpublished interview dated August 11, 1977, with Sara Kathryn Arledge, provided to the author in typescript by Terry Cannon, 13 pages.

Rice, Ron. "Note from Ron Rice to Jonas Mekas." *Film Culture* 70/71 (1983): 100–111.

Rich, B. Ruby. "Reflections of a Queer Screen." *Journal of Lesbian and Gay Studies* 1.1 (1993): 83–91.

Rothleder, Dianne. "From False Consciousness to Viral Consciousness." In *The Last Sex: Feminism and Outlaw Bodies*, ed. Arthur Kroker and Marilouise Kroker. New York: St. Martin's, 1993, 198–207.

Ruoff, Jeffrey K. "Movies of the Avant-Garde: Jonas Mekas and the New York Art World." *Cinema Journal* 30.3 (Spring 1991): 6–28.

Russo, Vito. *The Celluloid Closet: Homosexuality in the Movies*. 2nd edition. New York: Harper and Row, 1987.

Sarris, Andrew. "The Sub–New York Sensibility." *Cahiers du Cinema in English* 10 (May 1967): 43–45.

Sáurez, Juan, and Millicent Manglis. "Cinema, Gender and the Topography of Enigmas: A Conversation with Laura Mulvey." *Cinefocus* 3 (1995): 2–8.

Segal, Mark. "Hollis Frampton's *Zorn's Lemma.*" *Film Culture* 52 (Spring 1971): 88–95.

Seltzer, Mark. *Bodies and Machines.* New York: Routledge, 1992.

Shaviro, Steven. *The Cinematic Body.* Minneapolis: University of Minnesota Press, 1993.

Sitney, P. Adams. "Interview with George Landow." *Film Culture* 46 (Summer 1969): 10–12.

———. *Visionary Film: The American Avant-Garde, 1943–1978.* 2nd edition. Oxford: Oxford University Press, 1979.

Snead, James A. "Image of Blacks in Black Independent Films: A Brief Survey." In *Blackframes: Critical Perspectives on Black Independent Cinema,* ed. Mybe B. Cham and Claire Andrade-Watkins. Cambridge, MA: MIT Press, 1988, 16–25.

Snow, Michael. "*La Region Centrale.*" *Film Culture* 52 (Spring 1971): 58–63. Transcribed and edited by Charlotte Townsend.

———. Letter to Wheeler Winston Dixon dated October 12, 1995, with detailed film descriptions attached, 13 pages.

Sobchack, Vivian. *The Address of the Eye: A Phenomenology of Film Experience.* Princeton: Princeton University Press, 1992.

Sonbert, Warren. "Notes for a Brunch." Original typescript sent to Wheeler Winston Dixon, April 4, 1969.

———. Undated postcards to Wheeler Winston Dixon from Morocco and Europe, 1969–1973.

———. Undated letter from San Francisco to Wheeler Winston Dixon, circa 1974.

Springer, Gregory. "Barbara Hammer: The Leading Lesbian Behind the Lens." *Advocate* (February 7, 1980): 29, 35.

Stark, Scott. *The Flicker Pages.* Web address: <http://www.sirius.com/~sstark/welcome.html>

Stoneman, Rod. *London Filmmakers Cooperative Retrospective Notes on the Films of Vivienne Dick,* June 16, 1995 (pamphlet).

Strand, Chick. "Notes on Ethnographic Film by a Film Artist." *Wide Angle* 2.3 (1978): 45–51.

Suleiman, Susan Rubin. *Subversive Intent: Gender, Politics and the Avant-Garde.* Cambridge MA: Harvard University Press, 1990.

Tate, Greg. "Cinematic Sisterhood." *In the Black: The Women, the Men, the Critics of a Film Boom,* special centerfold section of *The Village Voice,* June 4, 1991: 77–78.

———. *Cinematic Sisterhood.* In the Black: The Women.

Taubin, Amy. "Warren Sonbert, 1947–1995." *The Village Voice,* June 20, 1995: 48.

Todorov, Tzvetan. *The Morals of History.* Trans. Alyson Waters. Minneapolis: University of Minnesota Press, 1995.

Tyler, Parker. *Underground Film: A Critical History.* New York: Grove, 1969.

Walsh, Martin. *The Brechtian Aspect of Radical Cinema.* Ed. Keith M. Griffiths. London: BFI, 1981.

Weinstein, Jeff. "The artist, the Artist, and the Pop Star." *The Village Voice,* March 3, 1987: 14.

———, ed. "Andy Warhol." Spring Art Supplement 3.1, *The Village Voice,* May 5, 1987: centerfold section, 12 pages.

Weiss, Andrea. *Vampires and Violets: Lesbians in Film.* New York: Penguin, 1993.

Whitney Museum of American Art. *Yoko Ono: Objects, Films.* New York: Whitney Museum of American Art, 1989.

Wieland, Joyce. "*True Patriot's Love.*" *Film Culture* 52 (Spring 1971): 64–72.

Wilkins, Timoleon. "Warren Sonbert 1947–1995." *Canyon Cinemanews* (July 1995): 6.

Willemen, Paul, and Jim Pines. *Questions of Third Cinema.* London: BFI Publishing, 1989.

Williams, Linda. *Hard Core: Power, Pleasure, and the "Frenzy of the Visible."* Berkeley: University of California Press, 1989.

Williamson, Judith. "Woman Is an Island: Femininity and Colonization." In *Studies in Entertainment: Critical Approaches to Mass Culture,* ed. Tania Modleski. Bloomington: Indiana University Press, 1986. 99–118.

Wilson, Colin *Poetry and Mysticism.* San Francisco: City Lights, 1969.

Women Make Movies. *Women Make Movies Catalogue.* New York: Women Make Movies, Inc. 1994.

Youngblood, Gene. *Expanded Cinema.* New York: Dutton, 1970.

Zavarzadeh, Mas'ud. *Seeing Films Politically.* Albany: SUNY Press, 1991.

Zita, Jacqueline. "Counter Currencies of a Lesbian Iconography: The Films of Barbara Hammer." *Jump Cut* 24 (1981): 26–30.

FILM RENTAL SOURCES

Most of the films discussed in this text are available for 16mm rental from either:

> The Filmmakers' Cooperative
> 175 Lexington Ave.
> New York, NY 10016
> (212) 889-3820

> or

> Canyon Cinema
> 2325 Third Street
> Suite 338
> San Francisco, CA 94107
> (415) 626-2255

ABOUT THE AUTHOR

■■

Wheeler Winston Dixon is the chairperson of the Film Studies Program at the University of Nebraska, Lincoln, and editor of the Cultural Studies in Cinema/Video Series from State University of New York Press. His most recent books include *It Looks at You: The Returned Gaze of Cinema* (State University of New York Press, 1995) and *The Films of Jean-Luc Godard* (State University of New York Press, 1997). Dixon is the author of more than fifty articles on film theory, history and criticism, which have appeared in *Cinéaste, Interview, Literature/Film Quarterly, Films in Review, Post Script, Journal of Film and Video, Film Criticism, New Orleans Review, Film and Philosophy*, and numerous other journals. His next book will be *The Transparency of Spectacle*, for the State University of New York Press series in Postmodern Culture, edited by Joseph Natoli.

225

INDEX

Brummer's (1966), 25
Brussels Film Festival, 29, 87
Brussels Loops (1958), 40
Bubuscio, Jack, 117
Buckingham, Matthew, 206
Buddha Again (1969), 84
Bullfight (1955), 40
Burch, Noel, 95, 117
Burckhardt, Jacob, 35
Burckhardt, Rudy, 35, 73
Burning Ear, The (1964), 65
Burroughs, William, 64
Bustin' Loose, 69
Bute, Mary Ellen, 35, 37, 53

Cairo Film Festival, 105
Cale, John, 63
California Spring (1965), 73
Callenbach, Ernest, 125
Cambridge Diary (1966), 108
Camp (1965), 155, 178
Canby, Vincent, 92
Cannes Film Festival, 137, 145
Cannon, Terry, 13, 14, 35
Cannon, William, 37–38
Canyon Cinema Cooperative, 15,
   16, 104, 203
Carabosse (1980), 87
Carillo, Tosh, 176
Carney, Raymond, 65
Carol (1970), 63
Carolyn and Me, 33
Carriage Trade (1968–72), 162
Carrots and Peas (1969), 64
Carruthers, Ben, 120
Casing Shelved, A (1970), 158
Cassavetes, John, 70
Castiglione, Contessa Angela Maria
   Andreacci, 38
Castro Street (1966), 17
Caswallon Trilogy (1986), 30
Caterpillar (1973), 35
Catfood (1967–68), 183
Cats Cradle Harp Wind Lock Heart
   (1967), 103
Cave of the Rainbow (1980), 16

Cayuga Run (1967), 44
Celebration #1 (1966), 120
Celery Stalks at Midnight, 181
Centennial Exposition (1964), 87
Centeno, Adolf, 38
Chafed Elbows (1966), 38, 62
Chamba Organization, 25
Changes, Myrna, 38
Chapelle, Pola, 38, 44
Charlatan (1976), 103
Charles, Ray, 73
Charlot, Martin, 38, 146
Charmides (1948), 112
Cheka, Mark, 88
Chelsea Girls, The (1966), 122, 146,
   178
Chicago Film Festival, 109
Chicken (1981), 33
Child (1965), 42
Child, Abigail, 206
Children (1969), 111
Children's Party, 87
Children's Television Workshop, 9
Choice Chance Woman Dance
   (1971), 63
Chomont, Tom, 38
Christmas Carol, A (1942), 112
Christmas on Earth, 137, 138, 140,
   172
Christopoulos, George, 113
Chromesthetic Response (1987),
   205
Chrysalis (1973), 63
Chumlum (1964), 134, 135, 155,
   172
Cineclub Estacao (Rio de Janeiro),
   28
City Pasture (1974), 35
Clarence (1965–68), 189, 193
Clarion, 25
Clark, Dan, 38
Clarke, Shirley, 38, 39, 40, 41
Climate of New York, The (1948),
   35
Cobra Woman, 155
Coburn, Kip, 40

21813698R00154

Made in the USA
Middletown, DE
11 July 2015

Great Slave Narratives

GREAT
SLAVE
NARRATIVES

Selected and Introduced by

ARNA BONTEMPS

❊ ❊ ❊ ❊ ❊ ❊ ❊ ❊ ❊

BEACON PRESS *BOSTON*

Introductions by Arna Bontemps copyright © 1969
Library of Congress catalog card number: 77–84792
All rights reserved
Beacon Press books are published under the auspices
of the Unitarian Universalist Association
Printed in the United States of America

Standard Book Numbers: 8070–5472–0 (casebound)

8070–5473–9 (paperback)

Second printing, March 1970

Contents

THE SLAVE NARRATIVE: An American Genre
BY ARNA BONTEMPS

In any debate between mind and conscience the omission of evidence is unforgivable. This remains partly true even when the evidence is not immediately at hand and must be sought, but the sin is compounded after it is found and treated with disdain.

When I was growing up, my teachers, as well as others unaware of what they were doing, gave me to understand that the only meaningful history of the Negro in the United States (possibly even in the world) began with the Emancipation Proclamation of 1863. In the half century since my school days, I have had a chance to observe the tenacity of this assumption. As evidence to the contrary is disclosed, I begin to suspect that the colossal omissions they perpetuated were more than inadvertent. They were deliberate. Many may have been vindictive.

One way or another, the considerable body of writing in the New World known as *slave narratives*, an influential contribution to American cultural history of the nineteenth century, has been allowed to languish. Only one title in a form that may have produced several hundred, by some estimates, was in print when the Supreme Court decision of 1954 made authentic the upsurge of feeling that produced the Civil Rights Revolution, and that title had escaped oblivion by disguising itself as something other than part of the genre in which it was first presented.

The Negro's suffering in his private hell of oppression was the point at which the narratives invariably began. Enduring this ordeal until he became desperate, or until he otherwise engaged the reader's interest or sympathy, the slave was eventually impelled to attempt the perils of escape. The stratagems used differed with the individuals, and the journeys varied as did the roads followed. A promised land and a chance to make a new life as a free man was always the goal, even though sometimes the realization fell short of the expectation. The recorded memoirs of the questing slaves were felt by many readers of the nineteenth century to epitomize the condition of man on the earth as it documented the personal history of the individual to whom bondage was real and freedom was more than a dream.

The disappearance of the slave narrative, unlike the phasing out of the minstrel show, deprived black people in the United States of a medium of self-expression for which there was no

vii

ready substitute. Decades of relative silence followed, insofar as protest was concerned; and this silence paralleled a growing hostility against Negroes. A crescendo of hatred, projected in the fiction of Thomas Dixon and Thomas Nelson Page on one hand and in motion picture films such as *The Birth of a Nation* on the other, began to fill the void. Mob violence against the Negro resulted in an appalling increase in the number of lynchings and waves of race riots that sometimes resembled massacres of the blacks.

To stem this tide Booker T. Washington tried conciliation. A man of enormous ability and high purpose, he was encouraged in his efforts for about five years, before it became clear to a certain number of other Negroes that his method was not doing what he hoped and probably could not prevail in the long run.

A small band of his opponents became significant later, but before they could group themselves and raise their voices in unison, Washington prepared a statement of his message in a format with which he was familiar and which, despite the passing of the institution of slavery, seemed remarkably appropriate in the heyday of angry reaction against Reconstruction. He wrote and published *The Story of My Life and Work.*

The reception accorded this edition of his autobiography in 1900 led to a subsequent rewriting of the same story and to its magazine serialization, which, in turn, was reissued by a more prominent publisher a couple of years later under the title *Up From Slavery;* and this time his book became a kind of landmark. Even those black men who had grown impatient after a decade and a half of unsuccessful conciliation effort were unable to find fault with a memoir such as *Up From Slavery.* Another year passed before W. E. B. Du Bois stirred up a storm, bringing the opponents to attention with his *The Souls of Black Folk,* which included the essay that eventually punctured the Washington balloon. Even so, the men around Du Bois showed no disposition to gainsay the touching account of the coming into freedom of the mulatto slave boy who had suffered every humiliation before achieving world fame. Here indeed was a slave narrative in the classic tradition, though most non-black readers began at once to think of it mainly as a fantastic example of New World success. Nor did it damage in any way the cause of Washington's critics when, three years later, they responded to Du Bois' call to initiate an organized movement to protest against their persecution and to assert with all their strength their manhood rights.

My own parents were not among the protesters when this sequence occurred. My mother had been a schoolteacher in Lake Providence, in Chaneyville, and in Alexandria, Louisiana, for five years, and my father was still a brick mason. They were moving to California at the time that Du Bois invited his dissenting black contemporaries to meet with him in Niagara Falls, on the Canadian side. By the time I discovered in the small bookcase in our living room a copy of the Booker T. Washington *The Story of My Life and Work,* the National Association for the Advancement of Colored People (NAACP) had been founded, and I was old enough to read books. I know I was in the fourth or fifth grade because I am sure of the house in which we were living at the time. Though I had previously thumbed through cookbooks, musical compendiums, and *The Book of Knowledge,* and read the several juveniles my parents bought for me, this was the first so-called adult book I read completely. It fairly hypnotized me. I was convinced that the adult world of letters had the books explicitly for children beat by a country mile, as my father might have stated it, for general interest.

Seeing my fascination, my father pointed to the picture of Emmett J. Scott among the illustrations in *My Life and Work* and told me proudly that he had met this young man in Alexandria and helped to entertain him on one of Scott's visits in the interest of Washington's school at Tuskegee. My mother approved of the book's story but didn't think much of the pen-and-ink drawings which were, she said, no better than she could have done. Neither touched the point that intrigued me most. I had not known before reading this book why I had been treated as someone special in the three schools I had attended from kindergarten to the present. Seeing the difference between young Booker's early life, as told in his story, and mine, I was simply amazed. The condition of slavery gripped my mind, and deliverance from slavery was a thought to transport the imagination.

While I was permanently affected by this reading experience, I did not learn till after college that *The Story of My Life and Work* was other than unique in literature. Actually, though neither the first nor the best of its genre, it does have the distinction of being the *last* in an altogether remarkable succession, and in this way it calls to mind high points in a great tradition.

As long ago as the Negro Renaissance of the 1920's, perceptive scholars and bibliophiles were bracketing Negro slave narratives with Negro music as the two most notable examples of
the black man's contribution to American culture. From the
spirituals came the cadences as well as the words and images
that awakened later poetic genius. From the narratives came the
spirit and the vitality and the angle of vision responsible for the
most effective prose writing by black American writers from
William Wells Brown to Charles W. Chesnutt, from W. E. B.
Du Bois to Richard Wright, Ralph Ellison, and James Baldwin.
Consciously or unconsciously, all of these reveal in their writing
a debt to the narratives, a debt that stands in marked contrast
to the relatively smaller obligations they owe the more recognized arbiters of fiction or autobiography in their time. If not
all of them had read slave narratives, they had heard them by
word of mouth or read or listened to accounts these had inspired. Thus when they put pen to paper, what came to light,
like emerging words first written in invisible ink, were their own
versions of bondage and freedom.

Neither historians nor literary critics troubled themselves very
much about slave narratives during the decades when the books
were in almost total eclipse and assumed to be as safely lost as
dead languages of antiquity. The neglect of the narratives is
now being felt, however, and the stages of their rediscovery may
be indicated.

Families such as ours may have kept association copies preserved for personal feeling or in some cases for actual genealogi-
cal links, but the significance of Negro history, much less
genealogy, had not yet registered, even on Negroes, when the
Renaissance of the twenties began to banish sleep. The bookseller Charles Tuttle of Rutland, Vermont, told me early in the
forties how his own interest in these narratives had been stimulated some twenty years earlier. Coming from a long line of
bookdealers, he had been fascinated and often thrilled by the
recorded experiences of slaves which had been plentiful in the
shops of his boyhood years. When as an adult bookseller, during
the twenties and thirties, he began to notice the intense interest
of two of his customers in these titles, he was surprised to discover that the books had become scarce since his youth. Thereafter he remained alert.

Nothing was more stimulating to a dealer in old books than
the friendly rivalry of two frantic bibliophiles such as Arthur

Schomburg and Arthur A. Spingarn, one black (or literally brown), the other white. These two were collecting Negroana long before their quest became a public challenge, and in so doing, using the slave narrative as a natural starting point· both acquired personal libraries that in the next decade formed the nuclei for the two most distinguished specialized collections of books by and about the Negro in America, possibly in the world. One is now owned by the New York Public Library, the other by the Library of Howard University in Washington, D.C. Spingarn and Schomburg also put collections into the libraries of U.C.L.A. and Fisk University, respectively.

When the Civil Rights Revolution erupted with renewed energy, following the long, patient, often heroic groundwork by the NAACP, it did not take long for militant blacks as well as enlightened Americans of other colors to realize the truth of Schomburg's remark made during the Harlem Renaissance that "The Negro must remake his past before he can begin to make his future." Nor did it take many years for individuals such as these to realize that this meant more than a chronology of constitutional and judicial actions as these related to Americans in bondage. It had to do with the black experience, how it felt to be black and a slave, how the world looked through the eyes of one who had achieved a measure of freedom by effort and suffering, who the people were who had passed through the ordeal, and how they had expressed their thoughts and feelings. By extension, and this did not have to be stated, it involved the light all this might cast on the human condition.

Many people knew and valued Negro muscle. But the capacity for living, for feeling, for exaltation, and perception did not so much require a new statement as a past revelation. Black voices needed to be heard. Gradually and to the astonishment of some it began to be realized that such voices had been raised often and in many ways over the past centuries in the New World and for more than a millennium in Africa. Black voices could still be evoked out of silence and suppression, as it were.

As in the case of those who were musical and those whose medium was motion, the articulate Negro was forced by oppression and denial to invent new formats for the expression of his thoughts and feelings. Intuition told him that the memoir was a natural medium in a period of great and varied personal distress, and he brought to it new vitality and a fresh angle of vision.

As we have suggested, the narratives that resulted gave a new name to the form. The first of them actually introduced the word. It was titled *A Narrative of the Uncommon Sufferings and Surprising Deliverance of Briton Hammon, a Negro Man,* and it was published in Boston in 1760. A double coincidence makes its date more than doubly interesting. It was in the same year that a broadside poetic composition by a slave writing under the same surname appeared. "An Evening Thought: Salvation by Christ, with Penitential Cries" was by Jupiter Hammon, a well-favored slave preacher on Long Island and sometimes assumed to have been the first black American ever to see his name in print. While one earlier effort in verse by a Negro slave in Massachusetts has been found, attributed to a "secondary" source, the distinction Jupiter Hammon has been allowed may be justified. And the fact that he is remembered for prose as well as verse publications puts him into a special category. Whether or not there was any relationship or connection between him and Briton Hammon, the inspiration for, if not the author of, *A Narrative of the Uncommon Sufferings and Surprising Deliverance* has not been established, so far as I know.

In the cases of both Hammons priority is the main reason for their places in the history of Negro self-expression in the New World. Both were succeeded, in poetry and in prose, by writers who had more to say and said it more effectively. Their successors, as it happens, were also Bostonians in at least two notable instances. Their wider and more lasting recognition is accordingly understandable.

In poetry it was Phillis Wheatley, a remarkable child kidnaped in Senegal and brought to Boston in a slave ship in 1761 at the age of seven and sold at the Boston slave market to John Wheatley to serve as a maid for his frail wife. Within sixteen months after her arrival, according to her owner, Phillis "attained the English Language," as he said, "to such a degree as to read the most difficult parts of the sacred Writings, to the great astonishment of all who heard her." Books were placed at her disposal in the home of the Wheatleys, and within six years after her kidnaping, when she was no more than fourteen, she wrote an attractive poem addressed "To the University of Cambridge, in New England." If the tone of the composition is too highly religious for most sons of Fair Harvard, it is unlikely they would find the lines lacking in grace.

The immediate successors of the two Hammons in prose also

dwarfed the originals. They were Olaudah Equiano or "Gustavus Vassa" and John Marrant, and here again the two authors are linked by a coincidence. Both published books in 1789 (in the case of John Marrant, two books), but Marrant's memoir *A Narrative of the Lord's Wonderful Dealings with J. Marrant, a Black, Taken Down from His Own Relation* actually appeared in London four years earlier. In 1789, when his *Sermon* as well as his *Journal* were issued in Boston and in London, respectively, he was serving as chaplain of the African Lodge of Masons in Boston.

Marrant had been born in New York in 1755, but he recounts a boyhood in the South and tells of his conversion under the preaching of Whitefield. There follow accounts of captivity among the Cherokees, of service with the British Navy in the Revolutionary War, and of his going to England, where he appears to have come under the protection of the Calvinistic Methodists. He appears to have had his *Narrative* prepared for the press at the instigation of the Countess of Huntington, and he states that it was she who persuaded him to go to Nova Scotia as a missionary in 1785. There his story breaks off, as far as records go, but the *Sermon* by him, preached in Boston on June 24, 1789, as indicated, was published there the same year.

Marrant's *Narrative*, as with many slave narratives after it, owed something to his amanuensis of record, in his case "the Rev. Mr. Aldridge," but this did not deprive it of what has been called "the simple ecstasy of a folk tale." It is this quality that convinced critics of a century later of its authenticity, reflecting, as they felt, a childlike instinct for sensing the marvelous and wonderful of the primitive Negro imagination. The description of his conversion in one of Whitefield's meetings in Charleston, South Carolina, is an instance. In the account Marrant turns cold and feels the grasp of an irresistible force when he hears the words "Prepare to meet thy God, O Israel." This throws him into a trance, and when he is given up as insane by his mother and sisters, he takes to wandering in the forests. He does not realize how far he has wandered on one of these sorties until he encounters an Indian hunter who leads him, after days of journeying, to a village of the Cherokees, where he is immediately taken prisoner and condemned to die. Visions of martyrdom for his newfound Christ enable him to face this prospect of doom with remarkable poise and assurance. Before his execution can be carried out, however, he is allowed to speak, and he is so effective (in *their* language, after just a few days, apparently) a young Pocahontas-like princess of the tribe intercedes for him, and the wrath of the Cherokees is miraculously turned to love and approbation.

Another engaging incident in the Marrant *Narrative* occurs during his experiences at sea. In a storm he is twice hurled into the high, raging waters and back to the deck again. After the second he ties himself to a mast, but the rope snaps and when he is washed into the sea again, he is attacked by sharks. If some of his close calls put a strain on credulity, there is no indication that Marrant's readers complained. Several editions of the *Narrative* appear to have been printed.

The first truly notable book in the genre now known as slave narratives, however, was *The Interesting Narrative of the Life of Olaudah Equiano, or Gustavus Vassa, the African*. It is a book that has had many lives and tends to be revived every time a black resurgence occurs. Bibliophiles in Harlem during the Renaissance of the twenties spoke of it with whispered pride as one of the most important books attributed to American Negro authorship. It was they who observed that with the exception of the folksongs, the Negro's worthiest contribution to American literature had been his personal memoirs.

Looking backward they noticed that the evolution of practically every black American, if he accomplished anything important, was likely to have been filled with drama. They realized, therefore, that pending the emergence of a Pushkin or a Dumas, whose rampant creativity might eclipse his own personality, there would continue to be more interest, more significance, in *how* a Negro achieved in the white world than in *what* he achieved. The brooding scholars moving among the young poets and artists of the New York enclave did not hesitate to suggest that in 1789, the year of its publication, few books had been produced in America with the vigor and sweep, the thrust and picturesqueness of Vassa's *Narrative*.

The success of Vassa's *Narrative* might be compared to that of a runaway best seller in contemporary terms. By 1794 it had gone into its eighth edition, and many more were to follow in America and in Europe. Despite other facets of interest in his odyssey, Vassa chose to highlight the opposition to slavery which is implicit in it. As early as the issue of 1790 he states in his dedication that he had that year presented to the Parliament in England a petition for the suppression of the slave trade. Nevertheless it was the book's naturalness, its wealth of fascinating detail and narrative events, that gave it strength.

With Briton Hammon, John Marrant, and Gustavus Vassa the seeds were planted, some might say the mold was set, for the literary genre which came to be known as the slave narrative. Actually the mold varied. *Memoirs of Eleanor Eldridge* (1838) and *Scenes in the Life of Harriet Tubman* (1869), for example, were presented as out-and-out autobiographies. *Slavery in the United States* by Charles Ball (1836) and a good many others in the same vein have at times been called "fictionized truth." Emily Pierson's *The Fugitive*, like Mattie Griffith's *Autobiography of a Female Slave*, by contrast was acknowledged fiction.

The list of the *Narratives* which, like *The Confession of Nat Turner* (1831), were offered as "told to" accounts is long. *The Narrative of Solomon Northup* (1857) belonged in this group and attracted widespread attention. Then there was the *Narrative of James Williams* (1839), told to John Greenleaf Whittier. Added interest is attached to the Williams narrative because of the name of the poet Whittier, but even more because the *Alabama Beacon* called it a "fraud." This led its publishers, the Anti-slavery Society, to suppress the book. A comparable publication by Harriet Jacobs called *Incidents in the Life of a Slave Girl* was presented as "edited" and "arranged" by the well-known Lydia Maria Child.

The true significance of the slave narrative and its influence on subsequent writing in various forms by white as well as black writers rests on the authentic autobiographies, however, recalling the bondage and freedom of black slaves and mulattoes. These writings identify the genre and justify its place in American literary and cultural history. The most representative of them followed the Vassa book by fifty years or more, a hiatus which can best be explained by a glance at the intervening history.

Slavery seemed to many people to be on the way out at the time of Vassa's writing. Thanks in part to misgivings about the institution by figures prominent in the formation of the new nation after the American Revolution, in part to a kind of spin-off from the French Revolution, as well as to the British antislavery movement, a feeling and a hope that slavery would die of itself, painlessly, was spreading. But then came the invention of the cotton gin, and the self-interest of those who stood to profit from the growth of cotton aroused the defenders of slavery. This was, of course, bitterly discouraging to sensitive and intelligent blacks, of whom there were many among the slaves as well as among the growing free black population, and their angry humors produced violence.

Overseas, in Europe and especially in the Caribbean, abolition campaigns rose to a fever pitch. In a successful, and thrillingly dramatic, revolution the island of Haiti won independence from France. In the former colony, now the state of Virginia, a young slave coachman led an attempt by slaves to accomplish something comparable, but he succeeded only in terrifying slaveholders. The backlash from this episode, described by me in my novel *Black Thunder,* was responsible for a changed attitude in dealing with the will to freedom by blacks. New codes, increasingly repressive, were adopted, ultimately by most of the slave states. An intensive effort to obscure, if not to blot out, the names and deeds of black people from the records of the time ensued.

Negroes appeared to become silent and invisible. Phillis Wheatley's *Poems* and Benjamin Banneker's *Almanacs* went out of print. Vassa's *Narrative* was too well known to be squelched, too many editions had been printed; but his death, when it occurred around 1801, passed without notice, as was to happen later in the cases of the great Ira Aldridge in 1867 and of James Bland ("Carry Me Back to Old Virginny," "O Dem Golden Slippers," "In the Evening by the Moonlight," etc.) in 1911. Few people as far from Raleigh, North Carolina, as Charleston, South Carolina, for example, heard of the remarkable career of John Chavis, educator. And since the new codes forbade the teaching of slaves, a generation of blacks deprived of the alphabet was growing up. A generation of whites who could not remember ever having seen a Negro who could read or write was gaining control.

This was the era in which self-expression by Negroes first went underground in the United States. Denied the ABC's, sensitive blacks fell back on the oral tradition of their forefathers in Africa and created folk music, the spirituals, and adapted to their new situation the folk tales from Africa. These seemed innocent enough to the masters of slaves and their families, as well as entertaining; and they satisfied for a time, at least, cravings of the spirit in the oppressed and the deprived.

Those people on both sides of the Atlantic to whom slavery was anathema were naturally outraged by the trend, and in 1808 the Abbé Henri Grégoire, staunch proponent of *Les Amis*

des Noirs, brought out his important *De la littérature des nègres.*
When the antislavery impulse began to shape up in the United
States in the 1820's, an early thought that occurred to its advo-
cates was to rescue from oblivion the works and the personalities
of gifted blacks like Phillis Wheatley, Benjamin Banneker, and
others whose talents might inspire Negroes and shame those
whites who had wished to belittle or obscure their humanity.
New editions of the significant earlier black writing began to
reappear under the auspices of the antislavery societies.

On this wave of feeling came the genuine slave narratives,
some of which can still be read with intense interest. The *Narrative of the Life of Frederick Douglass, an American Slave, Written by Himself* (Boston: 1845) was one that created drama.
Written to convince the boys at Harvard and others who had
called him an imposter or said that otherwise he demonstrated
that slavery could not have been so bad if it could produce such
outstanding figures as himself, it inadvertently disclosed his new
name and whereabouts to his former owner; and he was obliged
to flee the country to avoid being apprehended and returned to
slavery. In England, where he took refuge, he lectured and made
friends who purchased his freedom and enabled him to return
to the Abolitionist platform in his homeland. His *Narrative* sold
well, and twice later he expanded it, giving far more information
about his work but never exceeding the passion or eloquence
of the *Narrative* provoked by the Harvard students just five
years after Douglass' escape from harrowing bondage on the
eastern shore of Maryland.

The fate that befell Douglass' *Narrative* and others which can
be bracketed with it was not unlike the fading out of Wheatley,
Banneker, and those of their period after American Independence. All three editions of Douglass' autobiography disappeared
from print during the first half of the twentieth century. It took
the disorders of the Civil Rights Revolution of the 1950's and
1960's to bring it back, but many students of today find it almost as arresting as the autobiographies of Malcolm X and Richard Wright.

The wave that brought the Douglass *Narrative* before the
American public in the 1840's accounted for others by such of
his contemporaries in the antislavery movement as William Wells
Brown (updated twice) and Samuel Ringgold Ward, both suc-
cessful. Special interest attaches to *The Life of Josiah Henson,
Formerly a Slave Now an Inhabitant of Canada, as Narrated by*

Himself to Samuel Eliot (Boston: 1849). His sales were said to have been satisfactory, if not spectacular at first; but a later edition with an introduction by Harriet Beecher Stowe and re-titled *Truth Stranger Than Fiction, Father Henson's Story of His Own Life* did even better in 1858. The book was still selling well in 1879 when a new edition appeared as *An Autobiography of the Rev. Josiah Henson (Mrs. Harriet Beecher Stowe's "Uncle Tom")* with introductory notes by Wendell Phillips and John Greenleaf Whittier added to Mrs. Stowe's preface. The publish-ers stated that 100,000 copies of the book had been sold previ-ously. There had been French and Dutch translations as well as the English language editions.

Indeed, good sales had become the rule for slave narratives. *The Narrative of Solomon Northup* sold 27,000 copies in 1853 and 1854. *Narrative of the Life of William W. Brown, a Fugi-tive Slave, Written by Himself* went through four editions in its first year. According to a piece in the *Christian Examiner* of July 1849, the Frederick Douglass *Narrative* had achieved seven edi-tions since its publication in 1845. A narrative by Moses Roper was continuing to sell after its eleventh printing. By the 1850's the slave narrative had definitely caught the attention of Amer-ican readers. It is therefore not surprising that while the vogue lasted the number of the narratives published may have run into the hundreds.

Their popularity in the nineteenth century, all things consid-ered, was not unlike the vogue of the Western story in the twentieth. Like the Westerns, they also created a parable of the human condition, but with them the meaning was different. Their theme was the fetters of mankind and the yearning of all living things for freedom. In this context the perils of escape and the long journeys toward the North Star did not grow tiresome with repetition until a new myth, the Western, replaced the earlier one. Even so, slave narratives continued to be written and published occasionally until Booker T. Washington's *The Story of My Life and Work* and its somewhat revised follow-up under the title *Up From Slavery* brought the curtain down on the era and provided a denouement for the genre.

Hindsight may yet disclose the extent to which this writing, this impulse, has been influential on subsequent American writ-ing, if not indeed on America's view of itself. Certainly neither Mark Twain nor Herman Melville escaped its influence com-pletely, and writing by black authors from James Weldon Johnson to Richard Wright, Ralph Ellison, and James Baldwin shows a profound indebtedness to this tradition. The standard literary sources and the classics of modern fiction pale in comparison as a source of their strength.

The Fugitive Blacksmith, or Events in the History of James W. C. Pennington, Pastor of a Presbyterian Church, New York, Formerly a Slave in the State of Maryland, United States (1849) and *Running a Thousand Miles for Freedom, or the Escape of William and Ellen Craft from Slavery* (1860), together with the Vassa *Narrative*, it is hoped, will suggest the continuing relevance of these throbbing and frequently inspired chronicles of a half-forgotten history.

THE LIFE OF

OLAUDAH EQUIANO

OR

GUSTAVUS VASSA

THE AFRICAN

WRITTEN BY HIMSELF

❋   ❋   ❋   ❋   ❋   ❋   ❋   ❋   ❋

First published in London in 1789, *The Interesting Narrative of the Life of Olaudah Equiano, or Gustavus Vassa, the African* has sometimes been mentioned by critics in the same breath with the "continuous narrative" and "spontaneous variety" one associates with Bunyan or Defoe. It is a book for which Europe, Africa, and North America can all take a measure of credit; but a consensus of bibliographers, at least, appears to have favored its primary association with the United States. While Gustavus Vassa was born (he says, in 1745) and spent his early boyhood in Benin, now a part of Nigeria, and devoted the later period of his maturity in antislavery work in England, his slavery in Virginia and more important his years in the service of a Philadelphia owner, who saw to his education, such as it was, and put him to work on small trading vessels in the West Indies as well as on Caribbean plantations, were the years that shaped his thought and provided the frame of reference for this timeless *Narrative*.

Appreciated in his own day, as indicated by eight printings in its first five years, and at various times and places later, the career of the *Narrative* itself can be spliced together from occasional introductory notes in succeeding editions. The dedicatory remarks in a 1790 issue of the book, for example, states that Vassa that year presented to Parliament a petition for the suppression of the slave trade. An anonymous editor of an 1815 edition reveals that he (the editor) had been unable to determine where or when Vassa died, thus calling to mind a kind of veil that had already been drawn to obscure, if not to hide, the names and deeds of black men.

Nevertheless another edition had appeared in Leeds in 1814, and the Abbé Henri Grégoire had already undertaken to counteract this proslavery device by publishing a notable essay on black writing including treatment of such figures as Phillis Wheatley, Benjamin Banneker, and of course Vassa. Taking a lead from Grégoire in this regard, dedicated American Abolitionists undertook similar means to rescue from oblivion those Negroes whose works might raise the aspirations of other blacks, on one hand, while on the other, informing whites not yet committed to the struggle of the capacities of a people they had not properly judged. Under this general impulse the American antislavery societies reissued the *Poems* of Phillis Wheatley, the *Almanacs* of Benjamin Banneker, and the perennial *Narrative* of Gustavus Vassa, in the form reprinted herewith.

Vassa's commitment to freedom is unmistakable, and this was compatible with the romantic mood of his time as well as with the parallel attitude toward the noble savage or Grégoire's child-of-nature view. But the *Narrative* had more than this to sustain it. It had a style of its own. Others noted that Vassa remained an African throughout his life, a self-conscious African, and his bright imagination enabled him to see his adventures through African standards. His unquestioning acceptance of the strange, his genius for making the necessary personal adaptations, his remarkable insight into the characters of those around him, and above all his laughing resignation when his situation became impossible. Vassa thus becomes the first literary Negro caught in the act of laughing to keep from crying.

His *Narrative* is also unique, or almost unique, among the great slave narratives in that he recounts memories of a childhood in Africa. His pictures of life in "the kingdom of Benin" are both realistic and filled with warmth. Nor does his reluctance to dispense with his jungle superstitions, even after he has been Christianized, actually detract. Rather they may remind readers of today of Countee Cullen's "A Pagan Prayer" and other statements by this recent poet of his own vacillations between the religious attitudes of the two worlds to which he belonged.

A contemporary of Cullen's spoke of Vassa's *Narrative*, in the 1920's, as "one of the chief adornments of American Negro literature." Back in 1789 the *Monthly Review* (LXXXII, June 1789, pp. 551–552) had this to say about its original publication:

> We entertain no doubt of the general authenticity of this very intelligent African's interesting story. . . . The narrative wears an honest face: and we have conceived a good opinion of the man from the artless manner in which he has detailed the variety of adventures and vicissitudes which have befallen to his lot.

—ARNA BONTEMPS

✽   ✽   ✽   ✽   ✽   ✽   ✽   ✽   ✽

Chapter 1

The author's account of his country, and their manners and customs—Administration of justice—Embrenche—Marriage ceremony, and public entertainments—Mode of living—Dress—Manufactures—Buildings—Commerce—Agriculture—War and religion—Superstition of the natives—Funeral ceremonies of the priests or magicians—Curious mode of discovering poison—Some hints concerning the origin of the author's countrymen, with the opinions of different writers on that subject.

I BELIEVE it is difficult for those who publish their own memoirs to escape the imputation of vanity; nor is this the only disadvantage under which they labor: it is also their misfortune that what is uncommon is rarely, if ever, believed, and what is obvious we are apt to turn from with disgust, and to charge the writer with impertinence. People generally think those memoirs only worthy to be read or remembered which abound in great or striking events, those, in short, which in a high degree excite either admiration or pity; all others they consign to contempt and oblivion. It is therefore, I confess, not a little hazardous in a private and obscure individual, and a stranger too, thus to solicit the indulgent attention of the public, especially when I own I offer here the history of neither a saint, a hero, nor a tyrant. I believe there are few events in my life which have not happened to many; it is true the incidents of it are numerous, and, did I consider myself an European, I might say my sufferings were great; but when I compare my lot with that of most of my countrymen, I regard myself as a *particular favorite of heaven,* and acknowledge the mercies of Providence in every occurrence of my life. If, then, the following narrative does not appear sufficiently interesting to engage general attention, let my motive be some excuse for its publication. I am not so foolishly vain as to expect from it either immortality or literary reputation. If it affords any satisfaction to my numerous friends, at whose request it has been written, or in the smallest degree promotes the interests of humanity, the ends for which it was undertaken will be fully attained, and every wish of my heart gratified. Let it therefore be remembered, that, in wishing to avoid censure, I do not aspire to praise.

That part of Africa, known by the name of Guinea, to which

4

the trade for slaves is carried on, extends along the coast above 3400 miles, from Senegal to Angola, and includes a variety of kingdoms. Of these the most considerable is the kingdom of Benin, both as to extent and wealth, the richness and cultivation of the soil, the power of its king, and the number and warlike disposition of the inhabitants. It is situated nearly under the line, and extends along the coast about 170 miles, but runs back into the interior part of Africa to a distance hitherto, I believe, unexplored by any traveller, and seems only terminated at length by the empire of Abyssinia, near 1500 miles from its beginning. This kingdom is divided into many provinces or districts, in one of the most remote and fertile of which, I was born, in the year 1745, situated in a charming fruitful vale, named Essaka. The distance of this province from the capital of Benin and the sea coast must be very considerable, for I had never heard of white men or Europeans, nor of the sea; and our subjection to the king of Benin was little more than nominal, for every transaction of the government, as far as my slender observation extended, was conducted by the chief or elders of the place. The manners and government of a people who have little commerce with other countries are generally very simple, and the history of what passes in one family or village may serve as a specimen of the whole nation. My father was one of those elders or chiefs I have spoken of, and was styled Embrenche, a term, as I remember, importing the highest distinction, and signifying in our language a *mark* of grandeur. This mark is conferred on the person entitled to it, by cutting the skin across at the top of the forehead, and drawing it down to the eyebrows; and while it is in this situation applying a warm hand, and rubbing it until it shrinks up into a thick *weal* across the lower part of the forehead. Most of the judges and senators were thus marked; my father had long borne it; I had seen it conferred on one of my brothers, and I also was *destined* to receive it by my parents. Those Embrenche, or chief men, decided disputes and punished crimes, for which purpose they always assembled together. The proceedings were generally short, and in most cases the law of retaliation prevailed. I remember a man was brought before my father, and the other judges, for kidnapping a boy; and, although he was the son of a chief or senator, he was condemned to make recompense by a man or woman slave. Adultery, however, was sometimes punished with slavery or death, a punishment which I believe is inflicted on it throughout most of the nations of Africa,* so sacred among them is the honor of the marriage bed, and so jealous are they of the fidelity of their wives. Of this I recollect an instance—a woman was convicted before the judges of adultery, and delivered over, as the custom was, to her husband, to be punished. Accordingly he determined to put her to death; but it being found, just before her execution, that she had an infant at her breast, and no woman being prevailed on to perform the part of a nurse, she was spared on account of the child. The men, however, do not preserve the same constancy to their wives which they expect from them; for they indulge in a plurality, though seldom in more than two. Their mode of marriage is thus—both parties are usually betrothed when young by their parents (though I have known the males to betroth themselves). On this occasion a feast is prepared, and the bride and bridegroom stand up in the midst of all their friends, who are assembled for the purpose, while he declares she is henceforth to be looked upon as his wife, and that no other person is to pay any addresses to her. This is also immediately proclaimed in the vicinity, on which the bride retires from the assembly. Some time after, she is brought home to her husband, and then another feast is made, to which the relations of both parties are invited; her parents then deliver her to the bridegroom, accompanied with a number of blessings, and at the same time they tie round her waist a cotton string of the thickness of a goosequill, which none but married women are permitted to wear; she is now considered as completely his wife; and at this time the dowry is given to the new married pair, which generally consists of portions of land, slaves, and cattle, household goods, and implements of husbandry. These are offered by the friends of both parties; besides which the parents of the bridegroom present gifts to those of the bride, whose property she is looked upon before marriage; but after it she is esteemed the sole property of her husband. The ceremony being now ended, the festival begins, which is celebrated with bonfires and loud acclamations of joy, accompanied with music and dancing.

* See Benezet's "Account of Guinea," throughout.

We are almost a nation of dancers, musicians, and poets. Thus every great event, such as a triumphant return from battle or other cause of public rejoicing, is celebrated in public dances, which are accompanied with songs and music suited to the occasion. The assembly is separated into four divisions, which dance either apart or in succession, and each with a character peculiar to itself. The first division contains the married men, who in their dances frequently exhibit feats of arms and the representation of a battle. To these succeed the married women, who dance in the second division. The young men occupy the third, and the maidens the fourth. Each represents some interesting scene of real life, such as a great achievement, domestic employment, a pathetic story, or some rural sport; and as the subject is generally founded on some recent event, it is therefore ever new. This gives our dances a spirit and variety which I have scarcely seen elsewhere.* We have many musical instruments, particularly drums of different kinds, a piece of music which resembles a guitar, and another much like a stickado. These last are chiefly used by betrothed virgins, who play on them on all grand festivals.

As our manners are simple, our luxuries are few. The dress of both sexes is nearly the same. It generally consists of a long piece of calico, or muslin, wrapped loosely round the body, somewhat in the form of a highland plaid. This is usually dyed blue, which is our favorite color. It is extracted from a berry, and is brighter and richer than any I have seen in Europe. Besides this, our women of distinction wear golden ornaments, which they dispose with some profusion on their arms and legs. When our women are not employed with the men in tillage, their usual occupation is spinning and weaving cotton, which they afterwards dye, and make into garments. They also manufacture earthen vessels, of which we have many kinds. Among the rest, tobacco pipes, made after the same fashion, and used in the same manner, as those in Turkey.†

* When I was in Smyrna I have frequently seen the Greeks dance after this manner.

† The bowl is earthen, curiously figured, to which a long reed is fixed as a tube. This tube is sometimes so long as to be borne by one, and frequently out of grandeur, two boys.

Our manner of living is entirely plain; for as yet the natives
are unacquainted with those refinements in cookery which
debauch the taste; bullocks, goats, and poultry supply the greatest part of their food. (These constitute likewise the principal
wealth of the country, and the chief articles of its commerce.)
The flesh is usually stewed in a pan; to make it savory we sometimes use pepper, and other spices, and we have salt made of
wood ashes. Our vegetables are mostly plantains, eadas, yams,
beans, and Indian corn. The head of the family usually eats
alone; his wives and slaves have also their separate tables. Before we taste food we always wash our hands; indeed, our clean-
liness on all occasions is extreme, but on this it is an indispensable
ceremony. After washing, libation is made, by pouring out a
small portion of the drink on the floor, and tossing a small
quantity of the food in a certain place, for the spirits of departed
relations, which the natives suppose to preside over their conduct and guard them from evil. They are totally unacquainted
with strong or spirituous liquors; and their principal beverage is
palm wine. This is got from a tree of that name, by tapping it
at the top and fastening a large gourd to it; and sometimes one
tree will yield three or four gallons in a night. When just drawn
it is of a most delicious sweetness; but in a few days it acquires
a tartish and more spirituous flavor, though I never saw anyone
intoxicated by it. The same tree also produces nuts and oil. Our
principal luxury is in perfumes: one sort of these is an odoriferous
wood of delicious fragrance, the other a kind of earth, a small
portion of which thrown into the fire diffuses a most powerful
odor.* We beat this wood into powder, and mix it with palm oil,
with which both men and women perfume themselves.

In our buildings we study convenience rather than ornament.
Each master of a family has a large square piece of ground, surrounded with a moat or fence, or enclosed with a wall made of
red earth tempered, which, when dry, is as hard as brick. Within
this, are his houses to accommodate his family and slaves, which,
if numerous, frequently present the appearance of a village. In
the middle, stands the principal building, appropriated to the

---

* When I was in Smyrna I saw the same kind of earth, and brought
some of it with me to England; it resembles musk in strength, but is more
delicious in scent, and is not unlike the smell of a rose.

sole use of the master and consisting of two apartments; in one
of which he sits in the day with his family, the other is left apart
for the reception of his friends. He has besides these a distinct
apartment in which he sleeps, together with his male children.
On each side are the apartments of his wives, who have also their
separate day and night houses. The habitations of the slaves and
their families are distributed throughout the rest of the enclosure.
These houses never exceed one story in height; they are always
built of wood, or stakes driven into the ground, crossed with
wattles, and neatly plastered within and without. The roof is
thatched with reeds. Our day houses are left open at the sides;
but those in which we sleep are always covered, and plastered
in the inside, with a composition mixed with cow-dung, to keep
off the different insects, which annoy us during the night. The
walls and floors also of these are generally covered with mats.
Our beds consist of a platform, raised three or four feet from the
ground, on which are laid skins, and different parts of a spongy
tree, called plantain. Our covering is calico or muslin, the same
as our dress. The usual seats are a few logs of wood; but we
have benches, which are generally perfumed to accommodate
strangers: these compose the greater part of our household furniture. Houses so constructed and furnished require but little skill
to erect them. Every man is a sufficient architect for the purpose.
The whole neighborhood afford their unanimous assistance in
building them, and in return receive and expect no other recompense than a feast.

As we live in a country where nature is prodigal of her favors,
our wants are few and easily supplied; of course we have few
manufactures. They consist for the most part of calicoes, earthen
ware, ornaments, and instruments of war and husbandry. But
these make no part of our commerce, the principal articles of
which, as I have observed, are provisions. In such a state, money
is of little use; however, we have some small pieces of coin, if I
may call them such. They are made something like an anchor,
but I do not remember either their value or denomination. We
have also markets, at which I have been frequently with my
mother. These are sometimes visited by stout mahogany-colored
men from the south-west of us: we call them *Oye-Eboe,* which
term signifies red men living at a distance. They generally bring

us fire-arms, gun-powder, hats, beads, and dried fish. The last we esteemed a great rarity, as our waters were only brooks and springs. These articles they barter with us for odoriferous woods and earth, and our salt of wood ashes. They always carry slaves through our land; but the strictest account is exacted of their manner of procuring them before they are suffered to pass. Sometimes, indeed, we sold slaves to them, but they were only prisoners of war, or such among us as had been convicted of kidnapping, or adultery, and some other crimes, which we esteemed heinous. This practice of kidnapping induces me to think, that, notwithstanding all our strictness, their principal business among us was to trepan our people. I remember too, they carried great sacks along with them, which not long after, I had an opportunity of fatally seeing applied to that infamous purpose.

Our land is uncommonly rich and fruitful, and produces all kinds of vegetables in great abundance. We have plenty of Indian corn, and vast quantities of cotton and tobacco. Our pineapples grow without culture; they are about the size of the largest sugar-loaf, and finely flavored. We have also spices of different kinds, particularly pepper, and a variety of delicious fruits which I have never seen in Europe, together with gums of various kinds, and honey in abundance. All our industry is exerted to improve these blessings of nature. Agriculture is our chief employment; and everyone, even the children and women, are engaged in it. Thus we are all habituated to labor from our earliest years. Everyone contributes something to the common stock; and, as we are unacquainted with idleness, we have no beggars. The benefits of such a mode of living are obvious. The West India planters prefer the slaves of Benin or Eboe to those of any other part of Guinea, for their hardiness, intelligence, integrity, and zeal. Those benefits are felt by us in the general healthiness of the people, and in their vigor and activity; I might have added, too, in their comeliness. Deformity is indeed unknown amongst us, I mean that of shape. Numbers of the natives of Eboe now in London might be brought in support of this assertion: for, in regard to complexion, ideas of beauty are wholly relative. I remember while in Africa to have seen three Negro children who were tawny, and another quite white, who were universally regarded by myself, and the natives in general, as far as related to their complexions, as deformed. Our women, too, were, in my eye at least, uncommonly graceful, alert, and modest to a degree of bashfulness; nor do I remember to have heard of an instance of incontinence amongst them before marriage. They are also remarkably cheerful. Indeed, cheerfulness and affability are two of the leading characteristics of our nation.

Our tillage is exercised in a large plain or common, some hour's walk from our dwellings, and all the neighbors resort thither in a body. They use no beasts of husbandry; and their only instruments are hoes, axes, shovels, and beaks, or pointed iron, to dig with. Sometimes we are visited by locusts, which come in large clouds, so as to darken the air, and destroy our harvest. This, however, happens rarely, but when it does, a famine is produced by it. I remember an instance or two wherein this happened. This common is often the theatre of war; and therefore when our people go out to till their land, they not only go in a body, but generally take their arms with them for fear of a surprise; and when they apprehend an invasion, they guard the avenues to their dwellings, by driving sticks into the ground, which are so sharp at one end as to pierce the foot, and are generally dipt in poison. From what I can recollect of these battles, they appear to have been irruptions of one little state or district on the other, to obtain prisoners or booty. Perhaps they were incited to this by those traders who brought the European goods I mentioned, amongst us. Such a mode of obtaining slaves in Africa is common; and I believe more are procured this way, and by kidnapping, than any other.* When a trader wants slaves, he applies to a chief for them, and tempts him with his wares. It is not extraordinary, if on this occasion he yields to the temptation with as little firmness, and accepts the price of his fellow creature's liberty, with as little reluctance as the enlightened merchant. Accordingly he falls on his neighbors, and a desperate battle ensues. If he prevails and takes prisoners, he gratifies his avarice by selling them; but, if his party be vanquished, and he falls into the hands of the enemy, he is put to death; for, as he has been known to foment their quarrels, it is thought dangerous to let him survive, and no ransom can save him, though all other prisoners may be redeemed. We have fire-arms, bows and arrows, broad two-edged

* See Benezet's "Account of Africa," throughout.

swords and javelins; we have shields also which cover a man from
head to foot. All are taught the use of these weapons; even our
women are warriors, and march boldly out to fight along with the
men. Our whole district is a kind of militia: on a certain signal
given, such as the firing of a gun at night, they all rise in arms and
rush upon their enemy. It is perhaps something remarkable, that
when our people march to the field a red flag or banner is borne
before them. I was once a witness to a battle in our common. We
had been all at work in it one day as usual, when our people were
suddenly attacked. I climbed a tree at some distance, from which
I beheld the fight. There were many women as well as men on
both sides; among others my mother was there, and armed with
a broad sword. After fighting for a considerable time with great
fury, and many had been killed, our people obtained the victory,
and took their enemy's Chief a prisoner. He was carried off in
great triumph, and, though he offered a large ransom for his life,
he was put to death. A virgin of note among our enemies had
been slain in the battle, and her arm was exposed in our market-
place, where our trophies were always exhibited. The spoils were
divided according to the merit of the warriors. Those prisoners
which were not sold or redeemed, we kept as slaves; but how
different was their condition from that of the slaves in the West
Indies! With us, they do no more work than other members of the
community, even their master; their food, clothing, and lodging
were nearly the same as theirs (except that they were not permitted to eat with those who were free-born); and there was
scarce any other difference between them, than a superior degree
of importance which the head of a family possesses in our state,
and that authority which, as such, he exercises over every part of
his household. Some of these slaves have even slaves under them
as their own property, and for their own use.

As to religion, the natives believe that there is one Creator of
all things, and that he lives in the sun, and is girted round with
a belt; that he may never eat or drink, but, according to some, he
smokes a pipe, which is our own favorite luxury. They believe he
governs events, especially our deaths or captivity; but, as for the
doctrine of eternity, I do not remember to have ever heard of it;
some, however, believe in the transmigration of souls in a certain
degree. Those spirits which were not transmigrated, such as their

dear friends or relations, they believe always attend them, and guard them from the bad spirits or their foes. For this reason they always, before eating, as I have observed, put some small portion of the meat, and pour some of their drink, on the ground for them; and they often make oblations of the blood of beasts or fowls at their graves. I was very fond of my mother, and almost constantly with her. When she went to make these oblations at her mother's tomb, which was a kind of small solitary thatched house, I sometimes attended her. There she made her libations, and spent most of the night in cries and lamentations. I have been often extremely terrified on these occasions. The loneliness of the place, the darkness of the night, and the ceremony of libation, naturally awful and gloomy, were heightened by my mother's lamentations; and these concurring with the doleful cries of birds, by which these places were frequented, gave an inexpressible terror to the scene.

We compute the year, from the day on which the sun crosses the line, and on its setting that evening, there is a general shout throughout the land; at least, I can speak from my own knowledge, throughout our vicinity. The people at the same time make a great noise with rattles, not unlike the basket rattles used by children here, though much larger, and hold up their hands to heaven for a blessing. It is then the greatest offerings are made; and those children whom our wise men foretell will be fortunate are then presented to different people. I remember many used to come to see me, and I was carried about to others for that purpose. They have many offerings, particularly at full moons; generally two, at harvest, before the fruits are taken out of the ground; and when any young animals are killed, sometimes they offer up part of them as a sacrifice. These offerings, when made by one of the heads of a family, serve for the whole. I remember we often had them at my father's and my uncle's, and their families have been present. Some of our offerings are eaten with bitter herbs. We had a saying among us to anyone of a cross temper, "That if they were to be eaten, they should be eaten with bitter herbs."

We practised circumcision like the Jews, and made offerings and feasts on that occasion, in the same manner as they did. Like them also, our children were named from some event, some circumstance, or fancied foreboding, at the time of their birth. I was named *Olaudah,* which in our language signifies vicissitude, or fortunate; also, one favored, and having a loud voice and well spoken. I remember we never polluted the name of the object of our adoration; on the contrary, it was always mentioned with the greatest reverence; and we were totally unacquainted with swearing, and all those terms of abuse and reproach which find their way so readily and copiously into the language of more civilized people. The only expressions of that kind I remember were, "May you rot, or may you swell, or may a beast take you."

I have before remarked that the natives of this part of Africa are extremely cleanly. This necessary habit of decency was with us a part of religion, and therefore we had many purifications and washings; indeed almost as many, and used on the same occasions, if my recollection does not fail me, as the Jews. Those that touched the dead at any time were obliged to wash and purify themselves before they could enter a dwelling-house. Every woman, too, at certain times was forbidden to come into a dwelling-house, or touch any person, or anything we eat. I was so fond of my mother I could not keep from her, or avoid touching her at some of those periods, in consequence of which I was obliged to be kept out with her, in a little house made for that purpose, till offering was made, and then we were purified.

Though we had no places of public worship, we had priests and magicians, or wise men. I do not remember whether they had different offices, or whether they were united in the same persons, but they were held in great reverence by the people. They calculated our time, and foretold events, as their name imported, for we called them *Ah-affoe-way-cah,* which signifies calculators or yearly men, our year being called *Ah-affoe.* They wore their beards, and when they died, they were succeeded by their sons. Most of their implements and things of value were interred along with them. Pipes and tobacco were also put into the grave with the corpse, which was always perfumed and ornamented, and animals were offered in sacrifice to them. None accompanied their funerals, but those of the same profession or tribe. They buried them after sunset, and always returned from the grave by a different way from that which they went.

These magicians were also our doctors or physicians. They

practised bleeding by cupping, and were very successful in healing wounds and expelling poisons. They had likewise some extraordinary method of discovering jealousy, theft, poisoning, the success of which, no doubt, they derived from the unbounded influence over the credulity and superstition of the people. I do not remember what those methods were, except that as to poisoning; I recollect an instance or two, which I hope it will not be deemed impertinent here to insert, as it may serve as a kind of specimen of the rest, as is still used by the Negroes in the West Indies. A young woman had been poisoned, but it was not known by whom; the doctors ordered the corpse to be taken up by some persons, and carried to the grave. As soon as the bearers had raised it on their shoulders, they seemed seized with some* sudden impulse, and ran to and fro, unable to stop themselves. At last, after having passed through a number of thorns and prickly bushes unhurt, the corpse fell from them close to a house, and defaced it in the fall; and the owner being taken up, he immediately confessed the poisoning.†

The natives are extremely cautious about poison. When they buy any eatables, the seller kisses it all round before the buyer, to shew him it is not poisoned; and the same is done when any meat or drink is presented, particularly to a stranger. We have serpents of different kinds, some of which are esteemed ominous when they appear in our houses, and these we never molest. I

* See also Lieutenant Matthew's Voyage, p. 123.

† An instance of this kind happened at Montserrat, in the West Indies, in the year 1763. I then belonged to the *Charming Sally*, Capt. Doran. The chief mate, Mr. Mansfield, and some of the crew being one day on shore, were present at the burying of a poisoned Negro girl. Though they had often heard of the circumstance of the running in such cases, and had even seen it, they imagined it to be a trick of the corpse bearers. The mate therefore desired two of the sailors to take up the coffin, and carry it to the grave. The sailors, who were all of the same opinion, readily obeyed, but they had scarcely raised it to their shoulders before they began to run furiously about, quite unable to direct themselves, till at last, without intention, they came to the hut of him who had poisoned the girl. The coffin then immediately fell from their shoulders against the hut, and damaged part of the wall. The owner of the hut was taken into custody on this, and confessed the poisoning. I give this story as it was related by the mate and crew on their return to the ship. The credit which is due to it, I leave with the reader.

remember two of those ominous snakes, each of which was as
thick as the calf of a man's leg, and in color resembling a dolphin
in the water, crept at different times into my mother's night
house, where I always lay with her, and coiled themselves into
folds, and each time they crowed like a cock. I was desired by
some of our wise men to touch these, that I might be interested
in the good omens, which I did, for they were quite harmless,
and would tamely suffer themselves to be handled; and then they
were put into a large earthen pan, and set on one side of the highway. Some of our snakes, however, were poisonous; one of them
crossed the road one day as I was standing on it, and passed
between my feet without offering to touch me, to the great surprise of many who saw it; and these incidents were accounted by
the wise men, and likewise by my mother and the rest of the people, as remarkable omens in my favor.

Such is the imperfect sketch my memory has furnished me
with, of the manners and customs of a people among whom I first
drew my breath. And here I cannot forbear suggesting what has
long struck me very forcibly, namely, the strong analogy which
even by this sketch, imperfect as it is, appears to prevail in the
manners and customs of my countrymen and those of the Jews,
before they reached the land of promise, and particularly the
patriarchs while they were yet in that pastoral state which is described in Genesis—an analogy, which alone would induce me to
think that the one people had sprung from the other. Indeed, this
is the opinion of Dr. Gill, who, in his commentary on Genesis,
very ably deduces the pedigree of the Africans from Afer and
Afra, the descendents of Abraham by Keturah his wife and con-
cubine (for both these titles are applied to her). It is also con-
formable to the sentiments of Dr. John Clarke, formerly Dean of
Sarum, in his truth of the Christian religion; both these authors
concur in ascribing to us this original. The reasonings of those
gentlemen are still further confirmed by the scripture chronology;
and if any further corroboration were required, this resemblance
in so many respects, is a strong evidence in support of the
opinion. Like the Israelites in their primitive state, our government was conducted by our chiefs or judges, our wise men and
elders; and the head of a family with us enjoyed a similar authority over his household, with that which is ascribed to Abraham

and the other patriarchs. The law of retaliation obtained almost universally with us as with them: and even their religion appeared to have shed upon us a ray of its glory, though broken and spent in its passage, or eclipsed by the cloud with which time, tradition, and ignorance might have enveloped it; for we had our circumcision (a rule, I believe, peculiar to that people), we had also our sacrifices and burnt-offerings, our washings and purifications, and on the same occasions as they did.

As to the difference of color between the Eboan Africans and the modern Jews, I shall not presume to account for it. It is a subject which has engaged the pens of men of both genius and learning, and is far above my strength. The most able and Reverend Mr. T. Clarkson, however, in his much admired essay on the Slavery and Commerce of the Human Species, has ascertained the cause in a manner that at once solves every objection on that account, and, on my mind at least, has produced the fullest conviction. I shall therefore refer to that performance for the theory,* contenting myself with extracting a fact as related by Dr. Mitchel.† "The Spaniards, who have inhabited America, under the torrid zone, for any time, are become as dark colored as our native Indians of Virginia; of which *I myself have been a witness.*" There is also another instance‡ of a Portuguese settlement at Mitomba, a river in Sierra Leone, where the inhabitants are bred from a mixture of the first Portuguese discoverers with the natives, and are now become in their complexion, and in the woolly quality of their hair, *perfect Negroes,* retaining however a smattering of the Portuguese language.

These instances, and a great many more which might be adduced, while they show how the complexions of the same persons vary in different climates, it is hoped may tend also to remove the prejudice that some conceive against the natives of Africa on account of their color. Surely the minds of the Spaniards did not change with their complexions! Are there not causes enough to which the apparent inferiority of an African may be ascribed, without limiting the goodness of God, and supposing he forebore to stamp understanding on certainly his own image, be-

* Pages 178 to 216.
† Philos. Trans. No. 476, Sec. 4, cited by Mr. Clarkson, p. 205.
‡ Same page.

cause "carved in ebony." Might it not naturally be ascribed to
their situation? When they come among Europeans, they are
ignorant of their language, religion, manners, and customs. Are
any pains taken to teach them these? Are they treated as men?
Does not slavery itself depress the mind, and extinguish all its
fire and every noble sentiment? But, above all, what advantages
do not a refined people possess, over those who are rude and uncultivated? Let the polished and haughty European recollect that
his ancestors were once, like the Africans, uncivilized, and even
barbarous. Did Nature make *them* inferior to their sons? and
should *they too* have been made slaves? Every rational mind
answers, No. Let such reflections as these melt the pride of their
superiority into sympathy for the wants and miseries of their sable
brethren, and compel them to acknowledge that understanding is
not confined to feature or color. If, when they look round the
world, they feel exultation, let it be tempered with benevolence to
others, and gratitude to God, "who hath made of one blood all nations of men for to dwell on all the face of the earth";* "and
whose wisdom is not our wisdom, neither are our ways his ways."

* Acts 17:26.

Chapter 2

The author's birth and parentage—His being kidnapped with his sister—Their separation—Surprise at meeting again—Are finally separated—Account of the different places and incidents the author met with till his arrival on the coast—The effect the sight of a slave-ship had on him—He sails for the West Indies—Horrors of a slave-ship—Arrives at Barbadoes, where the cargo is sold and dispersed.

I HOPE THE READER will not think I have trespassed on his patience in introducing myself to him, with some account of the manners and customs of my country. They had been implanted in me with great care, and made an impression on my mind, which time could not erase, and which all the adversity and variety of fortune I have since experienced, served only to rivet and record: for, whether the love of one's country be real or imaginary, or a lesson of reason, or an instinct of nature, I still look back with pleasure on the first scenes of my life, though that pleasure has been for the most part mingled with sorrow.

I have already acquainted the reader with the time and place of my birth. My father, besides many slaves, had a numerous family, of which seven lived to grow up, including myself and sister, who was the only daughter. As I was the youngest of the sons, I became, of course, the greatest favorite with my mother, and was always with her; and she used to take particular pains to form my mind. I was trained up from my earliest years in the art of war: my daily exercise was shooting and throwing javelins, and my mother adorned me with emblems, after the manner of our greatest warriors. In this way I grew up till I had turned the age of eleven, when an end was put to my happiness in the following manner: Generally, when the grown people in the neighborhood were gone far in the fields to labor, the children assembled together in some of the neighboring premises to play; and commonly some of us used to get up a tree to look out for any assailant, or kidnapper, that might come upon us—for they sometimes took those opportunities of our parents' absence, to attack and carry off as many as they could seize. One day as I was watching at the top of a tree in our yard, I saw one of those people come into the yard of our next neighbor but one, to kidnap, there being many stout young people in it. Immediately on this I gave the alarm of the rogue, and he was surrounded by the stoutest of them, who entangled him with cords, so that he could not escape, till some of the grown people came and secured him. But, alas! ere long it was my fate to be thus attacked, and to be carried off, when none of the grown people were nigh. One day, when all our people were gone out to their works as usual, and only I and my dear sister were left to mind the house, two men and a woman got over our walls, and in a moment seized us both, and, without giving us time to cry out, or make resistance, they stopped our mouths, and ran off with us into the nearest wood. Here they tied our hands, and continued to carry us as far as they could, till night came on, when we reached a small house, where the robbers halted for refreshment, and spent the night. We were then unbound, but were unable to take any food; and, being quite overpowered by fatigue and grief, our only relief was some sleep, which allayed our misfortune for a short time. The next morning we left the house, and continued travelling all the day. For a long time we had kept the woods, but at last we came into a road which I believed I knew. I had now some hopes of being delivered; for we had advanced but a little way before I discovered some people at a distance, on which I began to cry out for their assistance; but my cries had no other effect than to make them tie me faster and stop my mouth, and then they put me into a large sack. They also stopped my sister's mouth, and tied her hands; and in this manner we proceeded till we were out of sight of these people. When we went to rest the following night, they offered us some victuals, but we refused it; and the only comfort we had was in being in one another's arms all that night, and bathing each other with our tears. But alas! we were soon deprived of even the small comfort of weeping together. The next day proved a day of greater sorrow than I had yet experienced; for my sister and I were then separated, while we lay clasped in each other's arms. It was in vain that we besought them not to part us; she was torn from me, and immediately carried away, while I was left in a state of distraction not to be described. I cried and grieved continually; and for several days did not eat anything but what they forced into my mouth. At length, after many days' travelling, during which I had often changed masters, I got into the hands of a chieftain, in a very pleasant country. This man had two wives and some children, and they all used me extremely well, and did all they could do to comfort me; particularly the first wife, who was something like my mother. Although I was a great many days' journey from my father's house, yet these people spoke exactly the same language with us. This first master of mine, as I may call him, was a smith, and my principal employment was working his bellows, which were the same kind as I had seen in my vicinity. They were in some respects not unlike the stoves here in gentlemen's kitchens, and were covered over with leather; and in the middle of that leather a stick was fixed, and a person stood up, and worked it in the same manner as is done to pump water out of a cask with a hand pump. I believe it was gold he worked, for it was of a lovely bright yellow color, and was worn by the women on their wrists and ankles. I was there I suppose about a month, and they at last used to trust me some little distance from the house. This liberty I used in embracing every opportunity to inquire the way to my own home; and I also sometimes, for the same purpose, went with the maidens, in the cool of the evenings, to bring pitchers of water from the springs for the use of the house. I had also remarked where the sun rose in the morning, and set in the evening, as I had travelled along; and I had observed that my father's house was towards the rising of the sun. I therefore determined to seize the first opportunity of making my escape, and to shape my course for that quarter; for I was quite oppressed and weighed down by grief after my mother and friends; and my love of liberty, ever great, was strengthened by the mortifying circumstance of not daring to eat with the free-born children, although I was mostly their companion. While I was projecting my escape one day, an unlucky event happened, which quite disconcerted my plan, and put an end to my hopes. I used to be sometimes employed in assisting an elderly slave to cook and take care of the poultry; and one morning, while I was feeding some chickens, I happened to toss a small pebble at one of them, which hit it on the middle, and directly killed it. The old slave, having soon after missed the chicken, inquired after it; and on my relating the accident (for I told her the truth, for my mother would never suffer me to tell a

lie), she flew into a violent passion, and threatened that I should
suffer for it; and, my master being out, she immediately went
and told her mistress what I had done. This alarmed me very
much, and I expected an instant flogging, which to me was uncommonly dreadful, for I had seldom been beaten at home. I
therefore resolved to fly; and accordingly I ran into a thicket
that was hard by, and hid myself in the bushes. Soon afterwards
my mistress and the slave returned, and, not seeing me, they
searched all the house, but not finding me, and I not making
answer when they called to me, they thought I had run away,
and the whole neighborhood was raised in the pursuit of me. In
that part of the country, as in ours, the houses and villages were
skirted with woods, or shrubberies, and the bushes were so thick
that a man could readily conceal himself in them, so as to elude
the strictest search. The neighbors continued the whole day
looking for me, and several times many of them came within a
few yards of the place where I lay hid. I expected every moment, when I heard a rustling among the trees, to be found out,
and punished by my master; but they never discovered me,
though they were often so near that I even heard their conjectures
as they were looking about for me; and I now learned from
them that any attempts to return home would be hopeless. Most
of them supposed I had fled towards home; but the distance was
so great, and the way so intricate, that they thought I could never
reach it, and that I should be lost in the woods. When I heard
this I was seized with a violent panic, and abandoned myself to
despair. Night, too, began to approach, and aggravated all my
fears. I had before entertained hopes of getting home, and had
determined when it should be dark to make the attempt; but I
was now convinced it was fruitless, and began to consider that,
if possibly I could escape all other animals, I could not those of
the human kind; and that, not knowing the way, I must perish
in the woods. Thus was I like the hunted deer—

> —— Every leaf and every whisp'ring breath,
> Convey'd a foe, and every foe a death.

I heard frequent rustlings among the leaves, and being pretty
sure they were snakes, I expected every instant to be stung by
them. This increased my anguish, and the horror of my situation

became now quite insupportable. I at length quitted the thicket, very faint and hungry, for I had not eaten or drank anything all the day, and crept to my master's kitchen, from whence I set out at first, which was an open shed, and laid myself down in the ashes with an anxious wish for death, to relieve me from all my pains. I was scarcely awake in the morning, when the old woman slave, who was the first up, came to light the fire, and saw me in the fireplace. She was very much surprised to see me, and could scarcely believe her own eyes. She now promised to intercede for me, and went for her master, who soon after came, and, having slightly reprimanded me, ordered me to be taken care of, and not ill treated.

Soon after this, my master's only daughter, and child by his first wife, sickened and died, which affected him so much that for sometime he was almost frantic, and really would have killed himself, had he not been watched and prevented. However, in a short time afterwards he recovered, and I was again sold. I was now carried to the left of the sun's rising, through many dreary wastes and dismal woods, amidst the hideous roarings of wild beasts. The people I was sold to used to carry me very often, when I was tired, either on their shoulders or on their backs. I saw many convenient well-built sheds along the road, at proper distances, to accommodate the merchants and travellers, who lay in those buildings along with their wives, who often accompany them; and they always go well armed.

From the time I left my own nation, I always found somebody that understood me till I came to the sea coast. The languages of different nations did not totally differ, nor were they so copious as those of the Europeans, particularly the English. They were therefore, easily learned; and, while I was journeying thus through Africa, I acquired two or three different tongues. In this manner I had been travelling for a considerable time, when, one evening, to my great surprise, whom should I see brought to the house where I was but my dear sister! As soon as she saw me, she gave a loud shriek, and ran into my arms—I was quite overpowered; neither of us could speak, but, for a considerable time, clung to each other in mutual embraces, unable to do anything but weep. Our meeting affected all who saw us; and, indeed, I must acknowledge, in honor of those sable destroyers of human

rights, that I never met with any ill treatment, or saw any offered
to their slaves, except tying them, when necessary, to keep them
from running away. When these people knew we were brother
and sister, they indulged us to be together; and the man, to whom
I supposed we belonged, lay with us, he in the middle, while she
and I held one another by the hands across his breast all night;
and thus for a while we forgot our misfortunes, in the joy of
being together; but even this small comfort was soon to have an
end; for scarcely had the fatal morning appeared when she was
again torn from me forever! I was now more miserable, if possible, than before. The small relief which her presence gave me
from pain, was gone, and the wretchedness of my situation was
redoubled by my anxiety after her fate, and my apprehensions
lest her sufferings should be greater than mine, when I could not
be with her to alleviate them. Yes, thou dear partner of all my
childish sports! thou sharer of my joys and sorrows! happy
should I have ever esteemed myself to encounter every misery
for you and to procure your freedom by the sacrifice of my own.
Though you were early forced from my arms, your image has been
always riveted in my heart, from which neither time nor fortune
have been able to remove it; so that, while the thoughts of your
sufferings have damped my prosperity, they have mingled with
adversity and increased its bitterness. To that Heaven which pro-
tects the weak from the strong, I commit the care of your innocence and virtues, if they have not already received their full
reward, and if your youth and delicacy have not long since fallen
victims to the violence of the African trader, the pestilential
stench of a Guinea ship, the seasoning in the European colonies,
or the lash and lust of a brutal and unrelenting overseer.

I did not long remain after my sister. I was again sold, and carried through a number of places, till after travelling a considerable time, I came to a town called Tinmah, in the most beautiful
country I had yet seen in Africa. It was extremely rich, and there
were many rivulets which flowed through it, and supplied a large
pond in the centre of the town, where the people washed. Here
I first saw and tasted cocoanuts, which I thought superior to any
nuts I had ever tasted before; and the trees, which were loaded,
were also interspersed among the houses, which had commodious
shades adjoining, and were in the same manner as ours, the insides

being neatly plastered and whitewashed. Here I also saw and tasted for the first time, sugar-cane. Their money consisted of little white shells, the size of the finger nail. I was sold here for one hundred and seventy-two of them, by a merchant who lived and brought me there. I had been about two or three days at his house, when a wealthy widow, a neighbor of his, came there one evening, and brought with her an only son, a young gentleman about my own age and size. Here they saw me; and, having taken a fancy to me, I was bought of the merchant, and went home with them. Her house and premises were situated close to one of those rivulets I have mentioned, and were the finest I ever saw in Africa: they were very extensive, and she had a number of slaves to attend her. The next day I was washed and perfumed, and when meal time came, I was led into the presence of my mistress, and ate and drank before her with her son. This filled me with astonishment; and I could scarce help expressing my surprise that the young gentleman should suffer me, who was bound, to eat with him who was free; and not only so, but that he would not at any time either eat or drink till I had taken first, because I was the eldest, which was agreeable to our custom. Indeed, every thing here, and all their treatment of me, made me forget that I was a slave. The language of these people resembled ours so nearly, that we understood each other perfectly. They had also the very same customs as we. There were likewise slaves daily to attend us, while my young master and I, with other boys, sported with our darts and bows and arrows, as I had been used to do at home. In this resemblance to my former happy state, I passed about two months; and I now began to think I was to be adopted into the family, and was beginning to be reconciled to my situation, and to forget by degrees my misfortunes, when all at once the delusion vanished; for, without the least previous knowledge, one morning early, while my dear master and companion was still asleep, I was awakened out of my reverie to fresh sorrow, and hurried away even amongst the uncircumcised.

Thus, at the very moment I dreamed of the greatest happiness, I found myself most miserable; and it seemed as if fortune wished to give me this taste of joy only to render the reverse more poignant. The change I now experienced was as painful as it was sudden and unexpected. It was a change indeed, from a state of bliss to a scene which is inexpressible by me, as it discovered to me an element I had never before beheld, and till then had no idea of, and wherein such instances of hardship and cruelty continually occurred, as I can never reflect on but with horror.

All the nations and people I had hitherto passed through, resembled our own in their manners, customs, and language; but I came at length to a country, the inhabitants of which differed from us in all those particulars. I was very much struck with this difference, especially when I came among a people who did not circumcise, and ate without washing their hands. They cooked also in iron pots, and had European cutlasses and cross bows, which were unknown to us, and fought with their fists among themselves. Their women were not so modest as ours, for they ate, and drank, and slept with their men. But above all, I was amazed to see no sacrifices or offerings among them. In some of those places the people ornamented themselves with scars, and likewise filed their teeth very sharp. They wanted sometimes to ornament me in the same manner, but I would not suffer them; hoping that I might some time be among a people who did not thus disfigure themselves, as I thought they did. At last I came to the banks of a large river which was covered with canoes, in which the people appeared to live with their household utensils, and provisions of all kinds. I was beyond measure astonished at this, as I had never before seen any water larger than a pond or a rivulet; and my surprise was mingled with no small fear when I was put into one of these canoes, and we began to paddle and move along the river. We continued going on thus till night, and when we came to land, and made fires on the banks, each family by themselves; some dragged their canoes on shore, others stayed and cooked in theirs, and laid in them all night. Those on the land had mats, of which they made tents, some in the shape of little houses; in these we slept; and after the morning meal, we embarked again and proceeded as before. I was often very much astonished to see some of the women, as well as the men, jump into the water, dive to the bottom, come up again, and swim about. Thus I continued to travel, sometimes by land, sometimes by water, through different countries and various nations, till, at the end of six or seven months after I had been kidnapped, I arrived at the sea coast. It would be tedious and uninteresting to relate all the incidents which befell me during this journey, and which I have not yet forgotten; of the various hands I passed through, and the manners and customs of all the different people among whom I lived—I shall therefore only observe, that in all the places where I was, the soil was exceedingly rich; the pumpkins, eadas, plantains, yams, &c. &c., were in great abundance, and of incredible size. There were also vast quantities of different gums, though not used for any purpose, and everywhere a great deal of tobacco. The cotton even grew quite wild, and there was plenty of red-wood. I saw no mechanics whatever in all the way, except such as I have mentioned. The chief employment in all these countries was agriculture, and both the males and females, as with us, were brought up to it, and trained in the arts of war.

The first object which saluted my eyes when I arrived on the coast, was the sea, and a slave ship, which was then riding at anchor, and waiting for its cargo. These filled me with astonishment, which was soon converted into terror, when I was carried on board. I was immediately handled, and tossed up to see if I were sound, by some of the crew; and I was now persuaded that I had gotten into a world of bad spirits, and that they were going to kill me. Their complexions, too, differing so much from ours, their long hair, and the language they spoke (which was very different from any I had ever heard), united to confirm me in this belief. Indeed, such were the horrors of my views and fears at the moment, that, if ten thousand worlds had been my own, I would have freely parted with them all to have exchanged my condition with that of the meanest slave in my own country. When I looked round the ship too, and saw a large furnace of copper boiling, and a multitude of black people of every description chained together, every one of their countenances expressing dejection and sorrow, I no longer doubted of my fate; and, quite overpowered with horror and anguish, I fell motionless on the deck and fainted. When I recovered a little, I found some black people about me, who I believed were some of those who had brought me on board, and had been receiving their pay; they talked to me in order to cheer me, but all in vain. I asked them if we were not to be eaten by those white men with horrible looks, red faces, and long hair. They told me I was not, and one of the crew brought me a small portion of spirituous liquor in a wine glass; but, being afraid of him, I would not take it out of his hand. One of the blacks, therefore, took it from him and gave it to me, and I took a little down my palate, which, instead of reviving me, as they thought it would, threw me into the greatest consternation at the strange feeling it produced, having never tasted any such liquor before. Soon after this, the blacks who brought me on board went off, and left me abandoned to despair.

I now saw myself deprived of all chance of returning to my native country, or even the least glimpse of hope of gaining the shore, which I now considered as friendly; and I even wished for my former slavery in preference to my present situation, which was filled with horrors of every kind, still heightened by my ignorance of what I was to undergo. I was not long suffered to indulge my grief; I was soon put down under the decks, and there I received such a salutation in my nostrils as I had never experienced in my life: so that, with the loathsomeness of the stench, and crying together, I became so sick and low that I was not able to eat, nor had I the least desire to taste anything. I now wished for the last friend, death, to relieve me; but soon, to my grief, two of the white men offered me eatables; and, on my refusing to eat, one of them held me fast by the hands, and laid me across, I think, the windlass, and tied my feet, while the other flogged me severely. I had never experienced anything of this kind before, and, although not being used to the water, I naturally feared that element the first time I saw it, yet, nevertheless, could I have got over the nettings, I would have jumped over the side, but I could not; and besides, the crew used to watch us very closely who were not chained down to the decks, lest we should leap into the water; and I have seen some of these poor African prisoners most severely cut, for attempting to do so, and hourly whipped for not eating. This indeed was often the case with myself. In a little time after, amongst the poor chained men, I found some of my own nation, which in a small degree gave ease to my mind. I inquired of these what was to be done with us? They gave me to understand, we were to be carried to these white people's country to work for them. I then was a little revived, and thought, if it were no worse than working, my situation was not so desperate; but still I feared I should be put to death, the white people looked and acted, as I thought, in so savage a manner; for I had never seen among any people such instances of brutal cruelty; and this not only shown towards us blacks, but also to some of the whites themselves. One white man in particular I saw, when we were permitted to be on deck, flogged so unmercifully with a large rope near the foremast, that he died in consequence of it; and they tossed him over the side as they would have done a brute. This made me fear these people the more; and I expected nothing less than to be treated in the same manner. I could not help expressing my fears and apprehensions to some of my countrymen; I asked them if these people had no country, but lived in this hollow place (the ship)? They told me they did not, but came from a distant one. "Then," said I, "how comes it in all our country we never heard of them?" They told me because they lived so very far off. I then asked where were their women? had they any like themselves? I was told they had. "And why," said I, "do we not see them?" They answered, because they were left behind. I asked how the vessel could go? They told me they could not tell; but that there was cloth put upon the masts by the help of the ropes I saw, and then the vessel went on; and the white men had some spell or magic they put in the water when they liked, in order to stop the vessel. I was exceedingly amazed at this account, and really thought they were spirits. I therefore wished much to be from amongst them, for I expected they would sacrifice me; but my wishes were vain—for we were so quartered that it was impossible for any of us to make our escape.

While we stayed on the coast I was mostly on deck; and one day, to my great astonishment, I saw one of these vessels coming in with the sails up. As soon as the whites saw it, they gave a great shout, at which we were amazed; and the more so, as the vessel appeared larger by approaching nearer. At last, she came to an anchor in my sight, and when the anchor was let go, I and my countrymen who saw it, were lost in astonishment to observe the vessel stop—and were now convinced it was done by magic. Soon after this the other ship got her boats out, and they came on board of us, and the people of both ships seemed very glad to see each other. Several of the strangers also shook hands with us black people, and made motions with their hands, signifying I suppose, we were to go to their country, but we did not understand them.

At last, when the ship we were in, had got in all her cargo, they made ready with many fearful noises, and we were all put under deck, so that we could not see how they managed the vessel. But this disappointment was the least of my sorrow. The stench of the hold while we were on the coast was so intolerably loathsome, that it was dangerous to remain there for any time, and some of us had been permitted to stay on the deck for the fresh air; but now that the whole ship's cargo were confined together, it became absolutely pestilential. The closeness of the place, and the heat of the climate, added to the number in the ship, which was so crowded that each had scarcely room to turn himself, almost suffocated us. This produced copious perspirations, so that the air soon became unfit for respiration, from a variety of loathsome smells, and brought on a sickness among the slaves, of which many died—thus falling victims to the improvident avarice, as I may call it, of their purchasers. This wretched situation was again aggravated by the galling of the chains, now became insupportable, and the filth of the necessary tubs, into which the children often fell, and were almost suffocated. The shrieks of the women, and the groans of the dying, rendered the whole a scene of horror almost inconceivable. Happily perhaps, for myself, I was soon reduced so low here that it was thought necessary to keep me almost always on deck; and from my extreme youth I was not put in fetters. In this situation I expected every hour to share the fate of my companions, some of whom were almost daily brought upon deck at the point of death, which I began to hope would soon put an end to my miseries. Often did I think many of the inhabitants of the deep much more happy than myself. I envied them the freedom they enjoyed, and as often wished I could change my condition for theirs. Every circumstance I met with, served only to render my state more painful, and heightened my apprehensions, and my opinion of the cruelty of the whites.

One day they had taken a number of fishes; and when they had killed and satisfied themselves with as many as they thought fit, to our astonishment who were on deck, rather than give any of them to us to eat, as we expected, they tossed the remaining fish into the sea again, although we begged and prayed for some as well as we could, but in vain; and some of my countrymen, being pressed by hunger, took an opportunity, when they thought no one saw them, of trying to get a little privately; but they were discovered, and the attempt procured them some very severe floggings. One day, when we had a smooth sea and moderate wind, two of my wearied countrymen who were chained together (I was near them at the time), preferring death to such a life of misery, somehow made through the nettings and jumped into the sea; immediately, another quite dejected fellow, who, on account of his illness, was suffered to be out of irons, also followed their example; and I believe many more would very soon have done the same, if they had not been prevented by the ship's crew, who were instantly alarmed. Those of us that were the most active, were in a moment put down under the deck; and there was such a noise and confusion amongst the people of the ship as I never heard before, to stop her, and get the boat out to go after the slaves. However, two of the wretches were drowned, but they got the other, and afterwards flogged him unmercifully, for thus attempting to prefer death to slavery. In this manner we continued to undergo more hardships than I can now relate, hardships which are inseparable from this accursed trade. Many a time we were near suffocation from the want of fresh air, which we were often without for whole days together. This, and the stench of the necessary tubs, carried off many.

During our passage, I first saw flying fishes, which surprised me very much; they used frequently to fly across the ship, and many of them fell on the deck. I also now first saw the use of the quadrant; I had often with astonishment seen the mariners make observations with it, and I could not think what it meant. They at last took notice of my surprise; and one of them, willing to increase it, as well as to gratify my curiosity, made me one day look through it. The clouds appeared to me to be land, which disappeared as they passed along. This heightened my wonder; and I was now more persuaded than ever, that I was in another world, and that every thing about me was magic. At last, we came in sight of the island of Barbadoes, at which the whites on board gave a great shout, and made many signs of joy to us. We did not know what to think of this; but as the vessel drew nearer, we plainly saw the harbor, and other ships of different kinds and sizes, and we soon anchored amongst them, off Bridgetown. Many

merchants and planters now came on board, though it was in the
evening. They put us in separate parcels, and examined us at-
tentively. They also made us jump, and pointed to the land,
signifying we were to go there. We thought by this, we should be
eaten by these ugly men, as they appeared to us; and, when soon
after we were all put down under the deck again, there was much
dread and trembling among us, and nothing but bitter cries to
be heard all the night from these apprehensions, insomuch, that
at last the white people got some old slaves from the land to
pacify us. They told us we were not to be eaten, but to work, and
were soon to go on land, where we should see many of our country people. This report eased us much. And sure enough, soon
after we were landed, there came to us Africans of all languages.

We were conducted immediately to the merchant's yard, where
we were all pent up together, like so many sheep in a fold, without regard to sex or age. As every object was new to me, everything I saw filled me with surprise. What struck me first, was,
that the houses were built with bricks and stories, and in every
other respect different from those I had seen in Africa; but I was
still more astonished on seeing people on horseback. I did not
know what this could mean; and, indeed, I thought these people
were full of nothing but magical arts. While I was in this
astonishment, one of my fellow prisoners spoke to a countryman
of his, about the horses, who said they were the same kind they
had in their country. I understood them, though they were from
a distant part of Africa; and I thought it odd I had not seen any
horses there; but afterwards, when I came to converse with different Africans, I found they had many horses amongst them, and
much larger than those I then saw.

We were not many days in the merchant's custody, before we
were sold after their usual manner, which is this: On a signal
given (as the beat of a drum), the buyers rush at once into the
yard where the slaves are confined, and make choice of that parcel
they like best. The noise and clamor with which this is attended,
and the eagerness visible in the countenances of the buyers, serve
not a little to increase the apprehension of terrified Africans, who
may well be supposed to consider them as the ministers of that
destruction to which they think themselves devoted. In this manner, without scruple, are relations and friends separated, most of

them never to see each other again. I remember, in the vessel in which I was brought over, in the men's apartment, there were several brothers, who, in the sale, were sold in different lots; and it was very moving on this occasion, to see and hear their cries at parting. O, ye nominal Christians! might not an African ask you —Learned you this from your God, who says unto you, Do unto all men as you would men should do unto you? Is it not enough that we are torn from our country and friends, to toil for your luxury and lust of gain? Must every tender feeling be likewise sacrificed to your avarice? Are the dearest friends and relations, now rendered more dear by their separation from their kindred, still to be parted from each other, and thus prevented from cheering the gloom of slavery, with the small comfort of being together, and mingling their sufferings and sorrows? Why are parents to lose their children, brothers their sisters, or husbands their wives? Surely, this is a new refinement in cruelty, which, while it has no advantage to atone for it, thus aggravates distress, and adds fresh horrors even to the wretchedness of slavery.

Chapter 3

The author is carried to Virginia—His distress—Surprise at seeing a picture and a watch—Is bought by Captain Pascal, and sets out for England—His terror during the voyage—Arrives in England—His wonder at a fall of snow—Is sent to Guernsey, and in some time goes on board a ship of war with his master—Some account of the expedition against Louisburg under the command of Admiral Boscawen, in 1758.

I NOW TOTALLY LOST the small remains of comfort I had enjoyed in conversing with my countrymen; the women too, who used to wash and take care of me were all gone different ways, and I never saw one of them afterwards.

I stayed in this island for a few days, I believe it could not be above a fortnight, when I, and some few more slaves, that were not saleable amongst the rest, from very much fretting, were shipped off in a sloop for North America. On the passage we were better treated than when we were coming from Africa, and we had plenty of rice and fat pork. We were landed up a river a good way from the sea, about Virginia county, where we saw few or none of our native Africans, and not one soul who could talk to me. I was a few weeks weeding grass and gathering stones in a plantation; and at last all my companions were distributed different ways, and only myself was left. I was now exceedingly miserable, and thought myself worse off than any of the rest of my companions, for they could talk to each other, but I had no person to speak to that I could understand. In this state, I was constantly grieving and pining, and wishing for death rather than anything else. While I was in this plantation, the gentleman, to whom I suppose the estate belonged, being unwell, I was one day sent for to his dwelling-house to fan him; when I came into the room where he was I was very much affrighted at some things I saw, and the more so as I had seen a black woman slave as I came through the house, who was cooking the dinner, and the poor creature was cruelly loaded with various kinds of iron machines; she had one particularly on her head, which locked her mouth so fast that she could scarcely speak; and could not eat nor drink. I was much astonished and shocked at this contrivance, which I afterwards learned was called the iron muzzle. Soon after

I had a fan put in my hand, to fan the gentleman while he slept; and so I did indeed with great fear. While he was fast asleep I indulged myself a great deal in looking about the room, which to me appeared very fine and curious. The first object that engaged my attention was a watch which hung on the chimney, and was going. I was quite surprised at the noise it made, and was afraid it would tell the gentleman anything I might do amiss; and when I immediately after observed a picture hanging in the room, which appeared constantly to look at me, I was still more affrighted, having never seen such things as these before. At one time I thought it was something relative to magic; and not seeing it move, I thought it might be some way the whites had to keep their great men when they died, and offer them libations as we used to do our friendly spirits. In this state of anxiety I remained till my master awoke, when I was dismissed out of the room, to my no small satisfaction and relief; for I thought that these people were all made up of wonders. In this place I was called Jacob; but on board the *African Snow,* I was called Michael. I had been some time in this miserable, forlorn, and much dejected state, without having anyone to talk to, which made my life a burden, when the kind and unknown hand of the Creator (who in very deed leads the blind in a way they know not) now began to appear, to my comfort; for one day the captain of a merchant ship, called the *Industrious Bee,* came on some business to my master's house. This gentleman, whose name was Michael Henry Pascal, was a lieutenant in the royal navy, but now commanded this trading ship, which was somewhere in the confines of the county many miles off. While he was at my master's house, it happened that he saw me, and liked me so well that he made a purchase of me. I think I have often heard him say he gave thirty or forty pounds sterling for me; but I do not remember which. However, he meant me for a present to some of his friends in England: and as I was sent accordingly from the house of my then master (one Mr. Campbell) to the place where the ship lay; I was conducted on horseback by an elderly black man (a mode of travelling which appeared very odd to me). When I arrived I was carried on board a fine large ship, loaded with tobacco, &c., and just ready to sail for England. I now thought my condition much mended; I had sails to lie on, and plenty of good victuals to eat; and everybody on board used me very kindly, quite contrary to what I had seen of any white people before; I therefore began to think that they were not all of the same disposition. A few days after I was on board we sailed for England. I was still at a loss to conjecture my destiny. By this time, however, I could smatter a little imperfect English; and I wanted to know as well as I could where we were going. Some of the people of the ship used to tell me they were going to carry me back to my own country, and this made me very happy. I was quite rejoiced at the idea of going back, and thought if I could get home what wonders I should have to tell. But I was reserved for another fate, and was soon undeceived when we came within sight of the English coast. While I was on board this ship, my captain and master named me *Gustavus Vassa*. I at that time began to understand him a little, and refused to be called so, and told him as well as I could that I would be called Jacob; but he said I should not, and still called me Gustavus: and when I refused to answer to my new name, which I at first did, it gained me many a cuff; so at length I submitted, and by which I have been known ever since. The ship had a very long passage; and on that account we had very short allowance of provisions. Towards the last, we had only one pound and a half of bread per week, and about the same quantity of meat, and one quart of water a day. We spoke with only one vessel the whole time we were at sea, and but once we caught a few fishes. In our extremities the captain and people told me in jest they would kill and eat me; but I thought them in earnest, and was depressed beyond measure, expecting every moment to be my last. While I was in this situation, one evening they caught, with a good deal of trouble, a large shark, and got it on board. This gladdened my poor heart exceedingly, as I thought it would serve the people to eat instead of their eating me; but very soon, to my astonishment, they cut off a small part of the tail, and tossed the rest over the side. This renewed my consternation; and I did not know what to think of these white people, though I very much feared they would kill and eat me. There was on board the ship a young lad who had never been at sea before, about four or five years older than myself: his name was Richard Baker. He was a native of America, had received an excellent education, and was of a most amiable temper. Soon after I went on board, he showed me a great deal of partiality and attention, and in return I grew extremely fond of him. We at length became inseparable; and, for the space of two years, he was of very great use to me, and was my constant companion and instructor. Although this dear youth had many slaves of his own, yet he and I have gone through many sufferings together on shipboard; and we have many nights lain in each other's bosoms when we were in great distress. Thus such a friendship was cemented between us as we cherished till his death, which, to my very great sorrow, happened in the year 1759, when he was up the Archipelago, on board his Majesty's ship the *Preston:* an event which I have never ceased to regret, as I lost at once a kind interpreter, an agreeable companion, and a faithful friend; who, at the age of fifteen, discovered a mind superior to prejudice; and who was not ashamed to notice, to associate with, and to be the friend and instructor of one who was ignorant, a stranger, of a different complexion, and a slave! My master had lodged in his mother's house in America; he respected him very much, and made him always eat with him in the cabin. He used often to tell him jocularly that he would kill and eat me. Sometimes he would say to me—the black people were not good to eat, and would ask me if we did not eat people in my country. I said, No; then he said he would kill Dick (as he always called him) first, and afterwards me. Though this hearing relieved my mind a little as to myself, I was alarmed for Dick, and whenever he was called I used to be very much afraid he was to be killed; and I would peep and watch to see if they were going to kill him; nor was I free from this consternation till we made the land. One night we lost a man overboard; and the cries and noise were so great and confused, in stopping the ship, that I, who did not know what was the matter, began, as usual, to be very much afraid, and to think they were going to make an offering with me, and perform some magic; which I still believed they dealt in. As the waves were very high, I thought the Ruler of the seas was angry, and I expected to be offered up to appease him. This filled my mind with agony, and I could not any more, that night, close my eyes again to rest. However, when daylight appeared, I was a little eased in my mind; but still, every time I was called, I used to think it was to be killed. Some time after this, we saw some very large fish, which

I afterwards found were called grampusses. They looked to me exceedingly terrible, and made their appearance just at dusk, and were so near as to blow the water on the ship's deck. I believed them to be the rulers of the sea; and as the white people did not make any offerings at any time, I thought they were angry with them; and, at last, what confirmed my belief was, the wind just then died away, and a calm ensued, and in consequence of it the ship stopped going. I supposed that the fish had performed this, and I hid myself in the fore part of the ship, through fear of being offered up to appease them, every minute peeping and quaking; but my good friend Dick came shortly towards me, and I took an opportunity to ask him, as well as I could, what these fish were. Not being able to talk much English, I could but just make him understand my question; and not at all, when I asked him if any offerings were to be made to them; however, he told me these fish would swallow anybody which sufficiently alarmed me. Here he was called away by the captain, who was leaning over the quarter-deck railing, and looking at the fish; and most of the people were busied in getting a barrel of pitch to light for them to play with. The captain now called me to him, having learned some of my apprehensions from Dick; and having diverted himself and others for some time with my fears, which appeared ludicrous enough in my crying and trembling, he dismissed me. The barrel of pitch was now lighted and put over the side into the water. By this time it was just dark, and the fish went after it; and, to my great joy, I saw them no more.

However, all my alarms began to subside when we got sight of land; and at last the ship arrived at Falmouth, after a passage of thirteen weeks. Every heart on board seemed gladdened on our reaching the shore, and none more than mine. The captain immediately went on shore, and sent on board some fresh provisions, which we wanted very much. We made good use of them, and our famine was soon turned into feasting, almost without ending. It was about the beginning of the spring 1757, when I arrived in England, and I was near twelve years of age at that time. I was very much struck with the buildings and the pavement of the streets in Falmouth; and, indeed, every object I saw, filled me with new surprise. One morning, when I got upon deck, I saw it covered all over with the snow that fell over night. As I had never seen anything of the kind before, I thought it was salt: so I immediately ran down to the mate, and desired him, as well as I could, to come and see how somebody in the night had thrown salt all over the deck. He, knowing what it was, desired me to bring some of it down to him. Accordingly I took up a handful of it, which I found very cold indeed; and when I brought it to him he desired me to taste it. I did so, and I was surprised beyond measure. I then asked him what it was; he told me it was snow, but I could not in anywise understand him. He asked me, if we had no such thing in my country; I told him, No. I then asked him the use of it, and who made it; he told me a great man in the heavens, called God. But here again I was to all intents and purposes at a loss to understand him; and the more so, when a little after I saw the air filled with it, in a heavy shower, which fell down on the same day. After this I went to church; and having never been at such a place before, I was again amazed at seeing and hearing the service. I asked all I could about it, and they gave me to understand it was worshipping God, who made us and all things. I was still at a great loss, and soon got into an endless field of inquiries, as well as I was able to speak and ask about things. However, my little friend Dick used to be my best interpreter; for I could make free with him, and he always instructed me with pleasure. And from what I could understand by him of this God, and in seeing these white people did not sell one another as we did, I was much pleased; and in this I thought they were much happier than we Africans. I was astonished at the wisdom of the white people in all things I saw; but was amazed at their not sacrificing, or making any offerings, and eating with unwashed hands, and touching the dead. I likewise could not help remarking the particular slenderness of their women, which I did not at first like; and I thought they were not so modest and shame-faced as the African women.

I had often seen my master and Dick employed in reading; and I had a great curiosity to talk to the books as I thought they did, and so to learn how all things had a beginning. For that purpose I have often taken up a book, and have talked to it, and then put my ears to it, when alone, in hopes it would answer me; and I have been very much concerned when I found it remained silent.

My master lodged at the house of a gentleman in Falmouth, who had a fine little daughter about six or seven years of age, and she grew prodigiously fond of me, insomuch that we used to eat together, and had servants to wait on us. I was so much caressed by this family that it often reminded me of the treatment I had received from my little noble African master. After I had been here a few days, I was sent on board of the ship; but the child cried so much after me that nothing could pacify her till I was sent for again. It is ludicrous enough, that I began to fear I should be betrothed to this young lady; and when my master asked me if I would stay there with her behind him, as he was going away with the ship, which had taken in the tobacco again, I cried immediately, and said I would not leave him. At last, by stealth, one night I was sent on board the ship again; and in a little time we sailed for Guernsey, where she was in part owned by a merchant, one Nicholas Doberry. As I was now amongst a people who had not their faces scarred, like some of the African nation where I had been, I was very glad I did not let them ornament me in that manner when I was with them. When we arrived at Guernsey, my master placed me to board and lodge with one of his mates, who had a wife and family there; and some months afterwards he went to England, and left me in care of this mate, together with my friend Dick. This mate had a little daughter, aged about five or six years, with whom I used to be much delighted. I had often observed that when her mother washed her face it looked very rosy, but when she washed mine it did not look so. I therefore tried oftentimes myself if I could not by washing make my face of the same color as my little play-mate, Mary, but it was all in vain; and I now began to be mortified at the difference in our complexions. This woman behaved to me with great kindness and attention, and taught me everything in the same manner as she did her own child, and, indeed, in every respect, treated me as such. I remained here till the summer of the year 1757, when my master, being appointed first lieutenant of his Majesty's ship the *Roebuck,* sent for Dick and me, and his old mate. On this we all left Guernsey, and set out for England in a sloop, bound for London. As we were coming up towards the Nore, where the *Roebuck* lay, a man-of-war's boat came along side to press our people, on which each man run to hide himself.

I was very much frightened at this, though I did not know what it meant, or what to think or do. However I went and hid myself also under a hencoop. Immediately afterwards, the press-gang came on board with their swords drawn, and searched all about, pulled the people out by force, and put them into the boat. At last I was found out also; the man that found me held me up by the heels while they all made their sport of me, I roaring and crying out all the time most lustily; but at last the mate, who was my conductor, seeing this, came to my assistance, and did all he could to pacify me; but all to very little purpose, till I had seen the boat go off. Soon afterwards we came to the Nore, where the *Roebuck* lay; and, to our great joy, my master came on board to us, and brought us to the ship. When I went on board this large ship, I was amazed indeed to see the quantity of men and the guns. However, my surprise began to diminish as my knowledge increased; and I ceased to feel those apprehensions and alarms which had taken such strong possession of me when I first came among the Europeans, and for some time after. I began now to pass to an opposite extreme; I was so far from being afraid of anything new which I saw, that after I had been some time in this ship, I even began to long for an engagement. My griefs, too, which in young minds are not perpetual, were now wearing away; and I soon enjoyed myself pretty well, and felt tolerably easy in my present situation. There was a number of boys on board, which still made it more agreeable; for we were always together, and a great part of our time was spent in play. I remained in this ship a considerable time, during which we made several cruises, and visited a variety of places; among others we were twice in Holland, and brought over several persons of distinction from it, whose names I do not now remember. On the passage, one day, for the diversion of those gentlemen, all the boys were called on the quarter-deck, and were paired proportionably, and then made to fight; after which the gentlemen gave the combatants from five to nine shillings each. This was the first time I ever fought with a white boy; and I never knew what it was to have a bloody nose before. This made me fight most desperately, I suppose considerably more than an hour; and at last, both of us being weary, we were parted. I had a great deal of this kind of sport afterwards, in which the captain and the ship's company used very much to encourage me. Sometime afterwards, the ship went to Leith in Scotland, and from thence to the Orkneys, where I was surprised in seeing scarcely any night; and from thence we sailed with a great fleet, full of soldiers, for England. All this time we had never come to an engagement, though we were frequently cruising off the coast of France; during which we chased many vessels, and took in all seventeen prizes. I had been learning many of the manœuvres of the ship during our cruise; and I was several times made to fire the guns. One evening, off Havre de Grace, just as it was growing dark, we were standing off shore, and met with a fine large French built frigate. We got all things immediately ready for fighting; and I now expected I should be gratified in seeing an engagement, which I had so long wished for in vain. But the very moment the word of command was given to fire, we heard those on board the other ship cry, "Haul down the jib"; and in that instant she hoisted English colors. There was instantly with us an amazing cry of— "Avast!" or stop firing; and I think one or two guns had been let off, but happily they did no mischief. We had hailed them several times, but they not hearing, we received no answer, which was the cause of our firing. The boat was then sent on board of her, and she proved to be the *Ambuscade*, man-of-war, to my no small disappointment. We returned to Portsmouth, without having been in any action, just at the trial of Admiral Byng (whom I saw several times during it); and my master having left the ship, and gone to London for promotion, Dick and I were put on board the *Savage*, sloop-of-war, and we went in her to assist in bringing off the *St. George*, man-of-war, that had run ashore somewhere on the coast. After staying a few weeks on board the *Savage*, Dick and I were sent on shore at Deal, where we remained some short time, till my master sent for us to London, the place I had long desired exceedingly to see. We therefore both with great pleasure got into a wagon, and came to London, where we were received by a Mr. Guerin, a relation of my master. This gentleman had two sisters, very amiable ladies, who took much notice and great care of me. Though I had desired so much to see London, when I arrived in it I was unfortunately unable to gratify my curiosity; for I had at this time the chilblains to such a degree that I could not stand for several months, and I was obliged to be sent to St. George's hospital. There I grew so ill that the doctors wanted to cut my left leg off, at different times, apprehending a mortification; but I always said I would rather die than suffer it, and happily (I thank God) I recovered without the operation. After being there several weeks, and just as I had recovered, the smallpox broke out on me, so that I was again confined; and I thought myself now particularly unfortunate. However, I soon recovered again; and by this time, my master having been promoted to be first lieutenant of the *Preston*, man-of-war, of fifty guns, then new at Deptford, Dick and I were sent on board her, and soon after, we went to Holland to bring over the late Duke of —— to England. While I was in the ship an incident happened, which, though trifling, I beg leave to relate, as I could not help taking particular notice of it, and considered it then as a judgment of God. One morning a young man was looking up to the foretop, and in a wicked tone, common on shipboard, d——d his eyes about something. Just at the moment some small particles of dirt fell into his left eye, and by the evening it was very much inflamed. The next day it grew worse, and within six or seven days he lost it. From this ship my master was appointed a lieutenant on board the *Royal George*. When he was going he wished me to stay on board the *Preston*, to learn the French horn; but the ship being ordered for Turkey, I could not think of leaving my master, to whom I was very warmly attached; and I told him if he left me behind, it would break my heart. This prevailed on him to take me with him; but he left Dick on board the *Preston*, whom I embraced at parting for the last time. The *Royal George* was the largest ship I had ever seen, so that when I came on board of her I was surprised at the number of people, men, women, and children, of every denomination; and the largeness of the guns, many of them also of brass, which I had never seen before. Here were also shops or stalls of every kind of goods, and people crying their different commodities about the ship as in a town. To me it appeared a little world, into which I was again cast without a friend, for I had no longer my dear companion Dick. We did not stay long here. My master was not many weeks on board before he got an appointment to the sixth lieutenant of the *Namur*, which was then at Spithead, fitting up for Vice-admiral Boscawen, who was going with a large

fleet on an expedition against Louisburg. The crew of the
Royal George were turned over to her, and the flag of that gallant
admiral was hoisted on board, the blue at the maintop gallant
mast head. There was a very great fleet of men-of-war of
every description assembled together for this expedition, and I
was in hopes soon to have an opportunity of being gratified with
a sea-fight. All things being now in readiness, this mighty fleet
(for there was also Admiral Cornish's fleet in company, destined
for the East Indies) at last weighed anchor, and sailed. The two
fleets continued in company for several days, and then parted;
Admiral Cornish, in the *Lenox,* having first saluted our Admiral
in the *Namur,* which he returned. We then steered for America;
but, by contrary winds, we were driven to Tenerife, where I was
struck with its noted peak. Its prodigious height, and its form,
resembling a sugar loaf, filled me with wonder. We remained in
sight of this island some days, and then proceeded for America,
which we soon made, and got into a very commodious harbor
called St. George, in Halifax, where we had fish in great plenty,
and all other fresh provisions. We were here joined by different
men-of-war and transport ships with soldiers; after which, our
fleet being increased to a prodigious number of ships of all kinds,
we sailed for Cape Breton in Nova Scotia. We had the good and
gallant General Wolfe on board our ship, whose affability made
him highly esteemed and beloved by all the men. He often
honored me, as well as other boys, with marks of his notice, and
saved me once a flogging for fighting with a young gentleman.
We arrived at Cape Breton in the summer of 1758; and here the
soldiers were to be landed, in order to make an attack upon
Louisburg. My master had some part in superintending the landing; and here I was in a small measure gratified in seeing an
encounter between our men and the enemy. The French were
posted on the shore to receive us, and disputed our landing for a
long time; but at last they were driven from their trenches, and
a complete landing was effected. Our troops pursued them as far
as the town of Louisburg. In this action many were killed on both
sides. One thing remarkable I saw this day. A lieutenant of the
Princess Amelia, who, as well as my master, superintended the
landing, was giving the word of command, and while his mouth
was open, a musket ball went through it, and passed out at his

cheek. I had that day, in my hand, the scalp of an Indian king, who was killed in the engagement; the scalp had been taken off by an Highlander. I saw the king's ornaments too, which were very curious, and made of feathers.

Our land forces laid siege to the town of Louisburg, while the French men-of-war were blocked up in the harbor by the fleet, the batteries at the same time playing upon them from the land. This they did with such effect, that one day I saw some of the ships set on fire by the shells from the batteries, and I believe two or three of them were quite burnt. At another time, about fifty boats belonging to the English men-of-war, commanded by Captain George Belfour, of the *Etna*, fire ship, and Mr. Laforey, another junior Captain, attacked and boarded the only two remaining French men-of-war in the harbor. They also set fire to a seventy-gun ship, but a sixty-four, called the *Bienfaisant*, they brought off. During my stay here, I had often an opportunity of being near Captain Belfour, who was pleased to notice me, and liked me so much that he often asked my master to let him have me, but he would not part with me; and no consideration could have induced me to leave him. At last, Louisburg was taken, and the English men-of-war came into the harbor before it, to my very great joy; for I had now more liberty of indulging myself, and I went often on shore. When the ships were in the harbor, we had the most beautiful procession on the water I ever saw. All the Admirals and Captains of the men-of-war, full dressed, and in their barges, well ornamented with pendants, came alongside of the *Namur*. The Vice-admiral then went on shore in his barge, followed by the other officers in order of seniority, to take possession, as I suppose, of the town and fort. Some time after this, the French governor and his lady, and other persons of note, came on board our ship to dine. On this occasion our ships were dressed with colors of all kinds, from the topgallant mast head to the deck; and this, with the firing of guns, formed a most grand and magnificent spectacle.

As soon as everything here was settled, Admiral Boscawen sailed with part of the fleet for England, leaving some ships behind with Rear-admirals Sir Charles Hardy and Durell. It was now winter; and one evening, during our passage home, about dusk, when we were in the channel, or near soundings, and were beginning to look for land, we descried seven sail of large men-of-war, which stood off shore. Several people on board of our ship said, as the two fleets were (in forty minutes from the first sight) within hail of each other, that they were English men-of-war; and some of our people even began to name some of the ships. By this time both fleets began to mingle, and our Admiral ordered his flag to be hoisted. At that instant, the other fleet, which were French, hoisted their ensigns, and gave us a broadside as they passed by. Nothing could create greater surprise and confusion among us than this. The wind was high, the sea rough, and we had our lower and middle deck guns housed in, so that not a single gun on board was ready to be fired at any of the French ships. However, the *Royal William* and the *Somerset,* being our sternmost ships, became a little prepared, and each gave the French ships a broadside as they passed by. I afterwards heard this was a French squadron, commanded by Monsieur Constans; and certainly, had the Frenchmen known our condition, and had a mind to fight us, they might have done us great mischief. But we were not long before we were prepared for an engagement. Immediately many things were tossed overboard, the ships were made ready for fighting as soon as possible, and about ten at night we had bent a new main-sail, the old one being split. Being now in readiness for fighting, we wore ship, and stood after the French fleet, who were one or two ships in number more than we. However we gave them chase, and continued pursuing them all night; and at day-light we saw six of them, all large ships of the line, and an English East Indiaman, a prize they had taken. We chased them all day till between three and four o'clock in the evening, when we came up with, and passed within a musket shot of one seventy-four–gun ship, and the Indiaman also, who now hoisted her colors, but immediately hauled them down again. On this we made a signal for the other ships to take possession of her; and, supposing the man-of-war would likewise strike, we cheered, but she did not; though if we had fired into her, from being so near we must have taken her. To my utter surprise, the *Somerset,* who was the next ship astern of the *Namur,* made way likewise; and, thinking they were sure of this French ship, they cheered in the same manner, but still continued to follow us. The French Commodore was about a gun-shot ahead of all, running from us with all speed; and about four o'clock he carried his foretopmast overboard. This caused another loud cheer with us; and a little after the topmast came close by us; but, to our great surprise, instead of coming up with her, we found she went as fast as ever, if not faster. The sea grew now much smoother; and the wind lulling, the seventy-four–gun ship we had passed, came again by us in the very same direction, and so near that we heard her people talk as she went by, yet not a shot was fired on either side; and about five or six o'clock, just as it grew dark, she joined her Commodore. We chased all night; but the next day we were out of sight, so that we saw no more of them; and we only had the old Indiaman (called *Carnarvon,* I think) for our trouble. After this we stood in for the channel, and soon made the land; and, about the close of the year 1758–9, we got safe to St. Helen's. Here the *Namur* ran aground, and also another large ship astern of us; but, by starting our water, and tossing many things overboard to lighten her, we got the ships off without any damage. We stayed for a short time at Spithead, and then went into Portsmouth harbor to refit. From whence the Admiral went to London; and my master and I soon followed, with a press-gang, as we wanted some hands to complete our complement.

Chapter 4

The author is baptized—Narrowly escapes drowning—Goes on an expedition to the Mediterranean—Incidents he met with there—Is witness to an engagement between some English and French ships—A particular account of the celebrated engagement between Admiral Boscawen and Monsieur Le Clue, off Cape Logas, in August 1759—Dreadful explosion of a French ship—The author sails for England—His master appointed to the command of a fire ship—Meets a Negro boy, from whom he experiences much benevolence—Prepares for an expedition against Belle Isle—A remarkable story of a disaster which befell his ship —Arrives at Belle Isle—Operations of the landing and siege—The author's danger and distress, with his manner of extricating himself—Surrender of Belle Isle—Transactions afterwards on the coast of France—Remarkable instance of kidnapping—The author returns to England—Hears a talk of peace, and expects his freedom—His ship sails for Deptford to be paid off, and when he arrives there he is suddenly seized by his master and carried forcibly on board a West India ship and sold.

IT WAS NOW between two and three years since I first came to England, a great part of which I had spent at sea; so that I became inured to that service, and began to consider myself as happily situated, for my master treated me always extremely well; and my attachment and gratitude to him were very great. From the various scenes I had beheld on shipboard, I soon grew a stranger to terror of every kind, and was, in that respect at least, almost an Englishman. I have often reflected with surprise that I never felt half the alarm at any of the numerous dangers I have been in, that I was filled with at the first sight of the Europeans, and at every act of theirs, even the most trifling, when I first came among them, and for some time afterwards. That fear, however, which was the effect of my ignorance, wore away as I began to know them. I could now speak English tolerably well, and I perfectly understood everything that was said. I not only felt myself quite easy with these new countrymen, but relished their society and manners. I no longer looked upon them as spirits, but as men superior to us; and therefore I had the stronger desire to resemble them, to imbibe their spirit, and imitate their manners. I therefore embraced every occasion of improvement, and every new thing that I observed I treasured up in my memory. I had long wished to be able to read and write; and for this purpose I took every opportunity to gain instruction, but had made as yet very little progress. However, when I went to London with my master, I had soon an opportunity of improving myself, which I gladly embraced. Shortly after my arrival, he sent me to wait upon the Miss Guerins, who had treated me with much kindness when I was there before; and they sent me to school.

While I was attending these ladies, their servants told me I could not go to Heaven unless I was baptized. This made me very uneasy, for I had now some faint idea of a future state. Accordingly I communicated my anxiety to the eldest Miss Guerin, with whom I was become a favorite, and pressed her to have me baptized; when to my great joy, she told me I should. She had formerly asked my master to let me be baptized, but he had refused. However she now insisted on it; and he being under some obligation to her brother, complied with her request. So I was baptized in St. Margaret's church, Westminster, in February 1759, by my present name. The clergyman at the same time, gave me a book, called *A Guide to the Indians,* written by the Bishop of Sodor and Man. On this occasion, Miss Guerin did me the honor to stand as god-mother, and afterwards gave me a treat. I used to attend these ladies about the town, in which service I was extremely happy; as I had thus many opportunities of seeing London, which I desired of all things. I was sometimes, however, with my master at his rendezvous house, which was at the foot of Westminster bridge. Here I used to enjoy myself in playing about the bridge stairs, and often in the waterman's wherries, with other boys. On one of these occasions there was another boy with me in a wherry, and we went out into the current of the river; while we were there, two more stout boys came to us in another wherry, and abusing us for taking the boat, desired me to get into the other wherry-boat. Accordingly, I went to get out of the wherry I was in, but just as I had got one of my feet into the other boat, the boys shoved it off, so that I fell into the Thames; and, not being able to swim, I should unavoidably have been drowned, but for the assistance of some watermen who providentially came to my relief.

The *Namur* being again got ready for sea, my master, with his gang, was ordered on board; and, to my no small grief, I was obliged to leave my school-master, whom I liked very much, and always attended while I stayed in London, to repair on board with my master. Nor did I leave my kind patronesses, the Miss Guerins, without uneasiness and regret. They often used to teach me to read, and took great pains to instruct me in the principles of religion and the knowledge of God. I therefore parted from those amiable ladies with reluctance, after receiving from them many friendly cautions how to conduct myself, and some valuable presents.

When I came to Spithead, I found we were destined for the Mediterranean, with a large fleet, which was now ready to put to sea. We only waited for the arrival of the Admiral, who soon came on board. And about the beginning of the spring of 1759, having weighed anchor, and got under way, sailed for the Mediterranean; and in eleven days, from the Land's End, we got to Gibraltar. While we were here I used to be often on shore, and got various fruits in great plenty, and very cheap.

I had frequently told several people, in my excursions on shore, the story of my being kidnapped with my sister, and of our being separated, as I have related before; and I had as often expressed my anxiety for her fate, and my sorrow at having never met her again. One day, when I was on shore, and mentioning these circumstances to some persons, one of them told me he knew where my sister was, and, if I would accompany him, he would bring me to her. Improbable as this story was, I believed it immediately, and agreed to go with him, while my heart leaped for joy; and, indeed, he conducted me to a black young woman, who was so like my sister, that at first sight, I really. thought it was her; but I was quickly undeceived. And, on talking to her, I found her to be of another nation.

While we lay here, the *Preston* came in from the Levant. As soon as she arrived, my master told me I should now see my old companion, Dick, who was gone in her when she sailed for Turkey. I was much rejoiced at this news, and expected every minute to embrace him; and when the captain came on board of our ship, which he did immediately after, I ran to inquire after my friend; but, with inexpressible sorrow, I learned from the boat's crew that the dear youth was dead! and that they had brought his chest, and all his other things, to my master. These he afterwards gave to me, and I regarded them as a memorial of my friend, whom I loved, and grieved for, as a brother.

While we were at Gibraltar, I saw a soldier hanging by the heels, at one of the moles.* I thought this a strange sight, as I had seen a man hanged in London by his neck. At another time I saw the master of a frigate towed to shore on a grating, by several of the men-of-war's boats, and discharged the fleet, which I understood was a mark of disgrace for cowardice. On board the same ship there was also a sailor hung up at the yard-arm.

After laying at Gibraltar for some time, we sailed up the Mediterranean, a considerable way above the Gulf of Lyons; where we were one night overtaken with a terrible gale of wind, much greater than any I had ever yet experienced. The sea ran so high, that, though all the guns were well housed, there was great reason to fear their getting loose, the ship rolled so much; and if they had, it must have proved our destruction. After we had cruised here for a short time, we came to Barcelona, a Spanish sea-port, remarkable for its silk manufactures. Here the ships were all to be watered; and my master, who spoke different languages, and used often to interpret for the Admiral, super-intended the watering of ours. For that purpose, he and the other officers of the ship, who were on the same service, had tents pitched in the bay; and the Spanish soldiers were stationed along the shore, I suppose to see that no depredations were committed by our men.

I used constantly to attend my master; and I was charmed with this place. All the time we stayed it was like a fair with the natives, who brought us fruits of all kinds, and sold them to us much cheaper than I got them in England. They used also to bring wine down to us in hog and sheep skins, which diverted me very much. The Spanish officers here treated our officers with great politeness and attention; and some of them, in particular, used to come often to my master's tent to visit him; where they would sometimes divert themselves by mounting me on the horses or mules, so that I could not fall, and setting them off at

---

* He had drowned himself in endeavoring to desert.

full gallop; my imperfect skill in horsemanship all the while affording them no small entertainment. After the ships were watered, we returned to our old station of cruising off Toulon, for the purpose of intercepting a fleet of French men-of-war that lay there. One Sunday, in our cruise, we came off a place where there were two small French frigates laying in shore; and our Admiral, thinking to take or destroy them, sent two ships in after them— the *Culloden* and the *Conqueror*. They soon came up to the Frenchmen, and I saw a smart fight here, both by sea and land; for the frigates were covered by batteries, and they played upon our ships most furiously, which they as furiously returned; and for a long time a constant firing was kept up on all sides at an amazing rate. At last, one frigate sunk; but the people escaped, though not without much difficulty. And soon after, some of the people left the other frigate also, which was a mere wreck. However, our ships did not venture to bring her away, they were so much annoyed from the batteries, which raked them both in going and coming. Their topmasts were shot away, and they were otherwise so much shattered, that the Admiral was obliged to send in many boats to tow them back to the fleet. I afterwards sailed with a man who fought in one of the French batteries during the engagement, and he told me our ships had done considerable mischief that day, on shore and in the batteries.

After this we sailed for Gibraltar, and arrived there about August 1759. Here we remained with all our sails unbent, while the fleet was watering and doing other necessary things. While we were in this situation, one day the Admiral, with most of the principal officers and many people of all stations, being on shore, about seven o'clock in the evening we were alarmed by signals from the frigates stationed for that purpose; and in an instant there was a general cry that the French fleet was out, and just passing through the straits. The Admiral immediately came on board with some other officers; and it is impossible to describe the noise, hurry, and confusion throughout the whole fleet, in bending their sails and shipping their cables; many people and ship's boats were left on shore in the bustle. We had two captains on board of our ship who came away in the hurry and left their ships to follow. We showed lights from the gun-wales to the main topmast head; and all our lieutenants were employed amongst the fleet to tell the ships not to wait for their captains, but to put the sails to the yards, slip their cables, and follow us; and in this confusion of making ready for fighting, we set out for sea in the dark after the French fleet. Here I could have exclaimed with Ajax,

> O Jove! O father! if it be thy will
> That we must perish, we thy will obey,
> But let us perish by the light of day.

They had got the start of us so far that we were not able to come up with them during the night; but at day light we saw seven sail of the line of battle some miles ahead. We immediately chased them till about four o'clock in the evening, when our ships came up with them; and, though we were about fifteen large ships, our gallant Admiral only fought them with his own division, which consisted of seven; so that we were just ship for ship. We passed by the whole of the enemy's fleet in order to come at their commander, Monsieur La Clue, who was in the *Ocean,* an eighty-four–gun ship. As we passed they all fired on us, and at one time three of them fired together, continuing to do so for some time. Notwithstanding which our Admiral would not suffer a gun to be fired at any of them, to my astonishment; but made us lie on our bellies on the deck until we came quite close to the *Ocean,* who was ahead of them all; when we had orders to pour the whole three tiers into her at once.

The engagement now commenced with great fury on both sides. The *Ocean* immediately returned our fire, and we continued engaged with each other for some time; during which I was frequently stunned with the thundering of the great guns, whose dreadful contents hurried many of my companions into awful eternity. At last the French line was entirely broken, and we obtained the victory, which was immediately proclaimed with loud huzzas and acclamations. We took three prizes, *La Modeste,* of sixty-four guns, and *Le Temeraire* and *Centaur,* of seventy-four guns each. The rest of the French ships took to flight with all the sail they could crowd. Our ship being very much damaged, and quite disabled from pursuing the enemy, the Admiral immediately quitted her, and went in the broken and only boat we had left on board the *Newark,* with which, and some other ships, he went after the French. The *Ocean,* and another large French ship, called the *Redoubtable,* endeavoring to escape, ran ashore at Cape Logas, on the coast of Portugal, and the French Admiral and some of the crew got ashore; but we, finding it impossible to get the ships off, set fire to them both. About midnight I saw the *Ocean* blow up, with a most dreadful explosion. I never beheld a more awful scene. In less than a minute, the midnight for a certain space seemed turned into day by the blaze, which was attended with a noise louder and more terrible than thunder, that seemed to rend every element around us.

My station during the engagement was on the middle deck, where I was quartered with another boy, to bring powder to the aftermost gun; and here I was a witness of the dreadful fate of many of my companions, who, in the twinkling of an eye, were dashed in pieces, and launched into eternity. Happily I escaped unhurt, though the shot and splinters flew thick about me during the whole fight. Towards the latter part of it, my master was wounded, and I saw him carried down to the surgeon; but though I was much alarmed for him, and wished to assist him, I dared not leave my post. At this station, my gun-mate (a partner in bringing powder for the same gun) and I ran a very great risk, for more than half an hour, of blowing up the ship. For, when we had taken the cartridges out of the boxes, the bottoms of many of them proving rotten, the powder ran all about the deck, near the match tub; we scarcely had water enough at the last to throw on it. We were also, from our employment, very much exposed to the enemy's shots; for we had to go through nearly the whole length of the ship to bring the powder. I expected, therefore, every minute to be my last, especially when I saw our men fall so thick about me; but, wishing to guard as much against the dangers as possible, at first I thought it would be safest not to go for the powder till the Frenchmen had fired their broadside; and then, while they were charging, I could go and come with my powder. But immediately afterwards I thought this caution was fruitless; and, cheering myself with the reflection that there was a time allotted for me to die, as well as to be born, I instantly cast off all fear or thought whatever of death, and went through the whole of my duty with alacrity; pleasing myself with the hope, if I survived the battle, of relating it and the dangers I had escaped to the Miss Guerins, and others, when I should return to London.

Our ship suffered very much in this engagement; for, besides the number of our killed and wounded, she was almost torn to pieces, and our rigging so much shattered, that our mizen-mast, main-yard, &c., hung over the side of the ship; so that we were obliged to get many carpenters, and others from some of the ships of the fleet, to assist in setting us in some tolerable order. And, notwithstand which, it took us some time before we were completely refitted; after which we left Admiral Broderick to command, and we, with the prizes, steered for England. On the passage, and as soon as my master was something recovered of his wounds, the Admiral appointed him Captain of the *Etna*, fire ship, on which, he and I left the *Namur*, and went on board of her at sea. I liked this little ship very much. I now became the captain's steward, in which situation I was very happy; for I was extremely well treated by all on board, and I had leisure to improve myself in reading and writing. The latter I had learned a little of before I left the *Namur*, as there was a school on board. When we arrived at Spithead, the *Etna* went into Portsmouth harbor to refit, which being done, we returned to Spithead and joined a large fleet that was thought to be intended against the Havannah; but about that time the king died. Whether that prevented the expedition, I know not, but it caused our ship to be stationed at Cowes, in the isle of Wight, till the beginning of the year sixty-one. Here I spent my time very pleasantly; I was much on shore, all about this delightful island, and found the inhabitants very civil.

While I was here, I met with a trifling incident, which surprised me agreeably. I was one day in a field belonging to a gentleman who had a black boy about my own size; this boy, having observed me from his master's house, was transported at the sight of one of his own countrymen, and ran to meet me with the utmost haste. I, not knowing what he was about, turned a little out of his way at first, but to no purpose. He soon came close to me, and caught hold of me in his arms, as if I had been his brother, though we had never seen each other before. After we had talked together for some time, he took me to his master's house, where I was treated very kindly. This benevolent boy and

I were very happy in frequently seeing each other, till about the month of March 1761, when our ship had orders to fit out again for another expedition. When we got ready, we joined a very large fleet at Spithead, commanded by Commodore Keppel, which was destined against Belle Isle; and, with a number of transport ships, with troops on board, to make a descent on the place, we sailed once more in quest of fame. I longed to engage in new adventures, and see fresh wonders.

I had a mind on which every thing uncommon made its full impression and every event which I considered as marvellous. Every extraordinary escape, or signal deliverance, either of myself or others, I looked upon to be effected by the interposition of Providence. We had not been above ten days at sea, before an incident of this kind happened; which, whatever credit it may obtain from the reader, made no small impression on my mind.

We had on board a gunner whose name was John Mondle, a man of very indifferent morals. This man's cabin was between the decks, exactly over where I lay, abreast of the quarter-deck ladder. One night, the 5th of April, being terrified with a dream, he awoke in so great a fright that he could not rest in his bed any longer, nor even remain in his cabin; and he went upon deck about four o'clock in the morning, extremely agitated. He immediately told those on the deck of the agonies of his mind, and the dream which occasioned it; in which he said he had seen many things very awful, and had been warned by St. Peter to repent, who told him time was short. This he said had greatly alarmed him, and he was determined to alter his life. People generally mock the fears of others, when they are themselves in safety, and some of his shipmates who heard him only laughed at him. However, he made a vow that he never would drink strong liquors again; and he immediately got a light, and gave away his sea-stores of liquor. After which, his agitation still continuing, he began to read the Scriptures, hoping to find some relief; and soon afterwards he laid himself down again on his bed, and endeavored to compose himself to sleep, but to no purpose; his mind still continuing in a state of agony. By this time it was exactly half after seven in the morning. I was then under the half-deck at the great cabin door; and, all at once I heard the people in the waist cry out, most fearfully—"The Lord have mercy upon us! We are all lost! The Lord have mercy upon us!" Mr. Mondle hearing the cries, immediately ran out of his cabin; and we were instantly struck by the *Lynne,* a forty-gun ship, Captain Clark, which nearly run us down. This ship had just put about, and was by the wind, but had not got full headway, or we must all have perished, for the wind was brisk. However, before Mr. Mondle had got four steps from his cabin door, she struck our ship with her cutwater, right in the middle of his bed and cabin, and ran it up to the combings of the quarter-deck hatchway, and above three feet below water, and in a minute there was not a bit of wood to be seen where Mr. Mondle's cabin stood; and he was so near being killed, that some of the splinters tore his face. As Mr. Mondle must inevitably have perished from this accident, had he not been alarmed in the very extraordinary way I have related, I could not help regarding this as an awful interposition of Providence for his preservation. The two ships for some time swung alongside of each other; for ours, being a fire ship, our grappling-irons caught the *Lynne* every way, and the yards and rigging went at an astonishing rate. Our ship was in such a shocking condition that we all thought she would instantly go down, and everyone run for their lives, and got as well as they could on board the *Lynne;* but our lieutenant, being the aggressor, he never quitted the ship. However, when we found she did not sink immediately, the captain came on board again, and encouraged our people to return to try to save her. Many, on this, came back, but some would not venture. Some of the ships in the fleet seeing our situation, immediately sent their boats to our assistance; but it took us the whole day to save the ship, with all their help. And, by using every possible means, particularly strapping her together with many hawsers, and putting a great quantity of tallow below water, where she was damaged, she was kept together. But it was well we did not meet with any gales of wind, or we must have gone to pieces; for we were in such a crazy condition, that we had ships to attend us till we arrived at Belle Isle, the place of our destination; and then we had all things taken out of the ship, and she was properly repaired. This escape of Mr. Mondle, which he, as well as myself, always considered as a singular act of Providence,

I believe had a great influence on his life and conduct ever afterwards.

Now that I am on this subject, I beg leave to relate another instance or two which strongly raised my belief of the particular interposition of Heaven, and which might not otherwise have found a place here, from their insignificance. I belonged, for a few days, in the year 1758, to the *Jason*, of fifty-four guns, at Plymouth; and one night, when I was on board, a woman, with a child at her breast, fell from the upper-deck down into the hold, near the keel. Everyone thought that the mother and child must be both dashed to pieces; but, to our great surprise, neither of them was hurt. I myself one day fell headlong from the upper deck of the *Etna*, down the after-hold, when the ballast was out; and all who saw me fall cried out I was killed, but I received not the least injury. And in the same ship a man fell from the mast-head on the deck, without being hurt. In these, and in many more instances, I thought I could plainly trace the hand of God, without whose permission a sparrow cannot fall. I began to raise my fear from man to him alone, and to call daily on his holy name with fear and reverence. And I trust he heard my supplications, and graciously condescended to answer me according to his holy word, and to implant the seeds of piety in me, even one of the meanest of his creatures.

When we had refitted our ship, and all things were in readiness for attacking the place, the troops on board the transports were ordered to disembark; and my master, as a junior captain, had a share in the command of the landing. This was on the 12th of April. The French were drawn up on the shore, and had made every disposition to oppose the landing of our men, only a small part of them this day being able to effect it; most of them, after fighting with great bravery, were cut off; and General Crawford, with a number of others, were taken prisoners. In this day's engagement we had also our lieutenant killed.

On the 21st of April we renewed our efforts to land the men, while all the men-of-war were stationed along the shore to cover it, and fired at the French batteries and breast-works from early in the morning till about four o'clock in the evening, when our soldiers effected a safe landing. They immediately attacked the French; and, after a sharp encounter, forced them from the batteries. Before the enemy retreated, they blew up several of them, lest they should fall into our hands. Our men now proceeded to besiege the citadel, and my master was ordered on board to superintend the landing of all the materials necessary for carrying on the siege; in which service I mostly attended him. While I was there, I went about to different parts of the island; and one day, particularly, my curiosity almost cost me my life. I wanted very much to see the mode of charging the mortars, and letting off the shells, and for that purpose I went to an English battery, that was but a very few yards from the walls of the citadel. There, indeed, I had an opportunity of completely gratifying myself in seeing the whole operation, and that not without running a very great risk, both from the English shells that burst while I was there, but likewise from those of the French. One of the largest of their shells bursted within nine or ten yards of me. There was a single rock close by, about the size of a butt; and I got instant shelter under it in time to avoid the fury of the shell. Where it burst, the earth was torn in such a manner that two or three butts might easily have gone into the hole it made, and it threw great quantities of stones and dirt to a considerable distance. Three shot were also fired at me and another boy, who was along with me, one of them in particular seemed

Wing'd with red lightning and impetuous rage;

for, with a most dreadful sound it hissed close by me, and struck a rock at a little distance, which it shattered to pieces. When I saw what perilous circumstances I was in, I attempted to return the nearest way I could find, and thereby I got between the English and the French sentinels. An English sergeant, who commanded the out-posts, seeing me, and surprised how I came there (which was by stealth along the seashore), reprimanded me very severely for it, and instantly took the sentinel off his post into custody, for his negligence in suffering me to pass the lines. While I was in this situation, I observed at a little distance a French horse, belonging to some islanders, which I thought I would now mount, for the greater expedition of getting off. Accordingly I took some cord, which I had about me, and making a kind of bridle of it, I put it round the horse's head, and the tame beast very quietly suffered me to tie him thus, and mount

him. As soon as I was on the horse's back, I began to kick and
beat him, and try every means to make him go quick, but all to
very little purpose; I could not drive him out of a slow pace.
While I was creeping along, still within reach of the enemy's
shot, I met with a servant well mounted on an English horse; I
immediately stopped, and crying, told him my case, and begged
of him to help me, and this he effectually did. For, having a fine
large whip, he began to lash my horse with it so severely that
he set off full speed with me towards the sea, while I was quite
unable to hold or manage him. In this manner I went along till
I came to a craggy precipice. I now could not stop my horse, and
my mind was filled with apprehensions of my deplorable fate,
should he go down the precipice, which he appeared fully disposed to do. I therefore thought I had better throw myself off
him at once, which I did immediately, with a great deal of
dexterity, and fortunately escaped unhurt. As soon as I found
myself at liberty, I made the best of my way for the ship, determined I would not be so foolhardy again in a hurry.

We continued to besiege the citadel till June, when it sur-
rendered. During the siege, I have counted above sixty shells
and carcases in the air at once. When this place was taken, I
went through the citadel, and in the bomb-proofs under it,
which were cut in the solid rock; and I thought it a surprising
place, both for strength and building. Notwithstanding which,
our shots and shells had made amazing devastation, and ruinous
heaps all around it.

After the taking of this island, our ships, with some others,
commanded by Commodore Stanhope, in the *Swiftsure*, went to
Basse road, where we blocked up a French fleet. Our ships were
there from June till February following; and in that time I saw a
great many scenes of war, and stratagems on both sides, to
destroy each other's fleet. Sometimes we would attack the French
with some ships of the line, at other times with boats, and frequently we made prizes. Once or twice the French attacked us
by throwing shells with their bomb-vessels; and one day, as a
French vessel was throwing shells at our ships, she broke from
her springs, behind the isle of I-de-Re. The tide being complicated, she came within a gun-shot of the *Nassau;* but the
Nassau could not bring a gun to bear upon her, and thereby the

Frenchman got off. We were twice attacked by their fire-floats, which they chained together, and then let them float down with the tide; but each time we sent boats with grapplings, and towed them safe out of the fleet.

We had different commanders while we were at this place, Commodores Stanhope, Dennis, Lord Howe, &c. From hence, before the Spanish war began, our ship and the *Wasp* sloop were sent to St. Sebastian, in Spain, by Commodore Stanhope; and Commodore Dennis afterwards sent our ship as a cartel, to Bayonne in France,* after which,† we went in February, in 1762, to Belle Isle, and there stayed till the summer, when we left it, and returned to Portsmouth.

After our ship was fitted out again for service, in September she went to Guernsey, where I was very glad to see my old hostess, who was now a widow, and my former little charming companion, her daughter. I spent some time here very happily with them, till October, when we had orders to repair to Portsmouth. We parted from each other with a great deal of affection; and I promised to return soon, and see them again, not knowing what all powerful fate had determined for me. Our ship having arrived at Portsmouth, we went into the harbor, and remained there till the latter end of November, when we heard great talk about a peace; and, to our very great joy, in the beginning of December we had orders to go up to London with our ship, to be paid off. We received this news with loud huzzas, and every other demonstration of gladness; and nothing but

* Amongst others whom we brought from Bayonne were two gentlemen who had been in the West Indies, where they sold slaves; and they confessed they had made at one time a false bill of sale, and sold two Portuguese white men among a lot of slaves.

† Some people have it, that sometimes shortly before persons die, their ward has been seen; that is, some spirit exactly in their likeness, though they are themselves at other places at the same time. One day while we were at Bayonne, Mr. Mondle saw one of our men, as he thought, in the gun-room; and a little after, coming on the quarter-deck, he spoke of some circumstances of this man to some of the officers. They told him that the man was then out of the ship, in one of the boats with the lieutenant; but Mr. Mondle would not believe it, and we searched the ship, when he found the man was actually out of her; and when the boat returned some time afterwards, we found the man had been drowned at the very time Mr. Mondle thought he saw him.

mirth was to be seen throughout every part of the ship. I too, was not without my share of the general joy on this occasion. I thought now of nothing but being freed, and working for myself, and thereby getting money to enable me to get a good education; for I always had a great desire to be able at least to read and write; and while I was on ship-board, I had endeavored to improve myself in both. While I was in the *Etna,* particularly, the captain's clerk taught me to write, and gave me a smattering of arithmetic, as far as the rule of three. There was also one Daniel Queen, about forty years of age, a man very well educated, who messed with me on board this ship, and he likewise dressed and attended the captain. Fortunately this man soon became very much attached to me, and took very great pains to instruct me in many things. He taught me to shave and dress hair a little, and also to read in the Bible, explaining many passages to me, which I did not comprehend. I was wonderfully surprised to see the laws and rules of my own country written almost exactly here; a circumstance which I believe tended to impress our manners and customs more deeply on my memory. I used to tell him of this resemblance, and many a time we have sat up the whole night together at this employment. In short, he was like a father to me, and some even used to call me after his name; they also styled me the black Christian. Indeed, I almost loved him with the affection of a son. Many things I have denied myself that he might have them; and when I used to play at marbles, or any other game, and won a few half-pence, or got any little money, which I sometimes did, for shaving anyone, I used to buy him a little sugar or tobacco, as far as my stock of money would go. He used to say, that he and I never should part; and that when our ship was paid off, as I was as free as himself, or any other man on board, he would instruct me in his business, by which I might gain a good livelihood. This gave me new life and spirits; and my heart burned within me, while I thought the time long till I obtained my freedom. For though my master had not promised it to me, yet, besides the assurances I had received, that he had no right to detain me, he always treated me with the greatest kindness, and reposed in me an unbounded confidence; he even paid attention to my morals, and would never suffer me to deceive him, or tell lies, of which he used to tell me the consequences; and that if I did so, God would not love me. So that, from all this tenderness, I had never once supposed, in all my dreams of freedom, that he would think of detaining me any longer than I wished.

In pursuance of our orders, we sailed from Portsmouth for the Thames, and arrived at Deptford the 10th of December, where we cast anchor just as it was high water. The ship was up about half an hour, when my master ordered the barge to be manned; and all in an instant, without having before given me the least reason to suspect anything of the matter, he forced me into the barge, saying, I was going to leave him, but he would take care I should not. I was so struck with the unexpectedness of this proceeding, that for some time I did not make a reply, only I made an offer to go for my books and chest of clothes, but he swore I should not move out of his sight, and if I did, he would cut my throat, at the same time taking his hanger. I began, however, to collect myself, and plucking up courage, I told him I was free, and he could not by law serve me so. But this only enraged him the more: and he continued to swear, and said he would soon let me know whether he would or not, and at that instant sprung himself into the barge from the ship, to the astonishment and sorrow of all on board. The tide, rather unluckily for me, had just turned downward, so that we quickly fell down the river along with it, till we came among some outward-bound West Indiamen; for he was resolved to put me on board the first vessel he could get to receive me. The boat's crew, who pulled against their will, became quite faint, different times, and would have gone ashore, but he would not let them. Some of them strove then to cheer me, and told me he could not sell me, and that they would stand by me, which revived me a little, and I still entertained hopes; for, as they pulled along, he asked some vessels to receive me, but they would not. But, just as we had got a little below Gravesend, we came alongside of a ship which was going away the next tide for the West Indies. Her name was the *Charming Sally*, Captain James Doran, and my master went on board, and agreed with him for me; and in a little time I was sent for into the cabin. When I came there, Captain Doran asked me if I knew him. I answered that I did not. "Then," said he, "you are now my slave." I told him my master could not sell me

to him, nor to anyone else. "Why," said he, "did not your master
buy you?" I confessed he did. "But I have served him," said I,
"many years, and he has taken all my wages and prize-money,
for I had only got one six pence during the war; besides this I
have been baptized, and by the laws of the land no man has a
right to sell me." And I added that I had heard a lawyer and
others at different times tell my master so. They both then said
that those people who told me so, were not my friends; but I
replied, "It was very extraordinary that other people did not
know the law as well as they." Upon this, Captain Doran said I
talked too much English; and if I did not behave myself well,
and be quiet, he had a method on board to make me. I was too
well convinced of his power over me to doubt what he said; and
my former sufferings in the slave-ship presenting themselves to
my mind, the recollection of them made me shudder. However,
before I retired I told them that, as I could not get any right
among men here, I hoped I should hereafter in Heaven; and I
immediately left the cabin, filled with resentment and sorrow.
The only coat I had with me my master took away with him,
and said, "If your prize money had been £10,000, I had a right
to it all, and would have taken it." I had about nine guineas,
which, during my long sea-faring life, I had scraped together
from trifling perquisites and little ventures; and I hid it at that
instant, lest my master should take that from me likewise, still
hoping that by some means or other I should make my escape to
the shore; and indeed some of my old shipmates told me not to
despair, for they would get me back again; and that, as soon as
they could get their pay, they would immediately come to Portsmouth to me, where the ship was going. But, alas! all my hopes
were baffled, and the hour of my deliverance as was yet far off.
My master, having soon concluded his bargain with the captain,
came out of the cabin, and he and his people got into the boat
and put off. I followed them with aching eyes as long as I could,
and when they were out of sight I threw myself on the deck,
with a heart ready to burst with sorrow and anguish.

Chapter 5

The author's reflections on his situation—Is deceived by a promise of being delivered—His despair at sailing for the West Indies—Arrives at Montserrat, where he is sold to Mr. King—Various interesting instances of oppression, cruelty, and extortion, which the author saw practised upon the slaves in the West Indies, during his captivity from the year 1763 to 1766—Address on it to the planters.

THUS, at the moment I expected all my toils to end, was I plunged, as I supposed, in a new slavery; in comparison of which, all my service hitherto had been perfect freedom; and whose horrors, always present to my mind, now rushed on it with tenfold aggravation. I wept very bitterly for some time, and began to think I must have done something to displease the Lord, that he thus punished me so severely. This filled me with painful reflections on my past conduct; I recollected that on the morning of our arrival at Deptford, I had rashly sworn that as soon as we reached London, I would spend the day in rambling and sport. My conscience smote me for this unguarded expression. I felt that the Lord was able to disappoint me in all things, and immediately considered my present situation as a judgment of Heaven, on account of my presumption in swearing. I therefore, with contrition of heart, acknowledged my transgression to God, and poured out my soul before him with unfeigned repentance, and with earnest supplications I besought him not to abandon me in my distress, nor cast me from his mercy forever. In a little time, my grief, spent with its own violence, began to subside, and after the first confusion of my thoughts was over, I reflected with more calmness on my present condition. I considered that trials and disappointments are sometimes for our good, and I thought God might perhaps have permitted this, in order to teach me wisdom and resignation; for he had hitherto shadowed me with the wings of his mercy, and by his invisible but powerful hand brought me the way I knew not. These reflections gave me a little comfort, and I rose at last from the deck with dejection and sorrow in my countenance, yet mixed with some faint hope that the Lord would appear for my deliverance.

Soon afterwards, as my new master was going on shore, he

called me to him, and told me to behave myself well, and do the business of the ship the same as any of the rest of the boys, and that I should fare the better for it; but I made him no answer. I was then asked if I could swim, and I said, No. However, I was made to go under the deck, and was well watched. The next tide the ship got under way, and soon after arrived at the Mother Bank, Portsmouth, where she waited a few days for some of the West India convoy. While I was here I tried every means I could devise, amongst the people of the ship, to get me a boat from the shore, as there was none suffered to come alongside of the ship; and their own, whenever it was used, was hoisted in again immediately. A sailor on board took a guinea from me on pretence of getting me a boat, and promised me, time after time, that it was hourly to come off. When he had the watch upon deck, I watched also, and looked long enough, but all in vain; I could never see either the boat or my guinea again. And what I thought was still the worst of all, the fellow gave information, as I afterwards found, all the while to the mates, of my intention to go off, if I could in any way do it; but, rogue-like, he never told them he had got a guinea from me to procure my escape. However, after we had sailed, and his trick was made known to the ship's crew, I had some satisfaction in seeing him detested and despised by them all, for his behavior to me. I was still in hopes that my old shipmates would not forget their promise to come for me at Portsmouth. And, indeed, at last, but not till the day before we sailed, some of them did come there, and sent me off some oranges, and other tokens of their regard. They also sent me word they would come off to me themselves the next day, or the day after; and a lady also, who lived in Gosport, wrote to me that she would come and take me out of the ship at the same time. This lady had been once very intimate with my former master. I used to sell and take care of a great deal of property for her, in different ships; and in return, she always showed great friendship for me, and used to tell my master that she would take me away to live with her. But, unfortunately for me, a disagreement soon afterwards took place between them; and she was succeeded in my master's good graces by another lady, who appeared sole mistress of the *Etna*, and mostly lodged on board. I was not so great a favorite with this lady as with the former;

she had conceived a pique against me on some occasion when she was on board, and she did not fail to instigate my master to treat me in the manner he did.*

However, the next morning, the 30th of December, the wind being brisk and easterly, the *Eolus* frigate, which was to escort the convoy, made a signal for sailing. All the ships then got up their anchors; and, before any of my friends had an opportunity to come off to my relief, to my inexpressible anguish, our ship had got under way. What tumultuous emotions agitated my soul when the convoy got under sail, and I a prisoner on board, now without hope! I kept my swimming eyes upon the land in a state of unutterable grief; not knowing what to do, and despairing how to help myself. While my mind was in this situation, the fleet sailed on, and in one day's time I lost sight of the wished-for land. In the first expression of my grief I reproached my fate, and wished I had never been born. I was ready to curse the tide that bore us, the gale that wafted my prison, and even the ship that conducted us. And I called on death to relieve me from the horrors I felt and dreaded, that I might be in that place

> Where slaves are free, and men oppress no more.
> Fool that I was, inur'd so long to pain,
> To trust to hope, or dream of joy again.
>
>   ❧   ❧   ❧   ❧   ❧   ❧
>
> Now dragg'd once more beyond the western main,
> To groan beneath some dastard planter's chain;
> Where my poor countrymen in bondage wait
> The long enfranchisement of a ling'ring fate.
> Hard ling'ring fate! while, ere the dawn of day,
> Rous'd by the lash they go their cheerless way;
> And as their souls with shame and anguish burn,
> Salute with groans unwelcome morn's return;
> And, chiding ev'ry hour the slow pac'd sun,

* Thus was I sacrificed to the envy and resentment of this woman for knowing that the lady whom she had succeeded in my master's good graces, designed to take me into her service; which, had I once got on shore, she would not have been able to prevent. She felt her pride alarmed at the superiority of her rival, in being attended by a black servant. It was not less to prevent this, than to be revenged on me, that she caused the captain to treat me thus cruelly.

Pursue their toils till all his race is run.
No eye to mark their suff'rings with a tear,
No friend to comfort, and no hope to cheer;
Then, like the dull unpity'd brutes, repair
To stalls as wretched, and as coarse a fare;
Thank heaven one day of misery was o'er,
Then sink to sleep, and wish to wake no more.*

The turbulence of my emotions, however, naturally gave way to calmer thoughts, and I soon perceived what fate had decreed no mortal on earth could prevent. The convoy sailed on without any accident, with a pleasant gale and smooth sea, for six weeks, till February, when one morning the *Eolus* ran down a brig, one of the convoy, and she instantly went down, and was engulfed in the dark recesses of the ocean. The convoy was immediately thrown into great confusion till it was day-light; and the *Eolus* was illumined with lights, to prevent any further mischief. On the 13th of February, 1763, from the mast-head, we descried our destined island, Montserrat; and soon after I beheld those

Regions of sorrow, doleful shades, where peace
And rest can rarely dwell. Hope never comes
That comes to all, but torture without end
Still urges.

At the sight of this land of bondage, a fresh horror ran through all my frame, and chilled me to the heart. My former slavery now rose in dreadful review to my mind, and displayed nothing but misery, stripes, and chains; and, in the first paroxysm of my grief, I called upon God's thunder, and his avenging power, to direct the stroke of death to me, rather than permit me to become a slave, and be sold from lord to lord.

In this state of my mind our ship came to anchor, and soon after discharged her cargo. I now knew what it was to work hard; I was made to help unload and load the ship. And, to com-

---

* "The Dying Negro," a poem originally published in 1773. Perhaps it may not be deemed impertinent here to add, that this elegant and pathetic little poem was occasioned, as appears by the advertisement prefixed to it, by the following incident. "A black, who, a few days before had run away from his master, and got himself christened, with intent to marry a white woman, his fellow-servant, being taken and sent on board a ship in the Thames, took an opportunity of shooting himself through the head."

fort me in my distress in that time, two of the sailors robbed me of all my money, and ran away from the ship. I had been so long used to a European climate, that at first I felt the scorching West India sun very painful, while the dashing surf would toss the boat and the people in it, frequently above high water mark. Sometimes our limbs were broken with this, or even attended with instant death, and I was day by day mangled and torn.

About the middle of May, when the ship was got ready to sail for England, I all the time believing that fate's blackest clouds were gathering over my head, and expecting their bursting would mix me with the dead, Captain Doran sent for me ashore one morning, and I was told by the messenger that my fate was then determined. With trembling steps and fluttering heart, I came to the captain, and found with him one Mr. Robert King, a Quaker, and the first merchant in the place. The captain then told me my former master had sent me there to be sold; but that he had desired him to get me the best master he could, as he told him I was a very deserving boy, which Captain Doran said he found to be true; and if he were to stay in the West Indies, he would be glad to keep me himself; but he could not venture to take me to London, for he was very sure that when I came there I would leave him. I at that instant burst out a crying, and begged much of him to take me to England with him, but all to no purpose. He told me he had got me the very best master in the whole island, with whom I should be as happy as if I were in England, and for that reason he chose to let him have me, though he could sell me to his own brother-in-law for a great deal more money than what he got from this gentleman. Mr. King, my new master, then made a reply, and said the reason he had bought me was on account of my good character; and as he had not the least doubt of my good behavior, I should be very well off with him. He also told me he did not live in the West Indies, but at Philadelphia, where he was going soon; and, as I understood something of the rules of arithmetic, when we got there he would put me to school, and fit me for a clerk. This conversation relieved my mind a little, and I left those gentlemen considerably more at ease in myself than when I came to them; and I was very thankful to Captain Doran, and even to my old master, for the character they had given me. A character which I afterwards found of infinite service to me. I went on board again, and took leave of all my ship-mates, and the next day the ship sailed. When she weighed anchor, I went to the waterside and looked at her with a very wishful and aching heart, and followed her with my eyes until she was totally out of sight. I was so bowed down with grief, that I could not hold up my head for many months; and if my new master had not been kind to me, I believe I should have died under it at last. And, indeed, I soon found that he fully deserved the good character which Captain Doran gave me of him, for he possessed a most amiable disposition and temper, and was very charitable and humane. If any of his slaves behaved amiss he did not beat or use them ill, but parted with them. This made them afraid of disobliging him; and as he treated his slaves better than any other man on the island, so he was better and more faithfully served by them in return. By this kind treatment I did at last endeavor to compose myself; and with fortitude, though money-less, determined to face whatever fate had decreed for me. Mr. King soon asked me what I could do; and at the same time said he did not mean to treat me as a common slave. I told him I knew something of seamanship, and could shave and dress hair pretty well; and I could refine wines, which I had learned on shipboard, where I had often done it; and that I could write, and understood arithmetic tolerably well, as far as the Rule of Three. He then asked me if I knew anything of gauging; and, on my answering that I did not, he said one of his clerks should teach me to gauge.

Mr. King dealt in all manner of merchandise, and kept from one to six clerks. He loaded many vessels in a year; particularly to Philadelphia, where he was born; and was connected with a great mercantile house in that city. He had, besides, many vessels and droggers, of different sizes, which used to go about the island; and others, to collect rum, sugar, and other goods. I understood pulling and managing those boats very well. And this hard work, which was the first that he set me to, in the sugar seasons used to be my constant employment. I have rowed the boat, and slaved at the oars, from one hour to sixteen in the twenty-four, during which I had fifteen pence sterling per day to live on, though sometimes only ten pence. However, this was considerably more than was allowed to other slaves that used to work often with me, and belonged to other gentlemen on the island. Those poor souls had never more than nine pence per day, and seldom more than six pence, from their masters or owners, though they earned them three or four pistareens.* For it is a common practice in the West Indies for men to purchase slaves, though they have not plantations themselves, in order to let them out to planters and merchants at so much a piece by the day, and they give what allowance they choose out of this product of their daily work to their slaves, for subsistence; this allowance is often very scanty. My master often gave the owners of the slaves two and a half of these pieces per day, and found the poor fellows in victuals himself, because he thought their owners did not feed them well enough according to the work they did. The slaves used to like this very well; and, as they knew my master to be a man of feeling, they were always glad to work for him, in preference to any other gentleman; some of whom, after they had been paid for these poor people's labors, would not give them their allowance out of it. Many times have I even seen these unfortunate wretches beaten for asking for their pay; and often severely flogged by their owners if they did not bring them their daily or weekly money exactly to the time; though the poor creatures were obliged to wait on the gentlemen they had worked for, sometimes more than half the day before they could get their pay; and this generally on Sundays, when they wanted the time for themselves. In particular, I knew a countryman of mine who once did not bring the weekly money directly that it was earned; and, though he brought it the same day to his master, yet he was staked to the ground for his pretended negligence, and was just going to receive a hundred lashes, but for a gentleman who begged him off with fifty. This poor man was very industrious; and by his frugality, had saved so much money by working on ship-board, that he had got a white man to buy him a boat, unknown to his master. Some time after he had this little estate, the governor wanted a boat to bring his sugar from different parts of the island; and, knowing this to be a Negro man's boat, he seized upon it for himself, and would not pay the owner a farthing. The man, on this, went to his master,

* These pistareens are of the value of a shilling.

and complained to him of this act of the governor; but the only satisfaction he received was to be damned very heartily by his master, who asked him how dared any of his Negroes to have a boat. If the justly merited ruin of the governor's fortune could be any gratification to the poor man he had thus robbed, he was not without consolation. Extortion and rapine are poor providers; and some time after this the governor died in the King's Bench in England, as I was told, in great poverty. The last war favored this poor Negro man, and he found some means to escape from his Christian master. He came to England, where I saw him afterwards several times. Such treatment as this often drives these miserable wretches to despair, and they run away from their masters at the hazard of their lives. Many of them, in this place, unable to get their pay when they have earned it, and fearing to be flogged, as usual, if they return home without it, run away where they can for shelter, and a reward is often offered to bring them in dead or alive. My master used sometimes, in these cases, to agree with their owners, and to settle with them himself; and thereby he saved many of them a flogging.

Once, for a few days, I was let out to fit a vessel, and I had no victuals allowed me by either party; at last I told my master of this treatment, and he took me away from it. In many of the estates, on the different islands where I used to be sent for rum or sugar, they would not deliver it to me, or any other Negro; he was therefore obliged to send a white man along with me to those places; and then he used to pay him from six to ten pistareens a day. From being thus employed, during the time I served Mr. King, in going about the different estates on the island, I had all the opportunity I could wish for, to see the dreadful usage of the poor men; usage that reconciled me to my situation, and made me bless God for the hands into which I had fallen.

I had the good fortune to please my master in every department in which he employed me; and there was scarcely any part of his business, or household affairs, in which I was not occasionally engaged. I often supplied the place of a clerk, in receiving and delivering cargoes to the ships, in tending stores, and delivering goods. And besides this, I used to shave and dress my master when convenient, and take care of his horse; and when it was necessary, which was very often, I worked likewise on board of different vessels of his. By these means I became very useful to my master, and saved him, as he used to acknowledge, above a hundred pounds a year. Nor did he scruple to say I was of more advantage to him than any of his clerks; though their usual wages in the West Indies are from sixty to a hundred pounds current a year.

I have sometimes heard it asserted that a Negro cannot earn his master the first cost; but nothing can be further from the truth. I suppose nine-tenths of the mechanics throughout the West Indies are Negro slaves; and I well know the coopers among them earn two dollars a day, the carpenters the same, and oftentimes more; as also the masons, smiths, and fishermen, &c. And I have known many slaves whose masters would not take a thousand pounds current for them. But surely this assertion refutes itself; for, if it be true, why do the planters and merchants pay such a price for slaves? And, above all, why do those who make this assertion exclaim the most loudly against the abolition of the slave trade? So much are men blinded, and to such inconsistent arguments are they driven by mistaken interest! I grant, indeed, that slaves are sometimes, by half-feeding, half-clothing, over-working, and stripes, reduced so low, that they are turned out as unfit for service, and left to perish in the woods, or expire on the dung-hill.

My master was several times offered, by different gentlemen, one hundred guineas for me, but he always told them he would not sell me, to my great joy. And I used to double my diligence and care, for fear of getting into the hands of those men who did not allow a valuable slave the common support of life. Many of them even used to find fault with my master for feeding his slaves so well as he did, although I often went hungry, and an Englishman might think my fare very indifferent; but he used to tell them he always would do it, because the slaves thereby looked better and did more work.

While I was thus employed by my master, I was often a witness to cruelties of every kind, which were exercised on my unhappy fellow slaves. I used frequently to have different cargoes of new Negroes in my care for sale; and it was almost a constant practice with our clerks, and other whites, to commit violent depredations on the chastity of the female slaves; and these I was, though with reluctance, obliged to submit to at all times, being unable to help them. When we have had some of these slaves on board my master's vessels, to carry them to other islands, or to America, I have known our mates to commit these acts most shamefully, to the disgrace, not of Christians only, but of men. I have even known them to gratify their brutal passion with females not ten years old; and these abominations, some of them practised to such scandalous excess, that one of our captains discharged the mate and others on that account. And yet in Montserrat I have seen a Negro man staked to the ground, and cut most shockingly, and then his ears cut off bit by bit, because he had been connected with a white woman, who was a common prostitute. As if it were no crime in the whites to rob an innocent African girl of her virtue, but most heinous in a black man only to gratify a passion of nature, where the temptation was offered by one of a different color, though the most abandoned woman of her species.

One Mr. D—— told me that he had sold 41,000 Negroes, and that he once cut off a Negro man's leg for running away. I asked him if the man had died in the operation, how he, as a Christian, could answer for the horrid act before God? and he told me, answering was a thing of another world, what he thought and did were policy. I told him that the Christian doctrine taught us to do unto others as we would that others should do unto us. He then said that his scheme had the desired effect—it cured that man and some others of running away.

Another Negro man was half hanged, and then burnt, for attempting to poison a cruel overseer. Thus, by repeated cruelties, are the wretched first urged to despair, and then murdered, because they still retain so much of human nature about them as to wish to put an end to their misery, and retaliate on their tyrants! These overseers are indeed for the most part persons of the worst character of any denomination of men in the West Indies. Unfortunately, many humane gentlemen, but not residing on their estates, are obliged to leave the management of them in the hands of these human butchers, who cut and mangle the slaves in a shocking manner on the most trifling occasions, and altogether treat them in every respect like brutes. They pay no regard to the situation of pregnant women, nor the least attention to the lodging of the field Negroes. Their huts, which ought to be well covered, and the place dry where they take their little repose, are often open sheds, built in damp places; so that when the poor creatures return tired from the toils of the field, they contract many disorders, from being exposed to the damp air in this uncomfortable state, while they are heated, and their pores are open. This neglect certainly conspires with many others to cause a decrease in the births as well as in the lives of the grown Negroes. I can quote many instances of gentlemen who reside on their estates in the West Indies, and then the scene is quite changed; the Negroes are treated with lenity and proper care, by which their lives are prolonged, and their masters profited. To the honor of humanity, I knew several gentlemen who managed their estates in this manner, and they found that benevolence was their true interest. And, among many I could mention in several of the islands, I knew one in Montserrat* whose slaves looked remarkably well, and never needed any fresh supplies of Negroes; and there are many other estates, especially in Barbadoes, which, from such judicious treatment, need no fresh stock of Negroes at any time. I have the honor of knowing a most worthy and humane gentleman, who is a native of Barbadoes, and has estates there.† This gentleman has written a treatise on the usage of his own slaves. He allows them two hours of refreshment at mid-day, and many other indulgencies and comforts, particularly in their lodging; and, besides this, he raises more provisions on his estate than they can destroy; so that by these attentions he saves the lives of his Negroes, and keeps them healthy, and as happy as the condition of slavery can admit. I myself, as shall appear in the sequel, managed an estate, where, by those attentions, the Negroes were uncommonly cheerful and healthy, and did more work by half than by the common mode of treatment they usually do. For want, therefore, of such care and attention to the poor Negroes, and otherwise oppressed as they are, it is no wonder that the decrease should require

* Mr. Dubury, and many others, Montserrat.
† Sir Phillip Gibbes, Baronet, Barbadoes.

20,000 new Negroes annually, to fill up the vacant places of the dead.

Even in Barbadoes, notwithstanding those humane exceptions which I have mentioned, and others I am acquainted with, which justly make it quoted as a place where slaves meet with the best treatment, and need fewest recruits of any in the West Indies, yet this island requires 1,000 Negroes annually to keep up the original stock, which is only 80,000. So that the whole term of a Negro's life may be said to be there but sixteen years!* And yet the climate here in every respect is the same as that from which they are taken, except in being more wholesome. Do the British colonies decrease in this manner? And yet what prodigious difference is there between an English and West India climate?

While I was in Montserrat I knew a Negro man, named Emanuel Sankey, who endeavored to escape from his miserable bondage, by concealing himself on board of a London ship, but fate did not favor the poor oppressed man; for, being discovered when the vessel was under sail, he was delivered up again to his master. This *Christian master* immediately pinned the wretch down to the ground at each wrist and ankle, and then took some sticks of sealing wax, and lighted them, and dropped it all over his back. There was another master who was noted for cruelty; and I believe he had not a slave but what had been cut, and had pieces fairly taken out of the flesh. And after they had been punished thus, he used to make them get into a long wooden box or case he had for that purpose, in which he shut them up during pleasure. It was just about the height and breadth of a man; and the poor wretches had no room, when in the case, to move.

It was very common in several of the islands, particularly in St. Kitts, for the slaves to be branded with the initial letters of their master's name; and a load of heavy iron hooks hung about their necks. Indeed, on the most trifling occasions, they were loaded with chains; and often instruments of torture were added. The iron muzzle, thumb-screws, &c., are so well known as not to need a description, and were sometimes applied for the slightest faults. I have seen a Negro beaten till some of his bones were broken, for only letting a pot boil over. Is it surprising that usage

* Benezet's Account of Guinea, p. 16.

like this should drive the poor creatures to despair, and make them seek a refuge in death from those evils which render their lives intolerable?—while,

> With shudd'ring horror pale, and eyes aghast,
> They view their lamentable lot, and find
> No rest!

This they frequently do. A Negro man, on board a vessel of my master, while I belonged to her, having been put in irons for some trifling misdemeanor, and kept in that state for some days, being weary of life, took an opportunity of jumping overboard into the sea; however, he was picked up without being drowned. Another, whose life was also a burden to him, resolved to starve himself to death, and refused to eat any victuals. This procured him a severe flogging; and he also, on the first occasion which offered, jumped overboard at Charleston, but was saved.

Nor is there any greater regard shown to the little property than there is to the persons and lives of the Negroes. I have already related an instance or two of particular oppression out of many which I have witnessed; but the following is frequent in all the islands. The wretched field slaves, after toiling all the day for an unfeeling owner, who gives them but little victuals, steal sometimes a few moments from rest or refreshment to gather some small portion of grass, according as their time will admit. This they commonly tie up in a parcel; either a bit's worth (six pence) or half a bit's worth, and bring it to town, or to the market, to sell. Nothing is more common than for the white people on this occasion to take the grass from them without paying for it; and not only so, but too often also, to my knowledge, our clerks, and many others, at the same time have committed acts of violence on the poor, wretched, and helpless females; whom I have seen for hours stand crying to no purpose, and get no redress or pay of any kind. Is not this one common and crying sin enough to bring down God's judgment on the islands? He tells us the oppressor and the oppressed are both in his hands; and if these are not the poor, the broken-hearted, the blind, the captive, the bruised, which our Saviour speaks of, who are they? One of these depredators once, in St. Eustatius, came on board of our vessel, and bought some fowls and pigs of me; and a whole day after his departure with the things, he returned again and wanted his money back. I refused to give it, and, not seeing my captain on board, he began the common pranks with me; and swore he would even break open my chest and take my money. I therefore expected, as my captain was absent, that he would be as good as his word. And was just proceeding to strike me, when fortunately a British seaman on board, whose heart had not been debauched by a West India climate, interposed and prevented him. But had the cruel man struck me I certainly should have defended myself at the hazard of my life; for what is life to a man thus oppressed? He went away, however, swearing, and threatened that whenever he caught me on shore, he would shoot me, and pay for me afterwards.

The small account in which the life of a Negro is held in the West Indies is so universally known that it might seem impertinent to quote the following extract, if some people had not been hardy enough of late to assert that Negroes are on the same footing in that respect as Europeans. By the 329th Act, page 125, of the Assembly of Barbadoes, it is enacted "That if any Negro, or other slave, under punishment by his master, or his order, for running away, or any other crime or misdemeanor towards his said master, unfortunately shall suffer in life or member, no person whatsoever shall be liable to a fine; but if any person shall, out of wantonness, or only of bloody-mindedness, or cruel intention, willfully kill a Negro, or other slave, of his own, he shall pay into the public treasury fifteen pounds sterling." And it is the same in most, if not all of the West India islands. Is not this one of the many acts of the islands which call loudly for redress? And do not the assembly which enacted it deserve the appellation of savages and brutes, rather than of Christians and men? It is an act at once unmerciful, unjust, and unwise; which for cruelty would disgrace an assembly of those who are called barbarians; and for its injustice and insanity would shock the morality and common sense of a Samaide or Hottentot.

Shocking as this and many other acts of the bloody West India code at first view appear, how is the iniquity of it heightened when we consider to whom it may be extended! Mr. James Tobin, a zealous laborer in the vineyard of slavery, gives an account of a French planter of his acquaintance, in the island of

Martinique, who showed him many mulattoes working in the field like beasts of burden; and he told Mr. Tobin these were all the produce of his own loins! And I myself have known similar instances. Pray, reader, are these sons and daughters of the French planter less his children by being the progeny of black women? And what must be the virtue of those legislators, and the feelings of those fathers, who estimate the lives of their sons, however begotten, at no more than fifteen pounds; though they should be murdered, as the act says, out of wantonness and bloody-mindedness! But is not the slave trade entirely at war with the heart of man? And surely that which is begun by breaking down the barriers of virtue, involves in its continuance destruction to every principle, and buries all sentiment in ruin!

I have often seen slaves, particularly those who were meagre, in different islands, put into scales and weighed, and then sold from three pence to six pence or nine pence a pound. My master, however, whose humanity was shocked at this mode, used to sell such by the lump. And at or after a sale, it was not uncommon to see Negroes taken from their wives, wives taken from their husbands, and children from their parents, and sent off to other islands, and wherever else their merciless lords choose; and probably never more during life see each other! Oftentimes my heart has bled at these partings, when the friends of the departed have been at the waterside, and with sighs and tears, have kept their eyes fixed on the vessel, till it went out of sight.

A poor Creole Negro, I knew well, who, after having been often thus transported from island to island, at last resided in Montserrat. This man used to tell me many melancholy tales of himself. Generally, after he had done working for his master, he used to employ his few leisure moments to go a fishing. When he had caught any fish, his master would frequently take them from him without paying him; and at other times some other white people would serve him in the same manner. One day he said to me, very movingly, "Sometimes when a white man take away my fish, I go to my maser, and he get me my right; and when my maser by strength take away my fishes, what me must do? I can't go to any body to be righted; then," said the poor man, looking up above, "I must look up to God Mighty, in the top, for right." This artless tale moved me much, and I could not

help feeling the just cause Moses had in redressing his brother
against the Egyptian. I exhorted the man to look up still to the
God on the top, since there was no redress below. Though I little
thought then that I myself should more than once experience
such imposition, and need the same exhortation hereafter, in my
own transactions in the islands, and that even this poor man and
I should some time after suffer together in the same manner, as
shall be related hereafter.

Nor was such usage as this confined to particular places or individuals, for in all the different islands in which I have been
(and I have visited no less than fifteen) the treatment of the slaves
was nearly the same; so nearly, indeed, that the history of an
island, or even a plantation, with a few such exceptions as I have
mentioned, might serve for a history of the whole. Such a
tendency has the slave trade to debauch men's minds, and harden
them to every feeling of humanity! For I will not suppose that
the dealers in slaves are born worse than other men—No; such
is the fatality of this mistaken avarice that it corrupts the milk of
human kindness and turns it into gall. And, had the pursuits of
those men been different, they might have been as generous, as
tender-hearted and just, as they are unfeeling, rapacious, and
cruel. Surely this traffic cannot be good, which spreads like a
pestilence, and taints what it touches! which violates that first
natural right of mankind, equality and independency, and gives
one man a dominion over his fellows which God could never
intend! For it raises the owner to a state as far above man as it
depresses the slave below it; and, with all the presumption of
human pride, sets a distinction between them, immeasurable in
extent, and endless in duration! Yet how mistaken is the avarice
even of the planters. Are slaves more useful by being thus hum-
bled to the condition of brutes than they would be if suffered to
enjoy the privileges of men? The freedom which diffuses health
and prosperity throughout Britain answers you—No. When you
make men slaves, you deprive them of half their virtue; you set
them, in your own conduct, an example of fraud, rapine, and
cruelty, and compel them to live with you in a state of war; and
yet you complain that they are not honest or faithful! You stupify
them with stripes, and think it necessary to keep them in a state
of ignorance. And yet you assert that they are incapable of

learning; that their minds are such a barren soil or moor that culture would be lost on them; and that they come from a climate where nature, though prodigal of her bounties in a degree unknown to yourselves, has left man alone scant and unfinished, and incapable of enjoying the treasures she has poured out for him! An assertion at once impious and absurd. Why do you use those instruments of torture? Are they fit to be applied by one rational being to another? And are ye not struck with shame and mortification, to see the partakers of your nature reduced so low? But, above all, are there no dangers attending this mode of treatment? Are you not hourly in dread of an insurrection? Nor would it be surprising; for when

> ——— No peace is given
> To us enslav'd, but custody severe,
> And stripes and arbitrary punishment
> Inflicted—What peace can we return?
> But to our power, hostility and hate;
> Untam'd reluctance, and revenge, though slow.
> Yet ever plotting how the conqueror least
> May reap his conquest, and may least rejoice
> In doing what we most in suffering feel.

But by changing your conduct, and treating your slaves as men, every cause of fear would be banished. They would be faithful, honest, intelligent, and vigorous; and peace, prosperity, and happiness would attend you.

Chapter 6

Some account of Brimstone Hill in Montserrat—Favorable change in the author's situation—He commences merchant with three pence—His various success in dealing in the different islands, and America, and the impositions he meets with in his transactions with Europeans—A curious imposition on human nature—Danger of the surfs in the West Indies—Remarkable instance of kidnapping a free mulatto—The author is nearly murdered by Doctor Perkins in Savannah.

In the preceding chapter I have set before the reader a few of those many instances of oppression, extortion, and cruelty which I have been a witness to in the West Indies; but were I to enumerate them all, the catalogue would be tedious and disgusting. The punishments of the slaves on every trifling occasion are so frequent, and so well known, together with the different instruments with which they are tortured, that it cannot any longer afford novelty to recite them; and they are too shocking to yield delight either to the writer or the reader. I shall therefore hereafter only mention such as incidentally befell myself in the course of my adventures.

In the variety of departments in which I was employed by my master, I had an opportunity of seeing many curious scenes in different islands; but, above all, I was struck with a celebrated curiosity called Brimstone Hill, which is a high and steep mountain, some few miles from the town of Plymouth, in Montserrat. I had often heard of some wonders that were to be seen on this hill, and I went once with some white and black people to visit it. When we arrived at the top, I saw under different cliffs great flakes of brimstone, occasioned by the streams of various little ponds, which were then boiling naturally in the earth. Some of these ponds were as white as milk, some quite blue, and many others of different colors. I had taken some potatoes with me, and I put them into different ponds, and in a few minutes they were well boiled. I tasted some of them, but they were very sulphurous; and the silver shoe buckles, and all the other things of that metal we had among us, were, in a little time turned as black as lead.

Sometime in the year 1763, kind Providence seemed to appear

rather more favorable to me. One of my master's vessels, a Bermudas sloop, about sixty tons burthen, was commanded by one captain Thomas Farmer, an Englishman, a very alert and active man, who gained my master a great deal of money by his good management in carrying passengers from one island to another; but very often his sailors used to get drunk and run away from the vessel, which hindered him in his business very much. This man had taken a liking to me, and many times begged of my master to let me go a trip with him as a sailor; but he would tell him he could not spare me, though the vessel sometimes could not go for want of hands, for sailors were generally very scarce in the island. However, at last, from necessity or force, my master was prevailed on, though very reluctantly, to let me go with this captain; but he gave him great charge to take care that I did not run away, for if I did he would make him pay for me. This being the case, the captain had for some time a sharp eye upon me whenever the vessel anchored; and as soon as she returned I was sent for on shore again. Thus was I slaving, as it were, for life, sometimes at one thing, and sometimes at another. So that the captain and I were nearly the most useful men in my master's employment. I also became so useful to the captain on ship-board, that many times, when he used to ask for me to go with him, though it should be but for twenty-four hours, to some of the islands near us, my master would answer he could not spare me, at which the captain would swear, and would not go the trip, and tell my master I was better to him on board than any three white men he had; for they used to behave ill in many respects, particularly in getting drunk; and then they frequently got the boat stove, so as to hinder the vessel from coming back as soon as she might have done. This my master knew very well; and at last, by the captain's constant entreaties, after I had been several times with him, one day to my great joy, told me the captain would not let him rest, and asked whether I would go aboard as a sailor, or stay on shore and mind the stores, for he could not bear any longer to be plagued in this manner. I was very happy at this proposal, for I immediately thought I might in time stand some chance by being on board to get a little money, or possibly make my escape if I should be used ill. I also expected to get better food, and in greater abundance; for I had oftentimes felt much hunger, though my master treated his slaves, as I have observed, uncommonly well. I therefore, without hesitation, answered him, that I would go and be a sailor if he pleased. Accordingly I was ordered on board directly. Nevertheless, between the vessel and the shore, when she was in port, I had little or no rest, as my master always wished to have me along with him. Indeed he was a very pleasant gentleman, and but for my expectations on ship-board, I should not have thought of leaving him. But the captain liked me also very much, and I was entirely his right hand man. I did all I could to deserve his favor, and in return I received better treatment from him than any other, I believe, ever met with in the West Indies, in my situation.

After I had been sailing for some time with this captain, at length I endeavored to try my luck, and commence merchant. I had but a very small capital to begin with; for one single half bit, which is equal to three pence in England, made up my whole stock. However, I trusted to the Lord to be with me; and at one of our trips to St. Eustatius, a Dutch island, I bought a glass tumbler with my half bit, and when I came to Montserrat, I sold it for a bit, or six pence. Luckily we made several successive trips to St. Eustatius (which was a general mart for the West Indies, about twenty leagues from Montserrat), and in our next, finding my tumbler so profitable, with this one bit I bought two tumblers more; and when I came back, I sold them for two bits, equal to a shilling sterling. When we went again, I bought with these two bits four more of these glasses, which I sold for four bits on our return to Montserrat. And in our next voyage to St. Eustatius, I bought two glasses with one bit, and with the other three I bought a jug of Geneva, nearly about three pints in measure. When we came to Montserrat, I sold the gin for eight bits, and the tumblers for two, so that my capital now amounted in all to a dollar, well husbanded and acquired in the space of a month or six weeks, when I blessed the Lord that I was so rich. As we sailed to different islands, I laid this money out in various things occasionally, and it used to turn out to very good account, especially when we went to Guadeloupe, Grenada, and the rest of the French islands. Thus was I going all about the islands upwards of four years, and ever trading as I went, during which I experienced many instances of ill usage, and have seen many injuries done to other Negroes in our dealings with whites. And, amidst our recreations, when we have been dancing and merry-making, they, without cause, have molested and insulted us. Indeed, I was more than once obliged to look up to God on high, as I had advised the poor fisherman some time before. And I had not been long trading for myself in the manner I have related above, when I experienced the like trial in company with him as follows: This man being used to the water, was upon an emergency put on board of us by his master, to work as another hand, on a voyage to Santa Cruz; and at our sailing he had brought his little all for a venture, which consisted of six bits' worth of limes and oranges in a bag; I had also my whole stock, which was about twelve bits' worth of the same kind of goods, separate in two bags, for we had heard these fruits sold well in that island. When we came there, in some little convenient time, he and I went ashore to sell them; but we had scarcely landed, when we were met by two white men, who presently took our three bags from us. We could not at first guess what they meant to do, and for some time we thought they were jesting with us; but they too soon let us know otherwise, for they took our ventures immediately to a house hard by, and adjoining the fort, while we followed all the way begging of them to give us our fruits, but in vain. They not only refused to return them, but swore at us, and threatened if we did not immediately depart they would flog us well. We told them these three bags were all we were worth in the world, and that we brought them with us to sell when we came from Montserrat, and showed them the vessel. But this was rather against us, as they now saw we were strangers, as well as slaves. They still therefore swore, and desired us to be gone, and even took sticks to beat us; while we, seeing they meant what they said, went off in the greatest confusion and despair. Thus, in the very minute of gaining more by three times than I ever did by any venture in my life before, was I deprived of every farthing I was worth. An unsupportable misfortune! but how to help ourselves we knew not. In our consternation we went to the commanding officer of the fort, and told him how we had been served by his people, but we obtained not the least redress. He answered our complaints only by a volley of imprecations against us, and immediately took a horse-whip, in order to chastise us, so that we were obliged to turn out much faster than we came in. I now, in the agony of distress and indignation, wished that the ire of God in his forked lightning might transfix these cruel oppressors among the dead. Still, however, we persevered; went back again to the house, and begged and besought them again and again for our fruits, till at last some other people that were in the house asked if we would be contented if they kept one bag and gave us the other two. We, seeing no remedy whatever, consented to this; and they, observing one bag to have both kinds of fruit in it, which belonged to my companion, kept that; and the other two, which were mine, they gave us back. As soon as I got them, I ran as fast as I could, and got the first Negro man I could to help me off. My companion, however, stayed a little longer to plead; he told them the bag they had was his, and likewise all that he was worth in the world; but this was of no avail, and he was obliged to return without it. The poor old man wringing his hands, cried bitterly for his loss; and, indeed, he then did look up to God on high, which so moved me in pity for him, that I gave him nearly one third of my fruits. We then proceeded to the markets to sell them; and Providence was more favorable to us than we could have expected, for we sold our fruits uncommonly well; I got for mine about thirty-seven bits. Such a surprising reverse of fortune in so short a space of time seemed like a dream, and proved no small encouragement for me to trust the Lord in any situation. My captain afterwards frequently used to take my part, and get me my right, when I have been plundered or used ill by these tender Christian depredators; among whom I have shuddered to observe the unceasing blasphemous execrations which are wantonly thrown out by persons of all ages and conditions, not only without occasion, but even as if they were indulgencies and pleasure.

At one of our trips to St. Kitts, I had eleven bits of my own; and my friendly captain lent me five more, with which I bought a Bible. I was very glad to get this book, which I scarcely could meet with anywhere. I think there was none sold in Montserrat; and, much to my grief, from being forced out of the *Etna* in the manner I have related, my Bible, and the *Guide to the Indians,* the two books I loved above all others, were left behind.

While I was in this place, St. Kitts, a very curious imposition on human nature took place: A white man wanted to marry in the church a free black woman, that had land and slaves in Montserrat; but the clergyman told him it was against the law of the place to marry a white and a black in the church. The man then asked to be married on the water, to which the parson consented, and the two lovers went in one boat, and the parson and clerk in another, and thus the ceremony was performed. After this, the loving pair came on board our vessel, and my captain treated them extremely well, and brought them safe to Montserrat.

The reader cannot but judge of the irksomeness of this situation to a mind like mine, in being daily exposed to new hardships and impositions, after having seen many better days, and been, as it were, in a state of freedom and plenty; added to which, every part of the world I had hitherto been in, seemed to me a paradise in comparison to the West Indies. My mind was therefore hourly replete with inventions and thoughts of being freed, and, if possible, by honest and honorable means; for I always remembered the old adage, and I trust it has ever been my ruling principle, that "honesty is the best policy"; and likewise that other golden precept—"To do unto all men as I would they should do unto me." However, as I was from early years a predestinarian, I thought whatever fate had determined must ever come to pass; and, therefore, if ever it were my lot to be freed, nothing could prevent me, although I should at present see no means or hope to obtain my freedom; on the other hand, if it were my fate not to be freed, I never should be so, and all my endeavors for that purpose would be fruitless. In the midst of these thoughts, I therefore looked up with prayers anxiously to God for my liberty; and at the same time used every honest means, and did all that was possible on my part to obtain it. In process of time, I became master of a few pounds, and in a fair way of making more, which my friendly captain knew very well; this occasioned him sometimes to take liberties with me; but whenever he treated me waspishly, I used plainly to tell him my mind, and

that I would die before I would be imposed upon as other Negroes were, and that to me life had lost its relish when liberty
was gone. This I said, although I foresaw my then well-being
or future hopes of freedom (humanly speaking) depended on
this man. However, as he could not bear the thoughts of my not
sailing with him, he always became mild on my threats. I therefore continued with him; and, from my great attention to his
orders and his business, I gained him credit, and through his
kindness to me, I at last procured my liberty. While I thus went
on, filled with the thoughts of freedom, and resisting oppression
as well as I was able, my life hung daily in suspense, particularly
in the surfs I have formerly mentioned, as I could not swim.
These are extremely violent throughout the West Indies, and I
was ever exposed to their howling rage and devouring fury in all
the islands. I have seen them strike and toss a boat right up on
end, and maim several on board. Once in the Grenada islands,
when I and about eight others were pulling a large boat with
two puncheons of water in it, a surf struck us, and drove the
boat, and all in it, about half a stone's throw, among some trees,
and above the high water mark. We were obliged to get all the
assistance we could from the nearest estate to mend the boat,
and launch it into the water again. At Montserrat, one night, in
pressing hard to get off the shore on board, the punt was overset
with us four times; the first time I was very near being drowned;
however, the jacket I had on kept me up above water a little
space of time, when I called on a man near me, who was a good
swimmer, and told him I could not swim; he then made haste to
me, and, just as I was sinking, he caught hold of me, and
brought me to sounding, and then he went and brought the punt
also. As soon as we had turned the water out of her, lest we
should be used ill for being absent, we attempted again three
times more, and as often the horrid surfs served us as at first;
but at last, the fifth time we attempted, we gained our point, at
the imminent hazard of our lives. One day also, at Old Road, in
Montserrat, our captain, and three men besides myself, were
going in a large canoe in quest of rum and sugar, when a single
surf tossed the canoe an amazing distance from the water, and
some of us, near a stone's throw from each other. Most of us
were very much bruised; so that I and many more often said,

and really thought, that there was not such another place under the heavens as this. I longed, therefore, much to leave it, and daily wished to see my master's promise performed, of going to Philadelphia.

While we lay in this place, a very cruel thing happened on board our sloop, which filled me with horror; though I found afterwards such practices were frequent. There was a very clever and decent free young mulatto man, who sailed a long time with us; he had a free woman for his wife, by whom he had a child, and she was then living on shore, and all very happy. Our captain and mate, and other people on board, and several elsewhere, even the natives of Bermudas, all knew this young man from a child that he was always free, and no one had ever claimed him as their property. However, as might too often overcomes right in these parts, it happened that a Bermudas captain, whose vessel lay there for a few days in the road, came on board of us, and seeing the mulatto man, whose name was Joseph Clipson, he told him he was not free, and that he had orders from his master to bring him to Bermudas. The poor man could not believe the captain to be in earnest, but he was very soon undeceived, his men laying violent hands on him; and although he showed a certificate of his being born free in St. Kitts, and most people on board knew that he served his time to boatbuilding, and always passed for a free man, yet he was forcibly taken out of our vessel. He then asked to be carried ashore before the Secretary or Magistrates, and these infernal invaders of human rights promised him he should; but instead of that, they carried him on board of the other vessel. And the next day, without giving the poor man any hearing on shore, or suffering him even to see his wife or child, he was carried away, and probably doomed never more in this world to see them again. Nor was this the only instance of this kind of barbarity I was a witness to. I have since often seen in Jamaica and other islands, free men, whom I have known in America, thus villainously trepanned and held in bondage. I have heard of two similar practices even in Philadelphia. And were it not for the benevolence of the Quakers in that city, many of the sable race, who now breathe the air of liberty, would, I believe, be groaning indeed under some planter's chains. These things opened my mind to a new scene of horror, to which I had been before a stranger. Hitherto I had thought slavery only dreadful, but the state of a free Negro appeared to me now equally so at least, and in some respects even worse, for they live in constant alarm for their liberty; which is but nominal, for they are universally insulted and plundered, without the possibility of redress; for such is the equity of the West Indian laws, that no free Negro's evidence will be admitted in their courts of justice. In this situation, is it surprising that slaves, when mildly treated, should prefer even the misery of slavery to such a mockery of freedom? I was now completely disgusted with the West Indies, and thought I never should be entirely free until I had left them.

> With thoughts like these, my anxious boding mind
> Recall'd those pleasing scenes I left behind;
> Scenes, where fair liberty, in bright array,
> Makes darkness bright, and e'en illumines day;
> Where, nor complexion, wealth, or station, can
> Protect the wretch who makes a slave of man.

I determined to make every exertion to obtain my freedom, and to return to old England. For this purpose, I thought a knowledge of navigation might be of use to me; for, though I did not intend to run away unless I should be ill used; yet, in such a case, if I understood navigation, I might attempt my escape in our sloop, which was one of the swiftest sailing vessels in the West Indies, and I could be at no loss for hands to join me. And if I should make this attempt, I had intended to have gone for England; but this, as I said, was only to be in the event of my meeting with any ill usage. I therefore employed the mate of our vessel to teach me navigation, for which I agreed to give him twenty-four dollars, and actually paid him part of the money down; though when the captain, some time after, came to know that the mate was to have such a sum for teaching me, he rebuked him, and said it was a shame for him to take any money from me. However, my progress in this useful art was much retarded by the constancy of our work. Had I wished to run away, I did not want opportunities, which frequently presented themselves; and particularly at one time, soon after this. When we were at the island of Guadeloupe, there was a large fleet of merchantmen bound for old France; and seamen then being very scarce, they gave from fifteen to twenty pounds a man for the run. Our mate and all the white sailors left our vessel on this account, and went on board of the French ships. They would have had me also to go with them, for they regarded me, and swore to protect me, if I would go. And, as the fleet was to sail the next day, I really believe I could have got safe to Europe at that time. However, as my master was kind, I would not attempt to leave him, still remembering the old maxim, that "honesty is the best policy," I suffered them to go without me. Indeed my captain was much afraid of my leaving him and the vessel at that time, as I had so fair an opportunity. But, I thank God, this fidelity of mine turned out much to my advantage hereafter, when I did not in the least think of it; and made me so much in favor with the captain, that he used now and then to teach me some parts of navigation himself; but some of our passengers, and others, seeing this, found much fault with him for it, saying it was a very dangerous thing to let a Negro know navigation; thus I was hindered again in my pursuits. About the latter end of the year 1764, my master bought a larger sloop, called the *Prudence,* about seventy or eighty tons, of which my captain had the command. I went with him in this vessel, and we took a load of new slaves for Georgia and Charleston. My master now left me entirely to the captain, though he still wished me to be with him; but I, who always much wished to lose sight of the West Indies, was not a little rejoiced at the thoughts of seeing any other country. Therefore, relying on the goodness of my captain, I got ready all the little venture I could; and, when the vessel was ready, we sailed, to my great joy. When we got to our destined places, Georgia and Charleston, I expected I should have an opportunity of selling my little property to advantage. But here, particularly in Charleston, I met with buyers, white men, who imposed on me as in other places. Notwithstanding, I was resolved to have fortitude, thinking no lot or trial too hard when kind Heaven is the rewarder.

We soon got loaded again, and returned to Montserrat; and there, amongst the rest of the islands, I sold my goods well; and in this manner I continued trading during the year 1764—meeting with various scenes of imposition, as usual. After this, my

master fitted out his vessel for Philadelphia, in the year 1765; and
during the time we were loading her, and getting ready for the
voyage, I worked with redoubled alacrity, from the hope of getting money enough by these voyages to buy my freedom, in
time, if it should please God; and also to see the town of Philadelphia, which I had heard a great deal about for some years
past. Besides which, I had always longed to prove my master's
promise the first day I came to him. In the midst of these elevated ideas, and while I was about getting my little stock of
merchandise in readiness, one Sunday my master sent for me to
his house. When I came there, I found him and the captain together; and, on my going in, I was struck with astonishment at
his telling me he heard that I meant to run away from him when
I got to Philadelphia. "And therefore," said he, "I must tell you
again, you cost me a great deal of money, no less than forty
pounds sterling; and it will not do to lose so much. You are a
valuable fellow," continued he, "and I can get any day for you
one hundred guineas, from many gentlemen in this island." And
then he told me of Captain Doran's brother-in-law, a severe
master, who ever wanted to buy me to make me his overseer. My
captain also said he could get much more than a hundred
guineas for me in Carolina. This I knew to be a fact; for the
gentleman that wanted to buy me came off several times on
board of us, and spoke to me to live with him, and said he would
use me well. When I asked him what work he would put me to,
he said, as I was a sailor, he would make me a captain of one of
his rice vessels. But I refused; and fearing at the same time, by a
sudden turn I saw in the captain's temper, he might mean to
sell me, I told the gentleman I would not live with him on any
condition, and that I certainly would run away with his vessel;
but he said he did not fear that, as he would catch him again,
and then he told me how cruelly he would serve me if I should
do so. My captain, however, gave him to understand that I knew
something of navigation, so he thought better of it; and, to my
great joy, he went away. I now told my master, I did not say I
would run away in Philadelphia; neither did I mean it, as he did
not use me ill, nor yet the captain; for if they did, I certainly
would have made some attempts before now; but as I thought
that if it were God's will I ever should be freed, it would be so,

and, on the contrary, if it was not his will, it would not happen. So I hoped if ever I were freed, whilst I was used well, it should be by honest means; but as I could not help myself, he must do as he pleased, I could only hope and trust to the God of heaven; and at that instant my mind was big with inventions, and full of schemes to escape. I then appealed to the captain, whether he ever saw any sign of my making the least attempt to run away, and asked him if I did not always come on board according to the time for which he gave me liberty; and, more particularly, when all our men left us at Guadeloupe, and went on board of the French fleet, and advised me to go with them, whether I might not, and that he could not have got me again. To my no small surprise, and very great joy, the captain confirmed every syllable that I had said, and even more; for he said he had tried different times to see if I would make any attempt of this kind, both at St. Eustatius and in America, and he never found that I made the smallest; but, on the contrary, I always came on board according to his orders; and he did really believe, if I ever meant to run away, that, as I could never have had a better opportunity, I would have done it the night the mate and all the people left our vessel at Guadeloupe. The captain then informed my master, who had been thus imposed on by our mate (though I did not know who was my enemy), the reason the mate had for imposing this lie upon him; which was, because I had acquainted the captain of the provisions the mate had given away or taken out of the vessel. This speech of the captain was like life to the dead to me, and instantly my soul glorified God; and still more so, on hearing my master immediately say that I was a sensible fellow, and he never did intend to use me as a common slave; and that but for the entreaties of the captain, and his character of me, he would not have let me go from the shores about as I had done. That also, in so doing, he thought by carrying one little thing or other to different places to sell, I might make money. That he also intended to encourage me in this, by crediting me with half a puncheon of rum and half a hogshead of sugar at a time; so that, from being careful, I might have money enough, in some time, to purchase my freedom; and, when that was the case, I might depend upon it he would let me have it for forty pounds sterling money, which was only the same price he gave for me. This sound gladdened my poor heart beyond measure; though indeed it was no more than the very idea I had formed in my mind of my master long before, and I immediately made him this reply: "Sir, I always had that very thought of you, indeed I had, and that made me so diligent in serving you." He then gave me a large piece of silver coin, such as I never had seen or had before, and told me to get ready for the voyage, and he would credit me with a tierce of sugar, and another of rum; he also said that he had two amiable sisters in Philadelphia, from whom I might get some necessary things. Upon this my noble captain desired me to go aboard; and, knowing the African metal, he charged me not to say any thing of this matter to anybody; and he promised that the lying mate should not go with him any more. This was a change indeed: in the same hour to feel the most exquisite pain, and in the turn of a moment the fullest joy. It caused in me such sensations as I was only able to express in my looks; my heart was so overpowered with gratitude, that I could have kissed both of their feet. When I left the room, I immediately went, or rather flew, to the vessel; which being loaded, my master, as good as his word, trusted me with a tierce of rum, and another of sugar, when we sailed, and arrived safe at the elegant town of Philadelphia. I sold my goods here pretty well; and in this charming place I found everything plentiful and cheap.

While I was in this place, a very extraordinary occurrence befell me. I had been told one evening of a wise woman, a Mrs. Davis, who revealed secrets, foretold events, &c. &c. I put little faith in this story at first, as I could not conceive that any mortal could foresee the future disposals of Providence, nor did I believe in any other revelation than that of the Holy Scriptures; however, I was greatly astonished at seeing this woman in a dream that night, though a person I never before beheld in my life. This made such an impression on me that I could not get the idea the next day out of my mind, and I then became as anxious to see her as I was before indifferent. Accordingly in the evening, after we left off working, I enquired where she lived, and being directed to her, to my inexpressible surprise, beheld the very woman in the very same dress she appeared to me to wear in the vision. She immediately told me I had dreamed of her the preceding night; related to me many things that had happened with a correctness that astonished me, and finally told me I should not be long a slave. This was the more agreeable news, as I believed it the more readily from her having so faithfully related the past incidents of my life. She said I should be twice in very great danger of my life within eighteen months, which, if I escaped, I should afterwards go on well. So, giving me her blessing, we parted. After staying here sometime till our vessel was loaded, and I had bought in my little traffic, we sailed from this agreeable spot for Montserrat, once more to encounter the raging surfs.

We arrived safe at Montserrat, where we discharged our cargo; and soon after that, we took slaves on board for St. Eustatius, and from thence to Georgia. I had always exerted myself, and did double work, in order to make our voyages as short as possible; and from thus overworking myself while we were at Georgia, I caught a fever and ague. I was very ill for eleven days, and near dying; eternity was now exceedingly impressed on my mind, and I feared very much that awful event. I prayed the Lord, therefore, to spare me; and I made a promise in my mind to God, that I would be good if ever I should recover. At length, from having an eminent doctor to attend me, I was restored again to health; and soon after, we got the vessel loaded, and set off for Montserrat. During the passage, as I was perfectly restored, and had much business of the vessel to mind, all my endeavors to keep up my integrity, and perform my promise to God, began to fail; and, in spite of all I could do, as we drew nearer and nearer to the islands, my resolutions more and more declined, as if the very air of that country or climate seemed fatal to piety. When we were safe arrived at Montserrat, and I had got ashore, I forgot my former resolutions. Alas! how prone is the heart to leave that God it wishes to love! and how strongly do the things of this world strike the senses and captivate the soul! After our vessel was discharged, we soon got her ready, and took in, as usual, some of the poor oppressed natives of Africa, and other Negroes; we then set off again for Georgia and Charleston. We arrived at Georgia, and, having landed part of our cargo, proceeded to Charleston with the remainder. While we were there, I saw the town illuminated; the guns were fired, and bon-

fires and other demonstrations of joy shown, on account of the
repeal of the stamp act. Here I disposed of some goods on my
own account; the white men buying them with smooth promises
and fair words, giving me, however, but very indifferent payment. There was one gentleman particularly, who bought a
puncheon of rum of me, which gave me a great deal of trouble;
and, although I used the interest of my friendly captain, I could
not obtain anything for it; for, being a Negro man, I could not
oblige him to pay me. This vexed me much, not knowing how
to act; and I lost some time in seeking after this Christian; and
though, when the Sabbath came (which the Negroes usually
make their holiday), I was much inclined to go to public worship,
I was obliged to hire some black men to help to pull a boat across
the water to go in quest of this gentleman. When I found him,
after much entreaty, both from myself and my worthy captain,
he at last paid me in dollars; some of them, however, were copper, and of consequence of no value; but he took advantage of
my being a Negro man, and obliged me to put up with those or
none, although I objected to them. Immediately after, as I was
trying to pass them in the market, amongst other white men, I
was abused for offering to pass bad coin; and, though I showed
them the man I got them from, I was within one minute of being
tied up and flogged without either judge or jury; however, by
the help of a good pair of heels, I ran off, and so escaped the
bastinadoes I should have received. I got on board as fast as I
could, but still continued in fear of them until we sailed, which
I thank God we did not long after; and I have never been
amongst them since.

We soon came to Georgia, where we were to complete our
landing, and here worse fate than ever attended me; for one
Sunday night, as I was with some Negroes in their master's yard,
in the town of Savannah, it happened that their master, one
Doctor Perkins, who was a very severe and cruel man, came in
drunk; and not liking to see any strange Negroes in his yard, he
and a ruffian of a white man, he had in his service, beset me in an
instant, and both of them struck me with the first weapons they
could get hold of. I cried out as long as I could for help and
mercy; but, though I gave a good account of myself, and he
knew my captain, who lodged hard by him, it was to no purpose.

They beat and mangled me in a shameful manner, leaving me near dead. I lost so much blood from the wounds I received, that I lay quite motionless, and was so benumbed that I could not feel anything for many hours. Early in the morning, they took me away to the jail. As I did not return to the ship all night, my captain, not knowing where I was, and being uneasy that I did not then make my appearance, made enquiry after me; and having found where I was, immediately came to me. As soon as the good man saw me so cut and mangled, he could not forbear weeping; he soon got me out of jail to his lodgings, and immediately sent for the best doctors in the place, who at first declared it as their opinion that I could not recover. My captain on this went to all the lawyers in the town for their advice, but they told him they could do nothing for me as I was a Negro. He then went to Doctor Perkins, the hero who had vanquished me, and menaced him, swearing he would be revenged on him, and challenged him to fight. But cowardice is ever the companion of cruelty—and the Doctor refused. However, by the skilfulness of one Dr. Brady of that place, I began at last to amend; but, although I was so sore and bad with the wounds I had all over me that I could not rest in any posture, yet I was in more pain on account of the captain's uneasiness about me, than I otherwise should have been. The worthy man nursed and watched me all the hours of the night; and I was, through his attention and that of the doctor, able to get out of bed in about sixteen or eighteen days. All this time I was very much wanted on board, as I used frequently to go up and down the river for rafts, and other parts of our cargo, and stow them, when the mate was sick or absent. In about four weeks, I was able to go on duty, and in a fortnight after, having got in all our lading, our vessel set sail for Montserrat; and in less than three weeks we arrived there safe towards the end of the year. This ended my adventures in 1764, for I did not leave Montserrat again till the beginning of the following year.

Chapter 7

The author's disgust at the West Indies—Forms schemes to obtain his freedom—Ludicrous disappointment he and his Captain met with in Georgia—At last, by several successful voyages, he acquires a sum of money sufficient to purchase it—Applies to his master, who accepts it, and grants his manumission, to his great joy—He afterwards enters as a freeman on board one of Mr. King's ships, and sails for Georgia—Impositions on free Negroes, as usual—His venture of turkies—Sails for Montserrat, and on his passage his friend, the Captain, falls ill and dies.

EVERY DAY now brought me nearer my freedom, and I was impatient till we proceeded again to sea, that I might have an opportunity of getting a sum large enough to purchase it. I was not long ungratified; for, in the beginning of the year 1766, my master bought another sloop, named the *Nancy*, the largest I had ever seen. She was partly laden, and was to proceed to Philadelphia; our captain had his choice of three, and I was well pleased he chose this, which was the largest; for, from his having a large vessel, I had more room, and could carry a larger quantity of goods with me. Accordingly, when we had delivered our old vessel, the *Prudence*, and completed the lading of the *Nancy*, having made near three hundred per cent. by four barrels of pork I brought from Charleston, I laid in as large a cargo as I could, trusting to God's providence to prosper my undertaking. With these views I sailed for Philadelphia. On our passage, when we drew near the land, I was for the first time surprised at the sight of some whales, having never seen any such large sea monsters before; and as we sailed by the land, one morning, I saw a puppy whale close by the vessel; it was about the length of a wherry boat, and it followed us all the day till we got within the Capes. We arrived safe, and in good time at Philadelphia, and I sold my goods there chiefly to the Quakers. They always appeared to be a very honest, discreet sort of people, and never attempted to impose on me; I therefore liked them, and ever after chose to deal with them in preference to any others.

One Sunday morning, while I was here, as I was going to church, I chanced to pass a meeting-house. The doors being open, and the house full of people, it excited my curiosity to go in. When I entered the house, to my great surprise, I saw a very tall woman standing in the midst of them, speaking in an audible voice something which I could not understand. Having never seen anything of this kind before, I stood and stared about me for some time, wondering at this odd scene. As soon as it was over, I took an opportunity to make inquiry about the place and people, when I was informed they were called Quakers. I particularly asked what that woman I saw in the midst of them had said, but none of them were pleased to satisfy me; so I quitted them, and soon after, as I was returning, I came to a church crowded with people; the church-yard was full likewise, and a number of people were even mounted on ladders looking in at the windows. I thought this a strange sight, as I had never seen churches, either in England or the West Indies, crowded in this manner before. I therefore made bold to ask some people the meaning of all this, and they told me the Rev. Mr. George Whitfield was preaching. I had often heard of this gentleman, and had wished to see and hear him; but I never before had an opportunity. I now therefore resolved to gratify myself with the sight, and pressed in amidst the multitude. When I got into the church, I saw this pious man exhorting the people with the greatest fervor and earnestness, and sweating as much as I ever did while in slavery on Montserrat beach. I was very much struck and impressed with this; I thought it strange I had never seen divines exert themselves in this manner before, and was no longer at a loss to account for the thin congregations they preached to.

When we had discharged our cargo here, and were loaded again, we left this fruitful land once more, and set sail for Montserrat. My traffic had hitherto succeeded so well with me, that I thought, by selling my goods when we arrived at Montserrat, I should have enough to purchase my freedom. But as soon as our vessel arrived there, my master came on board, and gave orders for us to go to St. Eustatius, and discharge our cargo there, and from thence proceed for Georgia. I was much disappointed at this; but thinking, as usual, it was of no use to encounter with the decrees of fate, I submitted without repining, and we went to St. Eustatius. After we had discharged our cargo there, we took in a live cargo (as we call a cargo of slaves).

Here I sold my goods tolerably well; but, not being able to lay out all my money in this small island to as much advantage as in many other places, I laid out only part, and the remainder I brought away with me net. We sailed from hence for Georgia, and I was glad when we got there, though I had not much reason to like the place from my last adventure in Savannah; but I longed to get back to Montserrat and procure my freedom, which I expected to be able to purchase when I returned. As soon as we arrived here, I waited on my careful doctor, Mr. Brady, to whom I made the most grateful acknowledgements in my power, for his former kindness and attention during my illness.

While we were here, an odd circumstance happened to the captain and me, which disappointed us both a great deal. A silversmith, whom we had brought to this place some voyage before, agreed with the captain to return with us to the West Indies, and promised at the same time to give the captain a great deal of money, having pretended to take a liking to him, and being, as we thought, very rich. But while we stayed to load our vessel, this man was taken ill in a house where he worked, and in a week's time became very bad. The worse he grew the more he used to speak of giving the captain what he had promised him, so that he expected something considerable from the death of this man, who had no wife or child, and he attended him day and night. I used also to go with the captain, at his own desire, to attend him; and especially when we saw there was no appearance of his recovery; and, in order to recompense me for my trouble, the captain promised me ten pounds, when he should get the man's property. I thought this would be of great service to me, although I had nearly money enough to purchase my freedom, if I should get safe this voyage to Montserrat. In this expectation I laid out above eight pounds of my money for a suit of superfine clothes to dance in at my freedom, which I hoped was then at hand. We still continued to attend this man, and were with him even on the last day he lived, till very late at night, when we went on board. After we were got to bed, about one or two o'clock in the morning, the captain was sent for, and informed the man was dead. On this he came to my bed, and, waking me, informed me of it, and desired me to get up and procure a light, and immediately go with him. I told him I was very sleepy, and wished he would take somebody else with him; or else, as the man was dead, and could want no further attendance, to let all things remain as they were till the next morning. "No, no," said he, "we will have the money tonight, I cannot wait till tomorrow, so let us go." Accordingly I got up and struck a light, and away we both went and saw the man as dead as we could wish. The captain said he would give him a grand burial, in gratitude for the promised treasure; and desired that all the things belonging to the deceased might be brought forth. Among others, there was a nest of trunks of which he had kept the keys, whilst the man was ill, and when they were produced we opened them with no small eagerness and expectation; and as there was a great number within one another, with much impatience we took them one out of the other. At last, when we came to the smallest, and had opened it, we saw it was full of papers, which we supposed to be notes, at the sight of which our hearts leapt for joy; and that instant the captain, clapping his hands, cried out, "Thank God, here it is." But when we took up the trunk, and began to examine the supposed treasure, and long looked-for bounty (alas! alas! how uncertain and deceitful are all human affairs!); what had we found? while we thought we were embracing a substance, we grasped an empty nothing. The whole amount that was in the nest of trunks, was only one dollar and a half; and all that the man possessed would not pay for his coffin. Our sudden and exquisite joy was now succeeded by as sudden and exquisite pain; and my captain and I exhibited, for some time, most ridiculous figures—pictures of chagrin and astonishment! We went away greatly mortified, and left the deceased to do as well as he could for himself, as we had taken so good care of him when alive for nothing. We set sail once more for Montserrat, and arrived there safe, but much out of humor with our friend the silversmith. When we had unladen the vessel, and I had sold my venture, finding myself master of about forty-seven pounds—I consulted my true friend, the captain, how I should proceed in offering my master the money for my freedom. He told me to come on a certain morning, when he and my master would be at breakfast together. Accordingly, on that morning I went, and met the captain there, as he had appointed. When I went in I made my obeisance to my master, and with my money in my hand, and many fears in my heart, I prayed him to be as good as his offer to me, when he was pleased to promise me my freedom as soon as I could purchase it. This speech seemed to confound him, he began to recoil, and my heart that instant sunk within me. "What," said he, "give you your freedom? Why, where did you get the money? Have you got forty pounds sterling?" "Yes, sir," I answered. "How did you get it?" replied he. I told him, very honestly. The captain then said he knew I got the money honestly, and with much industry, and that I was particularly careful. On which my master replied, I got money much faster than he did; and said he would not have made me the promise he did if he had thought I should have got the money so soon. "Come, come," said my worthy captain, clapping my master on the back, "Come, Robert (which was his name), I think you must let him have his freedom; you have laid your money out very well; you have received a very good interest for it all this time, and here is now the principal at last. I know Gustavus has earned you more than a hundred a year, and he will save you money, as he will not leave you. Come, Robert, take the money." My master then said he would not be worse than his promise; and, taking the money, told me to go to the Secretary at the Register Office, and get my manumission drawn up. These words of my master were like a voice from heaven to me. In an instant all my trepidation was turned into unutterable bliss; and I most reverently bowed myself with gratitude, unable to express my feelings, but by the overflowing of my eyes, and a heart replete with thanks to God, while my true and worthy friend, the captain, congratulated us both with a peculiar degree of heart-felt pleasure. As soon as the first transports of my joy were over, and that I had expressed my thanks to these my worthy friends, in the best manner I was able, I rose with a heart full of affection and reverence, and left the room, in order to obey my master's joyful mandate of going to the Register Office. As I was leaving the house I called to mind the words of the Psalmist, in the 126th Psalm, and like him, "I glorified God in my heart, in whom I trusted." These words had been impressed on my mind from the very day I was forced from Deptford to the present hour, and I now saw them, as I thought, fulfilled and verified. My imagination was all rapture as I flew to

the Register Office; and, in this respect, like the apostle Peter*
(whose deliverance from prison was so sudden and extraordinary
that he thought he was in a vision), I could scarcely believe I
was awake. Heavens! who could do justice to my feelings at this
moment! Not conquering heroes themselves, in the midst of a
triumph—Not the tender mother who has just regained her long
lost infant, and presses it to her heart—Not the weary hungry
mariner, at the sight of the desired friendly port—Not the lover,
when he once more embraces his beloved mistress, after she has
been ravished from his arms! All within my breast was tumult,
wildness, and delirium! My feet scarcely touched the ground,
for they were winged with joy; and, like Elijah, as he rose to
Heaven, they "were with lightning sped as I went on." Everyone
I met I told of my happiness, and blazed about the virtue of my
amiable master and captain.

When I got to the office and acquainted the Register with my
errand, he congratulated me on the occasion, and told me he
would draw up my manumission for half price, which was a
guinea. I thanked him for his kindness; and, having received it,
and paid him, I hastened to my master to get him to sign it, that
I might be fully released. Accordingly he signed the manumission
that day; so that, before night, I, who had been a slave in the
morning, trembling at the will of another, was become my own
master, and completely free. I thought this was the happiest day
I had ever experienced; and my joy was still heightened by the
blessings and prayers of many of the sable race, particularly the
aged, to whom my heart had ever been attached with reverence.

As the form of my manumission has something peculiar in it,
and expresses the absolute power and dominion one man claims
over his fellow, I shall beg leave to present it before my readers
at full length.

MONTSERRAT.

To all men unto whom these presents shall come: I, Robert
King, of the parish of St. Anthony, in the said island, merchant,
send greeting. Know ye, that I, the aforesaid Robert King, for
and in consideration of the sum of seventy pounds current
money of the said island, to me in hand paid, and to the intent
that a Negro man slave, named Gustavus Vassa, shall and may

* Acts 12:9.

become free, having manumitted, emancipated, enfranchised,
and set free, and by these presents do manumit, emancipate,
enfranchise, and set free, the aforesaid Negro man slave, named
Gustavus Vassa, for ever; hereby giving, granting, and releasing
unto him, the said Gustavus Vassa, all right, title, dominion,
sovereignty, and property, which, as lord and master over the
aforesaid Gustavus Vassa, I had, or now have, or by any means
whatsoever I may or can hereafter possibly have over him, the
aforesaid Negro, for ever. In witness whereof, I, the above said
Robert King, have unto these presents set my hand and seal,
this tenth day of July, in the year of our Lord one thousand
seven hundred and sixty-six.

                                           ROBERT KING
Signed, sealed, and delivered in the presence of Terry Legay,
Montserrat.
Registered the within manumission at full length, this eleventh
day of July 1766, in liber. D.

                                 TERRY LEGAY, Register

In short, the fair as well as the black people immediately styled
me by a new appellation, to me the most desirable in the world,
which was freeman; and at the dances I gave, my Georgia superfine blue clothes made no indifferent appearance, as I thought.
Some of the sable females, who formerly stood aloof, now began
to relax and appear less coy; but my heart was still fixed on
London, where I hoped to be ere long. So that my worthy
captain and his owner, my late master, finding that the bent of
my mind was towards London, said to me, "We hope you won't
leave us, but that you will still be with the vessels." Here
gratitude bowed me down; and none but the generous mind can
judge of my feelings, struggling between inclination and duty.
However, notwithstanding my wish to be in London, I obediently
answered my benefactors, that I would go in the vessel, and not
leave them; and from the day I was entered on board as an able-
bodied sailor, at thirty-six shillings per month, besides what
perquisites I could make. My intention was to make a voyage or
two, entirely to please these my honored patrons; but I determined that the year following, if it pleased God, I would see old
England once more, and surprise my old master, Captain Pascal,
who was hourly in my mind; for I still loved him, notwithstanding his usage of me, and pleased myself with thinking what he

would say, when he saw what the Lord had done for me in so short a time, instead of being, as he might perhaps suppose, under the cruel yoke of some planter. With these kind of reveries I used often to entertain myself, and shorten the time till my return; and now, being as in my original free African state, I embarked on board the *Nancy*, after having got all things ready for our voyage. In this state of serenity, we sailed for St. Eustatius; and having smooth seas and calm weather, we soon arrived there. After taking our cargo on board, we proceeded to Savannah, in Georgia, in August, 1766. While we were there, as usual, I used to go for the cargo up the rivers in boats; and on this business have been frequently beset by alligators, which were very numerous on that coast; and shot many of them when they have been near getting into our boats, which we have with great difficulty sometimes prevented, and have been very much frightened at them. I have seen a young one sold in Georgia alive for six pence.

During our stay at this place, one evening, a slave belonging to Mr. Read, a merchant of Savannah, came near our vessel, and began to use me very ill. I entreated him, with all the patience I was master of, to desist, as I knew there was little or no law for a free Negro here; but the fellow, instead of taking my advice, persevered in his insults, and even struck me. At this I lost all temper, and fell on him and beat him soundly. The next morning his master came to our vessel as we lay along side the wharf, and desired me to come ashore, that he might have me flogged all round the town, for beating his Negro slave. I told him he had insulted me, and given the provocation, by first striking me. I had told my captain also the whole affair that morning, and wished him to have gone along with me to Mr. Read, to prevent bad consequences; but he said that it did not signify, and if Mr. Read said any thing, he would make matters up, and desired me to go to work, which I accordingly did. The captain being on board when Mr. Read came and applied to him to deliver me up, he said he knew nothing of the matter, I was a free man. I was astonished and frightened at this, and thought I had better keep where I was than go ashore and be flogged round the town, without judge or jury. I therefore refused to stir; and Mr. Read went away, swearing he would bring all the constables in town, for he would have me out of the vessel. When he was gone, I thought his threat might prove too true to my sorrow; and as I was confirmed in this belief, as well by the many instances I had seen of the treatment of free Negroes, as from a fact that had happened within my own knowledge here a short time before.

There was a free black man, a carpenter, that I knew, who, for asking the gentleman that he worked for, for the money he had earned, was put into jail: and afterwards this oppressed man was sent from Georgia, with false accusations, of an intention to set the gentleman's house on fire, and run away with his slaves. I was therefore much embarrassed, and very apprehensive of a flogging at least. I dreaded, of all things, the thoughts of being striped, as I never in my life had the marks of any violence of that kind. At that instant a rage seized my soul, and for a little I determined to resist the first man that should offer to lay violent hands on me, or basely use me without a trial; for I would sooner die like a free man, than suffer myself to be scourged by the hands of ruffians, and my blood drawn like a slave. The captain and others, more cautious, advised me to make haste and conceal myself; for they said Mr. Read was a very spiteful man, and he would soon come on board with constables and take me. At first I refused this counsel, being determined to stand my ground; but at length, by the prevailing entreaties of the captain and Mr. Dixon, with whom he lodged, I went to Mr. Dixon's house, which was a little out of town, at a place called Yea-ma-chra. I was but just gone, when Mr. Read, with the constables, came for me, and searched the vessel; but, not finding me there, he swore he would have me dead or alive. I was secreted about five days; however, the good character which my captain always gave me, as well as some other gentlemen who also knew me, procured me some friends. At last some of them told my captain that he did not use me well, in suffering me thus to be imposed upon, and said they would see me redressed, and get me on board some other vessel. My captain, on this, immediately went to Mr. Read, and told him, that ever since I eloped from the vessel, his work had been neglected, and he could not go on with her loading, himself and mate not being well; and, as I had managed things on board for them, my absence must retard his voyage, and consequently hurt the owner; he therefore begged of him to forgive me, as he said he never heard any complaint of me before, during the several years I had been with him. After repeated entreaties, Mr. Read said I might go to hell, and that he would not meddle with me; on which my captain came immediately to me at his lodging, and telling me how pleasantly matters had gone on, desired me to go on board.

Some of my other friends then asked him if he had got the constable's warrant from them; the captain said, No. On this I was desired by them to stay in the house; and they said they would get me on board of some other vessel before the evening. When the captain heard this, he became almost distracted. He went immediately for the warrant, and, after using every exertion in his power, he at last got it from my hunters; but I had all the expenses to pay.

After I had thanked all my friends for their kindness, I went on board again to my work, of which I had always plenty. We were in haste to complete our lading, and were to carry twenty head of cattle with us to the West Indies, where they are a very profitable article. In order to encourage me in working, and to make up for the time I had lost, my captain promised me the privilege of carrying two bullocks of my own with me; and this made me work with redoubled ardor. As soon as I had got the vessel loaded, in doing which I was obliged to perform the duty of the mate as well my own work, and that the bullocks were near coming on board, I asked the captain leave to bring my two, according to his promise; but to my great surprise, he told me there was no room for them. I then asked him to permit me to take one; but he said he could not. I was a good deal mortified at this usage, and told him I had no notion that he intended thus to impose on me; nor could I think well of any man that was so much worse than his word. On this we had some disagreement, and I gave him to understand that I intended to leave the vessel. At this he appeared to be very much dejected; and our mate, who had been very sickly, and whose duty had long devolved upon me, advised him to persuade me to stay; in consequence of which, he spoke very kindly to me, making many fair promises, telling me, that, as the mate was so sickly, he could not do without me; and that, as the safety of the vessel and cargo depended greatly upon me, he therefore hoped that I would not be offended at what had passed between us, and swore he would make up all matters when we arrived in the West Indies; so I consented to slave on as before. Soon after this, as the bullocks were coming on board, one of them ran at the captain, and butted him so furiously in the breast, that he never recovered of the blow. In order to make me some amends for his treatment about the bullocks, the captain now pressed me very much to take some turkeys, and other fowls with me, and gave me liberty to take as many as I could find room for; but I told him he knew very well I had never carried any turkeys before, as I always thought they were such tender birds that they were not fit to cross the seas. However, he continued to press me to buy them for once; and what seemed very surprising to me, the more I was against it, the more he urged my taking them, insomuch that he ensured me from all losses that might happen by them, and I was prevailed on to take them; but I thought this very strange, as he had never acted so with me before. This, and not being able to dispose of my paper money any other way, induced me at length to take four dozen. The turkeys, however, I was so dissatisfied about, that I determined to make no more voyages to this quarter, nor with this captain; and was very apprehensive that my free voyage would be the worst I had ever made.

We set sail for Montserrat. The captain and mate had been both complaining of sickness when we sailed, and as we proceeded on our voyage they grew worse. This was about November, and we had not been long at sea before we began to meet with strong northerly gales and rough seas; and in about seven or eight days all the bullocks were near being drowned, and four or five of them died. Our vessel, which had not been tight at first, was much less so now. And, though we were but nine in the whole, including five sailors and myself, yet we were obliged to attend to the pumps every half or three quarters of an hour. The captain and mate came on deck as often as they were able, which was now but seldom; for they declined so fast, that they were not well enough to make observations above four or five times the whole voyage. The whole care of the vessel rested therefore upon me, and I was obliged to direct her by mere dint of reason, not being able to work a traverse. The captain was now very sorry he had not taught me navigation, and protested, if ever he should get well again, he would not fail to do so; but in about seventeen days his illness increased so much, that he was obliged to keep his bed, continuing sensible, however, till the last, constantly having the owner's interest at heart; for this just and benevolent man ever appeared much concerned about the welfare of what he was intrusted with. When this dear friend found the symptoms of death approaching, he called me by my name; and, when I came to him, he asked (with almost his last breath) if he had ever done me any harm? "God forbid I should think so," replied I, "I should then be the most ungrateful of wretches to the best of benefactors." While I was thus expressing my affection and sorrow by his bed side, he expired without saying another word; and the day following we committed his body to the deep. Every man on board loved him, and regretted his death; but I was exceedingly affected at it, and found that I did not know, till he was gone, the strength of my regard for him. Indeed, I had every reason in the world to be attached to him; for, besides that he was in general mild, affable, generous, faithful, benevolent, and just, he was to me a friend and father; and had it pleased Providence, that he had died about five months before, I verily believe I should not have obtained my freedom when I did; and it is not improbable that I might not have been able to get it at any rate afterwards.

The captain being dead, the mate came on the deck, and made such observations as he was able, but to no purpose. In the course of a few days more, the few bullocks that remained were found dead; but the turkeys I had, though on the deck, and exposed to so much wet and bad weather, did well, and I afterwards gained near three hundred per cent on the sale of them; so that in the event it proved a happy circumstance for me that I had not bought the bullocks I intended, for they must have perished with the rest; and I could not help looking on this otherwise trifling circumstance as a particular providence of God, and was thankful accordingly. The care of the vessel took up all my time, and engaged my attention entirely. As we were now out of the variable winds, I thought I should not be much puzzled to hit upon the islands. I was persuaded I steered right for Antigua, which I wished to reach, as the nearest to us; and in the course of nine or ten days we made the island, to our great joy, and the day after, we came safe to Montserrat.

Many were surprised when they heard of my conducting the sloop into the port, and I now obtained a new appellation, and was called Captain. This elated me not a little, and it was quite flattering to my vanity to be thus styled by as high a title as any freeman in this place possessed. When the death of the captain became known, he was much regretted by all who knew him, for he was a man universally respected. At the same time the sable captain lost no fame; for the success I had met with, increased the affection of my friends in no small measure.

Chapter 8

The author, to oblige Mr. King, once more embarks for Georgia
in one of his vessels—A new captain is appointed—They sail, and
steer a new course—Three remarkable dreams—The vessel is
shipwrecked on the Bahama Bank, but the crew are preserved,
principally by means of the author—He sets out from the island
with the captain, in a small boat, in quest of a ship—Their distress—Meet with a wrecker—Sail for Providence—Are overtaken
again by a terrible storm, and all are near perishing—Arrive
at New Providence—The author, after some time, sails from
thence to Georgia—Meets with another storm, and is obliged
to put back and refit—Arrives at Georgia—Meets new impositions—Two white men attempt to kidnap him—Officiates as a
person at a funeral ceremony—Bids adieu to Georgia, and sails
for Martinique.

As I HAD NOW, by the death of my captain, lost my great bene-
factor and friend, I had little inducement to remain longer in the
West Indies, except my gratitude to Mr. King, which I thought I
had pretty well discharged in bringing back his vessel safe, and
delivering his cargo to his satisfaction. I began to think of leaving this part of the world, of which I had been long tired, and
returning to England, where my heart had always been, but Mr.
King still pressed me very much to stay with his vessel; and he
had done so much for me that I found myself unable to refuse
his requests, and consented to go another voyage to Georgia, as
the mate, from his ill state of health, was quite useless in the
vessel. Accordingly a new captain was appointed, whose name
was William Phillips, an old acquaintance of mine; and, having
refitted our vessel, and taken several slaves on board, we set sail
for St. Eustatius, where we stayed but a few days; and on the
30th of January, 1767, we steered for Georgia. Our new captain
boasted strangely of his skill in navigation and conducting a
vessel; and in consequence of this he steered a new course,
several points more to the westward than we ever did before;
this appeared to me very extraordinary.

On the fourth of February, which was soon after we had got
into our new course, I dreamt the ship was wrecked amidst the
surfs and rocks, and that I was the means of saving everyone on
board; and on the night following I dreamed the very same

dream. These dreams, however, made no impression on my mind; and the next evening, it being my watch below, I was pumping the vessel, a little after eight o'clock, just before I went off the deck, as is the custom; and being weary with the duty of the day, and tired at the pump (for we made a good deal of water), I began to express my impatience, and uttered with an oath, "Damn the vessel's bottom out." But my conscience instantly smote me for the expression. When I left the deck I went to bed, and had scarcely fallen asleep, when I dreamed the same dream again about the ship as I had dreamed the two preceding nights. At twelve o'clock the watch was changed; and, as I had always the charge of the captain's watch, I then went upon deck. At half after one in the morning, the man at the helm saw something under the lee-beam that the sea washed against, and he immediately called to me that there was a grampus, and desired me to look at it. Accordingly I stood up and observed it for some time; but, when I saw the sea wash up against it again and again, I said it was not a fish but a rock. Being soon certain of this, I went down to the captain, and, with some confusion, told him the danger we were in, and desired him to come upon deck immediately. He said it was very well, and I went up again. As soon as I was upon deck, the wind, which had been pretty high, having abated a little, the vessel began to be carried sideways towards the rock, by means of the current. Still the captain did not appear. I therefore went to him again, and told him the vessel was then near a large rock, and desired he would come up with all speed. He said he would, and I returned to the deck. When I was upon the deck again, I saw we were not above a pistol shot from the rock, and I heard the noise of the breakers all around us. I was exceedingly alarmed at this, and the captain having not yet come on the deck, I lost all patience; and, growing quite enraged, I ran down to him again, and asked him why he did not come up, and what he could mean by all this? "The breakers," said I, "are round us, and the vessel is almost on the rock." With that he came on the deck with me, and we tried to put the vessel about, and get her out of the current, but all to no purpose, the wind being very small. We then called all hands up immediately; and after a little we got up one end of a cable, and fastened it to the anchor. By this time the surf was foamed round us, and made a dreadful noise on the breakers; and the very moment we let the anchor go, the vessel struck against the rocks. One swell now succeeded another, as it were one wave calling on its fellow; the roaring of the billows increased, and, with one single heave of the swells, the sloop was pierced and transfixed among the rocks! in a moment a scene of horror presented itself to my mind, such as I never had conceived or experienced before. All my sins stared me in the face; and especially, I thought that God had hurled his direful vengeance on my guilty head for cursing the vessel on which my life depended. My spirits at this forsook me, and I expected every moment to go to the bottom. I determined if I should still be saved, that I would never swear again. And in the midst of my distress, while the dreadful surfs were dashing with unremitting fury among the rocks, I remembered the Lord, though fearful that I was undeserving of forgiveness, and I thought that as he had often delivered he might yet deliver; and, calling to mind the many mercies he had shown me in times past, they gave me some small hope that he might still help me. I then began to think how we might be saved; and I believe no mind was ever like mine so replete with inventions, and confused with schemes, though how to escape death I knew not. The captain immediately ordered the hatches to be nailed down on the slaves in the hold, where there were about twenty, all of whom must unavoidably have perished if he had been obeyed. When he desired the man to nail down the hatches, I thought that my sin was the cause of this, and that God would charge me with these people's blood. This thought rushed upon my mind that instant with such violence, that it quite overpowered me, and I fainted. I recovered just as the people were about to nail down the hatches; perceiving which, I desired them to stop. The captain then said it must be done. I asked him why? He said that everyone would endeavor to get into the boat, which was but small, and thereby we should be drowned; for it would not have carried above ten at the most. I could no longer refrain my emotion, and told him he deserved drowning for not knowing how to navigate the vessel; and I believe the people would have tossed him overboard if I had given them the least hint of it. However, the hatches were not nailed down; and, as none of us could leave the vessel then on account of the darkness, and as we knew not where to go, and were convinced besides that the boat could not survive the surfs, we all said we would remain on the dry part of the vessel, and trust to God till daylight appeared, when we should know better what to do.

I then advised to get the boat prepared against morning, and some of us began to set about it; but others abandoned all care of the ship and themselves, and fell to drinking. Our boat had a piece out of her bottom near two feet long, and we had no materials to mend her; however, necessity being the mother of invention, I took some pump leather and nailed it to the broken part, and plastered it over with tallow-grease. And, thus prepared, with the utmost anxiety of mind, we watched for daylight, and thought every minute an hour till it appeared. At last it saluted our longing eyes, and kind Providence accompanied its approach with what was no small comfort to us, for the dreadful swells began to subside; and the next thing that we discovered to raise our drooping spirits, was a small key or desolate island, about five or six miles off. But a barrier soon presented itself; for there was not water enough for our boat to go over the reefs, and this threw us again into a sad consternation; but there was no alternative, we were therefore obliged to put but few in the boat at once. And, what was still worse, all of us were frequently under the necessity of getting out to drag and lift it over the reefs. This cost us much labor and fatigue; and, what was yet more distressing, we could not avoid having our legs cut and torn very much with the rocks. There were only four people that would work with me at the oars, and they consisted of three black men and a Dutch Creole sailor; and, though we went with the boat five times that day, we had no others to assist us. But, had we not worked in this manner, I really believe the people could not have been saved; for not one of the white men did anything to preserve their lives. Indeed, they soon got so drunk that they were not able, but lay about the deck like swine, so that we were at last obliged to lift them into the boat, and carry them on shore by force. This want of assistance made our labor intolerably severe; insomuch, that, by going on shore so often that day, the skin was partly stript off my hands.

However, we continued all the day to toil and strain our

exertions, till we had brought all on board safe to the shore, so that out of thirty-two people we lost not one.

My dream now returned upon my mind with all its force. It was fulfilled in every part, for our danger was the same I had dreamt of; and I could not help looking on myself as the principal instrument in effecting our deliverance; for, owing to some of our people getting drunk, the rest of us were obliged to double our exertions. And it was fortunate we did, for in a very little time longer the patch of leather on the boat would have been worn out, and she would have been no longer fit for service. Situated as we were, who could think that men should be so careless of the danger they were in? for, if the wind had but raised the swell as it was when the vessel struck, we must have bid a final farewell to all hopes of deliverance; and, though I warned the people who were drinking and entreated them to embrace the moment of deliverance, nevertheless they persisted, as if not possessed of the least spark of reason. I could not help thinking, that if any of these people had been lost, God would charge me with their lives; which, perhaps, was one cause of my laboring so hard for their preservation. And, indeed, every one of them afterwards seemed so sensible of the service I had rendered them, that while we were on the key I was a kind of chieftain amongst them. I brought some limes, oranges, and lemons ashore; and, finding it to be a good soil where we were, I planted several of them as a token to anyone that might be cast away hereafter. This key, as we afterwards found, was one of the Bahama islands, which consist of a cluster of large islands with smaller ones or keys, as they are called, interspersed among them. It was about a mile in circumference, with a white sandy beach running in a regular order along it. On that part of it where we first attempted to land, there stood some very large birds, called flamingoes. These, from the reflection of the sun, appeared to us at a little distance as large as men; and when they walked backwards and forwards, we could not conceive what they were. Our captain swore they were cannibals. This created a great panic among us, and we held a consultation how to act. The captain wanted to go to a key that was within sight, but a great way off; but I was against it, as in so doing we should not be able to save all the people. "And therefore," said I, "let

us go on shore here, and perhaps these cannibals may take to
the water." Accordingly we steered towards them; and when we
approached them, to our very great joy and no less wonder,
they walked off, one after the other very deliberately; and at
last they took flight and relieved us entirely from our fears.
About the key there were turtles and several sorts of fish in
such abundance that we caught them without bait, which was a
great relief to us after the salt provisions on board. There was
also a large rock on the beach, about ten feet high, which was in
the form of a punch-bowl at the top; this we could not help
thinking Providence had ordained to supply us with rain water;
and it was something singular, that, if we did not take the water
when it rained, in some little time after, it would turn as salt
as sea water.

Our first care after refreshment was to make ourselves tents
to lodge in, which we did as well as we could with some sails we
had brought from the ship. We then began to think how we
might get from this place, which was quite uninhabited; and
we determined to repair our boat, which was very much shattered, and to put to sea in quest of a ship or some inhabited
island. It took us up, however, eleven days before we could get
the boat ready for sea in the manner we wanted it, with a sail
and other necessaries. When we had got all things prepared, the
captain wanted me to stay on shore while he went to sea in
quest of a vessel to take all the people off the key. But this I
refused; and the captain and myself, with five more, set off in the
boat towards New Providence. We had no more than two musket
load of gun-powder with us, if anything should happen, and our
stock of provisions consisted of three gallons of rum, four of
water, some salt beef, and some biscuit; and in this manner we
proceeded to sea.

On the second day of our voyage, we came to an island called
Abaco, the largest of the Bahama islands. We were much in want
of water, for by this time our water was expended, and we were
exceedingly fatigued in pulling two days in the heat of the sun;
and it being late in the evening, we hauled the boat ashore to
try for water, and remain during the night. When we came
ashore we searched for water, but could find none. When it was
dark, we made a fire around us for fear of the wild beasts, as the

place was an entire thick wood, and we took it by turns to watch. In this situation we found very little rest, and waited with impatience for the morning. As soon as the light appeared we set off again with our boat, in hopes of finding assistance during the day. We were now much dejected and weakened by pulling the boat; for our sail was of no use, and we were almost famished for want of fresh water to drink. We had nothing left to eat but salt beef, and that we could not use without water. In this situation we toiled all day in sight of the island, which was very long; in the evening, seeing no relief, we made shore again, and fastened our boat. We then went to look for fresh water, being quite faint for the want of it; and we dug and searched about for some all the remainder of the evening, but could not find one drop, so that our dejection at this period became excessive, and our terror so great, that we expected nothing but death to deliver us. We could not touch our beef, which was salt as brine, without fresh water, and we were in the greatest terror from the apprehension of wild beasts. When unwelcome night came, we acted as on the night before; and the next morning we set off again from the island in hopes of seeing some vessel. In this manner we toiled as well as we were able till four o'clock, during which we passed several keys, but could not meet with a ship; and, still famishing with thirst, went ashore on one of those keys again, in hopes of finding some water. Here we found some leaves with a few drops of water in them, which we lapped with much eagerness; we then dug in several places, but without success. As we were digging holes in search of water, there came forth some very thick and black stuff; but none of us could touch it, except the poor Dutch Creole, who drank above a quart of it as eagerly as if it had been wine. We tried to catch fish, but could not; and we now began to repine at our fate, and abandon ourselves to despair, when, in the midst of our murmuring, the captain all at once cried out, "A sail! a sail! a sail!" This gladdening sound was like a reprieve to a convict, and we all instantly returned to look at it; but in a little time some of us began to be afraid it was not a sail. However, at a venture, we embarked and steered after it; and in half an hour to our unspeakable joy, we plainly saw that it was a vessel. At this our drooping spirits revived, and we made towards her with all the speed imaginable.

When we came near to her, we found she was a little sloop, about the size of a Gravesend hoy, and quite full of people; a circumstance which we could not make out the meaning of. Our captain, who was a Welshman, swore that they were pirates, and would kill us. I said, be that as it might, we must board her if we were to die by it; and if they should not receive us kindly, we must oppose them as well as we could, for there was no alternative between their perishing and ours. This counsel was immediately taken, and I really believe that the captain, myself, and the Dutchman would then have faced twenty men. We had two cutlasses and a musket, that I brought in the boat; and in this situation, we rowed alongside, and immediately boarded her. I believe there were about forty hands on board; but how great was our surprise, as soon as we got on board, to find that the major part of them were in the same predicament as ourselves.

They belonged to a whaling schooner that was wrecked two days before us, about nine miles to the north of our vessel. When she was wrecked, some of them had taken to their boats, and had left some of their people and property on the key, in the same manner as we had done; and were going like us to New Providence in quest of a ship, when they met with this little sloop, called a wrecker, their employment in those seas being to look after wrecks. They were then going to take the remainder of the people belonging to the schooner; for which the wrecker was to have all things belonging to the vessel, and likewise their people's help to get what they could out of her, and were then to carry the crew to New Providence.

We told the people of the wrecker the condition of our vessel, and we made the same agreement with them as the schooner's people; and, on their complying, we begged of them to go to our key directly, because our people were in want of water. They agreed, therefore, to go along with us first; and in two days we arrived at the key, to the inexpressible joy of the people that we had left behind, as they had been reduced to great extremities for want of water in our absence. Luckily for us, the wrecker had now more people on board than she could carry or victual for any moderate length of time; they therefore hired the schooner's people to work on the wreck, and we left them our boat, and embarked for New Providence.

Nothing could have been more fortunate than our meeting with this wrecker, for New Providence was at such a distance that we never could have reached it in our boat. The island of Abaco was much longer than we expected; and it was not till after sailing for three or four days that we got safe to the farther end of it, towards New Providence. When we arrived there we watered, and got a good many lobsters and other shell-fish; which proved a great relief to us, as our provisions and water were almost exhausted. We then proceeded on our voyage; but the day after we left the island, late in the evening, and whilst we were yet amongst the Bahama keys, we were overtaken by a violent gale of wind, so that we were obliged to cut away the mast. The vessel was very near foundering; for she parted from her anchors, and struck several times on the shoals. Here we expected every minute that she would have gone to pieces, and each moment to be our last; so much so, that my old captain and sickly, useless mate, and several others, fainted; and death stared us in the face on every side. All the swearers on board now began to call on the God of Heaven to assist them: and, sure enough, beyond our comprehension he did assist us, and in a miraculous manner delivered us! In the very height of our extremity the wind lulled for a few minutes; and, although the swell was high beyond expression, two men, who were expert swimmers, attempted to go to the buoy of the anchor, which we still saw on the water, at some distance, in a little punt that belonged to the wrecker, which was not large enough to carry more than two. She filled at different times in their endeavors to get into her alongside of our vessel; and they saw nothing but death before them, as well as we; but they said they might as well die that way as any other. A coil of very small rope, with a little buoy, was put in along with them; and, at last, with great hazard, they got the punt clear from the vessel; and these two intrepid water heroes paddled away for life towards the buoy of the anchor. Our eyes were fixed on them all the time, expecting every minute to be their last; and the prayers of all those that remained in their senses were offered up to God, on their behalf, for a speedy deliverance, and for our own, which depended on them; and he heard and answered us! These two men at last reached the buoy; and, having fastened the punt to it, they tied one end of their rope to the small buoy that they had in the punt, and sent it adrift towards the vessel. We on board, observing this, threw out boat-hooks and leads fastened to lines, in order to catch the buoy; at last we caught it, and fastened a hawser to the end of the small rope; we then gave them a sign to pull, and they pulled the hawser to them, and fastened it to the buoy, which being done we hauled for our lives; and, through the mercy of God, we got again from the shoals into the deep water, and the punt got safe to the vessel. It is impossible for any to conceive our heart-felt joy at this second deliverance from ruin, but those who have suffered the same hardships. Those whose strength and senses were gone came to themselves, and were now as elated as they were before depressed. Two days after this the wind ceased, and the water became smooth. The punt then went on shore, and we cut down some trees; and having found our mast and mended it, we brought it on board, and fixed it up. As soon as we had done this, we got up the anchor, and away we went once more for New Providence, which in three days more we reached safe, after having been above three weeks in a situation in which we did not expect to escape with life. The inhabitants here were very kind to us; and, when they learned our situation, shewed us a great deal of hospitality and friendship. Soon after this every one of our old fellow sufferers that were free parted from us, and shaped their course where their inclination led them. One merchant, who had a large sloop, seeing our condition, and knowing we wanted to go to Georgia, told four of us that his vessel was going there; and, if we would work on board and load her, he would give us our passage free. As we could not get any wages whatever, and found it very hard to get off the place, we were obliged to consent to his proposal; and we went on board and helped to load the sloop, though we had only our victuals allowed us. When she was entirely loaded, he told us she was going to Jamaica first, where we must go if we went in her. This, however, I refused; but my fellow sufferers not having any money to help themselves with, necessity obliged them to accept of the offer, and to steer that course, though they did not like it.

We stayed in New Providence about seventeen or eighteen days, during which time I met with many friends, who gave me encouragement to stay there with them, but I declined it; though, had not my heart been fixed on England I should have stayed, as I liked the place extremely, and there were some free black people here who were very happy, and we passed our time pleasantly together, with the melodious sound of the catguts, under the lime and lemon trees. At length Captain Phillips hired a sloop to carry him and some of the slaves that he could not sell to Georgia; and I agreed to go with him in this vessel, meaning now to take my farewell of that place. When the vessel was ready we all embarked; and I took my leave of New Providence, not without regret. We sailed about four o'clock in the morning with a fair wind, for Georgia; and about eleven o'clock the same morning, a sudden and short gale sprung up and blew away most of our sails; and, as we were still among the keys, in a very few minutes it dashed the sloop against the rocks. Luckily for us the water was deep; and the sea was not so angry, but that, after having for some time labored hard, and being many in number, we were saved, through God's mercy; and, by using our greatest exertions, we got the vessel off. The next day we returned to Providence, where we soon got her again refitted. Some of the people swore that we had spells set upon us by somebody in Montserrat; and others that we had witches and wizards amongst the poor helpless slaves; and that we never should arrive safe at Georgia. But these things did not deter me; I said, "Let us again face the winds and seas, and swear not, but trust to God, and he will deliver us." We therefore once more set sail; and with hard labor, in seven days' time, we arrived safe at Georgia.

After our arrival we went up to the town of Savannah; and the same evening I went to a friend's house to lodge, whose name was Mosa, a black man. We were very happy at meeting each other; and after supper we had a light till it was between nine and ten o'clock at night. About that time the watch or patrol came by, and, discerning a light in the house, they knocked at the door; we opened it, and they came in and sat down and drank some punch with us; they also begged some limes of me, as they understood I had some, which I readily gave them. A little after this they told me I must go to the watch house with them; this surprised me a good deal, after our kindness to them;

and I asked them, Why so? They said that all Negroes who had a light in their houses after nine o'clock were to be taken into custody, and either pay some dollars or be flogged. Some of those people knew that I was a free man; but, as the man of the house was not free, and had his master to protect him, they did not take the same liberty with him they did with me. I told them that I was a free man, and just arrived from Providence; that we were not making any noise, and that I was not a stranger in that place, but was very well known there: "Besides," said I, "what will you do with me?" "That you shall see," replied they, "but you must go to the watch house with us." Now, whether they meant to get money from me or not I was at a loss to know, but I thought immediately of the oranges and limes at Santa Cruz; and seeing that nothing would pacify them I went with them to the watch house, where I remained during the night. Early the next morning these imposing ruffians flogged a Negro man and woman that they had in the watch house, and then they told me that I must be flogged too. I asked why? and if there was any law for free men? and told them if there was I would have it put in force against them. But this only exasperated them the more, and instantly swore they would serve me as Doctor Perkins had done; and were going to lay violent hands on me; when one of them more humane than the rest, said that as I was a free man they could not justify striping me by law. I then immediately sent for Doctor Brady, who was known to be an honest and worthy man; and on his coming to my assistance they let me go.

This was not the only disagreeable incident I met with while I was in this place; for one day, while I was a little way out of the town of Savannah, I was beset by two white men, who meant to play their usual tricks with me in the way of kidnapping. As soon as these men accosted me, one of them said to the other, "This is the very fellow we are looking for, that you lost," and the other swore I was the identical person. On this they made up to me, and were about to handle me; but I told them to be still and keep off, for I had seen those kind of tricks played upon other free blacks, and they must not think to serve me so. At this they paused a little, and one said to the other—it will not do; and the other answered that I talked too good English. I replied,

I believed I did; and I had also with me a revengeful stick equal to the occasion; and my mind was likewise good. Happily, however, it was not used; and after we had talked together a little in this manner the rogues left me.

I stayed in Savannah some time, anxiously trying to get to Montserrat once more, to see Mr. King, my old master, and then to take a final farewell of the American quarter of the globe. At last I met with a sloop called the *Speedwell*, Captain John Bunton, which belonged to Grenada and was bound to Martinique, a French island, with a cargo of rice, and I shipped myself on board of her.

Before I left Georgia, a black woman who had a child lying dead, being very tenacious of the church burial service, and not able to get any white person to perform it, applied to me for that purpose. I told her I was no parson; and besides, that the service over the dead did not affect the soul. This however did not satisfy her; she still urged me very hard: I therefore complied with her earnest entreaties, and at last consented to act the parson for the first time in my life. As she was much respected, there was a great company both of white and black people at the grave. I then accordingly assumed my new vocation, and performed the funeral ceremony to the satisfaction of all present; after which, I bade adieu to Georgia, and sailed for Martinique.

Chapter 9

The author arrives at Martinique—Meets with new difficulties—
Gets to Montserrat, where he takes leave of his old master, and
sails for England—Meets Capt. Pascal—Learns the French horn
—Hires himself with Doctor Irving, where he learns to freshen
sea water—Leaves the Doctor, and goes a voyage to Turkey and
Portugal; and afterwards goes a voyage to Grenada, and another
to Jamaica—Returns to the Doctor, and they embark together on
a voyage to the North Pole, with the Hon. Captain Phipps—
Some account of that voyage, and the dangers the author was
in—He returns to England.

I THUS TOOK a final leave of Georgia, for the treatment I had received in it disgusted me very much against the place; and when
I left it and sailed for Martinique I determined never more to re-
visit it. My new captain conducted his vessel safer than any
former one; and, after an agreeable voyage, we got safe to our intended port. While I was on this island I went about a good deal,
and found it very pleasant; in particular, I admired the town of
St. Pierre, which is the principal one in the island, and built
more like an European town than any I had seen in the West
Indies. In general also, slaves were better treated, had more holidays, and looked better than those in the English islands. After
we had done our business here, I wanted my discharge, which was
necessary; for it was then the month of May, and I wished much
to be at Montserrat to bid farewell to Mr. King, and all my other
friends there, in time to sail for Old England in the July fleet.
But, alas! I had put a great stumbling block in my own way, by
which I was near losing my passage that season to England. I had
lent my captain some money which I now wanted to enable me
to prosecute my intentions. This I told him; but when I applied
for it, though I urged the necessity of my occasion, I met with
so much shuffling from him, that I began at last to be afraid of
losing my money, as I could not recover it by law; for I have
already mentioned that throughout the West Indies no black
man's testimony is admitted, on any occasion, against any white
person whatever, and therefore my own oath would have been
of no use. I was obliged, therefore, to remain with him till he
might be disposed to return it to me. Thus we sailed from
Martinique for the Grenadas, I frequently pressing the captain

for my money to no purpose; and to render my condition worse, when we got there, the captain and his owners quarrelled, so that my situation became daily more irksome: for besides that, we on board had little or no victuals allowed us, and I could not get my money nor wages, as I could then have gotten my passage free to Montserrat had I been able to accept it. The worst of all was, that it was growing late in July, and the ships in the islands must sail by the 26th of that month. At last, however, with a great many entreaties, I got my money from the captain, and took the first vessel I could meet with for St. Eustatius. From thence I went in another to Basse Terre in St. Kitts, where I arrived on the 19th of July. On the 22d, having met with a vessel bound to Montserrat, I wanted to go in her; but the captain and others would not take me on board until I should advertise myself, and give notice of my going off the island. I told them of my haste to be in Montserrat, and that the time then would not admit of advertising, it being late in the evening, and the vessel about to sail; but he insisted it was necessary, and otherwise he said he would not take me. This reduced me to great perplexity; for if I should be compelled to submit to this degrading necessity, which every black freeman is under, of advertising himself like a slave, when he leaves an island, and which I thought a gross imposition upon any freeman, I feared I should miss that opportunity of going to Montserrat, and then I could not get to England that year. The vessel was just going off, and no time could be lost; I immediately therefore set about with a heavy heart, to try who I could get to befriend me in complying with the demands of the captain. Luckily I found in a few minutes, some gentlemen of Montserrat whom I knew; and having told them my situation, I requested their friendly assistance in helping me off the island. Some of them, on this, went with me to the captain, and satisfied him of my freedom; and, to my very great joy, he desired me to go on board. We then set sail, and the next day, 23d, I arrived at the wished-for place, after an absence of six months, in which I had more than once experienced the delivering hand of Providence, when all human means of escaping destruction seemed hopeless. I saw my friends with a gladness of heart which was increased by my absence and the dangers I had escaped, and I was received with great friendship by them all, but particularly by

Mr. King, to whom I related the fate of his sloop, the *Nancy*, and the causes of her being wrecked. I now learned with extreme sorrow that his house was washed away during my absence, by the bursting of the pond at the top of a mountain that was opposite the town of Plymouth. It swept great part of the town away, and Mr. King lost a great deal of property from the inundation, and nearly his life. When I told him I intended to go to London that season, and that I had came to visit him before my departure, the good man expressed a great deal of affection for me, and sorrow that I should leave him, and warmly advised me to stay there, insisting, as I was much respected by all the gentlemen in the place, that I might do very well, and in a short time have land and slaves of my own. I thanked him for this instance of his friendship; but, as I wished very much to be in London, I declined remaining any longer there, and begged he would excuse me. I then requested he would be kind enough to give me a certificate of my behavior while in his service, which he very readily complied with, and gave me the following:

MONTSERRAT, JANUARY 26, 1767.

The bearer hereof, Gustavus Vassa, was my slave for upwards of three years, during which he has always behaved himself well, and discharged his duty with honesty and assiduity.

ROBERT KING

TO ALL WHOM THIS MAY CONCERN.

Having obtained this, I parted from my kind master, after many sincere professions of gratitude and regard, and prepared for my departure for London. I immediately agreed to go with one Capt. John Hamer, for seven guineas (the passage to London) on board a ship called the *Andromache;* and on the 24th and 25th, I had free dances, as they are called, with some of my countrymen, previous to my setting off; after which I took leave of all my friends, and on the 26th I embarked for London, exceedingly glad to see myself once more on board of a ship; and still more so, in steering the course I had long wished for. With a light heart I bade Montserrat farewell, and have never had my feet on it since; and with it I bade adieu to the sound of the cruel whip, and all other dreadful instruments of torture; adieu to the offensive sight of the violated chastity of the sable females, which has too often accosted my eyes; adieu to oppressions (although to me less severe than most of my countrymen); and adieu to the angry, howling, dashing surfs. I wished for a grateful and thankful heart to praise the Lord God on high for all his mercies! in this ecstasy, I steered the ship all night.

We had a most prosperous voyage, and, at the end of seven weeks, arrived at Cherry Garden stairs. Thus were my longing eyes once more gratified with the sight of London, after having been absent from it above four years. I immediately received my wages, and I never had earned seven guineas so quick in my life before; I had thirty-seven guineas in all, when I got cleared from the ship. I now entered upon a scene quite new to me, but full of hope. In this situation my first thoughts were to look out for some of my former friends, and amongst the first of those were the Miss Guerins. As soon, therefore, as I had regaled myself I went in quest of those kind ladies, whom I was very impatient to see; and with some difficulty and perseverance, I found them at May's-hill, Greenwich. They were most agreeably surprised to see me, and I quite overjoyed at meeting with them. I told them my history, at which they expressed great wonder, and freely acknowledged it did their cousin, Captain Pascal, no honor. He then visited there frequently; and I met him four or five days after in Greenwich park. When he saw me he appeared a good deal surprised, and asked me how I came back? I answered, "In a ship." To which he replied dryly, "I suppose you did not walk back to London on the water." As I saw, by his manner, that he did not seem to be sorry for his behavior to me, and that I had not much reason to expect any favor from him, I told him that he had used me very ill, after I had been such a faithful servant to him for so many years; on which, without saying any more, he turned about and went away. A few days after this I met Capt. Pascal at Miss Guerin's house, and asked him for my prize money. He said there was none due to me; for, if my prize money had been £10,000 he had a right to it all. I told him I was informed otherwise: on which he bade me defiance; and in a bantering tone, desired me to commence a law-suit against him for it: "There are lawyers enough," said he, "that will take the cause in hand, and you had better try it." I told him then that I would try it, which enraged him very much; however, out of regard to the ladies, I remained still, and never made any farther demand of my right. Some time afterwards these friendly ladies asked me what I meant to do with myself, and how they could assist me. I thanked them, and said, if they pleased, I would be their servant; but if not, I had thirty-seven guineas, which would support me for some time, I would be much obliged to them to recommend me to some person who would teach me a business whereby I might earn my living. They answered me very politely, that they were sorry it did not suit them to take me as their servant, and asked me what business I should like to learn? I said, hair dressing. They then promised to assist me in this; and soon after they recommended me to a gentleman, whom I had known before, one Capt. O'Hara, who treated me with much kindness, and procured me a master, a hair dresser, in Coventry court Haymarket, with whom he placed me. I was with this man from September till the February following. In that time we had a neighbor in the same court who taught the French horn. He used to blow it so well that I was charmed with it, and agreed with him to teach me to blow it. Accordingly he took me in hand, and began to instruct me, and I soon learned all the three parts. I took great delight in blowing on this instrument, the evenings being long; and besides that I was fond of it, I did not like to be idle, and it filled up my vacant hours innocently. At this time also I agreed with the Rev. Mr. Gregory, who lived in the same court, where he kept an academy and an evening school, to improve me in arithmetic. This he did as far as barter and alligation; so that all the time I was there I was entirely employed. In February 1768 I hired myself to Dr. Charles Irving, in Pallmall, so celebrated for his successful experiments in making sea water fresh; and here I had plenty of hair dressing to improve my hand. This gentleman was an excellent master; he was exceedingly kind and good tempered; and allowed me in the evenings to attend my schools, which I esteemed a great blessing; therefore I thanked God and him for it, and used all my diligence to improve the opportunity. This diligence and attention recommended me to the notice and care of my three preceptors, who, on their parts, bestowed a great deal of pains in my instruction, and besides, were all very kind to me. My wages, however, which were by two thirds less than ever I had in my life (for I had only £12 per annum), I soon found would not be sufficient to defray this extraordinary expense of masters, and my own necessary expenses; my old thirty-seven guineas had by this time worn all away to one. I thought it best, therefore, to try the sea again in quest of more money, as I had been bred to it, and had hitherto found the profession of it successful. I had also a very great desire to see Turkey, and I now determined to gratify it. Accordingly, in the month of May, 1768, I told the doctor my wish to go to sea again, to which he made no opposition; and we parted on friendly terms. The same day I went into the city in quest of a master. I was extremely fortunate in my inquiry, for I soon heard of a gentleman who had a ship going to Italy and Turkey, and he wanted a man who could dress hair well. I was overjoyed at this and went immediately on board of his ship, as I had been directed, which I found to be fitted up with great taste, and I already foreboded no small pleasure in sailing in her. Not finding the gentleman on board, I was directed to his lodgings, where I met with him the next day, and gave him a specimen of my dressing. He liked it so well that he hired me immediately, so that I was perfectly happy; for the ship, master, and voyage, were entirely to my mind. The ship was called the *Delaware,* and my master's name was John Jolly, a neat, smart, good humored man, just such an one as I wished to serve. We sailed from England in July following, and our voyage was extremely pleasant. We went to Villa Franca, Nice, and Leghorn; and in all these places I was charmed with the richness and beauty of the countries, and struck with the elegant buildings with which they abound. We had always in them plenty of extraordinary good wines and rich fruits, which I was very fond of; and I had frequent occasions of gratifying both my taste and curiosity; for my captain always lodged on shore in those places, which afforded me opportunities to see the country around. I also learned navigation of the mate, which I was very fond of. When we left Italy we had delightful sailing among the Archipelago islands, and from thence to Smyrna in Turkey. This is a very ancient city; the houses are built of stone, and most of them have graves adjoining to them; so that they sometimes present the appearance of church-yards. Provisions are very plentiful in this city, and good wine less than a penny a pint. The grapes, pomegranates, and many other fruits, were also the richest and largest I ever tasted. The natives are well looking and strong made, and treated me always with great civility. In general I believe they are fond of black people; and several of them gave me pressing invitations to stay amongst them, although they keep the franks, or Christians, separate, and do not suffer them to dwell immediately amongst them. I was astonished in not seeing women in any of their shops, and very rarely any in the streets; and whenever I did they were covered with a veil from head to foot, so that I could not see their faces, except when any of them out of curiosity uncovered them to look at me, which they sometimes did. I was surprised to see how the Greeks are, in some measure, kept under by the Turks, as the Negroes are in the West Indies by the white people. The less refined Greeks, as I have already hinted, dance here in the same manner as we do in our nation.

On the whole, during our stay here, which was about five months, I liked the place and the Turks extremely well. I could not help observing one very remarkable circumstance there: the tails of the sheep are flat and so very large that I have known the tail even of a lamb to weigh from eleven to thirteen pounds. The fat of them is very white and rich, and is excellent in puddings, for which it is much used. Our ship being at length richly loaded with silk and other articles, we sailed for England.

In May 1769, soon after our return from Turkey, our ship made a delightful voyage to Oporto, in Portugal, where we arrived at the time of the carnival. On our arrival, there were sent on board of us thirty-six articles to observe, with very heavy penalties if we should break any of them; and none of us even dared to go on board any other vessel or on shore, till the Inquisition had sent on board and searched for everything illegal, especially Bibles. Such as were produced, and certain other things, were sent on shore till the ships were going away; and any person, in whose custody a Bible was found concealed, was to be imprisoned and flogged, and sent into slavery for ten years. I saw here many very magnificent sights, particularly the garden of Eden, where many of the clergy and laity went in procession, in their several orders with the host, and sung Te Deum. I had a great curiosity to go into some of their churches, but could not gain admittance, without using the necessary sprinkling of holy water, at my entrance.

From curiosity, and a wish to be holy, I therefore complied with this ceremony, but its virtues were lost upon me, for I found myself nothing the better for it. This place abounds with plenty of all kinds of provisions. The town is well built and pretty, and commands a fine prospect. Our ship having taken in a load of wine, and other commodities, we sailed for London, and arrived in July following.

Our next voyage was to the Mediterranean. The ship was again got ready, and we sailed in September for Genoa. This is one of the finest cities I ever saw; some of the edifices were of beautiful marble, and made a most noble appearance; and many had very curious fountains before them. The churches were rich and magnificent, and curiously adorned, both in the inside and out. But all this grandeur was, in my eyes, disgraced by the galley slaves, whose condition, both there and in other parts of Italy, is truly piteous and wretched. After we had stayed there some weeks, during which we bought many different things we wanted, and got them very cheap, we sailed to Naples, a charming city, and remarkably clean. The bay is the most beautiful I ever saw; the moles for shipping are excellent. I thought it extraordinary to see grand operas acted here on Sunday nights, and even attended by their majesties. I too, like these great ones, went to those sights, and vainly served God in the day, while I thus served mammon effectually at night. While we remained here, there happened an eruption of Mount Vesuvius, of which I had a perfect view. It was extremely awful; and we were so near that the ashes from it, used to be thick on our deck. After we had transacted our business at Naples, we sailed with a fair wind, once more for Smyrna, where we arrived in December. A seraskier, or officer, took a liking to me here, and wanted me to stay, and offered me two wives; however, I refused the temptation, thinking one was as much as some could manage, and more than others would venture on. The merchants here travel in caravans or large companies. I have seen many caravans from India, with some hundreds of camels, laden with different goods. The people of these caravans are quite brown. Among other articles, they brought with them a great quantity of locusts, which are a kind of pulse, sweet and pleasant to the palate, and in shape resembling French beans, but longer. Each kind of goods is sold in a street by itself, and I always found the Turks very honest in their dealings. They let no Christians into their mosques or churches, for which I was very sorry; as I was always fond of going to see the different modes of worship, of the people wherever I went. The plague broke out while we were in Smyrna, and we stopped taking goods into the ship till it was over. She was then richly laden, and we sailed in about March 1770 for England. One day in our passage, we met with an accident, which was near burning the ship. A black cook, in melting some fat, overset the pan into the fire under the deck, which immediately began to blaze, and the flame went up very high under the foretop. With the fright, the poor cook became almost white, and altogether speechless. Happily, however, we got the fire out, without doing much mischief. After various delays in this passage, which was tedious, we arrived in Standgate creek in July; and, at the latter end of the year, some new event occurred, so that my noble captain, the ship, and I, all separated.

In April 1771, I shipped myself as steward, with Captain William Robertson, of the ship *Grenada Planter*, once more to try my fortune in the West Indies; and we sailed from London for Madeira, Barbadoes, and the Grenadas. When we were at this last place, having some goods to sell, I met once more with my former kind of West India customers.

A white man, an islander, bought some goods of me, to the amount of some pounds, and made me many fair promises as usual, but without any intention of paying me. He had likewise bought goods from some more of our people, whom he intended to serve in the same manner; but he still amused us with promises. However, when our ship was loaded, and near sailing, this honest buyer discovered no intention or sign of paying for anything he had bought of us; but on the contrary, when I asked him for my money, he threatened me and another black man he had bought goods of, so that we found we were like to get more blows than payment. On this, we went to complain to one Mr. M'Intosh, a justice of the peace; we told his worship of the man's villainous tricks, and begged that he would be kind enough to see us redressed; but being Negroes, although free, we could not get any remedy; and our ship being then just upon the point of sailing, we knew not how to help ourselves, though we thought it hard to lose our property in this manner. Luckily for us, however, this man was also indebted to three white sailors, who could not get a farthing from him; they therefore readily joined us, and we all went together in search of him. When we found where he was, I took him out of a house and threatened him with vengeance; on which, finding he was likely to be handled roughly, the rogue offered each of us some small allowance, but nothing near our demands. This exasperated us much more; and some were for cutting his ears off; but he begged hard for mercy, which was at last granted him, after we had entirely stripped him. We then let him go, for which he thanked us, glad to get off so easily, and ran into the bushes, after having wished us a good voyage. We then repaired on board, and shortly after set sail for England. I cannot help remarking here, a very narrow escape we had from being blown up, owing to a piece of negligence of mine. Just as our ship was under sail, I went down under the cabin, to do some business, and had a lighted candle in my hand, which, in my hurry, without thinking, I held in a barrel of gunpowder. It remained in the powder until it was near catching fire, when fortunately, I observed it, and snatched it out in time, and providentially no harm happened; but I was so overcome with terror that I immediately fainted at this deliverance.

In twenty-eight days' time, we arrived in England, and I got clear of this ship. But, being still of a roving disposition, and desirous of seeing as many different parts of the world as I could, I shipped myself soon after, in the same year, as steward on board of a fine large ship, called the *Jamaica*, Capt. David Watt; and we sailed from England in December 1771, for Nevis and Jamaica. I found Jamaica to be a very fine, large island, well peopled, and the most considerable of the West India islands. There was a vast number of Negroes here, whom I found as usual, exceedingly imposed upon by the white people, and the slaves punished as in the other islands. There are Negroes whose business is to flog slaves; they go about to different people for employment, and the usual pay is from one to four bits. I saw many cruel punishments inflicted on the slaves, in the short time I stayed here. In particular, I was present when a poor fellow was tied up and kept hanging by the wrists, at some distance from the ground, and then some half hundred weights were fixed to his ankles, in which posture, he was flogged most unmercifully. There was also, as I heard, two different masters, noted for cruelty on the island, who had staked up two Negroes naked, and in two hours the vermin stung them to death. I heard a gentleman, I well knew, tell my captain, that he passed sentence on a Negro man, to be burnt alive, for attempting to poison an overseer. I pass over numerous other instances, in order to relieve the reader, by a milder scene of roguery. Before I had been long on the island, one Mr. Smith, at Port Morant, bought goods of me to the amount of twenty-five pounds sterling; but when I demanded payment from him, he was going each time to beat me, and threatened that he would put me in jail. One time he would say, I was going to set his house on fire; at another, he would swear I was going to run away with his slaves. I was astonished at this usage, from a person who was in the situation of a gentleman, but I had no alternative, and was, therefore, obliged to submit. When I came to Kingston, I was surprised to see the number of Africans who were assembled together on Sundays, particularly at a large commodious place, called Spring Path. Here each different nation of Africa meet and dance after the manner of their own country. They still retain most of their native customs; they bury their dead, and put victuals, pipes, and tobacco, and other things, in the grave with the corpse, in the same manner as in Africa. Our ship having got her loading, we sailed for London, where we arrived in the August following. On my return to London, I waited on my old and good master, Dr. Irving, who made me an offer of his service again. Being now tired of the sea, I gladly accepted it. I was very happy in living with this gentleman once more, during which time we were daily employed in reducing old Neptune's dominions, by purifying the briny element and making it fresh. Thus I went on till May 1773, when I was roused by the sound of fame, to seek new adventures, and find, towards the North Pole, what our Creator never intended we should, a passage to India. An expedition was now fitting out to explore a north-east passage, conducted by the Honorable Constantine John Phipps, since Lord Mulgrave, in his Majesty's sloop-of-war, the *Race Horse*. My master being anxious for the reputation of this adventure, we therefore prepared everything for our voyage, and I attended him on board the *Race Horse,* the 24th day of May, 1773. We proceeded to Sheerness, where we were joined by his Majesty's sloop, the *Carcass,* commanded by Captain Lutwidge. On the 4th of June, we sailed towards our destined place, the Pole; and on the 15th of the same month, we were off Shetland. On this day I had a great and unexpected deliverance, from an accident which was near blowing up the ship and destroying the crew, which made me ever after, during the voyage, uncommonly cautious. The ship was so filled that there was very little room on board for anyone, which placed me in a very awkward situation. I had resolved to keep a journal of this singular and interesting voyage; and I had no other place for this purpose but a little cabin, or the doctor's store-room, where I slept. This little place was stuffed with all manner of combustibles, particularly with tow and aquafortis, and many other dangerous things. Unfortunately, it happened in the evening, as I was writing my journal, that I had occasion to take the candle out of the lanthorn, and a spark having touched a single thread of the tow, all the rest caught the flame, and immediately the whole was in a blaze. I saw nothing but present death before me, and expected to be the first to perish in the flames. In a moment the alarm was spread, and many people who were near, ran to assist in putting out the fire. All this time, I was in the very midst of the flames; my shirt and the handkerchief on my neck, were burnt, and I was almost smothered with the smoke. However, through God's mercy, as I was nearly giving up all hopes, some people brought blankets and mattresses, and threw them on the flames, by which means in a short time the fire was put out. I was severely reprimanded and menaced by such of the officers who knew it, and strictly charged never more to go there with a light; and, indeed, even my own fears made me give heed to this command for a little time; but at last, not being able to write my journal in any other part of the ship, I was tempted again to venture by stealth, with a light in the same cabin, though not without considerable fear and dread on . my mind. On the 20th of June, we began to use Dr. Irving's apparatus for making salt water fresh; I used to attend the distillery: I frequently purified from twenty-six to forty gallons a day. The water thus distilled was perfectly pure, well tasted, and free from salt, and was used on various occasions on board the

ship. On the 28th of June, being in latitude 78, we made Greenland, where I was surprised to see the sun did not set. The
weather now became extremely cold; and as we sailed between
north and east, which was our course, we saw many very high and
curious mountains of ice; and also a great number of very large
whales, which used to come close to our ship, and blow the water
up to a very great height in the air. One morning we had vast
quantities of sea horses about the ship, which neighed exactly
like any other horses. We fired some harpoon guns amongst them,
in order to take some, but we could not get any. The 30th, the
captain of a Greenland ship came on board, and told us of three
ships that were lost in the ice; however, we still held on our
course, till July the 11th, when we were stopt by one compact
and impenetrable body of ice. We ran along it from east to west
about ten degrees; and on the 27th, we got as far north as 80° 37';
and in 19 or 20 degrees, east longitude from London. On the 29th
and 30th of July, we saw one continued plain of smooth, unbroken ice, bounded only by the horizon; and we fastened to a
piece of ice that was eight yards eleven inches thick. We had
generally sunshine, and constant daylight; which gave cheerfulness and novelty to the whole of this striking, grand, and uncommon scene; and, to heighten it still more, the reflection of the
sun from the ice gave the clouds a most beautiful appearance. We
killed many different animals at this time, and among the rest
nine bears. Though they had nothing in their paunches but water,
yet they were all very fat. We used to decoy them to the ship
sometimes by burning feathers or skins. I thought them coarse
eating, but some of the ship's company relished them very much.
Some of our people, once in the boat, fired at and wounded a
sea horse, which dived immediately, and in a little time after,
brought up with it a number of others. They all joined in an attack upon the boat, and were with difficulty prevented from stav-
ing or oversetting her; but a boat from the *Carcass* having come
to assist ours, and joined it, they dispersed, after having wrested
an oar from one of the men. One of the ship's boats had before
been attacked in the same manner, but happily no harm was
done. Though we wounded several of these animals we never got
but one. We remained hereabouts until the 1st of August, when
the two ships got completely fastened in the ice, occasioned by

the loose ice that set in from the sea. This made our situation very dreadful and alarming; so that on the 7th day, we were in very great apprehension of having the ships squeezed to pieces. The officers now held a council to know what was best for us to do in order to save our lives; and it was determined that we should endeavor to escape by dragging our boats along the ice towards the sea, which, however, was farther off than any of us thought. This determination filled us with extreme dejection, and confounded us with despair, for we had very little prospect of escaping with life. However, we sawed some of the ice about the ships, to keep it from hurting them, and thus kept them in a kind of pond. We then began to drag the boats as well as we could towards the sea; but, after two or three days' labor, we made very little progress, so that some of our hearts totally failed us; and I really began to give up myself for lost, when I saw our surrounding calamities. While we were at this hard labor, I once fell into a pond we had made amongst some loose ice, and was very near being drowned; but providentially some people were near who gave me immediate assistance, and thereby I escaped drowning. Our deplorable condition, which kept up the constant apprehension of our perishing in the ice, brought me gradually to think of eternity, in such a manner as I never had done before. I had the fears of death hourly upon me, and shuddered at the thoughts of meeting the grim king of terrors in the natural state I then was in, and was exceedingly doubtful of a happy eternity if I should die in it. I had no hopes of my life being prolonged for any time; for we saw that our existence could not be long on the ice after leaving the ships, which were now out of sight, and some miles from the boats. Our appearance now became truly lamentable; pale dejection seized every countenance; many, who had been before blasphemers, in this our distress, began to call on the good God of Heaven for his help; and in the time of our utter need he heard us, and against hope or human probability, delivered us! It was the eleventh day of the ships' being thus fastened, and the fourth of our drawing the boats in this manner, that the wind changed to the E. N. E. The weather immediately became mild, and the ice broke towards the sea, which was to the S. W. of us. Many of us on this got on board again, and with all our might we hove the ships into every open water we could find, and made all the sail on them in our power; and now, having a prospect of success, we made signals for the boats, and the remainder of the people. This seemed to us like a reprieve from death, and happy was the man who could first get on board of any ship, or the first boat he could meet. We then proceeded in this manner, till we got into the open water again, which we accomplished in about thirty hours, to our infinite joy and gladness of heart. As soon as we were out of danger, we came to anchor and refitted; and on the 19th of August, we sailed from this uninhabited extremity of the world, where the inhospitable climate affords neither food nor shelter, and not a tree or a shrub of any kind grows amongst its barren rocks; but all is one desolate and expanded waste of ice, which even the constant beams of the sun for six months in the year cannot penetrate or dissolve. The sun now being on the decline, the days shortened as we sailed to the southward; and, on the 28th, in latitude 73, it was dark by ten o'clock at night. September 10th, in latitude 58, 59, we met a very severe gale of wind and high seas, and shipped a great deal of water in the space of ten hours. This made us work exceedingly hard at all our pumps a whole day; and one sea, which struck the ship with more force than anything I ever met with of the kind before, laid her under water for some time, so that we thought she would have gone down. Two boats were washed from the booms, and the long-boat from the chucks; all other moveable things on the decks were also washed away, among which were many curious things, of different kinds, which we had brought from Greenland; and we were obliged, in order to lighten the ship, to toss some of our guns overboard. We saw a ship at the same time, in very great distress, and her masts were gone; but we were unable to assist her. We now lost sight of the *Carcass,* till the 26th, when we saw land about Orfordness, of which place she joined us. From thence we sailed for London, and on the 30th came up to Deptford. And thus ended our Arctic voyage, to the no small joy of all on board, after having been absent four months, in which time, at the imminent hazard of our lives, we explored nearly as far towards the Pole as 81 degrees north, and 20 degrees east longitude; being much farther, by all accounts, that any navigator had ever ventured before; in which we fully proved the impracticability of finding a passage that way to India.

Chapter 10

The author leaves Doctor Irving, and engages on board a Turkey ship—Account of a black man's being kidnapped on board and sent to the West Indies, and the author's fruitless endeavors to procure his freedom—Some account of the manner of the author's conversion to the faith of Jesus Christ.

OUR VOYAGE TO THE NORTH POLE being ended, I returned to London with Doctor Irving, with whom I continued for some time, during which I began seriously to reflect on the dangers I had escaped, particularly those of my last voyage, which made a lasting impression on my mind, and, by the grace of God, proved afterwards a mercy to me; it caused me to reflect deeply on my eternal state, and to seek the Lord with full purpose of heart, ere it was too late. I rejoiced greatly; and heartily thanked the Lord for directing me to London, where I was determined to work out my own salvation, and, in so doing, procure a title to heaven; being the result of a mind blinded by ignorance and sin.

In process of time I left my master, Doctor Irving, the purifier of waters. I lodged in Coventry court, Haymarket, where I was continually oppressed and much concerned about the salvation of my soul, and was determined (in my own strength) to be a first-rate Christian. I used every means for this purpose; and, not being able to find any person amongst those with whom I was then acquainted that acquiesced with me in point of religion, or, in scripture language, that would show me any good, I was much dejected, and knew not where to seek relief; however, I first frequented the neighboring churches, St. James' and others, two or three times a day, for many weeks; still I came away dissatisfied: something was wanting that I could not obtain, and I really found more heart-felt relief in reading my Bible at home than in attending the church; and, being resolved to be saved, I pursued other methods. First I went among the Quakers, where the word of God was neither read or preached, so that I remained as much in the dark as ever. I then searched into the Roman Catholic principles, but was not in the least edified. I at length had recourse to the Jews, which availed me nothing, as the fear of eternity daily harassed my mind, and I knew not where to seek shelter from the wrath to come. However, this was my conclusion,

at all events, to read the four evangelists, and whatever sect or
party I found adhering thereto, such I would join. Thus I went
on heavily, without any guide to direct me the way that leadeth
to eternal life. I asked different people questions about the manner of going to heaven, and was told different ways. Here I was
much staggered, and could not find any at that time more righteous than myself, or indeed so much inclined to devotion. I
thought we should not all be saved (this is agreeable to the holy
scriptures) nor would all be damned. I found none among the
circle of my acquaintance that kept wholly the ten commandments. So righteous was I in my own eyes, that I was convinced
I excelled many of them in that point, by keeping eight out of ten;
and finding those who in general termed themselves Christians
not so honest or so good in their morals as the Turks, I really
thought the Turks were in a safer way of salvation than my neighbors; so that between hopes and fears I went on, and the chief
comforts I enjoyed were in the musical French horn, which I then
practised, and also dressing of hair. Such was my situation some
months, experiencing the dishonesty of many people here. I determined at last to set out for Turkey, and there to end my days. It
was now early in the spring, 1774. I sought for a master, and
found a Captain John Hughes, commander of a ship called *Angli-
canai*, fitting out in the river Thames, and bound to Smyrna, in
Turkey. I shipped myself with him as a steward; at the same
time I recommended to him a very clever black man, John Annis,
as a cook. This man was on board the ship near two months doing
his duty; he had formerly lived many years with Mr. William
Kirkpatrick, a gentleman of the island of St. Kitts, from whom
he parted by consent, though he afterwards tried many schemes
to inveigle the poor man. He had applied to many captains who
traded to St. Kitts to trepan him; and when all their attempts and
schemes of kidnapping proved abortive, Mr. Kirkpatrick came
to our ship at Union Stairs, on Easter Monday, April the fourth,
with two wherry boats and six men, having learned that the man
was on board, and tied, and forcibly took him away from the
ship, in the presence of the crew and the chief mate, who had
detained him after he had information to come away. I believe
this was a combined piece of business; but, be that as it may,
it certainly reflected great disgrace on the mate and captain also,

who, although they had desired the oppressed man to stay on board, yet this vile act on the man who had served him, he did not in the least assist to recover or pay me a farthing of his wages, which was about five pounds. I proved the only friend he had, who attempted to regain him his liberty if possible, having known the want of liberty myself. I sent as soon as I could to Gravesend, and got knowledge of the ship in which he was; but unluckily she had sailed the first tide after he was put on board. My intention was then immediately to apprehend Mr. Kirkpatrick, who was about setting off for Scotland; and, having obtained a habeas corpus for him and got a tipstaff to go with me to St. Paul's church-yard, where he lived, he, suspecting something of this kind, set a watch to look out. My being known to them obliged me to use the following deception: I whitened my face, that they might not know me; and this had the desired effect. He did not go out of his house that night, and next morning I contrived a well plotted stratagem, notwithstanding he had a gentleman in his house to personate him. My direction to the tipstaff, who got admittance into the house, was to conduct him to a judge, according to the writ. When he came there, his plea was, that he had not the body in custody, on which he was admitted to bail. I proceeded immediately to that well-known philanthropist, Granville Sharp, Esq., who received me with the utmost kindness, and gave me every instruction that was needful on the occasion. I left him in full hope that I should gain the unhappy man his liberty, with the warmest sense of gratitude towards Mr. Sharp, for his kindness; but alas! my attorney proved unfaithful; he took my money, lost me many months' employ, and did not do the least good in the cause; and when the poor man arrived at St. Kitts, he was, according to custom, staked to the ground with four pins through a cord, two on his wrists, and two on his ankles, was cut and flogged most unmercifully and afterwards loaded cruelly with irons about his neck. I had two very moving letters from him, while he was in this situation, and made attempts to go after him at a great hazard, but was sadly disappointed. I also was told of it by some very respectable families now in London, who saw him in St. Kitts, in the same state, in which he remained till kind death released him out of the hands of his tyrants. During this disagreeable business, I was under strong convictions of sin, and thought that my state was worse than any man's; my mind was unaccountably disturbed; I often wished for death, though at the same time convinced I was altogether unprepared for that awful summons. Suffering much by villains in the late cause, and being much concerned about the state of my soul, these things (but particularly the latter) brought me very low, so that I became a burden to myself and viewed all things around me as emptiness and vanity, which could give no satisfaction to a troubled conscience. I was again determined to go to Turkey, and resolved, at that time, never more to return to England. I engaged as a steward on board a Turkeyman (the *Wester Hall,* Captain Lina) but was prevented by means of my late captain, Mr. Hughes, and others. All this appeared to be against me, and the only comfort I then experienced was in reading the Holy Scriptures, where I saw that "there is no new thing under the sun" (Eccles. 1:9); and what was appointed for me I must submit to. Thus I continued to travel in much heaviness, and frequently murmured against the Almighty, particularly in his providential dealings; and, awful to think! I began to blaspheme, and wished often to be anything but a human being. In these severe conflicts the Lord answered me by awful "visions of the night, when deep sleep falleth upon men, in slumberings upon the bed" (Job 33:15). He was pleased, in much mercy, to give me to see, and in some measure understand, the great and awful scene of the judgment day, that "no unclean person, no unholy thing, can enter into the kingdom of God" (Eph. 5:5). I would then, if it had been possible, have changed my nature with the meanest worm on the earth; and was ready to say to the mountains and rocks "fall on me" (Rev. 6:16), but all in vain. I then, in the greatest agony, requested the divine Creator, that he would grant me a small space of time to repent of my follies and vile iniquities, which I felt were grievous. The Lord, in his manifold mercies, was pleased to grant my request, and, being yet in a state of time, the sense of God's mercies were so great on my mind when I awoke that my strength entirely failed me for many minutes, and I was exceedingly weak. This was the first spiritual mercy I ever was sensible of, and being on praying ground, as soon as I recovered a little strength, and got out of bed and dressed myself, I invoked heaven, from my inmost soul, and fervently begged

that God would never again permit me to blaspheme his most
holy name. The Lord, who is long-suffering and full of compassion to such poor rebels as we are, condescended to hear and
answer. I felt that I was altogether unholy, and saw clearly what
a bad use I had made of the faculties I was endowed with: they
were given me to glorify God with; I thought, therefore, I had
better want them here, and enter into life eternal, than abuse
them and be cast into hell fire. I prayed to be directed, if there
were any holier than those with whom I was acquainted, that the
Lord would point them out to me. I appealed to the Searcher of
hearts, whether I did not wish to love him more, and serve him
better. Notwithstanding all this, the reader may easily discern, if
a believer, that I was still in nature's darkness. At length I hated
the house in which I lodged, because God's most holy name was
blasphemed in it; then I saw the word of God verified, *viz.*, "Before they call, I will answer; and while they are yet speaking, I
will hear."

I had a great desire to read the Bible the whole day at home;
but not having a convenient place for retirement, I left the house
in the day, rather than stay amongst the wicked ones; and that
day, as I was walking, it pleased God to direct me to a house
where there was an old sea-faring man, who experienced much
of the love of God shed abroad in his heart. He began to discourse
with me; and, as I desired to love the Lord, his conversation rejoiced me greatly; and, indeed, I had never heard before the love
of Christ to believers set forth in such a manner, and in so clear
a point of view. Here I had more questions to put to the man
than his time would permit him to answer; and in that memorable hour there came in a dissenting minister; he joined our discourse, and asked me some few questions; among others, where I
heard the gospel preached? I knew not what he meant by hearing
the gospel; I told him I had read the gospel; and he asked where
I went to church, or whether I went at all or not? To which I
replied, "I attended St. James's, St. Martin's, and St. Ann's Soho."
"So, said he, "you are a churchman?" I answered, I was. He then
invited me to a love-feast at his chapel that evening. I accepted
the offer, and thanked him; and soon after he went away, I had
some further discourse with the old Christian, added to some
profitable reading, which made me exceedingly happy. When I

left him he reminded me of coming to the feast; I assured him I would be there. Thus we parted, and I weighed over the heavenly conversation that passed between these two men, which cheered my then heavy and drooping spirit more than anything I had met with for many months. However, I thought the time long in going to my supposed banquet. I also wished much for the company of these friendly men; their company pleased me much; and I thought the gentleman very kind in asking me, a stranger, to a feast; but how singular did it appear to me, to have it in a chapel! When the wished-for hour came I went, and happily the old man was there, who kindly seated me, as he belonged to the place. I was much astonished to see the place filled with people, and no signs of eating and drinking. There were many ministers in the company. At last they began by giving out hymns, and between the singing, the ministers engaged in prayer; in short, I knew not what to make of this sight, having never seen anything of the kind in my life before now. Some of the guests began to speak their experience, agreeable to what I read in the Scriptures; much was said by every speaker of the providence of God, and his unspeakable mercies, to each of them. This I knew in a great measure and could most heartily join them. But when they spoke of a future state, they seemed to be altogether certain of their calling and election of God; and that no one could ever separate them from the love of Christ, or pluck them out of his hands. This filled me with utter consternation, intermingled with admiration. I was so amazed as not to know what to think of the company; my heart was attracted, and my affections were enlarged. I wished to be as happy as them, and was persuaded in my mind that they were different from the world "that lieth in wickedness" (I John 5:19). Their language and singing, &c., did well harmonize; I was entirely overcome, and wished to live and die thus. Lastly, some persons in the place produced some neat baskets full of buns, which they distributed about; and each person communicated with his neighbor, and sipped water out of different mugs, which they handed about to all who were present. This kind of Christian fellowship I had never seen, nor ever thought of seeing on earth; it fully reminded me of what I had read in the Holy Scriptures, of the primitive Christians, who loved each other and broke bread, in partaking of it, even from house to house. This entertainment (which lasted about four hours) ended in singing and prayer. It was the first soul feast I ever was present at. This last twenty-four hours produced me things, spiritual and temporal, sleeping and waking, judgment and mercy, that I could not but admire the goodness of God, in directing the blind, blasphemous sinner in the path that he knew not of, even among the just; and, instead of judgment, he has shewed mercy, and will hear and answer the prayers and supplications of every returning prodigal:

> O! to grace how great a debtor
> Daily I'm constrained to be!

After this I was resolved to win Heaven if possible; and if I perished I thought it should be at the feet of Jesus, in praying to him for salvation. After having been an eye-witness to some of the happiness which attended those who feared God, I knew not how, with any kind of propriety, to return to my lodgings, where the name of God was continually profaned, at which I felt the greatest horror; I paused in my mind for some time, not knowing what to do; whether to hire a bed elsewhere, or go home again. At last fearing an evil report might arise, I went home, with a farewell to card playing and vain jesting, &c. I saw that time was very short, eternity long, and very near; and I viewed those persons alone blessed who were found ready at midnight call, or when the judge of all, both quick and dead, cometh.

The next day I took courage, and went to Holborn, to see my new and worthy acquaintance, the old man, Mr. C——; he, with his wife, a gracious woman, were at work, at silk weaving; they seemed mutually happy, and both quite glad to see me, and I more so to see them. I sat down and we conversed much about soul matters, &c. Their discourse was amazingly delightful, edifying, and pleasant. I knew not at last how to leave this agreeable pair, till time summoned me away. As I was going they lent me a little book, entitled *The Conversion of an Indian*. It was in questions and answers. The poor man came over the sea to London to inquire after the Christian's God, who (through rich mercy) he found and had not his journey in vain. The above book was of great use to me, and at that time was a means of strengthening my faith; however, in parting, they both invited me to call on them when I pleased. This delighted me, and I took care to

make all the improvement from it I could; and so far I thanked
God for such company and desires. I prayed that the many evils I
felt within might be done away, and that I might be weaned from
my former carnal acquaintances. This was quickly heard and
answered, and I was soon connected with those whom the scripture calls the excellent of the earth. I heard the gospel preached,
and the thoughts of my heart and actions were laid open by the
preachers, and the way of salvation by Christ alone was evidently
set forth. Thus I went on happily for near two months; and I
once heard, during this period, a reverend gentleman, Mr. G——,
speak of a man who had departed this life in full assurance of his
going to glory. I was much astonished at the assertion; and did
very deliberately inquire how he could get at this knowledge. I
was answered fully, agreeable to what I read in the oracles of
truth; and was told also that if I did not experience the new birth
and the pardon of my sins, through the blood of Christ, before I
died, I could not enter the kingdom of heaven. I knew not what to
think of this report, as I thought I kept eight commandments out
of ten; then my worthy interpreter told me I did not do it, nor
could I; and he added, that no man ever did or could keep the
commandments, without offending in one point. I thought this
sounded very strange, and puzzled me much for many weeks: for
I thought it a hard saying. I then asked my friend Mr. L——d,
who was a clerk in a chapel, why the commandments of God were
given, if we could not be saved by them? To which he replied,
"The law is a schoolmaster to bring us to Christ," who alone could
and did keep the commandments, and fulfilled all their requirements for his elect people, even those to whom he had given a
living faith, and the sins of those chosen vessels *were already*
atoned for and forgiven them whilst living; and if I did not experience the same before my exit, the Lord would say at that
great day to me, "Go, ye cursed," &c., &c., for God would appear
faithful in his judgments to the wicked, as he would be faithful
in shewing mercy to those who were ordained to it before the
world was; therefore Christ Jesus seemed to be all in all to that
man's soul. I was much wounded at this discourse, and brought
into such a dilemma as I never expected. I asked him, if *he* was
to die that moment, whether he was sure to enter the kingdom
of God? and added, "Do you *know* that your sins are forgiven

you?" He answered in the affirmative. Then confusion, anger, and discontent seized me, and I staggered much at this sort of doctrine; it brought me to a stand, not knowing which to believe, whether salvation by works, or by faith only in Christ. I requested him to tell me how I might know when my sins were forgiven me. He assured me he could not, and that none but God alone could do this. I told him it was very mysterious; but he said it was really matter of fact, and quoted many portions of scripture immediately to the point, to which I could make no reply. He then desired me to pray to God to shew me these things. I answered, that I prayed to God every day. He said, "I perceive you are a churchman." I answered, I was. He then entreated me to beg of God to shew me the true state of my soul. I thought the prayer very short and odd; so we parted for that time. I weighed all these things well over, and could not help thinking how it was possible for a man to know that his sins were forgiven him in this life. I wished that God would reveal this self-same thing unto me. In a short time after this I went to Westminster chapel; the Rev. Mr. P——— preached from Lam. 3:39. It was a wonderful sermon; he clearly shewed that a living man had no cause to complain for the punishments of his sins; he evidently justified the Lord in all his dealings with the sons of men; he also shewed the justice of God in the eternal punishment of the wicked and impenitent. The discourse seemed to me like a two-edged sword, cutting all ways; it afforded me much joy, intermingled with many fears about my soul; and when it was ended, he gave it out that he intended, the ensuing week, to examine all those who meant to attend the Lord's table. Now I thought much of my good works, and at the same time was doubtful of my being a proper object to receive the sacrament; I was full of meditation till the day of examining. However, I went to the chapel, and, though much distressed, I addressed the reverend gentleman, thinking if I was not right, he would endeavor to convince me of it. When I conversed with him, the first thing he asked me was, what I knew of Christ? I told him I believed in him, and had been baptized in his name. "Then," said he, "when were you brought to the knowledge of God? and how were you convinced of sin?" I knew not what he meant by these questions; I told him I kept eight commandments out of ten; but that I sometimes swore on board ship, and sometimes when on shore, and broke the Sabbath. He then asked me if I could read? I answered, "Yes." "Then," said he, "do you not read in the Bible, he that offends in one point is guilty of all?" I said, "Yes." Then he assured me, that one sin unatoned for was as sufficient to damn a soul as one leak was to sink a ship. Here I was struck with awe; for the minister exhorted me much, and reminded me of the shortness of time, and the length of eternity, and that no unregenerate soul, or anything unclean, could enter the kingdom of Heaven.

He did not admit me as a communicant, but recommended me to read the scriptures and hear the word preached, not to neglect fervent prayer to God, who has promised to hear the supplications of those who seek him in godly sincerity; so I took my leave of him, with many thanks, and resolved to follow his advice, so far as the Lord would condescend to enable me. During this time I was out of employ, nor was I likely to get a situation suitable for me, which obliged me to go once more to sea. I engaged as steward of a ship called the *Hope,* Captain Richard Strange, bound from London to Cadiz in Spain. In a short time after I was on board, I heard the name of God much blasphemed, and I feared greatly lest I should catch the horrible infection. I thought if I sinned again after having life and death set evidently before me, I should certainly go to hell. My mind was uncommonly chagrined, and I murmured much at God's providential dealings with me, and was discontented with the commandments, that I could not be saved by what I had done; I hated all things, and wished I had never been born; confusion seized me, and I wished to be annihilated. One day I was standing on the very edge of the stern of the ship, thinking to drown myself; but this scripture was instantly impressed on my mind—"That no murderer hath eternal life abiding in him" (I John 3:15). Then I paused and thought myself the unhappiest man living. Again I was convinced that the Lord was better to me than I deserved, and I was better off in the world than many. After this I began to fear death; I fretted, mourned, and prayed, till I became a burden to others, but more so to myself. At length I concluded to beg my bread on shore rather than go again to sea amongst a people who feared not God, and I entreated the captain three different times to discharge me; he would not, but each time gave me greater and greater encouragement to continue with him, and all on board shewed me very great civility: notwithstanding all this I was unwilling to embark again. At last some of my religious friends advised me, by saying it was my lawful calling, consequently it was my duty to obey, and that God was not confined to place, &c., &c. particularly Mr. G—— S——, the governor of Tothil-fields, Bridewell, who pitied my case, and read the eleventh chapter of the Hebrews to me, with exhortations. He prayed for me, and I believed that he prevailed on my behalf, as my burden was then greatly removed, and I found a heartfelt resignation to the will of God. The good man gave me a pocket Bible and Alleine's *Alarm to the Unconverted.* We parted, and the next day I went on board again. We sailed for Spain, and I found favor with the captain. It was the fourth of the month of September when we sailed from London; we had a delightful voyage to Cadiz, where we arrived the twenty-third of the same month. The place is strong, commands a fine prospect, and is very rich. The Spanish galleons frequent that port, and some arrived whilst we were there. I had many opportunities of reading the scriptures. I wrestled hard with God in fervent prayer, who had declared in his word that he would hear the groanings and deep sighs of the poor in spirit. I found this verified to my utter astonishment and comfort in the following manner.

On the morning of the 6th of October (I pray you to attend), all that day, I thought I should either see or hear something supernatural. I had a secret impulse on my mind of something that was to take place, which drove me continually for that time to a Throne of Grace. It pleased God to enable me to wrestle with him, as Jacob did: I prayed that if sudden death were to happen, and I perished, it might be at Christ's feet.

In the evening of the same day, as I was reading and meditating on the fourth chapter of Acts, twelfth verse, under the solemn apprehensions of eternity, and reflecting on my past actions, I began to think I had lived a moral life, and that I had a proper ground to believe I had an interest in the divine favor; but still meditating on the subject, not knowing whether salvation was to be had partly for our own good deeds or solely as the sovereign

gift of God; in this deep consternation the Lord was pleased to
break in upon my soul with his bright beams of heavenly light;
and in an instant, as it were, removing the veil, and letting light
into a dark place, I saw clearly with an eye of faith, the crucified
Saviour bleeding on the cross on mount Calvary; the scriptures
became an unsealed book; I saw myself a condemned criminal
under the law, which came with its full force to my conscience,
and when "the commandment came sin revived, and I died." I
saw the Lord Jesus Christ in his humiliation, loaded and bearing
my reproach, sin, and shame. I then clearly perceived that by the
deeds of the law no flesh living could be justified. I was then convinced that by the first Adam sin came, and by the second Adam
(the Lord Jesus Christ) all that are saved must be made alive. It
was given me at that time to know what it was to be born again
(John 3:5). I saw the eighth chapter to the Romans, and the
doctrines of God's decrees, verified agreeable to his eternal, ever-
lasting, and unchangeable purposes. The word of God was sweet
to my taste, yea, sweeter than honey and the honeycomb. Christ
was revealed to my soul as the chiefest among ten thousand.
These heavenly moments were really as life to the dead, and what
John calls an earnest of the Spirit.* This was indeed unspeakable,
and I firmly believe undeniable by many. Now every leading
providential circumstance that happened to me, from the day I
was taken from my parents to that hour, was then in my view, as
if it had but just then occurred. I was sensible of the invisible
hand of God, which guided and protected me, when in truth I
knew it not: still the Lord pursued me, although I slighted and
disregarded it; this mercy melted me down. When I considered
my poor wretched state I wept, seeing what a great debtor I was
to sovereign free grace. Now the Ethiopian was willing to be
saved by Jesus Christ, the sinner's only surety, and also to rely
on none other person or thing for salvation. Self was obnoxious,
and good works he had none, for it is God that worketh in us both
to will and to do. Oh! the amazing things of that hour can never
be told—it was joy in the Holy Ghost! I felt an astonishing change;
the burden of sin, the gaping jaws of hell, and the fears of death,
that weighed me down before, now lost their horror; indeed I
thought death would now be the best earthly friend I ever had.

* John 16:13, 14, &c.

Such were my grief and joy as I believe are seldom experienced. I was bathed in tears, and said, What am I that God should thus look on me, the vilest of sinners? I felt a deep concern for my mother and friends, which occasioned me to pray with fresh ardor; and in the abyss of thought, I viewed the unconverted people of the world in a very awful state, being without God and without hope.

It pleased God to pour out on me the spirit of prayer and the grace of supplication, so that in loud acclamations I was enabled to praise and glorify his most holy name. When I got out of the cabin, and told some of the people what the Lord had done for me, alas! who could understand me or believe my report! None but to whom the arm of the Lord was revealed. I became a barbarian to them in talking of the love of Christ: his name was to me as ointment poured forth, indeed it was sweet to my soul, but to them a rock of offense. I thought my case singular, and every hour a day until I came to London, for I much longed to be with some to whom I could tell of the wonders of God's love towards me, and join in prayer to him whom my soul loved and thirsted after. I had uncommon commotions within, such as few can tell aught about. Now the Bible was my only companion and comfort; I prized it much, with many thanks to God that I could read it for myself, and was not left to be tossed about or led by man's devices and notions. The worth of a soul cannot be told. May the Lord give the reader an understanding in this. Whenever I looked in the Bible I saw things new, and many texts were immediately applied to me with great comfort, for I knew that to me was the word of salvation sent. Sure I was that the Spirit which indited the word opened my heart to receive the truth of it as it is in Jesus—that the same Spirit enabled me to act faith upon the promises that were precious to me, and enabled me to believe to the salvation of my soul. By free grace I was persuaded that I had a part in the first resurrection, and was enlightened with the "light of the living" (Job 33:30). I wished for a man of God with whom I might converse: my soul was like the chariots of Amminadib (Canticles 6:12). These, among others, were the precious promises that were so powerfully applied to me. "All things whatsoever ye shall ask in prayer, believing, ye shall receive" (Mat. 21:22). "Peace I leave with you, my peace I give unto you" (John

14:27). I saw the blessed Redeemer to be the fountain of life, and the well of salvation. I experienced him to be all in all; he had brought me by a way that I knew not, and he had made crooked paths straight. Then in his name I set up my Ebenezer, saying, Hitherto he hath helped me: and could say to the sinners about me, Behold what a Saviour I have! Thus I was, by the teaching of that all-glorious Deity, the great One in Three, and Three in One, confirmed in the truths of the Bible, those oracles of ever-lasting truth, on which every soul living must stand or fall eternally, agreeable to Acts 4:12. "Neither is there salvation in any other, for there is none other name under heaven given among men whereby we must be saved, but only Christ Jesus." May God give the reader a right understanding in these facts! "To him that believeth, all things are possible, but to them that are unbelieving nothing is pure" (Titus 1:15).

During this period we remained at Cadiz until our ship got laden. We sailed about the fourth of November; and, having a good passage, we arrived in London the month following, to my comfort, with heartfelt gratitude to God for his rich and unspeakable mercies.

On my return I had but one text which puzzled me, or that the devil endeavored to buffet me with, *viz.*, Rom. 11:6, and, as I had heard of the Rev. Mr. Romaine, and his great knowledge in the scriptures, I wished much to hear him preach. One day I went to Blackfriars church, and, to my great satisfaction and surprise, he preached from that very text. He very clearly shewed the difference between human works and free election, which is according to God's sovereign will and pleasure. These glad tidings set me entirely at liberty, and I went out of the church rejoicing, seeing my spots were those of God's children. I went to Westminster Chapel, and saw some of my old friends, who were glad when they perceived the wonderful change that the Lord had wrought in me, particularly Mr. G—— S——, my worthy acquaintance, who was a man of a choice spirit and had great zeal for the Lord's service. I enjoyed his correspondence till he died, in the year 1784. I was again examined at that same chapel, and was received into church fellowship amongst them. I rejoiced in spirit, making melody in my heart to the God of all my mercies.

Now my whole wish was to be dissolved, and to be with Christ —but, alas! I must wait mine appointed time.

———————————◆─■◦■─◆———————————

MISCELLANEOUS VERSES:

OR,

Reflections on the state of my mind during my first Convictions, of the necessity of believing the Truth, and experiencing the inestimable benefits of Christianity.

> Well may I say my life has been
> One scene of sorrow and of pain;
> From early days I griefs have known,
> And as I grew my griefs have grown:
>
> Dangers were always in my path;
> And fear of wrath, and sometimes death:
> While pale dejection in me reign'd,
> I often wept, by grief constrained.
>
> When taken from my native land,
> By an unjust and cruel band,
> How did uncommon dread prevail!
> My sighs no more I could conceal.
>
> To ease my mind I often strove,
> And tried my trouble to remove;
> I sung, and utter'd sighs between—
> Assay'd to stifle guilt with sin.
>
> But O! not all that I could do
> Would stop the current of my woe:
> Conviction still my vileness shew'd;
> How great my guilt—how lost to good.
>
> "Prevented that I could not die,
> Nor could to one sure refuge fly:
> An orphan state I had to mourn—
> Forsook by all, and left forlorn."
>
> Those who beheld my downcast mien,
> Could not guess at my woes unseen;

They by appearance could not know
The troubles that I waded through.

Lust, anger, blasphemy, and pride,
With legions of such ills beside,
"Troubled my thoughts," while doubts and fears,
Clouded and darken'd most my years.

"Sighs now no more would be confin'd—
They breath'd the trouble of my mind:"
I wish'd for death, but check the word,
And often pray'd unto the Lord.

Unhappy more than some on earth,
I thought the place that gave me birth—
Strange thoughts oppress'd—while I replied
"Why not in Ethiopia died?"

And why thus spar'd when nigh to hell?—
God only knew—I could not tell!
"A tott'ring fence a bowing wall,"
"I thought myself ere since the fall."

Oft times I mus'd, and night despair,
While birds melodious fill'd the air:
"Thrice happy songsters, ever free,"
How blest were they, compar'd to me!

Thus all things added to my pain,
While grief compell'd me to complain!
When sable clouds began to rise
My mind grew darker than the skies.

The English nation call'd to leave,
How did my breast with sorrows heave!
I long'd for rest—cried, "Help me Lord;
Some mitigation, Lord, afford!"

Yet on, dejected, still I went—
Heart-throbbing woes within me pent;
Nor land, nor sea, could comfort give,
Nor aught my anxious mind relieve.

Weary with troubles yet unknown
To all but God and self alone,
Numerous months for peace I strove,
Numerous foes I had to prove.

Inur'd to dangers, griefs, and woes,
Train'd up 'midst perils, death, and foes,
I said, "Must it thus ever be?
No quiet is permitted me."

Hard hap, and more than heavy lot!
I pray'd to God "Forget me not—
What thou ordain'st help me to bear;
But O! deliver from despair!"

Strivings and wrestling seem'd in vain;
Nothing I did could ease my pain:
Then gave I up my work and will,
Confess'd and owned my doom was hell!

Like some poor pris'ner at the bar,
Conscious of guilt, of sin and fear,
Arraign'd, and self-condemned, I stood—
"Lost in the world and in my blood!"

Yet here, 'midst blackest clouds confin'd,
A beam from Christ, the day star shin'd:
Surely, thought I, if Jesus please,
He can at once sign my release.

I, ignorant of his righteousness,
Set up my labors in its place;
"Forgot for why his blood was shed,
And pray'd and fasted in its stead."

He died for sinners—I am one!
Might not his blood for me atone?
Tho' I am nothing else but sin,
Yet surely he can make me clean!

Thus light came in, and I believed;
Myself forgot, and help receiv'd!
My Saviour then I know I found,
For, eas'd from guilt no more I groan'd.

O, happy hour, in which I ceas'd
To mourn, for then I found a rest!
My soul and Christ were now as one—
Thy light, O Jesus, in me shone!

Bless'd be thy name, for now I know
I and my works can nothing do;

"The Lord alone can ransom man—
For this the spotless Lamb was slain!"

When sacrifices, works, and pray'r,
Prov'd vain, and ineffectual were—
"Lo, then I come!" the Saviour cried,
And bleeding, bow'd his head, and died!

He died for all who ever saw
No help in them, nor by the law:
I this have seen: and gladly own
"Salvation is by Christ alone!"*

* Acts 4:12.

Chapter 11

The author embarks on board a ship bound for Cadiz—Is near being ship-wrecked—Goes to Malaga—Remarkable fine cathedral there—The author disputes with a popish priest—Picking up eleven miserable men at sea in returning to England—Engages again with Doctor Irving to accompany him to Jamaica and the Mosquito Shore—Meets with an Indian Prince on board—The author attempts to instruct him in the truths of the Gospel—Frustrated by the bad example of some in the ship—They arrive on the Mosquito Shore with some slaves they purchased at Jamaica, and begin to cultivate a plantation—Some account of the manners and customs of the Mosquito Indians—Successful device of the author's to quell a riot among them—Curious entertainment given by them to Doctor Irving and the author, who leaves the shore and goes to Jamaica—Is barbarously treated by a man with whom he engaged for his passage—Escapes and goes to the Mosquito admiral, who treats him kindly—He gets another vessel and goes on board—Instances of bad treatment—Meets Dr. Irving—Gets to Jamaica—Is cheated by his captain—Leaves the Doctor and goes for England.

WHEN OUR SHIP was got ready for sea again, I was entreated by the captain to go in her once more; but as I felt myself now as happy as I could wish to be in this life, I for some time refused; however, the advice of my friends at last prevailed; and, in full resignation to the will of God, I again embarked for Cadiz, in March 1775. We had a very good passage, without any material accident, until we arrived off the Bay of Cadiz, when one Sunday, just as we were going into the harbor, the ship struck against a rock and knocked off a garboard plank, which is the next to the keel. In an instant all hands were in the greatest confusion, and began with loud cries to call on God to have mercy on them. Although I could not swim, and saw no way of escaping death, I felt no dread in my then situation, having no desire to live. I even rejoiced in spirit, thinking this death would be sudden glory. But the fulness of time was not yet come. The people near to me were much astonished in seeing me thus calm and resigned; but I told them of the peace of God, which, through sovereign grace I enjoyed, and these words were that instant in my mind:

Christ is my pilot wise, my compass is his word:
My soul each storm defies, while I have such a Lord
    I trust his faithfulness and power,
    To save me in the trying hour.
Though rocks and quicksands deep through all my passage lie,
Yet Christ shall safely keep and guide me with his eye,
    How can I sink with such a prop,
    That bears the world and all things up.

At this time there were many large Spanish flukers or passage
vessels, full of people crossing the channel; who seeing our condition, a number of them came alongside of us. As many hands as
could be employed began to work; some at our three pumps, and
the rest unloading the ship as fast as possible. There being only
a single rock, called the Porpus, on which we struck, we soon got
off of it, and providentially it was then high water, we therefore
run the ship ashore at the nearest place to keep her from sinking.
After many tides, with a great deal of care and industry, we got
her repaired again. When we had dispatched our business at
Cadiz we went to Gibraltar, and from thence to Malaga, a very
pleasant and rich city, where there is one of the finest cathedrals
I had ever seen. It had been above fifty years in building, as I
heard, though it was not then quite finished; great parts of the
inside, however, were completed and highly decorated with the
richest marble columns and many superb paintings; it was lighted
occasionally by an amazing number of wax tapers of different
sizes, some of which were as thick as a man's thigh: these, however, were only used on some of their grand festivals.

I was very much shocked at the custom of bull-baiting, and
other diversions which prevailed here on Sunday evenings, to the
great scandal of Christianity and morals. I used to express my
abhorrence of it to a priest whom I met with. I had frequent con-
tests about religion with the reverend father, in which he took
great pains to make a proselyte of me to his church; and I no less
to convert him to mine. On these occasions I used to produce my
Bible, and shew him in what points his church erred. He then said
he had been in England, and that every person there read the
Bible, which was very wrong; but I answered him that Christ desired us to search the scriptures. In his zeal for my conversion, he
solicited me to go to one of the universities in Spain, and declared

that I should have my education free; and told me, if I got myself made a priest, I might in time become even pope; and that Pope Benedict was a black man. As I was desirous of learning, I paused for some time upon this temptation; and thought by being crafty I might catch some with guile; but I began to think that it would be only hypocrisy in me to embrace his offer, as I could not in conscience conform to the opinions of his church. I was therefore enabled to regard the word of God, which says "Come out from amongst them," and refused Father Vincent's offer. So we parted without conviction on either side.

Having taken at this place some fine wines, fruits, and money, we proceeded to Cadiz, where we took about two tons more, of money, &c., and then sailed for England in the month of June. When we were about the north latitude 42, we had contrary wind for several days and the ship did not make in that time above six or seven miles strait course. This made the captain exceeding fretful and peevish, and I was very sorry to hear God's most holy name often blasphemed by him. One day as he was in that impious mood, a young gentleman on board who was a passenger, reproached him, and said he acted wrong; for we ought to be thankful to God for all things, as we were not in want of anything on board; and though the wind was contrary for us, yet it was fair for some others, who, perhaps stood in more need of it than we. I immediately seconded this young gentleman with some boldness, and said we had not the least cause to murmur, for that the Lord was better to us than we deserved, and that he had done all things well. I expected that the captain would be very angry with me for speaking, but he replied not a word. However, before that time on the following day, being the 21st of June, much to our great joy and astonishment, we saw the providential hand of our benign Creator, whose ways with his blind creatures are past finding out. The preceding night I dreamed that I saw a boat immediately off the starboard main shrouds; and exactly at half past one o'clock, the following day at noon, while I was below, just as we had dined in the cabin, the man at the helm cried out, A boat! which brought my dream that instant into my mind; I was the first man that jumped on the deck, and looking from the shrouds onward, according to my dream, I descried a little boat at some distance; but as the waves were high, it was as much as we could do sometimes to discern her; we however stopped the ship's way, and the boat, which was extremely small, came along-side with eleven miserable men, whom we took on board immedi-ately. To all human appearance, these people must have perished in the course of one hour or less; the boat being small, it barely contained them. When we took them up they were half drowned, and had no victuals, compass, water, or any other necessary whatsoever, and had only one bit of an oar to steer with, and that right before the wind; so that they were obliged to trust entirely to the mercy of the waves. As soon as we got them all on board, they bowed themselves on their knees, and, with hands and voices lifted up to heaven, thanked God for their deliverance; and I trust that my prayers were not wanting amongst them at the same time. This mercy of the Lord quite melted me, and I recol-lected his words which I saw thus verified in the 107th Psalm, "O give thanks unto the Lord, for he is good, for his mercy endureth for ever. Hungry and thirsty, their souls fainted in them. They cried unto the Lord in their trouble, and he delivered them out of their distresses. And he led them forth by the right way, that they might go to a city of habitation. O that men would praise the Lord for his goodness, and for his wonderful works to the chil-dren of men! For he satisfieth the longing soul, and filleth the hungry soul with goodness.

"Such as sit in darkness and in the shadow of death . . .

"Then they cried unto the Lord in their trouble, and he saved them out of their distresses. They that go down to the sea in ships, that do business in great waters: these see the works of the Lord and his wonders in the deep. Whoso is wise and will ob-serve these things, even they shall understand the lovingkindness of the Lord."

The poor distressed captain said, "that the Lord is good, for, seeing that I am not fit to die, he therefore gave me time to re-pent." I was very glad to hear this expression, and took an op-portunity when convenient, of talking to him on the providence of God. They told us they were Portuguese, and were in a brig loaded with corn, which shifted that morning at five o'clock, owing to which the vessel sunk that instant with two of the crew; and how these eleven got into the boat (which was lashed to the deck) not one of them could tell. We provided them with every necessary, and brought them all safe to London; and I hope the Lord gave them repentance unto life eternal.

I was happy once more amongst my friends and brethren, till November, when my old friend, the celebrated Doctor Irving, bought a remarkable fine sloop, about 150 tons. He had a mind for a new adventure in cultivating a plantation at Jamaica, and the Mosquito shore; asked me to go with him, and said that he would trust me with his estate in preference to anyone. By the advice, therefore, of my friends, I accepted of the offer, knowing that the harvest was fully ripe in those parts, and hoped to be an instrument under God, of bringing some poor sinner to my well beloved master, Jesus Christ. Before I embarked, I found with the Doctor four Mosquito Indians, who were chiefs in their own country, and were brought here by some English traders for some selfish ends. One of them was the Mosquito king's son; a youth of about eighteen years of age; and whilst he was here he was baptized by the name of George. They were going back at the government's expense, after having been in England about twelve months, during which they learned to speak pretty good English. When I came to talk to them, about eight days before we sailed, I was very much mortified in finding that they had not frequented any churches since they were here, to be baptized, nor was any attention paid to their morals. I was very sorry for this mock Christianity, and had just an opportunity to take some of them once to church before we sailed. We embarked in the month of November 1776, on board of the sloop *Morning Star,* Captain David Miller, and sailed for Jamaica. In our passage, I took all the pains that I could to instruct the Indian prince in the doctrines of Christianity, of which he was entirely ignorant; and, to my great joy he was quite attentive, and received with gladness the truths that the Lord enabled me to set forth to him. I taught him in the compass of eleven days all the letters, and he could even put two or three of them together and spell them. I had Fox's *Martyrology,* with cuts, and he used to be very fond of looking into it, and would ask many questions about the papal cruelties he saw depicted there, which I explained to him. I made such progress with this youth, especially in religion, that when I used to go to bed at different hours of the night, if he was in his bed, he would get up on purpose to go to prayer with me,

without any other clothes than his shirt; and before he would eat
any of his meals among the gentlemen in the cabin, he would
first come to me to pray, as he called it. I was well pleased at
this, and took great delight in him, and used much supplication
to God for his conversion. I was in full hope of seeing daily every
appearance of that change which I could wish; not knowing the
devices of satan, who had many of his emissaries to sow his tares
as fast as I sowed the good seed, and pull down as fast as I
built up. Thus we went on nearly four-fifths of our passage, when
Satan at last got the upper hand. Some of his messengers, seeing
this poor heathen much advanced in piety, began to ask him
whether I had converted him to Christianity, laughed and made
their jest at him, for which I rebuked them as much as I could;
but this treatment caused the prince to halt between two opinions. Some of the true sons of Belial, who did not believe that
there was any hereafter, told him never to fear the devil, for there
was none existing; and if ever he came to the prince, they desired
he might be sent to them. Thus they teased the poor innocent
youth, so that he would not learn his book any more! He would
not drink nor carouse with these ungodly actors, nor would he be
with me, even at prayers. This grieved me very much. I endeavored to persuade him as well as I could, but he would not
come; and entreated him very much to tell me his reasons for
acting thus. At last he asked me, "How comes it that all the
white men on board who can read and write, and observe the
sun, and know all things, yet swear, lie, and get drunk, only
excepting yourself?" I answered him, the reason was, that they
did not fear God; and that if any one of them died so they could
not go to, or be happy with God. He replied, that if these persons
went to hell he would go to hell too. I was sorry to hear this; and,
as he sometimes had the toothache, and also some other persons in
the ship at the same time. I asked him if their toothache made
his easy: he said, No. Then I told him if he and these people
went to hell together, their pains would not make his any lighter.
This answer had great weight with him; it depressed his spirits
much; and he became ever after, during the passage, fond of being alone. When we were in the latitude of Martinique, and near
making the land, one morning we had a brisk gale of wind, and,
carrying too much sail, the main-mast went over the side. Many

people were then all about the deck, and the yards, masts, and rigging came tumbling all about us, yet there was not one of us in the least hurt although some were within a hair's breadth of being killed; and, particularly, I saw two men who, by the providential hand of God, were most miraculously preserved from being smashed to pieces. On the fifth of January we made Antigua and Montserrat, and ran along the rest of the islands; and on the fourteenth we arrived at Jamaica. One Sunday, while we were there, I took the Mosquito Prince George to church, where he saw the sacrament administered. When we came out we saw all kinds of people, almost from the church door for the space of half a mile down to the waterside, buying and selling all kinds of commodities: and these acts afforded me great matter of exhortation to this youth, who was much astonished. Our vessel being ready to sail for the Mosquito shore, I went with the Doctor on board a Guinea-man, to purchase some slaves to carry with us, and cultivate a plantation; and I chose them all my own countrymen. On the 12th of February we sailed from Jamaica, and on the eighteenth arrived at the Mosquito shore, at a place called Dupeupy. All our Indian guests now, after I had admonished them, and a few cases of liquor given them by the Doctor, took an affectionate leave of us, and went ashore, where they were met by the Mosquito king, and we never saw one of them afterwards. We then sailed to the southward of the shore, to a place called Cape Gracias á Dios, where there was a large lagoon or lake, which received the emptying of two or three very fine large rivers, and abounded much in fish and land tortoise. Some of the native Indians came on board of us here; and we used them well, and told them we were come to dwell amongst them, which they seemed pleased at. So the Doctor and I, with some others, went with them ashore; and they took us to different places to view the land, in order to choose a place to make a plantation of. We fixed on a spot near a river's bank, in a rich soil; and, having got our necessaries out of the sloop, we began to clear away the woods, and plant different kinds of vegetables, which had a quick growth. While we were employed in this manner, our vessel went northward to Black River to trade. While she was there, a Spanish *guarda costa* met with and took her. This proved very hurtful, and a great embarrassment to us. However we went on with the culture of the land. We used to make fires every night all around us, to keep off wild beasts, which, as soon as it was dark, set up a most hideous roaring. Our habitation being far up in the woods, we frequently saw different kinds of animals; but none of them ever hurt us, except poisonous snakes, the bite of which the Doctor used to cure by giving to the patient as soon as possible, about half a tumbler of strong rum, with a good deal of Cayenne pepper in it. In this manner he cured two natives and one of his own slaves. The Indians were exceedingly fond of the Doctor, and they had good reason for it; for I believe they never had such an useful man amongst them. They came from all quarters to our dwelling; and some *woolwow* or flat-headed Indians, who lived fifty or sixty miles above our river, and this side of the South Sea, brought us a good deal of silver in exchange for our goods. The principal articles we could get from our neighboring Indians were turtle oil and shells, little silk grass, and some provisions; but they would not work at anything for us, except fishing; and a few times they assisted to cut some trees down, in order to build us houses; which they did exactly like the Africans, by the joint labor of men, women, and children. I do not recollect any of them to have had more than two wives. These always accompanied their husbands when they came to our dwelling, and then they generally carried whatever they brought to us, and always squatted down behind their husbands. Whenever we gave them anything to eat, the men and their wives eat separate. I never saw the least sign of incontinence amongst them. The women are ornamented with beads, and fond of painting themselves; the men also paint, even to excess, both their faces and shirts: their favorite color is red. The women generally cultivate the ground, and the men are all fishermen and canoe makers. Upon the whole, I never met any nation that were so simple in their manners as these people, or had so little ornament in their houses. Neither had they, as I ever could learn, one word expressive of an oath. The worst word I ever heard amongst them when they were quarrelling, was one that they had got from the English, which was "you rascal." I never saw any mode of worship among them; but in this they were not worse than their European brethren or neighbors, for I am sorry to say that there was not one white person in our dwelling, nor anywhere else, that

I saw, in different places I was at on the shore, that was better or more pious than those unenlightened Indians; but they either worked or slept on Sundays: and to my sorrow, working was too much Sunday's employment with ourselves, so much so, that in some length of time we really did not know one day from another. This mode of living laid the foundation of my decamping at last. The natives are well made and warlike; and they particularly boast of having never been conquered by the Spaniards. They are great drinkers of strong liquors when they can get them. We used to distil rum from pineapples, which were very plentiful here, and then we could not get them away from our place. Yet they seemed to be singular, in point of honesty, above any other nation I was ever amongst. The country being hot, we lived under an open shed, where we had all kinds of goods, without a door or a lock to any article; yet we slept in safety, and never lost anything, or were disturbed. This surprised us a good deal; and the Doctor, myself, and others, used to say if we were to lie in that manner in Europe we should have our throats cut the first night. The Indian Governor goes once in a certain time all about the province or district, and has a number of men with him as attendants and assistants. He settles all the differences among the people, like the judge here, and is treated with very great respect. He took care to give us timely notice before he came to our habitation, by sending his stick as a token, for rum, sugar, and gunpowder, which we did not refuse sending; and at the same time we made the utmost preparation to receive his honor and his train. When he came with his tribe, and all our neighboring chieftains, we expected to find him a grave, reverend judge, solid and sagacious; but instead of that, before he and his gang came in sight, we heard them very clamorous; and they even had plundered some of our good neighboring Indians, having intoxicated themselves with our liquor. When they arrived we did not know what to make of our new guests, and would gladly have dispensed with the honor of their company. However, having no alternative, we feasted them plentifully all the day till the evening, when the Governor, getting quite drunk, grew very unruly, and struck one of our most friendly chiefs who was our nearest neighbor, and also took his gold-laced hat from him. At this a great commotion took place; and the Doctor interfered to make peace, as we could all understand one another, but to no purpose; and at last they became so outrageous that the Doctor, fearing he might get into trouble, left the house, and made the best of his way to the nearest wood, leaving me to do as well as I could among them. I was so enraged with the Governor that I could have wished to have seen him tied fast to a tree and flogged for his behavior; but I had not people enough to cope with his party. I therefore thought of a stratagem to appease the riot. Recollecting a passage I had read in the life of Columbus, when he was amongst the Indians in Mexico or Peru, where on some occasion, he frightened them by telling them of certain events in the Heavens, I had recourse to the same expedient; and it succeeded beyond my most sanguine expectations. When I had formed my determination, I went in the midst of them and, taking hold of the Governor, I pointed up to the Heavens. I menaced him and the rest; I told them God lived there, and that he was angry with them, and they must not quarrel so; that they were all brothers, and if they did not leave off, and go away quietly, I would take the book (pointing to the Bible), read, and *tell* God to make them dead. This operated on them like magic. The clamor immediately ceased, and I gave them some rum and a few other things, after which they went away peaceably; and the Governor afterwards gave our neighbor, who was called Captain Plasmahy, his hat again. When the Doctor returned, he was exceedingly glad at my success in thus getting rid of our troublesome guests. The Mosquito people within our vicinity, out of respect to the Doctor, myself, and his people, made entertainments of the grand kind, called in their tongue *tourrie* or *dryckbot*. The English of this expression is, a feast of drinking about, of which it seems a corruption of language. The drink consisted of pineapples roasted, and casades chewed or beaten in mortars; which, after lying some time, ferments, and becomes so strong as to intoxicate, when drank in any quantity. We had timely notice given to us of the entertainment. A white family, within five miles of us, told us how the drink was made, and I and two others went before the time to the village, where the mirth was appointed to be held, and there we saw the whole art of making the drink, and also the kind of animals that were to be eaten there. I cannot say the sight of either the drink or the meat were enticing to me. They had some thousands of pine-apples roasting, which they squeezed, dirt and all, into a canoe they had there for the purpose. The casade drink was in beef barrels, and other vessels, and looked exactly like hog-wash. Men, women and children, were thus employed in roasting the pineapples, and squeezing them with their hands. For food they had many land torpins or tortoises, some dried turtle, and three large alligators alive, and tied fast to the trees. I asked the people what they were going to do with these alligators; and I was told they were to be eaten. I was much surprised at this, and went home not a little disgusted at the preparations. When the day of the feast was come, we took some rum with us, and went to the appointed place, where we found a great assemblage of these people, who received us very kindly. The mirth had begun before we came, and they were dancing with music; and the musical instruments were nearly the same as those of any other sable people, but, as I thought, much less melodious than any other nation I ever knew. They had many curious gestures in dancing, and a variety of motions and postures of their bodies, which to me were in no wise attracting. The males danced by themselves, and the females also by themselves, as with us. The Doctor shewed his people the example, by immediately joining the women's party, though not by their choice. On perceiving the women disgusted, he joined the males. At night there were great illuminations, by setting fire to many pine trees, while the dryckbot went round merrily by calabashes or gourds; but the liquor might more justly be called eating than drinking. One Owden, the oldest father in the vicinity, was dressed in a strange and terrifying form. Around his body were skins adorned with different kinds of feathers, and he had on his head a very large and high head piece, in the form of a grenadier's cap, with prickles like a porcupine; and he made a certain noise which resembled the cry of an alligator. Our people skipped amongst them out of complaisance, though some could not drink of their *tourrie;* but our rum met with customers enough, and was soon gone. The alligators were killed and some of them roasted. Their manner of roasting is by digging a hole in the earth, and filling it with wood, which they burn to coal, and then they lay sticks across, on which they set the meat. I had a raw piece of the

alligator in my hand; it was very rich: I thought it looked like
fresh salmon, and it had a most fragrant smell, but I could not
eat any of it. This merry-making at last ended, without the least
discord in any person in the company, although it was made up
of different nations and complexions.

The rainy season came on here about the latter end of May,
which continued till August very heavily; so that the rivers were
overflowed, and our provisions, then in the ground, were washed
away. I thought this was in some measure a judgment upon us for
working on Sundays, and it hurt my mind very much. I often
wished to leave this place and sail for Europe; for our mode of
procedure and living in this heathenish form was very irksome
to me. The word of God saith, "What does it avail a man if he
gain the whole world, and lose his own soul?" This was much
and heavily impressed on my mind; and, though I did not know
how to speak to the Doctor for my discharge, it was disagreeable
for me to stay any longer. But about the middle of June I took
courage enough to ask him for it. He was very unwilling at first
to grant my request; but I gave him so many reasons for it, that
at last he consented to my going, and gave me the following certificate of my behavior.

> The bearer, Gustavus Vassa, has served me several years with
> strict honesty, sobriety, and fidelity. I can therefore with justice
> recommend him for these qualifications; and indeed in every
> respect I consider him as an excellent servant. I do hereby cer-
> tify that he always behaved well, and that he is perfectly trust-
> worthy.
>
>   *CHARLES IRVING*
> MOSQUITO SHORE, JUNE 15, 1776.

Though I was much attached to the Doctor, I was happy
when he consented. I got everything ready for my departure,
and hired some Indians, with a large canoe, to carry me off. All
my poor countrymen, the slaves, when they heard of my leaving
them, were very sorry, as I had always treated them with care
and affection, and did everything I could to comfort the poor
creatures, and render their condition easy. Having taken leave of
my old friends and companions, on the 18th of June, accompanied by the Doctor, I left that spot of the world, and went
southward above twenty miles along the river. There I found a

sloop, the captain of which told me he was going to Jamaica. Having agreed for my passage with him and one of the owners, who was also on board, named Hughes, the Doctor and I parted, not without shedding tears on both sides. The vessel then sailed along the river till night, when she stopped in a lagoon within the same river. During the night a schooner belonging to the same owners came in, and, as she was in want of hands, Hughes, the owner of the sloop asked me to go in the schooner as a sailor, and said he would give me wages. I thanked him; but I said I wanted to go to Jamaica. He then immediately changed his tone, and swore, and abused me very much, and asked how I came to be freed. I told him, and said that I came into that vicinity with Dr. Irving, whom he had seen that day. This account was of no use; he still swore exceedingly at me, and cursed the master for a fool that sold me my freedom, and the Doctor for another in letting me go from him. Then he desired me to go in the schooner, or else I should not go out of the sloop as a freeman. I said this was very hard, and begged to be put on shore again; but he swore that I should not. I said I had been twice amongst the Turks, yet had never seen any such usage with them, and much less could I have expected anything of this kind among the Christians. This incensed him exceedingly; and with a volley of oaths and imprecations, he replied, "Christians! damn you, you are one of St. Paul's men; but by G——, except you have St. Paul's or St. Peter's faith, and walk upon the water to the shore, you shall not go out of the vessel," which I now learnt was going amongst the Spaniards towards Cartagena, where he swore he would sell me. I simply asked him what right he had to sell me? but, without another word, he made some of his people tie ropes round each of my ankles, and also to each wrist, and another rope around my body, and hoisted me up without letting my feet touch or rest upon anything. Thus I hung, without any crime committed, and without judge or jury; merely because I was a freeman, and could not by the law get any redress from a white person in those parts of the world. I was in great pain from my situation, and cried and begged very hard for some mercy, but all in vain. My tyrant, in a great rage, brought a musket out of the cabin and loaded it before me and the crew, and swore that he would shoot me if I cried any more. I had now no alternative; I therefore remained silent, seeing not one white man on board who said a word on my behalf. I hung in that manner from between ten and eleven o'clock at night till about one in the morning, when, finding my cruel abuser fast asleep, I begged some of his slaves to slack the rope that was round my body, that my feet might rest on something. This they did at the risk of being cruelly used by their master, who beat some of them severely at first for not tying me when he commanded them. Whilst I remained in this condition, till between five and six o'clock next morning, I trust I prayed to God to forgive this blasphemer who cared not what he did; but when he got up out of his sleep in the morning was of the very same temper and disposition as when he left me at night. When they got up the anchor, and the vessel was getting under way, I once more cried and begged to be released; and now, being fortunately in the way of their hoisting the sails, they released me. When I was let down, I spoke to one Mr. Cox, a carpenter whom I knew on board, on the impropriety of this conduct. He also knew the Doctor, and the good opinion he ever had of me. This man then went to the captain, and told him not to carry me away in that manner: that I was the Doctor's steward, who regarded me very highly, and would resent this usage when he should come to know it. On which he desired a young man to put me ashore in a small canoe I brought with me. This sound gladdened my heart, and I got hastily into the canoe and set off, whilst my tyrant was down in the cabin; but he soon spied me out, when I was not above thirty or forty yards from the vessel, and running upon the deck with a loaded musket in his hand, he presented it at me, and swore heavily and dreadfully, that he would shoot me that instant, if I did not come back on board. As I knew the wretch would have done as he said, without hesitation I put back to the vessel again; but, as the good Lord would have it, just as I was alongside he was abusing the captain for letting me go from the vessel, which the captain returned, and both of them soon got into a very great heat. The young man that was with me now got out of the canoe; the vessel was sailing on fast with a smooth sea: and I then thought it was neck or nothing, so at that instant I set off again, for my life, in the canoe, towards the shore; and fortunately the confusion was so great amongst them on board, that I got out of the musket shot unnoticed, while the vessel sailed on with a fair wind a different way; so that they could not overtake me without tacking: but even before that could be done I should have been on shore, which I soon reached, with many thanks to God for this unexpected deliverance. I then went and told the other owner, who lived near that shore (with whom I had agreed for my passage), of the usage I had met with. He was very much astonished and appeared sorry for it. After treating me with kindness, he gave me some refreshment, and three heads of roasted Indian corn, for a voyage of about 18 miles south to look for another vessel. He then directed me to an Indian chief of a district, who was also the Mosquito admiral, and had once been at our dwelling; after which I set off with the canoe across a large lagoon alone (for I could not get anyone to assist me), though I was much jaded, and had pains in my bowels, by means of the rope I had hung by the night before. I was therefore at different times unable to manage the canoe, for the paddling was very laborious. However, a little before dark I got to my destined place, where some of the Indians knew me and received me kindly. I asked for the admiral, and they conducted me to his dwelling. He was glad to see me, and refreshed me with such things as the place afforded; and I had a hammock to sleep in. They acted towards me more like Christians than those whites I was amongst the last night, though they had been baptized. I told the admiral I wanted to go to the next port to get a vessel to carry me to Jamaica, and requested him to send the canoe back which I then had, for which I was to pay him. He agreed with me, and sent five able Indians with a large canoe to carry my things to my intended place, about fifty miles; and we set off the next morning. When we got out of the lagoon and went along shore, the sea was so high that the canoe was oftentimes very near being filled with water. We were obliged to go ashore and drag across different necks of land; we were also two nights in the swamps, which swarmed with mosquito flies, and they proved troublesome to us. This tiresome journey of land and water ended, however, on the third day, to my great joy; and I got on board of a sloop commanded by one Captain Jenning. She was then partly loaded, and he told me he was expecting daily to sail for

Jamaica; and having agreed with me to work my passage, I went to work accordingly. I was not many days on board before we sailed; but to my sorrow and disappointment, though used to such tricks, we went to the southward along the Mosquito shore, instead of steering for Jamaica. I was compelled to assist in cutting a great deal of mahogany wood on the shore as we coasted along it, and load the vessel with it, before she sailed. This fretted me much; but, as I did not know how to help myself among these deceivers, I thought patience was the only remedy I had left, and even that was forced. There was much hard work and little victuals on board; except by good luck we happened to catch turtles. On this coast there was also a particular kind of fish called manatee, which is most excellent eating, and the flesh is more like beef than fish; the scales are as large as a shilling, and the skin thicker than I ever saw that of any other fish. Within the brackish waters along shore there were likewise vast numbers of alligators, which made the fish scarce. I was on board this sloop sixteen days, during which, in our coasting, we came to another place, where there was a smaller sloop called the *Indian Queen,* commanded by one John Baker. He also was an Englishman, and had been a long time along the shore trading for turtle shells and silver, and had got a good quantity of each on board. He wanted some hands very much; and, understanding I was a freeman, and wanted to go to Jamaica, he told me if he could get one or two, that he would sail immediately for that island: he also pretended to shew me some marks of attention and respect, and promised to give me forty-five shillings sterling a month if I would go with him. I thought this much better than cutting wood for nothing. I therefore told the other captain that I wanted to go to Jamaica in the other vessel; but he would not listen to me; and, seeing me resolved to go in a day or two, he got the vessel to sail, intending to carry me away against my will. This treatment mortified me extremely. I immediately, according to an agreement I had made with the captain of the *Indian Queen,* called for her boat, which was lying near us, and it came alongside; and, by the means of a North Pole shipmate which I met with in the sloop I was in, I got my things into the boat, and went on board the *Indian Queen,* July the 10th. A few days after I was there, we got all things ready and sailed: but again, to my great mortification, this vessel still went to the south, nearly as far as Cartagena, trading along the coast, instead of going to Jamaica, as the captain had promised me; and, what was worst of all, he was a very cruel and bloody-minded man, and was a horrid blasphemer. Among others, he had a white pilot, one Stoker, whom he beat often as severely as he did some Negroes he had on board. One night in particular, after he had beaten this man most cruelly, he put him into the boat, and made two Negroes row him to a desolate key, or small island, and he loaded two pistols, and swore bitterly that he would shoot the Negroes if they brought Stoker on board again. There was not the least doubt but that he would do as he said, and the two poor fellows were obliged to obey the cruel mandate; but, when the captain was asleep, the two Negroes took a blanket and carried it to the unfortunate Stoker, which I believe was the means of saving his life from the annoyance of insects. A great deal of entreaty was used with the captain the next day, before he would consent to let Stoker come on board; and when the poor man was brought on board he was very ill, from his situation during the night, and he remained so till he was drowned a little time after. As we sailed southward we came to many uninhabited islands, which were overgrown with fine large cocoanuts. As I was very much in want of provisions, I brought a boat load of them on board, which lasted me and others for several weeks, and afforded us many a delicious repast in our scarcity. One day, before this, I could not help observing the providential hand of God, that ever supplies all our wants, though in the way and manner we know not. I had been a whole day without food, and made signals for boats to come off, but in vain. I therefore earnestly prayed to God for relief in my need; and at the close of the evening I went off the deck. Just as I laid down I heard a noise on the deck, and, not knowing what it meant, I went directly on the deck again, when what should I see but a fine large fish about seven or eight pounds, which had jumped aboard! I took it, and admired, with thanks, the good hand of God; and, what I considered as not less extraordinary, the captain, who was very avaricious, did not attempt to take it from me, there being only him and I on board; for the rest were all gone ashore trading. Sometimes the people did not come off for some days; this used to fret the captain, and then he would vent his fury on me by beating me, or making me feel in other cruel ways. One day especially, in his wild, wicked, and mad career, after striking me several times with different things, and once across my mouth, even with a red burning stick out of the fire, he got a barrel of gunpowder on the deck, and swore that he would blow up the vessel. I was then at my wit's end, and earnestly prayed to God to direct me. The head was out of the barrel; and the captain took a lighted stick out of the fire to blow himself and me up, because there was a vessel then in sight coming in, which he supposed was a Spaniard, and he was afraid of falling into their hands. Seeing this I got an axe, unnoticed by him, and placed myself between him and the powder, having resolved in myself as soon as he attempted to put the fire in the barrel to chop him down that instant. I was more than an hour in this situation; during which he struck me often, still keeping the fire in his hand for this wicked purpose. I really should have thought myself justifiable in any other part of the world if I had killed him, and prayed to God, who gave me a mind which rested solely on himself. I prayed for resignation, that his will might be done: and the following two portions of his holy word, which occurred to my mind, buoyed up my hope, and kept me from taking the life of this wicked man. "He hath determined the times before appointed, and set bounds to our habitations" (Acts 17:26). And, "Who is there among you that feareth the Lord, that obeyeth the voice of his servant, that walketh in darkness and hath no light? let him trust in the name of the Lord, and stay upon his God" (Isaiah 50:10). And this by the grace of God I was enabled to do. I found him a present help in the time of need, and the captain's fury began to subside as the night approached: but I found,

> That he who cannot stem his anger's tide
> Doth a wild horse without a bridle ride.

The next morning we discovered that the vessel which had caused such a fury in the captain was an English sloop. They soon came to an anchor where we were, and, to my no small surprise, I learned that Doctor Irving was on board of her, on his way from the Mosquito shore to Jamaica. I was for going immediately to see this old master and friend, but the captain would not suffer me to leave the vessel. I then informed the Doctor, by letter, how I was treated, and begged that he would take me out of the sloop; but he informed me that it was not in his power, as he was a passenger himself; but he sent me some rum and sugar for my own use. I now learned that after I had left the estate which I managed for this gentleman on the Mosquito shore, during which the slaves were well fed and comfortable, a white overseer had supplied my place; this man through inhumanity and ill-judged avarice, beat and cut the poor slaves most unmercifully; and the consequence was, that everyone got into a large Puriogua canoe, and endeavored to escape; but not knowing where to go, or how to manage the canoe, they were all drowned; in consequence of which the Doctor's plantation was left uncultivated, and he was now returning to Jamaica to purchase more slaves, and stock it again.

On the 14th of October, the *Indian Queen* arrived at Kingston, in Jamaica. When we were unloaded I demanded my wages, which amounted to eight pounds five shillings sterling; but Captain Baker refused to give me one farthing, although it was the hardest earned money I ever worked for in my life. I found out Doctor Irving upon this, and acquainted him of the captain's knavery. He did all he could to help me to get my money; and we went to every magistrate in Kingston (and there were nine), but they all refused to do anything for me, and said my oath could not be admitted against a white man. Nor was this all; for Baker threatened that he would beat me severely, if he could catch me, for attempting to demand my money; and this he would have done, but that I got, by means of Doctor Irving, under the protection of Capt. Douglas, of the *Squirrel* man-of-war. I thought this exceeding hard usage, though indeed I found it to be too much the practice there, to pay free Negro men for their labor in this manner.

One day I went with a free Negro tailor, named Joe Diamond, to one Mr. Cochran, who was indebted to him some trifling sum; and the man, not being able to get his money, began to murmur. The other immediately took a horse-whip to pay him with it, but, by the help of a good pair of heels, the tailor got off. Such oppressions as these made me seek for a vessel to get off the island as fast as I could; and by the mercy of God, I found a ship in November bound for England, when I embarked with a convoy, after having taken a last farewell of Doctor Irving. When I left Jamaica he was employed in refining sugars; and some months after my arrival in England, I learned, with much sorrow, that this, my amiable friend, was dead, owing to his having eaten some poisoned fish.

We had many very heavy gales of wind in our passage, in the course of which no material incident occurred, except that an American privateer, falling in with the fleet, was captured and set fire to by his Majesty's ship, the *Squirrel*.

On January the seventh, 1777, we arrived at Plymouth. I was happy once more to tread upon English ground; and, after passing some little time at Plymouth and Exeter, among some pious friends whom I was happy to see, I went to London with a heart replete with thanks to God for past mercies.

Chapter 12

Different transactions of the author's life, till the present time—
His application to the late Bishop of London to be appointed a
missionary to Africa—Some account of his share in the conduct
of the late expedition to Sierra Leone—Petition to the Queen—
Conclusion.

SUCH WERE THE VARIOUS SCENES which I was a witness to, and the
fortune I experienced until the year 1777. Since that period, my
life has been more uniform, and the incidents of it fewer, than in
any other equal number of years preceding; I therefore hasten to
the conclusion of a narrative which I fear the reader may think
already sufficiently tedious.

I had suffered so many impositions in my commercial transactions in different parts of the world, that I became heartily disgusted with the sea-faring life, and was determined not to return
to it, at least for some time. I therefore once more engaged in
service shortly after my return, and continued for the most part
in this situation until 1784.

Soon after my arrival in London, I saw a remarkable circumstance relative to African complexion, which I thought so extraordinary that I beg leave just to mention it. A white Negro
woman, that I had formerly seen in London and other parts, had
married a white man, by whom she had three boys, and they
were every one mulattoes, and yet they had fine light hair. In
1779, I served Governor Macnamara, who had been a considerable time on the coast of Africa. In the time of my service, I used
to ask frequently other servants to join me in family prayer; but
this only excited their mockery. However, the Governor, understanding that I was of a religious turn, wished to know what
religion I was of; I told him I was a protestant of the church of
England, agreeable to the thirty-nine articles of that church; and
that whomsoever I found to preach according to that doctrine,
those I would hear. A few days after this, we had some more
discourse on the same subject; when he said he would, if I
chose, as he thought I might be of service in converting my
countrymen to the Gospel faith, get me sent out as missionary to
Africa. I at first refused going, and told him how I had been
served on a like occasion, by some white people, the last voyage

I went to Jamaica, when I attempted (if it were the will of God) to be the means of converting the Indian prince; and said I supposed they would serve me worse than Alexander, the coppersmith, did St. Paul, if I should attempt to go amongst them in Africa. He told me not to fear, for he would apply to the Bishop of London to get me ordained. On these terms I consented to the Governor's proposal, to go to Africa in hope of doing good, if possible, amongst my countrymen; so, in order to have me sent out properly, we immediately wrote the following letters to the late Bishop of London:

To the Right Reverend Father in God, ROBERT, *Lord Bishop of London:*

THE MEMORIAL OF GUSTAVUS VASSA

SHEWETH,

That your memorialist is a native of Africa, and has a knowledge of the manners and customs of the inhabitants of that country.

That your memorialist has resided in different parts of Europe for twenty-two years last past, and embraced the Christian faith in the year 1759.

That your memorialist is desirous of returning to Africa as a missionary, if encouraged by your Lordship, in hopes of being able to prevail upon his countrymen to become Christians; and your memorialist is the more induced to undertake the same, from the success that has attended the like undertakings when encouraged by the Portuguese through their different settlements on the Coast of Africa, and also by the Dutch; both governments encouraging the blacks, who, by their education are qualified to undertake the same, and are found more proper than European clergymen, unacquainted with the language and customs of the country.

Your memorialist's only motive for soliciting the office of a missionary is that he may be a means, under God, of reforming his countrymen and persuading them to embrace the Christian religion. Therefore your memorialist humbly prays your Lordship's encouragement and support in the undertaking.

GUSTAVUS VASSA

AT MR. GUTHRIE'S TAYLOR,
NO. 17, HEDGE LANE.

MY LORD,

I have resided near seven years on the coast of Africa, for most part of the time as commanding officer. From the knowledge I have of the country and its inhabitants, I am inclined to think that the within plan will be attended with great success, if countenanced by your Lordship. I beg leave further to represent to your Lordship, that the like attempts, when encouraged by other governments, have met with uncommon success; and at this very time I know a very respectable character, a black priest, at Cape Coast Castle. I know the within named Gustavus Vassa, and believe him a moral good man.

I have the honor to be, my Lord,
Your Lordship's
Humble and obedient servant,
MATT. MACNAMARA

GROVE, 11TH MARCH, 1779.

This letter was also accompanied by the following from Doctor Wallace, who had resided in Africa for many years, and whose sentiments on the subject of an African mission were the same with Governor Macnamara's.

MARCH 13, 1779.

MY LORD,

I have resided near five years on Senegambia, on the coast of Africa, and have had the honor of filling very considerable employments in that province. I do approve of the within plan, and think the undertaking very laudable and proper, and that it deserves your Lordship's protection and encouragement, in which case it must be attended with the intended success.

I am, my Lord, your Lordship's
Humble and obedient servant,
THOMAS WALLACE

With these letters, I waited on the Bishop by the Governor's desire, and presented them to his Lordship. He received me with much condescension and politeness; but from some certain scruples of delicacy, and saying the Bishops were not of opinion of sending a new missionary to Africa, he declined to ordain me.

My sole motive for thus dwelling on this transaction, or inserting these papers, is the opinion which gentlemen of sense and education, who are acquainted with Africa, entertain of the probability of converting the inhabitants of it to the faith of Jesus Christ, if the attempt were countenanced by the Legislature.

Shortly after this I left the Governor, and served a nobleman in the Dorsetshire militia, with whom I was encamped at Coxheath for some time; but the operations there were too minute and uninteresting to make a detail of.

In the year 1783, I visited eight counties in Wales, from motives of curiosity. While I was in that part of the country, I was led to go down into a coal-pit in Shropshire, but my curiosity nearly cost me my life; for while I was in the pit the coals fell in, and buried one poor man, who was not far from me: upon this, I got out as fast as I could, thinking the surface of the earth the safest part of it.

In the spring of 1784, I thought of visiting old ocean again. In consequence of this I embarked as steward on board a fine new ship called the *London,* commanded by Martin Hopkin, and sailed for New York. I admired this city very much; it is large and well built, and abounds with provisions of all kinds. While we lay here a circumstance happened which I thought extremely singular. One day a malefactor was to be executed on a gallows; but with a condition that if any woman, having nothing on but her shift, married the man under the gallows, his life was to be saved. This extraordinary privilege was claimed; a woman presented herself, and the marriage ceremony was performed.

Our ship having got laden, we returned to London in January 1785. When she was ready again for another voyage, the captain being an agreeable man, I sailed with him from hence in the spring, March 1785, for Philadelphia. On the 5th of April, we took our departure from the lands-end, with a pleasant gale; and about nine o'clock that night the moon shone bright, and the sea was smooth, while our ship was going free by the wind, at the rate of about four or five miles an hour. At this time another ship was going nearly as fast as we on the opposite point, meeting us right in the teeth; yet none on board observed either ship until we struck each other forcibly head and head, to the astonishment and consternation of both crews. She did us much damage, but I believe we did her more; for when we passed by each other, which we did very quickly, they called to us to bring to, and hoist out our boat, but we had enough to do to mind ourselves; and in about eight minutes we saw no more of her. We refitted as well as we could the next day, and proceeded on our voyage, and in May arrived at Philadelphia.

I was very glad to see this favorite old town once more; and my pleasure was much increased in seeing the worthy Quakers freeing and easing the burdens of many of my oppressed African brethren. It rejoiced my heart when one of these friendly people took me to see a free school they had erected for every denomination of black people, whose minds are cultivated here, and forwarded to virtue; and thus they are made useful members of the community. Does not the success of this practice say loudly to the planters, in the language of scripture—"Go ye and do likewise"?

In October 1785, I was accompanied by some of the Africans, and presented this address of thanks to the gentlemen called Friends or Quakers, in Grace Church Court, Lombard street:

GENTLEMEN,

By reading your book, entitled a Caution to Great Britain and her Colonies, concerning the calamitous state of the enslaved Negroes: We, part of the poor, oppressed, needy, and much degraded Negroes, desire to approach you with this address of thanks, with our inmost love and warmest acknowledgment; and with the deepest sense of your benevolence, unwearied labor, and kind interposition, towards breaking the yoke of slavery, and to administer a little comfort and ease to thousands and tens of thousands of very grievously afflicted, and too heavy burthened Negroes.

Gentlemen, could you, by perseverance, at last be enabled under God, to lighten in any degree the heavy burthen of the afflicted, no doubt it would in some measure, be the possible means, under God, of saving the souls of many of the oppressors; and if so, sure we are that the God, whose eyes are ever upon all his creatures, and always rewards every true act of virtue, and regards the prayers of the oppressed, will give to you and yours those blessings which it is not in our power to express or conceive, but which we, as a part of those captivated, oppressed, and afflicted people, most earnestly wish and pray for.

These gentlemen received us very kindly, with a promise to exert themselves on behalf of the oppressed Africans, and we parted.

While in town, I chanced once to be invited to a Quaker's wedding. The simple and yet expressive mode used at their solemnizations is worthy of note. The following is the true form of it:

After the company have met they have seasonable exhortations by several of the members; the bride and bridegroom stand up, and, taking each other by the hand in a solemn manner, the man audibly declares to this purpose: "Friends, in the fear of the Lord, and in the presence of this assembly, whom I desire to be my witnesses, I take this my friend, M—— N——, to be my wife; promising, through divine assistance, to be unto her a loving and faithful husband till death separate us," and the woman makes the like declaration. Then the two first sign their names to the record, and as many more witnesses as have a mind. I had the honor to subscribe mine to a register in Grace Church Court, Lombard street. My hand is ever free—if any female Debonair wishes to obtain it, this mode I recommend.

We returned to London in August; and our ship not going immediately to sea, I shipped as a steward in an American ship, called the *Harmony,* Captain John Willet, and left London in March 1786, bound to Philadelphia. Eleven days after sailing, we carried our foremast away. We had a nine weeks' passage, which caused our trip not to succeed well, the market for our goods proving bad; and to make it worse, my commander began to play me the like tricks as others too often practise on free Negroes in the West Indies. But, I thank God, I found many friends here, who in some measure prevented him.

On my return to London in August, I was very agreeably surprised to find that the benevolence of government had adopted the plan of some philanthropic individuals, to send the Africans from hence to their native quarter; and that some vessels were then engaged to carry them to Sierra Leone, an act which redounded to the honor of all concerned in its promotion, and filled me with prayers and much rejoicing. There was then in the city a select committee of gentlemen for the black poor, to some of whom I had the honor of being known; and as soon as they heard of my arrival, they sent for me to the committee. When I came there, they informed me of the intention of government; and as they seemed to think me qualified to superintend part of the undertaking, they asked me to go with the black poor to Africa. I pointed out to them many objections to my going; and particularly I expressed some difficulties on the account of the slave dealers, as I would certainly oppose their traffic in human species, by every means in my power. However, these objections were over-ruled by the gentlemen of the committee, who prevailed on me to consent to go; and recommended me to the honorable commissioners of his Majesty's Navy, as a proper person to act as commissary for government in the intended expedition; and they accordingly appointed me, in November 1786, to that office, and gave me sufficient power to act for the government, in the capacity of commissary, having received my warrant and the following order:

BY THE PRINCIPAL OFFICERS AND COMMISSIONERS OF HIS
MAJESTY'S NAVY

Whereas you were directed, by our warrant, of the 4th of last month, to receive into your charge from Mr. Joseph Irwin, the surplus provisions remaining of what was provided for the voyage, as well as the provisions for the support of the black poor, after the landing at Sierra Leone, with the clothing, tools, and all other articles provided at government's expense; and as the provisions were laid in at the rate of two months for the voyage, and for four months after the landing, but the number embarked being so much less than we expected, whereby there may be a considerable surplus of provisions, clothing, &c. These are in addition to former orders, to direct and require you to appropriate or dispose of such surplus to the best advantage you can for the benefit of government, keeping and rendering to us a faithful account of what you do herein. And for your guidance in preventing any white persons going, who are not intended to have the indulgence of being carried thither, we send you herewith a list of those recommended by the Committee for the black poor, as proper persons to be permitted to embark, and acquaint you that you are not to suffer any others to go who do not produce a

certificate from the Committee for the black poor, of their having
their permission for it. For which this shall be your warrant.
Dated at the Navy Office, Jan. 16, 1787.

J. HINSLOW
GEO. MARSH
W. PALMER

TO MR. GUSTAVUS VASSA, COMMISSARY
OF PROVISIONS AND STORES FOR THE
BLACK POOR GOING TO SIERRA LEONE.

I proceeded immediately to the executing of my duty on
board the vessels destined for the voyage, where I continued till
the March following.

During my continuance in the employment of government, I
was struck with the flagrant abuses committed by the agent, and
endeavored to remedy them, but without effect. One instance,
among many which I could produce, may serve as a specimen.
Government had ordered to be provided all necessaries (slops, as
they are called, included) for 750 persons; however, not being
able to muster more than 426, I was ordered to send the super-
fluous slops, &c., to the king's stores at Portsmouth; but, when I
demanded them for that purpose from the agent, it appeared
they had never been bought, though paid for by government.
But that was not all; government were not the only objects of
peculation; these poor people suffered infinitely more; their
accommodations were most wretched, many of them wanted
beds, and many more clothing and other necessaries. For the
truth of this, and much more, I do not seek credit from my own
assertion. I appeal to the testimony of Captain Thompson, of the
Nautilus, who conveyed us, to whom I applied in February 1787,
for a remedy, when I had remonstrated to the agent in vain, and
even brought him to be a witness of the injustice and oppression
I complained of. I appeal also to a letter written by these
wretched people, so early as the beginning of the preceding
January, and published in the *Morning Herald,* on the 4th of that
month, signed by twenty of their chiefs.

I could not silently suffer government to be thus cheated and
my countrymen plundered and oppressed, and even left destitute of the necessaries for almost their existence. I therefore informed the Commissioners of the Navy, of the agent's proceeding,

but my dismission was soon after procured, by means of a gentleman in the city, whom the agent, conscious of his peculation, had deceived by letter, and who, moreover, empowered the same agent to receive on board, at the government expense, a number of persons as passengers, contrary to the orders I received. By this I suffered a considerable loss in my property; however, the commissioners were satisfied with my conduct, and wrote to Captain Thompson, expressing their approbation of it.

Thus provided, they proceeded on their voyage; and at last, worn out by treatment, perhaps not the most mild, and wasted by sickness, brought on by want of medicine, clothes, bedding, &c., they reached Sierra Leone, just at the commencement of the rains. At that season of the year, it is impossible to cultivate the lands; their provisions therefore were exhausted before they could derive any benefit from agriculture; and it is not surprising that many, especially the Lascars, whose constitutions are very tender, and who had been cooped up in ships from October to June, and accommodated in the manner I have mentioned, should be so wasted by their confinement as not to survive it.

Thus ended my part of the long talked of expedition to Sierra Leone; an expedition which, however unfortunate in the event, was humane and politic in its design, nor was its failure owing to government; everything was done on their part; but there was evidently sufficient mismanagement attending the conduct and execution of it to defeat its success.

I should not have been so ample in my account of this transaction, had not the share I bore in it been made the subject of partial animadversion, and even my dismission from my employment thought worthy of being made by some a matter of public triumph.* The motives which might influence any person to descend to a petty contest with an obscure African, and to seek gratification by his depression, perhaps it is not proper here to inquire into or relate, even if its detection were necessary to my vindication, but I thank Heaven it is not. I wish to stand by my own integrity, and not to shelter myself under the impropriety of another; and I trust the behavior of the Commissioners of the Navy to me entitle me to make this assertion; for after I had been dismissed, March 24, I drew up a memorial thus:

* See the *Public Advertiser*, July 14, 1787.

To the Right Honorable the Lord's Commissioners of his Majesty's Treasury.

The Memorial and Petition of GUSTAVUS VASSA, a black man, late Commissary to the black poor going to Africa.

HUMBLY SHEWETH,

That your Lordship's memorialist was, by the Honorable the Commissioners of his Majesty's Navy, on the 4th of December last, appointed to the above employment by warrant from that board;

That he accordingly proceeded to the execution of his duty on board of the *Vernon,* being one of the ships appointed to proceed to Africa with the above poor;

That your memorialist, to his great grief and astonishment, received a letter of dismission from the Honorable Commissioners of the Navy, by your Lordships orders:

That, conscious of having acted with the most perfect fidelity and the greatest assiduity in discharging the trust reposed in him, he is altogether at a loss to conceive the reasons of your Lordships having altered the favorable opinion you were pleased to conceive of him, sensible that your Lordships would not proceed to so severe a measure without some apparent good cause; he therefore has every reason to believe that his conduct has been grossly misrepresented to your Lordships, and he is the more confirmed in his opinion, because, by opposing measures of others concerned in the same expedition, which tended to defeat your Lordship's humane intentions, and to put the government to a very considerable additional expense, he created a number of enemies, whose misrepresentations, he has too much reason to believe, laid the foundation of his dismission. Unsupported by friends, and unaided by the advantages of a liberal education, he can only hope for redress from the justice of his cause, in addition to the mortification of having been removed from his employment, and the advantage which he reasonably might have expected to have derived therefrom. He has had the misfortune to have sunk a considerable part of his little property in fitting himself out, and in other expenses arising out of his situation, an account of which he here annexes. Your memorialist will not trouble your Lordships with a vindication of any part of his conduct, because he knows not of what crimes he is accused; he, however, earnestly entreats that you will be pleased to direct an enquiry into his behavior during the time he acted in the public service; and, if it be found that his dismission arose from false representations, he is confident that in your Lord-ship's justice he shall find redress.

Your petitioner therefore humbly prays that your Lordships will take his case into consideration; and that you will be pleased to order payment of the above referred to account, amounting to 321.4s. and also the wages intended which is most humbly submitted.

LONDON, MAY 12, 1787.

The above petition was delivered into the hands of their Lord-ships, who were kind enough, in the space of some few months afterwards, without hearing, to order me 50l. sterling—that is, 18l. wages for the time (upwards of four months) I acted a faithful part in their service. Certainly the sum is more than a free Ne-gro would have had in the western colonies!!!

From that period, to the present time, my life has passed in an even tenor, and a great part of my study and attention has been to assist in the cause of my much injured countrymen.

March the 21st, 1788, I had the honor of presenting the Queen with a petition in behalf of my African brethren, which was re-ceived most graciously by Her Majesty.*

To the Queen's most Excellent Majesty:

MADAM,

Your Majesty's well known benevolence and humanity em-boldens me to approach your royal presence, trusting that the obscurity of my situation will not prevent your Majesty from attending to the sufferings for which I plead.

Yet I do not solicit your royal pity for my own distress; my sufferings, although numerous, are in a measure forgotten. I supplicate your Majesty's compassion for millions of my African countrymen, who groan under the lash of tyranny in the West Indies.

The oppression and cruelty exercised to the unhappy Negroes there, have at length reached the British Legislature, and they are now deliberating on its redress; even several persons of property in slaves in the West Indies, have petitioned Parliament against its continuance, sensible that it is as impolitic as it is unjust—and what is inhuman must ever be unwise.

Your Majesty's reign has been hitherto distinguished by pri-

* At the request of some of my most particular friends, I take the liberty of inserting it here.

vate acts of benevolence and bounty; surely the more extended
the misery is, the greater claim it has to your Majesty's compassion, and the greater must be your Majesty's pleasure in administering to its relief.

I presume, therefore, gracious Queen, to implore your interposition with your royal consort, in favor of the wretched Africans; that, by your Majesty's benevolent influence, a period may
now be put to their misery—and that they may be raised from
the condition of brutes, to which they are at present degraded,
to the rights and situation of freemen, and admitted to partake
of the blessings of your Majesty's happy government; so shall
your Majesty enjoy the heart-felt pleasure of procuring happiness to millions, and be rewarded in the grateful prayers of
themselves, and of their posterity.

And may the all-bountiful Creator shower on your Majesty,
and the Royal Family, every blessing that this world can afford,
and every fulness of joy which divine revelation has promised
us in the next.

I am your Majesty's
Most dutiful and devoted servant to command,

GUSTAVUS VASSA
The Oppressed Ethiopian

NO. 53, BALDWIN'S GARDENS

The Negro consolidated act, made by the assembly of Jamaica
last year, and the new act of amendment now in agitation there,
contain a proof of the existence of those charges that have been
made against the planters relative to the treatment of their slaves.

I hope to have the satisfaction of seeing the renovation of
liberty and justice, resting on the British government, to vindi-
cate the honor of our common nature. These are concerns which
do not perhaps belong to any particular office; but, to speak more
seriously, to every man of sentiment, actions like these are the
just and sure foundation of future fame; a reversion, though
remote, is coveted by some noble minds as a substantial good. It
is upon these grounds that I hope and expect the attention of
gentlemen in power. These are designs consonant to the elevation of their rank and the dignity of their stations; they are ends
suitable to the nature of a free and generous government, and,
connected with views of empire and dominion, suited to the
benevolence and solid merit of the legislature. It is a pursuit of

substantial greatness. May the time come—at least the specula-
tion to me is pleasing—when the sable people shall gratefully
commemorate the auspicious era of extensive freedom: then
shall those persons* particularly be named with praise and
honor who generously proposed and stood forth in the cause of
humanity, liberty, and good policy, and brought to the ear of
the legislature designs worthy of royal patronage and adoption.
May Heaven make the British senators the dispersers of light,
liberty, and science, to the uttermost parts of the earth: then
will be glory to God in the highest on earth peace, and good will
to men. Glory, honor, peace, &c. to every soul of man that
worketh good: to the Britons first (because to them the gospel
is preached), and also to the nations. "Those that honor their
Maker have mercy on the poor." It is "righteousness exalteth a
nation, but sin is a reproach to any people; destruction shall be
to the workers of iniquity, and the wicked shall fall by their
own wickedness." May the blessings of the Lord be upon the
heads of all those who commiserated the cases of the oppressed
Negroes, and the fear of God prolong their days; and may their
expectations be filled with gladness! "The liberal devise liberal
things, and by liberal things shall stand" (Isaiah 32:8). They can
say with pious Job, "Did not I weep for him that was in trouble?
was not my soul grieved for the poor?" (Job 30:25).

As the inhuman traffic of slavery is to be taken into the consideration of the British legislature, I doubt not, if a system of
commerce was established in Africa, the demand for manufactures will most rapidly augment, as the native inhabitants will
sensibly adopt the British fashions, manners, customs, &c. In proportion to the civilization, so will be the consumption of British
manufactures.

The wear and tear of a continent, nearly twice as large as
Europe and rich in vegetable and mineral production, is much
easier conceived than calculated.

A case in point. It cost the Aborigines of Britain little or nothing in clothing, &c. The difference between their forefathers and

---

* Granville Sharp, Esq., the Rev. Thomas Clarkson, the Rev. James
Ramsay, our approved friends, men of virtue, are an honor to their country, ornamental to human nature, happy in themselves, and benefactors to
mankind!

the present generation, in point of consumption, is literally infinite. The supposition is most obvious. It will be equally immense in Africa—The same, viz: civilization, will ever have the same effect.

It is trading upon safe grounds. A commercial intercourse with Africa opens an inexhaustible source of wealth to the manufacturing interest of Great Britain;* and to all which the slave trade is an objection.

If I am not misinformed, the manufacturing interest is equal, if not superior, to the landed interest, as to the value, for reasons which will soon appear. The abolition of slavery, so diabolical, will give a most rapid extension of manufactures, which is totally and diametrically opposite to what some interested people assert.

The manufactures of this country must and will, in the nature and reason of things, have a full and constant employ, by supplying the African markets.

Population, the bowels and surface of Africa, abound in valuable and useful returns; the hidden treasures of centuries will be brought to light and into circulation. Industry, enterprise, and mining will have their full scope, proportionably as they civilize. In a word, it lays open an endless field of commerce to the British manufacturers and merchant adventurer. The manufacturing interest and the general interests are synonymous. The abolition of slavery would be in reality an universal good.

Tortures, murder, and every other imaginable barbarity and iniquity, are practised upon the poor slaves with impunity. I

---

* "In the ship Trusty, lately for the new Settlement of Sierra Leona, in Africa, were 1,300 pair of shoes (an article hitherto scarcely known to be exported to that country) with several others equally new, as articles of export. Thus will it not become the interest, as well as the duty, of every artificer, mechanic, and tradesman, publicly to enter their protest against this traffic of the human species? What a striking—what a beautiful contrast is here presented to view, when compared with the cargo of a slave ship! Every feeling heart indeed sensibly participates of the joy, and with a degree of rapture reads of barrels of *flour* instead of *gunpowder—biscuits and bread* instead of *horse beans—implements of husbandry* instead of *guns* for destruction, rapine, and murder—and various articles of *usefulness* are the pleasing substitutes for the *torturing thumbscrew,* and the *galling chain,* &c."

hope the slave trade will be abolished. I pray it may be an event at hand. The great body of manufacturers, uniting in the cause, will considerably facilitate and expedite it; and has I have already stated, it is most substantially their interest and advantage, and as such the nation's at large (except those persons concerned in the manufacturing neck yokes, collars, chains, handcuffs, leg bolts, drags, thumb screws, iron muzzles, and coffins; cats, scourges, and other instruments of torture used in the slave trade). In a short time one sentiment will alone prevail, from motives of interest as well as justice and humanity. Europe contains one hundred and twenty millions of inhabitants. Query: How many millions doth Africa contain? Supposing the Africans, collectively and individually, to expend £5 a head in raiment and furniture yearly when civilized, &c., an immensity beyond the reach of imagination!

This I conceive to be a theory founded upon facts, and therefore an infallible one. If the blacks were permitted to remain in their own country, they would double themselves every fifteen years. In proportion to such increase will be the demand for manufactures. Cotton and indigo grow spontaneously in most parts of Africa; a consideration this of no small consequence to the manufacturing towns of Great Britain. It opens a most immense, glorious, and happy prospect—the clothing, &c., of a continent ten thousand miles in circumference, and immensely rich in productions of every denomination in return for manufactures.

Since the first publication of my Narrative, I have been in a great variety of scenes in many parts of Great Britain, Ireland, and Scotland, an account of which might not improperly be added here;* but this would swell the volume too much, I shall only observe in general, that in May 1791, I sailed from Liverpool to Dublin, where I was very kindly received, and from thence to Cork, and then travelled over many counties in Ireland. I was everywhere exceedingly well treated, by persons of all ranks. I found the people extremely hospitable, particularly in Belfast, where I took my passage on board of a vessel for Clyde,

---

* Viz. Some curious adventures beneath the earth, in a river in Manchester, and a most astonishing one under the Peak of Derbyshire—and in September 1792, I went 90 fathoms down St. Anthony's Colliery, at Newcastle, under the river Tyne, some hundreds of yards on Durham side.

on the 29th of January, and arrived at Greenock on the 30th. Soon after I returned to London, where I found persons of note from Holland and Germany, who requested me to go there; and I was glad to hear that an edition of my Narrative had been printed in both places, also in New York. I remained in London till I heard the debate in the House of Commons on the slave trade, April the 2d and 3d. I then went to Soham in Cambridge-shire, and was married on the 7th of April to Miss Cullen, daughter of James and Ann Cullen, late of Ely.*

I have only therefore to request the reader's indulgence, and conclude. I am far from the vanity of thinking there is any merit in this narrative: I hope censure will be suspended, when it is considered that it was written by one who was as unwilling as unable to adorn the plainness of truth by the coloring of imagi-nation. My life and fortune have been extremely checkered, and my adventures various. Nay even those I have related are con-siderably abridged. If any incident in this little work should ap-pear uninteresting and trifling to most readers, I can only say, as my excuse for mentioning it, that almost every event of my life made an impression on my mind, and influenced my conduct. I early accustomed myself to look at the hand of God in the minutest occurrence, and to learn from it a lesson of morality and religion; and in this light every circumstance I have related was to me of importance. After all, what makes any event im-portant, unless by its observation we become better and wiser, and learn "to do justly, to love mercy, and to walk humbly before God"? To those who are possessed of this spirit, there is scarcely any book or incident so trifling that does not afford some profit, while to others the experience of ages seems of no use; and even to pour out to them the treasures of wisdom is throwing the jewels of instruction away.

* See *Gentleman's Magazine* for April 1792, *Literary and Biographical Magazine,* and *British Review* for May 1792, and the *Edinburgh Historical Register* or *Monthly Intelligencer* for April 1792.

THE FUGITIVE BLACKSMITH

OR

EVENTS IN THE HISTORY OF

JAMES W. C. PENNINGTON

PASTOR OF A PRESBYTERIAN CHURCH

NEW YORK, FORMERLY A SLAVE IN THE

STATE OF MARYLAND

❉   ❉   ❉   ❉   ❉   ❉   ❉   ❉   ❉

While still legally a slave, James W. C. Pennington was honored
with the degree of Doctor of Divinity by the University of Heidelberg, one of the oldest and strongest of German universities.
Yale denied him admission as a regular student but did not interfere when he stood outside the doors of classrooms in order
to hear professors lecture. New York City had been even less
hospitable. At least two publications of the Abolitionist press
(*African Repository,* XXIX, March 1852, and the *National Anti-
Slavery Standard,* July 1, 1847) tell how Pennington was forced
to discharge his pastoral duties by walking over the great distances of New York City because colored people were not allowed to ride in public conveyances in those days. So he had
poignant experiences in the North as well as in the South to
look back on when he published his narrative in 1849. Pennington is remembered for other reasons as well as his narrative,
however.

One distinction that increases with time is his authorship of
the first history of the Negro by a black man in the New World,
A Text Book of the Origin and History of the Colored People
(1841). It was primarily intended for schoolchildren. Pennington
is credited with publication of an "Address on West Indian
Emancipation" that same year and later a sermon delivered in
the Fifth Congregational Church, Hartford, Thanksgiving Day,
November 17, 1842, on the subject, "Covenants Involving Moral
Wrong Are Not Obligatory upon Man." Three years later he

preached in the same church and published as a tract "A Two Years' Absence; or, A Farewell Sermon."

It apparently seemed worth mentioning during his career as minister and teacher in the middle of the nineteenth century, as it probably would not seem today, that he was of "unadulterated African blood." One gathers that apologists for slavery needed to be introduced to some black Abolitionists as well as to mulattos such as Frederick Douglass, William Wells Brown, and Ellen Craft. The United States Census marked the distinction, when Negroes were counted, and the unsophisticated public was often prompt to assume that talented Negroes owed their capacities to their white bloodlines. Pennington along with Henry Highland Garnet were cited as examples discrediting the assumption.

Ten years after publication of *The Fugitive Blacksmith*, Pennington was still writing and publishing. Essays and book reviews by him appeared in several issues of the *Anglo-African* magazine in 1859. Meanwhile he served five elected terms as a member of what was called the "General Convention for the Improvement of the Free Colored People," in which capacity he won warm approval from contemporary blacks.

Another aspect of his active life, not touched on in his narrative, is brought to light, however excusably, in the following paragraph which appeared in the church publication *The Rising Sun:*

In stature he was of the common size, slightly inclined to corpulency, with an athletic frame and a good constitution. The fact that Dr. Pennington was considered a good Greek, Latin, and German scholar, although his life was spent in slavery, is not more strange than that Henry Diaz, the black commander in Brazil, is extolled in all the histories of that country as one of the most sagacious and talented men and experienced officers of whom they can boast. Dr. Pennington died in 1871, his death being hastened by the excessive use of intoxicating liquors, which had impaired his usefullness in his latter days.

The *Liberator*, meanwhile, had reported much earlier another statement which may have contributed to the quandary in which this slave, scholar, teacher, preacher had lived and worked before succumbing. It is said to have been made by the conferring university at the time of granting his honorary doctorate:

You are the first African who has received this dignity from an European University, and it is the University of Heidelberg that thus pronounces the universal brotherhood of humanity.

—ARNA BONTEMPS

❊   ❊   ❊   ❊   ❊   ❊   ❊   ❊   ❊

MR. CHARLES GILPIN,

My Dear Sir,

The information just communicated to me by you, that another edition of my little book, *The Fugitive Blacksmith*, is called for, has agreeably surprised me. The British public has laid me under renewed obligations by this mark of liberality, which I hasten to acknowledge. I would avail myself of this moment also, to acknowledge the kindness of the gentlemen of the newspaper press for the many favorable reviews which my little book has received. It is to them I am indebted, in no small degree, for the success with which I have been favored in getting the book before the notice of the public.

Yours truly,

J. W. C. PENNINGTON

HOXTON, OCT. 15TH, 1849.

Preface

THE BRIEF NARRATIVE I here introduce to the public consists of outline notes originally thrown together to guide my memory when lecturing on this part of the subject of slavery. This will account for its style, and will also show that the work is not full.

The question may be asked, Why I have published anything so long after my escape from slavery? I answer I have been induced to do so on account of the increasing disposition to overlook the fact, that THE SIN of slavery lies in the chattel principle, or relation. Especially have I felt anxious to save professing Christians, and my brethren in the ministry, from falling into a great mistake. My feelings are always outraged when I hear them speak of "kind masters," "Christian masters," "the mildest form of slavery," "well fed and clothed slaves," as extenuations of slavery; I am satisfied they either mean to pervert the truth, or they do not know what they say. The being of slavery, its soul and body, lives and moves in the chattel principle, the property principle, the bill of sale principle; the cart-whip, starvation, and nakedness, are its inevitable consequences to a greater or less extent, warring with the dispositions of men.

There lies a skein of silk upon a lady's work-table. How smooth and handsome are the threads. But while that lady goes out to make a call, a party of children enter the apartment, and in amusing themselves, tangle the skein of silk, and now who can untangle it? The relation between master and slave is even as delicate as a skein of silk: it is liable to be entangled at any moment.

The mildest form of slavery, if there be such a form, looking at the chattel principle as the definition of slavery, is comparatively the worst form; for it not only keeps the slave in the most unpleasant apprehension, like a prisoner in chains awaiting his trial; but it actually, in a great majority of cases, where kind masters do exist, trains him under the most favorable circumstances the system admits of, and then plunges him into the worst of which it is capable.

It is under the mildest form of slavery, as it exists in Maryland, Virginia, and Kentucky, that the finest specimens of colored females are reared. There are no mothers who rear, and educate in the natural graces, finer daughters than the Ethiopian women, who have the least chance to give scope to their maternal affections. But what is generally the fate of such female slaves? When they are not raised for the express purpose of supplying the market of a class of economical Louisianan and Mississippi gentlemen, who do not wish to incur the expense of rearing legitimate families, they are, nevertheless, on account of their attractions, exposed to the most shameful degradation by the young masters in the families where it is claimed they are so well off. My master once owned a beautiful girl about twenty-four. She had been raised in a family where her mother was a great favorite. She was her mother's darling child. Her master was a lawyer of eminent abilities and great fame, but owing to habits of intemperance, he failed in business, and my master purchased this girl for a nurse. After he had owned her about a year, one of his sons became attached to her, for no honorable purposes; a fact which was not only well-known among all the slaves, but which became a source of unhappiness to his mother and sisters.

The result was, that poor Rachel had to be sold to Georgia. Never shall I forget the heart-rending scene, when one day one of the men was ordered to get "the one-horse cart ready to go into town"; Rachel, with her few articles of clothing, was placed in it, and taken into the very town where her parents lived, and there sold to the traders before their weeping eyes. That same son who had degraded her, and who was the cause of her being sold, acted as salesman, and bill-of-saleman. While this cruel business was being transacted, my master stood aside, and the girl's father, a pious member and exhorter in the Methodist Church, a venerable grey-headed man, with his hat off, besought that he might be allowed to get someone in the place to purchase his child. But no: my master was invincible. His reply was, "She has offended in my family, and I can only restore confidence by sending her out of hearing." After lying in prison a short time, her new owner took her with others to the far South, where her parents heard no more of her.

Here was a girl born and reared under the mildest form of slavery. Her original master was reputed to be even indulgent. He lived in a town, and was a high-bred gentleman, and a lawyer. He had but a few slaves, and had no occasion for an overseer, those Negro leeches, to watch and drive them; but when he became embarrassed by his own folly, the chattel principle doomed this girl to be sold at the same sale with his books, house, and horses. With my master she found herself under far more stringent discipline than she had been accustomed to, and finally degraded, and sold where her condition could not be worse, and where she had not the least hope of ever bettering it.

This case presents the legitimate working of the great chattel principle. It is no accidental result—it is the fruit of the tree. You cannot constitute slavery without the chattel principle—and with the chattel principle you cannot save it from these results. Talk not then about kind and Christian masters. They are not masters of the system. The system is master of them; and the slaves are their vassals.

These storms rise on the bosom of the calmed waters of the system. You are a slave, a being in whom another owns property. Then you may rise with his pride, but remember the day is at hand when you must also fall with his folly. Today you may be pampered by his meekness; but tomorrow you will suffer in the storm of his passions.

In the month of September 1848, there appeared in my study, one morning, in New York City, an aged colored man of tall and

slender form. I saw depicted on his countenance anxiety border-
ing on despair; still I was confident that he was a man whose
mind was accustomed to faith. When I learned that he was a
native of my own state, Maryland, having been born in the
county of Montgomery, I at once became much interested in
him. He had been sent to me by my friend, William Harned,
Esq., of the Anti-Slavery Office, 61 John Street. He put into my
hand the following bill of distress:

ALEXANDER, VIRGINIA, SEPTEMBER 5TH, 1848.

The bearer, Paul Edmondson, is the father of two girls, Mary
Jane and Emily Catherine Edmondson. These girls have been
purchased by us, and once sent to the South; and upon the positive assurance that the money for them would be raised if they
were brought back, they were returned. Nothing, it appears, has
as yet been done in this respect by those who promised, and we
are on the very eve of sending them south a second time; and
we are candid in saying, that if they go again, we will not regard any promises made in relation to them.

The father wishes to raise money to pay for them, and intends
to appeal to the liberality of the humane and the good to aid
him, and has requested us to state in writing *the condition upon
which we will sell his daughters.*

We expect to start our servants to the South in a few days;
if the sum of twelve hundred dollars be raised and paid us in
fifteen days, or we be assured of that sum, then we will retain
them for twenty-five days more, to give an opportunity for raising the other thousand and fifty dollars, otherwise we shall be
compelled to send them along with our other servants.

(Signed)

BRUIN AND *HILL*

The old man also showed me letters from other individuals,
and one from the Rev. Matthew A. Turner, pastor of Asbury
Chapel, where himself and his daughters were members. He was
himself free, but his wife was a slave. Those two daughters were
two out of fifteen children he had raised for the owner of his
wife. These two girls had been sold, along with four brothers, to
the traders, for an attempt to escape to the North, and gain their
freedom.

On the next Sabbath evening, I threw the case before my people, and the first fifty dollars of the sum was raised to restore the old man his daughters. Subsequently the case was taken up under the management of a committee of ministers of the Methodist Episcopal Church, consisting of the Rev. G. Peck, D.D., Rev. E. E. Griswold, and Rev. D. Curry, and the entire sum of $2,250 (£450) was raised for two girls, fourteen and sixteen years of age!

But why this enormous sum for two mere children? Ah, reader, they were reared under the mildest form of slavery known to the laws of Maryland! The mother is an invalid, and allowed to live with her free husband; but she is a woman of excellent mind, and has bestowed great pains upon her daughters. If you would know, then, why these girls were held at such a price, even to their own father, read the following extract of a letter from one who was actively engaged in behalf of them, and who had several interviews with the traders to induce them to reduce the price, but without success. Writing from Washington, D.C., September 12th, 1848, this gentleman says to William Harned, "The truth is, *and is confessed to be, that their destination is prostitution;* of this you would be satisfied on seeing them; they are of elegant form, and fine faces."

And such, dear reader, is the sad fate of hundreds of my young countrywomen, natives of my native state. Such is the fate of many who are not only reared under the mildest form of slavery, but of those who have been made acquainted with the milder system of the Prince of Peace.

When Christians, and Christian ministers, then, talk about the "mildest form of slavery," "Christian masters," &c., I say my feelings are outraged. It is a great mistake to offer these as an extenuation of the system. It is calculated to mislead the public mind. The opinion seems to prevail, that the Negro, after having toiled as a slave for centuries to enrich his white brother, to lay the foundation of his proud institutions, after having been sunk as low as slavery can sink him, needs now only a second-rate civilization, a lower standard of civil and religious privileges than the whites claim for themselves.

During the last year or two we have heard of nothing but revolutions and the enlargements of the eras of freedom, on both sides of the Atlantic. Our white brethren everywhere are reaching out their hands to grasp more freedom. In the place of absolute monarchies they have limited monarchies, and in the place of limited monarchies they have republics: so tenacious are they of their own liberties.

But when we speak of slavery, and complain of the wrong it is doing us, and ask to have the yoke removed, we are told, "O, you must not be impatient, you must not create undue excitement. You are not so badly off, for many of your masters are kind Christian masters." Yes, sirs, many of our masters are professed Christians; and what advantage is that to us? The grey heads of our fathers are brought down in scores to the grave in sorrow, on account of their young and tender sons, who are sold to the far South, where they have to toil without requite to supply the world's market with *cotton, sugar, rice, tobacco, &c.* Our venerable mothers are borne down with poignant grief at the fate of their children. Our sisters, if not by the law, are by common consent made the prey of vile men, who can bid the highest.

In all the bright achievements we have obtained in the great work of emancipation, if we have not settled the fact that the chattel principle is wrong, and cannot be maintained upon Christian ground, then we have wrought and triumphed to little purpose, and we shall have to do our first work over again.

It is this that has done all the mischief connected with slavery; it is this that threatens still further mischief. Whatever may be the ill or favored condition of the slave in the matter of mere personal treatment, it is the chattel relation that robs him of his manhood, and transfers his ownership in himself to another. It is this that transfers the proprietorship of his wife and children to another. It is this that throws his family history into utter confusion, and leaves him without a single record to which he may appeal in vindication of his character, or honor. And has a man no sense of honor because he was born a slave? Has he no need of character?

Suppose insult, reproach, or slander, should render it necessary for him to appeal to the history of his family in vindication of his character, where will he find that history? He goes to his native state, to his native county, to his native town; but nowhere does he find any record of himself *as a man.* On looking at the family record of his old, kind, Christian master, there he finds his name on a catalogue with the horses, cows, hogs, and dogs. However humiliating and degrading it may be to his feelings to find his name written down among the beasts of the field, *that* is just the place, and the *only* place assigned to it by the chattel relation. I beg our Anglo-Saxon brethren to accustom themselves to think that we need something more than mere kindness. We ask for justice, truth, and honor as other men do.

My colored brethren are now widely awake to the degradation which they suffer in having property vested in their persons, and they are also conscious of the deep and corrupting disgrace of having our wives and children owned by other men, men who have shown to the world that their own virtue is not infallible, and who have given us no flattering encouragement to entrust that of our wives and daughters to them.

I have great pleasure in stating that my dear friend W. W., spoken of in this narrative, to whom I am so deeply indebted, is still living. I have been twice to see him within four years, and have regular correspondence with him. In one of the last letters I had from him, he authorizes me to use his name in connection with this narrative in these words, "As for using my name, by reference or otherwise, in thy narrative, it is at thy service. I know thee so well, James, that I am not afraid of thy making a bad use of it, nor am I afraid or ashamed to have it known that I took thee in and gave thee aid, when I found thee travelling alone and in want.—W. W."

On the second page of the same sheet I have a few lines from his excellent lady, in which she says, "James, I hope thee will not attribute my long silence in writing to indifference. No such feeling can ever exist towards thee in our family. Thy name is mentioned almost every day. Each of the children claims the next letter from thee. It will be for thee to decide which shall have it. —P. W."

In a postscript following this, W. W. says again: "Understand me, James, that thee is at full liberty to use my name in any way thee wishes in thy narrative. We have a man here from the eastern shore of thy state. He is trying to learn as fast as thee did when here.—W. W."

I hope the reader will pardon me for introducing these extracts. My only apology is, the high gratification I feel in knowing that this family has not only been greatly prospered in health and happiness, but that I am upon the most intimate and pleasant terms with all its members, and that they all still feel a deep and cordial interest in my welfare.

There is another distinguished individual whose sympathy has proved very gratifying to me in my situation—I mean that true friend of the Negro, *Gerrit Smith, Esq.* I was well acquainted with the family in which Mr. Smith married in Maryland. My attention has been fixed upon him for the last ten years, for I have felt confident that God had set him apart for some great good to the Negro. In a letter dated Peterborough, November 7th, 1848, he says:

J. W. C. PENNINGTON,

Slight as is my *personal* acquaintance with you, I nevertheless am well acquainted with you. I am familiar with many passages in your history—all that part of your history extending from the time when, a sturdy blacksmith, you were running away from Maryland oppression, down to the present, when you are the successor of my lamented friend, Theodore S. Wright. Let me add that my acquaintance with you has inspired me with a high regard for your wisdom and integrity.

Give us a few more such men in America, and slavery will soon be numbered among the things that were. A few men who will not only have the moral courage to aim the severing blow at the chattel relation between master and slave, without parley, palliation, or compromise, but who have also the Christian fidelity to brave public scorn and contumely, to seize a colored man by the hand, and elevate him to the position from whence the avarice and oppression of the whites have degraded him. These men have the right view of the subject. They see that in every case where the relation between master and slave is broken, slavery is weakened, and that every colored man elevated, becomes a step in the ladder upon which his whole people are to ascend. They would not have us accept of some modified form of liberty, while the old mischief-working chattel relation remains unbroken, untouched, and unabrogated.

J. W. C. PENNINGTON

13 PRINCES SQUARE, LONDON

AUGUST 15TH, 1849

Preface to Third Edition

Mr. Charles Gilpin,

The rapid sale of the Sixth Thousand of *The Fugitive Black-smith* calls upon me for another acknowledgment of gratitude to the British public, and to yourself. In addition to favorable notices taken of the book originally by the news-presses, it has been my happiness to hear the most flattering opinions from all classes of readers. My object was to write an unexceptional book of the kind for children in point of matter, and for the masses in point of price. I believe both of these have been gained. I have been gratified also to find that my book has awakened a deep interest in the cause of the *American slave*. Since the second edition was printed, I have been constantly engaged in preaching and lecturing. I have spoken on an average five evenings weekly on slavery, temperance, missions, and Sabbath schools, and preached on an average three times each sabbath. In almost every instance where I have gone into a place, I have found the way prepared by the book. In some cases a single copy had been handed from one to another in the town, and some minister or leading gentleman has been prepared to speak of it at my meeting.

The fugitive slave question has assumed a painful interest in America within a few months. The masters have been for twenty years exerting themselves with increased vigilance to cut off the escape of the fugitives. Failing in this, and finding the stream regularly increasing, they *now* come out with the broad demand*

* In February last, the Honorable Henry Clay, a slaveholder and a senator from Kentucky, a slave-breeding state, offered the following among other resolutions in the Senate of the United States, "7th, Resolved, That more effectual provisions ought to be made by law, according to the requirement of the constitution, for the restitution and delivery of persons bound to service or labour in any state, who may escape into any other state or territory of this Union." And among other things, he said in support of it, "I do not say, sir, that a private individual is obliged to make the tour of his whole state, in order to assist the owner of a slave to recover his property, but I do say, if he is present when the owner of a slave is about to assert his rights and regain possession of his property, that he,

upon the free states to arrest and send back the flying bondman.
The North will hardly degrade herself by acceding to this.
Meanwhile, no power in this world will arrest the exodus of
the slaves from the South. Since the day I came out myself, I
have ever believed—and I believe it now more firmly than ever—
that this is the divinely ordered method for the effectual destruction of American slavery. For this I have been, and shall continue to exert my influence. The masters may legislate, rave like
madmen, pursue with bloodhounds, and offer rewards which
call to their aid the vile and the murderous. But we fear them
not. Things have been shaping for years in favor of a general
movement amongst the slaves. The conduct of the masters, the
state of the world, the providences of God have all tended to
this. We have the right of the question upon Christian principles.
We deny utterly and positively their claim to property in us, and
if as men they are determined to be so heartless, cruel, and
barbarous that we cannot dwell with them in peace—God, the
spirit of peace, the love of order, and the spirit of liberty say to
us, come out from among them.

I send forth the third edition of *The Fugitive Blacksmith* as
an humble harbinger to prepare and keep the way open; that the

---

that is every man present, whether officer or agent of the state or government, or private individual, is bound to assist in the execution of the laws
of their country."

The Honorable John C. Calhoun, also a slaveholder and a senator, from
South Carolina, who has since died, said in a speech on the occasion—"The
North has only to will, to do justice, and perform her duty, in order to
accomplish it; to do justice by conceding to the South an equal right in
the acquired territory; and to do her duty by causing the stipulations relative to the fugitive slave to be faithfully fulfilled; to cease the agitation of
the slave question, and provide for the insertion of a provision in the constitution, by an amendment, which will restore in substance the power she
possessed of protecting herself, before the equilibrium between the sections
destroyed by the action of the government. There will be no difficulty in
devising such a provision—one that will protect the South, and which at
the same time will improve and strengthen the government, instead of im-
pairing or weakening it."

This matter has gone so far that the compromise committee of thirteen,
of which Mr. Clay was chairman, has empowered him to frame a bill
in accordance with the above resolution.

world may be acquainted with the question, and that everyone may be well aware of the unreasonable claims urged by the American planters, and the utter impossibility of their maintaining them.

J. W. C. PENNINGTON

LONDON, JULY 30TH, 1850

Chapter 1. My Birth and Parentage—The Treatment of Slaves Generally in Maryland

I WAS BORN in the state of Maryland, which is one of the smallest and most northern of the slaveholding states; the products of this state are wheat, rye, Indian corn, tobacco, with some hemp, flax, &c. By looking at the map, it will be seen that Maryland, like Virginia her neighbor, is divided by the Chesapeake Bay into eastern and western shores. My birth-place was on the eastern shore, where there are seven or eight small counties; the farms are small, and tobacco is mostly raised.

At an early period in the history of Maryland, her lands began to be exhausted by the bad cultivation peculiar to slave states; and hence she soon commenced the business of breeding slaves for the more southern states. This has given an enormity to slavery, in Maryland, differing from that which attaches to the system in Louisiana, and equalled by none of the kind, except Virginia and Kentucky, and not by either of these in extent.

My parents did not both belong to the same owner: my father belonged to a man named ——; my mother belonged to a man named ——. This not only made me a slave, but made me the slave of him to whom my mother belonged; as the primary law of slavery is, that the child shall follow the condition of the mother.

When I was about four years of age, my mother, an older brother, and myself were given to a son of my master, who had studied for the medical profession, but who had now married wealthy, and was about to settle as a wheat planter in Washington County, on the western shore. This began the first of our family troubles that I knew anything about, as it occasioned a separation between my mother and the only two children she then had, and my father, to a distance of about two hundred miles. But this separation did not continue long; my father being a valuable slave, my master was glad to purchase him.

About this time, I began to feel another evil of slavery—I mean the want of parental care and attention. My parents were not able to give any attention to their children during the day. I often suffered much from *hunger* and other similar causes. To estimate the sad state of a slave child, you must look at it as a helpless human being thrown upon the world without the benefit of its natural guardians. It is thrown into the world without a social circle to flee to for hope, shelter, comfort, or instruction. The social circle, with all its heaven-ordained blessings, is of the utmost importance to the *tender child;* but of this, the slave child, however tender and delicate, is robbed.

There is another source of evil to slave children, which I cannot forbear to mention here, as one which early embittered my life; I mean the tyranny of the master's children. My master had two sons, about the ages and sizes of my older brother and myself. We were not only required to recognize these young sirs as our young masters, but *they* felt themselves to be such; and, in consequence of this feeling, they sought to treat us with the same air of authority that their father did the older slaves.

Another evil of slavery that I felt severely about this time was the tyranny and abuse of the overseers. These men seem to look with an evil eye upon children. I was once visiting a menagerie, and being struck with the fact, that the lion was comparatively indifferent to everyone around his cage, while he eyed with peculiar keenness a little boy I had; the keeper informed me that such was always the case. Such is true of those human beings in the slave states, called overseers. They seem to take pleasure in torturing the children of slaves, long before they are large enough to be put at the hoe, and consequently under the whip.

We had an overseer named Blackstone; he was an extremely cruel man to the working hands. He always carried a long hickory whip—a kind of pole. He kept three or four of these, in order that he might not at any time be without one.

I once found one of these hickories lying in the yard, and supposing that he had thrown it away, I picked it up, and boy-like, was using it for a horse; he came along from the field, and seeing me with it, fell upon me with the one he then had in his hand, and flogged me most cruelly. From that, I lived in constant dread of that man; and he would show how much he delighted in cruelty by chasing me from my play with threats and imprecations. I have lain for hours in a wood, or behind a fence, to hide from his eye.

At this time my days were extremely dreary. When I was nine

years of age, myself and my brother were hired out from home; my brother was placed with a pump-maker, and I was placed with a stonemason. We were both in a town some six miles from home. As the men with whom we lived were not slaveholders, we enjoyed some relief from the peculiar evils of slavery. Each of us lived in a family where there was no other Negro.

The slaveholders in that state often hire the children of their slaves out to non-slaveholders, not only because they save themselves the expense of taking care of them, but in this way they get among their slaves useful trades. They put a bright slave boy with a tradesman, until he gets such a knowledge of the trade as to be able to do his own work, and then he takes him home. I remained with the stonemason until I was eleven years of age; at this time I was taken home. This was another serious period in my childhood; I was separated from my older brother, to whom I was much attached; he continued at his place, and not only learned the trade to great perfection, but finally became the property of the man with whom he lived, so that our separation was permanent, as we never lived nearer, after, than six miles. My master owned an excellent blacksmith, who had obtained his trade in the way I have mentioned above. When I returned home at the age of eleven, I was set about assisting to do the mason work of a new smith's shop. This being done, I was placed at the business, which I soon learned, so as to be called a "first-rate blacksmith." I continued to work at this business for nine years, or until I was twenty-one, with the exception of the last seven months.

In the spring of 1828, my master sold me to a Methodist man, named ——, for the sum of seven hundred dollars. It soon proved that he had not work enough to keep me employed as a smith, and he offered me for sale again. On hearing of this, my old master re-purchased me, and proposed to me to undertake the carpentering business. I had been working at this trade six months with a white workman, who was building a large barn when I left. I will now relate the abuses which occasioned me to fly.

Three or four of our farm hands had their wives and families on other plantations. In such cases, it is the custom in Maryland to allow the men to go on Saturday evening to see their families, stay over the Sabbath, and return on Monday morning, not later than "half-an-hour by sun." To overstay their time is a grave fault, for which, especially at busy seasons, they are punished.

One Monday morning, two of these men had not been so fortunate as to get home at the required time; one of them was an uncle of mine. Besides these, two young men who had no families, and for whom no such provision of time was made, having gone somewhere to spend the Sabbath, were absent. My master was greatly irritated, and had resolved to have, as he said, "a general whipping-match among them."

Preparatory to this, he had a rope in his pocket, and a cowhide in his hand, walking about the premises, and speaking to everyone he met in a very insolent manner, and finding fault with some without just cause. My father, among other numerous and responsible duties, discharged that of shepherd to a large and valuable flock of Merino sheep. This morning he was engaged in the tenderest of a shepherd's duties: a little lamb, not able to go alone, lost its mother; he was feeding it by hand. He had been keeping it in the house for several days. As he stooped over it in the yard, with a vessel of new milk he had obtained, with which to feed it, my master came along, and without the least provocation, began by asking, "Bazil, have you fed the flock?"

"Yes, sir."

"Were you away yesterday?"

"No, sir."

"Do you know why these boys have not got home this morning yet?"

"No, sir, I have not seen any of them since Saturday night."

"By the Eternal, I'll make them know their hour. The fact is, I have too many of you; my people are getting to be the most careless, lazy, and worthless in the country."

"Master," said my father, "I am always at my post; Monday morning never finds me off the plantation."

"Hush Bazil! I shall have to sell some of you; and then the rest will have enough to do; I have not work enough to keep you all tightly employed; I have too many of you."

All this was said in an angry, threatening, and exceedingly insulting tone. My father was a high-spirited man, and feeling deeply the insult, replied to the last expression, "If I am one too many, sir, give me a chance to get a purchaser, and I am willing to be sold when it may suit you."

"Bazil, I told you to hush!" and suiting the action to the word, he drew forth the cowhide from under his arm, fell upon him with most savage cruelty, and inflicted fifteen or twenty severe stripes with all his strength, over his shoulders and the small of his back. As he raised himself upon his toes, and gave the last stripe, he said, "By the * * * I will make you know that I am master of your tongue as well as of your time!"

Being a tradesman, and just at that time getting my breakfast, I was near enough to hear the insolent words that were spoken to my father, and to hear, see, and even count the savage stripes inflicted upon him.

Let me ask any one of Anglo-Saxon blood and spirit, how would you expect a *son* to feel at such a sight?

This act created an open rupture with our family—each member felt the deep insult that had been inflicted upon our head; the spirit of the whole family was roused; we talked of it in our nightly gatherings, and showed it in our daily melancholy aspect. The oppressor saw this, and with the heartlessness that was in perfect keeping with the first insult, commenced a series of tauntings, threatenings, and insinuations, with a view to crush the spirit of the whole family.

Although it was some time after this event before I took the decisive step, yet in my mind and spirit, I never was a *Slave* after it.

Whenever I thought of the great contrast between my father's employment on that memorable Monday morning (feeding the little lamb) and the barbarous conduct of my master, I could not help cordially despising the proud abuser of my sire; and I believe he discovered it, for he seemed to have diligently sought an occasion against me. Many incidents occurred to convince me of this, too tedious to mention; but there is one I will mention, because it will serve to show the state of feeling that existed between us, and how it served to widen the already open breach.

I was one day shoeing a horse in the shop yard. I had been stooping for some time under the weight of the horse, which was large, and was very tired; meanwhile, my master had taken his position on a little hill just in front of me, and stood leaning back on his cane, with his hat drawn over his eyes. I put down the horse's foot, and straightened myself up to rest a moment, and without knowing that he was there, my eye caught his. This threw him into a panic of rage; he would have it that I was watching him. "What are you rolling your white eyes at me for, you lazy rascal?" He came down upon me with his cane, and laid on over my shoulders, arms, and legs, about a dozen severe blows, so that my limbs and flesh were sore for several weeks; and then after several other offensive epithets, left me.

This affair my mother saw from her cottage, which was near; I being one of the oldest sons of my parents, our family was now mortified to the lowest degree. I had always aimed to be trustworthy; and feeling a high degree of mechanical pride, I had aimed to do my work with dispatch and skill; my blacksmith's pride and taste was one thing that had reconciled me so long to remain a slave. I sought to distinguish myself in the finer branches of the business by invention and finish; I frequently tried my hand at making guns and pistols, putting blades in penknives, making fancy hammers, hatchets, swordcanes, &c., &c. Besides I used to assist my father at night in making straw hats and willow baskets, by which means we supplied our family with little articles of food, clothing, and luxury which slaves in the mildest form of the system never get from the master; but after this, I found that my mechanic's pleasure and pride were gone. I thought of nothing but the family disgrace under which we were smarting, and how to get out of it.

Perhaps I may as well extend this note a little. The reader will observe that I have not said much about my master's cruel treatment; I have aimed rather to shew the cruelties incident to the system. I have no disposition to attempt to convict him of having been one of the most cruel masters—that would not be true—his prevailing temper was kind, but he was a perpetualist. He was opposed to emancipation, thought free Negroes a great nuisance, and was, as respects discipline, a thorough slaveholder. He would not tolerate a look or a word from a slave like insubordination. He would suppress it at once, and at any risk. When he thought it necessary to secure unqualified obedience, he would strike a slave with any weapon, flog him on the bare back, and sell. And this was the kind of discipline he also empowered his overseers and sons to use.

I have seen children go from our plantations to join the chained-gang on its way from Washington to Louisiana; and I have seen men and women flogged—I have seen the overseers strike a man with a hayfork—nay, more, men have been maimed by shooting! Some dispute arose one morning between the overseer and one of the farm hands, when the former made at the slave with a hickory club; the slave taking to his heels, started for the woods; as he was crossing the yard, the overseer turned, snatched his gun which was near, and fired at the flying slave, lodging several shots in the calf of one leg. The poor fellow continued his flight, and got into the woods; but he was in so much pain that he was compelled to come out in the evening, and give himself up to his master, thinking he would not allow him to be punished as he had been shot. He was locked up that night; the next morning the overseer was allowed to tie him up and flog him; his master then took his instruments and picked the shot out of his leg, and told him, it served him just right.

My master had a deeply pious and exemplary slave, an elderly man, who one day had a misunderstanding with the overseer, when the latter attempted to flog him. He fled to the woods; it was noon; at evening he came home orderly. The next morning, my master, taking one of his sons with him, a rope and cowhide in his hand, led the poor old man away into the stable, tied him up, and ordered the son to lay on thirty-nine lashes, which he did, making the keen end of the cowhide lap around and strike him in the tenderest part of his side, till the blood sped out, as if a lance had been used.

While my master's son was thus engaged, the sufferer's little daughter, a child six years of age, stood at the door, weeping in agony for the fate of her father. I heard the old man articulating in a low tone of voice; I listened at the intervals between the stripes, and lo! he was praying!

When the last lash was laid on, he was let down; and leaving him to put on his clothes, they passed out of the door, and drove the man's weeping child away! I was mending a hinge to one of the barn doors; I saw and heard what I have stated. Six months after, this same man's eldest daughter, a girl fifteen years old, was sold to slave traders, where he never saw her more.

This poor slave and his wife were both Methodists; so was the wife of the young master who flogged him. My old master was an Episcopalian.

These are only a few of the instances which came under my own notice during my childhood and youth on our plantations; as to those which occurred on other plantations in the neighborhood, I could state any number.

I have stated that my master was watching the movements of our family very closely. Sometime after the difficulties began, we found that he also had a confidential slave assisting him in the business. This wretched fellow, who was nearly white, and of Irish descent, informed our master of the movements of each member of the family by day and by night, and on Sundays. This stirred the spirit of my mother, who spoke to our fellow slave, and told him he ought to be ashamed to be engaged in such low business.

Master hearing of this, called my father, mother, and myself before him, and accused us of an attempt to resist and intimidate his "confidential servant." Finding that only my mother had spoken to him, he swore that if she ever spoke another word to him, he would flog her.

I knew my mother's spirit and my master's temper as well. Our social state was now perfectly intolerable. We were on the eve of a general fracas. This last scene occurred on Tuesday; and on Saturday evening following, without counsel or advice from anyone, I determined to fly.

Chapter 2. The Flight

IT WAS THE SABBATH; the holy day which God in his infinite wisdom gave for the rest of both man and beast. In the state of Maryland, the slaves generally have the Sabbath, except in those districts where the evil weed, tobacco, is cultivated; and then, when it is the season for setting the plant, they are liable to be robbed of this only rest.

It was in the month of November, somewhat past the middle of the month. It was a bright day, and all was quiet. Most of the slaves were resting about their quarters; others had leave to visit their friends on other plantations, and were absent. The evening previous I had arranged my little bundle of clothing, and had secreted it at some distance from the house. I had spent most of the forenoon in my workshop, engaged in deep and solemn thought.

It is impossible for me now to recollect all the perplexing thoughts that passed through my mind during that forenoon; it was a day of heartaching to me. But I distinctly remember the two great difficulties that stood in the way of my flight: I had a father and mother whom I dearly loved, I had also six sisters and four brothers on the plantation. The question was, shall I hide my purpose from them? moreover, how will my flight affect them when I am gone? Will they not be suspected? Will not the whole family be sold off as a disaffected family, as is generally the case when one of its members flies? But a still more trying question was, how can I expect to succeed, I have no knowledge of distance or direction—I know that Pennsylvania is a free state, but I know not where its soil begins, or where that of Maryland ends? Indeed, at this time there was no safety in Pennsylvania, New Jersey, or New York, for a fugitive, except in lurking places, or under the care of judicious friends, who could be entrusted not only with liberty, but also with life itself.

With such difficulties before my mind, the day had rapidly worn away; and it was just past noon. One of my perplexing questions I had settled—I had resolved to let no one into my secret; but the other difficulty was now to be met. It was to be met without the least knowledge of its magnitude, except by imagination. Yet of one thing there could be no mistake, that the consequences of a failure would be most serious. Within my recollection no one had attempted to escape from my master; but I had many cases in my mind's eye, of slaves of other planters who had failed, and who had been made examples of the most cruel treatment, by flogging and selling to the far South, where they were never to see their friends more. I was not without serious apprehension that such would be my fate. The bare possibility was impressively solemn; but the hour was now come, and the man must act and be free, or remain a slave forever. How the impression came to be upon my mind I cannot tell; but there was a strange and horrifying belief that, if I did not meet the crisis that day, I should be self-doomed—that my ear would be nailed to the door post forever. The emotions of that moment I cannot fully depict. Hope, fear, dread, terror, love, sorrow, and deep melancholy were mingled in my mind together; my mental state was one of most painful distraction. When I looked at my numerous family—a beloved father and mother, eleven brothers and sisters, &c.; but when I looked at slavery as such; when I looked at it in its mildest form, with all its annoy- ances; and above all, when I remembered that one of the chief annoyances of slavery, in the most mild form, is the liability of being at any moment sold into the worst form, it seemed that no consideration, not even that of life itself, could tempt me to give up the thought of flight. And then when I considered the diffi- culties of the way—the reward that would be offered—the human bloodhounds that would be set upon my track—the weariness— the hunger—the gloomy thought, of not only losing all one's friends in one day, but of having to seek and to make new friends in a strange world. But, as I have said, the hour was come, and the man must act, or forever be a slave.

It was now two o'clock. I stepped into the quarter; there was a strange and melancholy silence mingled with the destitution that was apparent in every part of the house. The only morsel I could see in the shape of food, was a piece of Indian-flour bread, it might be half a pound in weight. This I placed in my pocket, and giving a last look at the aspect of the house, and at a few small children who were playing at the door, I sallied forth thoughtfully and melancholy, and after crossing the barnyard, a few moments' walk brought me to a small cave, near the mouth of which lay a pile of stones, and into which I had deposited my clothes. From this, my course lay through thick and heavy woods and back lands to ⸻ town, where my brother lived. This town was six miles distance. It was now near three o'clock, but my object was neither to be seen on the road nor to approach the town by daylight, as I was well-known there, and as any intelligence of my having been seen there would at once put the pursuers on my track. This first six miles of my flight, I not only travelled very slowly, therefore, so as to avoid carrying any daylight to this town; but during this walk another very perplexing question was agitating my mind. Shall I call on my brother as I pass through, and shew him what I am about! My brother was older than I, we were much attached; I had been in the habit of looking to him for counsel.

I entered the town about dark, resolved, all things in view, *not* to shew myself to my brother. Having passed through the town without being recognized, I now found myself under cover of night, a solitary wanderer from home and friends; my only guide was the *north star,* by this I knew my general course northward, but at what point I should strike Pennsylvania, or when and where I should find a friend I knew not. Another feeling now occupied my mind; I felt like a mariner who has gotten his ship outside of the harbor and has spread his sails to the breeze. The cargo is on board—the ship is cleared—and the voyage I must make; besides, this being my first night, almost everything will depend upon my clearing the coast before the day dawns. In order to do this my flight must be rapid. I therefore set forth in sorrowful earnest, only now and then I was cheered by the *wild* hope, that I should somewhere and at some time be free.

The night was fine for the season, and passed on with little interruption for want of strength, until, about three o'clock in the morning, I began to feel the chilling effects of the dew.

At this moment, gloom and melancholy again spread through my whole soul. The prospect of utter destitution which threatened me was more than I could bear, and my heart began to melt. What substance is there in a piece of dry Indian-bread? what nourishment is there in it to warm the nerves of one already chilled to the heart? Will this afford a sufficient sustenance after the toil of the night? But while these thoughts were agitating my mind, the day dawned upon me, in the midst of an open extent of country, where the only shelter I could find, without risking my travel by daylight, was a corn shock, but a few hundred yards from the road, and here I must pass my first day out. The day was an unhappy one; my hiding place was extremely precarious. I had to sit in a squatting position the whole day, without the least chance to rest. But, besides this, my scanty pittance did not afford me that nourishment which my hard night's travel needed. Night came again to my relief, and I sallied forth to pursue my journey. By this time, not a crumb of my crust remained, and I was hungry and began to feel the desperation of distress.

As I travelled I felt my strength failing and my spirits wavered; my mind was in a deep and melancholy dream. It was cloudy; I could not see my star, and had serious misgivings about my course.

In this way the night passed away, and just at the dawn of day I found a few sour apples, and took my shelter under the arch of a small bridge that crossed the road. Here I passed the second day in ambush.

This day would have been more pleasant than the previous, but the sour apples, and a draught of cold water, had produced anything but a favorable effect; indeed, I suffered most of the day with severe symptoms of cramp. The day passed away again without any further incident, and as I set out at nightfall I felt quite satisfied that I could not pass another twenty-four hours without nourishment. I made but little progress during the night, and often sat down, and slept frequently fifteen or twenty minutes. At the dawn of the third day I continued my travel. As I had found my way to a public turnpike road during the night, I came very early in the morning to a toll gate, where the only person I saw, was a lad about twelve years of age. I inquired of him where the road led to. He informed me it led to Baltimore. I asked him the distance, he said it was eighteen miles.

This intelligence was perfectly astounding to me. My master lived eighty miles from Baltimore. I was now sixty-two miles from home. That distance in the right direction would have placed me several miles across Mason and Dixon's line, but I was evidently yet in the state of Maryland.

I ventured to ask the lad at the gate another question— Which is the best way to Philadelphia? Said he, you can take a road which turns off about half-a-mile below this, and goes to Getsburgh, or you can go on to Baltimore and take the packet.

I made no reply, but my thought was, that I was as near Baltimore and Baltimore packets would answer my purpose.

In a few moments I came to the road to which the lad had referred, and felt some relief when I had gotten out of that great public highway, "The National Turnpike," which I found it to be.

When I had walked a mile on this road, and when it had now gotten to be about nine o'clock, I met a young man with a load of hay. He drew up his horses, and addressed me in a very kind tone, when the following dialogue took place between us.

"Are you travelling any distance, my friend?"

"I am on my way to Philadelphia."

"Are you free?"

"Yes, sir."

"I suppose, then, you are provided with free papers?"

"No, sir. I have no papers."

"Well, my friend, you should not travel on this road: you will be taken up before you have gone three miles. There are men living on this road who are constantly on the look-out for your people; and it is seldom that one escapes them who attempts to pass by day."

He then very kindly gave me advice where to turn off the road at a certain point, and how to find my way to a certain house, where I would meet with an old gentleman who would further advise me whether I had better remain till night, or go on.

I left this interesting young man; and such was my surprise and chagrin at the thought of having so widely missed my way, and my alarm at being in such a dangerous position, that in ten minutes I had so far forgotten his directions as to deem it unwise to attempt to follow them, lest I should miss my way, and get into evil hands.

I, however, left the road, and went into a small piece of wood, but not finding a sufficient hiding-place, and it being a busy part of the day, when persons were at work about the fields, I thought

I should excite less suspicion by keeping in the road, so I returned to the road; but the events of the next few moments proved that I committed a serious mistake.

I went about a mile, making in all two miles from the spot where I met my young friend, and about five miles from the toll gate to which I have referred, and I found myself at the twenty-four miles' stone from Baltimore. It was now about ten o'clock in the forenoon; my strength was greatly exhausted by reason of the want of suitable food; but the excitement that was then going on in my mind, left me little time to think of my *need* of food. Under ordinary circumstances as a traveller, I should have been glad to see the "Tavern," which was near the mile stone; but as the case stood with me, I deemed it a dangerous place to pass, much less to stop at. I was therefore passing it as quietly and as rapidly as possible, when from the lot just opposite the house, or signpost, I heard a coarse stern voice cry, "Halloo!"

I turned my face to the left, the direction from which the voice came, and observed that it proceeded from a man who was digging potatoes. I answered him politely, when the following occurred:

"Who do *you* belong to?"

"I am free, sir."

"Have you got papers?"

"No, sir."

"Well, you must stop here."

By this time he had got astride the fence, making his way into the road. I said,

"My business is onward, sir, and I do not wish to stop."

"I will see then if you don't stop, you black rascal."

He was now in the middle of the road, making after me in a brisk walk.

I saw that a crisis was at hand; I had no weapons of any kind, not even a pocketknife; but I asked myself, shall I surrender without a struggle. The instinctive answer was, "No." What will you do? continue to walk; if he runs after you, run; get him as far from the house as you can, then turn suddenly and smite him on the knee with a stone; that will render him, at least, unable to pursue you.

This was a desperate scheme, but I could think of no other,

and my habits as a blacksmith had given my eye and hand such mechanical skill, that I felt quite sure that if I could only get a stone in my hand, and have time to wield it, I should not miss his knee-pan.

He began to breathe short. He was evidently vexed because I did not halt, and I felt more and more provoked at the idea of being thus pursued by a man to whom I had not done the least injury. I had just begun to glance my eye about for a stone to grasp, when he made a tiger-like leap at me. This of course brought us to running. At this moment he yelled out "Jake Shouster!" and at the next moment the door of a small house standing to the left was opened, and out jumped a shoemaker girded up in his leather apron, with his knife in hand. He sprang forward and seized me by the collar, while the other seized my arms behind. I was now in the grasp of two men, either of whom were larger bodied than myself, and one of whom was armed with a dangerous weapon.

Standing in the door of the shoemaker's shop was a third man; and in the potato lot I had passed was still a fourth man. Thus surrounded by superior physical force, the fortune of the day it seemed to me was gone.

My heart melted away, I sunk resistlessly into the hands of my captors, who dragged me immediately into the tavern which was near. I ask my reader to go in with me, and see how the case goes.

Great Moral Dilemma

A few moments after I was taken into the bar-room, the news having gone as by electricity, the house and yard were crowded with gossipers, who had left their business to come and see "the runaway nigger." This hastily assembled congregation consisted of men, women, and children, each one had a look to give at, and a word to say about the "nigger."

But among the whole, there stood one v hose name I have never known, but who evidently wore the garb of a man whose profession bound him to speak for the dumb, but he, standing head and shoulders above all that were round about, spoke the first hard sentence against me. Said he, "That fellow is a runaway

I know; put him in jail a few days, and you will soon hear where he came from." And then fixing a fiend-like gaze upon me, he continued, "if I lived on this road, *you* fellows would not find such clear running as you do, I'd trap more of you."

But now comes the pinch of the case, the case of conscience to me even at this moment. Emboldened by the cruel speech just recited, my captors enclosed me, and said, "Come now, this matter may easily be settled without you going to jail; who do you belong to, and where did you come from?"

The facts here demanded were in my breast. I knew according to the law of slavery, who I belonged to and where I came from, and I must now do one of three things—I must refuse to speak at all, or I must communicate the fact, or I must tell an untruth. How would an untutored slave, who had never heard of such a writer as Archdeacon Paley, be likely to act in such a dilemma? The first point decided was, the facts in this case are my private property. These men have no more right to them than a highway robber has to my purse. What will be the consequence if I put them in possession of the facts. In forty-eight hours, I shall have received perhaps one hundred lashes, and be on my way to the Louisiana cottonfields. Of what service will it be to them? They will get a paltry sum of two hundred dollars. Is not my liberty worth more to me than two hundred dollars are to them?

I resolved, therefore, to insist that I was free. This not being satisfactory without other evidence, they tied my hands and set out, and went to a magistrate who lived about half a mile distant. It so happened, that when we arrived at his house he was not at home. This was to them a disappointment, but to me it was a relief; but I soon learned by their conversation, that there was still another magistrate in the neighborhood, and that they would go to him. In about twenty minutes, and after climbing fences and jumping ditches, we, captors and captive, stood before his door, but it was after the same manner as before—he was not at home. By this time the day had worn away to one or two o'clock, and my captors evidently began to feel somewhat impatient of the loss of time. We were about a mile and a quarter from the tavern. As we set out on our return, they began to parley. Finding it was difficult for me to get over fences with my hands tied, they untied me, and said, "Now John," that being the name they had given me, "if you have run away from anyone, it would be much better for you to tell us!" but I continued to affirm that I was free. I knew, however, that my situation was very critical, owing to the shortness of the distance I must be from home: my advertisement might overtake me at any moment.

On our way back to the tavern, we passed through a small skirt of wood, where I resolved to make an effort to escape again. One of my captors was walking on either side of me; I made a sudden turn, with my left arm sweeping the legs of one of my captors from under him; I left him nearly standing on his head, and took to my heels. As soon as they could recover they both took after me. We had to mount a fence. This I did most successfully, and making across an open field towards another wood; one of my captors being a long-legged man, was in advance of the other, and consequently nearing me. We had a hill to rise, and during the assent he gained on me. Once more I thought of self-defense. I am trying to escape peaceably, but this man is determined that I shall not.

My case was now desperate; and I took this desperate thought: "I will run him a little farther from his coadjutor; I will then suddenly catch a stone, and wound him in the breast." This was my fixed purpose, and I had arrived near the point on the top of the hill, where I expected to do the act, when to my surprise and dismay, I saw the other side of the hill was not only all ploughed up, but we came suddenly upon a man ploughing, who as suddenly left his plough and cut off my flight, by seizing me by the collar, when at the same moment my pursuer seized my arms behind. Here I was again in a sad fix. By this time the other pursuer had come up; I was most savagely thrown down on the ploughed ground with my face downward, the ploughman placed his knee upon my shoulders, one of my captors put his upon my legs, while the other tied my arms behind me. I was then dragged up and marched off with kicks, punches, and imprecations.

We got to the tavern at three o'clock. Here they again cooled down, and made an appeal to me to make a disclosure. I saw that my attempt to escape strengthened their belief that I was a fugitive. I said to them, "If you will not put me in jail, I will now tell you where I am from." They promised. "Well," said I, "a few weeks ago, I was sold from the eastern shore to a slave trader, who had a large gang, and set out for Georgia, but when he got to a town in Virginia, he was taken sick, and died with the smallpox. Several of his gang also died with it, so that the people in the town became alarmed, and did not wish the gang to remain among them. No one claimed us, or wished to have anything to do with us; I left the rest, and thought I would go somewhere and get work."

When I said this, it was evidently believed by those who were present, and notwithstanding the unkind feeling that had existed, there was a murmur of approbation. At the same time I perceived that a panic began to seize some, at the idea that I was one of a smallpox gang. Several who had clustered near me moved off to a respectful distance. One or two left the bar-room, and murmured, "better let the smallpox nigger go."

I was then asked what was the name of the slave trader. Without premeditation, I said, "John Henderson."

"John Henderson," said one of my captors, "I knew him; I took up a yaller boy for him about two years ago, and got fifty dollars. He passed out with a gang about that time, and the boy ran away from him at Frederickstown. What kind of a man was he?"

At a venture, I gave a description of him. "Yes," said he, "that is the man." By this time all the gossipers had cleared the coast; our friend, "Jake Shouster," had also gone back to his bench to finish his custom work, after having "lost nearly the whole day, trotting about with a nigger tied," as I heard his wife say as she called him home to his dinner. I was now left alone with the man who first called to me in the morning. In a sober manner, he made this proposal to me: "John, I have a brother living in Risterstown, four miles off, who keeps a tavern; I think you had better go and live with him, till we see what will turn up. He wants an ostler." I at once assented to this. "Well," said he, "take something to eat, and I will go with you."

Although I had so completely frustrated their designs for the moment, I knew that it would by no means answer for me to go into that town, where there were prisons, handbills, newspapers, and travellers. My intention was, to start with him, but not to enter the town alive.

I sat down to eat; it was Wednesday, four o'clock, and this was the first regular meal I had since Sunday morning. This over, we set out, and, to my surprise, he proposed to walk. We had gone about a mile and a half, and were approaching a wood through which the road passed with a bend. I fixed upon that as the spot where I would either free myself from this man, or die in his arms. I had resolved upon a plan of operation—it was this: to stop short, face about, and commence action; and neither ask or give quarters, until I was free or dead!

We had got within six rods of the spot, when a gentleman turned the corner, meeting us on horseback. He came up, and entered into conversation with my captor, both of them speaking in Dutch, so that I knew not what they said. After a few moments, this gentleman addressed himself to me in English, and I then learned that he was one of the magistrates on whom we had called in the morning; I felt that another crisis was at hand. Using his saddle as his bench, he put on an extremely stern and magisterial-like face, holding up his horse not unlike a field marshal in the act of reviewing troops, and carried me through a most rigid examination in reference to the statement I had made. I repeated carefully all I had said; at the close, he said, "Well, you had better stay among us a few months, until we see what is to be done with you." It was then agreed that we should go back to the tavern, and there settle upon some further plan. When we arrived at the tavern, the magistrate alighted from his horse, and went into the bar-room. He took another close glance at me, and went over some points of the former examination. He seemed quite satisfied of the correctness of my statement, and made the following proposition: that I should go and live with him for a short time, stating that he had a few acres of corn and potatoes to get in, and that he would give me twenty-five cents per day. I most cheerfully assented to this proposal. It was also agreed that I should remain at the tavern with my captor that night, and that he would accompany me in the morning. This part of the arrangement I did not like, but of course I could not say so. Things being thus arranged, the magistrate mounted his horse, and went on his way home.

It had been cloudy and rainy during the afternoon, but the western sky having partially cleared at this moment, I perceived that it was near the setting of the sun.

My captor had left his hired man most of the day to dig potatoes alone; but the wagon being now loaded, it being time to convey the potatoes into the barn, and the horses being all ready for that purpose, he was obliged to go into the potato field and give assistance.

I should say here, that his wife had been driven away by the smallpox panic about three o'clock, and had not yet returned; this left no one in the house, but a boy, about nine years of age.

As he went out, he spoke to the boy in Dutch, which I supposed, from the little fellow's conduct, to be instructions to watch me closely, which he certainly did.

The potato lot was across the public road, directly in front of the house; at the back of the house, and about 300 yards distant, there was a thick wood. The circumstances of the case would not allow me to think for one moment of remaining there for the night—the time had come for another effort—but there were two serious difficulties. One was, that I must either deceive or dispatch this boy who is watching me with intense vigilance. I am glad to say, that the latter did not for a moment seriously enter my mind. To deceive him effectually, I left my coat and went to the back door, from which my course would be direct to the wood. When I got to the door, I found that the barn, to which the wagon must soon come, lay just to the right, and overlooking the path I must take to the wood. In front of me lay a garden surrounded by a picket fence, to the left of me was a small gate, and that by passing through that gate would throw me into an open field, and give me clear running to the wood; but on looking through the gate, I saw that my captor, being with the team, would see me if I attempted to start before he moved from the position he then occupied. To add to my difficulty the horses had balked; while waiting for the decisive moment, the boy came to the door and asked me why I did not come in. I told him I felt unwell, and wished him to be so kind as to hand me a glass of water; expecting while he was gone to get it, the team would clear, so that I could start. While he was gone, another attempt was made to start the team but failed; he came with the water and I quickly used it up by gargling my throat and by drinking a part. I asked him to serve me by giving me another glass: he gave me a look of close scrutiny, but went in for the water. I

heard him fill the glass, and start to return with it; when the hind
end of the wagon cleared the corner of the house, which stood in
a range with the fence along which I was to pass in getting to the
wood. As I passed out the gate, I "squared my main-yard," and
laid my course up the line of fence, I cast a last glance over my
right shoulder, and saw the boy just perch his head above the
garden picket to look after me; I heard at the same time great
confusion with the team, the rain having made the ground
slippery, and the horses having to cross the road with a slant
and rise to get into the barn, it required great effort after they
started to prevent their balking. I felt some assurance that although the boy might give the alarm, my captor could not leave
the team until it was in the barn. I heard the horses' feet on the
barn-floor, just as I leaped the fence, and darted into the wood.

The sun was now quite down behind the western horizon, and
just at this time a heavy dark curtain of clouds was let down,
which seemed to usher in haste the night shade. I have never
before or since seen anything which seemed to me to compare
in sublimity with the spreading of the night shades at the close of
that day. My reflections upon the events of that day, and upon the
close of it, since I became acquainted with the Bible, have frequently brought to my mind that beautiful passage in the Book
of Job, "He holdeth back the face of His throne, and spreadeth
a cloud before it."

Before I proceed to the critical events and final deliverance of
the next chapter, I cannot forbear to pause a moment here for
reflection. The reader may well imagine how the events of the
past day affected my mind. You have seen what was done to me;
you have heard what was said to me—you have also seen what I
have done, and heard what I have said. If you ask me whether I
had expected before I left home, to gain my liberty by shedding
men's blood, or breaking their limbs? I answer, No! and as evidence of this, I had provided no weapon whatever; not so much
as a penknife—it never once entered my mind. I cannot say that I
expected to have the ill fortune of meeting with any human
being who would attempt to impede my flight.

If you ask me if I expected when I left home to gain my
liberty by fabrications and untruths? I answer, No! my parents,
slaves as they were, had always taught me, when they could, that

"truth may be blamed but cannot be ashamed"; so far as their example was concerned, I had no habits of untruth. I was arrested, and the demand made upon me, "Who do you belong to?" Knowing the fatal use these men would make of *my* truth, I at once concluded that they had no more right to it than a highwayman has to a traveller's purse.

If you ask me whether I now really believe that I gained my liberty by those lies? I answer, No! I now believe that I should be free, had I told the truth; but, at that moment, I could not see any other way to baffle my enemies, and escape their clutches.

The history of that day has never ceased to inspire me with a deeper hatred of slavery; I never recur to it but with the most intense horror at a system which can put a man not only in peril of liberty, limb, and life itself, but which may even send him in haste to the bar of God with a lie upon his lips.

Whatever my readers may think, therefore, of the history of events of the day, do not admire in it the fabrications; but *see* in it the impediments that often fall into the pathway of the flying bondman. *See* how human bloodhounds gratuitously chase, catch, and tempt him to shed blood and lie; how when he would do good, evil is thrust upon him.

Chapter 3. A Dreary Night in the Woods—Critical Situation the Next Day

ALMOST immediately on entering the wood, I not only found myself embosomed in the darkness of the night, but I also found myself entangled in a thick forest of undergrowth, which had been quite thoroughly wetted by the afternoon rain.

I penetrated through the wood, thick and thin, and more or less wet, to the distance I should think of three miles. By this time my clothes were all thoroughly soaked through; and I felt once more a gloom and wretchedness, the recollection of which makes me shudder at this distant day. My young friends in this highly favored Christian country, surrounded with all the comforts of home and parental care, visited by pastors and Sabbath-school teachers, think of the dreary condition of the blacksmith boy in the dark wood that night; and then consider that thousands of his brethren have had to undergo much greater hardships in their flight from slavery.

I was now out of the hands of those who had so cruelly teased me during the day; but a number of fearful thoughts rushed into my mind to alarm me. It was dark and cloudy, so that I could not see the *north star*. How do I know what ravenous beasts are in this wood? How do I know what precipices may be within its bounds? I cannot rest in this wood tomorrow, for it will be searched by those men from whom I have escaped; but how shall I regain the road? How shall I know when I am on the right road again?

These are some of the thoughts that filled my mind with gloom and alarm.

At a venture I struck an angle northward in search of the road. After several hours of zigzag and laborious travel, dragging through briars, thorns, and running vines, I emerged from the wood and found myself wading marshy ground and over ditches.

I can form no correct idea of the distance I travelled, but I came to a road, I should think about three o'clock in the morning. It so happened that I came out near where there was a fork in the road of three prongs.

Now arose a serious query—Which is the right prong for me? I was reminded by the circumstance of a superstitious proverb

among the slaves, that "the left-hand turning was unlucky," but
as I had never been in the habit of placing faith in this or any
similar superstition, I am not aware that it had the least weight
upon my mind, as I had the same difficulty with reference to the
right-hand turning. After a few moments parley with myself, I
took the central prong of the road and pushed on with all my
speed.

It had not cleared off, but a fresh wind had sprung up; it was
chilly and searching. This with my wet clothing made me very
uncomfortable; my nerves began to quiver before the searching
wind. The barking of mastiffs, the crowing of fowls, and the distant rattling of market wagons warned me that the day was approaching.

My British reader must remember that in the region where I
was, we know nothing of the long hours of twilight you enjoy
here. With us the day is measured more by the immediate presence of the sun, and the night by the prevalence of actual darkness.

The day dawned upon me when I was near a small house and
barn, situate close to the road-side. The barn was too near the
road, and too small to afford secure shelter for the day; but as I
cast my eye around by the dim light, I could see no wood, and
no larger barn. It seemed to be an open country to a wide
extent. The sun was travelling so rapidly from his eastern chamber that ten or fifteen minutes would spread broad daylight over
my track. Whether *my* deed was evil, *you* may judge, but I
freely confess that I did *then* prefer darkness rather than light;
I therefore took to the mow of the little barn at a great risk, as
the events of the day will shew. It so happened that the barn was
filled with corn fodder, newly cured and lately got in. You are
aware that however quietly one may crawl into such a bed, he is
compelled to make much more noise than if it were a feather-
bed; and also considerably more than if it were hay or straw.
Besides inflicting upon my own excited imagination the belief
that I made noise enough to be heard by the inmates of the
house who were likely to be rising at the time, I had the misfortune to attract the notice of a little house-dog, such as we call
in that part of the world a "fice," on account of its being not only
the smallest species of the canine race, but also because it is

the most saucy, noisy, and teasing of all dogs. This little creature commenced a fierce barking. I had at once great fears that the mischievous little thing would betray me; I fully apprehended that as soon as the man of the house arose, he would come and make search in the barn. It now being entirely daylight, it was too late to retreat from this shelter, even if I could have found another; I, therefore, bedded myself down into the fodder as best I could, and entered upon the annoyances of the day, with the frail hope to sustain my mind.

It was Thursday morning; the clouds that had veiled the sky during the latter part of the previous day and the previous night were gone. It was not until about an hour after the sun rose that I heard any outdoor movements about the house. As soon as I heard those movements, I was satisfied there was but one man about the house, and that he was preparing to go some distance to work for the day. This was fortunate for me; the busy movements about the yard, and especially the active preparations in the house for breakfast, silenced my unwelcome little annoyer, the fice, until after the man had gone, when he commenced afresh, and continued with occasional intermissions through the day. He made regular sallies from the house to the barn, and after smelling about, would fly back to the house, barking furiously; thus he strove most skilfully throughout the entire day to raise an alarm. There seemed to be no one about the house but one or two small children and the mother, after the man was gone. About ten o'clock my attention was gravely directed to another trial; how could I pass the day without food. The reader will remember it is Thursday, and the only regular meal I have taken since Sunday, was yesterday in the midst of great agitation, about four o'clock; that since that I have performed my arduous night's travel. At one moment, I had nearly concluded to go and present myself at the door, and ask the woman of the house to have compassion and give me food; but then I feared the consequences might be fatal, and I resolved to suffer the day out. The wind sprang up fresh and cool; the barn being small and the crevices large, my wet clothes were dried by it, and chilled me through and through.

I cannot now, with pen or tongue, give a correct idea of the feeling of wretchedness I experienced; every nerve in my system quivered, so that not a particle of my flesh was at rest. In this way I passed the day till about the middle of the afternoon, when there seemed to be an unusual stir about the public road, which passed close by the barn. Men seemed to be passing in parties on horseback, and talking anxiously. From a word which I now and then overheard, I had not a shadow of doubt that they were in search of me. One I heard say, "I ought to catch such a fellow, the only liberty he should have for one fortnight, would be ten feet of rope." Another I heard say, "I reckon he is in that wood now." Another said, "Who would have thought that rascal was so 'cute?" All this while the little fice was mingling his voice with those of the horsemen, and the noise of the horses' feet. I listened and trembled.

Just before the setting of the sun, the laboring man of the house returned, and commenced his evening duties about the house and barn; chopping wood, getting up his cow, feeding his pigs, &c., attended by the little brute, who continued barking at short intervals. He came several times into the barn below. While matters were passing thus, I heard the approach of horses again, and as they came up nearer, I was led to believe that all I had heard pass were returning in one party. They passed the barn and halted at the house, when I recognized the voice of my old captor; addressing the laborer, he asked, "Have you seen a runaway nigger pass here today?"

LABORER: "No; I have not been at home since early this morning. Where did he come from?"

CAPTOR: "I caught him down below here yesterday morning. I had him all day, and just at night he fooled me and got away. A party of us have been after him all day; we have been up to the line, but can't hear or see anything of him. I heard this morning where he came from. He is a blacksmith, and a stiff reward is out for him—two hundred dollars."

LAB.: "He is worth looking for."

CAP.: I reckon so. If I get my clutches on him again, I'll mosey* him down to —— before I eat or sleep."

Reader, you may if you can, imagine what the state of my mind was at this moment. I shall make no attempt to describe it to you; to my great relief, however, the party rode off, and the

---

* An expression which signifies to drive in a hurry.

laborer after finishing his work went into the house. Hope seemed now to dawn for me once more; darkness was rapidly approaching, but the moments of twilight seemed much longer than they did the evening before. At length the sable covering had spread itself over the earth. About eight o'clock I ventured to descend from the mow of the barn into the road. The little dog the while began a furious fit of barking, so much so, that I was sure that with what his master had learned about me, he could not fail to believe I was about his premises. I quickly crossed the road, and got into an open field opposite. After stepping lightly about two hundred yards, I halted, and on listening, I heard the door open. Feeling about on the ground, I picked up two stones, and one in each hand I made off as fast as I could, but I heard nothing more that indicated pursuit, and after going some distance I discharged my encumbrance, as from the reduced state of my bodily strength, I could not afford to carry ballast.

This incident had the effect to start me under great disadvantage to make a good night's journey, as it threw me at once off the road, and compelled me to encounter at once the tedious and laborious task of beating my way across marshy fields, and to drag through woods and thickets where there were no paths.

After several hours I found my way back to the road, but the hope of making anything like clever speed was out of the question. All I could do was to keep my legs in motion, and this I continued to do with the utmost difficulty. The latter part of the night I suffered extremely from cold. There came a heavy frost; I expected at every moment to fall on the road and perish. I came to a cornfield covered with heavy shocks of Indian corn that had been cut; I went into this and got an ear, and then crept into one of the shocks; ate as much of it as I could, and thought I would rest a little and start again, but weary nature could not sustain the operation of grinding hard corn for its own nourishment, and I sunk to sleep.

When I awoke, the sun was shining around; I started with alarm, but it was too late to think of seeking any other shelter; I therefore nestled myself down, and concealed myself as best I could from the light of day. After recovering a little from my fright, I commenced again eating my whole corn. Grain by grain

I worked away at it; when my jaws grew tired, as they often did, I would rest, and then begin afresh. Thus, although I began an early breakfast, I was nearly the whole of the forenoon before I had done.

Nothing of importance occurred during the day, until about the middle of the afternoon, when I was thrown into a panic by the appearance of a party of gunners, who passed near me with their dogs. After shooting one or two birds, however, and passing within a few rods of my frail covering, they went on, and left me once more in hope. Friday night came without any other incident worth naming. As I sallied out, I felt evident benefit from the ear of corn I had nibbled away. My strength was considerably renewed; though I was far from being nourished, I felt that my life was at least safe from death by hunger. Thus encouraged, I set out with better speed than I had made since Sunday and Monday night. I had a presentiment, too, that I must be near free soil. I had not yet the least idea where I should find a home or a friend, still my spirits were so highly elated, that I took the whole of the road to myself; I ran, hopped, skipped, jumped, clapped my hands, and talked to myself. But to the old slaveholder I had left, I said, "Ah! ah! old fellow, I told you I'd fix you."

After an hour or two of such freaks of joy, a gloom would come over me in connection with these questions, "But where are you going? What are you going to do? What will you do with freedom without father, mother, sisters, and brothers? What will you say when you are asked where you were born? You know nothing of the world; how will you explain the fact of your ignorance?

These questions made me feel deeply the magnitude of the difficulties yet before me.

Saturday morning dawned upon me; and although my strength seemed yet considerably fresh, I began to feel a hunger somewhat more destructive and pinching, if possible, than I had before. I resolved, at all risk, to continue my travel by daylight, and to ask information of the first person I met.

The events of the next chapter will shew what fortune followed this resolve.

THE RESOLUTION of which I informed the reader at the close of the last chapter, being put into practice, I continued my flight on the public road; and a little after the sun rose, I came in sight of a toll gate again. For a moment all the events which followed my passing a toll gate on Wednesday morning came fresh to my recollection, and produced some hesitation; but at all events, said I, I will try again.

On arriving at the gate, I found it attended by an elderly woman, whom I afterwards learned was a widow, and an excellent Christian woman. I asked her if I was in Pennsylvania. On being informed that I was, I asked her if she knew where I could get employ? She said she did not; but advised me to go to W. W., a Quaker, who lived about three miles from her, whom I would find to take an interest in me. She gave me directions which way to take; I thanked her, and bade her good morning, and was very careful to follow her directions.

In about half an hour I stood trembling at the door of W. W. After knocking, the door opened upon a comfortably spread table, the sight of which seemed at once to increase my hunger sevenfold. Not daring to enter, I said I had been sent to him in search of employ. "Well," said he, "come in and take thy breakfast, and get warm, and we will talk about it; thee must be cold without any coat." *"Come in and take thy breakfast, and get warm!"* These words spoken by a stranger, but with such an air of simple sincerity and fatherly kindness, made an overwhelming impression upon my mind. They made me feel, spite of all my fear and timidity, that I had, in the providence of God, found a friend and a home. He at once gained my confidence; and I felt that I might confide to him a fact which I had, as yet, confided to no one.

From that day to this, whenever I discover the least disposition in my heart to disregard the wretched condition of any poor or distressed persons with whom I meet, I call to mind these words—*"Come in and take thy breakfast, and get warm."* They invariably remind me of what I was at that time; my condition was as wretched as that of any human being can possibly be, with the exception of the loss of health or reason. I had but four pieces of clothing about my person, having left all the rest in the hands of my captors. I was a starving fugitive, without home or friends—a reward offered for my person in the public papers—pursued by cruel manhunters, and no claim upon him to whose door I went. Had he turned me away, I must have perished. Nay, he took me in, and gave me of his food, and shared with me his own garments. Such treatment I had never before received at the hands of any white man.

A few such men in slaveholding America, have stood, and even now stand, like Abrahams and Lots, to stay its forthcoming and well-earned and just judgment.

The limits of this work compel me to pass over many interesting incidents which occurred during my six months' concealment in that family. I must confine myself only to those which will show the striking providence of God, in directing my steps to the door of W. W., and how great an influence the incidents of that six months has had upon all my subsequent history. My friend kindly gave me employ to saw and split a number of cords of wood, then lying in his yard, for which he agreed with me for liberal pay and board. This inspired me with great encouragement. The idea of beginning to earn something was very pleasant. Next, we confidentially agreed upon the way and means of avoiding surprise, in case anyone should come to the house as a spy, or with intention to arrest me. This afforded still further relief, as it convinced me that the whole family would now be on the lookout for such persons.

The next theme of conversation was with reference to my education.

"Can thee read or write any, James?" was the question put to me the morning after my arrival, by W. W.

"No, sir, I cannot; my duties as a blacksmith have made me acquainted with the figures on the common mechanics' square. There was a day-book kept in the shop, in which the overseer usually charged the smithwork we did for the neighbors. I have spent entire Sabbaths looking over the pages of that book; knowing the names of persons to whom certain pieces of work were charged, together with their prices, I strove anxiously to learn to write in this way. I got paper, and picked up feathers about the yard, and made ink of —— berries. My quills being too soft, and my skill in making a pen so poor, that I undertook some years ago to make a steel pen.* In this way I have learnt to make a few of the letters, but I cannot write my own name, nor do I know the letters of the alphabet."

W. W. (*handing a slate and pencil*): "Let me see how thee makes letters; try such as thou hast been able to make easily."

A. B. C. L. G.

P. W. (*wife of W. W.*): "Why, those are better than I can make."

W. W.: "Oh, we can soon get thee in the way, James."

Arithmetic and astronomy became my favorite studies. W. W. was an accomplished scholar; he had been a teacher for some years, and was cultivating a small farm on account of ill health, which had compelled him to leave teaching. He is one of the most far-sighted and practical men I ever met with. He taught me by familiar conversations, illustrating his themes by diagrams on the slate, so that I caught his ideas with ease and rapidity.

I now began to see, for the first time, the extent of the mischief slavery had done to me. Twenty-one years of my life were gone, never again to return, and I was as profoundly ignorant, comparatively, as a child five years old. This was painful, annoying, and humiliating in the extreme. Up to this time, I recollected to have seen one copy of the New Testament, but the entire Bible I had never seen, and had never heard of the Patriarchs, or of the Lord Jesus Christ. I recollected to have heard two sermons, but had heard no mention in them of Christ, or the way of life by Him. It is quite easy to imagine, then, what was the state of my mind, having been reared in total moral midnight; it was a sad picture of mental and spiritual darkness.

As my friend poured light into my mind, I saw the darkness; it amazed and grieved me beyond description. Sometimes I sank down under the load, and became discouraged, and dared not hope that I could ever succeed in acquiring knowledge enough to make me happy, or useful to my fellow beings.

My dear friend, W. W., however, had a happy tact to inspire me with confidence; and he, perceiving my state of mind, exerted

* This attempt was as early as 1822.

himself, not without success, to encourage me. He cited to me various instances of colored persons, of whom I had not heard before, and who had distinguished themselves for learning, such as Bannicker, Wheatley, and Francis Williams.

How often have I regretted that the six months I spent in the family of W. W., could not have been six years. The danger of recapture, however, rendered it utterly imprudent that I should remain longer; and early in the month of March, while the ground was covered with the winter's snow, I left the bosom of this excellent family, and went forth once more to try my fortune among strangers.

My dear reader, if I could describe to you the emotions I felt when I left the threshold of W. W.'s door, you could not fail to see how deplorable is the condition of the fugitive slave, often for months and years after he has escaped the immediate grasp of the tyrant. When I left my parents, the trial was great, but I had now to leave a friend who had done more for me than parents could have done as slaves; and hence I felt an endearment to that friend which was heightened by a sense of the important relief he had afforded me in the greatest need, and hours of pleasant and highly profitable intercourse.

About a month previous to leaving the house of W. W., a small circumstance occurred one evening, which I only name to shew the harassing fears and dread in which I lived during most of the time I was there. He had a brother-in-law living some ten miles distant—he was a friend to the slave; he often came unexpectedly and spent a few hours—sometimes a day and a night. I had not however, ever known him to come at night. One night, about nine o'clock, after I had gone to bed (my lodging being just over the room in which W. W. and his wife were sitting), I heard the door open and a voice ask, "Where is the boy?" The voice sounded to me like the voice of my master; I was sure it must be his. I sprang and listened for a moment—it seemed to be silent; I heard nothing, and then it seemed to me there was a confusion. There was a window at the head of my bed, which I could reach without getting upon the floor: it was a single sash and opened upon hinges. I quickly opened this window and waited in a perfect tremor of dread for further development. There was a door at the foot of the stairs; as I heard that door open, I sprang for the window, and my head was just out, when the gentle voice of my friend W. W. said, "James?"* "Here," said I. "—— has come, and he would like to have thee put up his horse." I drew a breath of relief, but my strength and presence of mind did not return for some hours. I slept none that night; for a moment I could doze away, but the voice would sound in my ears, "Where is that boy?" and it would seem to me it must be the tyrant in quest of his weary prey, and would find myself starting again.

From that time the agitation of my mind became so great that I could not feel myself safe. Every day seemed to increase my fear, till I was unfit for work, study, or rest. My friend endeavored, but in vain, to get me to stay a week longer.

The events of the spring proved that I had not left too soon. As soon as the season for travelling fairly opened, active search was made, and my master was seen in a town, twenty miles in advance of where I had spent my six months.

The following curious fact also came out. That same brother-in-law who frightened me was putting up one evening at a hotel some miles off, and while sitting quietly by himself on one part of the room, he overheard a conversation between a travelling peddler and several gossipers of the neighborhood, who were lounging away the evening at the hotel.

PEDDLER: "Do you know one W. W. somewhere about here?"

GOSSIPER: "Yes, he lives —— miles off."

PED.: "I understand he had a black boy with him last winter, I wonder if he is there yet?"

GOS.: "I don't know, he most always has a runaway nigger with him."

PED.: "I should like to find out whether that fellow is there yet."

BROTHER-IN-LAW (turning about): "What does thee know about that boy?"

PED.: "Well he is a runaway."

BROTHER-IN-LAW: "Who did he run away from?"

PED.: "From Col. —— in ——."

BROTHER-IN-LAW: "How did thee find out that fact?"

PED.: "Well, I have been over there peddling."

* If W. W. had ascended the stairs without calling, I should certainly have jumped out of the window.

BROTHER-IN-LAW: "Where art thou from?"

PED.: "I belong in Conn."

BROTHER-IN-LAW: "Did thee see the boy's master?"

PED.: "Yes."

BROTHER-IN-LAW: "What did he offer thee to find the boy?"

PED.: "I agreed to find out where he was, and let him know, and if he got him, I was to receive ———."

BROTHER-IN-LAW: "How didst thou hear the boy had been with W. W.?"

PED.: "Oh, he is known to be a notorious rascal for enticing away, and concealing slaves; he'll get himself into trouble yet; the slaveholders are on the lookout for him."

BROTHER-IN-LAW: "W. W. is my brother-in-law; the boy of whom thou speakest is not with him, and to save thee the trouble of abusing him, I can moreover say, he is no rascal."

PED.: "He may not be there now, but it is because he has sent him off. His master heard of him, and from the description, he is sure it must have been his boy. He could tell me pretty nigh where he was; he said he was a fine healthy boy, twenty-one, a first-rate blacksmith; he would not have taken a thousand dollars for him."

BROTHER-IN-LAW: "I know not where the boy is, but I have no doubt he is worth more to himself than he ever was to his master, high as he fixes the price on him; and I have no doubt thee will do better to pursue thy peddling honestly, than to neglect it for the sake of serving Negro hunters at a venture."

All this happened within a month or two after I left my friend. One fact which makes this part of the story deeply interesting to my own mind is, that some years elapsed before it came to my knowledge.

Chapter 5. Seven Months' Residence in the Family of J. K., a
Member of the Society of Friends, in Chester County,
Pennsylvania—Removal to New York—Becomes a Convert to
Religion—Becomes a Teacher

ON LEAVING W. W., I wended my way in deep sorrow and melancholy, onward towards Philadelphia, and after travelling two days and a night, I found shelter and employ in the family of J. K., another member of the Society of Friends, a farmer.

The religious atmosphere in this family was excellent. Mrs. K. gave me the first copy of the Holy Scriptures I ever possessed; she also gave me much excellent counsel. She was a preacher in the Society of Friends; this occasioned her with her husband to be much of their time from home. This left the charge of the farm upon me, and besides put it out of their power to render me that aid in my studies which my former friend had. I, however, kept myself closely concealed, by confining myself to the limits of the farm, and using all my leisure time in study. This place was more secluded, and I felt less of dread and fear of discovery than I had before, and although seriously embarrassed for want of an instructor, I realized some pleasure and profit in my studies. I often employed myself in drawing rude maps of the solar system, and diagrams illustrating the theory of solar eclipses. I felt also a fondness for reading the Bible, and committing chapters, and verses of hymns to memory. Often on the Sabbath when alone in the barn, I would break the monotony of the hours by endeavoring to speak, as if I was addressing an audience. My mind was constantly struggling for thoughts, and I was still more grieved and alarmed at its barrenness; I found it gradually freed from the darkness entailed by slavery, but I was deeply and anxiously concerned how I should fill it with useful knowledge. I had a few books, and no tutor.

In this way I spent seven months with J. K., and should have continued longer, agreeably to his urgent solicitation, but I felt that life was fast wearing, and that as I was now free, I must adventure in search of knowledge. On leaving J. K., he kindly gave me the following certificate,

EAST NAUTMEAL, CHESTER COUNTY, PENNSYLVANIA
TENTH MONTH 5TH, 1828

I hereby certify, that the bearer, J. W. C. Pennington, has been in my employ seven months, during most of which time I have been from home, leaving my entire business in his trust, and that he has proved a highly trustworthy and industrious young man. He leaves with the sincere regret of myself and family; but as he feels it to be his duty to go where he can obtain education, so as to fit him to be more useful, I cordially commend him to the warm sympathy of the friends of humanity wherever a wise providence may appoint him a home.

Signed,   *J. K.*

Passing through Philadelphia, I went to New York, and in a short time found employ on Long Island, near the city. At this time, the state of things was extremely critical in New York. It was just two years after the general emancipation in that state. In the city it was a daily occurrence for slaveholders from the southern states to catch their slaves, and by certificate from Recorder Riker take them back. I often felt serious apprehensions of danger, and yet I felt also that I must begin the world somewhere.

I was earning respectable wages, and by means of evening schools and private tuition, was making encouraging progress in my studies.

Up to this time, it had never occurred to me that I was a slave in another and a more serious sense. All my serious impressions of mind had been with reference to the slavery from which I had escaped. Slavery had been my theme of thought day and night.

In the spring of 1829, I found my mind unusually perplexed about the state of the slave. I was enjoying rare privileges in attending a Sabbath school; the great value of Christian knowledge began to be impressed upon my mind to an extent I had not been conscious of before. I began to contrast my condition with that of ten brothers and sisters I had left in slavery, and the condition of children I saw sitting around me on the Sabbath, with their pious teachers, with that of 700,000, now 800,440, slave children, who had no means of Christian instruction.

The theme was more powerful than any my mind had ever

encountered before. It entered into the deep chambers of my soul, and stirred the most agitating emotions I had ever felt. The question was, what can I do for that vast body of suffering brotherhood I have left behind? To add to the weight and magnitude of the theme, I learnt, for the first time, how many slaves there were. The question completely staggered my mind; and finding myself more and more borne down with it, until I was in an agony, I thought I would make it a subject of prayer to God, although prayer had not been my habit, having never attempted it but once.

I not only prayed, but also fasted. It was while engaged thus, that my attention was seriously drawn to the fact that I was a lost sinner, and a slave to Satan; and soon I saw that I must make another escape from another tyrant. I did not by any means forget my fellow bondmen, of whom I had been sorrowing so deeply, and travailing in spirit so earnestly; but I now saw that while man had been injuring me, I had been offending God; and that unless I ceased to offend him, I could not expect to have his sympathy in my wrongs; and, moreover, that I could not be instrumental in eliciting his powerful aid in behalf of those for whom I mourned so deeply.

This may provoke a smile from some who profess to be the friends of the slave, but who have a lower estimate of experimental Christianity than I believe is due to it; but I am not the less confident that sincere prayer to God, proceeding from a few hearts deeply imbued with experimental Christianity about *that time*, has had much to do with subsequent happy results. At that time the 800,000 bondmen in the British Isles had not seen the beginning of the end of their sufferings—at that time, 20,000 who are now free in Canada, were in bonds—at that time, there was no Vigilance Committee to aid the flying slave—at that time, the two powerful Anti-Slavery Societies of America had no being.

I distinctly remember that I felt the need of enlisting the sympathy of God in behalf of my enslaved brethren; but when I attempted it day after day, and night after night, I was made to feel, that whatever else I might do, I was not qualified to do that, as I was myself alienated from him by wicked works. In short, I felt that I needed the powerful aid of some in my behalf with God, just as much as I did that of my dear friend in Penn-

sylvania, when flying from man. "If one man sin against another, the judge shall judge him, but if a man sin against God,
who shall entreat for him?"

Day after day, for about two weeks, I found myself more
deeply convicted of personal guilt before God. My heart, soul,
and body were in the greatest distress; I thought of neither food,
drink, or rest, for days and nights together. Burning with a
recollection of the wrongs man had done me—mourning for the
injuries my brethren were still enduring, and deeply convicted
of the guilt of my own sins against God. One evening, in the
third week of the struggle, while alone in my chamber, and after
solemn reflection for several hours, I concluded that I could
never be happy or useful in that state of mind, and resolved that
I would try to become reconciled to God. I was then living in the
family of an Elder of the Presbyterian Church. I had not made
known my feelings to anyone, either in the family or out of it;
and I did not suppose that anyone had discovered my feelings.
To my surprise, however, I found that the family had not only
been aware of my state for several days, but were deeply anxious
on my behalf. The following Sabbath Dr. Cox was on a visit in
Brooklyn to preach, and was a guest in the family; hearing of my
case, he expressed a wish to converse with me, and without knowing the plan, I was invited into a room and left alone with him.
He entered skilfully and kindly into my feelings, and after considerable conversation he invited me to attend his service that
afternoon. I did so, and was deeply interested.

Without detaining the reader with too many particulars, I will
only state that I heard the doctor once or twice after this, at his
own place of worship in New York City, and had several personal
interviews with him, as the result of which, I hope, I was
brought to a saving acquaintance with Him of whom Moses in
the Law and the Prophets did write; and soon connected myself
with the church under his pastoral care.

I now returned with all my renewed powers to the great theme
—slavery. It seemed now as I looked at it, to be more hideous
than ever. I saw it now as an evil under the moral government
of God—as a sin not only against man, but also against God. The
great and engrossing thought with me was, how shall I now
employ my time and my talents so as to tell most effectually

upon this system of wrong! As I have stated, there was no Anti-Slavery Society then—there was no Vigilance Committee. I had, therefore, to select a course of action, without counsel or advice from anyone who professed to sympathize with the slave. Many, many lonely hours of deep meditation have I passed during the years 1828 and 1829, before the great anti-slavery movement, on the questions, What shall I do for the slave? How shall I act so that he will reap the benefit of my time and talents? At one time I had resolved to go to Africa, and to react from there; but without bias or advice from any mortal, I soon gave up that, as looking too much like feeding a hungry man with a long spoon.

At length, finding that the misery, ignorance, and wretchedness of the free colored people was by the whites tortured into an argument for slavery; finding myself now among the free people of color in New York, where slavery was so recently abolished, and finding much to do for their elevation, I resolved to give my strength in that direction. And well do I remember the great movement which commenced among us about this time, for the holding of General Conventions, to devise ways and means for their elevation, which continued with happy influence up to 1834, when we gave way to anti-slavery friends, who had then taken up the laboring oar. And well do I remember that the first time I ever saw those tried friends, Garrison, Jocelyn, and Tappan, was in one of those Conventions, where they came to make our acquaintance, and to secure our confidence in some of their preliminary labors.

My particular mode of labor was still a subject of deep reflection, and from time to time I carried it to the Throne of Grace. Eventually my mind fixed upon the ministry as the desire of my whole heart. I had mastered the preliminary branches of English education, and was engaged in studying logic, rhetoric, and the Greek Testament, without a master. While thus struggling in my laudable work, an opening presented itself which was not less surprising than gratifying. Walking on the street one day, I met a friend who said to me, "I have just had an application to supply a teacher for a school, and I have recommended you." I said, "My dear friend, I am obliged to you for the kindness; but I fear I cannot sustain an examination for that station." "Oh," said he, "try." I said, "I will," and we separated. Two weeks afterwards, I met the trustees of the school, was examined, accepted, and agreed with them for a salary of two hundred dollars per annum; commenced my school, and succeeded. This was five years, three months, and thirteen days after I came from the South.

As the events of my life since that have been of a public professional nature, I will say no more about it. My object in writing this tract is now completed. It has been to shew the reader the hand of God with a slave; and to elicit your sympathy in behalf of the fugitive slave, by shewing some of the untold dangers and hardships through which he has to pass to gain liberty, and how much he needs friends on free soil; and that men who have felt the yoke of slavery, even in its mildest form, cannot be expected to speak of the system otherwise than in terms of the most unqualified condemnation.

There is one sin that slavery committed against me which I never can forgive. It robbed me of my education; the injury is irreparable; I feel the embarrassment more seriously now than I ever did before. It cost me two years' hard labor, after I fled, to unshackle my mind; it was three years before I had purged my language of slavery's idioms; it was four years before I had thrown off the crouching aspect of slavery; and now the evil that besets me is a great lack of that general information, the foundation of which is most effectually laid in that part of life which I served as a slave. When I consider how much now, more than ever, depends upon sound and thorough education among colored men, I am grievously overwhelmed with a sense of my deficiency, and more especially as I can never hope now to make it up. If I know my own heart, I have no ambition but to serve the cause of suffering humanity; all that I have desired or sought, has been to make me more efficient for good. So far I have some consciousness that I have done my utmost; and, should my future days be few or many, I am reconciled to meet the last account, hoping to be acquitted of any wilful neglect of duty; but I shall have to go to my last account with this charge against the system of slavery, "*Vile monster! thou hast hindered my usefulness, by robbing me of my early education.*"

Oh! what might I have been now, but for this robbery perpetrated upon me as soon as I saw the light. When the monster heard that a man child was born, he laughed, and said, "It is mine." When I was laid in the cradle, he came and looked on my face, and wrote down my name upon his barbarous list of chattels personal, on the same list where he registered his horses, hogs, cows, sheep, and even his *dogs!* Gracious Heaven, is there no repentance for the misguided men who do these things!

The only harm I wish to slaveholders is, that they may be speedily delivered from the guilt of a sin, which, if not repented of, must bring down the judgment of Almighty God upon their devoted heads. The least I desire for the slave is, that he may be speedily released from the pain of drinking a cup whose bitterness I have sufficiently tasted to know that it is insufferable.

Chapter 6. Some Account of the Family I Left in Slavery— Proposal to Purchase Myself and Parents—How Met by My Old Master

IT IS BUT NATURAL that the reader should wish to hear a word about the family I left behind.

There are frequently large slave families with whom God seems to deal in a remarkable manner. I believe my family is an instance.

I have already stated that when I fled, I left a father, mother, and eleven brothers and sisters. These were all, except my oldest brother, owned by the man from whom I fled. It will be seen at once then how the fear of implicating them embarrassed me in the outset. They suffered nothing, however, but a strong suspicion, until about six months after I had left; when the following circumstance took place:

When I left my friend W. W. in Pennsylvania to go on north, I ventured to write a letter back to one of my brothers, informing him how I was; and this letter was directed to the care of a white man who was hired on the plantation, who worked in the garden with my father, and who professed a warm friendship to our family; but instead of acting in good faith, he handed the letter to my master. I am sorry that truth compels me to say that that man was an Englishman.

From that day the family were handled most strangely. The history begins thus: they were all sold into Virginia, the adjoining state. This was done lest I should have some plan to get them off; but God so ordered that they fell into kinder hands. After a few years, however, their master became much embarrassed, so that he was obliged to pass them into other hands, at least for a term of years. By this change the family was divided, and my parents, with the greater part of their children, were taken to New Orleans. After remaining there several years at hard labor, my father being in a situation of considerable trust, they were again taken back to Virginia; and by this means became entitled by the laws of that state to their freedom. Before justice, however, could take its course, their old master in Maryland, as if intent to doom them forever to bondage, repurchased them; and in order to defeat a similar law in Maryland, by which they would have been entitled to liberty, he obtained from the General Assembly of that state the following special act. This will show not only something of his character as a slaveholder, but also his political influence in the state. It is often urged in the behalf of slaveholders, that the law interposes an obstacle in the way of emancipating their slaves when they wish to do so, but here is an instance which lays open the real philosophy of the whole case. They make the law themselves, and when they find the laws operate more in favor of the slaves than themselves, they can easily evade or change it. Maryland being a slave-exporting state, you will see why they need a law to prohibit the importation of slaves; it is a protection to that sort of trade. This law he wished to evade.

An act for the Relief of —— of —— County.
Passed January 17th, 1842.

Whereas it is represented to this General Assembly that —— of —— county, brought into this state from the state of Virginia, sometime in the month of March last, two negro slaves, to wit, —— and —— his wife, who are slaves for life, and who were acquired by the said —— by purchase, and whereas, the said —— is desirous of retaining said slaves in this state. THERE-FORE, BE IT ENACTED, *by the General Assembly* of Maryland, that the said —— be, and he is thereby authorized to retain said negroes as slaves for life within this state, provided that the said —— shall within thirty days after the passage of this act, file with the clerk of the —— county court, a list of said slaves so brought into this state, stating their ages, with an affidavit thereto attached, that the same is a true and faithful list of the slaves so removed, and that they were not brought into this state for the purpose of sale, and that they are slaves for life. And *provided also*, that the sum of fifteen dollars for each slave, between the ages of twelve and forty-five years, and the sum of five dollars for each slave above the age of forty-five years and under twelve years of age, so brought into this state, shall be paid to the said clerk of —— county court: to be paid over by him to the treasurer of the western shore, for the use and benefit of the Colonization Society of this state.

State of Connecticut.
Office of Secretary of State.

I hereby certify, that the foregoing is a true copy of an act passed by the General Assembly of Maryland, January 17th, 1842, as it appears in the printed acts of the said Maryland, in the Library of the state.

In testimony whereof, I have hereunto set my hand and seal of said state, at Hartford, this 17th day of August, 1846.

CHARLES W. BEADLEY,

(SEAL.)   Secretary of State.

Thus, the whole family after being twice fairly entitled to their liberty, even by the laws of two slave states, had the mortification of finding themselves again, not only recorded as slaves for life, but also a premium paid upon them, professedly to aid in establishing others of their fellow beings in a free republic on the coast of Africa; but the hand of God seems to have been heavy upon the man who could plan such a stratagem to wrong his fellows.

The immense fortune he possessed when I left him (bating one thousand dollars I brought with me in my own body), and which he seems to have retained till that time, began to fly, and in a few years he was insolvent, so that he was unable to hold the family, and was compelled to think of selling them again. About this time I heard of their state by an underground railroad passenger, who came from that neighborhood, and resolved to make an effort to obtain the freedom of my parents, and to relieve myself from liability. For this purpose, after arranging for the means to purchase, I employed counsel to make a definite offer for my parents and myself. To his proposal, the following evasive and offensive answer was returned.

JANUARY 12TH, 1846

J. H——, Esq.

Sir,—Your letter is before me. The ungrateful servant in whose behalf you write, merits no clemency from me. He was guilty of theft when he departed, for which I hope he has made due amends. I have heard he was a respectable man, and calculated to do some good to his fellow-beings. Servants are selling from five hundred and fifty to seven hundred dollars, I will take five hundred and fifty dollars, and liberate him. If my proposition is acceded to, and the money lodged in Baltimore, I will execute the necessary instrument, and deliver it in Baltimore, to be given up on payment being made.

Yours, &c.,

_____

Jim was a first-rate mechanic (blacksmith) and was worth to me one thousand dollars.

Here he not only refuses to account for my parents, by including them in his return and proposition, but he at the same time attempts to intimidate me by mooting the charge of theft.

I confess I was not only surprised, but mortified, at this result. The hope of being once more united to parents whom I had not seen for sixteen years, and whom I still loved dearly, had so excited my mind that I disarranged my business relations, disposed of a valuable library of four hundred volumes, and by additional aid obtained among the liberal people of Jamaica, I was prepared to give the extravagant sum of five hundred dollars each for myself, and my father and mother. This I was willing to do, not because I approve of the principle involved as a general rule. But supposing that, as my former master was now an old man not far from his grave (about which I was not mistaken), and as he knew, by his own shewing, that I was able to do some good, he would be inclined, whatever might have been our former relations and misunderstandings, to meet my reasonable desire to see my parents, and to part this world in reconciliation with each other, as well as with God. I should have rejoiced had his temper permitted him to accede to my offer. But I thought it too bad, a free man of Jesus Christ, living on "free soil," to give a man five hundred dollars for the privilege of being let alone, and to be branded as a thief into the bargain, and that too after I had served him twenty prime years, without the benefit of being taught so much as the alphabet.

I wrote him with my own hand, sometime after this, stating that no proposition would be acceded to by me, which did not include my parents; and likewise fix the sum for myself more reasonable, and also retract the offensive charge; to this he maintained a dignified silence. The means I had acquired by the contributions of kind friends to redeem myself, I laid by, in case the worst should come; and that designed for the purchase of my parents, I used in another kind of operation, as the result of which, my father and two brothers are now in Canada. My mother was sold a second time, south, but she was eventually found. Several of my sisters married free men, who purchased their liberty; and three brothers are owned, by what may be called conscience slaveholders, who hold slaves only for a term of years. My old master has since died; my mother and he are now in the other world together; she is at rest from him. Sometime after his death, I received information from a gentleman, intimate with his heirs (who are principally females), that the reduced state of the family, afforded not only a good opportunity to obtain a release upon reasonable terms, but also to render the children of my oppressor some pecuniary aid; and much as I had suffered, I must confess this latter was the stronger motive with me, for acceding to their offer made by him.

I have many other deeply interesting particulars touching our family history, but I have detailed as many as prudence will permit, on account of those members who are yet south of Mason and Dixon's line.

I have faith in the hand that has dealt with us so strangely, that all our remaining members will in time be brought together; and then the case may merit a reviewed and enlarged edition of this tract, when other important matter will be inserted.

Chapter 7. The Feeding and Clothing of the Slaves in the Part of Maryland Where I Lived, &c.

THE SLAVES are generally fed upon salt pork, herrings, and Indian corn.

The manner of dealing it out to them is as follows: Each working man, on Monday morning, goes to the cellar of the master where the provisions are kept, and where the overseer takes his stand with someone to assist him, when he, with a pair of steel-yards, weighs out to every man the amount of three and a half pounds, to last him till the ensuing Monday—allowing him just half a pound per day. Once in a few weeks there is a change made, by which, instead of the three and a half pounds of pork, each man receives twelve herrings, allowing two a day. The only bread kind the slaves have is that made of Indian meal. In some of the lower counties, the masters usually give their slaves the corn in the ear; and they have to grind it for themselves by night at hand mills. But my master had a quantity sent to the grist mill at a time, to be ground into coarse meal, and kept it in a large chest in his cellar, where the woman who cooked for the boys could get it daily. This was baked in large loaves, called "steel poun bread." Sometimes as a change it was made into "Johnny Cake," and then at others into mush.

The slaves had no butter, coffee, tea, or sugar; occasionally they were allowed milk, but not statedly; the only exception to this statement was the "harvest provisions." In harvest, when cutting the grain, which lasted from two to three weeks in the heat of summer, they were allowed some fresh meat, rice, sugar, and coffee; and also their allowance of whiskey.

At the beginning of winter, each slave had one pair of coarse shoes and stockings, one pair of pantaloons, and a jacket.

At the beginning of the summer, he had two pair of coarse linen pantaloons and two shirts.

Once in a number of years, each slave, or each man and his wife, had one coarse blanket and enough coarse linen for a "bed-tick." He never had any bedstead or other furniture kind. The men had no hats, waistcoats or handkerchiefs given them, or the women any bonnets. These they had to contrive for themselves. Each laboring man had a small "patch" of ground allowed him; from this he was expected to furnish himself and his boys hats, &c. These patches they had to work by night; from these, also, they had to raise their own provisions, as no potatoes, cabbage, &c., were allowed them from the plantation. Years ago the slaves were in the habit of raising broom-corn, and making brooms to supply the market in the towns; but now of later years great quantities of these and other articles, such as scrubbing brushes, wooden trays, mats, baskets, and straw hats, which the slaves made, are furnished by the shakers and other small manufacturers, from the free states of the north.

Neither my master or any other master, within my acquaintance, made any provisions for the religious instruction of his slaves. They were not worked on the Sabbath. One of the "boys" was required to stay at home and "feed," that is, take care of the stock, every Sabbath; the rest went to see their friends. Those men whose families were on other plantations usually spent the Sabbath with them; some would lie about at home and rest themselves.

When it was pleasant weather my master would ride "into town" to church, but I never knew him to say a word to one of us about going to church, or about our obligations to God, or a future state. But there were a number of pious slaves in our neighborhood, and several of these my master owned; one of these was an exhorter. He was not connected with a religious body, but used to speak every Sabbath in some part of the neighborhood. When slaves died, their remains were usually consigned to the grave without any ceremony; but this old gentleman, wherever he heard of a slave having been buried in that way, would send notice from plantation to plantation, calling the slaves together at the grave on the Sabbath, where he'd sing, pray, and exhort. I have known him to go ten or fifteen miles voluntarily to attend these services. He could not read, and I never heard him refer to any Scripture, and state and discourse upon any fundamental doctrine of the gospel; but he knew a number of "spiritual songs by heart," of these he would give two lines at a time very exact, set and lead the tune himself; he would pray with great fervor, and his exhortations were amongst the most impressive I have heard.

The Methodists at one time attempted to evangelize the slaves in our neighborhood, but the effort was sternly resisted by the masters. They held a Camp Meeting in the neighborhood, where many of the slaves attended. But one of their preachers, for addressing words of comfort to the slaves, was arrested and tried for his life.

My master was very active in this disgraceful affair, but the excellent man, Rev. Mr. G., was acquitted and escaped out of their hands. Still, it was deemed by his brethren to be imprudent for him to preach any more in the place, as some of the more reckless masters swore violence against him. This good man's name is remembered dearly, till this day, by slaves in that county. I met with a fugitive about a year ago, who remembered distinctly the words spoken by Mr. G., and by which his own mind was awakened to a sense of the value of his soul. He said, in the course of his preaching, addressing himself to the slaves, "You have precious immortal souls, that are worth far more to you than your bodies are to your masters"; or words to that effect. But while these words interested many slaves, they also made many masters exceedingly angry, and they tortured his words into an attempt to excite the slaves to rebellion.

Some of my master's slaves who had families were regularly married, and others were not; the law makes no provision for such marriages, and the only provision made by the master was, that they should obtain his leave. In some cases, after obtaining leave to take his wife, the slave would ask further leave to go to a minister and be married. I never knew him to deny such a request, and yet, in those cases where the slave did not ask it, he never required him to be married by a minister. Of course, no Bibles, Tracts, or religious books of any kind, were ever given to the slaves; and no ministers or religious instructors were ever known to visit our plantation at any time, either in sickness or in health. When a slave was sick, my master being himself a physician, sometimes attended, and sometimes he called other physicians. Slaves frequently sickened and died, but I never knew any provision made to administer to them the comforts, or to offer to them the hopes of the gospel, or to their friends after their death.

There is no one feature of slavery to which the mind recurs with more gloomy impressions, than to its disastrous influence upon the families of the masters, physically, pecuniarily, and mentally.

It seems to destroy families as by a powerful blight, large and opulent slaveholding families often vanish like a group of shadows at the third or fourth generation. This fact arrested my attention some years before I escaped from slavery, and of course before I had any enlightened views of the moral character of the system. As far back as I can recollect, indeed, it was a remark among slaves, that every generation of slaveholders are more and more inferior. There were several large and powerful families in our county, including that of my master, which affords to my mind a melancholy illustration of this remark. One of the wealthiest slaveholders in the county, was General R., a brother-in-law to my master. This man owned a large and highly valuable tract of land, called R.'s Manor. I do not know how many slaves he owned, but the number was large. He lived in a splendid mansion, and drove his coach and four. He was for some years a member of Congress. He had a numerous family of children.

The family showed no particular signs of decay until he had married a second time, and had considerably increased his number of children. It then became evident that his older children were not educated for active business, and were only destined to be a charge. Of sons (seven or eight), not one of them reached the eminence once occupied by the father. The only one that approached to it, was the eldest, who became an officer in the navy, and obtained the doubtful glory of being killed in the Mexican war.

General R. himself ran through his vast estate, died intemperate, and left a widow and large number of daughters, some minors, destitute, and none of his sons fitted for any employment but in the army and navy.

Slaves have a superstitious dread of passing the dilapidated dwelling of a man who has been guilty of great cruelties to his slaves, and who is dead, or moved away. I never felt this dread deeply but once, and that was one Sabbath about sunset, as I crossed the yard of General R.'s residence, which was about two miles from us, after he had been compelled to leave it.

To see the once fine smooth gravel walks, overgrown with grass—the redundances of the shrubbery neglected—the once finely painted pricket fences rusted and fallen down—a fine garden in splendid ruins—the lofty ceiling of the mansion thickly curtained with cobwebs—the spacious apartments abandoned, while the only music heard within as a substitute for the voices of family glee that once filled it, was the crying cricket and cockroaches! Ignorant slave as I was at that time, I could but pause for a moment, and recur in silent horror to the fact, that a strange reverse of fortune had lately driven from that proud mansion a large and once opulent family. What advantage was it now to the members of that family, that the father and head had for near half a century stood high in the counsels of the state, and had the benefit of the unrequited toil of hundreds of his fellow men, when they were already grappling with the annoyances of that poverty, which he had entailed upon others.

My master's family, in wealth and influence, was not inferior to General R.'s originally. His father was a member of the convention that framed the present constitution of the state; he was, also, for some years chief justice of the state.

My master was never equal to his father, although he stood high at one time. He once lacked but a few votes of being elected Governor of the state; he once sat in the Assembly, and was generally a leading man in his own county. His influence was found to be greatest when exerted in favor of any measure in regard to the control of slaves. He was the first mover in several cruel and rigid municipal regulations in the county, which prohibited slaves from going over a certain number of miles from their masters' places on the Sabbath, and from being seen about the town. He once instigated the authorities of the town where he attended service, to break up a Sabbath-school some humane members of the Methodist and Lutheran denominations had set up to teach the free Negroes, lest the slaves should get some benefit of it.

But there was still a wider contrast between my master and his own children, eight in number, when I left him. His eldest daughter, the flower of the family, married a miserable and reckless gambler. His eldest son was kind-hearted, and rather a favorite with the slaves on that account; but he had no strength of mind or weight of character. His education was limited, and he had no disposition or tact for business of any kind. He died at thirty-six, intestate, leaving his second wife (a sister to his father's second wife) with several orphan children, a widow with a small estate deeply embarrassed. The second son was once sent to West Point to fit for an officer. After being there a short time, however, he became unsteady, and commenced the study of medicine, but he soon gave that up and preferred to live at home and flog the slaves; and by them was cordially dreaded and disliked, and among themselves he was vulgarly nicknamed on account of his cruel and filthy habits.

These two families will afford a fair illustration of the gloomy history of many others that I could name. This decline of slave-holding families is a subject of observation and daily remark among slaves; they are led to observe every change in the pecuniary, moral, and social state of the families they belong to, from the fact, that as the old master declines, or as his children are married off, they are expecting to fall into their hands, or in case of insolvency on the part of the old master, they expect to be sold; in either case, it involves a change of master—a subject to which they cannot be indifferent. And it is very rarely the case that a slave's condition is benefited by passing from the old master into the hands of one of his children. Owing to the causes I have mentioned, the decline is so rapid and marked, in almost every point of view, that the children of slaveholders are universally inferior to themselves, mentally, morally, physically, as well as pecuniarily, especially so in the latter point of view; and this is a matter of most vital concern to the slaves. The young master not being able to own as many slaves as his father, usually works what he has more severely, and being more liable to embarrassment, the slaves' liability to be sold at an early day is much greater. For the same reason, slaves have a deep interest, generally, in the marriage of a young mistress. Very generally the daughters of slaveholders marry inferior men; men who seek to better their own condition by a wealthy connection. The slaves who pass into the hands of the young master has had some chance to become acquainted with his character, bad as it may be; but the young mistress brings her slaves a new, and sometimes an unknown master. Sometimes these are the sons of already broken-down slaveholders. In other cases they are adventurers from the North who remove to the South, and who readily become the most cruel masters.

Appendix

THESE TWO LETTERS are simply introduced to show what the state of my feeling was with reference to slavery at the time they were written. I had just heard several facts with regard to my parents, which had awakened my mind to great excitement.

TO MY FATHER, MOTHER, BROTHERS, AND SISTERS
The following was written in 1844:

DEARLY BELOVED IN BONDS,

About seventeen long years have now rolled away, since in the Providence of Almighty God, I left your embraces, and set out upon a daring adventure in search of freedom. Since that time, I have felt most severely the loss of the sun and moon and eleven stars from my social sky. Many, many a thick cloud of anguish has pressed my brow and sent deep down into my soul the bitter waters of sorrow in consequence. And you have doubtless had your troubles and anxious seasons also about your fugitive star.

I have learned that some of you have been sold, and again taken back by Colonel ———. How many of you are living and together, I cannot tell. My great grief is, lest you should have suffered this or some additional punishment on account of my *Exodus.*

I indulge the hope that it will afford you some consolation to know that your son and brother is yet alive. That God has dealt wonderfully and kindly with me in all my way. He has made me a Christian, and a Christian Minister, and thus I have drawn my support and comfort from that blessed Saviour, who came *to preach good tidings unto the meek, to bind up the broken hearted, to proclaim liberty to the captives, and the opening of the prison to them that are bound. To proclaim the acceptable year of the Lord and the day of vengeance of our God; to comfort all that mourn. To appoint unto them that mourn in Zion, to give unto them beauty for ashes, the oil of joy for mourning, the garment of praise for the spirit of heaviness, that they might be called trees of righteousness, the planting of the Lord that he might be glorified.*

If the course I took in leaving a condition which had become intolerable to me, has been made the occasion of making that condition worse to you in any way, I do most heartily regret such a change for the worse on your part. As I have no means, however, of knowing if such be the fact, so I have no means of making atonement, but by sincere prayer to Almighty God in your behalf, and also by taking this method of offering to you these consolations of the gospel to which I have just referred, and which I have found to be pre-eminently my own stay and support. My dear father and mother, I have very often wished, while administering the Holy Ordinance of Baptism to some scores of children brought forward by doting parents, that I could see you with yours among the number. And you, my brothers and sisters, while teaching hundreds of children and youths in schools over which I have been placed, what unspeakable delight I should have had in having you among the number; you may all judge of my feeling for these past years, when while preaching from Sabbath to Sabbath to congregations, I have not been so fortunate as even to see father, mother, brother, sister, uncle, aunt, nephew, niece, or cousin in my congregations. While visiting the sick, going to the house of mourning, and burying the dead, I have been a constant mourner for you. My sorrow has been that I know you are not in possession of those hallowed means of grace. I am thankful to you for those mild and gentle traits of character which you took such care to enforce upon me in my youthful days. As an evidence that I prize both you and them, I may say that at the age of thirty-seven, I find them as valuable as any lessons I have learned, nor am I ashamed to let it be known to the world, that I am the son of a bond man and a bond woman.

Let me urge upon you the fundamental truths of the Gospel of the Son of God. Let repentance towards God and faith in our Lord Jesus Christ have their perfect work in you, I beseech you. Do not be prejudiced against the gospel because it may be seemingly twisted into a support of slavery. The gospel rightly understood, taught, received, felt, and practised, is anti-slavery as it is anti-sin. Just so far and so fast as the true spirit of the gospel obtains in the land, and especially in the lives of the oppressed, will the spirit of slavery sicken and become powerless like the serpent with his head pressed beneath the fresh leaves of the prickly ash of the forest.

There is not a solitary decree of the immaculate God that has been concerned in the ordination of slavery, nor does any possible development of his holy will sanctify it.

He has permitted us to be enslaved according to the invention of wicked men, instigated by the devil, with intention to bring good out of the evil, but He does not, He cannot approve of it. He has no need to approve of it, even on account of the good which He will bring out of it, for He could have brought about that very good in some other way.

God is never straitened; He is never at a loss for means to work. Could He not have made this a great and wealthy nation without making its riches to consist in our blood, bones, and souls? And could He not also have given the gospel to us without making us slaves?

My friends, let us then, in our afflictions, embrace and hold fast the gospel. The gospel is the fulness of God. We have the glorious and total weight of God's moral character in our side of the scale.

The wonderful purple stream which flowed for the healing of the nations, has a branch for us. Nay, is Christ divided? "The grace of God that bringeth salvation hath appeared to (for) all men, teaching us that denying ungodliness and worldly lust, we should live soberly, righteously, and godly in this present world, looking for that blessed hope and glorious appearing of the great God and our Saviour Jesus Christ, who gave himself for us that he might redeem us from all iniquity, and purify unto himself a peculiar people, zealous of good works" (Titus 2:11–14).

But you say you have not the privilege of hearing of this gospel of which I speak. I know it; and this is my great grief. But you shall have it; I will send it to you by my humble prayer; I can do it; I will beg our heavenly Father, and he will preach this gospel to you in his holy providence.

You, dear father and mother, cannot have much longer to live in this troublesome and oppressive world; you cannot bear the yoke much longer. And as you approach another world, how desirable it is that you should have the prospect of a different destiny from what you have been called to endure in this world during a long life.

But it is the gospel that sets before you the hope of such a blessed rest as is spoken of in the word of God (Job 3:17, 19): "There the wicked cease from troubling, and there the weary be at rest; there the prisoners rest together; they hear not the voice of the oppressors. The small and great are there; and the servant is free from his master."

Father, I know that thy eyes are dim with age and weary with weeping, but look, dear father, yet a little while toward that haven. Look unto Jesus, "the author and finisher of thy faith," for the moment of thy happy deliverance is at hand.

Mother, dear mother, I know, I feel, mother, the pangs of thy bleeding heart, that thou hast endured, during so many years of vexation. Thy agonies are by a genuine son-like sympathy mine; I will, I must, I do share daily in those agonies of thine. But I sincerely hope that with me you bear your agonies to Christ who carries our sorrows.

O come then with me, my beloved family, of weary heart-broken and care-worn ones, to Jesus Christ, "casting all your care upon him, for he careth for you" (1 Peter 5:7).

With these words of earnest exhortation, joined with fervent prayer to God that He may smooth your rugged way, lighten your burden, and give a happy issue out of all your troubles, I must bid you adieu.

Your son and brother,

JAS. P.

Alias J. W. C. PENNINGTON

TO COLONEL F——— T———, OF H———, WASHINGTON COUNTY, MD. 1844

DEAR SIR,

It is now, as you are aware, about seventeen years since I left your house and service, at the age of twenty. Up to that time, I was, according to your rule and claim, your slave. Till the age of seven years, I was, of course, of little or no service to you. At that age, however, you hired me out, and for three years I earned my support; at the age of ten years, you took me to your place again, and in a short time after you put me to work at the blacksmith's trade, at which, together with the carpentering trade, &c., I served you peaceably until the day I left you with exception of the short time you had sold me to S——— H———, Esq., for seven hundred dollars. It is important for me to say to you, that I have no consciousness of having done you any wrong. I called you master when I was with you from the mere force of circumstances; but I never regarded you as my master. The nature which God gave me did not allow me to believe that you had any more right to me than I had to you, and that was just none at all. And from an early age, I had intentions to free myself from your claim. I never consulted anyone about it; I had no advisers or instigators; I kept my own counsel entirely concealed in my own bosom. I never meditated any evil to your person or property, but I regarded you as my oppressor, and I deemed it my duty to get out of your hands by peaceable means.

I was always obedient to your commands. I labored for you diligently at all times. I acted with fidelity in any matter which you entrusted me. As you sometimes saw fit to entrust me with considerable money, to buy tools or materials, not a cent was ever coveted or kept.

During the time I served you in the capacity of blacksmith, your materials were used economically, your work was done expeditiously, and in the very best style, a style second to no smith in your neighborhood. In short, sir, you know well that my habits from early life were advantageous to you. Drinking, gambling, fighting, &c., were not my habits. On Sabbaths, holidays, &c., I was frequently at your service, when not even your body servant was at home.

Times and times again, I have gone on Sunday afternoon to H——, six miles, after your letters and papers, when it was as much my privilege to be *"out of the way,"* as it was C——.

But what treatment did you see fit to return me for all this? You, in the most unfeeling manner, abused my father for no cause but speaking a word to you, as a man would speak to his fellow man, for the sake simply of a better understanding.

You vexed my mother, and because she, as a tender mother would do, showed solicitude for the virtue of her daughters, you threatened her in an insulting brutal manner.

You abused my brother and sister without cause, and in like manner you did to myself; you surmised evil against me. You struck me with your walking cane, called me insulting names, threatened me, swore at me, and became more and more wrathy in your conduct, and at the time I quitted your place, I had good reason to believe that you were meditating serious evil against me.

Since I have been out of your hands, I have been signally favored of God, whence I infer that in leaving you, I acted strictly in accordance with his holy will. I have a conscience void of offense towards God and towards all men, yourself not excepted. And I verily believe that I have performed a sacred duty to God and myself, and a kindness to you, in taking the blood of my soul peaceably off your soul. And now, dear sir, having spoken somewhat pointedly, I would, to convince you of my perfect good will towards you, in the most kind and respectful terms, remind you of your coming destiny. You are now over seventy years of age, pressing on to eternity with the weight of these seventy years upon you. Is not this enough without the blood of some half-score of souls?

You are aware that your right to property in man is now disputed by the civilized world. You are fully aware, also, that the question, whether the Bible sanctions slavery, has distinctly divided this nation in sentiment. On the side of Biblical Antislavery, we have many of the most learned, wise, and holy men in the land. If the Bible affords no sanction to slavery (and I claim that it cannot), then it must be a sin of the deepest dye; and can you, sir, think to go to God in hope with a sin of such magnitude upon your soul?

But admitting that the question is yet doubtful (which I do only for the sake of argument), still, sir, you will have the critical hazard of this doubt pressing, in no very doubtful way, upon your declining years, as you descend the long and tedious hill of life.

Would it not seem to be exceedingly undesirable to close an eventful probation of seventy or eighty years and leave your reputation among posterity suspended upon so doubtful an issue? But what, my dear sir, is a reputation among posterity, who are but worms, compared with a destiny in the world of spirits? And it is in light of that destiny that I would now have you look at this subject. You and I, and all that you claim as your slaves, are in a state of probation; our great business is to serve God under His righteous moral government. Master and slave are the subjects of that government, bound by its immutable requirements, and liable to its sanctions in the next world, though enjoying its forbearance in this. You will pardon me then for pressing this point in earnest good faith. You should, at this stage, review your life without political bias, or adherence to long cherished prejudices, and remember that you are soon to meet those whom you have held, and do hold in slavery, at the awful bar of the impartial Judge of all who doeth right. Then what will become of your own doubtful claims? What will be done with those doubts that agitated your mind years ago; will you answer for threatening, swearing, and using the cowhide among your slaves?

What will become of those long groans and unsatisfied complaints of your slaves, for vexing them with insulting words, placing them in the power of dogish and abusive overseers, or under your stripling, misguided, hot-headed son, to drive and whip at pleasure, and for selling parts or whole families to Georgia? They will all meet you at that bar. Uncle James True, Charles Cooper, Aunt Jenny, and the native Africans; Jeremiah, London, and Donmore, have already gone ahead, and only wait your arrival—Sir, I shall meet you there. The account between us for the first twenty years of my life, will have a definite character upon which one or the other will be able to make out a case.

Upon such a review as this, sir, you will, I am quite sure, see the need of seriousness. I assure you that the thought of meeting you in eternity and before the dread tribunal of God, with a complaint in my mouth against you, is to me of most weighty and solemn character. And you will see that the circumstances from which this thought arises are of equal moment to yourself. Can the pride of leaving your children possessed of long slave states, or the policy of sustaining in the state the institution of slavery, justify you in overlooking a point of moment to your future happiness?

What excuse could you offer at the bar of God, favored as you have been with the benefits of a refined education, and through a long life with the gospel of love, should you, when arraigned there, find that you have, all your life long, labored under a great mistake in regard to slavery, and that in this mistake you had died, and only lifted up your eyes in the light of eternity to be corrected, when it was too late to be corrected in any other way.

I could wish to address you (being bred, born, and raised in your family) *as a father in Israel, or as an older brother in Christ, but I cannot; mockery is a sin.* I can only say then, dear sir, farewell, till I meet you at the bar of God, where Jesus, who died for us, will judge between us. Now his blood can wash out our stain, break down the middle wall of partition, and reconcile us not only to God but to each other, then the word of his mouth, the sentence will set us at one. As for myself, I am quite ready to meet you face to face at the bar of God. I have done you no wrong; I have nothing to fear when we both fall into the hands of the just God.

I beseech you, dear sir, to look well and consider this matter soundly. In yonder world you can have no slaves—you can be no man's master—you can neither sell, buy, or whip, or drive. Are you then, by sustaining the relation of a slaveholder, forming a character to dwell with God in peace?

With kind regards,

I am, sir, yours respectfully,

J. W. C. PENNINGTON

RUNNING A THOUSAND MILES
FOR FREEDOM

OR

THE ESCAPE OF
WILLIAM AND ELLEN CRAFT
FROM SLAVERY

❖   ❖   ❖   ❖   ❖   ❖   ❖   ❖   ❖

The story of William and Ellen Craft had been told, repeated in fragments, and retold among proslavery people as well as by Abolitionists for at least a decade before the Crafts were in a position to publish their narrative. Apparently no two slaves in their flight for freedom ever thrilled the world so much as did this handsome young couple. It began, as the narrative indicates, when the near-white wife, disguised in man's clothes as a young planter, and her young black mate left Macon, Georgia, during the Christmas holidays of 1848. When the ruse succeeded, they became heroes, about whom speeches were made and poems written.

Remembering Héloise and Abelard, Tristram and Isolde, readers of historical fiction might have noted that here was romance with dimensions which Shakespeare might not have missed, and which President James K. Polk did not, altogether. Evidently infuriated, if we can believe the *Liberator*'s report, Polk declared after the passage of the Fugitive Slave Law that he would employ military force for their capture. By then, however, they were in England, where they were in a school founded by Lady Byron for the benefit of rural children. A story with enormous possibilities may thus have missed by the date of its publication the most favorable conjunction with historical events of the period, though its essential drama survives.

—ARNA BONTEMPS

Preface

HAVING HEARD while in slavery that "God made of one blood all nations of men," and also that the American Declaration of Independence says, that "We hold these truths to be self-evident, that all men are created equal, that they are endowed by their Creator with certain inalienable Rights, that among these are Life, Liberty, and the pursuit of Happiness"; we could not understand by what right we were held as "chattels." Therefore, we felt perfectly justified in undertaking the dangerous and exciting task of "running a thousand miles" in order to obtain those rights which are so vividly set forth in the Declaration.

I beg those who would know the particulars of our journey, to peruse these pages.

This book is not intended as a full history of the life of my wife, nor of myself; but merely as an account of our escape; together with other matter which I hope may be the means of creating in some minds a deeper abhorrence of the sinful and abominable practice of enslaving and brutifying our fellow-creatures.

Without stopping to write a long apology for offering this little volume to the public, I shall commence at once to pursue my simple story.

W. CRAFT

12 CAMBRIDGE ROAD
HAMMERSMITH
LONDON

Part 1

God gave us only over beast, fish, fowl,
Dominion absolute; that right we hold
By his donation. But man over man
He made not lord; such title to himself
Reserving, human left from human free.

MILTON.

MY WIFE AND MYSELF were born in different towns in the State of
Georgia, which is one of the principal slave States. It is true, our
condition as slaves was not by any means the worst; but the mere
idea that we were held as chattels, and deprived of all legal rights
—the thought that we had to give up our hard earnings to a
tyrant, to enable him to live in idleness and luxury—the thought
that we could not call the bones and sinews that God gave us
our own: but above all, the fact that another man had the power
to tear from our cradle the new-born babe and sell it in the
shambles like a brute, and then scourge us if we dared to lift
a finger to save it from such a fate, haunted us for years.

But in December 1848 a plan suggested itself that proved quite
successful, and in eight days after it was first thought of we were
free from the horrible trammels of slavery, rejoicing and praising
God in the glorious sunshine of liberty.

My wife's first master was her father, and her mother his slave,
and the latter is still the slave of his widow.

Notwithstanding my wife being of African extraction on her
mother's side, she is almost white—in fact, she is so nearly so
that the tyrannical old lady to whom she first belonged became
so annoyed, at finding her frequently mistaken for a child of the
family, that she gave her when eleven years of age to a daughter,
as a wedding present. This separated my wife from her mother,
and also from several other dear friends. But the incessant cruelty
of her old mistress made the change of owners or treatment so
desirable, that she did not grumble much at this cruel separation.

It may be remembered that slavery in America is not at all
confined to persons of any particular complexion; there are a very
large number of slaves as white as anyone; but as the evidence of
a slave is not admitted in court against a free white person, it is
almost impossible for a white child, after having been kidnapped

and sold into or reduced to slavery, in a part of the country where it is not known (as often is the case), ever to recover its freedom.

I have myself conversed with several slaves who told me that their parents were white and free; but that they were stolen away from them and sold when quite young. As they could not tell their address, and also as the parents did not know what had become of their lost and dear little ones, of course all traces of each other were gone.

The following facts are sufficient to prove, that he who has the power, and is inhuman enough to trample upon the sacred rights of the weak, cares nothing for race or color:

In March 1818, three ships arrived at New Orleans, bringing several hundred German emigrants from the province of Alsace, on the lower Rhine. Among them were Daniel Muller and his two daughters, Dorothea and Salomé, whose mother had died on the passage. Soon after his arrival, Muller, taking with him his two daughters, both young children, went up the river to Attakapas parish, to work on the plantation of John F. Miller. A few weeks later, his relatives, who had remained at New Orleans, learned that he had died of the fever of the country. They immediately sent for the two girls; but they had disappeared, and the relatives, notwithstanding repeated and persevering inquiries and researches, could find no traces of them. They were at length given up for dead. Dorothea was never again heard of; nor was anything known of Salomé from 1818 till 1843.

In the summer of that year, Madame Karl, a German woman who had come over in the same ship with the Mullers, was passing through a street in New Orleans, and accidentally saw Salomé in a wine-shop, belonging to Louis Belmonte, by whom she was held as a slave. Madame Karl recognized her at once, and carried her to the house of another German woman, Mrs. Schubert, who was Salomé's cousin and godmother, and who no sooner set eyes on her than, without having any intimation that the discovery had been previously made, she unhesitatingly exclaimed, "My God! here is the long-lost Salomé Muller."

The *Law Reported,* in its account of this case, says:

> As many of the German emigrants of 1818 as could be gathered together were brought to the house of Mrs. Schubert, and every

one of the number who had any recollection of the little girl upon the passage, or any acquaintance with her father and mother, immediately identified the woman before them as the long-lost Salomé Muller. By all these witnesses, who appeared at the trial, the identity was fully established. The family resemblance in every feature was declared to be so remarkable, that some of the witnesses did not hesitate to say that they should know her among ten thousand; that they were as certain the plaintiff was Salomé Muller, the daughter of Daniel and Dorothea Muller, as of their own existence.

Among the witnesses who appeared in Court was the midwife who had assisted at the birth of Salomé. She testified to the existence of certain peculiar marks upon the body of the child, which were found, exactly as described, by the surgeons who were appointed by the Court to make an examination for the purpose.

There was no trace of African descent in any feature of Salomé Muller. She had long, straight, black hair, hazel eyes, thin lips, and a Roman nose. The complexion of her face and neck was as dark as that of the darkest brunette. It appears, however, that, during the twenty-five years of her servitude, she had been exposed to the sun's rays in the hot climate of Louisiana, with head and neck unsheltered, as is customary with the female slaves, while laboring in the cotton or the sugar field. Those parts of her person which had been shielded from the sun were comparatively white.

Belmonte, the pretended owner of the girl, had obtained possession of her by an act of sale from John F. Miller, the planter in whose service Salomé's father died. This Miller was a man of consideration and substance, owning large sugar estates, and bearing a high reputation for honor and honesty, and for indulgent treatment of his slaves. It was testified on the trial that he had said to Belmonte, a few weeks after the sale of Salomé, "that she was white, and had as much right to her freedom as anyone, and was only to be retained in slavery by care and kind treatment." The broker who negotiated the sale from Miller to Belmonte, in 1838, testified in Court that he then thought, and still thought, that the girl was white!

The case was elaborately argued on both sides, but was at

length decided in favor of the girl, by the Supreme Court declaring that "she was free and white, and therefore unlawfully held in bondage."

The Rev. George Bourne, of Virginia, in his *Picture of Slavery,* published in 1834, relates the case of a white boy who, at the age of seven, was stolen from his home in Ohio, tanned and stained in such a way that he could not be distinguished from a person of color, and then sold as a slave in Virginia. At the age of twenty, he made his escape, by running away, and happily succeeded in rejoining his parents.

I have known worthless white people to sell their own free children into slavery; and, as there are good-for-nothing white as well as colored persons everywhere, no one, perhaps, will wonder at such inhuman transactions: particularly in the Southern States of America, where I believe there is a greater want of humanity and high principle amongst the whites than among any other civilized people in the world.

I know that those who are not familiar with the working of "the peculiar institution," can scarcely imagine anyone so totally devoid of all natural affection as to sell his own offspring into returnless bondage. But Shakespeare, that great observer of human nature, says:

> With caution judge of probabilities.
> Things deemed unlikely, e'en impossible,
> Experience often shows us to be true.

My wife's new mistress was decidedly more humane than the majority of her class. My wife has always given her credit for not exposing her to many of the worst features of slavery. For instance, it is a common practice in the slave States for ladies, when angry with their maids, to send them to the calaboose, sugar-house, or to some other place established for the purpose of punishing slaves, and have them severely flogged; and I am sorry it is a fact, that the villains to whom those defenseless creatures are sent, not only flog them as they are ordered, but frequently compel them to submit to the greatest indignity. Oh! if there is any one thing under the wide canopy of heaven horrible enough to stir a man's soul, and to make his very blood boil, it is the thought of his dear wife, his unprotected sister, or his young and virtuous daughters, struggling to save themselves from falling a prey to such demons!

It always appears strange to me that anyone who was not born a slaveholder, and steeped to the very core in the demoralizing atmosphere of the Southern States, can in any way palliate slavery. It is still more surprising to see virtuous ladies looking with patience upon, and remaining indifferent to, the existence of a system that exposes nearly two millions of their own sex in the manner I have mentioned, and that too in a professedly free and Christian country. There is, however, great consolation in knowing that God is just, and will not let the oppressor of the weak, and the spoiler of the virtuous, escape unpunished here and hereafter.

I believe a similar retribution to that which destroyed Sodom is hanging over the slaveholders. My sincere prayer is that they may not provoke God, by persisting in a reckless course of wickedness, to pour out his consuming wrath upon them.

I must now return to our history.

My old master had the reputation of being a very humane and Christian man, but he thought nothing of selling my poor old father and dear aged mother, at separate times, to different persons, to be dragged off never to behold each other again, till summoned to appear before the great tribunal of heaven. But, oh! what a happy meeting it will be on that great day for those faithful souls. I say a happy meeting, because I never saw persons more devoted to the service of God than they. But how will the case stand with those reckless traffickers in human flesh and blood, who plunged the poisonous dagger of separation into those loving hearts which God had for so many years closely joined together —nay, sealed as it were with his own hands for the eternal courts of heaven? It is not for me to say what will become of those heartless tyrants. I must leave them in the hands of an all-wise and just God, who will, in his own good time, and in his own way, avenge the wrongs of his oppressed people.

My old master also sold a dear brother and a sister, in the same manner as he did my father and mother. The reason he assigned for disposing of my parents, as well as of several other aged slaves, was, that "they were getting old, and would soon become valueless in the market, and therefore he intended to sell off all the old stock, and buy in a young lot." A most disgraceful conclusion for a man to come to, who made such great professions of religion!

This shameful conduct gave me a thorough hatred, not for true Christianity, but for slaveholding piety.

My old master, then, wishing to make the most of the rest of his slaves, apprenticed a brother and myself out to learn trades: he to a blacksmith, and myself to a cabinetmaker. If a slave has a good trade, he will let or sell for more than a person without one, and many slaveholders have their slaves taught trades on this account. But before our time expired, my old master wanted money; so he sold my brother, and then mortgaged my sister, a dear girl about fourteen years of age, and myself, then about sixteen, to one of the banks, to get money to speculate in cotton. This we knew nothing of at the moment; but time rolled on, the money became due, my master was unable to meet his payments; so the bank had us placed upon the auction stand and sold to the highest bidder.

My poor sister was sold first: she was knocked down to a planter who resided at some distance in the country. Then I was called upon the stand. While the auctioneer was crying the bids, I saw the man that had purchased my sister getting her into a cart, to take her to his home. I at once asked a slave friend who was standing near the platform, to run and ask the gentleman if he would please to wait till I was sold, in order that I might have an opportunity of bidding her good-bye. He sent me word back that he had some distance to go, and could not wait.

I then turned to the auctioneer, fell upon my knees, and humbly prayed him to let me just step down and bid my last sister farewell. But, instead of granting me this request, he grasped me by the neck, and in a commanding tone of voice, and with a violent oath, exclaimed, "Get up! You can do the wench no good; therefore there is no use in your seeing her."

On rising, I saw the cart in which she sat moving slowly off; and, as she clasped her hands with a grasp that indicated despair, and looked pitifully round towards me, I also saw the large silent tears trickling down her cheeks. She made a farewell bow, and buried her face in her lap. This seemed more than I could bear.

It appeared to swell my aching heart to its utmost. But before I could fairly recover, the poor girl was gone; gone, and I have never had the good fortune to see her from that day to this! Perhaps I should have never heard of her again, had it not been for the untiring efforts of my good old mother, who became free a few years ago by purchase, and, after a great deal of difficulty, found my sister residing with a family in Mississippi. My mother at once wrote to me, informing me of the fact, and requesting me to do something to get her free; and I am happy to say that, partly by lecturing occasionally, and through the sale of an engraving of my wife in the disguise in which she escaped, together with the extreme kindness and generosity of Miss Burdett Coutts, Mr. George Richardson of Plymouth, and a few other friends, I have nearly accomplished this. It would be to me a great and ever-glorious achievement to restore my sister to our dear mother, from whom she was forcibly driven in early life.

I was knocked down to the cashier of the bank to which we were mortgaged, and ordered to return to the cabinet shop where I previously worked.

But the thought of the harsh auctioneer not allowing me to bid my dear sister farewell, sent red-hot indignation darting like lightning through every vein. It quenched my tears, and appeared to set my brain on fire, and made me crave for power to avenge our wrongs! But, alas! we were only slaves, and had no legal rights; consequently we were compelled to smother our wounded feelings, and crouch beneath the iron heel of despotism.

I must now give the account of our escape; but, before doing so, it may be well to quote a few passages from the fundamental laws of slavery; in order to give some idea of the legal as well as the social tyranny from which we fled.

According to the law of Louisiana, "A slave is one who is in the power of a master to whom he belongs. The master may sell him, dispose of his person, his industry, and his labor; he can do nothing, possess nothing, nor acquire anything but what must belong to his master."—*Civil Code, art.* 35.

In South Carolina it is expressed in the following language: "Slaves shall be deemed, sold, taken, reputed and judged in law to be *chattels personal* in the hands of their owners and possessors, and their executors, administrators, and assigns, *to all intents, constructions, and purposes whatsoever.—2 Brevard's Digest,* 229.

The Constitution of Georgia has the following (Art. 4, sec. 12): "Any person who shall maliciously dismember or deprive a slave of life, shall suffer such punishment as would be inflicted in case the like offense had been committed on a free white person, and on the like proof, except in case of insurrection of such slave, and unless SUCH DEATH SHOULD HAPPEN BY ACCIDENT IN GIVING SUCH SLAVE MODERATE CORRECTION."—*Prince's Digest,* 559.

I have known slaves to be beaten to death, but as they died under "moderate correction," it was quite lawful; and of course the murderers were not interfered with.

"If any slave, who shall be out of the house or plantation where such slave shall live, or shall be usually employed, or without some white person in company with such slave, shall *refuse to submit* to undergo the examination of *any white* person (let him be ever so drunk or crazy), it shall be lawful for such white person to pursue, apprehend, and moderately correct such slave; and if such slave shall assault and strike such white person, such slave may be *lawfully killed.*"—*2 Brevard's Digest,* 231.

"Provided always," says the law, "that such striking be not done by the command and in the defense of the person or property of the owner, or other person having the government of such slave; in which case the slave shall be wholly excused."

According to this law, if a slave, by the direction of his overseer, strike a white person who is beating said overseer's pig, "the slave shall be wholly excused." But, should the bondman, of his own accord, fight to defend his wife, or should his terrified daughter instinctively raise her hand and strike the wretch who attempts to violate her chastity, he or she shall, saith the model republican law, suffer death.

From having been myself a slave for nearly twenty-three years, I am quite prepared to say that the practical working of slavery is worse than the odious laws by which it is governed.

At an early age we were taken by the persons who held us as property to Macon, the largest town in the interior of the State of Georgia, at which place we became acquainted with each other for several years before our marriage; in fact, our marriage was postponed for some time simply because one of the unjust and worse than Pagan laws under which we lived compelled all children of slave mothers to follow their condition. That is to say, the father of the slave may be the President of the Republic; but if the mother should be a slave at the infant's birth, the poor child is ever legally doomed to the same cruel fate.

It is a common practice for gentlemen (if I may call them such), moving in the highest circles of society, to be the fathers of children by their slaves, whom they can and do sell with the greatest impunity; and the more pious, beautiful, and virtuous the girls are, the greater the price they bring, and that too for the most infamous purposes.

Any man with money (let him be ever such a rough brute) can buy a beautiful and virtuous girl, and force her to live with him in a criminal connection; and as the law says a slave shall have no higher appeal than the mere will of the master, she cannot escape, unless it be by flight or death.

In endeavoring to reconcile a girl to her fate, the master sometimes says that he would marry her if it was not unlawful.* However, he will always consider her to be his wife, and will treat her as such; and she, on the other hand, may regard him as her lawful husband; and if they have any children, they will be free and well educated.

I am in duty bound to add, that while a great majority of such men care nothing for the happiness of the women with whom they live, nor for the children of whom they are the fathers, there are those to be found, even in that heterogeneous mass of licentious monsters, who are true to their pledges. But as the woman and her children are legally the property of the man, who stands in the anomalous relation to them of husband and father, as well as master, they are liable to be seized and sold for his debts, should he become involved.

There are several cases on record where such persons have been sold and separated for life. I know of some myself, but I have only space to glance at one.

---

* It is unlawful in the slave States for anyone of purely European descent to intermarry with a person of African extraction; though a white man may live with as many colored women as he pleases without materially damaging his reputation in Southern society.

I knew a very humane and wealthy gentleman, that bought a woman, with whom he lived as his wife. They brought up a family of children, among whom were three nearly white, well-educated, and beautiful girls.

On the father being suddenly killed it was found that he had not left a will; but, as the family had always heard him say that he had no surviving relatives, they felt that their liberty and property were quite secured to them, and, knowing the insults to which they were exposed, now their protector was no more, they were making preparations to leave for a free State.

But, poor creatures, they were soon sadly undeceived. A villain residing at a distance, hearing of the circumstance, came forward and swore that he was a relative of the deceased; and as this man bore, or assumed, Mr. Slator's name, the case was brought before one of those horrible tribunals, presided over by a second Judge Jeffreys, and calling itself a court of justice, but before whom no colored person, nor an abolitionist, was ever known to get his full rights.

A verdict was given in favor of the plaintiff, whom the better portion of the community thought had wilfully conspired to cheat the family.

The heartless wretch not only took the ordinary property, but actually had the aged and friendless widow, and all her father-less children, except Frank, a fine young man about twenty-two years of age, and Mary, a very nice girl, a little younger than her brother, brought to the auction stand and sold to the highest bidder. Mrs. Slator had cash enough, that her husband and master left, to purchase the liberty of herself and children; but on her attempting to do so, the pusillanimous scoundrel, who had robbed them of their freedom, claimed the money as his property; and, poor creature, she had to give it up. According to law, as will be seen hereafter, a slave cannot own anything. The old lady never recovered from her sad affliction.

At the sale she was brought up first, and after being vulgarly criticized, in the presence of all her distressed family, was sold to a cotton planter, who said he wanted the "proud old critter to go to his plantation, to look after the little woolly heads, while their mammies were working in the field."

When the sale was over, then came the separation, and

> O, deep was the anguish of that slave mother's heart,
> When called from her darlings for ever to part;
> The poor mourning mother of reason bereft,
> Soon ended her sorrows, and sank cold in death.

Antoinette, the flower of the family, a girl who was much beloved by all who knew her, for her Christ-like piety, dignity of manner, as well as her great talents and extreme beauty, was bought by an uneducated and drunken slave dealer.

I cannot give a more correct description of the scene, when she was called from her brother to the stand, than will be found in the following lines—

> Why stands she near the auction stand?
> That girl so young and fair;
> What brings her to this dismal place?
> Why stands she weeping there?
>
> Why does she raise that bitter cry?
> Why hangs her head with shame,
> As now the auctioneer's rough voice
> So rudely calls her name!
>
> But see! she grasps a manly hand,
> And in a voice so low,
> As scarcely to be heard, she says,
> "My brother, must I go?"
>
> A moment's pause: then, midst a wail
> Of agonizing woe,
> His answer falls upon the ear,—
> "Yes, sister, you must go!
>
> "No longer can my arm defend,
> No longer can I save
> My sister from the horrid fate
> That waits her as a SLAVE!"
>
> Blush, Christian, blush! for e'en the dark
> Untutored heathen see
> Thy inconsistency, and lo!
> They scorn thy God, and thee!

The low trader said to a kind lady who wished to purchase Antoinette out of his hands, "I reckon I'll not sell the smart critter for ten thousand dollars; I always wanted her for my own use." The lady, wishing to remonstrate with him, commenced by saying, "You should remember, Sir, that there is a just God." Hoskens not understanding Mrs. Huston, interrupted her by saying, "I does, and guess it's monstrous kind an' him to send such likely niggers for our convenience." Mrs. Huston finding that a long course of reckless wickedness, drunkenness, and vice, had destroyed in Hoskens every noble impulse, left him.

Antoinette, poor girl, also seeing that there was no help for her, became frantic. I can never forget her cries of despair, when Hoskens gave the order for her to be taken to his house, and locked in an upper room. On Hoskens entering the apartment, in a state of intoxication, a fearful struggle ensued. The brave Antoinette broke loose from him, pitched herself head foremost through the window, and fell upon the pavement below.

Her bruised but unpolluted body was soon picked up—restoratives brought—doctor called in; but, alas! it was too late: her pure and noble spirit had fled away to be at rest in those realms of endless bliss, "where the wicked cease from troubling, and the weary are at rest."

Antoinette like many other noble women who are deprived of liberty, still

> Holds something sacred, something undefiled;
> Some pledge and keepsake of their higher nature.
> And, like the diamond in the dark, retains
> Some quenchless gleam of the celestial light.

On Hoskens fully realizing the fact that his victim was no more, he exclaimed, "By thunder I am a used-up man!" The sudden disappointment, and the loss of two thousand dollars, was more than he could endure: so he drank more than ever, and in a short time died, raving mad with *delirium tremens.*

The villain Slator said to Mrs. Huston, the kind lady who endeavored to purchase Antoinette from Hoskens, "Nobody needn't talk to me 'bout buying them ar likely niggers, for I'm not going to sell em." "But Mary is rather delicate," said Mrs. Huston, "and, being unaccustomed to hard work, cannot do you much service on a plantation." "I don't want her for the field," replied Slator, "but for another purpose." Mrs. Huston understood what this meant, and instantly exclaimed, "Oh, but she is your cousin!" "The devil she is!" said Slator; and added, "Do you mean to insult me Madam, by saying that I am related to niggers?" "No," replied Mrs. Huston, "I do not wish to offend you, Sir. But wasn't Mr. Slator, Mary's father, your uncle?" "Yes, I calculate he was," said Slator; "but I want you and everybody to understand that I'm no kin to his niggers." "Oh, very well," said Mrs. Huston; adding, "Now what will you take for the poor girl?" "Nothin'," he replied; "for, as I said before, I'm not goin' to sell, so you needn't trouble yourself no more. If the critter behaves herself, I'll do as well by her as any man."

Slator spoke up boldly, but his manner and sheepish look clearly indicated that

> His heart within him was at strife
>   With such accursed gains;
> For he knew whose passions gave her life,
>   Whose blood ran in her veins.
>
> The monster led her from the door,
>   He led her by the hand,
> To be his slave and paramour
>   In a strange and distant land!

Poor Frank and his sister were handcuffed together, and confined in prison. Their dear little twin brother and sister were sold, and taken where they knew not. But it often happens that misfortune causes those whom we counted dearest to shrink away; while it makes friends of those whom we least expected to take any interest in our affairs. Among the latter class Frank found two comparatively new but faithful friends to watch the gloomy paths of the unhappy little twins.

In a day or two after the sale, Slator had two fast horses put to a large light van, and placed in it a good many small but valuable things belonging to the distressed family. He also took with him Frank and Mary, as well as all the money for the spoil; and after treating all his low friends and bystanders, and drinking deeply himself, he started in high glee for his home in South Carolina. But they had not proceeded many miles, before Frank and his sister discovered that Slator was too drunk to drive. But he, like most tipsy men, thought he was all right; and as he had with him some of the ruined family's best brandy and wine, such as he had not been accustomed to, and being a thirsty soul, he drank till the reins fell from his fingers, and in attempting to catch them he tumbled out of the vehicle, and was unable to get up. Frank and Mary there and then contrived a plan by which to escape. As they were still handcuffed by one wrist each, they alighted, took from the drunken assassin's pocket the key, undid the iron bracelets, and placed them upon Slator, who was better fitted to wear such ornaments. As the demon lay unconscious of what was taking place, Frank and Mary took from him the large sum of money that was realized at the sale, as well as that which Slator had so very meanly obtained from their poor mother. They then dragged him into the woods, tied him to a tree, and left the inebriated robber to shift for himself, while they made good their escape to Savannah. The fugitives being white, of course no one suspected that they were slaves.

Slator was not able to call anyone to his rescue till late the next day; and as there were no railroads in that part of the country at that time, it was not until late the following day that Slator was able to get a party to join him for the chase. A person informed Slator that he had met a man and woman, in a trap, answering to the description of those whom he had lost, driving furiously towards Savannah. So Slator and several slavehunters on horseback started off in full tilt, with their bloodhounds, in pursuit of Frank and Mary.

On arriving at Savannah, the hunters found that the fugitives had sold the horses and trap, and embarked as free white persons, for New York. Slator's disappointment and rascality so preyed upon his base mind, that he, like Judas, went and hanged himself.

As soon as Frank and Mary were safe, they endeavored to redeem their good mother. But, alas! she was gone; she had passed on to the realm of spirit life.

In due time Frank learned from his friends in Georgia where his little brother and sister dwelt. So he wrote at once to purchase them, but the persons with whom they lived would not sell them. After failing in several attempts to buy them, Frank cultivated large whiskers and moustachios, cut off his hair, put on a wig and glasses, and went down as a white man, and stopped in the neighborhood where his sister was; and after seeing her and also his little brother, arrangements were made for them to meet at a particular place on a Sunday, which they did, and got safely off.

I saw Frank myself, when he came for the little twins. Though I was then quite a lad, I well remember being highly delighted by hearing him tell how nicely he and Mary had served Slator.

Frank had so completely disguised or changed his appearance that his little sister did not know him, and would not speak till he showed their mother's likeness; the sight of which melted her to tears, for she knew the face. Frank might have said to her

> "O, Emma! O, my sister, speak to me!
> Dost thou not know me, that I am thy brother?
> Come to me, little Emma, thou shalt dwell
> With me henceforth, and know no care or want."
> Emma was silent for a space, as if
> 'Twere hard to summon up a human voice.

Frank and Mary's mother was my wife's own dear aunt.

After this great diversion from our narrative, which I hope, dear reader, you will excuse, I shall return at once to it.

My wife was torn from her mother's embrace in childhood, and taken to a distant part of the country. She had seen so many other children separated from their parents in this cruel manner, that the mere thought of her ever becoming the mother of a child, to linger out a miserable existence under the wretched system of American slavery, appeared to fill her very soul with horror; and as she had taken what I felt to be an important view of her condition, I did not, at first, press the marriage, but agreed to assist her in trying to devise some plan by which we might escape from our unhappy condition, and then be married.

We thought of plan after plan, but they all seemed crowded with insurmountable difficulties. We knew it was unlawful for any public conveyance to take us as passengers, without our masters' consent. We were also perfectly aware of the startling fact, that had we left without this consent the professional slave-hunters would have soon had their ferocious bloodhounds baying on our track, and in a short time we should have been dragged back to slavery, not to fill the more favorable situations which we had just left, but to be separated for life, and put to the very meanest and most laborious drudgery; or else have been tortured to death as examples, in order to strike terror into the hearts of others, and thereby prevent them from even attempting to escape from their cruel taskmasters. It is a fact worthy of remark, that nothing seems to give the slaveholders so much pleasure as the catching and torturing of fugitives. They had much rather take the keen and poisonous lash, and with it cut their poor trembling victims to atoms, than allow one of them to escape to a free country, and expose the infamous system from which he fled.

The greatest excitement prevails at a slavehunt. The slaveholders and their hired ruffians appear to take more pleasure in this inhuman pursuit than English sportsmen do in chasing a fox or a stag. Therefore, knowing what we should have been compelled to suffer, if caught and taken back, we were more than anxious to hit upon a plan that would lead us safely to a land of liberty.

But, after puzzling our brains for years, we were reluctantly driven to the sad conclusion, that it was almost impossible to escape from slavery in Georgia, and travel 1,000 miles across the slave States. We therefore resolved to get the consent of our owners, be married, settle down in slavery, and endeavor to make ourselves as comfortable as possible under that system; but at the same time ever to keep our dim eyes steadily fixed upon the glimmering hope of liberty, and earnestly pray God mercifully to assist us to escape from our unjust thraldom.

We were married, and prayed and toiled on till December 1848, at which time (as I have stated) a plan suggested itself that proved quite successful, and in eight days after it was first thought of we were free from the horrible trammels of slavery, and glorifying God who had brought us safely out of a land of bondage.

Knowing that slaveholders have the privilege of taking their slaves to any part of the country they think proper, it occurred to me that, as my wife was nearly white, I might get her to disguise herself as an invalid gentleman, and assume to be my master, while I could attend as his slave, and that in this manner we might effect our escape. After I thought of the plan, I suggested it to my wife, but at first she shrank from the idea. She thought it was almost impossible for her to assume that disguise, and travel a distance of 1,000 miles across the slave States. However, on the other hand, she also thought of her condition. She saw that the laws under which we lived did not recognize her to be a woman, but a mere chattel, to be bought and sold, or otherwise dealt with as her owner might see fit. Therefore the more she contemplated her helpless condition, the more anxious she was to escape from it. So she said, "I think it is almost too much for us to undertake; however, I feel that God is on our side, and with his assistance, notwithstanding all the difficulties, we shall be able to succeed. Therefore, if you will purchase the disguise, I will try to carry out the plan."

But after I concluded to purchase the disguise, I was afraid to go to anyone to ask him to sell me the articles. It is unlawful in Georgia for a white man to trade with slaves without the master's consent. But, notwithstanding this, many persons will sell a slave any article that he can get the money to buy. Not that they sympathize with the slave, but merely because his testimony is not admitted in court against a free white person.

Therefore, with little difficulty I went to different parts of the town, at odd times, and purchased things piece by piece (except the trousers which she found necessary to make) and took them home to the house where my wife resided. She being a ladies' maid, and a favorite slave in the family, was allowed a little room to herself; and amongst other pieces of furniture which I had made in my overtime, was a chest of drawers; so when I took the articles home, she locked them up carefully in these drawers. No one about the premises knew that she had anything of the kind. So when we fancied we had everything ready the time was fixed for the flight. But we knew it would not do to start off without first getting our masters' consent to be away for a few days. Had we left without this, they would soon have had us back into slavery, and probably we should never have got another fair opportunity of even attempting to escape.

Some of the best slaveholders will sometimes give their favorite slaves a few days' holiday at Christmas time; so, after no little amount of perseverance on my wife's part, she obtained a pass from her mistress, allowing her to be away for a few days. The cabinetmaker with whom I worked gave me a similar paper, but said that he needed my services very much, and wished me to return as soon as the time granted was up. I thanked him kindly; but somehow I have not been able to make it convenient to return yet; and, as the free air of good old England agrees so well with my wife and our dear little ones, as well as with myself, it is not at all likely we shall return at present to the "peculiar institution" of chains and stripes.

On reaching my wife's cottage she handed me her pass, and I showed mine, but at that time neither of us were able to read them. It is not only unlawful for slaves to be taught to read, but in some of the States there are heavy penalties attached, such as fines and imprisonment, which will be vigorously enforced upon anyone who is humane enough to violate the so-called law.

The following case will serve to show how persons are treated in the most enlightened slaveholding community.

INDICTMENT

COMMONWEALTH OF VIRGINIA, \ *In the Circuit Court.* The
    NORFOLK COUNTY, *ss.*   / Grand Jurors empannelled
and sworn to inquire of offences committed in the body of the said County on their oath present, that Margaret Douglass, being an evil disposed person, not having the fear of God before her eyes, but moved and instigated by the devil, wickedly, maliciously, and feloniously, on the fourth day of July, in the year of our Lord one thousand eight hundred and fifty-four, at Norfolk, in said County, did teach a certain black girl named Kate to read in the Bible, to the great displeasure of Almighty God, to the pernicious example of others in like case offending, contrary to the form of the statute in such case made and provided, and against the peace and dignity of the Commonwealth of Virginia.

VICTOR VAGABOND, Prosecuting Attorney

On this indictment Mrs. Douglass was arraigned as a necessary matter of form, tried, found guilty of course; and Judge Scalawag, before whom she was tried, having consulted with Dr. Adams, ordered the sheriff to place Mrs. Douglass in the prisoner's box, when he addressed her as follows: "Margaret Douglass, stand up. You are guilty of one of the vilest crimes that ever disgraced society; and the jury have found you so. You have taught a slave girl to read in the Bible. No enlightened society can exist where such offences go unpunished. The Court, in your case, do not feel for you one solitary ray of sympathy, and they will inflict on you the utmost penalty of the law. In any other civilized country you would have paid the forfeit of your crime with your life, and the Court have only to regret that such is not the law in this country. The sentence for your offence is, that you be imprisoned one month in the county jail, and that you pay the costs of this prosecution. Sheriff, remove the prisoner to jail." On the publication of these proceedings, the Doctors of Divinity preached each a sermon on the necessity of obeying the law; the *New York Observer* noticed with much pious gladness a revival of religion on Dr. Smith's plantation in Georgia, among his slaves; while the *Journal of Commerce* commended this political preaching of the Doctors of Divinity because it favoured slavery. Let us do nothing to offend our Southern brethren.

However, at first, we were highly delighted at the idea of having gained permission to be absent for a few days; but when the thought flashed across my wife's mind, that it was customary for travellers to register their names in the visitors' book at hotels, as well as in the clearance or Custom House book at Charleston, South Carolina—it made our spirits droop within us.

So, while sitting in our little room upon the verge of despair, all at once my wife raised her head, and with a smile upon her face, which was a moment before bathed in tears, said, "I think I have it!" I asked what it was. She said, "I think I can make a poultice and bind up my right hand in a sling, and with propriety ask the officers to register my name for me." I thought that would do.

It then occurred to her that the smoothness of her face might betray her; so she decided to make another poultice, and put it in a white handkerchief to be worn under the chin, up the cheeks, and to tie over the head. This nearly hid the expression of the countenance, as well as the beardless chin.

The poultice is left off in the engraving, because the likeness could not have been taken well with it on.

My wife, knowing that she would be thrown a good deal into the company of gentlemen, fancied that she could get on better if she had something to go over the eyes; so I went to a shop and bought a pair of green spectacles. This was in the evening.

We sat up all night discussing the plan, and making preparations. Just before the time arrived, in the morning, for us to leave,
I cut off my wife's hair square at the back of the head, and got
her to dress in the disguise and stand out on the floor. I found
that she made a most respectable looking gentleman.

My wife had no ambition whatever to assume this disguise, and
would not have done so had it been possible to have obtained our
liberty by more simple means; but we knew it was not customary
in the South for ladies to travel with male servants; and therefore, notwithstanding my wife's fair complexion, it would have
been a very difficult task for her to have come off as a free white
lady, with me as her slave; in fact, her not being able to write
would have made this quite impossible. We knew that no public
conveyance would take us, or any other slave, as a passenger,
without our masters' consent. This consent could never be obtained to pass into a free State. My wife's being muffled in the
poultices, &c., furnished a plausible excuse for avoiding general
conversation, of which most Yankee travellers are passionately
fond.

There are a large number of free Negroes residing in the
Southern States; but in Georgia (and I believe in all the slave
States) every colored person's complexion is *prima-facie* evidence
of his being a slave; and the lowest villain in the country, should
he be a white man, has the legal power to arrest, and question,
in the most inquisitorial and insulting manner, any colored person, male or female, that he may find at large, particularly at
night and on Sundays, without a written pass, signed by the
master or someone in authority; or stamped free papers, certify-
ing that the person is the rightful owner of himself.

If the colored person refuses to answer questions put to him,
he may be beaten, and his defending himself against this attack
makes him an outlaw, and if he be killed on the spot, the murderer will be exempted from all blame; but after the colored
person has answered the questions put to him, in a most humble
and pointed manner, he may then be taken to prison; and should
it turn out, after further examination, that he was caught where
he had no permission or legal right to be, and that he has not
given what they term a satisfactory account of himself, the master

will have to pay a fine. On his refusing to do this, the poor slave may be legally and severely flogged by public officers. Should the prisoner prove to be a free man, he is most likely to be both whipped and fined.

The great majority of slaveholders hate this class of persons with a hatred that can only be equalled by the condemned spirits of the infernal regions. They have no mercy upon, nor sympathy for, any Negro whom they cannot enslave. They say that God made the black man to be a slave for the white, and act as though they really believed that all free persons of color are in open rebellion to a direct command from heaven, and that they (the whites) are God's chosen agents to pour out upon them unlimited vengeance. For instance, a bill has been introduced in the Tennessee Legislature to prevent free Negroes from travelling on the railroads in that State. It has passed the first reading. The bill provides that the president who shall permit a free Negro to travel on any road within the jurisdiction of the State under his supervision shall pay a fine of five hundred dollars; any conductor permitting a violation of the act shall pay two hundred and fifty dollars; provided such free Negro is not under the control of a free white citizen of Tennessee, who will vouch for the character of said free Negro in a penal bond of one thousand dollars. The State of Arkansas has passed a law to banish all free Negroes from its bounds, and it came into effect on the 1st day of January, 1860. Every free Negro found there after that date will be liable to be sold into slavery, the crime of freedom being unpardonable. The Missouri Senate has before it a bill providing that all free Negroes above the age of eighteen years who shall be found in the State after September 1860 shall be sold into slavery; and that all such Negroes as shall enter the State after September 1861 and remain there twenty-four hours, shall also be sold into slavery forever. Mississippi, Kentucky, and Georgia, and in fact, I believe, all the slave States, are legislating in the same manner. Thus the slaveholders make it almost impossible for free persons of color to get out of the slave States, in order that they may sell them into slavery if they don't go. If no white persons travelled upon railroads except those who could get someone to vouch for their character in a penal bond of one thousand dollars, the rail-

road companies would soon go to the "wall." Such mean legislation is too low for comment; therefore I leave the villainous acts
to speak for themselves.

But the Dred Scott decision is the crowning act of infamous
Yankee legislation. The Supreme Court, the highest tribunal of
the Republic, composed of nine Judge Jeffreys, chosen both from
the free and slave States, has decided that no colored person, or
persons of African extraction, can ever become a citizen of the
United States, or have any rights which white men are bound to
respect. That is to say, in the opinion of this Court, robbery, rape,
and murder are not crimes when committed by a white upon a
colored person.

Judges who will sneak from their high and honorable position
down into the lowest depths of human depravity, and scrape up
a decision like this, are wholly unworthy the confidence of any
people. I believe such men would, if they had the power, and
were it to their temporal interest, sell their country's independence, and barter away every man's birthright for a mess of po-
tage. Well may Thomas Campbell say—

> United States, your banner wears,
>   Two emblems,—one of fame;
> Alas, the other that it bears
>   Reminds us of your shame!
> The white man's liberty in types
>   Stands blazoned by your stars;
> But what's the meaning of your stripes?
>   They mean your Negro-scars.

When the time had arrived for us to start, we blew out the
lights, knelt down, and prayed to our Heavenly Father mercifully
to assist us, as he did his people of old, to escape from cruel
bondage; and we shall ever feel that God heard and answered our
prayer. Had we not been sustained by a kind, and I sometimes
think special, providence, we could never have overcome the
mountainous difficulties which I am now about to describe.

After this we rose and stood for a few moments in breathless
silence—we were afraid that someone might have been about the
cottage listening and watching our movements. So I took my
wife by the hand, stepped softly to the door, raised the latch,

drew it open, and peeped out. Though there were trees all around the house, yet the foliage scarcely moved; in fact, everything appeared to be as still as death. I then whispered to my wife, "Come my dear, let us make a desperate leap for liberty!" But poor thing, she shrank back, in a state of trepidation. I turned and asked what was the matter; she made no reply, but burst into violent sobs, and threw her head upon my breast. This appeared to touch my very heart, it caused me to enter into her feelings more fully than ever. We both saw the many mountainous difficulties that rose one after the other before our view, and knew far too well what our sad fate would have been, were we caught and forced back into our slavish den. Therefore on my wife's fully realizing the solemn fact that we had to take our lives, as it were, in our hands, and contest every inch of the thousand miles of slave territory over which we had to pass, it made her heart almost sink within her, and, had I known them at that time, I would have repeated the following encouraging lines, which may not be out of place here—

> The hill, though high, I covet to ascend,
> The *difficulty will not me offend;*
> For I perceive the way to life lies here:
> Come, pluck up heart, let's neither faint nor fear;
> Better, though difficult, the right way to go,—
> Than wrong, though easy, where the end is woe.

However, the sobbing was soon over, and after a few moments of silent prayer she recovered her self-possession, and said, "Come, William, it is getting late, so now let us venture upon our perilous journey."

We then opened the door, and stepped as softly out as "moonlight upon the water." I locked the door with my own key, which I now have before me, and tiptoed across the yard into the street. I say tiptoed, because we were like persons near a tottering avalanche, afraid to move, or even breathe freely, for fear the sleeping tyrants should be aroused, and come down upon us with double vengeance, for daring to attempt to escape in the manner which we contemplated.

We shook hands, said farewell, and started in different directions for the railway station. I took the nearest possible way to the train, for fear I should be recognized by someone, and got into the Negro car in which I knew I should have to ride; but my *master* (as I will now call my wife) took a longer way round, and only arrived there with the bulk of the passengers. He obtained a ticket for himself and one for his slave to Savannah, the first port, which was about two hundred miles off. My master then had the luggage stowed away, and stepped into one of the best carriages.

But just before the train moved off I peeped through the window, and, to my great astonishment, I saw the cabinetmaker with whom I had worked so long, on the platform. He stepped up to the ticketseller, and asked some question, and then commenced looking rapidly through the passengers, and into the carriages. Fully believing that we were caught, I shrank into a corner, turned my face from the door, and expected in a moment to be dragged out. The cabinetmaker looked into my master's carriage, but did not know him in his new attire, and, as God would have it, before he reached mine the bell rang, and the train moved off.

I have heard since that the cabinetmaker had a presentiment that we were about to "make tracks for parts unknown"; but, not seeing me, his suspicions vanished, until he received the startling intelligence that we had arrived safely in a free State.

As soon as the train had left the platform, my master looked round in the carriage, and was terror-stricken to find a Mr. Cray—an old friend of my wife's master, who dined with the family the day before, and knew my wife from childhood—sitting on the same seat.

The doors of the American railway carriages are at the ends. The passengers walk up the aisle, and take seats on either side; and as my master was engaged in looking out of the window, he did not see who came in.

My master's first impression, after seeing Mr. Cray, was, that he was there for the purpose of securing him. However, my master thought it was not wise to give any information respecting himself, and for fear that Mr. Cray might draw him into conversation and recognize his voice, my master resolved to feign deafness as the only means of self-defense.

After a little while, Mr. Cray said to my master, "It is a very fine morning, sir." The latter took no notice, but kept looking out of the window. Mr. Cray soon repeated this remark, in a little louder tone, but my master remained as before. This indifference attracted the attention of the passengers near, one of whom laughed out. This, I suppose, annoyed the old gentleman; so he said, "I will make him hear"; and in a loud tone of voice repeated, "It is a very fine morning, sir."

My master turned his head, and with a polite bow said, "Yes," and commenced looking out of the window again.

One of the gentlemen remarked that it was a very great deprivation to be deaf. "Yes," replied Mr. Cray, "and I shall not trouble that fellow any more." This enabled my master to breathe a little easier, and to feel that Mr. Cray was not his pursuer after all.

The gentlemen then turned the conversation upon the three great topics of discussion in first-class circles in Georgia, namely, Niggers, Cotton, and the Abolitionists.

My master had often heard of abolitionists, but in such a connection as to cause him to think that they were a fearful kind of wild animal. But he was highly delighted to learn, from the gentlemen's conversation, that the abolitionists were persons who were opposed to oppression; and therefore, in his opinion, not the lowest, but the very highest, of God's creatures.

Without the slightest objection on my master's part, the gentlemen left the carriage at Gordon, for Milledgeville (the capital of the State).

We arrived at Savannah early in the evening, and got into an omnibus, which stopped at the hotel for the passengers to take tea. I stepped into the house and brought my master something on a tray to the omnibus, which took us in due time to the steamer, which was bound for Charleston, South Carolina.

Soon after going on board, my master turned in; and as the captain and some of the passengers seemed to think this strange, and also questioned me respecting him, my master thought I had better get out the flannels and opodeldoc which we had prepared for the rheumatism, warm them quickly by the stove in the gentleman's saloon, and bring them to his berth. We did this as an excuse for my master's retiring to bed so early.

While at the stove one of the passengers said to me, "Buck, what have you got there?" "Opodeldoc, sir," I replied. "I should think it's opo*devil*," said a lanky swell, who was leaning back in a chair with his heels upon the back of another, and chewing tobacco as if for a wager; "it stinks enough to kill or cure twenty men. Away with it, or I reckon I will throw it overboard!"

It was by this time warm enough, so I took it to my master's berth, remained there a little while, and then went on deck and asked the steward where I was to sleep. He said there was no place provided for colored passengers, whether slave or free. So I paced the deck till a late hour, then mounted some cotton bags, in a warm place near the funnel, sat there till morning, and then went and assisted my master to get ready for breakfast.

He was seated at the right hand of the captain, who, together with all the passengers, inquired very kindly after his health. As my master had one hand in a sling, it was my duty to carve his food. But when I went out the captain said, "You have a very attentive boy, sir; but you had better watch him like a hawk when you get on to the North. He seems all very well here, but he may act quite differently there. I know several gentlemen who have lost their valuable niggers among them d——d cut-throat abolitionists."

Before my master could speak, a rough slave dealer, who was sitting opposite, with both elbows on the table, and with a large piece of broiled fowl in his fingers, shook his head with emphasis, and in a deep Yankee tone, forced through his crowded mouth the words, "Sound doctrine, captain, very sound." He then dropped the chicken into the plate, leant back, placed his thumbs in the armholes of his fancy waistcoat, and continued, "I would not take a nigger to the North under no consideration. I have had a deal to do with niggers in my time, but I never saw one who ever had his heel upon free soil that was worth a d——n." "Now stranger," addressing my master, "if you have made up your mind to sell that ere nigger, I am your man; just mention your price, and if it isn't out of the way, I will pay for him on this board with hard silver dollars." This hard-featured, bristly-bearded, wire-headed, red-eyed monster, staring at my master as the serpent did at Eve, said, "What do you say, stranger?" He replied, "I don't wish to sell, sir; I cannot get on well without him."

"You will have to get on without him if you take him to the

North," continued this man; "for I can tell ye, stranger, as a friend, I am an older cove than you, I have seen lots of this ere world, and I reckon I have had more dealings with niggers than any man living or dead. I was once employed by General Wade Hampton, for ten years, in doing nothing but breaking 'em in; and everybody knows that the General would not have a man that didn't understand his business. So I tell ye, stranger, again, you had better sell, and let me take him down to Orleans. He will do you no good if you take him across Mason's and Dixon's line; he is a keen nigger, and I can see from the cut of his eye that he is certain to run away." My master said, "I think not, sir; I have great confidence in his fidelity." "Fi*devil*," indignantly said the dealer, as his fist came down upon the edge of the saucer and upset a cup of hot coffee in a gentleman's lap. (As the scalded man jumped up the trader quietly said, "Don't disturb yourself, neighbor; accidents will happen in the best of families.") "It always makes me mad to hear a man talking about fidelity in niggers. There isn't a d——d one on 'em who wouldn't cut sticks, if he had half a chance."

By this time we were near Charleston; my master thanked the captain for his advice, and they all withdrew and went on deck, where the trader fancied he became quite eloquent. He drew a crowd around him, and with emphasis said, "Cap'en, if I was the President of this mighty United States of America, the greatest and freest country under the whole univarse, I would never let no man, I don't care who he is, take a nigger into the North and bring him back here, filled to the brim, as he is sure to be, with d——d abolition vices, to taint all quiet niggers with the hellish spirit of running away. These air, cap'en, my flat-footed, every day, right up and down sentiments, and as this is a free country, cap'en, I don't care who hears 'em; for I am a Southern man, every inch on me to the backbone." "Good!" said an insignificant-looking individual of the slave dealer stamp. "Three cheers for John C. Calhoun and the whole fair sunny South!" added the trader. So off went their hats, and out burst a terrific roar of irregular but continued cheering. My master took no more notice of the dealer. He merely said to the captain that the air on deck was too keen for him, and he would therefore return to the cabin.

While the trader was in the zenith of his eloquence, he might as well have said, as one of his kit did, at a great Filibustering meeting, that "When the great American Eagle gets one of his mighty claws upon Canada and the other into South America, and his glorious and starry wings of liberty extending from the Atlantic to the Pacific, oh! then, where will England be, ye gentlemen? I tell ye, she will only serve as a pocket-handkerchief for Jonathan to wipe his nose with."

On my master entering the cabin he found at the breakfast table a young southern military officer, with whom he had travelled some distance the previous day.

After passing the usual compliments the conversation turned upon the old subject—niggers.

The officer, who was also travelling with a manservant, said to my master, "You will excuse me, Sir, for saying I think you are very likely to spoil your boy by saying 'thank you' to him. I assure you, Sir, nothing spoils a slave so soon as saying 'thank you' and 'if you please' to him. The only way to make a nigger toe the mark, and to keep him in his place, is to storm at him like thunder, and keep him trembling like a leaf. Don't you see, when I speak to my Ned, he darts like lightning; and if he didn't I'd skin him."

Just then the poor dejected slave came in, and the officer swore at him fearfully, merely to teach my master what he called the proper way to treat me.

After he had gone out to get his master's luggage ready, the officer said, "That is the way to speak to them. If every nigger was drilled in this manner, they would be as humble as dogs, and never dare to run away."

The gentleman urged my master not to go to the North for the restoration of his health, but to visit the Warm Springs in Arkansas.

My master said, he thought the air of Philadelphia would suit his complaint best; and, not only so, he thought he could get better advice there.

The boat had now reached the wharf. The officer wished my master a safe and pleasant journey, and left the saloon.

There were a large number of persons on the quay waiting the arrival of the steamer: but we were afraid to venture out for fear that someone might recognize me; or that they had heard that we were gone, and had telegraphed to have us stopped. However, after remaining in the cabin till all the other passengers were gone, we had our luggage placed on a fly, and I took my master by the arm, and with a little difficulty he hobbled on shore, got in and drove off to the best hotel, which John C. Calhoun, and all the other great southern fire-eating statesmen, made their headquarters while in Charleston.

On arriving at the house the landlord ran out and opened the door: but judging, from the poultices and green glasses, that my master was an invalid, he took him very tenderly by one arm and ordered his man to take the other.

My master then eased himself out, and with their assistance found no trouble in getting up the steps into the hotel. The proprietor made me stand on one side, while he paid my master the attention and homage he thought a gentleman of his high position merited.

My master asked for a bedroom. The servant was ordered to show a good one, into which we helped him. The servant returned. My master then handed me the bandages, I took them downstairs in great haste, and told the landlord my master wanted two hot poultices as quickly as possible. He rang the bell, the servant came in, to whom he said, "Run to the kitchen and tell the cook to make two hot poultices right off, for there is a gentleman upstairs very badly off indeed!"

In a few minutes the smoking poultices were brought in. I placed them in white handkerchiefs, and hurried upstairs, went into my master's apartment, shut the door, and laid them on the mantelpiece. As he was alone for a little while, he thought he could rest a great deal better with the poultices off. However, it was necessary to have them to complete the remainder of the journey. I then ordered dinner, and took my master's boots out to polish them. While doing so I entered into conversation with one of the slaves. I may state here, that on the sea-coast of South Carolina and Georgia the slaves speak worse English than in any other part of the country. This is owing to the frequent importation, or smuggling in, of Africans, who mingle with the natives. Consequently the language cannot properly be called English or African, but a corruption of the two.

The shrewd son of African parents to whom I referred said to me, "Say, brudder, way you come from, and which side you goin day wid dat ar little don up buckra" (white man)?

I replied, "To Philadelphia."

"What!" he exclaimed, with astonishment, "to Philumadelphy?"

"Yes," I said.

"By squash! I wish I was going wid you! I hears um say dat dare's no slaves way over in dem parts; is um so?"

I quietly said, "I have heard the same thing."

"Well," continued he, as he threw down the boot and brush, and, placing his hands in his pockets, strutted across the floor with an air of independence—"Gorra Mighty, dem is de parts for Pompey; and I hope when you get dare you will stay, and nebber follow dat buckra back to dis hot quarter no more, let him be eber so good."

I thanked him; and just as I took the boots up and started off, he caught my hand between his two, and gave it a hearty shake, and, with tears streaming down his cheeks, said:

"God bless you, broder, and may de Lord be wid you. When you gets de freedom, and sittin under your own wine and fig-tree, don't forget to pray for poor Pompey."

I was afraid to say much to him, but I shall never forget his earnest request, nor fail to do what little I can to release the millions of unhappy bondmen, of whom he was one.

At the proper time my master had the poultices placed on, came down, and seated himself at a table in a very brilliant dining-room, to have his dinner. I had to have something at the same time, in order to be ready for the boat; so they gave me my dinner in an old broken plate, with a rusty knife and fork, and said, "Here, boy, you go in the kitchen." I took it and went out, but did not stay more than a few minutes, because I was in a great hurry to get back to see how the invalid was getting on. On arriving I found two or three servants waiting on him; but as he did not feel able to make a very hearty dinner, he soon finished, paid the bill, and gave the servants each a trifle, which caused one of them to say to me, "Your massa is a big bug"— meaning a gentleman of distinction—"he is the greatest gentle-man dat has been dis way for dis six months." I said, "Yes, he is some pumpkins," meaning the same as "big bug."

When we left Macon, it was our intention to take a steamer at Charleston through to Philadelphia; but on arriving there we found that the vessels did not run during the winter, and I have no doubt it was well for us they did not; for on the very last voyage the steamer made that we intended to go by, a fugitive was discovered secreted on board, and sent back to slavery. However, as we had also heard of the Overland Mail Route, we were all right. So I ordered a fly to the door, had the luggage placed on; we got in, and drove down to the Custom House Office, which was near the wharf where we had to obtain tickets, to take a steamer for Wilmington, North Carolina. When we reached the building, I helped my master into the office, which was crowded with passengers. He asked for a ticket for himself and one for his slave to Philadelphia. This caused the principal officer—a very mean-looking, cheese-colored fellow, who was sitting there—to look up at us very suspiciously, and in a fierce tone of voice he said to me, "Boy, do you belong to that gentleman?" I quickly replied, "Yes, sir" (which was quite correct). The tickets were handed out, and as my master was paying for them the chief man said to him, "I wish you to register your name here, sir, and also the name of your nigger, and pay a dollar duty on him."

My master paid the dollar, and pointing to the hand that was in the poultice, requested the officer to register his name for him. This seemed to offend the "high-bred" South Carolinian. He jumped up, shaking his head, and, cramming his hands almost through the bottom of his trousers pockets, with a slave-bullying air, said, "I shan't do it."

This attracted the attention of all the passengers. Just then the young military officer with whom my master travelled and conversed on the steamer from Savannah stepped in, somewhat the worse for brandy; he shook hands with my master, and pretended to know all about him. He said, "I know his kin (friends) like a book"; and as the officer was known in Charleston, and was going to stop there with friends, the recognition was very much in my master's favor.

The captain of the steamer, a good-looking jovial fellow, seeing that the gentleman appeared to know my master, and perhaps not wishing to lose us as passengers, said in an off-hand sailor-like manner, "I will register the gentleman's name, and take the responsibility upon myself." He asked my master's name. He said, "William Johnson." The names were put down, I think, "Mr. Johnson and slave." The captain said, "It's all right now, Mr. Johnson." He thanked him kindly, and the young officer begged my master to go with him, and have something to drink and a cigar; but as he had not acquired these accomplishments, he excused himself, and we went on board and came off to Wilmington, North Carolina. When the gentleman finds out his mistake, he will, I have no doubt, be careful in future not to pretend to have an intimate acquaintance with an entire stranger. During the voyage the captain said, "It was rather sharp shooting this morning, Mr. Johnson. It was not out of any disrespect to you, sir; but they make it a rule to be very strict at Charleston. I have known families to be detained there with their slaves till reliable information could be received respecting them. If they were not very careful, any d——d abolitionist might take off a lot of valuable niggers."

My master said, "I suppose so," and thanked him again for helping him over the difficulty.

We reached Wilmington the next morning, and took the train for Richmond, Virginia. I have stated that the American railway carriages (or cars, as they are called) are constructed differently to those in England. At one end of some of them, in the South, there is a little apartment with a couch on both sides for the convenience of families and invalids; and as they thought my master was very poorly, he was allowed to enter one of these apartments at Petersburg, Virginia, where an old gentleman and two handsome young ladies, his daughters, also got in, and took seats in the same carriage. But before the train started, the gentleman stepped into my car, and questioned me respecting my master. He wished to know what was the matter with him, where he was from, and where he was going. I told him where he came from, and said that he was suffering from a complication of complaints, and was going to Philadelphia, where he thought he could get more suitable advice than in Georgia.

The gentleman said my master could obtain the very best advice in Philadelphia. Which turned out to be quite correct, though he did not receive it from physicians, but from kind abolitionists who understood his case much better. The gentleman also said, "I reckon your master's father hasn't any more such faithful and smart boys as you." "O, yes, sir, he has," I replied, "lots on 'em." Which was literally true. This seemed all he wished to know. He thanked me, gave me a ten-cent piece, and requested me to be attentive to my good master. I promised that I would do so, and have ever since endeavored to keep my pledge. During the gentleman's absence, the ladies and my master had a little cozy chat. But on his return, he said, "You seem to be very much afflicted, sir." "Yes, sir," replied the gentleman in the poultices. "What seems to be the matter with you, sir; may I be allowed to ask?" "Inflammatory rheumatism, sir." "Oh! that is very bad, sir," said the kind gentleman: "I can sympathize with you; for I know from bitter experience what the rheumatism is." If he did, he knew a good deal more than Mr. Johnson.

The gentleman thought my master would feel better if he would lie down and rest himself; and as he was anxious to avoid conversation, he at once acted upon this suggestion. The ladies politely rose, took their extra shawls, and made a nice pillow for the invalid's head. My master wore a fashionable cloth cloak, which they took and covered him comfortably on the couch. After he had been lying a little while the ladies, I suppose, thought he was asleep; so one of them gave a long sigh, and said, in a quiet fascinating tone, "Papa, he seems to be a very nice young gentleman." But before papa could speak, the other lady quickly said, "Oh! dear me, I never felt so much for a gentleman in my life!" To use an American expression, "they fell in love with the wrong chap."

After my master had been lying a little while he got up, the gentleman assisted him in getting on his cloak, the ladies took their shawls, and soon all were seated. They then insisted upon Mr. Johnson taking some of their refreshments, which of course he did, out of courtesy to the ladies. All went on enjoying themselves until they reached Richmond, where the ladies and their father left the train. But, before doing so, the good old Virginian gentleman, who appeared to be much pleased with my master, presented him with a recipe, which he said was a perfect cure

for the inflammatory rheumatism. But the invalid not being able
to read it, and fearing he should hold it upside down in pretend-
ing to do so, thanked the donor kindly, and placed it in his
waistcoat pocket. My master's new friend also gave him his card,
and requested him the next time he travelled that way to do
him the kindness to call, adding, "I shall be pleased to see you,
and so will my daughters." Mr. Johnson expressed his gratitude
for the proffered hospitality, and said he should feel glad to call
on his return. I have not the slightest doubt that he will fulfil the
promise whenever that return takes place. After changing trains
we went on a little beyond Fredericksburg, and took a steamer
to Washington.

At Richmond, a stout elderly lady, whose whole demeanor
indicated that she belonged (as Mrs. Stowe's Aunt Chloe expresses it) to one of the "firstest families," stepped into the carriage, and took a seat near my master. Seeing me passing quickly
along the platform, she sprang up as if taken by a fit, and exclaimed, "Bless my soul! there goes my nigger, Ned!"

My master said, "No; that is my boy."

The lady paid no attention to this; she poked her head out of
the window, and bawled to me, "You Ned, come to me, sir, you
runaway rascal!"

On my looking round she drew her head in, and said to my
master, "I beg your pardon, sir, I was sure it was my nigger; I
never in my life saw two black pigs more alike than your boy and
my Ned."

After the disappointed lady had resumed her seat, and the
train had moved off, she closed her eyes, slightly raising her
hands, and in a sanctified tone said to my master, "Oh! I hope,
sir, your boy will not turn out to be so worthless as my Ned has.
Oh! I was as kind to him as if he had been my own son. Oh! sir,
it grieves me very much to think that after all I did for him he
should go off without having any cause whatever."

"When did he leave you?" asked Mr. Johnson.

"About eighteen months ago, and I have never seen hair or hide
of him since."

"Did he have a wife?" enquired a very respectable-looking
young gentleman, who was sitting near my master and opposite
to the lady.

"No, sir; not when he left, though he did have one a little be-fore that. She was very unlike him; she was as good and as faith-ful a nigger as anyone need wish to have. But, poor thing! she became so ill, that she was unable to do much work; so I thought it would be best to sell her, to go to New Orleans, where the cli-mate is nice and warm."

"I suppose she was very glad to go South for the restoration of her health?" said the gentleman.

"No; she was not," replied the lady, "for niggers never know what is best for them. She took on a great deal about leaving Ned and the little nigger; but, as she was so weakly, I let her go."

"Was she good-looking?" asked the young passenger, who was evidently not of the same opinion as the talkative lady, and therefore wished her to tell all she knew.

"Yes; she was very handsome, and much whiter than I am; and therefore will have no trouble in getting another husband. I am sure I wish her well. I asked the speculator who bought her to sell her to a good master. Poor thing! she has my prayers, and I know she prays for me. She was a good Christian, and always used to pray for my soul. It was through her earliest prayers," continued the lady, "that I was first led to seek forgiveness of my sins, before I was converted at the great camp-meeting."

This caused the lady to snuffle and to draw from her pocket a richly embroidered handkerchief, and apply it to the corner of her eyes. But my master could not see that it was at all soiled.

The silence which prevailed for a few moments was broken by the gentleman's saying, "As your 'July' was such a very good girl, and had served you so faithfully before she lost her health, don't you think it would have been better to have emancipated her?"

"No, indeed I do not!" scornfully exclaimed the lady, as she impatiently crammed the fine handkerchief into a little work-bag. "I have no patience with people who set niggers at liberty. It is the very worst thing you can do for them. My dear husband just before he died willed all his niggers free. But I and all our friends knew very well that he was too good a man to have ever thought of doing such an unkind and foolish thing, had he been in his right mind, and, therefore we had the will altered as it should have been in the first place."

"Did you mean, madam," asked my master, "that willing the slaves free was unjust to yourself, or unkind to them?"

"I mean that it was decidedly unkind to the servants themselves. It always seems to me such a cruel thing to turn niggers loose to shift for themselves, when there are so many good masters to take care of them. As for myself," continued the considerate lady, "I thank the Lord my dear husband left me and my son well provided for. Therefore I care nothing for the niggers, on my own account, for they are a great deal more trouble than they are worth; I sometimes wish that there was not one of them in the world, for the ungrateful wretches are always running away. I have lost no less than ten since my poor husband died. It's ruinous, sir!"

"But as you are well provided for, I suppose you do not feel the loss very much," said the passenger.

"I don't feel it at all," haughtily continued the good soul, "but that is no reason why property should be squandered. If my son and myself had the money for those valuable niggers, just see what a great deal of good we could do for the poor, and in sending missionaries abroad to the poor heathen, who have never heard the name of our blessed Redeemer. My dear son who is a good Christian minister has advised me not to worry and send my soul to hell for the sake of niggers; but to sell every blessed one of them for what they will fetch, and go and live in peace with him in New York. This I have concluded to do. I have just been to Richmond and made arrangements with my agent to make clean work of the forty that are left."

"Your son being a good Christian minister," said the gentleman, "it's strange he did not advise you to let the poor Negroes have their liberty and go North."

"It's not at all strange, sir; it's not at all strange. My son knows what's best for the niggers; he has always told me that they were much better off than the free niggers in the North. In fact, I don't believe there are any white laboring people in the world who are as well off as the slaves."

"You are quite mistaken, madam," said the young man. "For instance, my own widowed mother, before she died, emancipated all her slaves, and sent them to Ohio, where they are getting along well. I saw several of them last summer myself."

"Well," replied the lady, "freedom may do for your ma's niggers, but it will never do for mine; and, plague them, they shall never have it; that is the word, with the bark on it."

"If freedom will not do for your slaves," replied the passenger, "I have no doubt your Ned and the other nine Negroes will find out their mistake, and return to their old home."

"Blast them!" exclaimed the old lady, with great emphasis, "if I ever get them, I will cook their infernal hash, and tan their accursed black hides well for them! God forgive me," added the old soul, "the niggers will make me lose all my religion!"

By this time the lady had reached her destination. The gentleman got out at the next station beyond. As soon as she was gone, the young Southerner said to my master, "What a d——d shame it is for that old whining hypocritical humbug to cheat the poor Negroes out of their liberty! If she has religion, may the devil prevent me from ever being converted!"

For the purpose of somewhat disguising myself, I bought and wore a very good second-hand white beaver, an article which I had never indulged in before. So just before we arrived at Washington, an uncouth planter, who had been watching me very closely, said to my master, "I reckon, stranger, you are *'spiling'* that ere nigger of yourn, by letting him wear such a devilish fine hat. Just look at the quality on it; the President couldn't wear a better. I should just like to go and kick it overboard." His friend touched him, and said, "Don't speak so to a gentleman." "Why not?" exclaimed the fellow. He grated his short teeth, which appeared to be nearly worn away by the incessant chewing of tobacco, and said, "It always makes me itch all over, from head to toe, to get hold of every d——d nigger I see dressed like a white man. Washington is run away with *spiled* and free niggers. If I had my way I would sell every d——d rascal of 'em way down South, where the devil would be whipped out on 'em."

This man's fierce manner made my master feel rather nervous, and therefore he thought the less he said the better; so he walked off without making any reply. In a few minutes we were landed at Washington, where we took a conveyance and hurried off to the train for Baltimore.

We left our cottage on Wednesday morning, the 21st of December, 1848, and arrived at Baltimore, Saturday evening, the 24th (Christmas Eve). Baltimore was the last slave port of any note at which we stopped.

On arriving there we felt more anxious than ever, because we knew not what that last dark night would bring forth. It is true we were near the goal, but our poor hearts were still as if tossed at sea; and, as there was another great and dangerous bar to pass, we were afraid our liberties would be wrecked, and, like the ill-fated *Royal Charter,* go down forever just off the place we longed to reach.

They are particularly watchful at Baltimore to prevent slaves from escaping into Pennsylvania, which is a free State. After I had seen my master into one of the best carriages, and was just about to step into mine, an officer, a full-blooded Yankee of the lower order, saw me. He came quickly up, and, tapping me on the shoulder, said in his unmistakable native twang, together with no little display of his authority, "Where are you going, boy?" "To Philadelphia, sir," I humbly replied. "Well, what are you going there for?" "I am travelling with my master, who is in the next carriage, sir." "Well, I calculate you had better get him out; and be mighty quick about it, because the train will soon be starting. It is against my rules to let any man take a slave past here, unless he can satisfy them in the office that he has a right to take him along."

The officer then passed on and left me standing upon the platform, with my anxious heart apparently palpitating in the throat. At first I scarcely knew which way to turn. But it soon occurred to me that the good God, who had been with us thus far, would not forsake us at the eleventh hour. So with renewed hope I stepped into my master's carriage, to inform him of the difficulty. I found him sitting at the farther end, quite alone. As soon as he looked up and saw me, he smiled. I also tried to wear a cheerful countenance, in order to break the shock of the sad news. I knew what made him smile. He was aware that if we were fortunate we should reach our destination at five o'clock the next morning, and this made it the more painful to communicate what the officer had said; but, as there was no time to lose, I went up to him and asked him how he felt. He said, "Much better," and that he thanked God we were getting on so nicely.

I then said we were not getting on quite so well as we had anticipated. He anxiously and quickly asked what was the matter. I told him. He started as if struck by lightning, and exclaimed, "Good Heavens! William, is it possible that we are, after all, doomed to hopeless bondage?" I could say nothing, my heart was too full to speak, for at first I did not know what to do. However we knew it would never do to turn back to the "City of Destruction," like Bunyan's Mistrust and Timorous, because they saw lions in the narrow way after ascending the hill Difficulty; but press on, like noble Christian and Hopeful, to the great city in which dwelt a few "shining ones." So, after a few moments, I did all I could to encourage my companion, and we stepped out and made for the office: but how or where my master obtained sufficient courage to face the tyrants who had power to blast all we held dear, heaven only knows! Queen Elizabeth could not have been more terror-stricken, on being forced to land at the traitors' gate leading to the Tower, than we were on entering that office. We felt that our very existence was at stake, and that we must either sink or swim. But, as God was our present and mighty helper in this as well as in all former trials, we were able to keep our heads up and press forwards.

On entering the room we found the principal man, to whom my master said, "Do you wish to see me, sir?" "Yes," said this eagle-eyed officer; and he added, "It is against our rules, sir, to allow any person to take a slave out of Baltimore into Philadelphia, unless he can satisfy us that he has a right to take him along." "Why is that?" asked my master, with more firmness than could be expected. "Because, sir," continued he, in a voice and manner that almost chilled our blood, "if we should suffer any gentleman to take a slave past here into Philadelphia; and should the gentleman with whom the slave might be travelling turn out not to be his rightful owner, and should the proper master come and prove that his slave escaped on our road, we shall have him to pay for; and, therefore, we cannot let any slave pass here without receiving security to show, and to satisfy us, that it is all right."

This conversation attracted the attention of the large number of bustling passengers. After the officer had finished, a few of them said, "Chit, chit, chit"; not because they thought we were slaves endeavoring to escape, but merely because they thought my master was a slaveholder and invalid gentleman, and therefore it was wrong to detain him. The officer, observing that the passengers sympathized with my master, asked him if he was not acquainted with some gentleman in Baltimore that he could get to endorse for him, to show that I was his property, and that he had a right to take me off. He said, "No," and added, "I bought tickets in Charleston to pass us through to Philadelphia, and therefore you have no right to detain us here." "Well, sir," said the man, indignantly, "right or no right, we shan't let you go." These sharp words fell upon our anxious hearts like the crack of doom, and made us feel that hope only smiles to deceive.

For a few moments perfect silence prevailed. My master looked at me, and I at him, but neither of us dared to speak a word, for fear of making some blunder that would tend to our detection. We knew that the officers had power to throw us into prison, and if they had done so we must have been detected and driven back, like the vilest felons, to a life of slavery, which we dreaded far more than sudden death.

We felt as though we had come into deep waters and were about being overwhelmed, and that the slightest mistake would clip asunder the last brittle thread of hope by which we were suspended, and let us down forever into the dark and horrible pit of misery and degradation from which we were straining every nerve to escape. While our hearts were crying lustily unto Him who is ever ready and able to save, the conductor of the train that we had just left stepped in. The officer asked if we came by the train with him from Washington; he said we did, and left the room. Just then the bell rang for the train to leave, and had it been the sudden shock of an earthquake it could not have given us a greater thrill. The sound of the bell caused every eye to flash with apparent interest, and to be more steadily fixed upon us than before. But, as God would have it, the officer all at once thrust his fingers through his hair, and in a state of great agitation said, "I really don't know what to do; I calculate it is all right." He then told the clerk to run and tell the conductor to "let this gentleman and slave pass," adding, "As he is not well, it is a pity to stop him here. We will let him go." My master thanked him, and stepped out and hobbled across the platform as quickly as possible. I tumbled him unceremoniously into one of the best carriages, and leaped into mine just as the train was gliding off towards our happy destination.

We thought of this plan about four days before we left Macon; and as we had our daily employment to attend to, we only saw each other at night. So we sat up the four long nights talking over the plan and making preparations.

We had also been four days on the journey; and as we travelled night and day, we got but very limited opportunities for sleeping. I believe nothing in the world could have kept us awake so long but the intense excitement, produced by the fear of being retaken on the one hand, and the bright anticipation of liberty on the other.

We left Baltimore about eight o'clock in the evening; and not being aware of a stopping place of any consequence between there and Philadelphia, and also knowing that if we were fortunate we should be in the latter place early the next morning, I thought I might indulge in a few minutes' sleep in the car; but I, like Bunyan's Christian in the arbor, went to sleep at the wrong time, and took too long a nap. So, when the train reached Havre de Grace, all the first-class passengers had to get out of the carriages and into a ferry boat, to be ferried across the Susquehanna river, and take the train on the opposite side.

The road was constructed so as to be raised or lowered to suit the tide. So they rolled the luggage vans on to the boat, and off on the other side; and as I was in one of the apartments adjoining a baggage car, they considered it unnecessary to awaken me, and tumbled me over with the luggage. But when my master was asked to leave his seat, he found it very dark, and cold, and raining. He missed me for the first time on the journey. On all previous occasions, as soon as the train stopped, I was at hand to assist him. This caused many slaveholders to praise me very much: they said they had never before seen a slave so attentive to his master; and therefore my absence filled him with terror and confusion; the children of Israel could not have felt more troubled on arriving at the Red Sea. So he asked the conductor if he had seen anything of his slave. The man being somewhat of an abolitionist, and believing that my master was really a slaveholder, thought he would tease him a little respecting me. So he said, "No, sir; I haven't seen anything of him for some time: I have no doubt he has run away, and is in Philadelphia, free, long before now." My master knew that there was nothing in this, so he asked the conductor if he would please to see if he could find me. The man indignantly replied, "I am no slavehunter; and as far as I am concerned everybody must look after their own niggers." He went off and left the confused invalid to fancy whatever he felt inclined. My master at first thought I must have been kidnapped into slavery by someone, or left, or perhaps killed on the train. He also thought of stopping to see if he could hear anything of me, but he soon remembered that he had no money. That night all the money we had was consigned to my own pocket, because we thought, in case there were any pickpockets about, a slave's pocket would be the last one they would look for. However, hoping to meet me some day in a land of liberty, and as he had the tickets, he thought it best upon the whole to enter the boat and come off to Philadelphia, and endeavor to make his way alone in this cold and hollow world as best he could. The time was now up, so he went on board and came across with feelings that can be better imagined than described.

After the train had got fairly on the way to Philadelphia, the guard came into my car and gave me a violent shake, and bawled out at the same time, "Boy, wake up!" I started, almost frightened out of my wits. He said, "Your master is scared half to death about you." That frightened me still more—I thought they had found him out; so I anxiously inquired what was the matter. The guard said, "He thinks you have run away from him." This made me feel quite at ease. I said, "No, sir; I am satisfied my good master doesn't think that." So off I started to see him. He had been fearfully nervous, but on seeing me he at once felt much better. He merely wished to know what had become of me.

On returning to my seat, I found the conductor and two or three other persons amusing themselves very much respecting my running away. So the guard said, "Boy, what did your master want?"* I replied, "He merely wished to know what had become of me." "No," said the man, "that was not it; he thought you had taken French leave, for parts unknown. I never saw a fellow so badly scared about losing his slave in my life. Now," continued the guard, "let me give you a little friendly advice. When you get to Philadelphia, run away and leave that cripple, and have your liberty." "No, ·sir," I indifferently replied, "I can't promise to do that." "Why not?" said the conductor, evidently much surprised, "don't you want your liberty?" "Yes, sir," I replied; "but I shall never run away from such a good master as I have at present."

One of the men said to the guard, "Let him alone; I guess he will open his eyes when he gets to Philadelphia, and see things in another light." After giving me a good deal of information, which I afterwards found to be very useful, they left me alone.

I also met with a colored gentleman on this train, who recommended me to a boarding house that was kept by an abolitionist, where he thought I would be quite safe, if I wished to run away from my master. I thanked him kindly, but of course did not let him know who we were. Late at night, or rather early in the morning, I heard a fearful whistling of the steam engine; so I opened the window and looked out, and saw a large number of flickering lights in the distance, and heard a passenger in the next carriage—who also had his head out of the window—say to his companion, "Wake up, old horse, we are at Philadelphia!"

The sight of those lights and that announcement made me feel almost as happy as Bunyan's Christian must have felt when he first caught sight of the cross. I, like him, felt that the straps that bound the heavy burden to my back began to pop, and the load to roll off. I also looked, and looked again, for it appeared very wonderful to me how the mere sight of our first city of refuge should have all at once made my hitherto sad and heavy heart become so light and happy. As the train speeded on, I rejoiced and thanked God with all my heart and soul for his great kind-

---

* I may state here that every man slave is called boy till he is very old, then the more respectable slaveholders call him uncle. The women are all girls till they are aged, then they are called aunts. This is the reason why Mrs. Stowe calls her characters Uncle Tom, Aunt Chloe, Uncle Tiff, &c.

ness and tender mercy, in watching over us, and bringing us
safely through.

As soon as the train had reached the platform, before it had
fairly stopped, I hurried out of my carriage to my master, whom
I got at once into a cab, placed the luggage on, jumped in myself, and we drove off to the boarding house which was so kindly
recommended to me. On leaving the station, my master—or
rather my wife, as I may now say—who had from the commencement of the journey borne up in a manner that much surprised
us both, grasped me by the hand, and said, "Thank God, William,
we are safe!" then burst into tears, leant upon me, and wept like
a child. The reaction was fearful. So when we reached the house,
she was in reality so weak and faint that she could scarcely
stand alone. However, I got her into the apartments that were
pointed out, and there we knelt down, on this Sabbath, and
Christmas Day—a day that will ever be memorable to us—and
poured out our heartfelt gratitude to God, for his goodness in
enabling us to overcome so many perilous difficulties, in escaping
out of the jaws of the wicked.

Part 2

AFTER MY WIFE had a little recovered herself, she threw off the disguise and assumed her own apparel. We then stepped into the sitting room, and asked to see the landlord. The man came in, but he seemed thunderstruck on finding a fugitive slave and his wife, instead of a "young cotton planter and his nigger." As his eyes travelled round the room, he said to me, "Where is your master?" I pointed him out. The man gravely replied, "I am not joking, I really wish to see your master." I pointed him out again, but at first he could not believe his eyes; he said "he knew that was not the gentleman that came with me."

But, after some conversation, we satisfied him that we were fugitive slaves, and had just escaped in the manner I have described. We asked him if he thought it would be safe for us to stop in Philadelphia. He said he thought not, but he would call in some persons who knew more about the laws than himself. He then went out, and kindly brought in several of the leading abolitionists of the city, who gave us a most hearty and friendly welcome amongst them. As it was in December, and also as we had just left a very warm climate, they advised us not to go to Canada as we had intended, but to settle at Boston in the United States. It is true that the constitution of the Republic has always guaranteed the slaveholders the right to come into any of the so-called free States, and take their fugitives back to southern Egypt. But through the untiring, uncompromising, and manly efforts of Mr. Garrison, Wendell Phillips, Theodore Parker, and a host of other noble abolitionists of Boston and the neighborhood, public opinion in Massachusetts had become so much opposed to slavery and to kidnapping, that it was almost impossible for anyone to take a fugitive slave out of that State.

So we took the advice of our good Philadelphia friends, and settled at Boston. I shall have something to say about our sojourn there presently.

Among other friends we met with at Philadelphia, was Robert Purves, Esq., a well-educated and wealthy colored gentleman, who introduced us to Mr. Barkley Ivens, a member of the Society of Friends, and a noble and generous-hearted farmer, who lived at some distance in the country.

This good Samaritan at once invited us to go and stop quietly with his family, till my wife could somewhat recover from the fearful reaction of the past journey. We most gratefully accepted the invitation, and at the time appointed we took a steamer to a place up the Delaware river, where our new and dear friend met us with his snug little cart, and took us to his happy home. This was the first act of great and disinterested kindness we had ever received from a white person.

The gentleman was not of the fairest complexion, and therefore, as my wife was not in the room when I received the information respecting him and his anti-slavery character, she thought of course he was a quadroon like herself. But on arriving at the house, and finding out her mistake, she became more nervous and timid than ever.

As the cart came into the yard, the dear good old lady, and her three charming and affectionate daughters, all came to the door to meet us. We got out, and the gentleman said, "Go in, and make yourselves at home; I will see after the baggage." But my wife was afraid to approach them. She stopped in the yard, and said to me, "William, I thought we were coming among colored people?" I replied, "It is all right; these are the same." "No," she said, "it is not all right, and I am not going to stop here; I have no confidence whatever in white people, they are only trying to get us back to slavery." She turned round and said, "I am going right off." The old lady then came out, with her sweet, soft, and winning smile, shook her heartily by the hand, and kindly said, "How art thou, my dear? We are all very glad to see thee and thy husband. Come in, to the fire; I dare say thou art cold and hungry after thy journey."

We went in, and the young ladies asked if she would like to go upstairs and "fix" herself before tea. My wife said, "No, I thank you; I shall only stop a little while." "But where art thou going this cold night?" said Mr. Ivens, who had just stepped in. "I don't know," was the reply. "Well, then," he continued, "I think thou hadst better take off thy things and sit near the fire; tea will soon be ready." "Yes, come Ellen," said Mrs. Ivens, "let me assist thee" (as she commenced undoing my wife's bonnet-strings); "don't be frightened, Ellen, I shall not hurt a single hair of thy head. We have heard with much pleasure of the marvellous escape of thee and thy husband, and deeply sympathize with thee in all that thou hast undergone. I don't wonder at thee, poor thing, being timid; but thou needs not fear us; we would as soon send one of our own daughters into slavery as thee; so thou mayest make thyself quite at ease!" These soft and soothing words fell like balm upon my wife's unstrung nerves, and melted her to tears; her fears and prejudices vanished, and from that day she has firmly believed that there are good and bad persons of every shade of complexion.

After seeing Sally Ann and Jacob, two colored domestics, my wife felt quite at home. After partaking of what Mrs. Stowe's Mose and Pete called a "busting supper," the ladies wished to know whether we could read. On learning we could not, they said if we liked they would teach us. To this kind offer, of course, there was no objection. But we looked rather knowingly at each other, as much as to say that they would have rather a hard task to cram anything into our thick and matured sculls.

However, all hands set to and quickly cleared away the tea things, and the ladies and their good brother brought out the spelling and copy books and slates, &c., and commenced with their new and green pupils. We had, by stratagem, learned the alphabet while in slavery, but not the writing characters; and, as we had been such a time learning so little, we at first felt that it was a waste of time for anyone at our ages to undertake to learn to read and write. But, as the ladies were so anxious that we should learn, and so willing to teach us, we concluded to give our whole minds to the work, and see what could be done. By so doing, at the end of the three weeks we remained with the good family we could spell and write our names quite legibly. They all begged us to stop longer; but, as we were not safe in the State of Pennsylvania, and also as we wished to commence doing something for a livelihood, we did not remain.

When the time arrived for us to leave for Boston, it was like parting with our relatives. We have since met with many very kind and hospitable friends, both in America and England; but we have never been under a roof where we were made to feel more at home, or where the inmates took a deeper interest in our well-being, than Mr. Barkley Ivens and his dear family. May God ever bless them, and preserve each one from every reverse of fortune!

We finally, as I have stated, settled at Boston, where we remained nearly two years, I employed as cabinetmaker and furniture broker, and my wife at her needle; and, as our little earnings in slavery were not all spent on the journey, we were getting on very well, and would have made money, if we had not been compelled by the General Government, at the bidding of the slaveholders, to break up business, and fly from under the Stars and Stripes to save our liberties and our lives.

In 1850, Congress passed the Fugitive Slave Bill, an enactment too infamous to have been thought of or tolerated by any people in the world, except the unprincipled and tyrannical Yankees. The following are a few of the leading features of the above law; which requires, under heavy penalties, that the inhabitants of the *free* States should not only refuse food and shelter to a starving, hunted human being, but also should assist, if called upon by the authorities, to seize the unhappy fugitive and send him back to slavery.

In no case is a person's evidence admitted in Court, in defense of his liberty, when arrested under this law.

If the judge decides that the prisoner is a slave, he gets ten dollars; but if he sets him at liberty, he only receives five.

After the prisoner has been sentenced to slavery, he is handed over to the United States Marshal, who has the power, at the expense of the General Government, to summon a sufficient force to take the poor creature back to slavery, and to the lash, from which he fled.

Our old masters sent agents to Boston after us. They took out warrants, and placed them in the hands of the United States Marshal to execute. But the following letter from our highly esteemed and faithful friend, the Rev. Samuel May, of Boston, to our equally dear and much lamented friend, Dr. Estlin of Bristol, will show why we were not taken into custody.

21 CORNHILL, BOSTON
NOVEMBER 6th, 1850

My dear Mr Estlin,

I trust that in God's good providence this letter will be handed to you in safety by our good friends, William and Ellen Craft. They have lived amongst us about two years, and have proved themselves worthy, in all respects, of our confidence and regard.

The laws of this republican and Christian land (tell it not in Moscow, nor in Constantinople) regard them only as slaves—chattels—personal property. But they nobly vindicated their title and right to freedom, two years since, by winning their way to it; at least, so they thought. But now, the slave power, with the aid of Daniel Webster and a band of lesser traitors, has enacted a law, which puts their dearly-bought liberties in the most imminent peril; holds out a strong temptation to every mercenary and unprincipled ruffian to become their kidnapper; and has stimulated the slaveholders generally to such desperate acts for the recovery of their fugitive property, as have never before been enacted in the history of this government.

Within a fortnight, two fellows from Macon, Georgia, have been in Boston for the purpose of arresting our friends William and Ellen. A writ was served against them from the United States District Court; but it was not served by the United States Marshal; why not, is not certainly known: perhaps through fear, for a general feeling of indignation, and a cool determination not to allow this young couple to be taken from Boston into slavery, was aroused, and pervaded the city. It is understood that one of the judges told the Marshal that he would not be authorised in breaking the door of Craft's house. Craft kept himself close within the house, armed himself, and awaited with remarkable composure the event. Ellen, in the meantime, had been taken to a retired place out of the city. The Vigilance Committee (appointed at a late meeting in Fanueil Hall) enlarged their numbers, held an almost permanent session, and appointed various subcommittees to act in different ways. One of these committees called repeatedly on Messrs. Hughes and Knight, the slave-catchers, and requested and advised them to leave the city. At first they peremptorily refused to do so, " 'til they got hold of the niggers." On complaint of different persons, these two fellows were several times arrested, carried before one of our county courts, and held to bail on charges of "conspiracy to kidnap," and of "defamation," in calling William and Ellen *slaves.*" At length, they became so alarmed, that they left the city by an indirect route, evading the vigilance of many persons who were on the look-out for them. Hughes, at one time, was near losing his life at the hands of an infuriated colored man. While these men remained in the city, a prominent whig gentleman sent word to William Craft, that if he would submit peaceably to an arrest, he and his wife should be bought from their owners,

cost what it might. Craft replied, in effect, that he was in a
measure the representative of all the other fugitives in Boston,
some 200 or 300 in number; that, if he gave up, they would all
be at the mercy of the slave-catchers, and must fly from the city
at any sacrifice; and that, if his freedom could be bought for
two cents, he would not consent to compromise the matter in
such a way. This event has stirred up the slave spirit of the
country, south and north; the United States government is determined to try its hand in enforcing the Fugitive Slave law;
and William and Ellen Craft would be prominent objects of the
slaveholders' vengeance. Under these circumstances, it is the almost unanimous opinion of their best friends, that they should
quit America as speedily as possible, and seek an asylum in England! Oh! shame, shame upon us, that Americans, whose fathers
fought against Great Britain, in order to be FREE, should have to
acknowledge this disgraceful fact! God gave us a fair and goodly
heritage in this land, but man has cursed it with his devices and
crimes against human souls and human rights. Is America the
"land of the free, and the home of the brave?" God knows it is
not; and we know it too. A brave young man and a virtuous
young woman must fly the American shores, and seek, under the
shadow of the British throne, the enjoyment of "life, liberty, and
the pursuit of happiness."

But I must pursue my plain, sad story. All day long, I have
been busy planning a safe way for William and Ellen to leave
Boston. We dare not allow them to go on board a vessel, even in
the port of Boston; for the writ is yet in the Marshal's hands,
and he *may* be waiting an opportunity to serve it; so I am expecting to accompany them to-morrow to Portland, Maine, which
is beyond the reach of the Marshal's authority; and there I hope
to see them on board a British steamer.

This letter is written to introduce them to you. I know your
infirm health; but I am sure, if you were stretched on your bed
in your last illness, and could lift your hand at all, you would
extend it to welcome these poor hunted fellow-creatures. Henceforth, England is their nation and their home. It is with real regret for our personal loss in their departure, as well as burning
shame for the land that is not worthy of them, that we send
them away, or rather allow them to go. But, with all the resolute
courage they have shown in a most trying hour, they themselves
see it is the part of a foolhardy rashness to attempt to stay here
longer.

I must close; and with many renewed thanks for all your kind words and deeds towards us,

I am, very respectfully yours,

SAMUEL MAY, JUN.

Our old masters, having heard how their agents were treated at Boston, wrote to Mr. Filmore, who was then President of the States, to know what he could do to have us sent back to slavery. Mr. Filmore said that we should be returned. He gave instructions for military force to be sent to Boston to assist the officers in making the arrest. Therefore we, as well as our friends (among whom was George Thompson, Esq., late M.P. for the Tower Hamlets—the slave's long-tried, self-sacrificing friend, and eloquent advocate) thought it best, at any sacrifice, to leave the mock-free Republic, and come to a country where we and our dear little ones can be truly free. "No one daring to molest or make us afraid." But, as the officers were watching every vessel that left the port to prevent us from escaping, we had to take the expensive and tedious overland route to Halifax.

We shall always cherish the deepest feelings of gratitude to the Vigilance Committee of Boston (upon which were many of the leading abolitionists), and also to our numerous friends, for the very kind and noble manner in which they assisted us to preserve our liberties and to escape from Boston, as it were, like Lot from Sodom, to a place of refuge, and finally to this truly free and glorious country; where no tyrant, let his power be ever so absolute over his poor trembling victims at home, dare come and lay violent hands upon us or upon our dear little boys (who had the good fortune to be born upon British soil), and reduce us to the legal level of the beast that perisheth. Oh! may God bless the thousands of unflinching, disinterested abolitionists of America, who are laboring through evil as well as through good report, to cleanse their country's escutcheon from the foul and destructive blot of slavery, and to restore to every bondman his God-given rights; and may God ever smile upon England and upon England's good, much-beloved, and deservedly honored Queen, for the generous protection that is given to unfortunate refugees of every rank, and of every color and clime.

On the passing of the Fugitive Slave Bill, the following

learned doctors, as well as a host of lesser traitors, came out strongly in its defense.

The Rev. Dr. Gardiner Spring, an eminent Presbyterian clergyman of New York, well known in this country by his religious publications, declared from the pulpit that, "if by one prayer he could liberate every slave in the world he would not dare to offer it."

The Rev. Dr. Joel Parker, of Philadelphia, in the course of a discussion on the nature of slavery, says, "What, then, are the evils inseparable from slavery? There is not one that is not equally inseparable from depraved human nature in other lawful relations."

The Rev. Moses Stuart, D.D. (late professor in the Theological College of Andover), in his vindication of this Bill, reminds his readers that "many Southern slaveholders are true *Christians.*" That "sending back a fugitive to them is not like restoring one to an idolatrous people." That "though we may *pity* the fugitive, yet the Mosaic Law does not authorize the rejection of the claims of the slaveholders to their stolen or strayed *property.*"

The Rev. Dr. Spencer, of Brooklyn, New York, has come forward in support of the "Fugitive Slave Bill," by publishing a sermon entitled the "Religious Duty of Obedience to the Laws," which has elicited the highest encomiums from Dr. Samuel H. Cox, the Presbyterian minister of Brooklyn (notorious both in this country and America for his sympathy with the slaveholder).

The Rev. W. M. Rogers, an orthodox minister of Boston, delivered a sermon in which he says, "When the slave asks me to stand between him and his master, what does he ask? He asks me to murder a nation's life; and I will not do it, because I have a conscience—because there is a God." He proceeds to affirm that if resistance to the carrying out of the "Fugitive Slave Law" should lead the magistracy to call the citizens to arms, their duty was to obey and "if ordered to take human life, in the name of God to take it"; and he concludes by admonishing the fugitives to "hearken to the Word of God, and to count their own masters worthy of all honor."

The Rev. William Crowell, of Waterfield, State of Maine, printed a Thanksgiving sermon of the same kind, in which he calls upon his hearers not to allow "excessive sympathies for a few hundred fugitives to blind them so as that they may risk increased suffering to the millions already in chains."

The Rev. Dr. Taylor, an Episcopal Clergyman of New Haven, Connecticut, made a speech at a union meeting, in which he deprecates the agitation on the law, and urges obedience to it, asking, "Is that article in the Constitution contrary to the law of Nature, of nations, or to the will of God? Is it so? Is there a shadow of reason for saying it? I have not been able to discover it. Have I not shown you it is lawful to deliver up, in compliance with the laws, fugitive slaves, for the high, the great, the momentous interests of those [Southern] States?"

The Right Rev. Bishop Hopkins, of Vermont, in a lecture at Lockport, says, "It was warranted by the Old Testament"; and inquires, "What effect had the Gospel in doing away with slavery? None whatever." Therefore he argues, as it is expressly permitted by the Bible, it does not in itself involve any sin; but that every Christian is authorized by the Divine Law to own slaves, provided they were not treated with unnecessary cruelty.

The Rev. Orville Dewey, D.D., of the Unitarian connection, maintained in his lectures that the safety of the Union is not to be hazarded for the sake of the African race. He declares that, for his part, he would send his own brother or child into slavery, if needed to preserve the Union between the free and the slave-holding States; and, counselling the slave to similar magnanimity, thus exhorts him: *"Your right to be free is not absolute, unqualified, irrespective of all consequences.* If my espousal of your claim is likely to involve your race and mine together in disasters infinitely greater than your personal servitude, then you ought not to be free. In such a case personal rights ought to be sacrificed to the general good. You yourself ought to see this, and be willing to suffer for a while—one for many."

If the Doctor is prepared, he is quite at liberty to sacrifice his "personal rights to the general good." But, as I have suffered a long time in slavery, it is hardly fair for the Doctor to advise me to go back. According to his showing, he ought rather to take my place. That would be practically carrying out his logic, as respects "suffering awhile—one for many."

In fact, so eager were they to prostrate themselves before the

great idol of slavery, and, like Baalam, to curse instead of blessing the people whom God had brought out of bondage, that they
in bringing up obsolete passages from the Old Testament to
justify their downward course, overlooked, or would not see, the
following verses, which show very clearly, according to the
Doctor's own textbook, that the slaves have a right to run away,
and that it is unscriptural for anyone to send them back.

In the 23rd chapter of Deuteronomy, 15th and 16th verses, it
is thus written: "Thou shalt not deliver unto his master the
servant which is escaped from his master unto thee. He shall
dwell with thee, even among you, in that place which he shall
choose in one of thy gates, where it liketh him best: thou
shalt not oppress him."

"Hide the outcast. Bewray not him that wandereth. Let mine
outcasts dwell with thee. Be thou a covert to them from the
face of the spoiler" (Isa. 16:3, 4).

The great majority of the American ministers are not content
with uttering sentences similar to the above, or remaining wholly
indifferent to the cries of the poor bondman; but they do all
they can to blast the reputation, and to muzzle the mouths, of
the few good men who dare to beseech the God of mercy "to
loose the bonds of wickedness, to undo the heavy burdens, and
let the oppressed go free." These reverend gentlemen pour a
terrible cannonade upon "Jonah," for refusing to carry God's
message against Nineveh, and tell us about the whale in which
he was entombed; while they utterly overlook the existence of
the whales which trouble their republican waters, and know not
that they themselves are the "Jonahs" who threaten to sink their
ship of state, by steering in an unrighteous direction. We are
told that the whale vomited up the runaway prophet. This
would not have seemed so strange, had it been one of the above
lukewarm Doctors of Divinity whom he had swallowed; for
even a whale might find such a morsel difficult of digestion.

> I venerate the man whose heart is warm,
> Whose hands are pure; whose doctrines and whose life
> Coincident, exhibit lucid proof
> That he is honest in the sacred cause.

But grace abused brings forth the foulest deeds,
As richest soil the most luxuriant weeds.

I must now leave the reverend gentlemen in the hands of Him who knows best how to deal with a recreant ministry.

I do not wish it to be understood that all the ministers of the States are of the Baalam stamp. There are those who are as uncompromising with slaveholders as Moses was with Pharaoh, and, like Daniel, will never bow down before the great false God that has been set up.

On arriving at Portland, we found that the steamer we intended to take had run into a schooner the previous night, and was lying up for repairs; so we had to wait there, in fearful suspense, for two or three days. During this time, we had the honor of being the guest of the late and much lamented Daniel Oliver, Esq., one of the best and most hospitable men in the State. By simply fulfilling the Scripture injunction, to take in the stranger, &c., he ran the risk of incurring a penalty of two thousand dollars, and twelve months' imprisonment.

But neither the Fugitive Slave Law, nor any other Satanic enactment, can ever drive the spirit of liberty and humanity out of such noble and generous-hearted men.

May God ever bless his dear widow, and eventually unite them in His courts above!

We finally got off to St. John, New Brunswick, where we had to wait two days for the steamer that conveyed us to Windsor, Nova Scotia.

On going into a hotel at St. John, we met the butler in the hall, to whom I said, "We wish to stop here tonight." He turned round, scratching his head, evidently much put about. But thinking that my wife was white, he replied, "We have plenty of room for the lady, but I don't know about yourself; we never take in colored folks." "Oh, don't trouble about me," I said; "if you have room for the lady, that will do; so please have the luggage taken to a bedroom." Which was immediately done, and my wife went upstairs into the apartment.

After taking a little walk in the town, I returned, and asked to see the "lady." On being conducted to the little sitting room, where she then was, I entered without knocking, much to the surprise of the whole house. The "lady" then rang the bell, and ordered dinner for two. "Dinner for two, mum!" exclaimed the waiter, as he backed out of the door. "Yes, for two," said my wife. In a little while the stout, red-nosed butler, whom we first met, knocked at the door. I called out, "Come in." On entering, he rolled his whisky eyes at me, and then at my wife, and said, in a very solemn tone, "Did you order dinner for two, mum?" "Yes, for two," my wife again replied. This confused the chubby butler more than ever; and, as the landlord was not in the house, he seemed at a loss what to do.

When dinner was ready, the maid came in and said, "Please mum, the Missis wishes to know whether you will have dinner up now, or wait till your friend arrives?" "I will have it up at once, if you please." "Thank you, mum," continued the maid, and out she glided.

After a good deal of giggling in the passage, someone said, "You are in for it, butler, after all; so you had better make the best of a bad job." But before dinner was sent up, the landlord returned, and having heard from the steward of the steamer by which we came that we were bound for England, the proprietor's native country, he treated us in the most respectful manner.

At the above house, the boots (whose name I forget) was a fugitive slave, a very intelligent and active man, about forty-five years of age. Soon after his marriage, while in slavery, his bride was sold away from him, and he could never learn where the poor creature dwelt. So after remaining single for many years, both before and after his escape, and never expecting to see again, nor even to hear from, his long-lost partner, he finally married a woman at St. John. But, poor fellow, as he was passing down the street one day, he met a woman; at the first glance they nearly recognized each other; they both turned round and stared, and unconsciously advanced, till she screamed and flew into his arms. Her first words were, "Dear, are you married?" On his answering in the affirmative, she shrank from his embrace, hung her head, and wept. A person who witnessed this meeting told me it was most affecting.

This couple knew nothing of each other's escape or whereabouts. The woman had escaped a few years before to the free States, by secreting herself in the hold of a vessel; but as they tried to get her back to bondage, she fled to New Brunswick for that protection which her native country was too mean to afford.

The man at once took his old wife to see his new one, who was also a fugitive slave, and as they all knew the workings of the infamous system of slavery, they could (as no one else can) sympathize with each other's misfortune.

According to the rules of slavery, the man and his first wife were already divorced, but not morally; and therefore it was arranged between the three that he should live only with the lastly married wife, and allow the other one so much a week, as long she requested his assistance.

After staying at St. John two days, the steamer arrived, which took us to Windsor, where we found a coach bound for Halifax. Prejudice against color forced me on the top in the rain. On arriving within about seven miles of the town, the coach broke down and was upset. I fell upon the big crotchety driver, whose head stuck in the mud; and as he "always objected to niggers riding inside with white folks," I was not particularly sorry to see him deeper in the mire than myself. All of us were scratched and bruised more or less. After the passengers had crawled out as best they could, we all set off, and paddled through the deep mud and cold and rain, to Halifax.

On leaving Boston, it was our intention to reach Halifax at least two or three days before the steamer from Boston touched there, *en route* for Liverpool; but, having been detained so long at Portland and St. John, we had the misfortune to arrive at Halifax at dark, just two hours after the steamer had gone; consequently we had to wait there a fortnight, for the *Cambria*.

The coach was patched up, and reached Halifax with the luggage, soon after the passengers arrived. The only respectable hotel that was then in the town had suspended business, and was closed; so we went to the inn, opposite the market, where the coach stopped: a most miserable, dirty hole it was.

Knowing that we were still under the influence of the low Yankee prejudice, I sent my wife in with the other passengers, to engage a bed for herself and husband. I stopped outside in the rain till the coach came up. If I had gone in and asked for a bed they would have been quite full. But as they thought my wife was white, she had no difficulty in securing apartments, into which the luggage was afterwards carried. The landlady, observing that I took an interest in the baggage, became somewhat uneasy, and went into my wife's room, and said to her, "Do you know the dark man downstairs?" "Yes, he is my husband." "Oh! I mean the black man—the *nigger?*" "I quite understand you; he is my husband." "My God!" exclaimed the woman as she flounced out and banged to the door. On going upstairs, I heard what had taken place: but, as we were there, and did not mean to leave that night, we did not disturb ourselves. On our ordering tea, the landlady sent word back to say that we must take it in the kitchen, or in our bedroom, as she had no other room for "niggers." We replied that we were not particular, and that they could send it up to our room—which they did.

After the pro-slavery persons who were staying there heard that we were in, the whole house became agitated, and all sorts of oaths and fearful threats were heaped upon the "d——d niggers, for coming among white folks." Some of them said they would not stop there a minute if there was another house to go to.

The mistress came up the next morning to know how long we wished to stop. We said a fortnight. "Oh! dear me, it is impossible for us to accommodate you, and I think you had better go: you must understand, I have no prejudice myself; I think a good deal of the colored people, and have always been their friend; but if you stop here we shall lose all our customers, which we can't do nohow." We said we were glad to hear that she had "no prejudice," and was such a staunch friend to the colored people. We also informed her that we would be sorry for her "customers" to leave on our account; and as it was not our intention to interfere with anyone, it was foolish for them to be frightened away. However, if she would get us a comfortable place, we would be glad to leave. The landlady said she would go out and try. After spending the whole morning in canvassing the town, she came to our room and said, "I have been from one end of the place to the other, but everybody is full." Having a little foretaste of the vulgar prejudice of the town, we did not wonder at this result. However, the landlady gave me the address of some respectable colored families, whom she thought, "under the circumstances," might be induced to take us. And, as we were not at all comfortable—being compelled to sit, eat, and sleep, in the same small room—we were quite willing to change our quarters.

I called upon the Rev. Mr. Cannady, a truly good-hearted Christian man, who received us at a word; and both he and his kind lady treated us handsomely, and for a nominal charge.

My wife and myself were both unwell when we left Boston, and, having taken fresh cold on the journey to Halifax, we were laid up there under the doctor's care, nearly the whole fortnight. I had much worry about getting tickets, for they baffled us shamefully at the Cunard office. They at first said that they did not book till the steamer came; which was not the fact. When I called again, they said they knew the steamer would come full from Boston, and therefore we had "better try to get to Liverpool by other means." Other mean Yankee excuses were made; and it was not till an influential gentleman, to whom Mr. Francis Jackson, of Boston, kindly gave us a letter, went and rebuked them, that we were able to secure our tickets. So when we went on board my wife was very poorly, and was also so ill on the voyage that I did not believe she could live to see Liverpool.

However, I am thankful to say she arrived; and, after laying up at Liverpool very ill for two or three weeks, gradually recovered.

It was not until we stepped upon the shore at Liverpool that we were free from every slavish fear.

We raised our thankful hearts to Heaven, and could have knelt down, like the Neapolitan exiles, and kissed the soil; for we felt that from slavery

> Heaven sure had kept this spot of earth uncurs'd,
> To show how all things were created first.

In a few days after we landed, the Rev. Francis Bishop and his lady came and invited us to be their guests; to whose unlimited kindness and watchful care my wife owes, in a great degree, her restoration to health.

We enclosed our letter from the Rev. Mr. May to Mr. Estlin, who at once wrote to invite us to his house at Bristol. On arriving there, both Mr. and Miss Estlin received us as cordially as did our first good Quaker friends in Pennsylvania. It grieves me much to have to mention that he is no more. Everyone who knew him can truthfully say—

> Peace to the memory of a man of worth,
> A man of letters, and of manners too!
> Of manners sweet as Virtue always wears
> When gay Good-nature dresses her in smiles.

It was principally through the extreme kindness of Mr. Estlin, the Right Hon. Lady Noel Byron, Miss Harriet Martineau, Mrs. Reid, Miss Sturch, and a few other good friends, that my wife and myself were able to spend a short time at a school in this country, to acquire a little of that education which we were so shamefully deprived of while in the house of bondage. The school is under the supervision of the Misses Lushington, daughters of the Right Hon. Stephen Lushington, D.C.L. During our stay at the school we received the greatest attention from everyone; and I am particularly indebted to Thomas Wilson, Esq., of Bradmore House, Chiswick (who was then the master) for the deep interest he took in trying to get me on in my studies. We shall ever fondly and gratefully cherish the memory of our endeared and departed friend, Mr. Estlin. We, as well as the Anti-Slavery cause, lost a good friend in him. However, if departed spirits in Heaven are conscious of the wickedness of this world, and are allowed to speak, he will never fail to plead in the presence of the angelic host, and before the great and just Judge, for down-trodden and outraged humanity.

> Therefore I cannot think thee wholly gone;
>   The better part of thee is with us still;
> Thy soul its hampering clay aside hath thrown,
>   And only freer wrestles with the ill.
>
> Thou livest in the life of all good things;
>   What words thou spak'st for Freedom shall not die;
> Thou sleepest not, for now thy Love hath wings
>   To soar where hence thy hope could hardly fly.
>
> And often, from that other world, on this
>   Some gleams from great souls gone before may shine,
> To shed on struggling hearts a clearer bliss,
>   And clothe the Right with lustre more divine.

Farewell! good man, good angel now! this hand
  Soon, like thine own, shall lose its cunning, too;
Soon shall this soul, like thine, bewildered stand,
  Then leap to thread the free unfathomed blue.

JAMES RUSSELL LOWELL.

In the preceding pages I have not dwelt upon the great barbarities which are practised upon the slaves, because I wish to present the system in its mildest form, and to show that the "tender mercies of the wicked are cruel." But I do now, however, most solemnly declare, that a very large majority of the American slaves are over-worked, under-fed, and frequently unmercifully flogged.

I have often seen slaves tortured in every conceivable manner. I have seen them hunted down and torn by bloodhounds. I have seen them shamefully beaten, and branded with hot irons. I have seen them hunted, and even burned alive at the stake, frequently for offenses that would be applauded if committed by white persons for similar purposes.

In short, it is well known in England, if not all over the world, that the Americans, as a people, are notoriously mean and cruel towards all colored persons, whether they are bond or free.

Oh, tyrant, thou who sleepest
On a volcano, from whose pent-up wrath,
Already some red flashes bursting up,
Beware!

DATE DUE
